Lecture Notes in Computer Science   8533

Commenced Publication in 1973
Founding and Former Series Editors:
Gerhard Goos, Juris Hartmanis, and Jan van Leeuwen

Theo Tryfonas   Ioannis Askoxylakis (Eds.)

Human Aspects of Information Security, Privacy, and Trust

Second International Conference, HAS 2014
Held as Part of HCI International 2014
Heraklion, Crete, Greece, June 22-27, 2014
Proceedings

 Springer

Volume Editors

Theo Tryfonas
University of Bristol
Cryptography Group
Bristol, BS8 1UB, UK
E-mail: theo.tryfonas@bristol.ac.uk

Ioannis Askoxylakis
Foundation for Research and Technology - Hellas (FORTH)
Institute of Computer Science
N. Plastira 100, Vassilika Vouton, 70013 Heraklion, Crete, Greece
E-mail: asko@ics.forth.gr

ISSN 0302-9743   e-ISSN 1611-3349
ISBN 978-3-319-07619-5   e-ISBN 978-3-319-07620-1
DOI 10.1007/978-3-319-07620-1
Springer Cham Heidelberg New York Dordrecht London

Library of Congress Control Number: 2014939518

LNCS Sublibrary: SL 3 – Information Systems and Application, incl. Internet/Web
and HCI

Typesetting: Camera-ready by author, data conversion by Scientific Publishing Services, Chennai, India

Printed on acid-free paper

Springer is part of Springer Science+Business Media (www.springer.com)

Volume Editors

Theo Tryfonas
University of Bristol
Cryptography Group
Bristol, BS8 1UB, UK
E-mail: theo.tryfonas@bristol.ac.uk

Ioannis Askoxylakis
Foundation for Research and Technology - Hellas (FORTH)
Institute of Computer Science
N. Plastira 100, Vassilika Vouton, 70013 Heraklion, Crete, Greece
E-mail: asko@ics.forth.gr

ISSN 0302-9743   e-ISSN 1611-3349
ISBN 978-3-319-07619-5   e-ISBN 978-3-319-07620-1
DOI 10.1007/978-3-319-07620-1
Springer Cham Heidelberg New York Dordrecht London

Library of Congress Control Number: 2014939518

LNCS Sublibrary: SL 3 – Information Systems and Application, incl. Internet/Web
and HCI

Typesetting: Camera-ready by author, data conversion by Scientific Publishing Services, Chennai, India

Printed on acid-free paper

Springer is part of Springer Science+Business Media (www.springer.com)

Theo Tryfonas   Ioannis Askoxylakis (Eds.)

Human Aspects of Information Security, Privacy, and Trust

Second International Conference, HAS 2014
Held as Part of HCI International 2014
Heraklion, Crete, Greece, June 22-27, 2014
Proceedings

 Springer

Foreword

The 16th International Conference on Human–Computer Interaction, HCI International 2014, was held in Heraklion, Crete, Greece, during June 22–27, 2014, incorporating 14 conferences/thematic areas:

Thematic areas:

- Human–Computer Interaction
- Human Interface and the Management of Information

Affiliated conferences:

- 11th International Conference on Engineering Psychology and Cognitive Ergonomics
- 8th International Conference on Universal Access in Human–Computer Interaction
- 6th International Conference on Virtual, Augmented and Mixed Reality
- 6th International Conference on Cross-Cultural Design
- 6th International Conference on Social Computing and Social Media
- 8th International Conference on Augmented Cognition
- 5th International Conference on Digital Human Modeling and Applications in Health, Safety, Ergonomics and Risk Management
- Third International Conference on Design, User Experience and Usability
- Second International Conference on Distributed, Ambient and Pervasive Interactions
- Second International Conference on Human Aspects of Information Security, Privacy and Trust
- First International Conference on HCI in Business
- First International Conference on Learning and Collaboration Technologies

A total of 4,766 individuals from academia, research institutes, industry, and governmental agencies from 78 countries submitted contributions, and 1,476 papers and 225 posters were included in the proceedings. These papers address the latest research and development efforts and highlight the human aspects of design and use of computing systems. The papers thoroughly cover the entire field of human–computer interaction, addressing major advances in knowledge and effective use of computers in a variety of application areas.

This volume, edited by Theo Tryfonas and Ioannis Askoxylakis, contains papers focusing on the thematic area of Human Aspects of Information Security, Privacy and Trust, addressing the following major topics:

- Usable security
- Authentication and passwords

- Security policy and awareness
- Human behaviour in cybersecurity
- Privacy issues

The remaining volumes of the HCI International 2014 proceedings are:

- Volume 1, LNCS 8510, Human–Computer Interaction: HCI Theories, Methods and Tools (Part I), edited by Masaaki Kurosu
- Volume 2, LNCS 8511, Human–Computer Interaction: Advanced Interaction Modalities and Techniques (Part II), edited by Masaaki Kurosu
- Volume 3, LNCS 8512, Human–Computer Interaction: Applications and Services (Part III), edited by Masaaki Kurosu
- Volume 4, LNCS 8513, Universal Access in Human–Computer Interaction: Design and Development Methods for Universal Access (Part I), edited by Constantine Stephanidis and Margherita Antona
- Volume 5, LNCS 8514, Universal Access in Human–Computer Interaction: Universal Access to Information and Knowledge (Part II), edited by Constantine Stephanidisand MargheritaAntona
- Volume 6, LNCS 8515, Universal Access in Human–Computer Interaction: Aging and Assistive Environments (Part III), edited by Constantine Stephanidis and Margherita Antona
- Volume 7, LNCS 8516, Universal Access in Human–Computer Interaction: Design for All and Accessibility Practice (Part IV), edited by Constantine Stephanidis and Margherita Antona
- Volume 8, LNCS 8517, Design, User Experience, and Usability: Theories, Methods and Tools for Designing the User Experience (Part I), edited by Aaron Marcus
- Volume 9, LNCS 8518, Design, User Experience, and Usability: User Experience Design for Diverse Interaction Platforms and Environments (Part II), edited by Aaron Marcus
- Volume 10, LNCS 8519, Design, User Experience, and Usability: User Experience Design for Everyday Life Applications and Services (Part III), edited by Aaron Marcus
- Volume 11, LNCS 8520, Design, User Experience, and Usability: User Experience Design Practice (Part IV), edited by Aaron Marcus
- Volume 12, LNCS 8521, Human Interface and the Management of Information: Information and Knowledge Design and Evaluation (Part I), edited by Sakae Yamamoto
- Volume 13, LNCS 8522, Human Interface and the Management of Information: Information and Knowledge in Applications and Services (Part II), edited by Sakae Yamamoto
- Volume 14, LNCS 8523, Learning and Collaboration Technologies: Designing and Developing Novel Learning Experiences (Part I), edited by Panayiotis Zaphiris and Andri Ioannou
- Volume 15, LNCS 8524, Learning and Collaboration Technologies: Technology-rich Environments for Learning and Collaboration (Part II), edited by Panayiotis Zaphiris and Andri Ioannou

- Volume 16, LNCS 8525, Virtual, Augmented and Mixed Reality: Designing and Developing Virtual and Augmented Environments (Part I), edited by Randall Shumaker and Stephanie Lackey
- Volume 17, LNCS 8526, Virtual, Augmented and Mixed Reality: Applications of Virtual and Augmented Reality (Part II), edited by Randall Shumaker and Stephanie Lackey
- Volume 18, LNCS 8527, HCI in Business, edited by Fiona Fui-Hoon Nah
- Volume 19, LNCS 8528, Cross-Cultural Design, edited by P.L. Patrick Rau
- Volume 20, LNCS 8529, Digital Human Modeling and Applications in Health, Safety, Ergonomics and Risk Management, edited by Vincent G. Duffy
- Volume 21, LNCS 8530, Distributed, Ambient, and Pervasive Interactions, edited by Norbert Streitz and Panos Markopoulos
- Volume 22, LNCS 8531, Social Computing and Social Media, edited by Gabriele Meiselwitz
- Volume 23, LNAI 8532, Engineering Psychology and Cognitive Ergonomics, edited by Don Harris
- Volume 25, LNAI 8534, Foundations of Augmented Cognition, edited by Dylan D. Schmorrow and Cali M. Fidopiastis
- Volume 26, CCIS 434, HCI International 2014 Posters Proceedings (Part I), edited by Constantine Stephanidis
- Volume 27, CCIS 435, HCI International 2014 Posters Proceedings (Part II), edited by Constantine Stephanidis

I would like to thank the Program Chairs and the members of the Program Boards of all affiliated conferences and thematic areas, listed below, for their contribution to the highest scientific quality and the overall success of the HCI International 2014 Conference.

This conference could not have been possible without the continuous support and advice of the founding chair and conference scientific advisor, Prof. Gavriel Salvendy, as well as the dedicated work and outstanding efforts of the communications chair and editor of *HCI International News*, Dr. Abbas Moallem.

I would also like to thank for their contribution towards the smooth organization of the HCI International 2014 Conference the members of the Human–Computer Interaction Laboratory of ICS-FORTH, and in particular George Paparoulis, Maria Pitsoulaki, Maria Bouhli, and George Kapnas.

April 2014   Constantine Stephanidis
                                                    General Chair, HCI International 2014

Organization

Human–Computer Interaction

Program Chair: Masaaki Kurosu, Japan

Jose Abdelnour-Nocera, UK
Sebastiano Bagnara, Italy
Simone Barbosa, Brazil
Adriana Betiol, Brazil
Simone Borsci, UK
Henry Duh, Australia
Xiaowen Fang, USA
Vicki Hanson, UK
Wonil Hwang, Korea
Minna Isomursu, Finland
Yong Gu Ji, Korea
Anirudha Joshi, India
Esther Jun, USA
Kyungdoh Kim, Korea

Heidi Krömker, Germany
Chen Ling, USA
Chang S. Nam, USA
Naoko Okuizumi, Japan
Philippe Palanque, France
Ling Rothrock, USA
Naoki Sakakibara, Japan
Dominique Scapin, France
Guangfeng Song, USA
Sanjay Tripathi, India
Chui Yin Wong, Malaysia
Toshiki Yamaoka, Japan
Kazuhiko Yamazaki, Japan
Ryoji Yoshitake, Japan

Human Interface and the Management of Information

Program Chair: Sakae Yamamoto, Japan

Alan Chan, Hong Kong
Denis A. Coelho, Portugal
Linda Elliott, USA
Shin'ichi Fukuzumi, Japan
Michitaka Hirose, Japan
Makoto Itoh, Japan
Yen-Yu Kang, Taiwan
Koji Kimita, Japan
Daiji Kobayashi, Japan

Hiroyuki Miki, Japan
Shogo Nishida, Japan
Robert Proctor, USA
Youngho Rhee, Korea
Ryosuke Saga, Japan
Katsunori Shimohara, Japan
Kim-Phuong Vu, USA
Tomio Watanabe, Japan

Engineering Psychology and Cognitive Ergonomics

Program Chair: Don Harris, UK

Guy Andre Boy, USA	Axel Schulte, Germany
Shan Fu, P.R. China	Siraj Shaikh, UK
Hung-Sying Jing, Taiwan	Sarah Sharples, UK
Wen-Chin Li, Taiwan	Anthony Smoker, UK
Mark Neerincx, The Netherlands	Neville Stanton, UK
Jan Noyes, UK	Alex Stedmon, UK
Paul Salmon, Australia	Andrew Thatcher, South Africa

Universal Access in Human–Computer Interaction

Program Chairs: Constantine Stephanidis, Greece, and Margherita Antona, Greece

Julio Abascal, Spain	Georgios Kouroupetroglou, Greece
Gisela Susanne Bahr, USA	Patrick Langdon, UK
João Barroso, Portugal	Barbara Leporini, Italy
Margrit Betke, USA	Eugene Loos, The Netherlands
Anthony Brooks, Denmark	Ana Isabel Paraguay, Brazil
Christian Bühler, Germany	Helen Petrie, UK
Stefan Carmien, Spain	Michael Pieper, Germany
Hua Dong, P.R. China	Enrico Pontelli, USA
Carlos Duarte, Portugal	Jaime Sanchez, Chile
Pier Luigi Emiliani, Italy	Alberto Sanna, Italy
Qin Gao, P.R. China	Anthony Savidis, Greece
Andrina Granić, Croatia	Christian Stary, Austria
Andreas Holzinger, Austria	Hirotada Ueda, Japan
Josette Jones, USA	Gerhard Weber, Germany
Simeon Keates, UK	Harald Weber, Germany

Virtual, Augmented and Mixed Reality

Program Chairs: Randall Shumaker, USA, and Stephanie Lackey, USA

Roland Blach, Germany	Hirokazu Kato, Japan
Sheryl Brahnam, USA	Denis Laurendeau, Canada
Juan Cendan, USA	Fotis Liarokapis, UK
Jessie Chen, USA	Michael Macedonia, USA
Panagiotis D. Kaklis, UK	Gordon Mair, UK

Jose San Martin, Spain
Tabitha Peck, USA
Christian Sandor, Australia

Christopher Stapleton, USA
Gregory Welch, USA

Cross-Cultural Design

Program Chair: P.L. Patrick Rau, P.R. China

Yee-Yin Choong, USA
Paul Fu, USA
Zhiyong Fu, P.R. China
Pin-Chao Liao, P.R. China
Dyi-Yih Michael Lin, Taiwan
Rungtai Lin, Taiwan
Ta-Ping (Robert) Lu, Taiwan
Liang Ma, P.R. China
Alexander Mädche, Germany

Sheau-Farn Max Liang, Taiwan
Katsuhiko Ogawa, Japan
Tom Plocher, USA
Huatong Sun, USA
Emil Tso, P.R. China
Hsiu-Ping Yueh, Taiwan
Liang (Leon) Zeng, USA
Jia Zhou, P.R. China

Online Communities and Social Media

Program Chair: Gabriele Meiselwitz, USA

Leonelo Almeida, Brazil
Chee Siang Ang, UK
Aneesha Bakharia, Australia
Ania Bobrowicz, UK
James Braman, USA
Farzin Deravi, UK
Carsten Kleiner, Germany
Niki Lambropoulos, Greece
Soo Ling Lim, UK

Anthony Norcio, USA
Portia Pusey, USA
Panote Siriaraya, UK
Stefan Stieglitz, Germany
Giovanni Vincenti, USA
Yuanqiong (Kathy) Wang, USA
June Wei, USA
Brian Wentz, USA

Augmented Cognition

Program Chairs: Dylan D. Schmorrow, USA, and Cali M. Fidopiastis, USA

Ahmed Abdelkhalek, USA
Robert Atkinson, USA
Monique Beaudoin, USA
John Blitch, USA
Alenka Brown, USA

Rosario Cannavò, Italy
Joseph Cohn, USA
Andrew J. Cowell, USA
Martha Crosby, USA
Wai-Tat Fu, USA

Rodolphe Gentili, USA
Frederick Gregory, USA
Michael W. Hail, USA
Monte Hancock, USA
Fei Hu, USA
Ion Juvina, USA
Joe Keebler, USA
Philip Mangos, USA
Rao Mannepalli, USA
David Martinez, USA
Yvonne R. Masakowski, USA
Santosh Mathan, USA
Ranjeev Mittu, USA

Keith Niall, USA
Tatana Olson, USA
Debra Patton, USA
June Pilcher, USA
Robinson Pino, USA
Tiffany Poeppelman, USA
Victoria Romero, USA
Amela Sadagic, USA
Anna Skinner, USA
Ann Speed, USA
Robert Sottilare, USA
Peter Walker, USA

Digital Human Modeling and Applications in Health, Safety, Ergonomics and Risk Management

Program Chair: Vincent G. Duffy, USA

Giuseppe Andreoni, Italy
Daniel Carruth, USA
Elsbeth De Korte, The Netherlands
Afzal A. Godil, USA
Ravindra Goonetilleke, Hong Kong
Noriaki Kuwahara, Japan
Kang Li, USA
Zhizhong Li, P.R. China

Tim Marler, USA
Jianwei Niu, P.R. China
Michelle Robertson, USA
Matthias Rötting, Germany
Mao-Jiun Wang, Taiwan
Xuguang Wang, France
James Yang, USA

Design, User Experience, and Usability

Program Chair: Aaron Marcus, USA

Sisira Adikari, Australia
Claire Ancient, USA
Arne Berger, Germany
Jamie Blustein, Canada
Ana Boa-Ventura, USA
Jan Brejcha, Czech Republic
Lorenzo Cantoni, Switzerland
Marc Fabri, UK
Luciane Maria Fadel, Brazil
Tricia Flanagan, Hong Kong
Jorge Frascara, Mexico

Federico Gobbo, Italy
Emilie Gould, USA
Rüdiger Heimgärtner, Germany
Brigitte Herrmann, Germany
Steffen Hess, Germany
Nouf Khashman, Canada
Fabiola Guillermina Noël, Mexico
Francisco Rebelo, Portugal
Kerem Rızvanoğlu, Turkey
Marcelo Soares, Brazil
Carla Spinillo, Brazil

Distributed, Ambient and Pervasive Interactions

Program Chairs: Norbert Streitz, Germany, and Panos Markopoulos, The Netherlands

Juan Carlos Augusto, UK
Jose Bravo, Spain
Adrian Cheok, UK
Boris de Ruyter, The Netherlands
Anind Dey, USA
Dimitris Grammenos, Greece
Nuno Guimaraes, Portugal
Achilles Kameas, Greece
Javed Vassilis Khan, The Netherlands
Shin'ichi Konomi, Japan
Carsten Magerkurth, Switzerland

Ingrid Mulder, The Netherlands
Anton Nijholt, The Netherlands
Fabio Paternó, Italy
Carsten Röcker, Germany
Teresa Romao, Portugal
Albert Ali Salah, Turkey
Manfred Tscheligi, Austria
Reiner Wichert, Germany
Woontack Woo, Korea
Xenophon Zabulis, Greece

Human Aspects of Information Security, Privacy and Trust

Program Chairs: Theo Tryfonas, UK, and Ioannis Askoxylakis, Greece

Claudio Agostino Ardagna, Italy
Zinaida Benenson, Germany
Daniele Catteddu, Italy
Raoul Chiesa, Italy
Bryan Cline, USA
Sadie Creese, UK
Jorge Cuellar, Germany
Marc Dacier, USA
Dieter Gollmann, Germany
Kirstie Hawkey, Canada
Jaap-Henk Hoepman, The Netherlands
Cagatay Karabat, Turkey
Angelos Keromytis, USA
Ayako Komatsu, Japan
Ronald Leenes, The Netherlands
Javier Lopez, Spain
Steve Marsh, Canada

Gregorio Martinez, Spain
Emilio Mordini, Italy
Yuko Murayama, Japan
Masakatsu Nishigaki, Japan
Aljosa Pasic, Spain
Milan Petković, The Netherlands
Joachim Posegga, Germany
Jean-Jacques Quisquater, Belgium
Damien Sauveron, France
George Spanoudakis, UK
Kerry-Lynn Thomson, South Africa
Julien Touzeau, France
Theo Tryfonas, UK
João Vilela, Portugal
Claire Vishik, UK
Melanie Volkamer, Germany

HCI in Business

Program Chair: Fiona Fui-Hoon Nah, USA

Andreas Auinger, Austria
Michel Avital, Denmark
Traci Carte, USA
Hock Chuan Chan, Singapore
Constantinos Coursaris, USA
Soussan Djamasbi, USA
Brenda Eschenbrenner, USA
Nobuyuki Fukawa, USA
Khaled Hassanein, Canada
Milena Head, Canada
Susanna (Shuk Ying) Ho, Australia
Jack Zhenhui Jiang, Singapore
Jinwoo Kim, Korea
Zoonky Lee, Korea
Honglei Li, UK
Nicholas Lockwood, USA
Eleanor T. Loiacono, USA
Mei Lu, USA

Scott McCoy, USA
Brian Mennecke, USA
Robin Poston, USA
Lingyun Qiu, P.R. China
Rene Riedl, Austria
Matti Rossi, Finland
April Savoy, USA
Shu Schiller, USA
Hong Sheng, USA
Choon Ling Sia, Hong Kong
Chee-Wee Tan, Denmark
Chuan Hoo Tan, Hong Kong
Noam Tractinsky, Israel
Horst Treiblmaier, Austria
Virpi Tuunainen, Finland
Dezhi Wu, USA
I-Chin Wu, Taiwan

Learning and Collaboration Technologies

Program Chairs: Panayiotis Zaphiris, Cyprus, and Andri Ioannou, Cyprus

Ruthi Aladjem, Israel
Abdulaziz Aldaej, UK
John M. Carroll, USA
Maka Eradze, Estonia
Mikhail Fominykh, Norway
Denis Gillet, Switzerland
Mustafa Murat Inceoglu, Turkey
Pernilla Josefsson, Sweden
Marie Joubert, UK
Sauli Kiviranta, Finland
Tomaž Klobučar, Slovenia
Elena Kyza, Cyprus
Maarten de Laat, The Netherlands
David Lamas, Estonia

Edmund Laugasson, Estonia
Ana Loureiro, Portugal
Katherine Maillet, France
Nadia Pantidi, UK
Antigoni Parmaxi, Cyprus
Borzoo Pourabdollahian, Italy
Janet C. Read, UK
Christophe Reffay, France
Nicos Souleles, Cyprus
Ana Luísa Torres, Portugal
Stefan Trausan-Matu, Romania
Aimilia Tzanavari, Cyprus
Johnny Yuen, Hong Kong
Carmen Zahn, Switzerland

External Reviewers

Ilia Adami, Greece
Iosif Klironomos, Greece
Maria Korozi, Greece
Vassilis Kouroumalis, Greece

Asterios Leonidis, Greece
George Margetis, Greece
Stavroula Ntoa, Greece
Nikolaos Partarakis, Greece

HCI International 2015

The 15th International Conference on Human–Computer Interaction, HCI International 2015, will be held jointly with the affiliated conferences in Los Angeles, CA, USA, in the Westin Bonaventure Hotel, August 2–7, 2015. It will cover a broad spectrum of themes related to HCI, including theoretical issues, methods, tools, processes, and case studies in HCI design, as well as novel interaction techniques, interfaces, and applications. The proceedings will be published by Springer. More information will be available on the conference website: http://www.hcii2015.org/

General Chair
Professor Constantine Stephanidis
University of Crete and ICS-FORTH
Heraklion, Crete, Greece
Email: cs@ics.forth.gr

Table of Contents

Usable Security

Authentication and Passwords

Security Policy and Awareness

Human Behaviour in Cybersecurity

Privacy Issues

Usable Security

On Supporting Security and Privacy-Preserving Interaction through Adaptive Usable Security

Marios Belk[1], Christos Fidas[1,2], Panagiotis Germanakos[1,3], and George Samaras[1]

[1] Department of Computer Science, University of Cyprus, CY-1678 Nicosia, Cyprus
{belk,cssamara}@cs.ucy.ac.cy
[2] Interactive Technologies Lab, HCI Group, Electrical and Computer Engineering Department,
University of Patras, GR-26504, Patras, Greece
fidas@upatras.gr
[3] SAP AG, Dietmar-Hopp-Allee 16, 69190 Walldorf, Germany
panagiotis.germanakos@sap.com

Abstract. The purpose of this paper is to propose a preliminary framework for supporting usable security on the World Wide Web through adaptivity in user interface designs. In particular we elaborate the concept of "Adaptive Usable Security" and suggest that it is a promising research area aiming to organize and present information and functionalities in an adaptive format to diverse user groups, by using different levels of abstractions through appropriate interaction styles, terminology, information presentation and user modeling techniques related to security and/or privacy preserving tasks. Furthermore, we present components of a preliminary framework aiming to provide guidance in developing "adaptive usable secure" interactive systems. The results and implications of this paper can be considered valuable in elaborating a common architecture for future deployment of adaptive usable security systems on a variety of application areas and services through the World Wide Web.

Keywords: Adaptive Interactive Systems, User Modeling, Usable Security.

1 Introduction

Security and privacy issues of today's interactive systems are considered of paramount importance as it is known that the consequences of a security breach can harm the credibility and legal liability of an organization, decreases users' trust and acceptance while it exponentially increases maintenance and support costs. In this context, one of the most important and challenging issues is to support users, engaged on tasks related to security and privacy, through usable computer human interface designs.

In 2009, the U.S. Government acknowledged "usable security" as one of the eleven hard problems to be researched for achieving cyber security; usable security is a cross-layer issue correlating with all other hard problems related to cyber security which are: scalable trustworthy systems (including system architectures and requisite development methodology), enterprise-level metrics (including measures of overall system trustworthiness), system evaluation life cycle (including approaches for sufficient assurance), combatting insider threats, combatting malware and botnets,

T. Tryfonas and I. Askoxylakis (Eds.): HAS 2014, LNCS 8533, pp. 3–10, 2014.

global-scale identity management, survivability of time-critical systems, situational understanding and attack attribution, provenance (relating to information, systems, and hardware) and privacy-aware security [1]. Usable security is therefore pronounced as the cornerstone of future online services and applications which are expected to offer a rich set of computing and communication services to users in a broader context representing unprecedented opportunities to access, manipulate, and share information as well as to accomplish tasks through heterogeneous devices and contexts of use. Within this realm, adapting functionality and content, of an interactive system, into an assemblance that specific users are able to understand and use intuitively in order to perform specific tasks related to security or privacy issues is a challenging endeavor. It entails understanding and modeling human behavior for diverse user groups and stakeholders, with regards to structural and functional user requirements, which needs to be translated into usable computer human interaction designs and workflows, whilst minimizing user cognitive loads, perceptual and learning efforts aiming to minimize erroneous interactions. Indeed, an erroneous user decision related to security and privacy issues can unarm the most sophisticated security architecture.

Taken into consideration that users of the World Wide Web do not necessarily share common conventions, cultural, and cognitive backgrounds; tools and resources; and contexts in which security and privacy decisions are required to be taken we suggest that adaptive user interfaces [2] (Figure 1) provide a viable alternative in order to ensure usable security and privacy offering equal chances for participation by all. Adaptive user interfaces in the context of usable security provide an alternative to the "one-size-fits-all" approach of static user interfaces by adapting the interactive system's structure, navigation, terminology, functionalities and presentation of content to users' perceptions and level of knowledge with regards to security and privacy related tasks, aiming to increase the usability and provide a positive user experience.

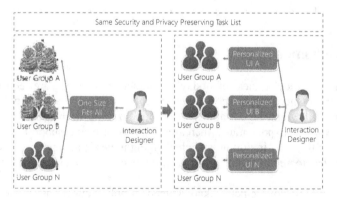

Fig. 1. Adaptive User Interfaces in Usable Secure Systems

The paper is organized as follows: Section 2 elaborates on the notion of adaptive usable security. Section 3 proposes a preliminary framework and presents an example of applying the framework in the frame of an online banking system. Finally, Section 4 concludes the paper and describes directions of future work.

2   Adaptive Usable Security

The notion of usable security has been the subject of numerous research papers since the World Wide Web's exponential growth, and user interface experts have performed several attempts to provide an intuitive way of computer human interaction related to security and privacy preserving tasks [3-7]. However, usable security is still an open research area mainly due to lack of understanding in depth security and privacy tasks and integrating them intuitively in the user interface design process by following a User Centered Approach [7]. User-centered design approaches focus on interacting iteratively with the end-users, especially for identifying and validating user requirements, designing system prototypes as well as for evaluating them. The aim is to investigate thoroughly what users require from a system design and how the system can support them in accomplishing specific tasks effectively, efficiently, and with a certain degree of user satisfaction. An important aspect of this process is to model a user interaction with a user interface. A good design practice aims to establish a common ground among designers and users related to aspects of user-system interaction by formalizing the information architecture of the interactive system and specify the interaction flow for accomplishing specific tasks. A well-used and simple approach to modeling interactive systems is to analyze the user actions in several levels of abstractions and identify on each level the most appropriate terminology, content presentation and interaction flow.

Ineffective practice of usable security, ignore to naturally embed in the system's design, security and privacy issues, and usually adopts a "one size fits all" approach when concerning user interface designs ignoring the fact that different users develop different structural and functional mental models and thus need individual scaffolding. Forming a mental model related to system interaction embraces a seven step iteration cycle [8]. The users form a conceptual intention related to their goal and try to adapt the intention to the features provided by the system and from these, user-perceived features the users try to perform their actions. Subsequently, the users attempt to understand the outcome of their actions by evaluating the system response. The last three stages help the users develop and refine their mental models of the system. The whole process is repeated in iterations of user actions and evaluations which results in developing and refining their mental models by interpreting the system's response. The development and maintenance of user mental models is a dynamic and continuous process, especially related to novice and average users who are still in the process of developing these models based on empirical system interaction. Once these models are created, then the users interact with the system in more automated ways, faster, and more efficiently.

Within this context, supporting usable security of interactive systems with user-adaptive technologies is based on the promise that understanding and modeling human behavior in terms of structural and functional user requirements related to security or privacy preserving tasks can provide an alternative to the "one size fit all" approach aiming to formalize and specify appropriate user modeling that deals with what information is important to be incorporated in the user model and how to represent and extract this information, as well as formalize and specify appropriate adaptation types and mechanisms, and how to communicate them to the adaptive user interfaces in order to improve the system's usable security and user experience.

3   A Preliminary Framework for Adaptive Usable Security

Following a User-Centered Design (UCD) approach the first step of a framework which utilizes the development of an adaptive usable secure interactive system is to identify the user categories and group them according to predefined criteria which are considered to affect interaction design related to usable security. These grouping criteria, can be related with the static or dynamic part of the user or context information model, and need to be identified and specified for each application area as each specific domain embraces its own constructs, user affordances and custom requirements and thus requires to be modeled explicitly. This is further strengthened taking into consideration that usable security has different semantics and specifications in various application areas on the World Wide Web, e.g., e-banking, e-government, e-health, e-gaming, e-entertainment. As an example, providing an adaptive usable security solution to an on-line banking system is a different challenge than providing an adaptive usable security solution to an on-line stock exchange system as in both systems tasks, user groups, terminology and affordances are very different. Thus, it becomes obvious that supporting this attribute needs a modular approach embracing different levels of abstractions related to security and privacy issues that needs to be modeled in each application area explicitly.

Taking into consideration that security and/or privacy preserving tasks are usually secondary tasks which are performed by the users combined with the primary tasks, it becomes mandatory to scaffold this tasks with more sophisticated approaches. In this context, defining appropriate information architecture together with efficient, and effective user interface designs are necessary steps for allowing users to navigate logically through an interactive system and performing intuitively security or privacy preserving tasks in an efficient and effective way with respect to their own individual preferences. This is achieved at early stages of user requirements analysis by defining an appropriate information architecture in terms of organizing, grouping and presenting information, data and results in an understandable format to diverse user groups, by using adaptive content presentation with different levels of abstractions through appropriate interaction styles, terminology and information presentation techniques related to security or privacy preserving tasks. For each task, which affects the security and/or privacy policy, it is proposed to enrich the user interface with valuable information aiming to improve the level of information security awareness for each user category in an appropriate approach based on user and context information.

The proposed framework consists of three main layers; *the security application layer*, *the adaptation layer*, and *the adaptive user interface layer*.

The security application layer identifies specific and important attributes that are dependent on each application domain. As mentioned previously, each application domain has customized requirements with regards to adaptive usable security. In this respect, the security application layer includes the identification of *user categories*, *user model features* (i.e., user and/or context information), *tasks* and *security and privacy implications*, and *adaptation goals* of the adaptive usable security system.

The *user category* dimension supports the classification of user groups according to predefined criteria which are considered to affect interaction design related to usable security.

The *user model* dimension indicates what characteristics of the user could be used as a source of adaptation, i.e., to what characteristics of the user the system can adapt its behavior. The *security and privacy related tasks* indicate what could be adapted in the system, i.e., which features of the system can be different for different users. It is argued that system designers should list the tasks the users are supposed to accomplish through system interaction and analyze these tasks through task analysis techniques, taking into consideration the security and privacy aspects of interaction in order to understand cognitive processes that take place during task completion and may affect security and privacy issues. Given this analysis, the *adaptation goals* should be identified aiming to offer personalized adaptation effects related to security awareness information to specific user categories through appropriate adaptation mechanisms.

The adaptation layer specifies which mechanisms are appropriate for the adaptation of security and privacy related tasks. Simple user customization and rule-based mechanisms could be used to decide what adaptation will be performed on the content and functionality of the system. For example, users could customize the structure and complexity of privacy related tasks. Furthermore, it is argued that collaborative mechanisms [9] could assist the adaptation process by modeling the behaviour of users with similar preferences.

The adaptive user interface layer is responsible for deciding which features of the interface (information architecture or functionality) should be adapted and how the adaptation effect should be transformed into a usable user interface design for improving the system's security. Various adaptive content presentation techniques could be used to provide personalized tasks to the users, such as, expanding/collapsing content fragments based on the user's level of knowledge on security/privacy terminology, or altering the presentation of content based on users' cognitive styles (i.e., Imager/Verbal styles) [10]. Adaptive navigation support could also assist security and privacy related tasks by guiding the user through a security related task, by restricting navigation space to complex tasks, or by augmenting security related tasks with additional information about the task, with appropriate annotations.

3.1   Example of Applying the Framework in an Online Banking System

World Wide Web services and applications entail in their interaction design high quality and extensive security measures aiming to protect themselves and their users from miscellaneous interactions. This includes, for example, ensuring that confidential data sent over the internet cannot be accessed or modified by unauthorized third parties. Typical threats in such contexts are related to deleting or tampering data while they are being transmitted or gaining unauthorized access to system resources or accounts through a variety of techniques such as viruses, trojans, phishing, or hacking.

Within this context, users are expected to perform various tasks related to security, which include, among others, properly configure an antivirus or firewall software, configure browser's security settings, installing certificates, confirm the credentials of the Web server by an independent certificate authority, be aware of hacking tricks such as phishing ("password fishing"), choose secure, difficult to remember passwords. In this realm, user studies revealed the average users either ignore security indicators, such as absence or invalidity of SSL certificates [11] or cannot easily detect and understand this practice and its consequences [12].

We next present and discuss an example of applying the framework for adaptive usable security in an online banking system. In this context, user categories are grouped formed on the user's level of experience in online commercial transactions, such as novice users that use online banking tasks rarely, and expert users that use online banking tasks more often as we assume that expert users have already built their mental models relating to the system usage and need thus less scaffolding and education relating to security tasks.

Table 1. Specification of online banking attributes

Task	Security/Privacy Implications	User Model	Adaptation Goals	Adaptation Mechanism
Login	User Authentication and Authorization	Location, Expertise, Interaction History	Additional support	Rule-based
Configuration	Security/Privacy Configuration	Goals, Knowledge, Background	Increase comprehension	Rule-based, Collaborative
Monetary Transaction	Security Certificates	Goals, Knowledge, Background	Provide security information awareness on certificates	Rule-based, Content-based
Login, Forum	CAPTCHA	Lingual/cultural context	Improve CAPTCHA usability	User customization, Rule-based

The user model incorporates user and context information such as the level of knowledge and background on security and privacy related tasks, individual traits (e.g., cognitive styles), platform characteristics (e.g., device characteristics, bandwidth) and lingual and cultural context characteristics. Primary security and privacy tasks of online banking systems include among others login mechanisms, configuration of security and privacy related settings, and monetary transactions. Table 1 summarizes the attributes of the framework for some of the tasks related to online banking interactions aiming to provide a proof of concept of the proposed framework. It is beyond the aim of this paper to provide an extensive and detailed paradigm on how the proposed framework can be applied in the online banking domain.

In this context some important user tasks related to security are the user authentication and authorization tasks which entail a rule-based adaptation mechanism that is used to assess the user's expertise and interaction history with the system by tracking the number of login attempts. The number of login attempts indicates the system to automatically offer security information awareness to the user or appropriate live customer support option to users who could not succeed to login in the system for several times. Furthermore, CAPTCHA [13] challenges which are required during failed login attempts aiming to provide a high confidence proof that it is a human being trying to gain access to the system, are adapted to user's lingual and cultural context [14] by utilizing simple user customization techniques and rule-based mechanisms (i.e., user indicates through a checkbox that (s)he prefers localized CAPTCHAs).

During monetary transactions, security certificate installation processes take into consideration the user's current goal or level of knowledge on certificates with the use of a weighed knowledge model that indicates the level of knowledge on specific security/privacy related terms. Based on this information about the user, the certificate is augmented with additional information, in the form of annotations in order to increase the comprehension of the security certificate. Content-based mechanisms [15] are also used to create a vector of keywords of the certificate and compare them with the user's weighed knowledge model to augment the security/privacy terms, that the user is not familiar, with additional information.

4   Conclusions and Future Work

In this paper a preliminary framework is proposed for supporting the design and deployment of usable and secure interactive systems driven primarily by the need to define more effective and efficient User-Centered Design (UCD) techniques related to usable security. It is argued that for supporting efficient and effective usable security, research in this area should partially move its focus away from the technical issues towards understanding the end users and developing approaches which can be applied in offering better awareness on security and privacy issues on an application domain, user and task level.

Within this realm the concept of adaptive usable security is elaborated with the aim to offer personalized security information awareness, to specific group of users who are engaged in accomplishing specific tasks within certain application domains, by rendering the information architecture and adapting its functionality based on user preferences and contexts of use. Adaptive usable security implies the ability of an interactive system to support its end users, who are engaged in security and/or privacy related tasks, based on user models which describe in a holistic way what constitutes the user's physical, cognitive and social context in which computation takes place. Such an approach facilitates, among others, reasoning of context-based rules which describe in a declarative way conditions which are considered important and need further investigation, scaffolding or detailed analysis by the designer.

The added value of the proposed framework relies on the fact that it speeds up the integration and adaption process of usable security by separating domain knowledge from the operational knowledge by describing a multilayer formal context model aiming to provide a common representation of contextual information, facilitating thus usable security aspects of an interactive system.

The aim of this paper is to increase our understanding and knowledge on supporting usable security interaction design through user modeling, and adaptivity in user interfaces based on adaptation mechanisms. Taking into consideration that future World Wide Web interactive systems will embrace a variety of factors affecting security and privacy issues across various application domains (like e-banking, e-government, e-health etc.) approaches like the proposed one can be of general value. Achieving usable security in future interactive systems will have wider social and economic impact by helping citizens to understand and familiarize with secure services and best practices for security and privacy on interactive systems which will offer a rich set of computation and communication services.

Future work, consist in developing suite of methods and techniques for understanding user attitudes and perceptions towards security and privacy issues in various application areas, transforming them into software specifications, designing and finally evaluating appropriate adaptive user interface designs in different contexts of use.

Acknowledgements. The work is co-funded by the PersonaWeb project under the Cyprus Research Promotion Foundation (ΤΠΕ/ΠΛΗΡΟ/0311(BIE)/10), and the EU project SocialRobot (285870).

References

1. Department of Homeland Security: A Roadmap for Cybersecurity Research (2009), http://www.cyber.st.dhs.gov/docs/DHS-Cybersecurity-Roadmap.pdf
2. Brusilovsky, P., Kobsa, A., Nejdl, W.: The Adaptive Web: Methods and Strategies of Web Personalization. Springer, Heidelberg (2007)
3. Adams, A., Sasse, M.A.: Users Are Not the Enemy: Why Users Compromise Security Mechanisms and How to Take Remedial Measures. J. Communications of the ACM. 42(12), 40–46 (1999)
4. Cranor, L., Garfinkel, S.: O'Reilly Media, Inc. (2005)
5. Shay, R., Kelley, P., Komanduri, S., Mazurek, M., Ur, B., Vidas, T., Bauer, L., Christin, N., Cranor, L.: Correct Horse Battery Staple: Exploring the Usability of System-assigned Passphrases. In: ACM Symposium on Usable Privacy and Security, Article 7, 20 pages. ACM Press, New York (2012)
6. Biddle, R., Chiasson, S., van Oorschot, P.: Graphical Passwords: Learning from the First Twelve Years. J. ACM Computing Surveys 44(4), 41 pages (2012)
7. Fidas, C.A., Voyiatzis, A.G., Avouris, N.M.: When security meets usability: A user-centric approach on a crossroads priority problem. In: Proc. of Panhellenic Conference on Informatics, PCI 2010, pp. 112–117. IEEE Computer Society (2010)
8. Norman, D.: The Design of Everyday Things. Psychology of Everyday Action. New York (1988)
9. Su, X., Khoshgoftaar, T.: A Survey of Collaborative Filtering Techniques. J. Advances in Artificial Intelligence, Article 4, 19 pages (2009)
10. Riding, R., Cheema, I.: Cognitive Styles – An Overview and Integration. J. Educational Psychology 11(3-4), 193–215 (1991)
11. Schecter, S.E., Dhamija, R., Ozment, A., Fischer, I.: The Emperor's New Security Indicators: An evaluation of website authentication and the effect of role playing on usability studies. In: Proc. of IEEE Symposium on Security and Privacy (2007)
12. Falk, L., Prakash, A., Borders, K.: Analyzing Websites for User-Visible Security Design Flaws. In: Proc. of Symposium on Usable Privacy and Security, pp. 117–126. ACM Press (2008)
13. von Ahn, L., Blum, M., Langford, J.: Telling Humans and Computers Apart Automatically. J. Communications of the ACM 47, 56–60 (2004)
14. Fidas, C., Voyiatzis, A., Avouris, N.: On the Necessity of User-friendly CAPTCHA. In: Proc. of Human Factors in Computing Systems, CHI 2011, pp. 2623–2626. ACM Press (2011)
15. Smyth, B.: Case-based recommendation. In: Brusilovsky, P., Kobsa, A., Nejdl, W. (eds.) Adaptive Web 2007. LNCS, vol. 4321, pp. 342–376. Springer, Heidelberg (2007)

A Network Telescope for Early Warning Intrusion Detection

Panos Chatziadam, Ioannis G. Askoxylakis, and Alexandros Fragkiadakis

FORTHcert, Institute of Computer Science Foundation for Research & Technology –
Hellas (FORTH)
{panosc,asko,alfrag}@ics.forth.gr

Abstract. Proactive cyber-security tools provide basic protection as today's cyber-criminals utilize legitimate traffic to perform attacks and remain concealed quite often until it is too late. As critical resources, hidden behind layers of cyber-defenses, can still become compromised with potentially catastrophic consequences, it is of paramount significance to be able to identify cyber-attacks and prepare a proper defense as early as possible. In this paper we will go over the architecture, deployment and usefulness of a distributed network of honeypots that relies on darknets to obtain its data. As we have envisioned that such a system has the potential to detect large scale events as early as possible we have adopted the name Early Warning Intrusion System (EWIS).

Keywords: Human aspects of intelligence-driven cybersecurity.

1 Introduction

Honeypots (HP) can capture and identify not only known but also emerging cyber-attacks. As a HP is not generating any network activity, any traffic that is directed toward it, it is considered to be malicious. An active HP can interact with the attacking system and capture the data flow so that it can be analyzed at a later point. The attack can then be classified as a known attack with an established approach for resolution, or a new kind of attack that has to be analyzed in order to produce a way to act upon it. Honeypots that interact with the attacking system can be classified either as low-interaction or high-interaction. Low-interaction HPs will interact with the attacking system by realistically emulating specific Operating Systems (OS) and services thus allowing the full capture of the attack in progress. Beyond this emulation they will not allow further control to the attackers thus posing little security risk. High-interaction HP on the other hand, become fully exposed to Internet attacks. This method can provide a full view of the specifics of the attack as well as the technique the attacker has used to perform the attack but it's also quite risky as an attacker can establish control of them just like with any other real system. Often security analysts consider them unsafe to use as they pose a risk to real production systems should they be breached by an attacker [1].

T. Tryfonas and I. Askoxylakis (Eds.): HAS 2014, LNCS 8533, pp. 11–22, 2014.

While HPs can provide extensive information about an attack carried out to a specific system, utilizing specific methods and resources, they lack the capability of observing the big picture. Consequently, large scale events go unnoticed by HPs that can only focus on attacks carried out on them. If an attack is initiated towards an organization, unless it is directed to the HP itself first, there will be so little knowledge regarding the attack, that by the time it reaches the HP it may have affected many systems. A large deployment of HPs enhances the probability of the attacker hitting one of them; however, managing many HPs has been proven to be a prohibited affair [1].

Network telescopes (NT) allow the capture of attacking data on a wider scale. In principle, a NT allows the observation of large scale events by capturing traffic from dark (unutilized) Internet address spaces. The more dark address spaces a NT monitors, the higher its resolution is [1] thus making it capable of detecting a wider range of events. A NT is also safe to use as it passively captures traffic without interacting with it. A distributed NT [2] may consist of many devices (sensors) that reside on remote networks capturing traffic from dark address spaces and relaying it back to a central server so that it can be classified and analyzed. This is the approach we have adopted for our system which has been largely influenced, in regards to its architecture and implementation, by project NoAH [3]. This work will be presented as follows. Section 2 offers implementation insights whereas Section 3 goes through the components of the system. In Section 4 we present visualizations of the collected data, while Section 5 offers a discussion on EWIS' benefits and future potential. Lastly, we summarize in Section 6.

2   Concepts and Implementation

Our vision was to establish a system that would be cost effective to implement, easy to deploy and provide us with sufficient data to create an Early Warning System that could potentially detect large scale events on a global scale. A potential implementation of a NT was found to exceed our needs and expectations. As it operates on unused address spaces, all traffic reaching it can be classified as malicious thus avoiding unnecessary filtering of legitimate traffic. While there are two major types of NTs we have adopted our design to be of a passive NT as opposed to an active implementation. A passive NT can capture data from UDP and ICMP attacks making it possible to detect DoS attacks [4] and UDP worms. Nevertheless, it is incapable of detecting malicious traffic as a result of application exploitation of captured TCP traffic since it does not complete a TCP handshake [5].

As it is very difficult for an organization to dedicate a large number of IPv4 addresses to the NT, our design had to include a number of smaller NTs that would be combined to create a large NT. These smaller telescopes (sensors) would have to be easily deployable, fit easily within an organization's network infrastructure and be robust enough to continuously capture traffic and relay it back for analysis. As security is a major concern, the sensors would have to be built on a secured OS platform, run the bare minimum and be protected by a firewall. The fact that our sensors utilize a passive approach to data collection is also a favorable point by an organization that certainly doesn't need any devices within their infrastructure to be talking back to a potential attacker. From a network topology point of view, the sensors should be positioned outside the organization's network on the Demilitarized Zone (DMZ) or even the public section of the network just outside the organization's firewall (Fig.1)

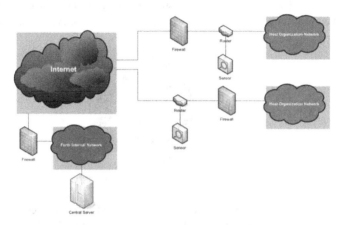

Fig. 1. Possible scenarios for sensor deployment

Isolating the sensor from the organization's Intranet and at the same time fully exposing it to the outside world is the best way for deployment. Should the sensor be compromised there would be no posed threat to the internal network of the host organization. In such an unlikely case, we can simply replace the sensor.

3   Architecture and Deployment

The previous sections have offered several hints as to how our NT is architected and implemented. We will look further into that in this section.

3.1   The Sensors

The initial sensor rollout consisted of small, inexpensive PCs preconfigured and ready to use (Fig.2). Recently, we are experimenting in utilizing very small computing platforms [6] as sensors, such as the Raspberry Pi [7]. A deployable bootable image is also under development. Software cost has also been minimized by utilizing in-house built applications and running them on a Linux-based open source OS.

Prior to deployment, each sensor is assigned a dark network space that could span from a few IPs to entire subnets. Assigning the dark space addresses to the network interface of the sensor was proven to be impractical and time consuming. Instead, we utilized a redirection on the ARP level [1]. When traffic arrives for a specific IP address the router broadcasts an ARP request for discovering the host. When the host replies to the ARP request as the owner of the corresponding IP address, the router directs all traffic to this host. To utilize this methodology of traffic direction we used a daemon called *farpd*. For *farpd* to function, it has to be assigned the IP addresses it will respond for when receiving the gateway's ARP request. While this method is the most non-intrusive when deploying a sensor to an organization's network, it may prove to be inefficient and resource consuming when monitoring very large blocks of dark space networks [1]. In this case, a static redirection on the router level, for all traffic of the monitored dark addresses would be a more effective solution [1].

Fig. 2. Hardware used for initial versions of the sensor

Next, the *monitoring* daemon captures the received traffic and records a subset of the popular format NetFlow [8] to the database. This in-house developed daemon uses the *pcap* library to capture information such as the source and destination IP addresses, the source and destination ports, the flow payload size, the protocol type (number), the TCP flag (in case the flow is of TCP type) and the associated timestamp. As with *farpd* the *monitoring* daemon is also assigned the IP addresses that it should be recording traffic for, as well as the network interface in case the sensor has multiple interfaces (we would utilize multiple physical interfaces to place the sensor itself on a different network subnet than the dark space network it will monitor).

On a timely interval, the sensor will initiate a reverse SSH tunnel so that the central server will pull the collected data from the sensor's database. We utilize strong encryption and password-less shared key authentication for the tunnel. The reverse tunnel utilizes a predefined port and triggers a component on the server side that will perform the data collection. The sensor utilizes a number of PHP and BASH scripts for automating the process of daemon startup, tunnel opening, information transfer as well as database maintenance. SSH access is restricted to the IP of the central server as well to a specific IP of the host organization should they request remote access to the sensor. For this, as well as console operations in case of an emergency, the host organization is given access to a local user account on the sensor.

3.2   Central Server

The EWIS central server is where all data collected by the sensors is stored, processed, analyzed and presented. It is hosted at FORTH's main datacenter and it is maintained as a high priority system by FORTH's Systems and Networks team. The hardware we are using for the central server is of server class with all possible redundancies for continuous operation and high availability. The server's PostgreSQL [9] database has been tuned to be able to cope with the volume of data downloaded from the sensors as well as to quickly respond to concurrent queries for the purpose of displaying the collected data. At the time that this document is written the *packets* table in the server's database has over 900 million records.

Every download from each of the sensors is logged and its timestamp is recorded so that downloads resume from that point forward. Each downloaded set consists of the captured traffic that has been recorded since the last download as well as the list of IPs the sensor monitors. This is useful to have in the database as it is used in filtering data when performing certain queries. Similarly to the sensors, PHP and BASH scripts are used for the automation of procedures such as the process of data transfer from the sensor, the parsing and commitment of data to the server's database, the monitoring of the sensors, the issue of alerts etc.

The sensors are monitored in regards to their ability to connect with the server and the integrity of the downloaded data set. If the sensor's communication is late, the state of the sensor is changed to potentially down while if the sensor fails to connect to the server the sensor's state is changed to down. If a sensor is flagged down, the support team will attempt to access the sensor to investigate the issue. If the sensor is not accessible from the server side, the issue will be communicated to a contact on the host organization so that the sensor's situation can be assessed from the console. Both the sensors and the server are monitored on a 24 hour basis so to provide an uninterrupted flow of data to the system.

4   Visualization Dashboard

The central server is utilizing a web interface for the users to interact with the data collected as well as perform some administrative functions. The web interface is comprised of a collection of PHP scripts that provide a functional and versatile environment. Access to this facility is given to the organizations that host a sensor as well as other individuals that may need access to the data for research purposes. Typically the host organization would only be allowed access to the data of their own sensor(s) while an admin type user will have access to the entire range of information stored.

The current implementation of this interface is rather minimalistic; however, a more comprehensive implementation is work in progress. There are several views that offer real-time queries to the statistics downloaded from the sensors.

4.1   Sum of Packets

The following three plots (Fig.3, Fig.4 and Fig.5) provide a trend of incoming traffic to the dark address spaces allocated to the sensor. Sudden changes observed from hour to hour (Fig.3) is an indication that an attack is likely to be taking place. The second and third graphs (Fig.4, Fig.5) display days of the week and weeks of the year respectfully and are meant more for statistical than alerting purposes.

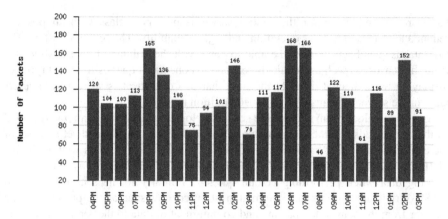

Fig. 3. The number of packets the sensor has received for each of the past 24 hours

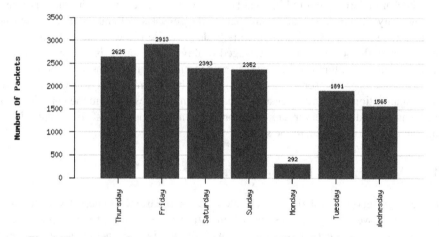

Fig. 4. The number of packets the sensor has received for each of the last 7 days

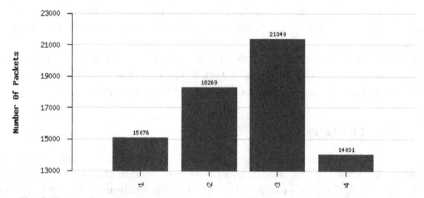

Fig. 5. The number of packets the sensor has received for each of the past 4 weeks

4.2   Top Statistics

This view has three tables that provide an assortment of top 10 statistics within a defined timeframe (Fig.6). For all three tables the user has the option to select the timeframe and top count option.

Source IP Addresses			Destination TCP/UDP Ports			Countries		
Source IP	Packet Count	Country	Destination Port	Packet Count	Trend	Total Packets	Country	Top IP
94.23.188.195 (?)	960		22 (?)	7991	▲	5153		61.147.103.142 (?)
188.138.125.48 (?)	944		5060 (?)	793	▼	2948		54.193.47.198 (?)
186.216.174.39 (?)	288		80 (?)	650	▼	1929		188.138.125.48 (?)
192.95.15.21 (?)	216		1433 (?)	509	▼	1140		94.23.188.195 (?)
54.193.47.198 (?)	204		8080 (?)	365	▼	698		186.216.174.39 (?)
61.147.103.142 (?)	200		3389 (?)	298	▼	501		89.248.172.195 (?)
218.2.22.107 (?)	192		23 (?)	291	▲	416		77.40.50.146 (?)
183.62.118.142 (?)	190		53 (?)	251	▼	396		192.95.15.21 (?)
89.248.172.195 (?)	168		21320 (?)	201	▼	316		180.225.203.220 (?)
207.244.66.108 (?)	151		443 (?)	148	▼	314		210.61.135.104 (?)

Fig. 6. Three tables providing statistics based on selected timeframe and top count

The left table, labeled *Source IP Addresses*, offers a list of the top 10 source IP addresses within the past 7 days. Next to each IP address is the accumulated number of packets the IP sent on the selected timeframe, as well as its country of origin. The flags displayed are the result of a match between the result of geoiplookup [10] and a local cache of flag icons. Selecting one of the source IP addresses the user will be presented with a list of all the IP flows received within the timeframe (Fig.7).

Source PORT	Destination IP	Destination PORT	Protocol	TCP Flags	Payload Size	Timestamp (sec)
6884		5060	UDP	******	406	2014-01-25T08:38:00+02:00
6884		5060	UDP	******	408	2014-01-25T08:38:00+02:00
6884		5060	UDP	******	408	2014-01-27T07:45:41+02:00
6884		5060	UDP	******	405	2014-01-25T08:38:00+02:00
6884		5060	UDP	******	408	2014-01-27T07:45:41+02:00
6884		5060	UDP	******	407	2014-01-25T08:38:00+02:00
6884		5060	UDP	******	407	2014-01-25T08:38:00+02:00
6884		5060	UDP	******	409	2014-01-27T07:45:41+02:00
6884		5060	UDP	******	404	2014-01-25T08:38:00+02:00
6884		5060	UDP	******	405	2014-01-27T07:45:41+02:00

Fig. 7. Truncated list of IP flows received within the past 7 day from the selected IP

Selecting the question mark next to the IP will perform a reverse DNS lookup and display the associated FQDN if one exists (Fig.8).

Hostname for IP 207.244.66.108 = hosted-by.leaseweb.com.

Fig. 8. FQDN name of selected IP

Selecting the source or destination port on the table of Fig.7 will result on a lookup of the port on an online resource database. If there are known applications that use the specific port, their names will be displayed (Fig.9).

| sip | 5060 | TCP | IANA | SIP |
| sip | 5060 | UDP | IANA | SIP |

Fig. 9. Destination port 5060 lookup

The table in the center of Fig.6, labeled *Destination TCP/UDP ports*, offers a list of the top 10 destination ports for the selected timeframe. Next to each port is the total packet count received for that timeframe and in the last column an indicator of the traffic trend. By selecting one of the ports, a list of all the IP flows received within the selected timeframe (Fig.10) is provided. The selection of the traffic trend indicator, offers a plot that illustrates the traffic trend of received packets for the selected destination port within the selected timeframe (Fig.11). This provides an explicit view of how incoming traffic changes for a specific timeframe while sudden rises suggest that perhaps a major event is taking place.

Source IP	Source PORT	Destination IP	Destination PORT	Protocol	Flags	Timestamp (sec)
85.25.199.95	5263		5060	UDP	0	2014-01-23T15:50:07+02:00
85.25.199.95	5263		5060	UDP	0	2014-01-23T15:50:07+02:00
85.25.199.95	5263		5060	UDP	0	2014-01-23T15:50:07+02:00
85.25.199.95	5263		5060	UDP	0	2014-01-23T15:50:07+02:00
85.25.199.95	5263		5060	UDP	0	2014-01-23T15:50:07+02:00
85.25.199.95	5263		5060	UDP	0	2014-01-23T15:50:07+02:00
85.25.199.95	5263		5060	UDP	0	2014-01-23T15:50:07+02:00
85.25.199.95	5263		5060	UDP	0	2014-01-23T15:50:07+02:00
85.25.199.95	5263		5060	UDP	0	2014-01-23T15:50:07+02:00
85.25.199.95	5263		5060	UDP	0	2014-01-23T15:50:07+02:00

Fig. 10. Truncated list of IP flows received within the past 7 days for the selected port

The rightmost table on Fig.6, labeled *Countries*, presents a top list of countries sorted by total packet number and the top source IP address from that country. This enables the viewer to quickly identify the top attacking country/IP address combination for a quick action against the attacking pair, such as submitting the information to the national CERT of the country in question. Selecting an IP address from the table will display a list of all the IP flows received from the selected source IP within the selected timeframe (Fig.7). As previously mentioned, selecting the question mark next to the IP will perform a reverse DNS lookup of the IP and display the associated FQDN if one exists (Fig.8).

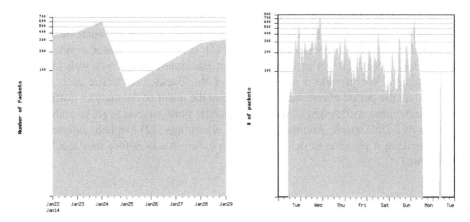

Fig. 11. 7 day traffic trend to destination port

Fig. 12. 7 day trend of backscatter traffic

4.3   Protocol and Backscatter

The third view provides protocol breakdown statistics in three separate graphs (Fig.13). The left graph, labeled *Incoming TCP Traffic*, offers a view of the top ten destination ports and the total number of packets received for each port within the last 24 hours. In a similar manner, the right graph labeled *Incoming UDP Traffic*, offers a view of the top ten destination ports and the total number of packets received for each port within the last 24 hours. The bottom graph illustrates a breakdown of percentages of TCP, UDP and ICMP traffic received during the last 24 hours.

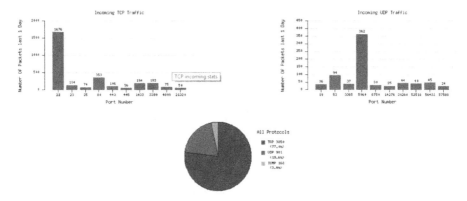

Fig. 13. Protocol Breakdown Statistics

By selecting the bar of a charted port on either the TCP or UDP graph the traffic trend of that port (Fig.11) is displayed. This provides a further understanding as to whether an attack is taking place or the activity of the port is normal as usual.

The sensors also receive responses from hosts that have received packets spoofed with sender's address to be one of the monitored dark space addresses. This unsolicited traffic, also known as Backscatter [11], is a known indicator or side-effect of a spoofed DoS attack. An ascending trend of Backscatter traffic is a well justified cause for alert. We provide a plot (Fig.12) of the Backscatter traffic each sensor receives over the period of one week. Associating the result of Backscatter traffic on a specific timeframe with spikes of traffic on specific ports we can begin to realize the detection of a DoS attack. Anomaly detection algorithms [12] can help automate the process making it possible to detect upcoming cyber-attacks before they reach their full potential.

4.4   Sensor Information

The Sensors view provides information on the sensor location and availability (Fig.14). This section is only available to admin users as it discloses privileged information regarding each sensor such as its IP address, geographical location and host organization. On the left side of Fig.14 there is a table showing the sensor names (hidden for privacy) and their availability status. As mentioned previously, should a sensor fail to contact the server an escalation to the EWIS support team takes place by utilizing email and SMS [13]. If needed, the host organization is contacted to provide hands on assistance to the hardware of the sensor.

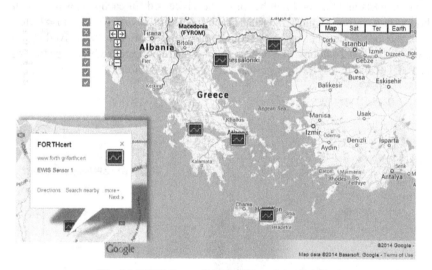

Fig. 14. EWIS Sensor Information and Availability

5   Discussion

EWIS provides a scalable platform for detecting emerging network threats on a large scale. By increasing the number of sensors the resolution of our NT also increases providing more accurate results and less false positives when predicting upcoming attacks [1]. A large number of sensors will provide the resolution necessary to create an international Network Alert Weather Map.

Current means of visualization of the captured data provides a basic platform of analysis at a satisfactory level. We envision an automated procedure that will be able to correlate past and present data and provide results without human intervention. Algorithms of pattern recognition and anomaly detection [12] can further enhance the predictive capability and even provide an early warning alert of a large scale event at its early stages. An alerting system can subsequently inform our sensor hosts of an upcoming threat such as a Worm or Distributed DoS (DDoS) attack. DDoS attacks are considered a product of SYN Floods received from compromised hosts (zombies) [14] and can be detected by monitoring the backscatter traffic [11]. Worms can be detected by monitoring for excessively large portions of traffic. Known examples are Conficker [15], Blaster [16] and Nimda [16], all utilizing port 445/TCP used by CIFS [17].

At the time this document was compiled, a total of 7 sensors have been installed to an assortment of organizations ranging from small to large and from government operated to public sector. Although all functioning sensors are installed within Greece, a sensor was once hosted by the Computer Emergency Response Team of Austria (cert.at) [18] as part of a joined project with FORTHcert. To further expand the functionality of the EWIS NT we envision a merge with other NTs and Darknets [19] already functioning on the Internet such as the UCSD NT [20], the CCIED NT project[21], Oxford University's Darknet Mesh project [19] and Team Cymru's Darknet project[22]. We are also exploring the possibility of enhancing EWIS's capabilities by adding sensors that detect attacks on wireless networks[23].

6   Conclusion

The current deployment of EWIS has served well as an operational pilot and has provided an interesting assortment of data. Our main goal was to create a functional framework that would work as the basis of a distributed NT that could scale well beyond our national borders. The passive sensors deployed seamlessly on a host organization's infrastructure pave the road for a topologically diverse deployment. The security utilized for sensor to server transfers combined with tight software integration and a scalable database, makes EWIS a competent platform. The functional traffic analysis interface provides the means of basic data exploitation while the implementation of more advanced visualization tools is work in progress. The use of advanced backend data processing by utilizing anomaly detection algorithms [12] will assist in uncovering large scale malicious events such as DDoS attacks and worms.

By forming alliances with other organizations operating their own NTs we will be able to create a very large NT of global scale that could provide us and our partners the ability to have an aggregate view of Internet traffic across operational boundaries.

References

1. Irwin, B.: A framework for the application of network telescope sensors in a global IP network (January 2011)
2. Pouget, F., Dacier, M., Pham, V.: Vh: Leurre.com: on the advantages of deploying a large scale distributed honeypot platform. In: ECCE 2005, E-Crime and Computer Evidence, pp. 1–13 (2005)
3. Final Report - NoAH (NoAH: a European Network of Affined Honeypots) (2008)
4. Spyridopoulos, T., Karanikas, G., Tryfonas, T., Oikonomou, G.: A game theoretic defence framework against DoS/DDoS cyber attacks. Computers & Security 38, 39–50 (2013)
5. Cooke, E., Bailey, M., Watson, D., Jahanian, F., Nazario, J.: The Internet motion sensor: A distributed global scoped Internet threat monitoring system, 1–16 (2004)
6. Akram, R.N., Markantonakis, K., Mayes, K.: User centric security model for tamper-resistant devices. In: Proceedings - 2011 8th IEEE International Conference on e-Business Engineering, ICEBE 2011, pp. 168–177 (2011)
7. Raspberry Pi, http://www.raspberry.org
8. Bailey, M., Cooke, E., Jahanian, F., Myrick, A., Sinha, S.: Practical Darknet Measurement. In: 40th Annual Conference on Information Sciences and Systems (2006)
9. PostgreSQL, http://www.postgresql.org
10. Maxmind, http://www.maxmind.com
11. Moore, D., Shannon, C., Brown, D.: Inferring internet denial-of-service activity. ACM Transactions (2006)
12. Bhuyan, M.H., Bhattacharyya, D.K., Kalita, J.K.: Surveying Port Scans and Their Detection Methodologies. The Computer Journal 54(10), 1565–1581 (2011)
13. Akram, R., Markantonakis, K. (n.d.): Smart Cards: State-of-the-Art to Future Directions. crow.org.nz
14. Cooke, E., Jahanian, F., McPherson, D.: The zombie roundup: Understanding, detecting, and disrupting botnets. In: USENIX SRUTI Workshop (2005)
15. Symantec, W32.downadup, http://www.symantec.com
16. Cisco, Branch router QoS design, http://www.cisco.com
17. Internet file system, http://www.snia.org
18. Computer Emergency Response Team of Austria, cert.at
19. Oxford University, The Darknet Mesh Project, projects.oucs.ox.ac.uk
20. Caida, The UCSD Network Telescope, http://www.caida.org/projects/network_telescope/
21. ICSI, CCIED Network Telescope, http://www.icir.org/vern/telescope.html
22. Team Cymru, The Darknet Project, http://www.team-cymru.org
23. Fragkiadakis, A.G., Tragos, E.Z., Tryfonas, T., Askoxylakis, I.G.: Design and performance evaluation of a lightweight wireless early warning intrusion detection prototype. EURASIP Journal on Wireless Communications and Networking (1), 73 (2012)

Visualization of System Log Files for Post-incident Analysis and Response

John Haggerty and Thomas Hughes-Roberts

School of Science and Technology, Nottingham Trent University, Clifton Campus,
Clifton Lane, Nottingham, NG11 8NS
{john.haggerty,thomas.hughesroberts}@ntu.ac.uk

Abstract. Post-incident analysis of a security event is a complex task due to the volume of data that must be assessed, often within tight temporal constraints. System software, such as operating systems and applications, provide a range of opportunities to record data in log files about interactions with the computer that may provide evidence during an investigation. Data visualization can be used to aid data set interpretation and improve the ability of the analyst to make sense of information. This paper posits a novel methodology that visualizes data from a range of log files to aid the investigation process. In order to demonstrate the applicability of the approach, a case study of identification and analysis of attacks is presented.

Keywords: Visualization, system logs, triage, intrusion detection.

1   Introduction

Post-incident analysis of a security event is a complex task due to the amount of data that must be triaged and analyzed from multiple sources. This analysis may involve just one computer, for example a Web server on the perimeter of the network boundary, or many computers within a large, interconnected system. Depending on the attack itself, evidence will be resident on the victim system in a variety of locations that may help the security analyst understand the attacker's actions and thus enable the organization to secure their systems.

In order to identify attacks against our systems and their perpetrators, system log files may be used as one form of evidence during an investigation. Current operating systems contain various log files that record a wide range of data and contain a wealth of information for the security analyst. For example, dependent on system configuration, log files may record information such as network nodes that have (or are) connected with the system under investigation, failed login attempts to a user account or interactions remote nodes have had with a victim system. However, the volume, diversity and format of system logs make this evidence source intractable for post-incident analysis and response.

The textual format of log files often results in such data rarely being analyzed despite the wealth of information that they may contain. For example, whilst an organization may invest a considerable sum of money in perimeter-based protections,

T. Tryfonas and I. Askoxylakis (Eds.): HAS 2014, LNCS 8533, pp. 23–32, 2014.
© Springer International Publishing Switzerland 2014

such as a firewalls and Intrusion Detection Systems (IDS), it is rare that the logs that these systems produce are accessed and routinely analyzed. This paper therefore posits a novel approach to the visualization of system logs to encourage users to interact with such files on a regular basis. Moreover, as will be demonstrated by the case study in this paper, the results of these visualizations can be used to identify attacks against our systems.

This paper is organized as follows. Section 2 discusses related work. Section 3 posits the methodology for visualization of log files for post-incident analysis and response. Section 4 presents the results of a case study to demonstrate the applicability of the approach. Finally, we make our conclusions and discuss further work.

2   Related Work

Due to the complexity and volume of information available today, there is much interest in data visualization outside the security domain. The applications of data visualization are wide and varied. For example, Changbo Wang et al (2013) propose *SentiView*, a visualization system to analyze multiple attributes and relationships within demographics of interest and the sentiments of participants on popular topics. Alternatively, Guerra-Gomez et al (2013) propose a system for the analysis of data change over time by creating dynamic hierarchies based on the data attributes. Schmidt et al (2013) focus on the requirement for image comparison through *VAICo*, a system which visualizes differences and similarities in large sets of images and preserves contextual information. Another application of data visualization has been proposed by Krishnan et al (2012) for the representation of anatomic and time-varying flow data sets within the health sector.

The benefits of data visualization and interaction for large data sets have ensured that such approaches have been adopted within the security and forensics domains. Visualization enables an analyst to gain an overview of data during an investigation (Schrenk and Poisel, 2011). For example, Haggerty et al (2014) propose *TagSNet*, an approach for the quantitative and qualitative analysis of email data to enable a forensics examiner to analyze not only actor relationships but also visualize discourse between those actors. Koniaris et al (2013) present visualizations of their results of detecting attackers utilizing SSH vulnerabilities to attack honeypot systems. Promrit et al (2011) propose an approach that analyzes simulated network traffic and their features to identify a variety of attacks through visualization. Ando et al (2010) propose *Blink*, an approach for the monitoring and visualization of peer-to-peer traffic to identify security incidents that may arise in such network architectures. Giacobe and Xen Su (2011) propose an approach to visually represent security data in a geographical sphere based on IP address rather than physical location. These visualization schemes have in common that they are only targeted at a particular type of investigation or attack rather than providing a systemic overview of available data to aid the security effort.

Visualization can play an important role in informing security decisions regardless of the relative skill and knowledge of the user. For example, Stoll et al (2008) propose *Sesame*, a user interface aimed at conceptualizing security such that users will be motivated and informed enough to take appropriate action. Furthermore, it is well highlighted that network security often deals with large amounts data that humans can find difficult to cope with and visualization of that data provides a clears means of streamlining the analysis process (Dunlop et al, 2012) for all potential stakeholders. Hence, the visualization of data from seemingly complex, and often underused, log files may provide a method of analysis that is relevant to range of end-users.

Recent work has posited schemes for the analysis of security device, such as firewalls and IDS, log files for post-incident analysis and response. For example, Schmerl et al (2010) propose an approach to visualize system audit information to develop IDS signatures in order to respond to network attacks. An approach proposed by Nishioka et al (2011) attempts to identify system data leakage or incorrect system operations that may be related to security incidents. Mantoro et al (2013) propose a system to detect SQL injection attacks by visualizing traffic and intrusion detection logs. Thomson et al (2013) propose *Pianola*, a system for visualizing and understanding the contents of intrusion detection logs. The use of security system logs as the basis for post-incident analysis and visualization remains problematic for two reasons. First, the logs that are produced by such systems are diverse in format. Therefore, data would have to be interpreted or re-formatted for incident analysis, thus violating digital forensics principles which prevent evidence tampering. Second, security device logs implement only partial logging, i.e. attacks that are detected according to the system configuration, and therefore potential data of interest during a post-incident analysis may be missing. This will affect the success of any security response mechanism.

3   Log File Visualization

The volume of data that an investigator may encounter during the post-incident analysis and response process may be considerable. The key challenges encountered include: the high volume of data that may contain evidence, evidence identification and analysis, identification of further potential security issues, and representation of the data under investigation. However, data visualization may be used by analysts to alleviate the overheads of interpreting data sets and improve the ability of users to make sense of activity patterns in event logs (Thomson et al, 2013).This section outlines the use and visualization of system log files for post-incident analysis and response.

A log file is data recorded by the operating system or other software in response to events or messages from software to a human user. For example, network log files record information about incoming and/or outgoing connections to remote hosts. The information that these may contain varies according to operating system or software. These may also be targeted for a particular use, such as firewall and IDS logs that detail suspected attacks against computer systems. Other logs may take the form of personal messages and therefore are more entropic for a user. For example, the Windows operating system records information such as programs that fail to start properly or updates that are downloaded automatically in user-friendly system messages. Both types of log provide a wealth of information that may be used during post-incident analysis and response as they record what has happened to the system during an incident under investigation. However, as Schmerl et al (2010) suggest, much of this data is represented in textual form so remains suboptimal for providing a holistic view of system behavior.

Schrenk and Poisel (2011) suggest that data for visualization in forensics investigations can be classified in a number of ways. For example, data categorization ranges from one- to multi-dimensional data, to traffic captures and traffic flow analysis. However, this paper posits that the information that may be retrieved from system log files falls into two categories; quantitative and qualitative. Quantitative information refers to the network events that may be inferred from log data. For example, host A receives data across the Internet from host B which is an event in the network. From this event, we may infer that host A and host B have some form of relationship in that there is communications between them. With the multiple events that occur in the network over time, a forensics examiner may derive relational information between a number of network nodes, for example by using statistical techniques. Qualitative information refers to the content of more entropic log files recording a single event. For example, the Windows operating system security centre records logins and logouts from the system. Analyzing this information, either as an individual message or as a series of messages, provides qualitative data.

As discussed above, security countermeasures provide system logs for audit purposes. However, these are of minimum use during a post-incident investigation for two reasons. First, firewalls and IDS only provide a minimal logging facility. Once a suspected attack has been detected, the system only records information about the suspicious packet or anomalous behavior. Second, the logs themselves will only record data according to their security rules, and therefore, if there is a log entry, a potential attack has already been detected and thwarted by the security system. However, in post-incident analysis investigations, it is probable that the security countermeasures have not detected the attack and would therefore hold little or no information for the investigator.

Operating systems provide a wide range of log files. However, it may be necessary for a system administrator to create additional log files, for example to record network activity of users. This should be defined within the organizational security policies. There is also an issue with the reliance on system logs during post-incident analysis and response in that during the incident, the attacker may have tampered with these files to avoid detection. Log file tampering may occur in a number of ways, for example, missing logs where system files have been completely removed, counterfeit logs where the system files have been replaced by those created by the attacker, or logs replaced with nonsensical data. However, visualization of the log files may be used to detect these occurrences. For example, no data will be visualized in the case of missing logs or inconsistent data representations where logs are replaced with nonsensical entries.

As illustrated in figure 1, the software developed by the authors has, at its most basic level, three main areas of functionality; file reading and processing (data mining), visualization, and graphical output. These functional points are covered in more detail below.

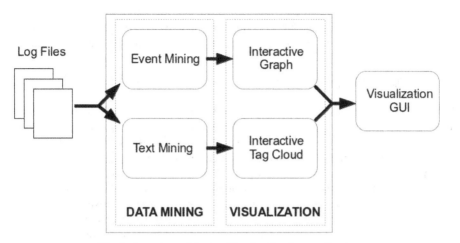

Fig. 1. Overview of the log file visualization application

The log files are processed in two ways dependent on the type of data to be investigated. Event mining analyses the file for information relevant to quantitative investigations, such as events and IP addresses. Text mining applies simple statistical measures against the data input. For example, in the case of investigations involving data theft, the log files would be analyzed using the event mining feature to identify outward network connections from the host computer. However, in the case of failed logon attempts, a textual analysis is performed to identify key words in qualitative data associated with this type of event. The results of this analysis are then passed to their respective visualization functions. For network events, such as relationships with other networked hosts, an interactive graph is produced. For textual analysis, an interactive tag cloud is visualized. It is posited that the occurrence of words (or lack of) suggests their concern to the incident. As such, commonly occurring words, such as 'the', 'a', 'to', etc. are ignored during this process. These words provide a useful function in language but their commonality adds noise to the visualizations without aiding the analysis. However, this function could be extended to a user-defined dictionary of words to include or exclude in a search.

The results of this data mining are passed to the two visualization functions. A network graph is constructed from the data passed from the event mining function. This graph-building element visualizes events or IP addresses as network nodes and produces lines to represent relationships between them. A tag cloud is created from the textual analysis results to produce a narrative view of qualitative data. This view sizes words in the log file text by frequency of occurrence and these are placed using a random layout. Various sensitivity levels, or thresholds, can be applied to the data, based on popularity of words, to reduce noise, and highlight key concerns within the text. These visualizations together form an appropriate output within the visualization graphical user interface (GUI). Both these visualizations are interactive in that the examiner may move both network nodes and text around the interface. This enhances the visualization by ensuring that the results can be explored and that the best layout can be chosen, for example to enhance analysis of the data or for presentation to a management team who may not be well versed in such data analysis.

This section has provided an overview to the log file approach for post-incident analysis and response. In the next section, we demonstrate the applicability of the approach for evidence analysis by applying it to three different case studies of attacks.

4   Case Study and Results

In order to demonstrate the application of log file visualization for post-incident analysis and response, three cases will be considered; a history of failed logins, analysis of network connections and a Denial of Service attack. The logs are taken from a computer running the Ubuntu 12.04 operating system.

Linux-based systems provide many log files under the /var/log directory. For example, /var/log/messages records general system messages, /var/log/auth.log provides authentication logs, and /var/log/wtmp provides a history of logins. Windows logs may be accessed through the Control Panel's Event Viewer application. Logs relating to Windows applications, security, setup, system and forwarded events may be viewed within this program. It should be noted that certain functionality for logging that would be useful during an investigation may not be invoked as default, and therefore, the organization's security policies should detail how logging is to be set.

Figure 2 illustrates a visualization of the /var/log/auth.log file. This log file contains system authorization information, such as commands in the terminal run as administrator, *iptables* entry changes, and records of system logins (successful or not). Font size in the visualization is by occurrence; the more that a word occurs, the greater the font size.

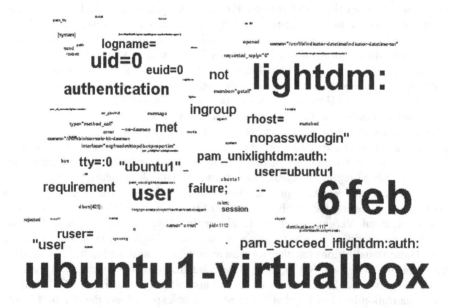

Fig. 2. Visualization of the /var/log/auth.log file

As figure 2 demonstrates, the piece of data that is recorded most often is the machine name, *ubuntu1-virtualbox* followed by the date. *Lightdm* refers the X Window display which uses various front-ends to draw login interfaces. However, of interest to post-incident analysis and response are the words *authentication, failure, ubuntu1, ingroup* and *nopasswdlogin*. These are from the following log entries; `logname= uid=0 euid=0 tty=:0 ruser= rhost= user=ubuntu1` and `requirement "user ingroupnopasswdlogin" not met by user "ubuntu1"`. These entries are records of failed user logins to the system for the ubuntu1 user account and are clearly discernible within the visualization. Their presence within the visualization would suggest to the examiner that a user has attempted to login to the system without authorization.

Figure 3 illustrates network connections that a computer has with other devices and such visualizations may be used to identify computers of interest, such as those involved in data theft. There are no standard log files that collect IP addresses of computers to which the victim device has been connected. Therefore, in this case, log files are created to monitor recent connections using the `netstat -natp` command and the data recorded to a file. The log file in this case has been parsed to return only destination IP addresses and port numbers to simplify the graph output.

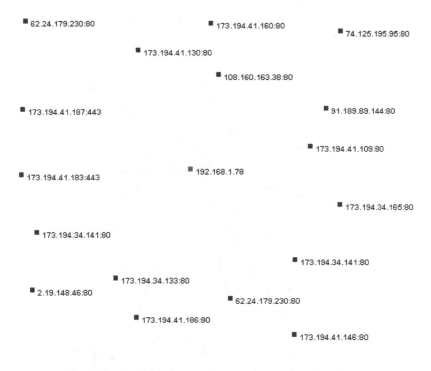

Fig. 3. Graph output of network connections and port numbers

The outputs of the log file in figure 3 shows the victim machine in the centre and colored red and IP addresses of machines to which it has been connected in blue. Unexpected IP addresses and port numbers would be of interest of interest during an incident, as well as connections to online file repositories where protected data may be stored. As can be seen in figure 3, many of the connections are to Web servers indicated by port 80 (http) and port 443 (https). However, one of these, 108.160.163.38:80, is a connection to a Dropbox account which may be used to store files belonging to the organization. IP addresses that would be of interest to the examiner would be dependent on the nature of the investigation, the network configuration and organizational security policies. Visualizations such as that in figure 3 can be further enhanced by visualizing statistical information. For example, thicker of thinner lines between networked nodes can be used to indicate frequency of contact or colorization to indicate other information, such as protocols used or geographic location.

Figure 4 visualizes a TCP SYN flood Denial of Service (DoS) attack against a network host. As with the above example, network logs do not monitor all traffic on a network by default. However, dependent on an organization's requirements, logs can be created using the *tcpdump* application and the results written to a file. This type of attack can be visualized in either of the two ways as illustrated in figures 2 and 3. However, the impact of such an attack can be clearly discerned using a similar approach to figure 2. The log file in this case has been parsed to return only source IP addresses of incoming connections.

Fig. 4. Visualization of a TCP SYN flood attack

In figure 4, the IP address of a legitimate connection on the internal network is clearly visible at the bottom of the image. As with figure 2, font size reflects the number of occurrences in the log file. However, it is immediately obvious that there are a large number of connection requests from a range of IP addresses, which is an indicator of this type of attack. A TCP SYN flood is an effective attack as it requires a computer(s) to send packets from spoofed source addresses in order to subvert the TCP three-way handshake for establishing a session. Hence, in the visualization above, there are apparently many hundreds of individual computers attempting to establish a TCP session with the victim host without completing the three-way handshake.

This section has demonstrated that visualization may be used as a tool in post-incident analysis and response. The visualizations are able to automatically mine various log file types and identify a number of attacks. This, combined with a knowledge of the context surrounding the attack and the organizational security policies, enable the examiner to effectively triage data from a wide range of sources to effectively secure their systems.

5   Conclusions and Further Work

Post-incident analysis of a security event is a complex task due to the volume of data that must be assessed, often within tight temporal constraints. System software, such as operating systems and applications, provide a variety of opportunities to record data in log files about interactions with the computer that may provide evidence during an investigation. The range of information that may be recorded will be defined within the organization's security policies. The use of a variety of log file sources for post-incident analysis overcomes issues associated with the reliance on perimeter-based security countermeasures' data. This paper has presented a novel approach for the visualization of log files to aid post-incident analysis and response. To illustrate the methodology's applicability to the investigation process, it has been applied to system logs and the resulting visualizations demonstrate the use of the approach.

The methodology and software has been tested on a small number of users using different data. However, future work will test the approach with a larger, statistically representative sample to fully understand the advantages and disadvantages of visualization as a tool for post-incident analysis and response. Furthermore, the authors plan to extend the approach to assess visualization as an approach for the analysis of a range of attacks. Finally, the applicability of log file correlation will be assessed.

References

1. Ando, R., Kadobayashi, Y., Shinoda, Y.: Blink: Large-scale P2P network monitoring and visualization system using VM introspection. In: Proceedings of the Sixth International Conference on Networked Computing and Advanced Information Management, Seoul, South Korea, August 16-18, pp. 351–358 (2010)

2. Wang, C., Xiao, Z., Li, Y., Xu, Y., Zhou, A., Zhang, K.: SentiView: Sentiment Analysis and Visualization for Internet Popular Topics. IEEE Transactions on Human-Machine Systems 43(6), 620–630 (2013)

3. Dunlop, M., Urbanski, W., Marchany, R., Tront, J.: Leveraging Cognitive Principles to Improve Security Visualization. In: Proceedings of Networked Digital Technologies, Dubai, UAE, April 24-26, pp. 262–276 (2012)

4. Giacobe, N.A., Xu, S.: Geovisual analytics for cyber security: Adopting the GeoViz Toolkit. In: Proceedings of the IEEE Conference on Visual Analytics Science and Technology, Providence, RI, USA, October 23-28, pp. 315–316 (2011)

5. Guerra-Gomez, J., Pack, M.L., Plaisant, C., Shneiderman, B.: Visualizing Change over Time Using Dynamic Hierarchies: TreeVersity2 and the StemView. IEEE Transactions on Visualization and Computer Graphics 19(12), 2566–2575 (2013)

6. Haggerty, J., Haggerty, S., Taylor, M.: Forensic Triage of Email Network Narratives through Visualisation. Journal of Information Management and Computer Security (forthcoming, 2014)

7. Koniaris, I., Papadimitriou, G., Nicopolitidis, P.: Analysis and Visualization of SSH Attacks Using Honeypots. In: Proceedings of EuroCon, Zagreb, Croatia, July 1-4, pp. 65–72 (2013)

8. Krishnan, H., Garth, C., Guhring, J., Gulsun, M.A., Greiser, A., Joy, K.I.: Analysis of Time-Dependent Flow-Sensitive PC-MRI Data. IEEE Transactions on Visualization and Computer Graphics 18(6), 966–977 (2012)

9. Mantoro, T., Aziz, N.A., Yusoff, N.D.M., Talib, N.A.A.: Log Visualization of Intrusion and Prevention Reverse Proxy Server against Web Attacks. In: Proceedings of the International Conference on Informatics and Creative Multimedia, Kuala Lumpur, Malaysia, September 3-6, pp. 325–329 (2013)

10. Nishioka, C., Kozaki, M., Okada, K.: Visualization System for Log Analysis with Probabilities of Incorrect Operation. In: Proceedings of the IEEE 17th International Conference on Parallel and Distributed Systems, Tainan, Taiwan, December 7-9, pp. 929–934 (2011)

11. Promrit, N., Mingkhwan, A., Simcharoen, S., Namvong, N.: Multi-dimensional visualization for network forensic analysis. In: Proceedings of the 7th International Conference on Networked Computing, Gumi, South Korea, September 26-28, pp. 68–73 (2011)

12. Schmerl, S., Vogel, M., Rietz, R., König, H.: Explorative Visualization of Log Data to support Forensic Analysis and Signature Development. In: Proceedings of the Fifth International Workshop on Systematic Approaches to Digital Forensic Engineering, Oakland, CA, USA, pp. 109–118 (May 10, 2010)

13. Schmidt, J., Groller, M.E., Bruckner, S.: VAICo: Visual Analysis for Image Comparison. IEEE Transactions on Visualization and Computer Graphics 19(12), 2090–2099 (2013)

14. Schrenk, G., Poisel, R.: A Discussion of Visualization Techniques for the Analysis of Digital Evidence. In: Proceedings of the Sixth International Conference on Availability, Reliability and Security, Vienna, Austria, August 22-26, pp. 758–763 (2011)

15. Stoll, J., Tashman, C.S., Edwards, W.K., Spafford, K.: Sesame: informing user security decisions with system visualization. In: Proceedings of the SIGCHI Conference on Human Factors in Computing Systems, Florence, Italy, April 5-10, pp. 1045–1054 (2008)

16. Thomson, A., Graham, M., Kennedy, J.: Pianola - Visualization of Multivariate Time-Series Security Event Data. In: Proceedings of the 17th International Conference on Information Visualisation, London, UK, July 15-18 (2013)

An Assessment Framework for Usable-Security Based on Decision Science

Yasser M. Hausawi and William H. Allen

Department of Computer Sciences,
Florida Institute of Technology,
Melbourne, FL 32901, USA
{yhausawi@my.,wallen@}fit.edu

Abstract. The balance between security and usability must be addressed as early as possible in the Software Development Life Cycle (SDLC) to ensure the inclusion of usable-security in software products. Unfortunately, there has been little research on assessing and integrating security, usability, and usable-security during the requirements engineering phase of the SDLC. To address that deficiency, this paper proposes an Assessment Framework for Usable-Security (AFUS) based on two well-known techniques from the decision science field.

Keywords: Security, Usability, Human Computer Interaction, HCI, HCI-SEC, Usable-Security, Quality Attributes Assessment, Decision Science.

1 Introduction

Security and usability are two important software quality attributes that should be incorporated into software projects during the requirements phase [10,15]. However, implementing both in a particular product is problematic because the goals of security and usability are often in conflict [1,8,24,25]. Much research has been done by HCI and security specialists to bring security and usability into a synergetic integration [7,18] and a more recent approach to resolving these potential conflicts is to employ a hybrid attribute, namely: usable-security [14,16,19]. However, most of the research on usable-security has focused on the design phase of the SDLC, resulting in a usable-security assessment gap in the requirements phase [5]. A recent literature survey found no current usable-security assessment methodology that addresses the requirements phase.

The field of Decision Science provides tools and techniques for resolving conflicts between differing objectives [6]. In this paper, we propose an Assessment Framework for Usable-Security (AFUS) that explores the benefits of using two well-known techniques from Decision Science, namely Utility Functions and Decision Trees, for assessing the balance between security, usability and usable-security represented in the set of requirements for a particular software product.

The goal of this work is not to produce an objective measure for comparing two products, but rather to generate a metric that developers can use to gauge the balance between the attributes. We assume that the developers of a product

T. Tryfonas and I. Askoxylakis (Eds.): HAS 2014, LNCS 8533, pp. 33–44, 2014.

are aware of the balance between security and usability that is appropriate for their product, thus the proposed technique is intended to assist in reaching that desired balance. As changes to the requirements are made, reassessment using AFUS can indicate if the product has shifted to a greater emphasis on one attribute at the expense of the others, or if all attributes have moved towards the developer's preferred equilibrium.

Next section (Section 2 presents background information about security, usability, and usable-security; and presents the related assessment research work. Section 3 introduces our usable-security assessment framework (AFUS). Section 5 discusses the results, and Section 6 concludes this article.

2   Background

2.1   Security

There are various definitions of the term "security". Garfinkel and Spafford define a computer as secure, "if you can depend on it and its software to behave as you expect it to" [14]. Pfleeger and Pfleeger define computer security as, "preventing the weaknesses from being exploited and understanding preventive measures that make the most sense" [21]. Essentially, system security is a set of methods and techniques that work together to generate what is called *security mechanisms*. The security mechanisms are used to prevent weaknesses of computer systems from being exploited by applying three main security properties: 1) confidentiality, 2) integrity, and 3) availability [21].

2.2   Usability

Usability is defined by the International Standard Organization (ISO) as the limit that a product can be used by legitimate users to satisfactorily perform specific tasks in an effective, efficient, and specified way [17]. Usability specialists have developed various techniques to achieve three main usability properties: 1) effectiveness, 2) efficiency, and 3) user satisfaction.

2.3   Usable-Security

In 2003, a multi-discipline group of researchers formed a working group called *Human-Computer Interaction and Security (HCI-SEC)* [12]. This group was formed to bridge the gap between usability and security under the main goal of "Usable-Security". In other words their goal was to come up with usable-security mechanisms to secure computer systems. Usable-security is defined by Whitten and Tygar [26] as a software product that makes its users: 1) reliably aware of the needed security tasks, 2) able to figure out how to successfully perform such tasks, 3) able to avoid dangerous errors when performing their tasks, and 4) sufficiently comfortable to use and be happy with the software interface.

Unfortunately, much of the recent research on the assessment of quality attributes does not consider assessing the results of aligning two or more attributes.

As a result, each researcher focused on assessing one attribute. However, the Security Usability Symmetry "SUS" [4] is a novel subjective metrics-based usability inspection design model proposed to design, inspect, and evaluate the usability of security systems through identifying and then subjectively rating security-usability related problems according to the three-level severity rating (low, medium, and high). One disadvantage of the SUS is that, like many other usability and security evaluation techniques, it adopts the subjective (qualitative) evaluation methodology rather than the objective (quantitative) one.

Therefore, in this paper, we propose a framework that uses a mathematical modeling assessment [3] through application of utility functions and decision trees. Moreover, our framework reduces the subjective-based assessment to produce a more objective-based assessment.

3   Assessment Framework for Usable-Security (AFUS)

The proposed framework (see Figure 1) has three main components: 1) requirements filtering and merging using the OWASP Risk Rating Methodology [20] for security and the SALUTA Attribute Preference Table [13] for usability as guides, 2) utility functions, and 3) a decision tree.

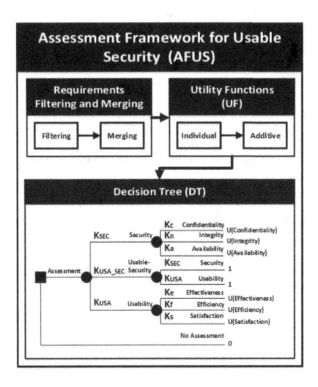

Fig. 1. Assessment Framework for Usable-Security (AFUS)

The framework was evaluated by using case studies based on three real-world scenarios. Scenarios are often used in software engineering to gather and validate non-functional requirements [5] and in HCI to improve communication between stakeholders and developers [2]. The first scenario was based directly on the non-functional usability, humanity, and security requirements from the Volere Requirements Specification Template [22]. Two additional scenarios were produced with different specifications for their non-functional requirements. We should note that the usable-security requirements were derived from the other non-functional requirements, as the Volere template does not have a usable-security section.

3.1   Requirements Filtering and Merging

Requirements engineering is the first phase of the SDLC [23] . In this phase, the stakeholders meet together to set the project requirements and analyze the generated requirements [23]. Among those requirements are security, usability, and other requirements. The scope of the AFUS is limited to the requirements that are related to security, usability, and usable-security. Therefore, the intended system requirements are filtered to select and gather the requirements that are within the scope of the AFUS, and then they are grouped into three main groups, namely: security requirements, usability requirements, and usable-security requirements. The requirements of each of the three groups are rated according to their importance as the following processes:

Security Requirements Group (SR). The OWASP Risk Rating Methodology (OWASP RRM) [20] has been adapted for use as the foundation for assessing security requirements. The importance of each security requirement is rated on each security property [21] (confidentiality (CI), integrity (NI), and availability (AI)) based on Table 1. We observed that OWASP does not use standardized rating values, as each security property has its own rating. Also, there are some gaps in rating some properties. For example, OWASP uses the values (1, 5, 7, and 9) to estimate the impact of availability loss on the system if vulnerability is exploited. Such estimation values may experience lack of accuracy, because an estimated impact between 1 and 5, let us say 3, cannot be accurately given. This may force the estimator to choose between 1 or 5. Therefore, we adapted the OWASP rating methodology to fill in those rating gaps to better align it with the usability requirement ratings, as will be explained later in the next section. The security rate of each requirement (SecR) is calculated through averaging the rates of the three security properties. The calculation formula is shown as the following:

$$SecR_i = \frac{CI_i + NI_i + AI_i}{3} \tag{1}$$

The overall security rate (SEC) for the requirements set is derived by:

$$SEC = \sum_i^{SR} SecR_i \tag{2}$$

Moreover, to assess the shares (SH) of each security property (confidentiality (SH_c), integrity (SH_n), and availability (SH_a)), summing of each property importance is calculated from all of the security requirements and divided by overall security rate (SEC) as depicted on the following three formulae respectively:

$$SH_c = \frac{\sum_i^{SR} CI_i}{SEC}, SH_n = \frac{\sum_i^{SR} NI_i}{SEC}, SH_a = \frac{\sum_i^{SR} AI_i}{SEC} \tag{3}$$

Table 1. Security and Usability Properties Importance Rating Guidance

Requirement Importance on Properties	[9] Critical
	[7] Very Important
	[6] Important
	[3] Some Important
	[1] Not Important

Usability Requirements Group (UR). SALUTA [13] is a usability assessment technique used to rate usability based on assigning quantitative values for usability preferences. An adapted rating methodology based on SAULTA Attribute Preference Table [13] is used to rate usability requirements. The same rating values that were used to rate the security requirements group are used to rate the importance of each usability property [17] (effectiveness (EI), efficiency (FI), and satisfaction (SI)) for the usability requirements. It is worthwhile to note that having unified rating values for both security and usability requirements provides a consistent qualification strategy for measuring the requirements. Table 1 is used as a guide for the rating process. A five-value rating is used (1, 3, 6, 7, and 9). This rating can be justified as the most appropriate for usability requirements rating process, because it efficiently helps rating any usability requirement on the three usability properties where the evaluator is not forced to give an inappropriate rate. Although SAULTA uses a four-value rating (1, 2, 3 and 4), as it ranks scenarios based on four usability properties (each property gets one ranking value), our framework rates requirements, but does not rank them, and the rating guidance should work with all of the requirements. The usability rate of each requirement (UsaR) is calculated through averaging the rates of the three usability properties. The calculation formula is:

$$UsaR_j = \frac{EI_j + FI_j + SI_j}{3} \tag{4}$$

The overall usability rate (USA) for the requirements set is derived by:

$$USA = \sum_j^{UR} UsaR_j \tag{5}$$

To assess the shares (SH) of each usability property (effectiveness (SH_e), efficiency (SH_f), and satisfaction (SH_s)), summing of each property importance is calculated from all of the usability requirements and divided by overall usability rate, USA, as depicted on the following three formulae respectively:

$$SH_e = \frac{\sum_j^{UR} EI_j}{USA}, SH_f = \frac{\sum_j^{UR} FI_j}{USA}, SH_s = \frac{\sum_j^{UR} SI_j}{USA} \qquad (6)$$

Hence, after rating the requirements of both security and usability (based on the modified OWASP and the SALUTA methods) to produce overall static ratings for both attributes (SEC and USA), a static assessment is calculated for the two attributes (SEC_{static} and USA_{static}) by applying the following formulae:

$$SEC_{static} = \frac{SEC}{SEC + USA}, USA_{static} = \frac{USA}{SEC + USA} \qquad (7)$$

Usable-Security Requirements Group (USR). This requirements group has two sub-groups, namely: 1) initial usable-security requirements sub-group ($IUSR$), and 2) merged usable-security requirements sub-group ($MUSR$). The overall usable-security rate (USA_SEC) is calculated by summing the two sub-groups. The following sections describe each sub-group.

Initial Usable-Security Requirements Sub-Group (IUSR). The requirements of this sub-group are rated by a different rating methodology, as usable-security does not have standard properties like those associated with security and usability and a usable-security requirement may mix security and usability properties. Moreover, the requirements that are based on the Human-Computer Interaction and Security (HCI-SEC) are considered as IUSR [9,11]. Therefore,

Table 2. Initial $Usable - Security$ Importance Rating Guidance

Importance (I)	[9] Critical
	[7] Very Important
	[6] Important
	[3] Some Important
	[1] Not Important

each initial usable-security requirement is rated based on Table 2, then multiplied by 2, and then divided by 3 as illustrated on this formula:

$$IUsa\_SecR_k = \frac{I_k * 2}{3} \qquad (8)$$

The overall initial usable-security rate ($IUSA\_SEC$) is calculated from the following formula:

$$IUSA\_SEC = \sum_k^{IUSR} IUsa\_SecR_k \qquad (9)$$

Merged Usable-Security Requirements Sub-Group (MUSR). To assess usable-security in the most appropriate manner, both security and usability requirements must be analyzed with merging and alignment in mind [14,16]. If the requirements are merged successfully, the security-usability alignment can be balanced to achieve usable-security. Therefore, the requirements of the two groups, security requirements and usability requirements, are visited again and analyzed to prepare them for merging. Once new usable-security requirements are derived from the existing security and usability requirements, they are rated ($MUsa\_SecR$) through averaging the security and usability rates (SecR ,UsaR) of all contributing requirements (CSR and CUR) multiplied by 2 as the following:

$$MUsa\_SecR_l = \frac{\left(\left(\frac{\sum_i^{CSR} SecR_i + \sum_j^{CUR} UsaR_j}{CSR+CUR}\right) * 2\right)}{3} \tag{10}$$

The overall merged usable-security rate ($MUSA\_SEC$) is calculated from the following formula:

$$MUSA\_SEC = \sum_l^{MUSR} MUsa\_SecR_l \tag{11}$$

The overall prediction of usable-security rate (USA_SEC) for the entire system is calculated by the following formula:

$$USA\_SEC = IUSA\_SEC + MUSA\_SEC. \tag{12}$$

3.2 Utility Functions

Utility Functions (UF) are a relatively straightforward methodology for dealing with conflicting objectives and can capture stakeholders' attitudes about predictive assessment and the evaluation of trade-offs [6]. Utility functions are often used in systems engineering and management for decision and risk analysis purposes. There are various models of utility function. One is the Additive Utility Function (AUF) that is used to estimate total utility of conflicting objectives. Another utility function model is the Individual Utility Function (IUF). The IUF is used to predictively estimate utilities for subjectively measurable/non-measurable objectives. More details about the above utility function models are available in [6]. Usable-security is a subjectively measurable hybrid software quality attribute that is based on two conflicting quality attributes, namely: security and usability, along with consideration of HCI-SEC principles [11,16]. Therefore, the utility function models can be adapted for usable-security assessment during the requirements engineering phase. Assessing usable-security during the requirements phase can provide clear prediction about the balance between security and usability early in software development process. Based on the requirements filtering and merging component's process, both the IUF and AUF models can be used to assess usable-security.

First, the ratio-based IUF is used to calculate weights for the software quality attributes: security, usability, and usable-security. The ratios of security (R_{SEC}), usability (R_{USA}), and usable-security ($R_{USA-SEC}$) are derived by the following calculation, where α represents an attribute (security, usability, or usable-security) and β represents another attribute: α is $\frac{\alpha}{\beta}$ times as important as β. For instance, the ratio of security over usability is calculated based on the above calculation as follows: Security is $\frac{SEC}{USA}$ times as important as usability. The attribute's accumulative ratio is calculated through summing its ratios over all the attributes. For instance, the security accumulative ratio is calculated by summing the security ratios over all the attributes as in the following:

$$R_{SEC} = \frac{SEC}{SEC} + \frac{SEC}{USA} + \frac{SEC}{USA\_SEC} \tag{13}$$

After the accumulative ratios of the attributes are derived, each attribute is weighted on the following formulae, where security, usability, and usable-security weights are $K_{SEC}, K_{USA}, and K_{USA\_SEC}$ respectively [6], i represents a quality attribute, and QA represents the number of all the quality attributes :

$$K_{SEC} = \frac{1}{\sum_i^{QA} R_i}*R_{SEC}, K_{USA} = \frac{1}{\sum_i^{QA} R_i}*R_{USA}, K_{USA\_SEC} = \frac{1}{\sum_i^{QA} R_i}*R_{USA\_SEC} \tag{14}$$

Second, the IUF is used to calculate weights of each of security and usability properties based on their ratios (R) and pointing (P), where the starting pointing value is five (5). The following formulae are used to calculate the weights of security properties: confidentiality (K_c), integrity (K_n), and availability (K_a) [6], i represents a property, and SP represents the number of all properties. The weights calculation is applied as follows:

$$K_c = \frac{1}{\sum_i^{SP} P_i} * P_c, K_n = \frac{1}{\sum_i^{SP} P_i} * P_n, K_a = \frac{1}{\sum_i^{SP} P_i} * P_a \tag{15}$$

The following formulae are used to calculate the weights of usability properties: effectiveness (K_e), efficiency (K_f), and satisfaction (K_s) [6], j represents a property, and UP represents the number of all properties. The weights calculation is applied as follows:

$$K_e = \frac{1}{\sum_j^{UP} P_j} * P_e, K_f = \frac{1}{\sum_j^{UP} P_j} * P_f, K_s = \frac{1}{\sum_j^{UP} P_j} * P_s \tag{16}$$

Third, the IUF is used to calculate utilities of each of security and usability properties based on the ratios (R), pointing (P) where the starting pointing value is five (5), and the following equations are used to find values of constants a and b for each of security and usability individually [6]:

$$b = \frac{1}{(-1) * minP_{properties} + maxP_{properties}}, a = ((-1) * minP_{properties}) * b \tag{17}$$

Based on the values of the constants a and b on security, the following formulae are used to calculate the utilities (U) of security properties: confidentiality (U_c), integrity (U_n), and availability (U_a):

$$U_c = a + (b * P_c), U_n = a + (b * P_n), U_a = a + (b * P_a) \tag{18}$$

Similarly, based on the values of the constants a and b on usability, the following formulae are used to calculate the utilities (U) of usability properties: effectiveness (U_e), efficiency (U_f), and satisfaction (U_s) [6]:

$$U_e = a + (b * P_e), U_f = a + (b * P_f), U_s = a + (b * P_s) \tag{19}$$

Fourth, the AUF is used to calculate the overall utility of the quality attributes based on their properties' weights and utility values. The following formulae represent the AUF for the security and usability quality attributes:

$$U_{SEC}(c,n,a) = K_c*U_c + K_n*U_n + K_a*U_a, U_{USA}(e,f,s) = K_e*U_e + K_f*U_f + K_s*U_s \tag{20}$$

Usable-security utility (U_{USA_SEC}) differs from the utility of the above two attributes because usable-security does not have properties. However, it is a result of merging the two quality attributes, namely: security and usability. Therefore, the following formula is used to calculate the utility of usable-security:

$$U_{USA\_SEC}(SEC, USA) = K_{SEC} * U_{SEC} + K_{USA} * U_{USA} \tag{21}$$

3.3   Decision Trees

The Decision Tree (DT) is a tool used during the process of modeling decisions [6]. It is a method of structuring different objectives' elements in order to make decisions for using the objectives based on displaying all of the minute details. Quality attributes in general, and security, usability, and usable-security in particular, are objectives of software development within the scope of our framework. More information about decision trees is available in [6].

To get the overall utility value of the Decision Tree for the three quality attributes, the weights and utilities of each attribute are calculated by the following formulae. It is important to mention that to get the overall utility for usable-security, we subtracted the gap between security and usability utilities as one important factor that plays a role in assessing the usability-security interaction (usable-security):

$$DTU_{SEC} = K_{SEC} * U_{SEC} \tag{22}$$

$$DTU_{USA} = K_{USA} * U_{USA} \tag{23}$$

$$DTU_{USA\_SEC} = (K_{USA\_SEC} * U_{USA\_SEC}) - |DTU_{SEC} - DTU_{USA}| \tag{24}$$

Finally, to get the final assessment value for the three quality attributes, the resulted Decision Tree utility value of each attribute is divided by the total summing of the three Decision Tree utilities of all the three attributes as in the following formulae, where the sum of the results must equal 1:

$$ASS_{SEC} = \frac{DTU_{SEC}}{(DTU_{SEC} + DTU_{USA} + DTU_{USA\_SEC})} \qquad (25)$$

$$ASS_{USA} = \frac{DTU_{USA}}{(DTU_{SEC} + DTU_{USA} + DTU_{USA\_SEC})} \qquad (26)$$

$$ASS_{USA\_SEC} = \frac{DTU_{USA\_SEC}}{(DTU_{SEC} + DTU_{USA} + DTU_{USA\_SEC})} \qquad (27)$$

4   Results and Discussion

For each of the three scenarios (see Figure 2), we first created a baseline by applying the static OWASP RRM [20] and SALUTA APT [13] assessments for security and usability requirements respectively, using predetermined values for rating each of the two attributes' requirements. Then, we applied the AFUS approach to reassess the balance between the three attributes.

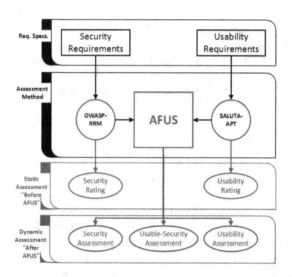

Fig. 2. The "Before" and "After" Assessment Results

The table below shows the outcomes from the static assessments ("before") and after applying the AFUS. As seen in Table 3, the results of all three scenarios show moderate differences in assessing security and usability attributes before and after applying AFUS. Moreover, usable-security weight was only incorporated after applying AFUS. The AFUS assessment of the first two scenarios show a moderate to small range of assessment gap between the security and usability attributes, 16.96% and 10.44% respectively. The third scenario showed a very little assessment gap between the security and usability attributes, 0.80%. Therefore, it provided a higher weight for usable-security.

Table 3. Assessment for Scenarios 1, 2, and 3

Scenario	Assessment	Security	Usable-Security	Usability
Scenario 1	Before applying AFUS	0.364	No Assessment	0.636
	After applying AFUS	0.365	0.197	0.439
Scenario 2	Before applying AFUS	0.432	No Assessment	0.568
	After applying AFUS	0.348	0.338	0.315
Scenario 3	Before applying AFUS	0.504	No Assessment	0.496
	After applying AFUS	0.251	0.500	0.249

5   Conclusion

We proposed an Assessment Framework for Usable-Security (AFUS) that employs two well-known techniques from Decision Science to assess the balance between security, usability and usable-security represented in the set of requirements for a particular software product. We demonstrated that this approach can extend the work of the currently available techniques in order to produce objective results, but more work is needed to determine how responsive this approach is to changes in requirements and how accurately it measures the balance between the three attributes. Unfortunately, the lack of prior work on assessing usable-security requirements complicates this task.

References

1. Adams, A., Sasse, M.A.: Users are not the enemy. Communications of the ACM 42(12), 40–46 (1999)
2. Anton, A.I., Carter, R.A., Dagnino, A., Dempster, J.H., Siege, D.F.: Deriving goals from a use-case based requirements specification. Requirements Engineering 6(1), 63–73 (2001)
3. Bosch, J.: Design and use of software architectures: adopting and evolving a product-line approach. Pearson Education (2000)
4. Braz, C., Seffah, A., M'Raihi, D.: Designing a trade-off between usability and security: A metrics based-model. In: Baranauskas, C., Abascal, J., Barbosa, S.D.J. (eds.) INTERACT 2007. LNCS, vol. 4663, pp. 114–126. Springer, Heidelberg (2007)
5. Chung, L., do Prado Leite, J.C.S.: On non-functional requirements in software engineering. In: Borgida, A.T., Chaudhri, V.K., Giorgini, P., Yu, E.S. (eds.) Conceptual Modeling: Foundations and Applications. LNCS, vol. 5600, pp. 363–379. Springer, Heidelberg (2009)
6. Clemens, R.T., Reilly, T.: Making hard decisions with decision tools® (2001)
7. Cranor, L.F., Garfinkel, S.: Guest editors' introduction: Secure or usable? IEEE Security & Privacy 2(5), 16–18 (2004)
8. DeWitt, A.J., Kuljis, J.: Is usable security an oxymoron? Interactions 13(3), 41–44 (2006)
9. Dhamija, R., Dusseault, L.: The seven flaws of identity management: Usability and security challenges. IEEE Security & Privacy 6(2), 24–29 (2008)

10. Ferre, X.: Integration of usability techniques into the software development process. In: International Conference on Software Engineering (Bridging the gaps between software engineering and human-computer interaction), pp. 28–35 (2003)

11. Ferreira, A., Rusu, C., Roncagliolo, S.: Usability and security patterns. In: Second International Conferences on Advances in Computer-Human Interactions, ACHI 2009, pp. 301–305. IEEE (2009)

12. Flechais, I., Mascolo, C., Sasse, A.: Integrating security and usability into the requirements and design process. International Journal of Electronic Security and Digital Forensics 1(1), 12–26 (2007)

13. Folmer, E., van Gurp, J., Bosch, J.: Scenario-based assessment of software architecture usability. In: ICSE Workshop on SE-HCI, Citeseer, pp. 61–68 (2003)

14. Garfinkel, S.: Design Principles and Patterns for Computer Systems that are Simultaneously Secure and Usable. PhD thesis, Massachusetts Institute of Technology (2005)

15. Gorton, I.: Software quality attributes. In: Essential Software Architecture, pp. 23–38 (2011)

16. Hausawi, Y.M., Mayron, L.M.: Towards usable and secure natural language processing systems. In: Stephanidis, C. (ed.) HCII 2013, Part I. CCIS, vol. 373, pp. 109–113. Springer, Heidelberg (2013)

17. WD ISO. 9241-11. ergonomic requirements for office work with visual display terminals (VDTs). In: The International Organization for Standardization (1998)

18. Lampson, B.: Privacy and security usable security: How to get it. Communications of the ACM 52(11), 25–27 (2009)

19. Mayron, L.M., Hausawi, Y., Bahr, G.S.: Secure, usable biometric authentication systems. In: Stephanidis, C., Antona, M. (eds.) UAHCI 2013, Part I. LNCS, vol. 8009, pp. 195–204. Springer, Heidelberg (2013)

20. OWASP. Risk rating methodology (2013)

21. Pfleeger, C.P., Pfleeger, S.L.: Security in Computing. Prentice Hall PTR (2006)

22. Robertson, J., Robertson, S.: Volere requirements specification template: Edition January 14 (2009)

23. Sommerville, I., Sawyer, P.: Requirements engineering: a good practice guide. John Wiley & Sons, Inc. (1997)

24. Weir, C.S., Douglas, G., Carruthers, M., Jack, M.: User perceptions of security, convenience and usability for e-banking authentication tokens. Computers & Security 28(1), 47–62 (2009)

25. Whitten, A.: Making Security Usable. PhD thesis, Princeton University (2004)

26. Whitten, A., Tygar, D.: Why johnny can't encrypt: A usability evaluation of pgp 5.0. In: Proceedings of the 8th USENIX Security Symposium, vol. 99, McGraw-Hill (1999)

On Designing Usable Policy Languages for Declarative Trust Aggregation

Michael Huth and Jim Huan-Pu Kuo

Department of Computing, Imperial College London,
London, SW7 2AZ, United Kingdom
{m.huth,jimhkuo}@imperial.ac.uk

Abstract. We argue that there will be an increasing future need for the
design and implementation of declarative languages that can aggregate
trust evidence and therefore inform the decision making of IT systems
at run-time. We first present requirements for such languages. Then we
discuss an instance of such a language, Peal$^+$, which extends an early prototype Peal that was researched by others in collaboration with us. Next,
we formulate the intuitive semantics of Peal$^+$, present a simple use case
of it, and evaluate to what extent Peal$^+$ meets our formulated requirements. In this evaluation, particular attention is given to the usability
aspects of declarative languages that mean to aggregate trust evidence.

1   Introduction

There is little doubt that the advances in computing and information technology
are transforming the manner in which we conduct our business and lead our
personal lives. The use of small devices such as tablets and smart phones, the
rapid pace with which such technologies evolve, and the increased reach of these
technologies – to name smart meters for electric power supply – are prominent
examples of this.

One consequence of this is that ever more things have programmable interfaces
to which other things and processes may connect. In this *Internet of Things*, designers, programmers, and users alike need to be able to formulate constraints on
the interactions across such interfaces that adequately reflect implicit trust assumptions, risk appetite, and other intentions. We think that trust management
will play a key role in the articulation of such interaction constraints. Let us first
state what we mean by the term "trust" in this paper. We say that an agent A (a
program, a user, a system, etc.) trusts another agent B for a planned interaction
I with B, when agent A has collected and inspected evidence that leads agent
A to believe that engaging in the interaction I with B is worth taking any risk
reflected in the studied evidence. This asymmetric view of trust can be made
symmetric by letting agent B perform a similar inspection and decision process
regarding the interaction I with agent A – typically based on evidence pertinent
to agent B. If we think of the symmetric view as a *logical and* of the asymmetric
view (a trust-mediated interaction would only take place if both agents agree to
it), we can focus on the asymmetric view subsequently.

T. Tryfonas and I. Askoxylakis (Eds.): HAS 2014, LNCS 8533, pp. 45–56, 2014.

In this paper, we investigate how declarative languages can help with formalizing the process of collecting and studying indicators of trust in context-dependent interactions with other agents. We posit that such languages will be increasingly needed, and formulate requirements that they should satisfy. For sake of illustration, we will study an extension of a trust-aggregation language that we have designed with others [8,2,7,9] and assess its suitability against the requirements we will formulate further below. This will in part make use of a toy example written in that language. The paper concludes by identifying future work for the design of more usable trust aggregation languages.

2   Declarative Trust Aggregation through Policies

We refer to *trust aggregation* as a process in which agent A first collects observable indicators of trust in an interaction I with agent B, and then systematically combines such indicators to more compact or abstract expressions that can directly inform the decision making of agent A (e.g. whether or not to commit to interaction I with agent B). Note that observable indicators may also be estimates, for example, the estimated uncertainty in the computed reputation of an agent. Such indicators may themselves be talking about perceived trust, reputation scores, risk levels, or about things that influence trust perceptions indirectly – for example the financial risk to agent A in interaction I with agent B. We note that existing approaches to computing trust or reputation scores (including those that have only binary scores as in "trust" or "don't trust") acknowledge that such computations benefit from incorporating context-dependent information in the aggregation of trust evidence. For example, reputation systems for online trading sites that base reputation scores on the number of successful past interactions without taking into account the monetary values of these transactions are subject to active attacks. Such attacks can indeed be prevented or mitigated against by making reputation scores dependent on transaction values as well – see for example the nice discussion in [11].

We posit that the future Internet of Things will have an increased need for using such trust aggregations at many interfaces, and that this creates the need for a sort of *trust calculus* as the basis of computing the perceived trust in interactions across interfaces, which can then be enforced at run-time. No doubt will this lead to many dialects or variants of such a calculus. But there is evolutionary pressure to standardize such aggregation languages in order to get portability across platforms and technologies. Additionally, the creation of a more generic trust calculus will facilitate the development of robust analyses of aggregations formulated in such a calculus. It will also allow the decoupling of executable and analyzable such core languages from user-facing and domain-specific languages for expressing trust aggregation. With such a separation of concerns, one would for example only have to compile user-facing domain-specific languages into a (not user-facing) core language that can be implemented in systems and for which the desired analyses can be performed.

Such a core trust calculus has to be able to collect indicators of trust that have different semantic types, for example, the location of an agent, the past interaction history with agent B, and the nature of the intended next interaction with B. This need adds cognitive complexity to the aggregation of such indicators. We believe that such cognitive complexity cannot be eliminated by formal foundations of a core calculus and its aggregation mechanisms, even though such foundations will have many other benefits discussed further below. For example, the interaction of indicators of trust with indicators of distrust may be non-obvious or unintuitive and so harder to understand. In mathematical terms, the introduction of distrust indicators moves from simpler semi-rings of values to rings in which negative and positive information gets combined.

Many reputation systems and related approaches hardwire the aggregation of indicators and its possible state-change semantics through mathematical formulas that express scoring functions. This allows for easy implementations and supports the formal analysis of the mathematical system being described. However, we claim that future IT systems will require more expressive and more adaptable mechanisms for specifying, implementing, and analyzing such evidence aggregation and state-transformation mechanisms. For example, the management of trust and risk across different logical, physical or legal domains can no longer rely on scoring functions that implicitly assume a closed system with observable boundaries. There are also systems for which not enough prior information might be available and yet some form of trust evidence is present and perhaps the only basis for decision making. An example thereof are processes by which parties of arms reduction treaties can confirm to each other that specific arms have indeed been destroyed.

We propose to use *policy languages* to attain such declarative flexibility and adaptability. Policy languages have already been used successfully in trust management (e.g. for public-key systems [1]) and access control (see e.g. [3]). Such languages have often a means of composing simple rules into global policies, something we feel to be desirable from a usability perspective.

3   Requirements for Declarative Trust Aggregation

We now describe requirements that we deem to be important for the design of policy languages $\mathcal{L}$ for declarative trust aggregation:

Expressiveness: Such a language $\mathcal{L}$ needs to be able to declare aggregations and state changes as they occur or are needed in a wide range of real systems, at least up to an acceptable degree of abstraction.

Scalable analysis: Declarations made in such a language $\mathcal{L}$ should be subject to formal analysis that aids in the validation of these declarations, and such analyses should scale up to realistic declaration sizes.

Interface-facing: Such a language $\mathcal{L}$ should be designed so that it can interface easily with other languages down-stream (by using those other languages) and up-stream (by being used by other languages). Down-stream, we need to be able to plug into $\mathcal{L}$ desired expressions from other languages that specify indicators of trust, distrust, risk, etc.. Up-stream, we want to be able to take $\mathcal{L}$ expressions that declare trust aggregation or state-changes based on such aggregation, and plug them into other languages (e.g. as conditions) to be used for decision making or further computation.

Usability: Declarations made in $\mathcal{L}$ should be easy to formulate, should support the intuitions of a specifier, and should also have easily specifiable and intuitive analyses used to validate such declarations. Equally, the feedback provided by analyses should be easy to understand and be presented at the same cognitive layer as the analyzed declarations. This may require that syntactic patterns of language fragments of a core calculus be identified (so called embedded domain-specific languages). Or it may require the development of application-specific user-facing languages that have efficient and transparent translations into a core language $\mathcal{L}$. Language choices such as "embedded" versus "compiled" will typically be made based on external factors and will therefore vary.

4   A Core Language for Trust Aggregation

We now sketch a language Peal$^+$ that may serve as a core calculus for trust aggregation. This language supports aggregation but not yet declarations of state changes based on computed trust. We leave such aspects to future work. The language Peal$^+$ is depicted in Figure 1. Its most abstract expressions are conditions *cond*, which are Boolean combinations of two sorts of formulas: predicates q as indicators of trust, risk, value, etc., and inequalities $pSet1 \leq pSet2$ which declare that the score computed by a policy set $pSet1$ is not larger than the score computed by policy set $pSet2$. Note that we can derive language expressions *cond* $||$ *cond* (for disjunction) and $pSet < pSet$ (for strict inequality of scores) as syntactic sugar of Peal$^+$ since the latter contains the dual constructors conjunction for conditions (&&) and less-than-or-equal comparison for policy sets ($\leq$), as well as the negation operator for conditions ($\neg$).

In language Peal$^+$, the language of predicates q itself is left unspecified. This omission is intentional as this is how we want to ensure that we can interface with down-stream languages that may express such indicators in whichever way. The decision to use Boolean variables means we require that interfaces to such other languages render their trust indicators in Boolean form. Examples of such a down-stream languages would be first-order or higher-order logic, where predicates q would be defined or bound to formulas of such logics.

In Peal$^+$, predicates are used to build rules, rules are used to build policies, and policies are used to build policy sets. Finally, predicates and policy sets are used to build conditions. These conditions can then be used as stand-alone expressions to support decision making, or they may serve as Boolean expressions in up-stream languages. A condition such as $0.5 < pSet$ might model whether or not there is sufficient trust in committing to a risky interaction, where 0.5 acts

$$op ::= min \mid max \mid + \mid *$$
$$raw\_score ::= real\_const \mid real\_var \mid real\_const * real\_var$$
$$score ::= raw\_score \mid raw\_score \, [real\_const, \, real\_const]$$
$$rule ::= if \, (cond) \, score$$
$$pol ::= op \, (rule^*) \, default \, score$$
$$pSet ::= score \mid pol \mid op \, (pSet, \, pSet)$$
$$cond ::= q \mid pSet \le pSet \mid \neg cond \mid cond \, \&\& \, cond$$

Fig. 1. Syntax of Peal$^+$ where q ranges over some language of predicates, and the constants and variables in *score* range over real numbers (potentially restricted by domains or analysis methods)

as a strict trust threshold and *pSet* captures the aggregation of trust evidence. Note that the language Peal$^+$ does not explicitly assign such conditions to specific agents. Such designations would indeed be expected to happen in an up-stream language that were to use such conditions to regulate and enforce trust-mediated interactions in a multi-agent system. Note further that conditions *cond* might also appeal to agents and their states through predicates q that have meaning in a suitable logic, and so down-stream languages may also reflect agency if needed.

Policy sets of Peal$^+$ are either atomic, in which case they are scores or policies, or they are composite objects, in which case they are recursively composed from policy sets through composition operators listed under syntactic clause *op*. The composition choices for *op* supported in *core* are minimum, maximum, addition and multiplication of scores – but one can well image extensions of this.

Let us now discuss the two forms of atomic policy sets, beginning with scores. A score is defined to be either a raw score or a raw score annotated with a real interval. A raw score is either a real constant, a real variable, or the product of a real constant with a real variable. For example 0.56, y_2, and $-1.4 * z$ could all be declared as raw scores and so as scores as well. The annotation of an interval allows us to write expressions such as $0.456 * x \, [-0.1, 0.2]$ as a score. The role of the interval $[-0.1, 0.2]$ is to express *non-deterministic uncertainty* in the value of $0.456 * x$. The intuition is that, no matter what value x has, the value of the score will be in the set $\{0.456 * x + u \mid -0.1 \le u \le 0.2\}$. One advantage of having such an annotation is that it allows the specifier to make uncertainty in the true value of the score explicit (said value may be a best-effort estimate of a probability, for example). And the analysis of conditions *cond* written in Peal$^+$ can then reflect such non-deterministic choices, and may so validate conditions so that they are robust under any sensitivity changes within the ranges of these declared intervals.

It remains to explain the syntax for declaring policies and rules. A rule *if* (*cond*) *score* evaluates a condition *cond*. If the latter is true, the rule evaluates to the value of *score*; otherwise, the rule does not evaluate to anything. A policy consists of zero or more rules, a composition operator for rules (ranging over the same operators as for composition of policy sets), and the specification of a default score:

$$p_i = op\left(if\left(c_1\ s_1\right)\ldots if\left(c_n\ s_n\right)\right) default\ s \qquad \text{or} \qquad p_i = op\left(\right) default\ s \quad (1)$$

The intuitive semantics of a policy p_i as in (1) in Peal^+ is then as follows. First, determine which rules in policy p_i have a true condition c_i: this is the set $X = \{s_i \mid c_i \text{ true and occurs in } p_i\}$. Second, if X is non-empty, return $op(X)$; otherwise, return default score s as meaning of p_i. This semantics requires that we can reliably determine the truth values of all predicates within a policy.

The language Peal^+ is an extension of the language Peal which was developed in the papers [8,2,7,9]. Let us therefore quickly state what new features Peal^+ contains over the version of Peal described in [7,9]. In Peal^+, composition operators are now unified in that they are the same for policies and policy sets, meaning that we now can also combine policy sets with addition and multiplication. Scores in Peal^+ may not just be raw scores but may be annotated with a constant real-valued interval, and scores can now also be casted into policy sets. Finally, the condition expressions $score < pSet$ and $pSet \leq score$ of Peal are generalized in Peal^+ to $pSet1 < pSet2$ and $pSet1 \leq pSet2$. The justification for such extensions from Peal to Peal^+ is that it allows for more expressive score calculations, for the modelling of score uncertainty, but at the same time won't complicate much the *symbolic* generation of analysis code in the Z3 SMT solver as described for Peal in detail in [7,9].

Let us see how Peal^+ can be used to plug into up-stream languages. For example, an expression of form $0.9 < min(pSet1, pSet2)$ is a Boolean condition in which 0.9 acts as a strict threshold for the score of a declared policy set, where the *min* composition means that the scores of both policy sets $pSet1$ and $pSet2$ have to be above 0.9. This condition may aggregate evidence for trusting a request to some resource and were we combine two policy sets in a conservative manner as both policy sets have to attain sufficient evidence for the threshold constraint $0.9 < x$. If we plug this condition into an access-control language that supports rules such as `grant if (cond) else deny`, then using $0.9 < min(pSet1, pSet2)$ in place of `cond` articulates the circumstances under which access would be granted. Note that conditions in Peal^+ are agnostic as to whether or not they support positive (as in this example) or negative decisions. This depends on the up-stream context into which such conditions are placed, and this is a potential usability issues.

5   Usability Issues of Peal^+

We provide a small example of condition declarations in the language Peal^+. The example captures a fictional setting in which a car rental company might assess the trust it places in US rental agreements within a variety of contexts, and it shows that trust declarations may have ethical or legal dimensions as well.

Example 1. The policies, policy sets, and conditions for this example are depicted in Figure 2, using concrete syntax very close to that of the tool PEALT that implements language Peal [9]. These declarations specify four policies:

- Policy b1 classifies the type of car to be rented, and associates with it a monetary value, where the default value is higher than that of a compact car. The composition operator is maximum here.
- Policy b2 classifies the driver who wishes to rent the car by assigning a trust score based on the country of origin of the driver's license. US Licences are trusted more than European ones, and European ones are trusted somewhat more than UK ones (as Europeans and Americans drive on the same side of the road). Licences from other parts of the world are trusted less and there is uncertainty about their trustworthiness coded in the interval $[-0.1, 0.1]$. Drivers with no licence are not trusted at all (default of 0). The composition operator is here minimum (seeking the least trust).
- Policy b3 classifies the risk of the car rental in terms of the type of intended car usage: there is the highest risk if some off road driving is planned, followed by city driving as the next highest risk, whereas long distance driving has the lowest risk (lower than the default risk of 0.3). A mixed usage of long distance and city driving has an intermediate risk associated with it. The composition operator is maximum (going for the highest risk).
- Finally, policy b4 accumulates evidence for trusting to rent out the car, based on evidence aggregated from driver information: a trust score that is linear in the number x of years driven accident-free within the past years from now is one source, as is the indication of being able to speak English (e.g. so that road signs can be read and understood), and the fact that the driver is female. Note that negative trust evidence is included when the driver would travel alone. The composition operator is addition here, accumulating trust and distrust.

These policies are composed into policy sets in condition c_1, where we take the asset value of the case in b1 and multiply this with the perceived risk – which is the trust score of b2 "inverted" to $1 - b2$ in order to capture such risk:

- Condition c0 limits the credit for number of years driven without accidents to 10 and forces x to be non-negative.
- Condition c1 stipulates that this weighted risk be no larger than 50,000.
- Condition c2, on the other hand, specifies that the accumulative trust evidence collected about the driver be strictly larger than 0.4.
- The next three conditions express, using propositional connectives, that the events listed in the three respective policies b1 up to b3 are mutually exclusive (but not necessarily *across* such policies).
- Condition c5 captures a logical constraint (company policy), that no luxury car is rented out if the intended usage includes some off road driving.
- Finally, the condition for trusting the rental arrangement (from the point of view of the rental company) is expressed in condition cond, that specifies that all seven conditions already discussed have to be met.

Let us now illustrate usability issues of trust aggregation languages, by appealing to the above example and its use of the language Peal$^+$ when and where appropriate. One concern is the intuitive meaning and appropriateness of composition operators *op*. In policy b1, for example, the operator is the maximum.

```
b1 = max ((isLuxuryCar) 150,000) (isSedan 60,000)
          (isCompact 30,000)) default 50,000
b2 = min ((hasUSLicense 0.9) (hasUKLicense 0.6)
          (hasEULicence 0.7) (hasOtherLicense 0.4 [-0.1,0.1])) default 0
b3 = max ((someOffRoadDriving 0.8) (OnlyCityUsage 0.4)
          (onlyLongDistance 0.2) (mixedUsage 0.25)) default 0.3
b4 = + ((accidentFreeForYears 0.05*x) (speaksEnglish 0.05)
        (travelsAlone -0.2) (femaleDriver 0.1)) default 0
c0 = (0 <= x <= 10)
c1 = (* b1 (+ b2 (-1))) <= 50,000
c2 = 0.4 < b4
c3 = "all events in b1 are mutually exclusive"
c4 = "all events in b2 are mutually exclusive"
c5 = "all events in b3 are mutually exclusive"
c6 = !isLuxuryCar || !someOffRoadDriving
cond = c0 && c1 && c2 && c3 && c4 && c5 && c6
```

Fig. 2. Declarations in Peal$^+$ that specify criteria for a car rental company to trust renting out cars in certain usage scenarios

This conveys a false sense of purpose for this composition, as condition $c3$ stipulates that all events within that policy are mutually exclusive. So an operator such as *sole* (which would return the score of the only true event or the default score if no or more than one event were true) may seem more intuitive. In fact, operator *sole* would also be usable for policy $b2$. Although it is interesting to note that policy $b1$ uses maximum as it conservatively wants to estimate the value of assets under risk, whereas policy $b2$ uses minimum as a conservative estimate of a trust score.

Another potential problem with policy $b1$ is that the default score is not smaller than all scores within the policy body. This means that the policy is *not monotone*: all its events might be false, but when we then make more events true by making just `isCompact` true, the score of the policy *decreases*. This might be intended by the specifier but it could lead to "attacks" of these specifications by which conditions for trust could be made true by making some events false. Similarly, one might hide attributes in attribute-based access control to get unintended access. The presence of such attacks can be statically analyzed. For example, for the attribute-based language PTaCL [3] a tool ATRAP was developed in [6] that automatically searches for such attacks and – in their absence – constructs a formal proof of their absence.

Furthermore, language Peal$^+$ does not contain types or similar annotations that might indicate whether policies, policy sets or conditions intent to express risk, trust, monetary values or any other modality. For example, we might expect that risk and trust are inversely proportionate. Similarly, the language does not say whether these modalities are specified with a pessimistic, optimistic, averaging or some other cognitive stance.

Language Peal$^+$ also has a simple but implicit scoping: there are no syntactic blocks that can rebind declared names of predicates, policies, etc. Such names refer to the same entities in all declared conditions. We think that the introduction of local names and their static scoping would introduce unwanted cognitive complexity to using Peal$^+$. On the other hand, the language does not have a direct means of defining condition names that contain parameter headers. For example, condition c1 has policies b1 and b2 as parameters and so it would be convenient to write c1(b1, b2) and to be able to replace formal parameters b1 and b2 with actual parameters in other condition expressions.

Another interesting usability issue is the fact that rules may contain complex conditions *cond* and not just predicates *q*. This may mostly just be for convenience so that predicates *q* can reflect their propositional logical structure explicitly in Peal$^+$ as opposed to through an interface to a down-stream language. But expressions *cond* used in rules may themselves talk about policy sets. This allows richer aggregation mechanisms, yet it also introduces an apparent circularity: consider policy b1 = (if (c1) 0.3) default 0 and condition c1 = 0.2 < max(b1, b2) for some policy b2. The meaning of b1 (its score) depends on the meaning of c1 (a truth value), which in turn depends on the score of b1. Fortunately, this is not a genuine circularity as it merely constrains the possible truth values of c1 and scores of b1 in analyses. However, a user-facing language may want to prevent or flag up such circularities as they are most likely due to typos or reflect unintended consequences.

A general usability issue of languages such as Peal$^+$ is how we aid specifiers in validating that the conditions they express in these languages reflect the intentions that they have in managing assets, risks, reputations, and trust. We believe that specifiers should be able to subject conditions to a variety of automated analyses that can boost their confidence in that intentions have been met in specified conditions. In [2] such analyses were proposed, and some of these analyses were implemented in the tool PEALT [9] for the smaller language Peal. For example, in PEALT one can ask whether a condition is always true or always false – both would typically indicate that intentions are not met; one can ask whether a condition of form *score* < *pSet* changes when *score* is changed by a specified value; etc. These analyses are rendered as push-button technology through automated translation of conditions and the desired analysis to code for the SMT solver Z3, where the execution of that code performs that analysis and gives feedback. We believe that this automated means of performing analyses and getting their feedback is crucial for gaining acceptance for the use of trust-aggregation languages in real systems.

6   Evaluation of Peal$^+$ against Remaining Requirements

We now assess to what extent our language Peal$^+$ meets the requirements we formulated above, and how these requirements interact with usability issues. We begin with **Expressiveness**. Language Peal$^+$ is certainly very expressive in that predicates *q* may provide plugs to very rich languages for providing the exact meaning of such predicates. Conditions have intuitive structure: propositional logic over the input language for predicates plus the comparison of policy sets. A source of cognitive complexity is whether we understand a comparison to be true in all scenarios or to be true in at least one scenario. For example, when we write $pSet1 \leq pSet2$ do we mean that the score of the first expression is always no larger than that of the second expression or that is can be no larger? Answering such questions depends on how such conditions are used in up-stream languages (or even in Peal^+ conditions). Again, analyses can be used to provide needed sanity checks that intended usage of conditions matches their semantics. Additionally, user-facing languages that compile into Peal^+ could be designed in which patterns and types make clear the intentional stances of policies and their composition (e.g. whether a policy aggregates trust scores, asset values, etc.). Use of such patterns would be expected to prevent a lot of misinterpretations that would therefore not be flagged up in analyses and so reduce the number of "condition refinement steps".

The stratification of policy sets into rules, policies, and policy sets should help with structuring more complex aggregation meachanisms. The structure of rules seems intuitive enough, but one may object to its behavior when its condition is false. For example, one might want a rule that says "if q, then 0.9 else 0.1" for expressing trust, suggesting that q indicates trust whereas $\neg q$ indicates distrust. But this is not a good language primitive as not all trust indicators suggest distrust in their absence. Moreover, we can build expressions such as the above as a policy $op\,(if\,(q)\,0.9)\,default\,0.1$.

Let us discuss **Scalable Analysis** next. In [9], we showed experimentally that language Peal allows analyses of fairly large conditions (with hundreds or thousands of rules and policies) within seconds or minutes, where the marked bottleneck is an extensive use of multiplication in policies. Given the specifics of symbolic code generation for these analyses in the Z3 SMT solver, we anticipate that similar scalability will be achievable for the richer language Peal^+, and we plan to investigate this in future work. A nice aspect of using back-ends such as Z3 is that this approach will benefit from whatever future optimizations or marked improvements will be made in SMT solving.

One important usability aspect of these analyses is that their output consists of the description of a scenario (some true predicates, some false predicates, and values of variables that support such truth values). We are currently developing techniques for the independent verification of the correctness of such output. In general, this is needed because the method of code generation for analysis may be flawed or because the reasoning about real numbers in some back-end tool may be imprecise. By correctness of computed output we mean that the reported information is statically sufficient for explaining that the conditions supplied as arguments to an analysis have the claimed truth values. Verification of this claim involves the solution of 2-person games and fairly simple static analyses of policy expressions. It would be interesting to investigate how this algorithmic certification of correctness could be communicated to users in a form that goes beyond *"Independent verification of analysis outputs was successful"* but renders the insights of this verification process in an abstract yet still more informative form – by hiding some of the complexity of that verification process.

As for **Interfacing**, we think that the addition of parameterized headers to Peal$^+$ would help in defining clear interfaces to down-stream and up-stream languages. In Peal$^+$, we don't explicitly manage name spaces across domains. But existing naming convention could enforce globally unique names for predicates and variables within Peal$^+$. Also, Peal$^+$ can use any down-stream language that returns Booleans as predicates q; and Peal$^+$ can plug into any up-stream language that expects real values (for policy sets $pSet$) or Booleans (for conditions $cond$).

7   Related Work

We refer to the extant literature, see for example [13] and [4], for a more thorough discussion of trust mechanisms and their role in general system design. Empirical work done by social scientists in the general space of trust perceptions and its support in decision making is an important source of information for the design of user-facing trust aggregation languages.

In [5], it was studied how software engineers evaluate the trustworthiness of software components and how they decide to use such components in their software development. It was shown that these technical people used the same socio-cognitive processes as non-technical ones and also employ a "leap of faith" in which their trust decision may not reflect their trust evaluation. Interestingly, the decision to trust was *negatively* impacted by contact with component developers (since such contact was often the result of problems in said component).

The book chapter [14] recalls that a lot of research focussed on trust symbols (e.g. on web sites) that may influence the trust perceptions of users but that the effectiveness of such trust signals cannot be empirically validated [10]. In fact, technical systems need to consider trustworthiness of services already at the design phase of such systems. They also stress the need to move from mere trust symbols to trust *symptons* that can form the basis of trust assessment heuristics. In that context, we point out that the credit card industry has a history of using and modifying statistics that form the basis of so called *score cards* with which the creditworthiness of an applicant is evaluated against a history of past clients and their attributes and performance. For example, [12] studies how one might account for "population drift" in consumer credit classification – something of great importance in times of high migration and fast societal changes. Therefore, there could be of interest to investigate whether that research in statistics may offer insights in the design of trust assessment heuristics for executable IT systems.

Acknowledgements: We are grateful that this work was supported by funding from Intel® Corporation within its *Trust Evidence* research project.

References

1. Blaze, M., Feigenbaum, J., Keromytis, A.D.: KeyNote: Trust management for public-key infrastructures. In: Christianson, B., Crispo, B., Harbison, W.S., Roe, M. (eds.) Security Protocols 1998. LNCS, vol. 1550, pp. 59–63. Springer, Heidelberg (1999)
2. Crampton, J., Huth, M., Morisset, C.: Policy-based access control from numerical evidence. Technical Report 2013/6, Imperial College London, Department of Computing (October 2013) ISSN 1469-4166 (Print)
3. Crampton, J., Morisset, C.: PTaCL: A language for attribute-based access control in open systems. In: Degano, P., Guttman, J.D. (eds.) Principles of Security and Trust. LNCS, vol. 7215, pp. 390–409. Springer, Heidelberg (2012)
4. Flechais, I., Riegelsberger, J., Sasse, M.A.: Divide and conquer: the role of trust and assurance in the design of secure socio-technical systems. In: Proceedings of the 2005 Workshop on New security Paradigms, NSPW 2005, pp. 33–41. ACM, New York (2005)
5. Fugard, A.J.B., Beck, E., Gärtner, M.: How Will Software Engineers of the Internet of Things Reason about Trust? In: Wichert, R., Van Laerhoven, K., Gelissen, J. (eds.) AmI 2011. CCIS, vol. 277, pp. 274–279. Springer, Heidelberg (2012)
6. Griesmayer, A., Morisset, C.: Automated certification of authorisation policy resistance. In: Crampton, J., Jajodia, S., Mayes, K. (eds.) ESORICS 2013. LNCS, vol. 8134, pp. 574–591. Springer, Heidelberg (2013)
7. Huth, M., Kuo, J.H.-P.: PEALT: A reasoning tool for numerical aggregation of trust evidence. Technical Report 2013/7, Imperial College London, Department of Computing (2013) ISSN 1469-4166 (Print)
8. Huth, M., Kuo, J.H.-P.: Towards verifiable trust management for software execution - (extended abstract). In: Huth, M., Asokan, N., Čapkun, S., Flechais, I., Coles-Kemp, L. (eds.) TRUST 2013. LNCS, vol. 7904, pp. 275–276. Springer, Heidelberg (2013)
9. Huth, M., Kuo, J.H.-P.: PEALT: An automated reasoning tool for numerical aggregation of trust evidence. In: Ábrahám, E., Havelund, K. (eds.) TACAS 2014 (ETAPS). LNCS, vol. 8413, pp. 109–123. Springer, Heidelberg (2014)
10. Kirlappos, I., Sasse, M.A., Harvey, N.: Why trust seals don't work: A study of user perceptions and behavior. In: Katzenbeisser, S., Weippl, E., Camp, L.J., Volkamer, M., Reiter, M., Zhang, X. (eds.) Trust 2012. LNCS, vol. 7344, pp. 308–324. Springer, Heidelberg (2012)
11. Mui, L.: Computational Models of Trust and Reputation: Agents, Evolutionary Games, and Social Networks. PhD thesis. MIT (2002)
12. Pavlidis, N.G., Tasoulis, D.K., Adams, N.M., Hand, D.J.: Adaptive consumer credit classification. Journal of the Operational Research Society 63(12), 1645–1654 (2012)
13. Riegelsberger, J., Sasse, M.A., McCarthy, J.D.: The mechanics of trust: A framework for research and design. Int. J. Hum.-Comput. Stud. 62(3), 381–422 (2005)
14. Sasse, A., Kirlappos, I.: Trust, Computing, and Society, chapter Design for trusted and truthworthy services: why we must do better. Cambridge University Press (in press, 2014)

An Image-Based CAPTCHA
Using Sophisticated Mental Rotation

Yuki Ikeya, Masahiro Fujita, Junya Kani, Yuta Yoneyama, and Masakatsu Nishigaki

Graduate School of Informatics, Shizuoka University, Japan
nisigaki@inf.shizuoka.ac.jp

Abstract. As one of the advanced Completely Automated Public Turing tests to tell Computers and Humans Apart (CAPTCHAs), the CAPTCHA using mental rotation has been proposed. Mental rotation is an advanced human-cognitive-processing ability to rotate mental representations of "one" single 2D/3D object. However, as have already been reported, the mental rotation CAPTCHA can be overcome by pattern matching and/or machine learning. Therefore, this paper proposes to enhance the mental rotation CAPTCHA by using "two" distinct 3D objects in the task of mental rotation, which we call "sophisticated mental rotation". We implemented a prototype of the sophisticated mental rotation CAPTCHA, and carried out basic experiments to confirm its usability. Also, we conducted a comparison between the proposed CAPTCHA and existing CAPTCHAs. The obtained results were satisfactory.

Keywords: CAPTCHA, Mental Rotation, 3DCG.

1 Introduction

With the expansion of Web services, denial of service (DoS) attacks by malicious automated programs (malwares) are becoming a serious problem. Thus, the Turing test is becoming a necessary technique to discriminate humans from malicious automated programs and the Completely Automated Public Turing test to tell Computers and Humans Apart (CAPTCHA) [1] system developed by Carnegie Mellon University has been widely used. The simplest CAPTCHA presents distorted or noise added text (Fig. 1) to users who visit Web sites and want to use their services. We refer to this simple CAPTCHA as text recognition based-CAPTCHA. If they can read the given text, they are certified as human. If they cannot read the text, they are certified to be malwares.

However, many researchers have recently pointed out that automated programs with optical character reader (OCR) and/or machine learning can answer those conventional text recognition based-CAPTCHA [2]. Indeed, these sophisticated malwares have been spreading and they have cracked the text recognition based-CAPTCHA [3, 4]. It can be made more difficult for automated programs to pass tests (i.e. read texts) by increasing the distortion or noise. However, it also becomes more difficult for humans to read such texts. We therefore need to adopt even more advanced human cognitive processing capabilities to enhance CAPTCHA to overcome this problem.

T. Tryfonas and I. Askoxylakis (Eds.): HAS 2014, LNCS 8533, pp. 57–68, 2014.
© Springer International Publishing Switzerland 2014

Fig. 1. CAPTCHA used by Google   **Fig. 2.** Asirra

Image recognition based-CAPTCHA such as Asirra [6] (Fig. 2) is known as one of the effective solutions for enhancing CAPTCHA, because image recognition is a much more difficult problem for automated programs than character recognition [5]. Labeled images are used in the image recognition based-CAPTCHA to confirm that a user can recognize the meaning of the image. In Asirra, several photos of animals (e.g. images of cats and dogs with diverse backdrops, angles, poses, and lighting) are presented to a user, and the user is then asked to select a specific animal in a test. For example, suppose that the user is asked to select "cat"; if he/she can select all photos labeled as cat in the test, then he/she is certified to be human. If not, he/she is certified to be an automated program.

However, a technique that has effectively been used to breach the image recognition based-CAPTCHA has been reported and shocked researchers [7, 8]. Advancements to cracking capabilities (CAPTCHA cracking algorithms and CPU processing speeds) will continue indefinitely. No matter how advanced malicious automated programs are, a CAPTCHA that will not pass automated programs is required. Hence, we have to find another human cognitive processing capability to tackle this challenge.

As one of the interesting possibilities to deal with this challenge, mental rotation has been used in YUNiTi's CAPTCHA [11] (Fig. 3). Mental rotation [9, 10] is the advanced human-cognitive-processing ability to rotate mental representations of two-dimensional (2D) and/or three-dimensional (3D) objects. In YUNiTi's CAPTCHA, Web page visitors need to choose an appropriate object from a candidate image list matching the same 3D object as the question image. However, a report suggested that this 3D CAPTCHA could be vulnerable to template matching attack [12]. The CAPTCHA using only simple rotation of "one" single 3D object is not safe enough.

Therefore, this paper proposes to enhance the mental rotation CAPTCHA. The approach taken in this paper is make the task of mental rotation more complex by using "two" distinct 3D objects. We call this enhanced mental task "sophisticated mental rotation". Our CAPTCHA is expected to improve the decrypting tolerance for automated programs without noticeable degradation in understandability for humans.

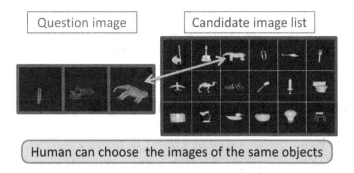

Fig. 3. YUNiTi's 3D CAPTCHA

2   Mental Rotation and YUNiTi's CAPTCHA

Humans are good at spatial reasoning capacity. For this reason, it is not difficult for humans to understand the three-dimensional (3D) shape of the object from the two-dimensional (2D) image. This kind of "ability to recognize 3D objects from 2D image" is considered to be an advanced human-cognitive-processing ability [14]. Also, it is possible for humans to rotate 2D/3D objects in an imagination and to recognize the shape figure, which has been photographed from a different point of view. This human ability is called "mental rotation" [9, 10]. Therefore, by looking at the 2D images of the two sheets of copies from different viewpoints of one single 3D object, humans infer the shape of the 3D object in the 2D images, and understand the change of the viewpoint.

Mental rotation is used in YUNiTi's CAPTCHA [11] (Fig. 3). In this CAPTCHA, Web page visitors need to choose appropriate objects from a candidate image list (containing 18 objects) by matching the same 3D objects as the question image (containing 3 objects). If they can choose all the correct 3D objects corresponding to each of three question images, they are certified as human. If they cannot, they are rejected as automated programs. The question images are automatically generated by randomly selecting a 3D object from the candidate image list and then photo shooting the object from different viewpoints.

However, it has been reported that this 3D CAPTCHA could be vulnerable to template matching attack [12]. In YUNiTi's CAPTCHA, all 3D objects which are used in the candidate image list are unchanged and immutable. Therefore, an attacker can collect a variety of question images shot from all angles for each object in a limited number of CAPTCHA trials, and exploit them for template matching attack and/or machine learning attack. Additionally, automated programs (malwares) can utilize the technology of three-dimensional object recognition. In the current technology, it is possible to figure out almost exactly the 3D shape of the 3D object from two images, which are taken of a 3D object from two viewpoints [13]. In YUNiTi's CAPTCHA, the response to the CAPTCHA test is to select an answer image among the candidate images. This means that malwares may be able to identify the correct object by restoring the 3D shape of the correct object from two images displayed in a CAPTCHA test (a question image and the corresponding image in the candidate image list). That is why the CAPTCHA using only simple rotation of one single 3D object is not safe enough.

3   Sophisticated Mental Rotation CAPTCHA

3.1   Concept

In this paper, we propose to use two distinct 3D objects in the task of mental rotation (which is referred to as "sophisticated mental rotation" in this paper). As long as these two distinct objects are the semantically same as each other, it is expected that this task is still not too difficult for humans, but enhances the safety by increasing complexity of analysis by automated programs (malwares).

Fig. 4 and Fig. 5 show the overview of the sophisticated mental rotation CAPTCHA. Sophisticated mental rotation CAPTCHA is presented with a pair of 2D images (the "question image" and its "response image") of two distinct 3D objects shot from two different viewpoints. In the question image, a marker (like a red sphere) is added to any portion of the 3D object. There is no marker in the response image. The user is then asked to click the location on the response image, which is corresponding to the position where the marker in the question image is located. If the user is a human, he/she can use (sophisticated) mental rotation to identify the correct position of the response image.

On the other hand, malware can utilize the technologies of pattern matching, machine learning, and three-dimensional recognition. However, these technologies are all basically designed for finding the "visually identical" object to a target object. In contrast, in the sophisticated mental rotation proposed here, two different 3D objects (to be more precise, two objects are semantically same but "visually different" from each other) are being used. Therefore, it can be expected that it is still difficult even for these technologies to overcome the task of sophisticated mental rotation. Alternatively, if an appropriate level of transformation/deformation is applied against two images, it is also expected that three-dimensional shape identification for malwares become markedly difficult. Therefore, in this paper, we consider two types of systems; two distinct 3D objects are produced by deforming one 3D model (type-α) (Fig. 4), or by two different 3D models (type-β) (Fig. 5).

Generally speaking, for automated programs, producing 2D images from the 3D object is significantly easier than identification of 3D objects from a 2D image. In (sophisticated) mental rotation CAPTCHA, this "one-way property" contributes to the automatic generation of a pair of the question image and its response image. As shown in Fig. 6, automated programs (Web servers) can generate new images using 3D computer graphic technology every time and achieve the automatic generation of the pair of images. The pair of images can be generated innumerably by registering a large number of 3D models with a system and changing some parameters such as the object, size of the object, marker position, viewpoint, and so on.

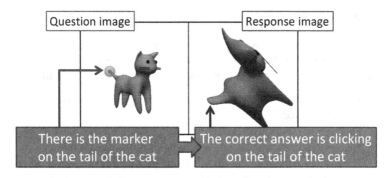

Fig. 4. Sophisticated mental rotation CAPTCHA (type-α)
(Left: question image; Right: response image)

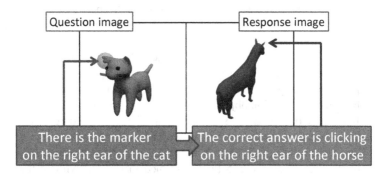

Fig. 5. Sophisticated mental rotation CAPTCHA (type-β)
(Left: question image; Right: response image)

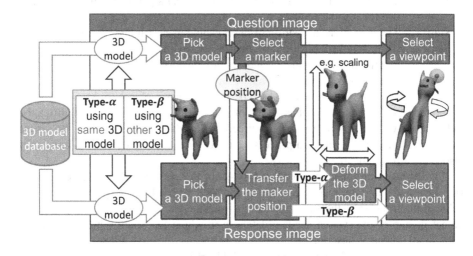

Fig. 6. Automatic generation procedure in sophisticated mental rotation CAPTCHA

3.2   Authentication Procedure

Authentication procedure of the sophisticated mental rotation CAPTCHA is as follows. It is here assumed that the sophisticated mental rotation CAPTCHA system has a 3D model database, in which enough number of 3D models are archived.

Step1.   The system picks up a 3D model for the question image (defined to as "question object") at random.

Step2.   The system randomly selects a marker position on the question object.

Step3.   The system randomly selects a viewpoint of the question image.

Step4.   The system generates the question image, by photo shooting the question object (selected in step 1) with the marker (selected in step 2) from the viewpoint (selected in step 3).

Step5.   The system picks up the question object (selected in step 1) again as a 3D object for the response image (defined to as "response object") (type-α), or the system picks up another 3D model for the response object at random (type-β).

Step6.   The marker position (selected in step 2) in the question object is transferred to the response object (selected in step 5). That is, the marker positions are quite identical (type-α), or semantically identical (type-β) between the question object and the response object.

Step7.   In the case of type-α, the system deforms the response object randomly.

Step8.   The system randomly selects a viewpoint of the response image.

Step9.   The system generates the response image, by photo shooting the response object (selected in step 5 (and deformed in step 7)) without the marker from the viewpoint (selected in step 8). Note that the response object has the marker (set in step 6), but no marker is visually shown.

Step10.   The system shows a user (Web page visitor) a pair of the question image and the response image.

Step11.   The user clicks a position of the invisible marker in the response image.

Step12.   If the clicked position of the response image is correct, the user is identified as a human, and if the position is incorrect, the user is identified as a malware.

Fig. 4 shows an image example of type-α. A response object (right of Fig. 4) is generated from the question object (left of Fig. 4) by scaling at any magnification independently in each of the x/y/z direction. In this paper we use the affine transformation as a deformation processing in step 7, but some other deforming may also be able be applicable.

Fig. 5 shows an image example of type-β. In Fig. 5, the question object is a cat (left of Fig. 5), and the response object is replaced with a horse (right of Fig. 5). To achieve the transfer of the marker position from the question object to the response object in step 6, the system needs a database in which the relationship between the parts of all objects is described.

In the sophisticated mental rotation CAPTCHA, it is difficult for malwares to identify the invisible marker position in the response image by using only the question image (with a marker) and response image (without a marker). On the other hand, our system knows the marker position in the response image in step 6. Because this knowledge forms a trapdoor, our system (Web server) can automatically generate the challenges that malwares cannot answer, and then the system can determine whether the user (Web page visitor) clicked the correct position. By randomly choosing the object, the position of the marker, and the position of the viewpoint every time of the authentication, the system with a large amount of 3D models can automatically generate a myriad of challenges. Therefore, the sophisticated mental rotation CAPTCHA is expected to be also resistant to template matching attack and/or machine learning attack.

3.3   Implementation

We implemented a prototype sophisticated mental rotation CAPTCHA (type-α). Fig. 7 shows an authentication screen example of our CAPTCHA: the question image is in the left of Fig. 7; the response image is the right of Fig. 7. The red sphere that is drawn on the question image is the marker. The Web page visitor needs to identify and click the location on the response image, which corresponds to the position of the marker on the question image. If the distance between the clicked position and the correct position is the threshold value or less, he/she is certified as human. In the example of Fig. 7, as the marker is pointing to the right ear of the cat in the question image, it is correct if the visitor clicks the right ear of the cat in the response image.

Note here that the coordinate of the (invisible) maker position in the response object is a 3D data, whereas a mouse click by the user is a 2D data (because it is obtained as the coordinate information on the display). Therefore, the system computes the 2D coordinates of the marker on the display from the 3D marker position. In this implementation, the correct answer range (threshold value) is a circle with a 30-pixel radius.

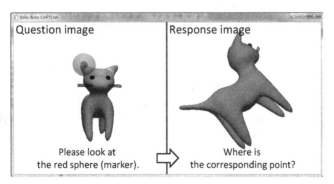

Fig. 7. Prototype sophisticated mental rotation CAPTCHA (type-α)
(Left: question image; Right: response image)

4   Verification Experiment

We conducted basic experiments to evaluate the authentication rate of the proposed method (type-α). In addition, after the experiment, we did a survey on subjects for usability. Due to time constraints, the prototype system implementation and the experiment have yet to be performed on the sophisticated mental rotation CAPTCHA (type-β).

4.1   Experiment Method

The subjects included twenty volunteers, subjects 01-20, who all are college students in the Faculty of Informatics and Faculty of Engineering at Shizuoka University. Each subject solved five challenges of the sophisticated mental rotation CAPTCHA in a row. In this experiment, the first and the second trials were treated as a tutorial. We only evaluated the remaining three trials.

Five 3D objects (A - E) were used in the experiment. In the tutorial, the object A and B were shown in this order. In the following three trials, the object C – E appeared in random order. The subjects were told to answer according to the center of the sphere (the small opaque sphere inside rather than the big translucent outer sphere). For each challenge, we recorded success or failure, response time, and the click position.

After completing all of the CAPTCHA challenges, we had the subjects respond to the following questionnaires. Question 1, 3, 5 were answered on a 5-point scale.

Question 1.   Is it easy solving the CAPTCHA? (Easy) : Yes (5) – No (1)
Question 2.   If you chose 1 or 2 in Question 1, please write why you think that it is not easy.
Question 3.   Is it user-friendly? (User-friendly) : Yes (5) – No (1)
Question 4.   If you chose 1 or 2 in Question 3, please write why you think that it is not user-friendly.
Question 5.   Is it pleasant? (Pleasant) : Yes (5) – No (1)
Question 6.   If you chose 4 or 5 in Question 5, please write why you think that it is pleasant.
Question 7.   How many challenges would you be able to consecutively solve? Also, please write why you think that.
Question 8.   Which would you choose: text recognition based-CAPTCHA or sophisticated mental rotation CAPTCHA in at real Web service? Also, please write your reason.

4.2   Experiment Results

Correct Response Rate and Response Time. The experiment results are shown in Table 1, which summarizes the correct response rate and the average response time for each subject. Because the order of the 3D object was random in this experiment, we show the results summarized in experimental order in Table 2 and by object in Table 3.

Table 1. The experiment results for each subject

	Subject									
	01	02	03	04	05	06	07	08	09	10
Correct response rate	2/3	2/3	3/3	3/3	3/3	2/3	3/3	2/3	1/3	3/3
Average response time [sec]	6.7	5.3	3.9	8.7	3.9	8.9	6.5	4.6	4.3	5.4
	Subject									
	11	12	13	14	15	16	17	18	19	20
Correct response rate	2/3	2/3	2/3	3/3	2/3	3/3	2/3	1/3	1/3	2/3
Average response time [sec]	7.1	3.9	3.2	3.7	4.8	6.4	3.4	5.9	6.1	4.5

	Average
Correct response rate	73.3% (44/60)
Average response time [sec]	5.4

Table 2. The experiment result of each order

	First time	Second time	Third time
Average correct response rate	60.0% (12/20)	80.0% (16/20)	80.0% (16/20)
Average response time [sec]	5.9	5.5	5.2

Table 3. The experiment result of each 3D object

	Object C	Object D	Object E
Average correct response rate	80.0% (16/20)	55.0% (11/20)	85.0% (17/20)
Average response time [sec]	6.1	4.6	5.4

From Table 1, the correct response rate of the sophisticated mental rotation CAPTCHA is 77.3% on average (a total of 60 times, 44 successes, 16 failures). The correct response rate is too low for practical use. Future improvements are necessary. As can be seen from Table 2, the correct answer rate for the first trial is the lowest. Thus the correct response rate is expected to increase, as a user gains familiarity. As Table 3 shows, the correct response rate depends strongly on which 3D object is used.

We analyzed why the subjects failed. There are three main reasons. The first is a mistake due to confusing left and right sides of the 3D object shown in the response image. There were five failures by this reason among the 16 total failures. The second reason is a slight deviation of the click position. There were four failures by this reason. If we increase the radius of the correct answer range (threshold value) to 35 pixels from 30 pixels, then the correct response rate rises to 80.0%. In the future, we will consider the appropriate correct answer range. The third reason is a difficulty in the recognition of the depth information of the image. In particular, when the 3D object is viewed from just in front, behind, above, beside, or under, the depth is difficult to be grasped and it is more likely to make a mistake. Since incorrect recognition of depth is associated with the other two reasons, further examination is required on the selection of viewpoint.

From Table 1, the average response time per challenge is 5.4 seconds; the shortest time is 3.2 seconds, and the maximum time is 8.9 seconds. The expected response time for the text recognition based-CAPTCHAs is around 10 seconds at the most. Therefore, it can be said that the proposed CAPTCHA can be solved in a shorter time compared with the text recognition based-CAPTCHA. As Table 2 shows, the response time is not dependent on the execution order. As can be seen from Table 3, there is a difference in response time by 3D object. We will study the trends of 3D objects that can be solved in a short time.

Usability. The results of the survey are shown in Table 4.

In Questions 1, most subjects answered 4 (5 if easy), and the average value was 3.3. The subjects who answered difficult (1 or 2) were asked to write the reason in Question 2. Several reasons are as follows: viewing in three dimensions is difficult; understanding of left and right of object is difficult; it is difficult as the place to click (in the response image) is not visible.

In Questions 3, most subjects answered 5 (5 if user-friendly), and the average value was 4.3. The subjects who answered user-hostile (1 or 2) wrote the following reasons in Question 4: considering the structure of the solid object is troublesome; it is troublesome if it has to be solved every time.

In Questions 5, most subjects answered 4 (5 if pleasant), and the average value was 4.3. The subjects who answered pleasant (4 or 5) wrote the following reasons in Question 5: using the image is fun; it is fun like a game; it is interesting because it tests spatial reasoning capacity.

In Question 7, most subjects, 13 people, answered "three challenges". The second most common answer, chosen by five subjects, was "two challenges". There was one subject who answered one and four challenges respectively. This result indicates that many subjects do not feel like solving the CAPTCHA four or more times consecutively. The primary reasons include the following: "I would fail if there are too many", "It is troublesome and takes too long". In addition, there were also opinions saying, "An appropriate number of challenges will vary with the importance of Web services", and "I think even one challenge is painful if I grow older".

Table 4. Result of survey

	Subject														
	01	02	03	04	05	06	07	08	09	10	11	12	13	14	15
Q1	2	2	4	4	4	5	4	4	2	2	4	3	3	4	2
Q3	4	4	4	2	5	5	4	5	5	1	5	5	5	3	5
Q5	4	4	4	4	4	3	5	3	5	4	5	4	4	4	5
Q7	3	3	2	1	3	2	4	2	2	2	3	3	3	3	3
Q8	T	T	M	M	M	M	M	M	M	M	M	M	T	T	M

	Subject					Average	Q1. Easy: Yes (5) – No (1)
	16	17	18	19	20		Q3. User-friendly: Yes (5) – No (1)
Q1	4	4	3	2	3	3.3	Q5. Pleasant: Yes (5) – No (1)
Q3	5	4	5	4	5	4.3	Q7. How many questions?
Q5	5	5	5	4	5	4.3	Q8. Which would you choose?
Q7	3	3	3	3	3	2.7	(T: Text recognition based-CAPTCHA,
Q8	M	M	M	T	M	-	M: proposed CAPTCHA)

In Question 8, five subjects chose the text recognition based-CAPTCHA, while 15 subjects chose the sophisticated mental rotation CAPTCHA. We believe subjects who felt inconvenience of the text recognition based-CAPTCHA chose the sophisticated mental rotation CAPTCHA. The main reasons for choosing the text recognition based-CAPTCHA are as follows: text recognition based-CAPTCHA is easier to understand; it can be done with only the keyboard; the sophisticated mental rotation CAPTCHA requires time in order to answer correctly. The main reasons for choosing the sophisticated mental rotation CAPTCHA are as follows: text recognition based-CAPTCHA is more difficult; it can be done with only the mouse; it is pleasant to use a picture.

5   Conclusion and Future Work

In this paper, we propose the sophisticated mental rotation CAPTCHA, which is an image recognition based-CAPTCHA focusing on the advanced human-cognitive-processing ability of mental rotation. We implemented a prototype of our CAPTCHA, and the system was evaluated in a verification experiment. Twenty human subjects solved the challenges of our CAPTCHA in the experiment. The results show that the correct response rate is 77.3% and the average response time per one challenge is 5.4 seconds. Although the response time required per question is short, the correct response rates have to be improved. Our survey of the results of usability is satisfactory.

At present, there is still room for improvement in terms of both security and usability, so we plan to make improvements to the proposed method based on the knowledge obtained through the experimental results in this paper. For example, we are planning to consider 3D objects, which are more suitable for (sophisticated) mental rotation CAPTCHA, and improve selection of the viewpoint and threshold value of the correct answer range. In addition, we plan to use our results in the implementation and evaluation of type-β.

It is expected that sophisticated mental rotation is one of difficult tasks for automated programs (malwares). However, the attack techniques of malware vary, and the sophisticated mental rotation CAPTCHA's resistance to decipherment is not proven theoretically. We will conduct studies to determine whether our CAPTCHA is truly resistant to malware attacks.

References

1. The Official CAPTCHA Site, http://www.captcha.net
2. PWNtcha-Captcha Decoder, http://caca.zoy.org/wiki/PWNtcha
3. Yan, J., Ahmad, A.S.E.: Breaking Visual CAPTCHAs with Naïve Pattern Recognition Algorithms. In: 2007 Computer Security Applications Conference, pp. 279–291 (2007)
4. Elson, J., Douceur, J., Howela, J., Saul, J.: Asirra: a CAPTCHA that exploit interest-aligned manual image categorization. In: 2007 ACM CSS, pp. 366–374 (2007)

5. Chellapilla, K., Larson, K., Simard, P., Czerwinski, M.: Computers beat humans at single character recognition in reading-based Human Interaction Proofs (HIPs). In: 2nd Conference on Email and Anti-Spam (CEAS) (2005)
6. MSR Asirra Project, http://research.microsoft.com/asirra/
7. Golle, P.: Machine Learning Attacks Against the ASIRRA CAPTCHA. In: 2008 ACM CSS, pp. 535–542 (2008)
8. Vaughan-Nichols, S.J.: How CAPTCHA got trashed, Computerworld (July 15, 2008), http://www.computerworld.com.au/article/253015/how_captcha_got_trashed/
9. Shepard, R., Cooper, L.: Mental images and their transformations. MIT Press, Cambridge (1982)
10. Shepard, R., Metzler, J.: Mental rotation of three dimensional objects. Science, New Series 171(3972), 701–703 (1971)
11. YUNiTi.com, http://www.yuniti.com/
12. TechnoBabble Pro: How they'll break the 3D CAPTCHA, http://technobabblepro.blogspot.jp/2009/04/how-theyll-break-3d-captcha.html
13. Hartley, R., Zisserman, A.: Multiple View Geometry in Computer Vision. Cambridge University Press, Cambridge (2000)
14. Stafford, T., Webb, M.: Mind Hacks. Oreilly & Associates Inc. (2004)

What Usable Security Really Means:
Trusting and Engaging Users

Iacovos Kirlappos and M. Angela Sasse

University College London, Department of Computer Science,
London, United Kingdom
{i.kirlappos,a.sasse}@cs.ucl.ac.uk

Abstract. Non-compliance with security mechanisms and processes poses a significant risk to organizational security. Current approaches focus on designing systems that restrict user actions to make them 'secure', or providing user interfaces to make security tools 'easy to use'. We argue that an important but often-neglected aspect of compliance is trusting employees to 'do what's right' for security. Previous studies suggest that most employees are intrinsically motivated to behave securely, and that contextual elements of their relationship with the organization provide further motivation to stay secure. Drawing on research on trust, usable security, and economics of information security, we outline how the organization-employee trust relationship can be leveraged by security designers.

Keywords: trust, usable security, information security management.

1 Current State of Security Implementations in Organizations

For most people, the term 'information security' evokes technical mechanisms - such as authentication and access control - implemented to protect organizational assets [1]. Over the past two decades, awareness has been growing that many information security breaches were results of human error and social engineering; Bruce Schneier described people as the "weakest link" in the security chain [2]. Whilst some security experts have, unhelpfully, described users as stupid or careless [3], others have tried to increase compliance by providing 'more usable' security in some form. An implicit assumption of this work has been that - if people are *able* to use a security mechanism correctly, they would be *motivated* to do so [4-9]. But work by usability researchers who listen closely to users [10],[11] and economics-inspired researchers looking at cost and benefits of security mechanisms [12],[13] suggests that the assumption that 'users want security, provided it's not too difficult to use' may be wide off the mark [11],[12],[14]. Users look for efficiencies in their daily lives, and that means 'the less I have to think about security, the better'. And given that is the case, trust becomes important. The traditional "command-and-control" approach to information security management treats employees as untrustworthy components, whose behavior has to be constrained [4]. But recent research has revealed that even

T. Tryfonas and I. Askoxylakis (Eds.): HAS 2014, LNCS 8533, pp. 69–78, 2014.
© Springer International Publishing Switzerland 2014

employees who do not comply with some security policies are motivated and act responsible when they recognize a security risk, and the cost to them is reasonable [10],[11],[15].

Thus, designers of security mechanisms should consider how trust between an organization and its employees affects security behaviors. The role of trust in technology design has been examined by research aiming to create technology platforms that enable the development of trust relationships in online commerce and gaming [16-21]. In this paper we take a different path, building on the trust model by Riegelsberger et al. [16] to explain the benefits of treating employees as trusted entities in organizational security implementations. We (1) use the model explain the creation of a trust relationship between employees and organization, (2) analyze how that affects employee compliance decisions with security policies and mechanisms, and (3) present how the organization-employee trust relationship can be leveraged by security designers to create usable and effective security implementations.

2   Trust in the Organization-Employee Security Relationships

Trust is defined as the "willingness to be vulnerable based on positive expectations about the actions of others" [22] and is only required in interactions where risk and uncertainty about the outcome exist. Risk usually arises from the potential losses a *trustor* (trusting actor) suffers if the *trustee* (trusted actor) does not behave as expected, whilst uncertainty arises from the lack of information about the ability and motivation of the trustee [16]. Both risk and uncertainty leave trustors vulnerable. The trustee's decision to behave in a trustworthy manner depends on a number of factors called *trust-warranting* properties, which can be distinguished between *intrinsic* and *contextual* [16].

- *Intrinsic properties (ability and motivation)*: These provide incentives for trustworthy behaviors internal to an individual. In the interaction of an employee with a security mechanism ability stems from the mechanism's usability and an individual's knowledge, while motivation comes from internalized norms and benevolence that dictate doing what they perceive to be "the right thing" in order to protect the organization they work for.
- *Contextual properties (temporal, social and institutional embeddedness)*: These depend on the context of the interaction and trustworthy behavior incentives for employees emerge from external factors:
  - *Temporal embeddedness* – When the prospect of repeated future interactions exist (e.g. long term future in the organization), employees are motivated to preserve the trust relationship.
  - *Social embeddedness* – When a compliant social environment exists, new employees try to fit in and mimic the behavior of others. If the majority behaves in a trustworthy manner, violations can become socially unacceptable, providing incentive to individuals to exhibit trustworthy behavior.

   – *Institutional embeddedness* – The strictness, severity and potential of punishment imposed upon an employee, together with high probability of misbehavior detection, acts as a deterrent factor to trust defection.

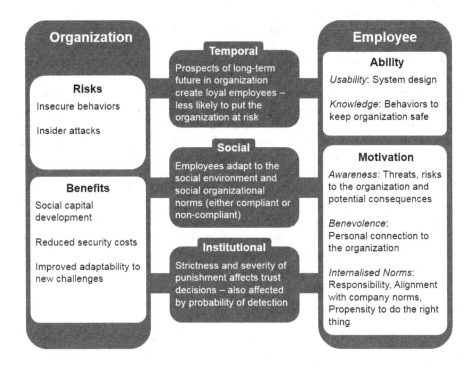

Fig. 1. The organization-employee trust relationship model (adapted from Riegelsberger et al. [16])

3 Treating Users as Untrustworthy Components

Traditionally, information security focused on creating contextually-incentivized trustworthy behavior: imposed restrictions, controls and policies aim to create incentives for security compliance. This approach assumes users do not possess intrinsic motives to behave securely. But most employees in most organizations are trustworthy, and suggesting and they are not is counterproductive [11],[15],[23]: (i) it increases security enforcement costs, (ii) makes employees feeling untrusted, (iii) encourages creation of non-compliant environments, and (iv) negatively impacts security experts' ability to detect violations.

3.1 Enforcement Is Expensive

Attempts to enforce desired behaviors upon employees increase the need for *architectural means* (security mechanisms) and *formal procedures* (policies) [24], which restrict and monitor employee actions. This increases the workload for both security experts and employees:

1. The increasing complexity of the threat landscape means defining, communicating and enforcing policy-compliant behavior to employees for all existing security challenges becomes monumental. Any attempts to achieve this become uneconomic for security experts, constrained by finite investment resources (workforce, time and budget) and may lead to security experts compromising with sub-optimal solutions [24],[25].
2. It is equally impossible for employees to memorize all approved behaviors and exhibit those in the organizational environment. Security designers, who distrust users, ask them to expend significant effort on security mechanisms. Not adopting a genuine user-centered perspective, they do not accept that security from the user's perspective is a secondary task, and that time and effort consumed eats into the users' primary task performance – and ultimately, that of the organization [12]. More often than not, users circumvent security because it gets in the way of their main job [23],[26]: users are focused on their primary work tasks and have a limited *compliance budget* for security [10] - so they try to avoid security that poses a significant obstacle to the completion of their day-to-day activities [12]. This leads to the development of insecure *informal rules* [24] and non-compliance becomes organizational security culture.

3.2   Enforcement Leads to Distrust

Treating employees as a potential threat leads to security implementations that protect from the actions of employees, who never showed any intention to damage the organization. Their non-compliance, however, stems from the difficulty to comply with security solutions that have high workload and interfere with their primary tasks [10]. For example, employees may share authentication credentials because of clear business needs: a colleague needs access to complete an urgent task, but there is no way to get credentials quickly [27]. When employees report that mechanisms are difficult or impossible to comply with, security experts tend to dismiss those reports with *'you just do to not understand the risks'* [11]. This leads to employees feeling distrusted by the security experts. Employees who are frustrated with high security overhead and do not feel trusted are likely to develop a negative attitude towards security. This leads to the creation of a *value gap* between security and production parts of an organization, and reduces employee's willingness to collaborate to keep the organization secure [28]. When that negative attitude becomes prominent, it leads to widespread non-compliance [32], insider attacks [14] and valuable employees that feel untrusted leaving organization (loss of human capital) [29].

3.3   Non-compliance becomes the Norm

In many organizations, non-compliance has become prevalent behavior. Managers who trust their employees tolerate bending and circumvention of burdensome security policies and mechanisms. This does not mean that security is ignored: rather, employees create their own ways of keeping things they value secure, creating a *shadow security* environment [11]. This may have no resemblance to the organization's official rules, and cannot manage risks effectively, because employees do not have an accurate understanding of the risks and countermeasures. When security violations become a norm, the effects of social embeddedness on exhibiting trustworthy behavior are eliminated: new employees that try to "fit in" are more likely to follow suit to their colleague's non-compliance [30].

3.4   Ability to Detect Violations Is Reduced

When rule-bending or breaking becomes an organizational norm, detection of malicious activity becomes difficult. Organization-wide rule breaking introduces significant amounts of noise in any attempts to detect suspicious activity as observed non-compliant behaviors can be both legitimate and malicious. This reduces the ability of security experts to detect and take remediating actions before the problems escalate [14]. It also makes security more expensive, requiring further investment to distinguish between 'good' and 'bad' non-compliant behaviors, further increasing the cost of architectural means to keep the organization secure [24].

3.5   Need for Trust in Security Design

The aforementioned problems suggest the need for security design to re-consider the intrinsic propensity of employees to be trustworthy: the current "command-and-control" approach does more harm than the attacks it seeks to prevent [7]. Employees possess the intrinsic properties required to behave securely: they are motivated and willing to participate in security, as long as their ability to complete their primary tasks is not significantly hindered by burdensome security implementations [11],[14],[15],[23]. They are also capable of taking actions to protect the organization, without excessive restrictions on their systems and information access. In addition they can participate in security re-thinking as long as the experts listen to their feedback and use it to implement visible changes to the organizational security policies and mechanisms [11]. The high trust that can emerge from such an environment has social and economic benefits for the organization: it reduces the costs of compliance enforcement [24] and disgruntlement [17] (which is the starting point for most insider attacks [14] and improves organizational adaptability to the changing nature of modern security challenges [32]).

4   Incorporating Trust in Security Design

Genuine engagement of employees in security protection can have a positive effect for the organization. Collaboration builds social capital[1], creating mutual beliefs and

---

[1] Expected collective benefits derived from cooperation between individuals or groups [31].

norms which can be leveraged to improve organizational security performance [33],[34]: organizations where employees have increased responsibilities are more likely to establish a high-level of security awareness and improved understanding about the need for security. This can inject security-conscious behavior in the psychological contracts[2] that dictate employee-employer relationships, increasing the overall workforce engagement in security, and improving the effectiveness of security implementations. The emerging security consciousness also has positive economic effects on the security implementation: compliance comes from employees motivated to behave securely, based on norms developed by the existence of 'informal rules' that are significantly cheaper to enforce than formal rules and architectural means [24]. The emergent trusted environment also reduces potential disgruntlement from employees and all the potential negative effects of it (loss of human capital, insider attacks). The new dynamics that emerge can aid the organization grow especially in the new era of distributed workforce with looser and' more rapidly changing organizational environments [32]. In the remainder of this section we discuss how trust can be incorporated in designing or improving security implementations, touching on four elements that currently appear to require improvements: *usability* (improving employee ability to behave in a trustworthy way), *awareness* (improving motivation to do so), *participation* (improving organizational ability to identify problems) and *punishment* (providing contextual incentives for compliance). Effective security design should aim to combine all four to balance assurance (based on architectural means and formal rules) and trust (informal rules) to create cheaper and more effective security implementations [30].

4.1   Improving Usability by Learning from Circumventions

A key requirement for employees to behave securely is the usability of security mechanisms they have to use. Security mechanisms that are difficult or impossible to use drive even trustworthy users to non-compliance [15]. Security designers and organizations need to think about usable security as a key factor of organizational *security hygiene*: rules should not have to be broken for productivity reasons. Flexibility may be available for urgent situations (e.g. give a password to a colleague who was locked out of a system), but employees should have to report these violations using an approved *controlled circumvention* system [27]. Some organizations already have *self-reporting mechanisms* that offer amnesty from sanctions to employees who self-report, but these are not helpful if self-reporting just becomes an additional task employees have to do. The causes for non-compliance have to be investigated and removed. Rules that need to be circumvented often should then be considered as unfit to support the organization. Re-designing such rules and mechanisms should be seen as essential *security hygiene,* part of an ongoing process of adapting security to fit with users' primary task and business processes [11].

---

[2] Mutual beliefs, perceptions, and informal obligations between employers and employees [35].

4.2   Improving Awareness and Education

When security hygiene is in place, security design should build on trustworthy behavior enabled by genuinely usable security. Once that is in place, appropriate awareness campaigns to increase employee motivation to behave securely can be considered. Security designers need to identify and target current employee perceptions with context specific examples drawn from the work environment, which may differ across various employee groups [15]. The emerging communication should aim to change the perception of information security as something that protects the business process, thus presenting it as an integral part of it. This can be done by: (i) stressing the importance of security in protecting the organization and the resources that enable primary task completion and (ii) explaining the critical role employees can play in it [36]. Any education and training material used should always be easily available for employees that need to refer back to it.

4.3   Engaging with Line Managers

Line managers need to be encouraged to shape an organization's security. Security experts need to draw on their knowledge of business processes to (1) learn from circumventions and (2) get help with tailoring security awareness and make it relevant to their staff. Managers have a considerable influence on their staff's security decisions [11], and with help from security experts, they can assess the role-related risks within their teams and communicate desired behaviors. Increased awareness and ability to connect with the risks presented by their managers can provide additional motivation for employees to behave securely and can trigger internalized norms and benevolence-related compliance by employees that feel they are acting to the organization's interest. This can lead to the creation of security conscious informal rules and a security implementation based on a *bottom up* collaborative approach where employees feel trusted and motivated to collaborate in the emergent *participatory security* environment [11].

4.4   Balancing Trust and Assurance

Improvements of the trust relationship do not mean that an organization should completely abandon its deployed security mechanisms: contextual properties are also important to employees exhibiting trustworthy behavior [30]. When the ground that allows for intrinsic trustworthy behavior is created (employees are able and motivated to do so), employees should be discouraged breaking trust relationships by appropriate assurance mechanisms. Employees that are caught to abuse trust should then be visibly punished; high risk of being caught together with severe consequences has a dissuading effect for potential trust violators. In other words, organizations need to balance trust-based trustworthy behavior (based on ability and motivation) and assurance-based trustworthy behavior (based on contextual properties).

Organizations also need to recognize that, in addition to context dependent, trust is also conditional [37]: employees that have been in the organization for longer may feel more loyal, thus motivated to behave securely. Instead of all employees having to deal with the same procedures from day 1, increased levels of assurance can be implemented for new employees, with the restrictions gradually reduced the longer an employee stays in the organization – assurance should evolve to trust over time. Reducing the need for productivity-driven violations also improves the security experts' ability to protect the organization: reduction of the 'noise' introduced by productivity-driven 'legitimate' violations enables the implementation of clever monitoring implementations to identify malicious activity (insider or outsider attacks) [38].

5   Conclusion

Treating employees as a trusted entity when designing (new or improved) security processes and mechanisms can significantly benefit the organization and its security experts. It reduces the organization's exposure to information security risks by improving its security hygiene. Improved efficiency of deployed security approaches also reduces the overhead impact of security on the production tasks and employee frustration with security, creating a more positive, participatory approach to keeping the organization secure. This increases an organization's ability to depend on the human defenses (in this case employees) to manage its information security risks. Trust also improves employee attitudes, work behaviors and job satisfaction and makes security management economically more efficient, as implementation and maintenance of many cumbersome mechanisms becomes obsolete.

Improved trust relationships can emerge through: (i) improved usability of security mechanisms to improve on employee ability to comply, (ii) improved awareness to provide motivation, (iii) participatory security and middle management involvement to improve on the security designers' ability to identify and deploy improvements and (iv) monitoring and punishment to provide contextual compliance incentives – balancing all four creates an environment where trustworthy behavior is cheap for employees to exhibit and untrustworthy behavior is easily detected by the organization. This leverages employees as an additional layer of defense and improves the overall security of the organization.

References

1. Von Solms, B.: Information security–the fourth wave. Computers & Security 25(3), 165–168 (2006)
2. Schneier, B.: Secrets and lies: digital security in a networked world. Wiley (2000)
3. Sasse, M.A.: Designing for Homer Simpson - D'Oh! Interfaces: The Quarterly Magazine of the BCS Interaction Group 86, 5–7 (2011)
4. Adams, A., Sasse, M.A.: Users Are Not The Enemy: Why users compromise security mechanisms and how to take remedial measures. Communications of the ACM 42(12), 40–46 (1999)

5. Sasse, M.A., Brostoff, S., Weirich, D.: Transforming the "weakest link": a human-computer interaction approach to usable and effective security. BT Technology Journal 19(3), 122–131 (2001)
6. Egelman, S., Cranor, L.F., Hong, J.: You've been warned: an empirical study of the effectiveness of web browser phishing warnings. In: Proceeding of the Twenty-Sixth Annual SIGCHI Conference on Human Factors in Computing Systems, pp. 1065–1074. ACM, New York (2008)
7. Weirich, D.: Persuasive password Security, PhD thesis, University College London (2005)
8. Faily, S., Fléchais, I.: Eliciting Policy Requirements for Critical National Infrastructure Using the IRIS Framework. International Journal of Secure Software Engineering (IJSSE) 2(4), 1–18 (2011)
9. Kirlappos, I., Sasse, M.A.: Security Education against Phishing: A Modest Proposal for a Major Rethink. IEEE Security & Privacy 10(2), 24–32 (2012)
10. Beautement, A., Sasse, M.A., Wonham, M.: The compliance budget: managing security behavior in organizations. In: Proceedings of the 2008 New Security Paradigms Workshop, pp. 47–58. ACM (2008)
11. Kirlappos, I., Parkin, S., Sasse, M.A.: Learning from "Shadow security": Why understanding non-compliant behaviors provides the basis for effective security (in press, 2014)
12. Herley, C.: So long, and no thanks for the externalities: the rational rejection of security advice by users. In: Proceedings of the 2009 Workshop on New Security Paradigms Workshop (NSPW 2009), pp. 133–144. ACM, New York (2009)
13. Herley, C.: More is Not the Answer. IEEE Security & Privacy Magazine (2014)
14. Cappelli, D., Moore, A., Trzeciak, R., Shimeall, T.J.: Common sense guide to prevention and detection of insider threats, 3rd edn. version 3.1. CERT, Software Engineering Institute, Carnegie Mellon University (2009), http://www.cert.org
15. Kirlappos, I., Beautement, A., Sasse, M.A.: "Comply or die" is dead: Long live security-aware principal agents. In: Adams, A.A., Brenner, M., Smith, M. (eds.) FC 2013. LNCS, vol. 7862, pp. 70–82. Springer, Heidelberg (2013)
16. Riegelsberger, J., Sasse, M.A., McCarthy, J.D.: The mechanics of trust: a framework for research and design. International Journal of Human-Computer Studies 62(3), 381–422 (2005)
17. Hu, X.R., Lin, Z.X., Zhang, H.: Myth or reality: effect of trust promoting seals in electronic markets. In: Proceeding of the Eleventh Annual Workshop on Information Technologies and Systems (WITS), New Orleans, Louisiana, pp. 65–70 (2001)
18. Resnick, P., Zeckhauser, R., Friedman, E., Kuwabara, K.: Reputation systems: facilitating trust in internet interactions. Communications of the ACM 43(12), 45–48 (2000)
19. Kim, D., Ferrin, D., Rao, H.: A trust-based consumer decision-making model in electronic commerce: The role of trust, perceived risk, and their antecedents. Decision Support Systems 44(2), 544–564 (2008)
20. Ba, S., Whinston, A.B., Zhang, H.: Building trust in online auction markets through an economic incentive mechanism. Decis. Support Syst. 35(3), 273–286 (2003)
21. Nielsen, J., Molich, R., Snyder, S., Farrell, C.: E-Commerce User Experience: Trust. Nielsen Norman Group, Fremont (2000)
22. Mayer, R., Davis, J., Schoorman, F.D.: An integrative model of organizational trust. Academy of Management Review 20(3), 709–734 (1995)
23. Blythe, J., Koppel, R., Smith, S.W.: Circumvention of Security: Good Users Do Bad Things. IEEE Security & Privacy 11(5), 80–83 (2013)

24. Pallas, F.: Information Security inside organizations, PhD Thesis, technical University of Berlin (2009
25. Björck, F.: Security Scandinavian style. PhD diss., Stockholm University (2001)
26. Sasse, M.A.: Computer security: Anatomy of a usability disaster, and a plan for recovery. In: Proceedings of CHI 2003 Workshop on HCI and Security Systems (2003)
27. Bartsch, S., Sasse, M.A.: How Users Bypass Access Control and Why: The Impact of Authorization Problems on Individuals and the Organization. In: ECIS 2013: The 21st European Conference in Information Systems (2013)
28. Albrechtsen, E., Hovden, J.: The information security digital divide between information security managers and users. Computers & Security 28(6), 476–490 (2009)
29. Morrison, E.W., Robinson, S.L.: When employees feel betrayed: A model of how psychological contract violation develops. Academy of Management Review 22(1), 226–256 (1997)
30. Flechais, I., Riegelsberger, J., Sasse, M.A.: Divide and conquer: the role of trust and assurance in the design of secure socio-technical systems. In: Proceedings of the 2005 Workshop on New Security Paradigms (NSPW 2005), pp. 33–41. ACM, New York (2005)
31. Hanifan, L.J.: The rural school community center. Annals of the American Academy of Political and Social Science 67, 130–138 (1916)
32. Tyler, T.R.: Trust within organizations. Personnel Review 32(5), 556–568 (2003)
33. Bussing, A.: Trust and its relations to commitment and involvement in work and organizations. SA Journal of Industrial Psychology 28(4) (2002)
34. Tsai, W., Ghoshal, S.: Social capital and value creation: The role of intrafirm networks. Academy of Management Journal 41(4), 464–476 (1998)
35. Rousseau, D.M.: Psychological and implied contracts in organizations. Employee Responsibilities and Rights Journal 2(2), 121–139 (1989)
36. Von Solms, B., von Solms, R.: From information security to business security. Computers & Security 24(4), 271–273 (2005)
37. Castelfranchi, C., Falcone, R.: Trust theory: A socio-cognitive and computational model, vol. 18. John Wiley & Sons (2010)
38. Caputo, D., Maloof, M., Stephens, G.: Detecting insider theft of trade secrets. IEEE Security & Privacy 7(6), 14–21 (2009)

QR Code Security: A Survey of Attacks and Challenges for Usable Security

Katharina Krombholz, Peter Frühwirt, Peter Kieseberg, Ioannis Kapsalis,
Markus Huber, and Edgar Weippl

SBA Research, Vienna
[1stletterfirstname][lastname]@sba-research.org

Abstract. QR (Quick Response) codes are two-dimensional barcodes
with the ability to encode different types of information. Because of their
high information density and robustness, QR codes have gained popularity in various fields of application. Even though they offer a broad range
of advantages, QR codes pose significant security risks. Attackers can encode malicious links that lead e.g. to phishing sites. Such malicious QR
codes can be printed on small stickers and replace benign ones on billboard advertisements. Although many real world examples of QR code
based attacks have been reported in the media, only little research has
been conducted in this field and almost no attention has been paid on
the interplay of security and human-computer interaction. In this work,
we describe the manifold use cases of QR codes. Furthermore, we analyze the most significant attack scenarios with respect to the specific
use cases. Additionally, we systemize the research that has already been
conducted and identified usable security and security awareness as the
main research challenges. Finally we propose design requirements with
respect to the QR code itself, the reader application and usability aspects
in order to support further research into to making QR code processing
both secure and usable.

Keywords: qr codes, security, hci, usability.

1 Introduction

QR (Quick Response) codes are two-dimensional matrix barcodes that are used
to encode information. In recent years, they have more and more found their way
into our everyday lives. They were initially invented to track automotive parts
during the production process. Nowadays, they have been adapted for a variety of use cases. QR codes are cheap to produce and easy to deploy. Therefore,
they became the medium of choice in billboard advertising to access potential
customers. One of the most commonly found use case is URL encoding to make
information instantly available. Besides a broad range of advantages, QR codes
have been misused as attack vector for social engineers. Attackers encode malicious links that lead e.g. to phishing sites or to execute fraudulent code. These
malicious QR codes can be printed on small stickers and pasted over already

T. Tryfonas and I. Askoxylakis (Eds.): HAS 2014, LNCS 8533, pp. 79–90, 2014.

existing QR codes. Furthermore, attackers can modify selected modules from white to black and vice-versa in order to override the originally encoded content as proposed in [22]. Even though many real world examples have been reported in the media [24], there has been little research conducted on human-computer interaction and security aspects of QR code based attacks. In this work, we provide a comprehensive overview of the most relevant use cases of QR codes and the associated attack vector with an emphasis on phishing. To do so, we conducted a comprehensive literature survey to determine the state of the art regarding user studies and exemplary attacks. Additionally we identified the major research challenges to improve the security of QR codes and contribute questions and directions toward secure and usable QR code processing. The main contributions of this paper are as follows:

- We provide a comprehensive overview on the most relevant use cases and identify associated attack vectors.
- We systemize the state of the art in the research community.
- We identify the major research challenges to improve QR code security with an emphasis on usability and security aspects.

The remainder of this paper is structured as follows: In Section 2 we provide an introduction to the QR code standard and an overview of the use cases. In Section 3 we systemize attack scenarios with QR codes as attack vector and discuss related user studies. In Section 4 we describe reported real world examples and Section 5 discusses related user studies.In Section 6, we identify open research challenges with respect to security and usability aspects. Section 7 concludes our work.

2   The QR Code Standard

In this section, we provide a brief introduction to the QR standard as well as an overview of the manifold use cases of QR codes. QR (Quick Response) codes are two-dimensional bar codes that encode information in both vertical and horizontal direction. To access the encoded data from a QR code, a built-in smartphone camera captures an image of the QR code and then decodes it using QR code reader software. There are 40 different versions of QR codes with different data capacities. Version 1 consists of 21 X 21 modules from which 133 can be used for storing the encoded data. Version 40, which produces the largest QR code, has 23,648, hence 4296 alphanumeric characters [32], [37] can be encoded. Figure 1 shows an example of a version 2 QR code, which is the most commonly used one [27], [34], [40], [15]. In addition to alphanumeric characters, QR codes can encode binaries, Kanjis[1] or control codes. Furthermore, QR codes are readable from different angles and the data can be decoded successfully even if the code is partially covered or damaged [12]. This is because of robust error correction that is based on Reed-Solomon Codes [19]. There are four different error correction

---

[1] Japanese characters of Chinese origin.

levels namely L(Low 7%), M(Medium 15%), Q(Quartile 25%) and H(High 30%) Error correction level L tolerates up to 7% unreadable modules respectively [31]. Higher error correction levels increases the area, which is reserved for error correction codewords and decreases the area reserved for the actual data. Therefore, error correction level L is usually preferred. An additional feature to stabilize the decoding process is masking. Masking ensures an equal distribution between black and white modules. The appropriate mask is automatically chosen by the encoding software when the code is created.

Fig. 1. Example QR Code Version 2 [27]

2.1 Uses of QR Codes

QR codes have been invented to track automotive parts in manufacturing plants and have more and more found their way into urban spaces and mobile devices.

Advertising. The most common use case in advertising is encoding URLs or contact information, geo-locations and text to make them instantly available to the user [7]. Billboard advertisements with QR codes can be found in most urban spaces [25] to deliver information to potential future customers, obviating the need to type in the URL manually to visit a webpage. According to [16], the chain supermarket *Tesco* used QR codes to boost online shopping and to penetrate further into the South Korean market. Another innovative and cost efficient marketing campaign was launched by a shampoo company by cutting QR codes into hairstyles [23]. People with these haircuts acted as moving advertisement for shampoo since their "hair tattoos" redirected to the company's web site after scanning.

Mobile Payments. QR codes are also used to process mobile payments and provide opportunities to purchase a product or a service by solely scanning a QR code. This is referred to as "one-click" payment [30], [26], [20]. After scanning the respective QR code, the user is redirected to an intermediate payment agent or the company's web page. PayPal, which is one of the biggest payment companies has already adopted this payment practice in some countries [11].

Access Control. According to [44], QR codes are used for physical access control in combination with other security enhancing methods. Kao et al. [44] proposed a safe authentication system by combining QR codes and the One Time Password technique (OTP [28]). The user information is stored at a main server, which holds the user information, a mobile application that generates QR codes, and a client PC with a camera to scan the QR code. In order to authenticate, the user generates a QR code with an encrypted password encoded, which is then scanned by the client PC.

Augmented Reality and Navigation. QR codes are also used in digital government services to effectively distribute valuable information to the public. According to [9], QR codes are used to increase citizen participation and to navigate users through park trails and museums [33], [41]. Furthermore they are used as supplementary material for education and within games. QR codes are also used to share information between people who participate in the same social event [10] or to share information in order to support the learning process. Furthermore, interesting and creative uses of QR codes are presented in [2] and [21] where QR Codes are used as a surface on which an augmented reality application is deployed and as a result, impressive 3D virtual objects are produced and displayed to the user.

3   QR Codes as Attack Vectors

In this section we describe different attack scenarios based on QR codes. In the media, the most frequently reported attack scenario is social engineering [24]. In Information Technology (IT) security, social engineering refers to the art of manipulating people to reveal confidential information to the social engineer and it is mainly used to steal data. One of the most popular practices in social engineering is phishing. Attackers use malicious QR codes to direct users to fraudulent web sites, which masquerade as legitimate web sites aiming to steal sensitive personal information such as usernames, passwords or credit card information. There are two main attack vectors to exploit QR codes:

The attacker replaces the entire QR code. This attack is simple yet effective. An attacker creates a new QR code with a malicious link encoded and pastes it over an already existing one on e.g. a billboard advertisement.

The attacker modifies individual modules of a QR code. The main idea of this modification is that the encoded content is modified solely by changing the color of specific modules of the QR Code to which the user will be directed after scanning the code as proposed in [27].

4   Real World Examples

In 2012 security expert Ravi Borgaonkar demonstrated how Man-Machine-Interface (MMI) codes can be used to run different attacks against Samsung

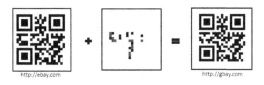

Fig. 2. The modification attack as proposed by Kieseberg et al. [27]

devices [6], e.g. by making the phone dial the MMI code *2767*3855# to wipe the phone. Attackers encoded this MMI code into a QR code with the prefix *tel:* to trigger the execution of the MMI code which erases all data from the mobile device. Sharma et al. [36] outlined different attacks against the automated processes of the scanning library or the scanning software. If a scanning application uses a database to store scanned entires, it is possible to execute a sql injection by scanning values such as *1' OR 1=1* – in order to circumvent authentication mechanisms. Furthermore, he outlined the threat of browser-based exploits, XSS attacks and command injections via QR codes. Jester et al. [29] changed his profile picture on his twitter account to a QR code with a shortened URL encoded. The QR Code directed victims to a webpage, which hosted hidden code exploiting a known browser vulnerability on iOS and Android. Apart from the WebKit [1] secondary exploits exposed the device to the attacker. The attacker claims that he successfully trapped 500 victims that executed the OS-specific payload. Even though researchers and security specialists are questioning the success of this attack, they confirm that this kind of attack is feasible. In [39] Moore and Edelman present a method to identify typosquatting. Typosquatting is the intentional registration of misspellings of popular website addresses. In 2010, it was estimated that there are at least 938,000 typosquatting domains targeting the top 3,264 ".com" sites, and most of these sites supported the pay-per-click ads. This information is fundamental proof that attacking a QR code in order to produce a misspelled and misleading domain name is an effective phishing attack.

5   Related User Studies

The importance of human-computer interaction aspects in QR code security has been acknowledged by the research of Seeburger et al. [35] and Vidas et al. [42]. Seeburger et al. [35] investigated how users interact with QR code stickers in urban spaces with so called *PlaceTagz*. These *PlaceTagz* were deployed in different locations in Melbourne such as cafeterias, libraries and public toilets. When a dweller scans a *PlaceTag*, he is taken to a dialog box where he can read comments from previous visitors but also leave his own comments. Their results suggest that curiosity is the main motive for a user to scan non-contextual QR codes. With curiosity being the main motivation to interact with an unknown source, users are ignoring the security threats associated with QR codes from unverified sources or are unaware of them. Vidas et al. [42] described QR code-initiated phishing attacks by conducting two experiments in the city of Pittsburgh, a *surveillance* and a *QRishing* experiment. Within their surveillance experiment, they observed how users interacted with the code and if they scanned the codes or not. Furthermore, they observed the proportion of users who scanned the code but refused to visit the encoded URL by visually monitoring user interactions with QR codes. To do so, they deployed a poster with a QR code and a camera to record the user interactions. In the *QRishing* experiment, they deployed QR codes on three different types of posters and flyers to assess the susceptibility of such a phishing attack. In their deployed QR codes, a link to a survey was encoded. This survey contained a set of questions to identify the initiatives and the behavior of the people that scanned the QR codes. Similar to Seeburger et al. [35], Vidas et al. [42] found that curiosity is the main motivation for smartphone users to scan a code. Their findings highlight the need for further research on adequate tools to support the user in detecting potential threats as they are mostly scanning unverified codes because of their curiosity. Their research also highlights that most QR code readers do not provide feasible tools to automatically detect attacks and to minimize the impact on the user's privacy and security.

6   Open Research Challenges

Despite the fact that the use of QR codes is gaining popularity, many users are still not able to distinguish between QR codes from trusted and untrusted sources. As the results by Seeburger et al. [35] and Vidas et al. [42] suggest, scanning a QR code is not a safe practice. One of the main reasons for this is that users need to decode the QR code at first in order to decide whether the content is trusted because they are not human-readable. Even after decoding, users find it difficult to judge the trustworthiness of an encoded URL. Therefore we identify the major research challenges with respect to usability and security with QR codes and describe them in this section.

6.1   Security Awareness Challenges

Bellman et al. [4] determined that there are significant differences in how Internet users perceive privacy challenges and security vulnerabilities. Their findings alongside with the differences in consumer acceptance of QR codes amongst different nationalities suggest that people have different concerns regarding security vulnerabilities when interacting with QR codes. Based on the studies by Seeburger et al. [35] and Vidas et al. [42], another important challenge is to investigate intercultural differences in security awareness. To do so, the deployment of stickers with QR codes (similar to *PlaceTagz* [35]) in public places like university cafeterias, bus stops and public toilets would be beneficial to investigate the differences between European and Asian users. A detailed understanding of the intercultural differences would significantly contribute to the scientific community in order to enhance awareness raising tools and support the adoption of successful security enhancements worldwide.

6.2 Usable Security Design Guidelines

Yao et al. [45] analyzed the most frequently downloaded QR code readers for Android and found that most of the readers are not able to successfully detect phishing attacks. However, a more detailed analysis on security, privacy and usability factors is necessary in order to design software that supports the user's decision making process about the trustworthiness of a URL. To support the development of a secure and usable multi-layer framework for QR code processing another important challenge is to develop design guidelines. These design guidelines should be developed in a way to harden the QR code itself, the reader software and to furthermore support the user to detect potential threats. In this section, we propose a set of requirements to support research in the areas of security and human-computer interaction with respect to the attack scenarios described in 3. We suggest to distribute the requirements in the following three categories: *(1) Secure QR Code Requirements, (2) Service Layer Requirements* and *(3) Usability Requirements*.

QR Code Requirements. In this section, we identify security requirements to secure the QR coding scheme. We consider coding scheme improvements as invariant to the QR code reader application.

Visual QR Codes. In case of an attack scenario (as described in Section 3) visual QR codes significantly support the user in detecting modified or replaced QR codes in urban spaces. The more complex the theme, the harder it becomes for an attacker to modify QR codes in an unobtrusive way. To make it more expensive for an attacker to replace the original QR code (e.g. in billboard advertising), we suggest to investigate the impact of complex color schemes embedded into the color scheme of the whole advertisement on the user's ability to detect malicious modifications.

Digital Signatures. In other domains, digital signatures have proven to be an effective means to improve security as shown in [17]. Therefore, we recommend to place emphasis on the integration of digital signatures in the QR code standardization to verify the originator of the code and to thereby check if the QR code has been modified. A digital signature significantly complicates QR code based attacks as the attacker needs to modify the checksum and the verification process accordingly. However, the increased amount of data to encode reduces the area to encode actual data. Furthermore, QR code readers have to be adapted in a way to verify the digital signatures and to indicate whether the verification was successful, similar to SSL. We suggest to develop the integration of digital signatures in order to propose a specification update.

Service Layer Requirements. The challenges highlighted in this section place emphasis on securing the QR code reader application and are intended to harden secure QR codes. The overall purpose of service layer improvements is to enrich the security features embedded in the QR codes themselves and to determine whether the user's decision is necessary to obviate a malicious code.

Masking. The distribution of black and white modules in a specification-compliant QR code follows a specific pattern. This pattern is determined by the mask that is used to specify whether or not to change the color of the considered module. Due to its robustness provided by the error-correcting Reed-Solomon codes, a certain degree of corrupt pixels does not have a negative impact on decoding the QR code. The higher the deviation from an even distribution of black and white modules is, the higher the probability that the QR code is modified. A detailed analysis on the trade-off between error rate and security would be beneficial in order to use masking aspects to secure reader software.

Malicious URL Detection. In general, there are different approaches to successfully distinguish potentially malicious URLs from benign ones. However, shortened URLs can be used by an attacker to obfuscate malicious URLs. The trustworthiness of an URL can be determined by metrics as proposed by Choi et al. [8]. Furthermore, URL black- or whitelists can be used to verify the originator of encoded URLs.

Usability Requirements. In this section, we describe research challenges with respect to the user's decision making process on the trustworthiness of a QR code.

Content Display. As QR codes are non human-readable, content display is essential to inform the user about the actually encoded content. We suggest to use the findings of [13,14] as a starting point for further research on the usability of this feature.

Content Preprocessing. In case of shortened URLs or redirects, simply displaying the encoded content does not provide enough information for the user to determine whether the encoded content is malicious or benign (as shown in [13,14]). Therefore we emphasize the need for usable content preprocessing tools. Shortened URLs e.g. could be executed in the background in order to display the final URL to the user.

Anti-Phishing Tools. As discussed in Section 3, one of the major problems of manipulated QR codes is phishing. Zhang et al. [46] evaluated different Anti-Phishing solutions that can be further used in QR code reader software. In context of usability it is important that the verification process is transparent to the user. However similar to SSL [5,38,43] the main challenge is to properly inform the user about an incident [18].

Content Verification. In addition to content preprocessing before display, verification tools should be emphasized such as e.g. blacklists as proposed in [45]. As the results from [14] and [3] suggest, warnings are in many cases not effective to inform the user about possible threats and the implications of the actions they will perform. These findings highlight the need for further research regarding usable tools to indicate verified and unverified content.

7   Conclusion

In this paper, we provided a comprehensive overview of the state of the art research regarding QR code security and usability. We identified the most significant use cases and the attack vectors associated with them. To do so, we conducted an extensive literature survey. In the media, the most commonly reported fraud conducted with QR codes as attack vector is social engineering and phishing in particular. QR codes have found their way from automotive manufacturing plants into our everyday smartphone usage. They are used in advertising, authentication and even for monetary transactions where sensitive data is transferred. However, very little research has been conducted in this field. Therefore, the major goal of this work was to identify and systemize the major research challenges in the area of security and human-computer-interaction. Based on our systematization, we defined specific requirements to develop multi-layer guidelines as a first step toward the development of a secure QR code processing environment.

Acknowledgements. The research was funded by COMET K1, FFG - Austrian Research Promotion Agency and by the Josef Ressel Center for User-Friendly Secure Mobile Environments (Usmile).

References

1. The WebKit Open Source Project (2013), `http://www.webkit.org` (last accessed on July 2, 2014)
2. Agusta, G.M., Hulliyah, K., Bahaweres, R.B., et al.: Qr code augmented reality tracking with merging on conventional marker based backpropagation neural network. In: 2012 International Conference on Advanced Computer Science and Information Systems (ICACSIS), pp. 245–248. IEEE (2012)
3. Akhawe, D., Felt, A.P.: Alice in Warningland: A Large-scale Field Study of Browser Security Warning Effectiveness. In: Proceedings of the 22Nd USENIX Conference on Security (SEC 2013), pp. 257–272 (2013)
4. Bellman, S., Johnson, E.J., Kobrin, S.J., Lohse, G.L.: International differences in information privacy concerns: A global survey of consumers 20(5), 313–324 (2004)
5. Biddle, R., van Oorschot, P.C., Patrick, A.S., Sobey, J., Whalen, T.: Browser interfaces and extended validation ssl certificates: an empirical study. In: Proceedings of the 2009 ACM Workshop on Cloud Computing Security, pp. 19–30. ACM (2009)
6. Borgaonkar, R.: Dirty use of ussd codes in cellular network (2012), `http://www.youtube.com/watch?v=Q2-0B04HPhs` (last accessed on July 2, 2014)

7. Dow, C., Lee, Y., Yang, H., Koo, W., Liao, J.: A location-based mobile advertisement publishing system for vendors. In: Eighth International Conference on Information Technology: New Generations, pp. 24–29 (2011)
8. Choi, H., Zhu, B.B., Lee, H.: Detecting Malicious Web Links and Identifying Their Attack Types. In: Proceedings of the 2Nd USENIX Conference on Web Application Development (WebApps 2011), p. 11. USENIX Association, Berkeley (2011)
9. Lorenzi, D.: B Shafiq, J. Vaidya, G. Nabi, S. Chun, V. Atluri. Using QR codes for enhancing the scope of digital government services. In: Proceedings of the 13th Annual International Conference on Digital Government Research, pp. 21–29 (2012)
10. Pirrone, D., Andolina, S., Santangelo, A., Gentile, A., Takizava, M.: Platforms for human-human interaction in large social events. In: Seventh International Conference on Broadband, Wireless Computing, Communication and Applications, pp. 545–551 (2012)
11. Moth, D.: PayPal trials QR code shop in Singapore subway (2012), http://econsultancy.com/at/blog/8983-paypal-trials-qr-code-shop-in-singapore-subway (last accessed on July 2, 2014)
12. DENSO Wave Incorporated. What is a QR Code (2013), http://www.qrcode.com/en/ (last accessed on July 2, 2014)
13. Downs, J.S., Holbrook, M., Cranor, L.F.: Behavioral Response to Phishing Risk. In: Proceedings of the Anti-Phishing Working Groups 2Nd Annual eCrime Researchers Summit (eCrime 2007), pp. 37–44. ACM, New York (2007)
14. Egelman, S., Cranor, L.F., Hong, J.: You'Ve Been Warned: An Empirical Study of the Effectiveness of Web Browser Phishing Warnings. In: Proceedings of the 2008 SIGCHI Conference on Human Factors in Computing Systems (CHI 2008), pp. 1065–1074 (2008)
15. Esponce. Innovative QR Code campaigns (About QR codes) (2013), http://www.esponce.com/about-qr-codes (last accessed on July 2, 2014)
16. Esponce. Innovative, Q.R.: Esponce. Innovative QR Code campaigns (Real world case studies) (2013), http://www.esponce.com/case-studies (last accessed on July 2, 2014)
17. Hanser, C., Slamanig, D.: Blank digital signatures. In: Proceedings of the 8th ACM SIGSAC Symposium on Information, Computer and Communications Security (ASIA CCS 2013), pp. 95–106. ACM, New York (2013)
18. Harbach, M., Fahl, S., Muders, T., Smith, M.: Towards measuring warning readability. In: Proceedings of the 2012 ACM Conference on Computer and Communications Security, pp. 989–991. ACM (2012)
19. Reed, I., Solomon, G.: Polynomial Codes Over Certain Finite Fields 8(2):300–304 (1960)
20. Gao, J., Kulkarni, V., Ranavat, H.: Lee Chang Hsing Mei. A 2D barcode-based mobile payment system. In: Third International Conference on Multimedia and Ubiquitous Engineering, pp. 320–329 (2009)
21. Wang, J., Shyi, C., Hou, T.-W., Fong, C.P.: Design and implementation of augmented reality system collaborating with QR code. In: International Computer Symposium (ICS), pp. 414–418 (2010)
22. Kieseberg, P., Leithner, M., Mulazzani, M., Munroe, L., Schrittwieser, S., Sinha, M., Weippl, E.: Qr code security. In: Proceedings of the 8th International Conference on Advances in Mobile Computing and Multimedia, pp. 430–435. ACM (2010)
23. Korkidis, J.: The world's first qr-code hair cut (2014), http://www.complex.com/art-design/2011/11/the-worlds-first-qr-code-hair-cut (last accessed February 4, 2014)

24. Leyden, J.: That square QR barcode on the poster? Check it's not a sticker
25. Ebling, M., Caceres, R.: Bar Codes Everywhere You Look 9(2), 4–5 (2010)
26. Talbot, M.: QR Codes: Scanning For Loyalty And Payment (2013),
    http://blogs.sap.com/innovation/industries/qr-codes-scanning-for-
    loyalty-and-payment-3-025064 (last accessed on July 2, 2014)
27. Kieseberg, P., Leithner, M., Mulazzani, M., Munroe, L., Schrittwieser, S., Sinha,
    M., Weippl, E.: Qr code security. In: Proceedings of the 8th International Con-
    ference on Advances in Mobile Computing and Multimedia (MoMM 2010), pp.
    430–435 (2010)
28. Paterson, K.G., Stebila, D.: One-time-password-authenticated key exchange. In:
    Steinfeld, R., Hawkes, P. (eds.) ACISP 2010. LNCS, vol. 6168, pp. 264–281.
    Springer, Heidelberg (2010)
29. Wagenseil, P.: Anti-Anonymous hacker threatens to expose them (2012),
    http://www.nbcnews.com/id/46716942/ns/technology_and_science-security/
    (accessed July 2, 2014)
30. Pay, Q.: Qr pay - scan, pay, done (2014), http://www.qrpay.com/ (last accessed
    on July 2, 2014)
31. QRStuff. QR Code Error Correction (2011),
    http://www.qrstuff.com/blog/2011/12/14/qr-code-error-correction   (last
    accessed on July 2, 2014)
32. QRStuff. What's a QR Code (2011), http://www.qrstuff.com/qr_codes.html
    (last accessed on July 2, 2014)
33. Rouillard, J., Laroussi, M.: Perzoovasive: contextual pervasive qr codes as tool
    to provide an adaptive learning support. In: Proceedings of the 5th International
    Conference on Soft Computing as Transdisciplinary Science and Technology, pp.
    542–548. ACM (2008)
34. Russ Cox. QArt Codes (2012), http://research.swtch.com/qart (last accessed
    on July 2, 2014)
35. Seeburger, J.: No cure for curiosity: linking physical and digital urban layers. In:
    Proceedings of the 7th Nordic Conference on Human-Computer Interaction: Mak-
    ing Sense Through Design, pp. 247–256. ACM (2012)
36. Sharma, V.: A study of malicious qr codes 3(3) (May 2012)
37. Steeman, J.: QR code data capacity (2004),
    http://blog.qr4.nl/page/QR-Code-Data-Capacity.aspx (last accessed on July
    2, 2014)
38. Sunshine, J., Egelman, S., Almuhimedi, H., Atri, N., Cranor, L.F.: Crying wolf:
    An empirical study of ssl warning effectiveness, 399–416 (2009)
39. Moore, T., Edelman, B.: Measuring the perpetrators and funders of typosquatting.
    In: Sion, R. (ed.) FC 2010. LNCS, vol. 6052, pp. 175–191. Springer, Heidelberg
    (2010)
40. Thonky.com. QR Code Tutorial (2012),
    http://www.thonky.com/qr-code-tutorial/ (last accessed on July 2, 2014)
41. Ceipidor, U.B., Medaglia, C.M., Perrone, A., De Marsico, M., Di Romano, G.:
    A museum mobile game for children using QR-codes. In: Proceedings of the 8th
    International Conference on Interaction Design and Children, IDC 2009, pp. 282–
    283 (2009)
42. Vidas, T., Owusu, E., Wang, S., Zeng, C., Cranor, L.F., Christin, N.: QRishing:
    The susceptibility of smartphone users to QR code phishing attacks. In: Adams,
    A.A., Brenner, M., Smith, M. (eds.) FC 2013. LNCS, vol. 7862, pp. 52–69. Springer,
    Heidelberg (2013)

43. Vratonjic, N., Freudiger, J., Bindschaedler, V., Hubaux, J.-P.: The Inconvenient Truth about Web Certificates, pp. 79–117 (2013)
44. Kao, Y., Luo, G., Lin, H., Huang, Y., Yuani, S.: Physical access control based on QR code. In: International Conference on Cyber-Enabled Distributed Computing and Knowledge Discovery, pp. 285–288 (2011)
45. Yao, H., Shin, D.: Towards preventing qr code based attacks on android phone using security warnings. In: Proceedings of the 8th ACM SIGSAC Symposium on Information, Computer and Communications Security, pp. 341–346. ACM (2013)
46. Zhang, Y., Egelman, S., Cranor, L., Hong, J.: Phinding phish: Evaluating anti-phishing tools. In: Proceedings of the 14th Annual Network and Distributed System Security Symposium (NDSS 2007) (2007)

Designing Mobile Security Apps; a Paradigm Shift: A User Experience Case Study with Emerging Markets like India

Rutuja More and Abhishek Bora

Clarice Technologies, Baner, Pune, India
{rutuja.more,abhishek.bora}@claricetechnologies.com

Abstract. This case study talks about a mobile security app design that we worked on for one of our clients. In this project we made an attempt at to look at design as a game changer for the product's strategy; and not just a mere tool for beautification of the UI. Through research and design we have tried to find an answer to the apprehensions that users have about mobile security. We have tried to create a security app that has a warm and friendly look and feel; and we hope this might reduce the anxiety on a non tech savvy user's mind while engaging with it. We have attempted to raise the product's emotional design quotient by integrating product's UI and content strategy with very simple gamification elements. With this change in product perception we hope to drive the ROI in terms of a rise in user adoption, conversion and retention rates.

Keywords: Balancing user friendliness and strong security, User security and privacy by design, mobile security, virus applications, user experience design, usability.

1   Introduction

A recent McKinsey & Company research stated that - with a user base of around 120 million, India has become the third largest market for internet users, in the world. Low cost handsets and access to low cost & high speed internet connectivity; smart phones are rapidly penetrating the rural and semi-urban India; it has been predicted that the user base could project to 330million to 370 million by 2015 which will be second largest in the world and largest in terms of incremental growth.[1]

An average Indian in the age group of 18 to 35 who has on an average 30 third party apps on their phones spends almost 8 hours of the day on the internet. Though an Indian user spends less time online per capita than users in developed countries; their pattern of online behavior is converging. With the rise in digital awareness & literacy, the market for mobile security apps is also slowly maturing and is forecasted to rise from a mere 4 % in 2011 to 20 % by 2015. Leveraging this untapped market IT security companies are also investing in creating mobile security products for the Indian audience. [1]

T. Tryfonas and I. Askoxylakis (Eds.): HAS 2014, LNCS 8533, pp. 91–101, 2014.

One such leading IT security company in India approached us at Clarice to revamp their existing mobile security app. Though the existing app had a decent traction and download rates on play store the stakeholders felt that the UI needs to be redesigned for the following:

1. Upgrades in Android OS versions
2. Updates in android design patterns
3. Product evolution life cycle
4. Introduction of new value propositions like cloud service

2 Design Approach

The client requirement was a standard redesign and the expectations were to revamp the existing user interface with the latest android interaction and visual styles. We thought as design consultants; instead of redesigning the existing app wearing only a designer's hat, lets observe how do end users use the existing app; understand their stated as well as unstated goals and then take that learning as a cue for the design phase. The project plan thus consisted of three major buckets:

Formative Research, Detailed Interaction & Visual Design and Summative Research.

2.1 Formative Research

Formative research consisted of two activities competitor analysis and usability tests with end users.

Competitor Analysis. Competitor analysis as the first step of the research gave us an idea what does the mobile security product's landscape looks like and helped in our domain onboarding process.   Through the activity we were looking for answers to the following questions:

1. Who the competitors (direct and indirect if any) are?
2. What is there market share?
3. What are the services that they offer?
4. What is their unique selling point?
5. What are their strengths and weakness?
6. What are the potential threats that the competitors might pose?
7. What are the various opportunities that you may take advantage of?
8. What are the user opinions about these products?

We collected & studied data from Google Play store for 6 competitors; which helped us in reaching the following observations:

Insights

1.*Cost of the product counts*

In India, children stay with their parents till they start earning generally by their mid-twenties and it is the parents who pay for their education as well. So many youngsters preferred opting for free apps even with basic functionalities as cost was a primary factor that affected their buying decision.

2. *Local language support is preferred*

The download trend for apps with nominal functionalities but supporting as many as 19 local languages was higher than apps which were feature packed but supported only English. So in countries where language of communication is not English, products supporting native languages work better than feature rich English products.

3. *Users want an integrated solution*

New ventures that offered a feature packed one stop shop for mobile security apps had a bigger user base than industry veterans who made dedicated apps for various user needs. We feel that users preferred an integrated solution over a bunch of dedicated apps.

Usability Testing. We conducted formal usability test sessions with a good mix of 20 users further categorizing them into 4 groups of 5 users each.

Group 1 consisted of repeat users for the existing mobile security app whereas group 2 consisted of users who opted for the existing app but didn't continue beyond the license cycle. These users helped us in understanding what were the factors that decided the retention rates as well as the reasons for customer drop offs.

Groups 3 & 4 were non users. Group 3 contained people who used security apps of competitors on their phones. This gave us a user perspective about why did they prefer a competitor over the existing app and the last group consisted of users who had never used any mobile security product till now which let us look into a novice user's mind and give us insights on what are the anxieties that users have about having or not having a security app. We also thought that this was our window of opportunity to upsell the existing app to non-users.

Usability Setup & Preparation. The tests were conducted in a controlled environment for a week with 3-4 sessions per day and each session lasted from 60 to 90 minutes. Through the tests we were trying to validate the following goals:

- Understand user conceptual model about mobile security
- Goals for using/ not using anti-virus security on their mobile phones
- Factors that affect user's decision for buying the existing app
- Sales channel preferred by the users and why
- Product positives, pain points and deadlocks
- User likes and dislikes
- User wish list

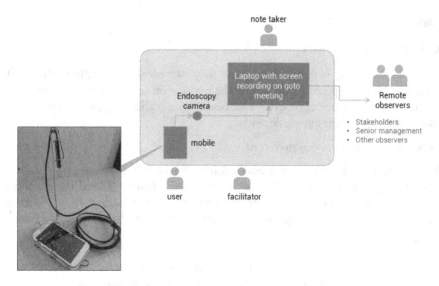

Fig. 1. Usability test setup

Insights

— *Mobile security product is meant for tech-savvy people & require domain expertise to use it*

As some of the terminology used in the app like spam, malware etc. sounds technical; users felt that security products are targeted for tech savvy people by tech-savvy people and are not meant for general consumers. Hence they tend to defended themselves by saying that they do not belong to the software or IT sector (which is considered a tech-savvy job profile in India) if they made any errors during the usability test session.

— *Security products require domain expertise to use it*

Indian non-tech savvy users are apprehensive to use security apps on mobile phones as they feel these apps require domain expertise to use. This may be mainly because of the jargons that are used and also the tonality of the content which feels very technical. Users though buy security apps for features like anti-theft and contact block never use them because of this anxiety.

Users thus tend to excuse a bad user experience offered by the app for their lack in the domain knowledge and don't mind exploring.

— *Feature discovery and user need go hand in hand*

Users generally do not explore beyond the basic features (like virus protection and contact blocking) unless there is an explicit need or the feature is apparent.

It was observed that users install an app as a utility for their expensive smart phone and then totally forget about it. When probed, many of the users knew the security app by its brand and not the name.

2.2   Detailed Interaction and Visual Design

Translating Usability Findings into Design Goals

1. Create a consumerish look & feel for the product

Our design strategy for the app was to break the user mental model; that security apps are not meant for general consumers. Considering the look and feel of the existing apps is very geeky and technical.

Our primary goal was to make the app look & feel consumerish, so that even a novice user can use it with as much ease as a tech savvy power consumer.

2. Increase the user engagement and create transparency between feature & functionality

The current product usage was passive and need based. Users didn't use the value propositions of the app to the fullest, but stuck to using very basic features like scanning a device or blocking contacts. This user behavior helped us to decide our second goal which was to ensure that users would be exposed to not just a laundry list of the features provided by service provider but the values add that feature would provide.

Thus by letting the users understand feature functionality along with how will they benefit by using the same would encourage them to use it.

3. Create a feeling of security by minimizing the user anxiety

During the research it was observed that users bought security apps for a 360^0 protection of their smart phones; but they there still hesitant to use or activate these advance features like anti-theft or panic alarms. This behavior could be because; people buy high end smartphones and install security apps on them but lack the digital literacy to use them. Due to which they are apprehensive to activate these features as they fear that if they commit any errors in the activation process they might harm their expensive phone.

Reducing this anxiety and make the users feel comfortable & secure while using even advance features became a goal for us.

2.3   Design Considerations

While designing the app we had to address two questions: 1: how to make an app look consumerish and 2: how to make it feel consumerish? While creating this experience we needed to define a brand voice for the mobile app, we had to define what the app should communicate and what it shouldn't. Keywords for the visual and content strategy were:

— Funny but not silly
— Smart but not Stupid
— Friendly but not bossy
— Helpful but not demanding
— Understanding but not Unforgiving

How to make a security app look consumerish?. To create a consumerish looking app create and fit the defined visual strategy within constraints like: target user demographics, market positioning of the current as well as redesigned product, communication goals, stakeholder expectations, project timelines and existing branding guidelines.

We started with creating a mood board which would help in consolidating different ideas relevant to the nature and usage of the product. Mood boarding helped in finding metaphors which could be used to define the visual language. We derived the following keywords which communicated the idea of security (in direct as well as an abstract manner) through discussions with stakeholders and secondary research:

— Secure
— Protect
— Safe
— Sheltered

These words acted as starting points for us to explore the visual metaphors for the product. Apt images which portrayed the ideas and emotions related to the sense of security and protection was compiled into a photo montage.

Fig. 2. Mood board for the visual strategy

Images representing similar concepts were then categorized further into two sets. Each set of images depicted few characteristics based on their syntactic properties.

First set were objects that directly depicted a sense of high security like pictures of safe deposit lockers, surveillance cameras and window/ door grills. Keywords like hi-tech, dark, aggressive, sleek could define its characteristics. From these images, certain visual attributes were derived like glow, contrast, texture, sharpness that would form the basis of visual elements for the design as well as the color palette which was blues and greys that made the visual layer look techy.

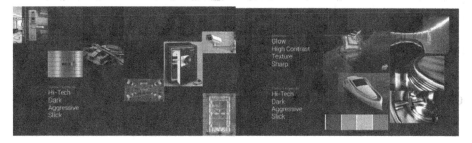

Fig. 3. First theme for the visual strategy

The second group described the concept of security in a more humane way. Mood board contained pictures of umbrellas, hand bags, blankets and quilts. Keywords like bright, friendly, personalized and modern quickly mapped the visual attributes of roundness, transparency, layered with a blend of bright colors like hues of orange, green and blue.

Fig. 4. Second theme for the visual strategy

The final visual language was created for both the themes by juxtaposing the attributes from the mood board with the latest android UI guidelines. The second theme was chosen over the other and taken forward for the visual design of the app.

How to make a security app feel consumerish?. After working on the detailed tasks and interactions of the product; this consumerish "feel" of the app was the emotional, pleasurable layer that was superimposed on top of a usable product. The goal of the emotional layer was to connect with users and evoke positive feelings. Positive feelings would instill positive experiences and thus make users want to interact with the product in the future.[3]

As stated in the device comfort premise by S. Marsh [2] the security design strategy for mobiles should be to advice, encourage, warn and proscribe actions to enable a foreground trust with the device.

Table 1. Foreground trust for the app

Area	Impact
Homepage	An opportunity to break ice with the user & create a first impression
Alerts	Drive user to take a certain actions
Success messages	Gives a chance to praise the user. Make them feel happy
Notifications	Inform the user
Tips	To show users how they can use specific features

Creating a personalized foreground through creative messaging. Creative messaging would strike a two-way conversation with the user rather than being a one-way monologue with the user and be more human than a mere functional app.

Table 2. Few samples for creative messaging used in the app

Messaging Area	User emotions	Messaging tips	Sample message
Landing page	• Curious to know the health of his phone • User wants to know if it is safe & secure	• Show the user the current security status • Tell the user security can be improved in case it in case it is low	• Make your device 100% secure. Care for it as you do care for your loved ones!
When threat is detected	• Tensed • Wants to know how to resolve it or Where did the threat come from	• Show the user what can be done to resolve the threat • Inform the user to take action to solve the issue & show him the step	• You don't have to panic. All you need to do is scan your device to resolve the threat
When device is secured	• Happy, Content, Relaxed • User is happy about taking care of the device	• Give user a pat on the back & appreciate him • Use casual language & feel free to be friendly	• You show care towards the device. Guessing it is your most prized possession!
When device is not completely secured	• Curious • Wants to know how to completely secure the device	• Guide the user & explain how secure the device • Inform the user to keep device security at optimum level at all time	• Use the security measures & your device will be ready in no time to fight any possible threat

— Balancing automation & empowerment

One of the design considerations was to understand to what extent the app could violate the user's privacy and take control of the phone. There could be certain advance features that could run in the background while the others could be triggered by the user. Maintaining this balance was important because we did not want the users to feel that the app is taking control over their phone which would make them anxious and leading in distrust

2.4   Solution Summary

The final concept was a minimal dashboard that shows the user how secure the device is. This level of security would be directly proportional to the features that are used by the user. So the security level would rise as the user activates/ engages with features on the app. The emotional design layer was to communicate and highlight these security propositions contextually and using the right tone of messaging to provide a consumerish experience whilst using a security app.

The design strategy was to use a hub and spoke task based model. So tasks would be the entry points for the user instead of a feature list. As a user would use the app with a predefined task in his/her mind the app would map the user's mental model and feature discoverability would be quicker. This would also lessen the cognitive load on the user as they would not have to map the feature label with the task/ functionality to be used.

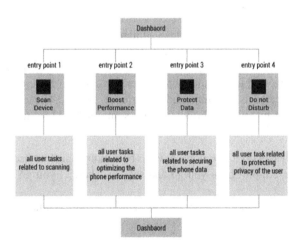

Fig. 5. Illustration of the hub and spoke task based model

Thus the solution would provide an all-round protection to the user but still keep the user in control of the phone. We hope that this sense of empowerment would reduce the anxiety and motivate them to use it to the fullest rather than having it just installed on their phones.

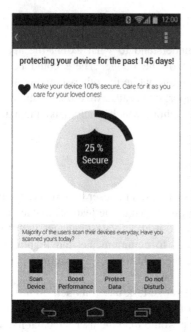

Fig. 6. Sample Dashboard for the redesigned app (landing screen has been tweaked to protect the client IP)

2.5   Summative Research

The redesigned app was evaluated with a similar demographic mix of users, to nip any minor user experience bugs and to ensure near-perfect product out in the market before getting in the development phase. These users were asked to perform the same tasks as the previous usability evaluation sessions to check if have we addressed the pain points and created a differentiated experience or not. The evaluation results endorsed our design hypothesis. Following are some of the user statement from the actual sessions:

- Simple, anybody can do it you don't have to be a mobile geek to use it!
- It's like Google, simple! Like you go and search… here… you go read it and you get it
- Purpose is wonderful, its user friendly, easy and it is self-explanatory

3   Conclusion

Through a "consumerish" user interface and a crude gamification of device security we hope to engage users in the domain of mobile security which was considered to be very technical and geeky and increase the product adoption, conversion and retention rates. In this paper we want to highlight that design has the power drive a product's ROI and also can influence the end user's mind and affect product adoption.

We would like to thank Anish Bhuwania for reviewing our work throughout the project and also for reviewing the paper and proof reading the abstract and Siddhesh Naik for help us with creating the content strategy in the design solution.

References

1. Gnanasambandam, C., Madgavkar, A., Noshir, K., Manyika, J., Chui, M., Bughin, J., Gomes, M.: Online and Upcoming: The Internet's Impact on India. In: Technology, Media and Telecom Practice. McKinsey& Company (2012)
2. Marsh, S., Basu, A., Dywer, N.: Security Enhancement With Foreground Trust, Comfort, And Ten Commandments For Real People. In: Mayem, A., Meinel, C. (eds.) Theories and Intricacies of Information Security Problems, University of Potsdam, pp. 2–5 (2013)
3. Smashing Magazine,
   http://uxdesign.smashingmagazine.com/2012/07/18/the-personality-layer/

Discrete Hardware Apparatus and Method for Mobile Application and Communication Security

Paschalis Papagrigoriou[1], Anargyros Plemenos[1], and Ioannis G. Askoxylakis[2]

[1] EMPELOR GmbH, Zug, Switzerland
{papagrigoriou,plemenos}@empelor.com
http://www.empelor.com, http://www.secocard.com
[2] Institute of Computer Science, Foundation for Research and Technology - Hellas, Heraklion, Greece
asko@ics.forth.gr

Abstract. With the dramatic shift of internet use away from desktop and laptop PCs toward smartphones and tablets, protection thresholds for application, device and communication security have significantly lowered. Most attempts on reversing this situation by means of converting standard mobile devices into tamper-proof equipment have proven to leave ample space for vulnerability of mobile processes and communication content. The only high efficacy method of sheltering against spying and fraud is seen in a new approach where a dedicated piece of discrete hardware is tasked with all security related operations while the standard cell phone or tablet remains unchanged, providing only its connectivity capabilities. The increasing cost caused by e.g. fraud in the area of mobile banking provides the background to economically justify this effort, which can in parallel support many other areas of mobile security.

Keywords: Mobile, internet, security, espionage, fraud, hardware.

1 Challenges for Mobile Application and Communication Security

Smartphones and tablet computers are on a very large scale in use for mobile internet access. Global user groups consist of consumers as well as enterprise and public sector employees. The ongoing use progression has been ignited and still is driven by aggressive offerings of internet and mobile network service providers, by declining cost of mobile communication due to increased competition, by people's growing desire for improved flexibility, competitive advantages and location independence, as well as by omnipresent promotions which are individually tailored to the consumers as a result of advanced monitoring mechanisms of their communication behaviors and patterns.

Media scientist Mark Andrejevic says "We are communicating in a context that uses us as advertising platforms for each other"[1]. Andrejevic characterizes this situation as a formal subordination of social behavior to commercial requirements.

T. Tryfonas and I. Askoxylakis (Eds.): HAS 2014, LNCS 8533, pp. 102–112, 2014.

Mobile IT infrastructure users with their craving for increased mobility and dynamic use of resources for the purposes of accelerating communication, optimizing cost and gaining competitive advantages, seem to be willing to sacrifice their privacy. Especially younger people show an increasing tendency to "publish" their lives towards larger internet communities, thus making their personal information easily accessible for anyone. It may not be surprising at all that this promptness to publicly display personal information including photo material in social networks is thankfully welcomed by public authorities in their pursuit of alleged traffic offenders as a both legal and very cost-effective identification method.

It appears by far more worrying how simply and easily one can get access not only to publicly available information, but also to non-public information and communication. Such possibilities are offered by a tremendously high number of malicious "apps" for smartphones[2]. Recent studies[3] show how dangerous smartphone apps have become. The widespread use of so-called IMSI-catcher equipment, available by online order[4], is definitely to be considered a criminal act[5]. The associated potential risk may have a wide variety of forms and manifestations for the user of mobile communication or services provided via the mobile internet such as mobile commerce, mobile banking and mobile payment, starting from privacy intrusion, spying on intellectual property and business secrets, to classic identity theft for fraudulent purposes.

In the wake of revelations of state agency spying on consumers, business people and politicians from other nations, we can rest assured that even if criminals may lack the excessive resources which have been allocated to state spying agencies, we need to be aware that both groups of privacy intruders, those with a legal background and those without, are out there doing their jobs. Since data and voice communication have been mobilized through fast miniaturization and mobilization of devices, rapid expansion of mobile networks and growing availability of all types of services over these networks, data privacy can be compromised in ways not only available to criminal forces, but also to legal or semi-legal entities and forces[6]. All this considered, risk awareness is still at a rather low level with enterprises and consumers.

2   Conventional Approach and Failure

For the purpose of establishing the obviously missing security for the public sector, for enterprises and consumers, many contributions have been made, with mostly discouraging results: None of the mainstream service providers currently offer appropriate mechanisms, procedures or devices which could ensure sufficient security for those who need to be secured[7].

Technically, information technology has a long history of creating and offering protection. Unfortunately, this is mainly true for the immobile IT the pre-cellphone world consisting of PCs, server farms, and closed circuit networks.

Existing security means which are mainly used by enterprises and in the public sector, include defense mechanisms such as firewalls, VPN tunnels, end-to-end encryption, two-factor authentication, strong passwords, and certificate-based logon[8]. Practically all of these protection mechanisms developed for the pre-mobile IT world can be overcome.

Privacy intrusion is possible for state-empowered forces as well as for ethical hackers. Consequently, we can rest assured that any defense can as well be overcome by terrorists, enemy states, competitors, criminals, and whoever is willing to spend enough time and energy to "hack" into privacy protection systems of the sort as it is in use today[9].

Mobile IT specialists such as providers of device management software have a tendency of creating the illusion that there is no risk in using arbitrary private end user devices in the context of confidential business processes ("BYOD"). The same can be said about providers of antivirus solutions and about device manufacturers who want to make bank customers believe that their online transactions will be executed exactly as shown on their device and a user can trust what she sees with regard to the recipient and the amount being transferred.

According to a recent study published by PwC, "Information Security Breaches Survey 2013", 50% of large (meaning enterprise level) organizations have implemented mobile device management (MDM) solutions in an effort to mitigate risks connected with BYOD or with the overall use of mobile communication devices to access enterprise resources like email, hosted applications, and file servers. These software-only protection tools give enterprises the security of "having done something". Any security breach committed by someone more malign than an ignorant employee cannot be prevented by these systems. The logic behind this mismatch is quite simple: the axiomatic paradigm "Software cannot be protected by software" prevails more than ever in the mobile sphere [5].

When it comes to hardware security, the incumbent approach of "device hardening" is basically in contradiction with the device producers' philosophy, and therefore becoming increasingly inappropriate. The shorter life cycles of consumer devices combined with the tendency of allowing use of privately owned consumer devices in a business or public administration environment represent a serious obstacle for establishing sufficient security mechanisms for all possible usage scenarios.

Public sector employees in Germany and other countries have been equipped with special versions of cellphones and smartphones to enable use of classified material on their mobile device. These devices, heaviest price tags, were ordered by the domestic IT security industry, and some of the vendors even delivered a job well done. Phones featuring virtualized operating systems and interfaces as well as customized boot ROMs requiring consent from the device manufacturer to avoid copyright infringement, can successfully prevent tapping or other forms of intrusion yet at a high cost. Besides the hefty investment for the procurement itself, the unfortunate users were gifted with devices at least three generations older than those of their peers without a phone authorized for confidential information because of the lengthy evaluation and authorization processes. In addition to this reputation affecting side effect, the "trusted" phones provide a lot less battery life and show painfully limited overall computational power.

3 A New Solution Concept

A different approach on fighting existing threats to data and communication security is the exclusive use of dedicated hardware for all security functions. There are several reasons why this approach was found more likely to achieve all safety objectives.

The solution for providing increased and sufficient mobile application and communication security in all environments where this is a fundamental requirement is the introduction of a separate security device. This device will be used in parallel with a smartphone or tablet, where the latter will provide connectivity, and the former adds the necessary security mechanisms to all activities related to the use of mobile devices.

It was found that minimum requirements for such security devices include:

- Affordability, i.e. a purchasing price within a reasonable proportion ratio to the cost of the standard mobile device it will accompany for protective purposes. Possible fraud damage prevention numbers should be left out of the equation. A recent study by PwC found that in the UK, 18% of IT spend was allocated to security in areas where security is a high priority. In other areas, the percentage spent on IT security was only 10% of the IT budget [10].
- Ease of use, i.e. an extra device which a majority of potential users will view as a discomfort should be as small and lightweight as possible to achieve maximum acceptance.
- Compatibility with widespread standardized interfaces; in the sense of fast and easy proliferation, the security device needs to provide the ability to interact with the largest possible variety of end-user devices via standard interfaces and thus maintain the greatest independency from device manufacturers and proprietary communication methods and protocols.
- Versatility in security applications; as a minimum, high-security online banking should be supported by providing a secure means of data display and input.
- For more security applications such as supporting a more secure use of credit cards and other payment types, existing processes must remain intact. A new POS device needs to be deployable without requiring changes to remainder of the existing infrastructure. This applies to the use of state of the art POS related back-end infrastructure and includes other security areas such as time and attendance control, physical access control, closed group payment systems, and the overall use of corporate and civic ID cards.
- Ideally, the device should be able to provide a wide range of security mechanisms such as storing and handling PKI-certificates for secure email, secure access to a company VPN, as well as secure voice communication with encrypted VoIP including gateways to fixed-line networks.
- It should be considered to add the function of creating a protected data area inside the smartphone or tablet, which must not be accessible without the security device in place and the authentication of the authorized user properly checked.

The challenge lies in combining the appropriate technology with the required functionality, at the same time exhibiting comfortable usability for the potential users.

3.1 Framework Architecture and State of Development

Basic Secocard Functionality. Secocard [11], developed by [12], in the first place acts as a card reader when a smartcard (ICC) is inserted into the device. The smartcard will actively trigger the ICC in-service register (ISR), which in turn notifies the ICC task about the presence of the card. The ICC task sets the card status to "PRESENT" and forwards the status to the application management task. The application management task checks the card type by means of the ICC task which returns the ATR of the ICC to the application management task which then will select the standard compliant application, i.e. it will run EMVCo Terminal or Secoder-2, etc.. The actually selected application will be communicated to the display and keypad tasks, prompting the user for confirmation.

An incoming command APDU is processed under the leadership of the application task in collaboration with the display and keypad tasks, the communication tasks, and the ICC task or NFC task[13], respectively. The framework provides a generic way of processing an incoming command APDU, and of finally sending the appropriate response APDU back to the command APDU sender.

Secocard can also act as a smartcard or ICC (acc. ISO 14443) after being switched into card emulation mode, an operating mode of the NFC framework. This mode is generally used for contactless payment and ticketing applications. An NFC enabled module is capable of storing different contactless smartcard applications in one device.

State of the Art Systems. The present state of smartcard or ICC terminal architecture   mostly POS (point of sale) or card reader terminals - calls for connecting an external terminal device via USB or Bluetooth with a host system, generally a desktop or notebook PC or a smartphone or tablet computing device, using T=0, T=1 or a proprietary communication protocol[14].

This architecture is characterized by the fact that relevant data need to be signed and/or decrypted by secret information stored on the smartcard or ICC, whereas after decryption or access granted through a verified digital signature by the rightful card owner, mostly by entering the correct Personal Identification Number (PIN) on the terminal, the same data will be handled shown on a screen, altered by a keyboard inside a system environment which is not trustworthy, namely a PC or smartphone which can be subject to the presence of Trojan horse software and many other forms of malice attacks.

3.2 Secocard Architecture

Security-relevant hardware is presented as a hardware abstraction layer which can be accessed by an internet access or connectivity device via middleware.

Thus, the Secocard architecture makes use of specific hardware components, such as an embedded secure element, a capacitive touch screen, audio support, as well as all relevant communication mechanisms required to connect to a large range of mobile devices currently on the market. The types of communication links to mobile devices or to cards and card readers include NFC, Bluetooth, Smart Bluetooth or Bluetooth Low Energy, and USB. The Secocard firmware provides a framework for an open set of security applications by offering basic functionality for application management, internet access via the internet connectivity of mobile devices, and accessing smartcards, using the relevant protocols.

Not present in the Secocard architecture is a radio module for direct access to a cellular network. The same is true for WLAN . These protocols have proven insufficient for reliable intrusion protection. Higher layer protocols, though, are implemented in the Secocard framework architecture to ensure its capability to establish, maintain and use a secured IP communication with e.g. a banks back-end data center or a secure email service.

Secocard architecture, unlike standard smartphones, PCs and tablet computational devices, does not comprise an operating system capable of running an arbitrary number of applications. As a result, it cannot be made subject to intrusion or any form of exploitation. The software consists of single tasks with task interactions implemented by means of message queues and semaphores. Tasks may also be triggered by interrupts via the corresponding interrupt service routine (ISR).

The Bluetooth pairing is a service that manages the discovery process and the Bluetooth-enabled device pairing process. It provides an interface to control the discovery and pairing process, and to manage the set of paired Bluetooth-enabled devices. It also maintains a database of Bluetooth profile information for each of the paired devices.

Figure 1 gives an overview on the Secocard architecture.

Related Work. Similar approaches of using dedicated hardware are not completely new to mobile IT security. Rohde & Schwarz SIT have introduced TopSec Mobile in 2009 to support voice encryption over GSM networks in an external hardware device which at that time communicated with standard GSM phones over the speaker jack, a connection which was later replaced by Bluetooth, and VoIP support was added. While the beauty of this setting voice is transported by the standard phone and over the mobile network only in encrypted mode was evenly invulnerable to all known tapping and intrusion methods, it lacked hugely in versatility. The device was so dedicated to its only application that even something undemanding as SMS encryption could not be integrated in a form that earned user acceptance. Similarly User Centric Temper-Resistant Device[15] enables a user control security and privacy[16] preserving device that can provide a secure and trusted execution and storage platform.

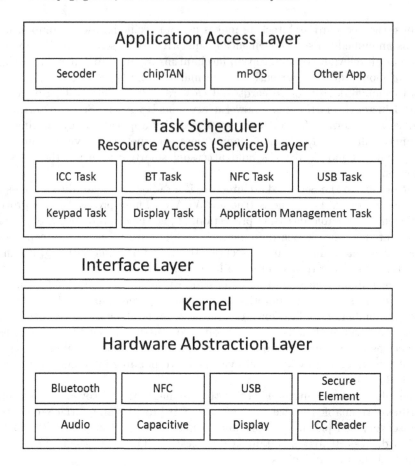

Fig. 1. Secocard architecture overview

3.3   Use Case: Online Banking

Online banking in Germany is a widespread form of handling a bank account through a web-based portal provided by a bank or a group of associated banks. It is used on a regular basis by almost 50% of all bank customers[17]. Generally, secure access to the web portal is being provided by requiring the entry of a pre-registered user name and a password. Once logged on successfully, for the transaction of wiring money or transferring funds to another account, different banks offer different varieties and methods to be used.

In almost all cases of online banking, a 6 digit transaction number (TAN) which is basically a one-time password is generated either in advance by the bank and given to the customer in printed form, where during the transaction dialog the customer is informed which exact position of the numbered TAN list must be used for the current transaction, or it is generated by a TAN generator device the bank hands out to their customers for a small fee. The TAN generator device needs to read a certificate safely stored on the bank customer's money card, and is given the transfer information either by manual input or by reading a "flicker code" from the users PC screen.

Other methods in wider use comprise Mobile TAN (mTAN). mTANs are used by banks in Austria, Bulgaria, Czech Republic, Germany, Hungary, the Netherlands, Poland, Russia, South Africa, Spain, Switzerland and some in New Zealand, Australia and Ukraine. When the user initiates a transaction, a TAN is generated by the bank and sent to the user's mobile phone by SMS. The SMS may also include transaction data, allowing the user to verify that the transaction has not been modified in transmission to the bank.

The security level of this scheme depends on the security of the mobile phone system. It has become common in a variety of countries to attack the bank customer by obtaining a replacement SIM card for their phone either by cloning if the card data can be accessed or by ordering a replacement or multi-card from the mobile network operator if the victim's user name and password can be obtained by keylogging or phishing. As long as the victim has yet to detect that text messages are directed to anther card - as a basic function of the GSM standard, SMS will only be transferred to one card per subscriber - the attacker can transfer/extract the victim's funds from their accounts.[Wikipedia]

The mTAN online banking procedure in its vulnerability can entirely be replaced with "girocard" payment using the chipTAN standard as defined by the German credit industry. When using Secocard, keylogging and use of Trojan horses is successfully prevented, while phishing victimization unfortunately escapes technology based security solutions and instead requires the user to apply common sense.

Figure 2 provides an overview on how well-designed security standards allow safe mobile and online banking, and figure 3 presents how they were implemented on Secocard.

4   Discussion

The idea behind Secocard as a secure means of supporting protected online banking transactions and mobile payment services is that the same device with its secure architecture can also shield the dialog between bank and customer from eavesdropping and tapping. There is no need to exchange the small and lightweight device which is not really bigger than a few credit cards stacked on one another in case the bank customer subscribes to a new bank service or decides to change the way she wants to operate her account from her desk or any other place through remotely using the mobile internet - as long as the service is protected by a protocol and application which has been standardized according to the requirements of e.g. the German credit industry, and as such has been implemented beforehand. Even if an extra piece of hardware may be resented by many potential smartphone and tablet users, this may boost acceptance as the device is definitely compatible with all the smartphones, tablets and PCs. So as a result of the combinational logic, users will not have to worry whether or

chipTAN, Bluetooth bidirectional communication

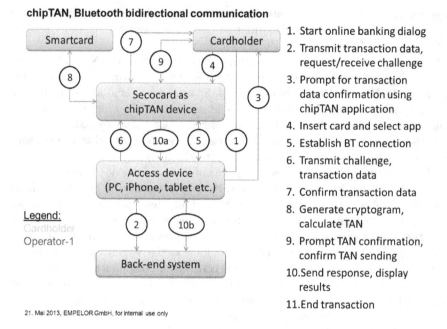

1. Start online banking dialog
2. Transmit transaction data, request/receive challenge
3. Prompt for transaction data confirmation using chipTAN application
4. Insert card and select app
5. Establish BT connection
6. Transmit challenge, transaction data
7. Confirm transaction data
8. Generate cryptogram, calculate TAN
9. Prompt TAN confirmation, confirm TAN sending
10. Send response, display results
11. End transaction

Fig. 2. Online banking process using chipTAN application on Secocard

not the next service a bank may promote could be something that will become corrupted within a few months or weeks following its introduction, as it has been the case with earlier banking applications designed to support mobile device use for online banking.

5   Conclusion and Outlook on More Supported Use Cases

Cost is definitely an issue when selecting the ideal equipment for retail card reading and transaction performing. Credit card schemes and banks are well advised to add more value to POS equipment for less cost. Secocard enables credit card schemes and acquirers to provide their merchants with full protection of a dedicated POS hardware solution which works well with their fancy smartphones and tablets. Also, the merchant can exchange the cell phone practically every day at random the POS device will remain the same and will not only run protected mobile payment and card acceptance services, but also online banking transactions and, if needed, it can also shield the dialog between the shop and a bank or a business partner, even a shop client, effectively from eavesdropping and tapping.

Reasonable manufacturing costs combined with a broad and growing selection of beneficial security functions from secure online banking and secure mobile POS to voice and email protection will contribute to making this development

Secoder & online banking (advanced signature)

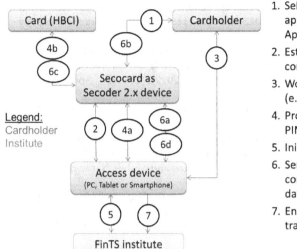

1. Select Secoder 2.x application (Secocard App)
2. Establish BT or USB connection
3. Work on online banking (e.g.)
4. Prompt for card & PIN, PIN verify
5. Initialize dialog
6. Send data for confirmation, confirm data, compute signature
7. Encrypt & send transaction data

Fig. 3. Online banking process using Secoder application on Secocard

a real asset to wider user groups searching for higher levels of application and communication security. The robust architecture will show its resistance against all forms and powers of intrusion in official tests upon request by public sector customers.

In a dialog with the German public sector, support for the new electronic ID card is currently discussed as this could significantly contribute to an overall mobile data and voice privacy protection for the population.

References

1. Andrejevic, M.: Facebook als neue Produktionsweise. In: Leistert, O., Rohle, T. (eds.) Generation Facebook: Uber das leben im social net, pp. 31–49 (2011)
2. Zhou, Y., Wang, Z., Zhou, W., Jiang, X.: Hey, you, get off of my market: Detecting malicious apps in official and alternative android markets. In: Proceedings of the 19th Annual Network and Distributed System Security Symposium, pp. 5–8 (2012)
3. Suarez-Tangil, G., Tapiador, J.E., Peris-Lopez, P., Ribagorda, A.: Evolution, Detection and Analysis of Malware for Smart Devices. IEEE Communications Surveys & Tutorials, 1–27 (2013)
4. Frick, J., Rainer, B.: Method for identifying a mobile phone user or for eavesdropping on outgoing calls. Patent: EP1051053

5. Texas Criminal Lawyer Blog. Devices that Track Cell Phone Signals Violate Fourth Amendment, Say Privacy Advocates (2013),
   https://www.gov.uk/government/uploads/system/uploads/attachment_data/
   file/200455/bis-13-p184-2013-information-security-breaches-survey-
   technical-report.pdf
6. Andriotis, P., Oikonomou, G., Tryfonas, T.: Forensic Analysis of Wireless Networking Evidence of Android Smartphones. In: Proc. IEEE International Workshop on Information Forensics and Security (WIFS 2012), Tenerife, Spain, pp. 109–114. IEEE (December 2012)
7. Internet Service Providers. Guiding Principles on Cyber Security. Guidance for Internet Service Providers and Government (December 2013)
8. Andriotis, P., Tryfonas, T., Oikonomou, G., Yildiz, C.: A pilot study on the security of pattern screen-lock methods and soft side channel attacks. In: Proc. 6th ACM Conference on Security and Privacy in Wireless and Mobile Networks (WiSec 2013), pp. 1–6. ACM Press (2013)
9. Petroulakis, N.E., Tragos, E.Z., Fragkiadakis, A.G., Spanoudakis, G.: A lightweight framework for secure life-logging in smart environments. Information Security Technical Report 17(3), 58–70 (2013); Security and Privacy for Digital Ecosystems
10. Department for Business Innovation and Skills. Information Security Breaches Survey (2013)
11. Secocard. The security Platform, http://www.secocard.ch
12. EMPELOR GmbH, http://www.empelor.ch
13. Akram, R.N., Markantonakis, K., Mayes, K.: Coopetitive Architecture to Support a Dynamic and Scalable NFC based Mobile Services Architecture. In: Chim, T.W., Yuen, T.H. (eds.) ICICS 2012. LNCS, vol. 7618, pp. 214–227. Springer, Heidelberg (2012)
14. Akram, R.N., Markantonakis, K.: Smart Cards: State-of-the-Art to Future Directions. In: IEEE International Symposium on Signal Processing and Information Technology (ISSPIT 2013) (December 2013)
15. Akram, R.N., Markantonakis, K., Mayes, K.: User Centric Security Model for Tamper-Resistant Devices. In: 8th IEEE International Conference on e-Business Engineering (ICEBE 2011). IEEE Computer Society (October 2011)
16. Petroulakis, N.E., Askoxylakis, I.G., Traganitis, A., Spanoudakis, G.: A privacy-level model of user-centric cyber-physical systems. In: Marinos, L., Askoxylakis, I. (eds.) HAS 2013. LNCS, vol. 8030, pp. 338–347. Springer, Heidelberg (2013)
17. E-Banking Snapshot 39. Deutsche Bank Research (2012)
18. Courtois, N.T.: Computer Security at the Low, Hardware/Process/Memory Level. University College London (2009)
19. Leibholz, S.W., Frankel, C.T.L.: Tracking Inappropriate Data Exfiltration: Dealing with the Ubiquitous Insider Threat via Zero-Knowledge Proof (2013)

Authentication and Passwords

Complexity Metrics and User Strength Perceptions of the Pattern-Lock Graphical Authentication Method

Panagiotis Andriotis, Theo Tryfonas, and George Oikonomou

University of Bristol, Merchant Venturers Building, Bristol, BS8 1UB, U.K.
{p.andriotis,theo.tryfonas,g.oikonomou}@bristol.ac.uk

Abstract. One of the most popular contemporary graphical password approaches is the Pattern-Lock authentication mechanism that comes integrated with the Android mobile operating system. In this paper we investigate the impact of password strength meters on the selection of a perceivably secure pattern. We first define a suitable metric to measure pattern strength, taking into account the constraints imposed by the Pattern-Lock mechanism's design. We then implement an app via which we conduct a survey for Android users, retaining demographic information of responders and their perceptions on what constitutes a pattern complex enough to be secure. Subsequently, we display a pattern strength meter to the participant and investigate whether this additional prompt influences the user to change their pattern to a more effective and complex one. We also investigate potential correlations between our findings and results of a previous pilot study in order to detect any significant biases on setting a Pattern-Lock.

Keywords: Security, Android, password, bias, usability, feedback.

1 Introduction

Innovation in the smartphone industry is now focused on novel user authentication methods. Apple recently launched their new flagship device with a built-in fingerprint identity sensor and the new trend has been set. Other smartphone manufacturers will include this feature to their products but there must exist devices that should be more affordable to the wide public. This is why traditional user authentication methods have to be enhanced with security precautions in order to make them solid against various types of attacks.

Mobile devices are playing a major role to the way we communicate with others. They are valuable assets to our personal and professional life because they integrate the most usable and popular applications. Despite the fact that a smartphone is a telephone device, it can also store sensitive information like text messages, electronic mail, notes and calendar events. It can record and play various multimedia files such as photos, audio and video. We can connect to the Internet, browse web pages, navigate to our social media accounts and extend its internal capacity by using cloud storage services. All these capabilities imprint

T. Tryfonas and I. Askoxylakis (Eds.): HAS 2014, LNCS 8533, pp. 115–126, 2014.

important personal information on their internal storage. Thus, user protection and authentication schemes should provide usability and security in a balanced mixture.

Traditional user authentication is achieved by utilizing text-based methods. These methods include Personal Identification Numbers (PIN) and text passwords. A PIN is usually (but not limited to) a four-digit code and a password is a sequence of characters. Over the years, alphanumeric and textual passwords have shown significant disadvantages because they are vulnerable to dictionary attacks. When it comes to the right proportion between usability and security people tend to prefer usability. Humans usually provide passwords that are easy to remember and add no complexity to their daily routine. This choice leads them to use poor and memorable passwords making the defense against intruders easy to break.

The problems textual passwords might cause to the protection of personal data stored in a mobile device were partially solved when graphical passwords were introduced. These types of security measures were also deployed by the need of commercial identification of Operating Systems against their competitors. Graphical passwords use pictures, images or patterns to create authentication schemes, which are easy to remember, fun to use and provide a sense of uniqueness, while at the same time aiming to be secure enough to prevent attackers from breaking them. The Android community introduced a popular graphical authentication method, which is called Android Pattern-Lock. The Android Pattern-Lock is a 3x3 grid of nodes. In order to unlock their phone, users swipe their fingers connecting nodes and formulate a memorable shape that acts as a password. Vision is also engaged in the particular process and this makes the password easier to remember.

Since the Android Pattern-Lock mechanism was introduced, numerous attempts were made by researchers to decode the way people responded to the new protection scheme. These studies tried to exploit psychological or physical biases that might occur when humans try to form a secure or a usable password. One of the problems we can identify to the graphical password authentication methods is the lack of interaction between the user and the device while the password is been generated. Thus, when setting a pattern users are not informed about its strength. On the other hand, our daily interaction with computers and web sites that require user identification, projects the importance of providing feedback to the users that the passwords they chose are not secure enough. A characteristic example of this concept is the coloured bars next to the password fields when we create a new account for a web site or when we update our details.

In this paper we investigate whether such feedback prompts actually have any impact on user perception about the security of an Android pattern. To this end, we developed an application and collected data from 120 Android users who participated in a survey about their understanding of Android Pattern-Lock security. We therefore confirm previous results highlighting that there exist specific heuristic rules that define pattern formation. Finally, we propose a password strength assessment methodology for the Android Pattern-Lock and evaluate its impact on survey participant responses.

In Sect. 2 we discuss the relevant research on the field of textual and graphical password security and mention some of the methods used in the past to exploit potential vulnerabilities present in these schemes. Section 3 provides a dissection of the experimental methodology we used and defines our metrics. Results and an evaluating discussion are been presented in Sect. 4. We draw our conclusions in Sect. 5 and propose future directions for further research.

2   Background and Related Work

Authenticating a user is among the most critical tasks in the area of computer security and especially when we are dealing with cases with high risk, including bank transactions, accessing personal information or logging into ad-hoc networks [2]. The common form of user authentication, when there is no need for sophisticated security measures, is a text-based password. Sometimes individuals have to balance between security and usability [13] and the outcome can be a choice of a weak password because a strong one is difficult to recall [5]. Numerous exploits of text-based passwords have been proposed including dictionary attacks. A well-known tool that performs such type of guessing is 'John The Ripper' [10].

As an alternative to the vulnerable textual passwords, other schemes have been proposed, known as graphical passwords [4], given the fact that the human brain reacts better when it has to deal with visual and graphical information [14] [17]. The variety of graphical passwords makes them distinct. Various processes like clicking points on an image or drawing a line can define their formation principles. An example of a graphical authentication is the PassFaces algorithm [9] that was studied and evaluated for its usability by [6]. However, human behavioural heuristic rules may affect the efficiency of a graphical password and make it vulnerable to image-based dictionary attacks [12]. Other types of graphical authentication include 'face selection' mechanisms or 'point harvesting' by clicking on specific areas of an image. Studies demonstrated that as users, we tend to pick faces that attract us [7] and we select distinct regions of interest on images [16], resulting to high levels of password predictability [11].

In the smartphone universe there exists a very popular and easy to use graphical password identification method called Android Pattern-Lock. This is a two-dimensional square grid of nine nodes that serves as a drawing canvas. The smartphone user has to form a shape that links between four and nine nodes, and this shape is the formal password that allows access to the phone. This is actually a specialized version of the Pass-Go [15] authentication system focused on the standardized size of mobile devices. Pass-Go could be considered as an algorithm that followed the concept of Draw-a-Secret (DaS) scheme [8]. In the Pass-Go paradigm we have a grid of nxn dots but the password does not need to be a cohesive line like the Android Pattern-Lock. The Pattern-Lock is a line connecting nodes in a 3x3 grid. There are also some basic rules users must have in mind when they come up with their patterns: At least four nodes should be lit to form a password, a node cannot be used twice and jumps across unlit nodes are prohibited. These rules restrict the password space and allow only for 389,112 unique patterns to be drawn [3].

The special characteristics of the aforementioned password scheme make it an interesting topic for research. Aspects of its usability against security have been studied in [17]. In a relevant case study [3] researchers demonstrated the vulnerabilities of touchscreens and conducted attacks (known as smudge attacks) on graphical passwords using the residues that were left on the screen. This information, in conjunction with behavioural biases traced from a pilot web survey, was used in [1] to perform attacks on the Android Pattern-Lock providing promising results. Our intention here is to confirm those results and examine how the users would react if they had the ability to be informed by the smartphone about the strength of the graphical password they chose.

3   Experimental Setup and Definitions

In this section we will present the methodology we used to collect our data and evaluate them according to the objectives of this study. We want to measure the password strength of patterns the participants provide and also evaluate their responses to a feedback tool that informs them if they used a weak or a strong password.

3.1   Methodology

We developed an application and distributed it through the official channel for Android apps (Play Store). We were aiming to get feedback by Android users who had the chance to draw their patterns on a real device, simulating the original user identification method of the phone. First, the participants had to answer some demographic questions. Then we asked them if they would change their password if their device gave them feedback that it was a weak one. Two more questions followed, asking their opinion if the pattern they were about to draw is usable and secure. The final stage prompted them to draw the actual pattern. After the pattern was formed, the device calculated and informed the users about its strength, subsequently asking if they would like to change it or keep it. They had the right either to change the chosen pattern and draw a new one or keep it and finish the survey by submitting the results.

The survey was fully anonymized and we also took precautions to avoid duplicates. We designed the application to be unambiguous and the participants should not spend more than a few minutes to complete it. The survey was publicized through the social media in various groups of interest.

3.2   Definitions

The calculation of the password strength was one of the most critical parts of our study. We based our assumptions and definitions on our pilot study [1] which

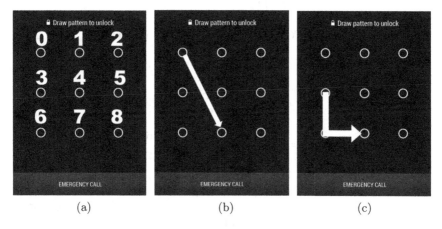

Fig. 1. (a) The topography of the grid, (b) a knight move, (c) a direction change

illustrated that there exist behavioural biases when humans create their graphical passwords. The basic heuristic rules we derived by the study are: (a) More than 50% of users start their patterns from the top left node, (b) a pattern that consists of less than 6 nodes is considered as not secure enough, (c) a secure password is the one that has more than 2 direction changes. Taking these observations into account, we also included two more features to our password strength assessment algorithm. The first is the presence of one or more knight moves and the other is the existence of overlapping nodes. (In Fig. 1 we demontrate the topology of nodes (a), we show an example of a knight move (b) and provide an example of a direction change (c).) We therefore provide the following definitions.

Let G be a set (representing the Android Pattern-Lock Grid) such that:
$G = \{n : n \in \mathbb{N} \text{ and } 0 \leq n \leq 8\}$.
A pattern P is an ordered set:
$P \subseteq G : P = \{a_i : i \in \mathbb{N} \text{ and } 0 \leq i < |P|, \ 4 \ \leq \ |P| \ \leq \ 9\}$,
($|P|$ is the cardinallity of the set.)
A direction change (abbr. c) happens when there is an angle in the shape three consecutive nodes form or when we revisit an already visited node. For example, 367 or 364 constitute a direction change and 2435 define two direction changes.

A knight move (abbr. k) is an edge that connects two distant nodes, e.g. 07, 05, 16, 15, etc.

An overlapping node (abbr. o) is an already visited node. For instance, the pattern 0124357 has an overlapping node (the node 4), which gets visited for a second time when the user moves from node 5 towards node 3.

$\|\cdot\|$ defines the number of knight moves or overlapping nodes.

Let X be a 5x1 matrix: $X = \begin{bmatrix} x_1 \\ x_2 \\ x_3 \\ x_4 \\ x_5 \end{bmatrix}$ and N the 1x5 matrix $N = \begin{bmatrix} 1 & 1 & 1 & 1 & 1 \end{bmatrix}$

where

$$x_1 = \begin{cases} 1 & , \quad \text{if } a_0 \neq 0 \\ 0 & , \quad \text{else} \end{cases}$$

$$x_2 = \begin{cases} |P| - 5 & , \quad \text{if } |P| \geq 6 \\ 0 & , \quad \text{else} \end{cases}$$

$$x_3 = \begin{cases} 1 & , \quad \text{if } c \geq 2 \\ 0 & , \quad \text{else} \end{cases}$$

$$x_4 = \|k\| \text{ and } x_5 = \|o\|$$

x_1 evaluates if the starting point of the patten is 0, x_2 contributes to the score if the pattern consists of more than 6 nodes, x_3 is used to highlight if there are more than 2 direction changes and x_4, x_5 evaluate the presence of knight moves and overlapping nodes.

Thus, the pattern-lock strength Δ is defined as: $\Delta = N \cdot X$ \qquad (1)

The feedback Φ is given to the user in a form of textual information (Weak, Medium, Strong). There are three scales of security defined from the following equation.

$$\Phi = \begin{cases} \text{Weak} & , \quad \text{if } 0 \leq \Delta \leq 1 \\ \text{Medium} & , \quad \text{if } \Delta = 2 \\ \text{Strong} & , \quad \text{if } \Delta \geq 3 \end{cases} \qquad (2)$$

4   Results and Discussion

Table 1 provides a generic presentation of the survey results. Most of the participants were male aged between 18-29 years old. As discussed previously, the survey was publicized through university related channels; hence the education level of the participants is quite high. The vast majority of the people that took the survey are smartphone owners, and they currently have devices running the Android OS. They prefer to use the Pattern-Lock mechanism to protect personal information, prevent others fiddling with the phone or protect data if someone steals their phone (Question 9). One of the most interesting questions for the current study is Question 10. We wanted to know if they would change their chosen password if they were informed by some kind of feedback, provided by the device, that their password is weak; 77.5% of them answered affirmatively. Finally, most of the replies suggest that the users believe that their chosen pattern is usable as well as secure.

Table 1. Survey results

Number	Question	Category	Percentage
Q1	Gender	Male	60.0%
		Female	34.2%
		Didn't say	5.8%
Q2	Age	18 - 29 y.o.	60.8%
		30 - 39 y.o.	35.0%
		40+ y.o.	4.2%
Q3	Ethnicity	African-American	39.2%
		White	25.8%
		Asian	21.7%
		Hispanic/Latin	11.7%
		Others	1.6%
Q4	Education	Bachelor's	40.0%
		Master's	40.0%
		Doctorate	11.7%
		High School & Other	8.3%
Q5	Smartphone user	Yes	99.2%
		No	0.8%
Q6	Smartphone usage	6 - 12 months	45.1%
		1 - 6 years	30.1%
		less than 6 months	24.8%
		more than 6 years	1.7%
Q7	Smartphone OS	Android	82.5%
		iOS	30.1%
		Blackberry	4.2%
		Windows Phone OS	1.7%
Q8	Preferred password type	Pattern Lock	53.3%
		PIN	39.2%
		Others	7.5%
Q10	Password meter effect	Yes	77.5%
		No	22.5%
Q11	Usable pattern provided	Yes	81.7%
		No	18.3%
Q12	Secure pattern provided	Yes	86.7%
		No	13.3%

Table 2. Direction changes in the set of patterns

Changes	Number	Frequency
1	13	10.8%
2	26	21.7%
3	31	25.8%
4	33	27.5%
5	14	11.6%
6	2	1.6%
7	1	$\approx 1\%$

4.1   Analysing Pattern Characteristics

The analysis of certain characteristics the patterns had (direction changes and pattern length, which is measured by the number of nodes that constitute the shape) provided the results we demonstrate in Tables 2 and 3. In Table 2 for example we can see that for the majority of patterns, their shape introduces 2 - 4 direction changes. Also, Table 3 shows that even if we use a feedback method to engage users to a better understanding of security, the outcome will still be patterns that basically consist of 5 - 7 nodes.

We believe that this is an observation that diversifies the users and keep the authentication method reliable from being predictable. If we force the user to provide stronger passwords that consist of 8 - 9 nodes (to be considered as stronger and safe) and loop around the nodes to produce a lot of direction changes, we eventually minimize the already limited password space of the Android Pattern-Lock method. Thus, a very strict feedback schema would probably have the opposite results than making the authentication method stronger and this is reflected in the definition of our strength criteria (Equation 2).

Table 3. Pattern length in the set of patterns

Length	Number	Frequency
4	17	14.2%
5	23	19.2%
6	25	20.8%
7	24	20.0%
8	13	10.8%
9	18	15.0%

4.2   Comparison with Previous Results

One of our objectives when we designed the experiment was to evaluate previous results we presented during a pilot study which examined (in a similar way) if there exist any heuristic rules that are responsible for specific biases in the provided patterns [1]. The experiments in this study were conducted using a web application, thus, the participants were not really interacting with a smartphone device but with the monitor of their computer. In addition, they were not using their fingers to form their passwords on the screen because it was an online survey and the interaction medium of the application and the user was the mouse. These characteristics and the fact that the whole procedure was a simulation of the original user authentication method, could force people to answer in a different way when they were interacting with a smartphone.

Figures 2 and 3 demonstrate that user reactions are quite similar in both experiments. We must underline here that the participants in both experiments were different and the second study took place two years after the first. In Fig. 2

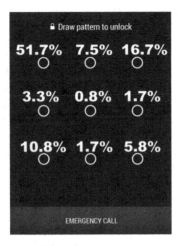

Fig. 2. Frequency of starting points

we can see that more than 50% chose to start their patterns from node 0. Nodes 2 and 6 are also popular starting points and we can conclude that participants preferred to begin their drawings from the corners of the grid. Figure 3 illustrates the most common bigrams, trigrams and fourgrams. These are sub-patterns that exist in the password and provide information about the most common edges that were formed during the drawing of the pattern. A comparison with [1] shows that indeed the upper nodes are heavily utilized during password formation.

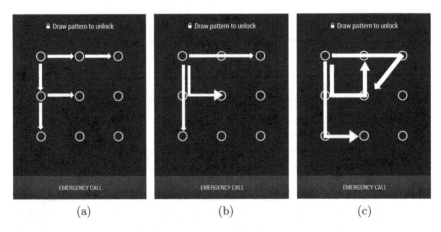

Fig. 3. The most common: (a) Bigrams, (b) trigrams, (c) fourgrams

4.3   Evaluating the Feedback Responses

Table 4 concatenates the results of our research describing user perceptions about the security of the Android Pattern-Lock method and their responses to our feedback prompt. The findings we highlight in Table 4 evaluate the responses after the feedback prompt was shown to the participants. Hence, these are the final choices the users of our proposed scheme made. The password strength of the resulting patterns is almost equally distributed among the three scales. As expected, the 'Weak' passwords were fewer after the feedback was propounded. One observation we can make is that the majority of male users came up with stronger passwords in contrast to the patterns females chose.

In addition, 23.3% of the participants changed their choice of pattern when they were informed about the valence of their password. This means that almost one out of five users changed their pattern to make it stronger when the feedback underlined the lack of security of their initial choice. Another interesting finding that strengthens the importance of such a feedback mechanism is the fact that 10.7% of the people that finally changed their graphical password had said before (in Question 10) that they would not take into account any evaluation of their password strength from the device. Thus, one out of nine people paid attention to the feedback mechanism and changed the pattern they chose even though they had said (seconds before) that they would not do that.

Table 4. Password strength assesment

Scale	Number	Percentage	Gender	Number	Percentage
Weak	32	26.6%	Male	15	46.9%
			Female	12	37.5%
			Didn't say	5	15.6%
Medium	44	36.7%	Male	28	63.6%
			Female	16	36.4%
Strong	44	36.7%	Male	29	66.0%
			Female	13	29.5%
			Didn't say	2	4.5%

Remarks	Number	Percentage
Changed Pattern	28/120	23.3%
Changed despite their 'No' at Q10	3/28	10.7%
Didn't Change 'Weak' despite their 'Yes'	26/120	21.7%
Changed from 'Weak' to 'Weak'	2/28	7.1%

On the contrary 21.7%, meaning one out of five users, did not change their 'Weak' passwords although they had answered that they would consider a feedback from the device. Perhaps a more aggressive design strategy and a more exhorting message would be sufficient to change this feature. Finally, one out of fourteen participants that changed their patterns, they chose 'Weak' passwords again. An explanation to this observation might be that there is a small part of users that prefer a very usable pattern ignoring the security a more complex drawing provides.

5   Conclusion and Future Work

In this study we compared our results with previous knowledge justifying that there are specific behavioural biases that define the formation of graphical patterns. We proposed a scheme, which measures the strength of Android Pattern-Lock instances and reported the effects a feedback prompt would have to users. We demonstrated that the majority of people that participated in our experiments were positively affected by the suggestions about security our proposed algorithm produced. They finally changed their passwords and this outcome resulted to stronger user authentication paradigms.

Further work should include the investigation of the impact other features might have at the calculation of the password strength. The password valence assessment criteria could include ending points, bigrams, trigrams and dexterity; the algorithm could also assign different weights to the final evaluation criteria of the password strength. Another issue we should take into consideration is how aggressive and persuasive a feedback prompt could be in order to provide to the user a better understanding of security without decreasing the password space of the Android Pattern-Lock method.

Acknowledgements. This work has been supported by the European Union's Prevention of and Fight against Crime Programme "Illegal Use of Internet" - ISEC 2010 Action Grants, grant ref. HOME/2010/ISEC/AG/INT-002 and the Systems Centre of the University of Bristol. We are grateful to Etelaowoni Queeneth Ogbeche for her contribution to data collection.

References

1. Andriotis, P., Tryfonas, T., Oikonomou, G., Yildiz, C.: A pilot study on the security of pattern screen-lock methods and soft side channel attacks. In: 6th ACM Conference on Security and Privacy in Wireless and Mobile Networks, WiSec 2013, pp. 1–6. ACM (2013)
2. Askoxylakis, I.G., Kastanis, D.D., Traganitis, A.: Elliptic curve and password based dynamic key agreement in wireless ad-hoc networks. In: Communication, Network, and Information Security, pp. 50–60 (2006)
3. Aviv, A.J., Gibson, K., Mossop, E., Blaze, M., Smith, J.M.: Smudge attacks on smartphone touch screens. In: 4th USENIX Conference on Offensive Technologies, pp. 1–7. USENIX Association (2010)
4. Biddle, R., Chiasson, S., Van Oorschot, P.C.: Graphical passwords: Learning from the first twelve years. ACM Computing Surveys 44(4), 1–41 (2012)
5. Bonneau, J.: The science of guessing: analyzing an anonymized corpus of 70 million passwords. In: 2012 IEEE Symposium Security and Privacy (SP), pp. 538–552. IEEE (2012)

6. Brostoff, S., Sasse, A.: Are Passfaces More Usable Than Passwords? A Field Trial Investigation. In: People and Computers XIV Usability or Else!. Springer, London (2000)
7. Davis, D., Monrose, F., Reiter, M.: On user choice in graphical password schemes. In: USENIX Assosiation Proceedings of the 13th USENIX Security Symposium, pp. 151–163. USENIX Association (2004)
8. Jermyn, I., Mayer, A., Monrose, F., Reiter, M.K., Rubin, A.D.: The Design and Analysis of Graphical Passwords. In: 8th USENIX Security Symposium, pp. 1–14 (1999)
9. Passfaces Corporation.: The Science Behind Passfaces. White paper, http://www.passfaces.com/enterprise/resources/white_papers.htm
10. Solar Designer. John the Ripper, http://www.openwall.com/john/
11. van Oorschot, P.C., Thorpe, J.: Exploiting Predictability in Click-based Graphical Passwords. Journal of Computer Security 19(4), 669–702 (2011)
12. van Oorschot, P.C., Thorpe, J.: On predictive models and user-drawn graphical passwords. ACM Trans. Inf. Syst. Secur. 10(4), 5:1–5:33 (2008)
13. Sasse, M.A., Brostoff, S., Weirich, D.: Transforming the 'weakest link' - a human/computer interaction approach to usable and effective security. BT Technology Journal 19(3), 122–131 (2001)
14. Standing, L., Conezio, J., Haber, R.N.: Perception and Memory for Pictures: Single-trial Learning of 2500 Visual Stimuli. Psychonomic Science 19(2), 73–74 (1970)
15. Tao, H., Adams, C.: Pass-Go: A Proposal to Improve the Usability of Graphical Passwords. International Journal of Network Security 7(2), 273–292 (2008)
16. Thorpe, J., van Oorschot, P.C.: Human-seeded attacks and exploiting hot-spots in graphical passwords. In: USENIX Assosiation Proceedings of the 16th USENIX Security Symposium, pp. 103–118. USENIX Association (2007)
17. Uellenbeck, S., Dürmuth, M., Wolf, C., Holz, T.: Quantifying the security of graphical passwords: the case of android unlock patterns. In: 2013 ACM SIGSAC Conference on Computer & Communications Security, pp. 161–172. ACM (2013)

A Cognitive-Behavioral Framework of User Password Management Lifecycle[*]

Yee-Yin Choong

National Institute of Standards and Technology,
100 Bureau Drive, Gaithersburg, MD 20899, USA
yee-yin.choong@nist.gov

Abstract. Passwords are the most commonly used mechanism in controlling users' access to information systems. Little research has been established on the entire user password management lifecycle from the start of generating a password, maintaining the password, using the password to authenticate, then to the end of the lifespan of the password when it needs to be changed. We develop a cognitive-behavioral framework depicting the cognitive activities that users perform within each stage, and how the stages interact with the human information processor, i.e. memory and attention resources. Individual factors are also represented in the framework such as attitudes, motivations, and emotions that can affect users' behaviors during the password management lifecycle. The paper discusses cognitive and behavioral activities throughout the lifecycle as well as the associated economics. We show the importance of a holistic approach in understanding users' password behaviors and the framework provides guidance on future research directions.

Keywords: password, password management lifecycle, cyber security, password policy, usability, cognitive-behavioral framework, economics of passwords.

1   Introduction

Text-based passwords are the most commonly used mechanism in controlling users' access to information systems. Arguably, passwords are currently the best fit for many authentication needs as passwords allow access from anywhere assuming only a simple browser and revocation is as simple as changing passwords [1]. Users often possess multiple account-password pairs for work, school and private use. For example, it is reported that an average user has 25 web accounts requiring passwords [2], and employees of organizations have about 4 [3] to 9 passwords [4] at work.

Users are often viewed by IT security professionals as the weakest link of cyber security [5,6]. Users are also blamed for employing insecure behaviors such as selecting bad and simple-easy-to-guess passwords, reusing passwords, writing down or sharing their passwords, and, whenever possible, not changing their passwords on a

---

[*] The rights of this work are transferred to the extent transferable according to title 17 U.S.C. 105.

T. Tryfonas and I. Askoxylakis (Eds.): HAS 2014, LNCS 8533, pp. 127–137, 2014.
© Springer International Publishing Switzerland 2014

regular basis. For example, in a recent major security breach in which 150 million user accounts were compromised, "123456" was used the most as the password by over 2 million users, followed by a little more complicated password "123456789", and the word "password" ranked 3rd used by 345,000 users [7].

On the other hand, for users, usability of passwords is their main concern. Users have to juggle multiple passwords for work, school or personal use and often are forced to comply with password policies that they view as burdensome [4,8]. Frustration with login problems such as forgetting or mistyping passwords increase greatly with the number of passwords that users must manage [1,4]. Users perceive that security measures hinder their productivity and sometimes use workarounds to break the security protocol [4,8].

Research focusing on human factors and usability of passwords has been challenging the view that users are the primary cause for cyber security issues and pointing out that security policies are often imposing unreasonable requirements and pushing users' cognitive limits. For example, a typical enterprise password policy can require its employees create complicated passwords, not write down or store them, change passwords every 90 days, and not reuse the last 10 passwords. It is almost impossible for employees to comply with this stringent policy especially with multiple passwords as there are fundamental limitations on human memory (e.g. limited memory span, memory decay, recognition vs. recall, and memory interferences) as summarized by Sasse et al. [9]. Many studies have investigated the construct of users' selection of "good" or "bad" passwords [10-12]. Researchers also challenge the necessity and true effectiveness of using aggressive password policies for security and sacrificing usability that forces users to adopt insecure practices and may eventually compromise security [13-15].

As shown, studies are abundant on password usability and its implications on cyber security. However, little research has been established on the cognitive and behavioral aspects of the entire user password management lifecycle, i.e. from the start of generating a password to the end of the lifespan of the password when it needs to be changed due to events such as forgetting, expiration, or compromise. While performing research on a particular stage of the lifecycle provides valuable insight on users' experiences during that stage, it does not offer complete understanding of the entire process and could miss opportunities for identifying potential interactions and interdependencies among various stages during the password management lifecycle. This paper focuses on the holistic view of the end-to-end password management lifecycle and proposes a framework connecting the dots of users' activities during the lifecycle. This framework serves as a foundation in guiding future research directions.

2   The Cognitive-Behavioral Framework

We develop a framework to represent the cognitive process and user behaviors in the end-to-end password management lifecycle and to guide our future research. The user password management lifecycle consists of three stages: *Generation, Maintenance,* and *Authentication*. The framework depicts the cognitive activities that users perform within each stage, and how the stages interact with the human information processor, i.e. memory and attention resources. In addition, individual factors such as attitudes, motivations, and emotions are also included that can affect users' decision-making and behaviors during the password management lifecycle. The framework is illustrated in Figure 1 and each stage in the user password management lifecycle is described in detail in the sections below.

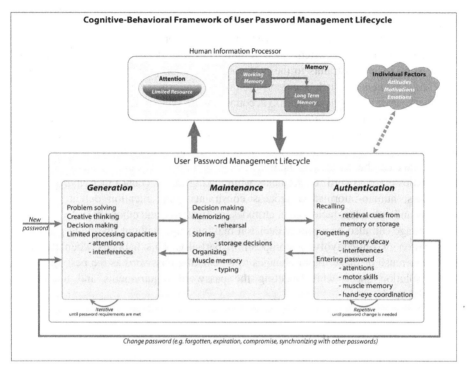

Fig. 1. A Cognitive-Behavioral Framework of User Password Management Lifecycle

2.1   Password Generation

In the first stage of the password management lifecycle, i.e. *Generation*, users have to generate a plausible text string by combining various characters to satisfy the requirements for accessing the associated account or system. The requirements, known as composition rules, are a common organizational approach aimed at forcing users to select stronger passwords. The contents and wordings of those composition rules vary greatly from system to system, but they generally consist of rules on: password length (minimum and/or maximum), use (allowed or prohibited) of certain characters (uppercase or lowercase alphabets, numerical digits, special characters), use (allowed or prohibited) of common names, dictionary words, birthdays or other personal information. Composition rules can be presented as just password selection guidelines in some systems, whereas for other systems, the rules can be programmatically enforced such that users have to create compliant passwords in order to gain access to the systems.

This password generating and composing process is similar to a writing process that usually starts with the writer setting up the goals of the writing, understanding the constraints (e.g. grammar, target audience), generating ideas, selecting and arranging words, constructing text, and finally refining the written text [16]. This process, in essence, is a problem solving process that includes higher mental functions and creative thinking [17]. Password composition progresses in a similar way with the user first setting the goals of what account/system the password is for, understanding the constraints, choosing characters, then refining the text string to meet the password requirements. The constraints to the password generation problem can be categorized as: (1) *Environmental* – such as composition rules, platforms (e.g. desktop and/or laptop computers, and/or mobile devices), account/system type (e.g. web, application, or hardware access); (2) *Cognitive* – such as memory load and attention resources, rule comprehension ability; (3) *Individual* – such as attitudes, motivation, and perception of the criticality and sensitivity of the account and potential security threats.

This stage can be iterative as the user tries to find the best combination of characters that satisfies the password requirements while taking into account other environmental constraints, human-information process constraints (e.g. attention deficit, memory capacity) and individual factors (e.g. attitudes, motivations, and emotions).

This stage can also be a purely decision making stage without involving password composition or only involving composition partially. This happens when the user decides to reuse or make minor changes to an existing password as the best approach in the solution space while meeting the password requirements and the user's individual needs.

2.2   Password Maintenance

Once the user generates a satisfactory password for a specific account/system, the password moves into its second stage of the lifecycle, *Maintenance*. The user makes decisions on how he/she will keep track of the newly generated password, by memorizing or storing using some mechanism; and he/she also needs to decide how best to organize – mentally or physically – the newly generated password along with other existing and active passwords to minimize memory interferences at a later stage. If the user decides to memorize the password, he/she needs to employ some strategies (e.g. mnemonic device, rote rehearsing, or typing multiple times to establish muscle memory) to make sure the password has been encoded properly into the long-term memory. If the user decides to store the password, he/she needs to decide the storage mechanism, for example, writing down (in its entirety, partially, or disguised), recording electronically (file, devices, etc.), or utilizing some password management software. Sometimes, there may be an organizational policy on how passwords should be maintained by limiting maintenance options to users. For example, "Passwords should never be written down or stored on-line without encryption." is the most common policy set by many organizations.

It should be noted that there can be interactions and interdependencies between the *Generation* and *Maintenance* stages as the user may hold an *a priori* preference on whether to memorize or to store the password which can impact the user's password composing process with the thought that he/she has to memorize the text for later use. Also, the memorability of a text string can impact the user's decision on how to maintain the password.

2.3   Authentication

The last stage in the lifecycle is *Authentication* in which the password is used to gain access to the associated account/system. The authentication stage is repetitive as the password will be used multiple times for its entire lifespan until a change event occurs such as forgotten, expiration, password compromised, or user's desire to synchronize multiple passwords for different accounts. In each authentication instance, the user needs to retrieve the correct password either by recalling from memory or by looking up from stored media that matches the associated account/system for access, at the same time struggles with forgetting due to memory decay or interferences from other passwords, and needs to enter the password correctly which requires attentions, motor skills, muscle memory, and hand-eye coordination.

There are many factors that can affect a user's authentication experience with a password such as authentication frequency, how the password is maintained, memorability and type-ability of the account/password pair, or interferences from other passwords. The authentication experience (positive or negative) can then influence how the user creates new passwords when he/she moves out from the authentication stage and starts the next password management lifecycle.

3   Holistic Research Approach on User Password Behaviors Guided by the Framework

The framework serves as a constant reminder in research approaches to always consider users' password behaviors in a holistic manner that, at any point of time, the users are going through a stage in the password management lifecycle and their behaviors are a reflection of the interactions among stages in the lifecycle, the capabilities and limitations of the human information processor, and the individual factors.

In the following sections, we discuss the importance of employing a holistic approach and some misconceptions in the literature on user password behaviors research. We also review relevant research and point out areas for further research.

3.1   Password Generation – More than a Selection Task

The most common misconception of password generation in the literature is the notion of users' selecting passwords. It is often described that users *select* bad and insecure passwords [11,18,19]. However, generating passwords is more than a selection task in that the word "selection" implies choosing from a set of readily available password options. Users only *select* passwords when they decide to reuse existing passwords. In password generating tasks, users employ high-level cognitive, problem-solving tasks when they are faced with the task of composing text strings to satisfy password requirements of combining and arranging various characters with length limits while trying to make sense of the text strings and meeting their own personal needs.

3.2   Password Composition – Problem Solving

As noted earlier, password composition is in essence problem solving in that it involves goals defining, ideas searching/planning, and refining/finalizing. There have been few studies investigating password generation under restrictive composition rules [11,20,21]. However, those studies focused only on the outcomes of the password generation, i.e. the characteristics of the passwords generated, and the impacts of the restrictions, but did not investigate the entire generation process.

Password research has seldom recognized that composition is not a trivial task. There is a need for research on how users solve the "password generation" problem from the beginning when users first encounter and perceive the problem domain; comprehend the constraints (*Environmental*, *Cognitive*, and *Individual*); explore the solution space; verify solution feasibility; refine/narrow solution space; and make decisions on the best-fit solution. By researching password generation as a problem solving effort with the framework, it enables us to investigate topics such as the differences among the "problem solvers" (e.g. experts vs. novices); the impacts of password constraints on the solution space; the most important factor(s) leading to the best-fit solution; and the influences of the maintenance decision on password generation.

3.3   The Economics – Password Management Lifecycle

The cost of passwords appears low at a glance from the service providers' perspective as deploying a functional password system is relatively simple compared to other authentication alternatives such as biometrics or smart cards. From the users' perspective, it doesn't seem to cost much, either, since passwords allow instantaneous account setup and are readily understood [1]. However, there are significant costs associated with the password authentication mechanism for both the service providers and the end users. It is shown qualitatively [15] that an unusable password policy can degrade employees' productivity, and ultimately affect the organization's overall productivity. It is reported that more than 30% of IT support center calls were related to password resets [22]. On average, each call lasts about 5 minutes and the cost of support per incident is \$ 25[1] on average [23]. In addition to the support center cost, there are also costs associated with a user's time and productivity loss when making calls to the support center.

Of the three stages in the user password management lifecycle, *Generation* and *Authentication* are the most effort- and time-consuming stages for the users. It is imperative for researchers to start investigating the associated costs for these two stages from the users' perspective.

---

[1] All cost estimates in this paper are based on the United States dollar, i.e. USD or US\$.

The Cost of Password Generation

Besides composition rules, organizations often include other requirements such as password expiration, password reuse limitations, and password uniqueness in their organizational policies. It will be difficult to quantify the direct impacts of the password policies on users' cognitive activities and behaviors and translate the impacts into associated costs. One way to estimate the costs is to look at the number of passwords generated and the time it takes to generate those passwords.

In the study performed by Choong et al. [4], it is reported that an employee has on average 9 work-related passwords. An organizational password policy commonly looks like:

— Password **must be**
  o Changed at least every 60 days
  o At least 12 characters long
  o Consistent with the complexity requirements (mixed-case characters, numbers, and special characters)
— Password **must not**
  o Be written down or stored on-line on non-organization systems
  o Reuse any password of the last 24 prior passwords
  o Use the same password on multiple systems, applications or websites

If a new employee acquires his/her 9 passwords in the first months on the job, by following the policy, it means that the new employee will have to generate 54 unique passwords within the first year of employment, which means that a unique and complex password is generated on average every week throughout the year. The constant password generation task puts a huge amount of burden on employees who only see managing passwords as a secondary task enabling access to their primary task [24]. This estimate does not take into account other password generation events outside of the regular changing cycle due to unplanned incidents such as forgotten passwords or password compromises.

It is also reported that the longest time it takes to generate passwords for work is, on average, 98.5 minutes for frequent passwords and 86.6 minutes for occasionally passwords [4]. The worst scenario: if every password takes the longest time to generate, an employee can spend 18.6 hours (or 2 ¼ business days) at a 60-day cycle each year generating passwords for their work. If the average annual wage of $81,704 (or $39.15/hour) of federal civilian workers is used [25], we can estimate an annual cost of $728.19 per employee being pulled away from work to generate passwords.

The Cost of Authentication

Users interact with authentication systems on a daily basis for work, school, or for personal use. As shown in Figure 1, each authentication instance involves retrieving the correct password (from memory or from stored media) and typing the password to gain access. This authentication instance can be iterative in itself if any step fails in the sequence, e.g. incorrect password retrieved – forgetting or interferences, typing errors, or system failure.

Research investigating real-life user authentication experience includes diary studies, e.g. [15,24,26,27], and longitudinal studies, e.g. [2,28]. The number of authentication instances varies greatly in those studies, ranging from typing 8.11 passwords per day [2], 75 password events in a two-week span [27], to 23 authentication events in a day with 46.9% (~11 times) being password logins [24]. Users expressed frustration and time wasted from various login problems such as mistyping passwords, forgetting passwords, mismatching account and password, and getting locked out [4]. When entering passwords from memory, it is reported that the most common error is incorrect capitalization (shifting), followed by missing character(s) [29].

While it is difficult to estimate the full costs of users' authentication experience with passwords, we can start with a simplified way to calculate the costs associated with password entry. In the diary study done at the National Institute of Standards and Technology (NIST) [24], employees entered passwords about 11 times in a day and the NIST's password policy requires passwords being 12 characters or longer. As reported in [21], it takes roughly14 seconds to type a password of 8 characters long. Estimating conservatively (as the NIST required passwords are longer than 8 characters), a typical full-time employee can spend 10.27 hours a year on typing passwords for authentication[2]. The estimate should be doubled, i.e. 20.54 hours, as a complete authentication often includes typing the user name besides the password. Using the same wage information (i.e. $39.15/hour) in [25], the annual cost per employee on entering user name and password pairs for authentication is roughly $804.14.

For an organization with 100 employees, a rough estimate of $153,000 annually can be spent on employees' basic password management activities (*Maintenance* not included), i.e. *Generation* ($728.19) and *Authentication* ($802.58), aside from productivity. For large organizations with 1,000 employees or more, this cost of basic password management can be more than $ 1,500,000 each year.

Hidden Costs

Beyond the two costs for basic password management demonstrated earlier, there are other hidden costs associated with the password management lifecycle. For example, it is not uncommon for organizations to enforce timeouts and screen locking to mitigate opportunistic misuse of an unattended computer [15,24]. It creates constant task interruptions and requires users to recover from interruptions that will also translate to productivity loss.

More and more users' computing experiences happen on mobile devices such as laptop computers, tablets, and smart phones. The cognitive and behavioral framework will provide us a foundation to explore the impacts on password entering experience with different keyboards and layouts. It will also allow us to investigate the potential interferences on users' muscle memory of a well-practiced password and the increase on recall errors or typing errors due to transitioning from one platform to another or having to switch back and forth between platforms. Research is needed to understand the associated costs of users' mobile authentication experience.

---

[2] Total of 240 workdays assuming 5 days a week, 52 weeks, and minus two vacation weeks and 10 federal holidays.

3.4   Positive Attitudes = Better Security Behaviors and Less Frustration?

In general, users are concerned with security, but they often are forced to develop less secure coping strategies (e.g. reuse passwords, or write down passwords) when they are unable to comply with password policies that are too restrictive and inflexible to match users' capabilities [15].

However, in a large-scale survey study [4], the researchers found that users' attitudes toward organizational password requirements are related to their password behaviors and experiences across all three stages in the password management lifecycle. Users holding positive attitudes toward password requirements value more in creating compliant and strong passwords, write down passwords less often, feel less frustration with authentication problems, better understand and respect the significance of security, as compared to users with negative attitudes.

The findings on attitudes lead us to more research questions on searching for plausible means to encourage positive user attitudes and to provide user support addressing the negative thoughts.

4   Conclusion

Are cyber security and usability two parallel lines that never meet? Or, are they cross roads where the intersection is yet to be reached? We believe that, though it may not be easily seen, the intersection does exist among the theoretical, technical, and usability aspects of cyber security. It requires collaboration from researchers and practitioners with multi-disciplinary backgrounds in finding the right balance to reach that intersection that will provide acceptable security and usability.

More research is needed on users' cognitive and behavioral activities regarding interrelationships among the three stages in the password management lifecycle. What can be done more on the technology side to ensure security and protect information assets, and alleviate the burden on users so they will think more positively about security measures? Future research should use a holistic approach with the goal of providing data to enable the policy makers to make informed decisions on security policies that are both secure and usable, and to provide guidance in user support and education to promote positive attitudes.

References

1. Herley, C., van Oorschot, P.: A Research Agenda Acknowledging the Persistence of Passwords. IEEE Security & Privacy 10(1), 28–36 (2012)
2. Florêncio, D., Herley, C.: A Large-Scale Study of Web Password Habits. In: Proceedings of the 16th International Conference on World Wide Web, pp. 657–666. ACM (2007)
3. Hoonakker, P., Bornoe, N., Carayon, P.: Password Authentication from a Human Factors Perspective: Results of a Survey among End-Users. In: Proceedings of the Human Factors and Ergonomics Society Annual Meeting, vol. 53(6), pp. 459–463. SAGE Publications (2009)

4. Choong, Y.-Y.T.M., Liu, H.-K.: A Large-Scale Survey of Employees' Password Behaviors. Manuscript submitted for publication (2014)
5. Goverance, I.T.: Boardroom Cyber Watch 2013 – Report (2013), http://www.itgovernance.co.uk/what-is-cybersecurity/boardroom-cyber-watch.aspx
6. Haskins, W.: Network Security: Gullible Users Are the Weakest Link. TechNewsWorld (November 29, 2007), http://www.technewsworld.com/story/60520.html (retrieved)
7. Malenkovich, S.: 10 Worst Password Ideas (As Seen In the Adobe Hack). Kaspersky Lab Daily (November 21, 2013), http://blog.kaspersky.com/10-worst-password-ideas-as-seen-in-the-adobe-hack/ (retrieved)
8. MeriTalk.: Cyber Security Experience: Security Pros from Mars, Users from Mercury (2013), http://www.meritalk.com/cybersecurityexperience (retrieved)
9. Sasse, M.A., Brostoff, B., Weirich, D.: Transforming the 'weakest link' — a human/computer interaction approach to usable and effective security. BT Technology Journal 19(3), 122–131 (2001)
10. Brown, A.S., Bracken, E., Zoccoli, S., Douglas, K.: Generating and remembering passwords. Applied Cognitive Psychology 18(6), 641–651 (2004)
11. Campbell, J., Ma, W., Kleeman, D.: Impact of restrictive composition policy on user password choices. Behaviour & Information Technology 30(3), 379–388 (2011)
12. Yan, J., Blackwell, A., Anderson, R., Grant, A.: Password Memorability and Security: Empirical Results. IEEE Security & Privacy 2(5), 25–31 (2004)
13. Florêncio, D., Herley, C., Coskun, B.: Do Strong Web Passwords Accomplish Anything? In: Proceedings of the 2nd USENIX Workshop on Hot Topics in Security, pp. 1–6 (2007)
14. Herley, C.: So Long, And No Thanks for the Externalities: The Rational Rejection of Security Advice by Users. In: NSPW 2009 Proceedings of the 2009 Workshop on New Security Paradigms Workshop, pp. 133–144 (2009)
15. Inglesant, P., Sasse, M.A.: The True Cost of Unusable Password Policies: Password Use in the Wild. In: Proceedings of the SIGCHI Conference on Human Factors in Computing Systems, pp. 383–392 (2010)
16. Flower, L.H., Hayes, J.R.: A Cognitive Process Theory of Writing. College Composition and Communication 32(4), 365–387 (1981)
17. Flower, L.H., Hayes, J.R.: Problem-solving strategies and the writing process. College English 39(4), 449–461 (1977)
18. Imerva Application Defense Center (ADC).: Consumer Password Worst Practices. Imperva White Paper (2009), http://www.imperva.com/docs/wp_consumer_password_worst_practices.pdf (retrieved)
19. Zhang, Y., Monrose, F., Reiter, M.K.: The Security of Modern Password Expiration: An Algorithmic Framework and Empirical Analysis. In: Proceedings of the 17th ACM Conference on Computer and Communications Security, pp. 176–186 (2010)
20. Proctor, R.W., Lien, M.-C., Vu, K.-P.L., Schultz, E.E., Salvendy, G.: Improving computer security for authentication of users: Influence of proactive password restrictions. Behavior Research Methods, Instruments, & Computers 34(2), 163–169 (2002)
21. Vu, K.-P.L., Bhargav, A., Proctor, R.W.: Imposing Password Restrictions for Multiple Accounts: Impact on Generation and Recall of Passwords. In: Proceedings of the Human Factors and Ergonomics Society Annual Meeting, vol. 47(11), pp. 1331–1335. SAGE Publications (2003)

22. Pratt, M.K.: 5 Annonying Help Desk Calls - And How to Banish Them. PCWorld (April 3, 2012), http://www.pcworld.com/article/253073/5_annoying_help_desk_calls_and_how_to_banish_them.html (retrieved)

23. Abel, S.: Industry Average Help Desk Support Costs. The Content Wrangler (April 28, 2011),
http://thecontentwrangler.com/2011/04/28/industry-average-help-desk-support-costs/ (retrieved)

24. Steves, M., Chisnell, D., Sasse, M.A., Krol, K., Theofanos, M., Wald, H.: Report: Authentication Diary Study. NISTIR 7983. National Institute of Standards and Technology, Gaithersburg, MD (2014)

25. U.S. Bureau of Economic Analysis: National Income and Product Accounts, Tables 6.6D, Wages and Salaries Per Full-Time Equivalent Employee by Industry (August 7, 2013), http://www.bea.gov/national/nipaweb (retrieved)

26. Grawemeyer, B., Johnson, H.: Using and managing multiple passwords: A week to a view. Interacting with Computers 23(3), 256–267 (2011)

27. Hayashi, E., Hong, J.I.: A Diary Study of Password Usage in Daily Life. In: Proceedings of the SIGCHI Conference on Human Factors in Computing Systems, pp. 2627–2630. ACM (2011)

28. Keith, M., Shao, B., Steinbart, P.: A Behavioral Analysis of Passphrase Design and Effectiveness. Journal of the Association for Information Systems 10(2), 63–89 (2009)

29. Stanton, B., Greene, K.K.: Character Strings, Memory and Passwords: What a Recall Study Can Tell Us. In: Proceedings of the 16th International Conference on Human-Computer Interaction (in press, 2014)

Do Graphical Authentication Systems Solve the Password Memorability Problem?

Soumyadeb Chowdhury, Ron Poet, and Lewis Mackenzie

School of Computing Science, University of Glasgow
soumc@dcs.gla.ac.uk,
{Ron.Poet,Lewis.Mackenzie}@glasgow.ac.uk

Abstract. Passwords are the most common form of authentication. The password memorability problem is magnified with increasing number of systems users have to access. Graphical authentication systems (GASs) have received significant attention as one potential alternative to alphanumeric passwords to provide more usable authentication. In this paper we review all the existing work which had explored the memorability of multiple graphical passwords. The review reveals that human memory capabilities should not be overestimated and the password memorability problem remains unsolved, even when graphical passwords are employed. Hence we propose a novel graphical authentication system with certain new security features which could solve the problem. This paper will be of interest to Human Computer Interaction-Security researchers investigating approaches to usable and secure authentication techniques.

Keywords: graphical authentication, memorability, password problem.

1 Introduction

In the current practice, alphanumeric passwords are the most widely used mechanism to authenticate users. According to Adams and Sasse, as the number of passwords per user increases, the rate of forgetting them also increases [1]. In order to cope with multiple passwords, users tend to adopt unsafe strategies, which include writing them down, reusing the same passwords and sharing them with others [1, 2].

An alternative approach that has received significant attention is that of graphical authentication [3-11], which uses images to form passwords. The motivating idea is that humans can supposedly remember images better than alphanumeric text [12], so use of the former may be a way of devising more memorable passwords. In this context, GASs can be categorized as follows.

- *Cognometrics*: During registration users can either choose their password images from a collection presented by the system [4,5 and 6] or the passwords are issued by the system [7] to the users. The users can also provide their own images to be used as password too [9 and 10]. Each password is a combination of certain number of target images. During authentication, users must recognize each target image among a collection of decoys (figure 1). The work reported in [12] suggests that human beings have exceptional ability to recognize images that they have previously seen, even if the image has been viewed for a very short period of time.

T. Tryfonas and I. Askoxylakis (Eds.): HAS 2014, LNCS 8533, pp. 138–148, 2014.

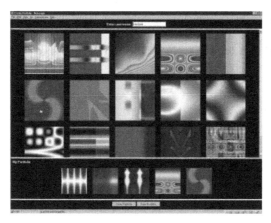

Fig. 1. Authentication screen for Dejavu system [6]

- *Locimetrics:* In these systems, specific points in an image that is either selected by the user or issued by the system form the password (figure 2). An example of such a system is Passpoints [3]. These systems are often referred to as cued recall based systems. The cognitive studies in the past have explained that items in human memory may be available, but not accessible for retrieval at a later time [13]. Ideally, a cue should be helpful only to the legitimate users and not to intruders to break into the system. In graphical authentication systems using this approach, the users don't have to remember the image, but remember specific points in the image that has been selected by them as their password.

Fig. 2. Authentication screen for Click-based password [3]

- Drawmetrics: In these systems, users must draw an image during the password creation stage and they have to reproduce that same image during authentication (figure 3). This is same as pure recall, where the users are asked to retrieve their password from memory, which they have used or chosen in the past without any cues. Unaided recall is considered to be the least accurate type of memories because the accuracy would decay after a considerable amount of time, if the password is not used frequently [14]. In case of graphical passwords, the users have to reproduce their passwords without any cues. It is a difficult memory task and the users may sometimes use the interface as the cues, even if it is not intended as such. Examples of systems include DAS [15] and Pass go [11]

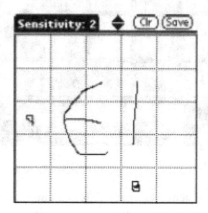

Fig. 3. Authentication screen for DAS [15]

Given the need for more usable authentication and the existing interest of the research community in graphical passwords as a potential solution, an important limitation of the existing work is: most studies in the field of GASs have focused on the use of single password. We believe that people will need to remember and use graphical passwords in the same way as they currently use alphanumeric passwords. In this paper we will review all the studies that have explored the memorability of multiple graphical passwords. This review to our knowledge is first of its kind which will help to understand, whether graphical passwords in their current form had been able to solve the issue of remembering multiple passwords.

2   Survey of Multiple Graphical Password Studies

In the last fifteen years, only four studies [3, 4, 7 and 8] in the field of GASs had explored the memorability of multiple graphical passwords. We will review them and draw our inferences for each study based upon the results reported by the respective authors. This review will not discuss the conclusions and claims made by the authors.

2.1   Pictures at the ATM: Exploring the Usability of Multiple Graphical Passwords (CHI 2007) –Moncur and Leplatre [8]

The first study with multiple graphical passwords was conducted by Moncur & LePlâtre [8]. They compared the memorability of multiple graphical passwords to multiple PINs. Photographic images of food, music, sports, flowers etc. were used as the visual cue in case of graphical passwords.

System. Each user was assigned five numerical or graphical passwords, depending upon their respective group. The assignment of password to the user was done on a random basis. In case of graphical password, each of the passwords comprised of four colourful and meaningful photographic image. During authentication, a challenge set was displayed to the participants containing 10 images (figure 4). The participants had to select four target images in the correct order, among a collection of 6 decoy images. In case of PINs the 0-9 numerals were displayed on the screen and the participants had to click on the numbers in correct order that formed the digits of their PIN.

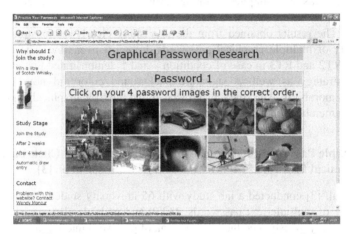

Fig. 4. Challenge set reported in Moncur and Leplatre [8]

User Study. The study examined the memorability of five system-issued passwords with 172 university students, who were assigned randomly to one of the five conditions given below:

- Condition 1: four digit pin;
- Condition 2: graphical passwords;
- Condition 3: graphical password + signature colour background;
- Condition 4: graphical password + mnemonic strategy;
- Condition 5: graphical password + signature colour background + mnemonic strategy.

Three memorability rests (RT1, RT2, and RT3) were conducted, with a gap of two weeks between each one of them. The dropout rate in the user study was 64.91%, which made it difficult to analyze the results.

Results. According to the statistics presented in the paper [13, figure 5], the mean login success percentages are discussed below:

- Condition 1: RT1 was 15%, dropped to almost 5% after 2 weeks and remained almost the same for RT3;
- Condition 2: RT1 was 55%, dropped to 10% after 2 weeks and remained almost the same for RT3;

- Condition 3: RT1 was close to 70%, dropped to almost 10% after two weeks and was slightly more than 10% in RT3;
- Condition 4: RT1 was almost 90%, dropped to 15% after two weeks and was almost 20% in RT3;
- Condition 5: 80% in RT1, dropped to 10% in RT2 and close to 20% in RT3.

However, the mean values reported in the paper are high because the retention just after the passwords were supplied (training session) was taken in to account.

Inferences. The results obtained from the user study clearly demonstrated that the memorability of multiple graphical passwords drops off over time. The mean login success for RT2 and RT3 in case of condition 4 and 5 demonstrated that employing a mnemonic strategy as well as signature background color did not improve the password memorability. The study also revealed that multiple graphical passwords are difficult to remember, when they are issued by the system.

2.2   Multiple Password Interference in Text Passwords and Click-Based Graphical Passwords (ACM CCS 2009) – Chiasson et al. [3]

Chiasson et al. [3] conducted a lab study with 65 university students to compare the memorability of multiple text passwords (MTP) and multiple click-based passwords (MCP). The study investigated the phenomenon of password interference, i.e. whether remembering a password for one system might affect the user's memory of a password for another system.

System. The participants were randomly divided into two groups:

- Members of the first group were required to remember six text passwords created by them during the registration stage;
- Members of the second group created six click-based passwords. Each password comprised of five click points on an image. The users were provided with six distinct images to create each of their passwords.

User Study. The lab study was divided into two sessions:

- Session1: All the participants registered with six passwords depending upon their group. After completing the registration, they were asked to login, once they have performed a distraction task. The distraction tasks were conducted to clear the textual and visual working memory. The login success for each of the participants in the session was obtained and reported as recall1.
- Session 2: The second session was conducted two weeks after the first session and 26 participants took part in it. There were no practice sessions between the two sessions. The login success was collected and reported as recall 2. The authors did not report the number of participants in each group, who took part in session 2.

Results. The mean login success percentages for each session reported in the paper are discussed below:

- Recall 1: The mean login success percentage was 95% for MCP and 68% for MTP during the training session, when the participants logged in successfully in the first attempt. The mean login success for multiple attempts was 88% in case of MTP and 99% in the case of MCP. However, these are the mean success percentages in the training session, just after the passwords were created. Hence the results do not reveal much in context to the long term memorability of multiple graphical passwords.
- Recall 2: The mean login success percentage was 38% for MCP and 30% for MTP, when the participants logged in successfully in the first attempt. The mean login success for multiple attempts was 70% for MTP and 57% for MCP and this was found to be statistically insignificant.

Inferences. The results of recall 1 reveal that the short term memory for MCP is significantly better than MTP. However, the results for recall 2 revealed that users find it difficult to remember multiple click-based passwords over a longer term. Since the participation rate in the second session was low, the results may not be an actual reflection of the phenomenon of memory interference.

2.3 A Comprehensive Study of Frequency, Interference and Training of Multiple Graphical Passwords (CHI 2009) – Everitt et al. [7]

Everitt et al. [7] conducted a user study with 100 university students over a period of five weeks to examine the memorability of multiple facial passwords.

System. Each participant was assigned x number of passwords by the system. Each password comprised of five faces. During authentication, participants had to select the correct face from a sequence of 3x3 grids of decoy faces, at each step of a five step login process (figure 5).

Fig. 5. Authentication screen reported in [7]

User Study. The user study was conducted using a between subject design where each participant was randomly assigned to one of the five conditions as given below:

- Condition 1: Participants used one facial graphical password (5 faces) once a week for a period of 5 weeks.
- Condition 2: Participants used one facial graphical password (5 faces) thrice a week for a period of 5 weeks.
- Condition 3: Participants used two facial graphical passwords (10 faces). One facial password was used thrice a week for a period of 5 weeks and the other was used once a week for a period of 5 weeks.
- Condition 4: Participants used four facial graphical passwords (20 faces). Each facial password was used once a week for a period of 5 weeks. Hence all the 4 different facial passwords were used at least once during the week.
- Condition 5: Participants used four facial graphical passwords (20 faces). In this condition only one password was used 4 times in a week. In the second week a different password was used. Thus distinct passwords were used during each week.

Results

- It was found that the participants using one facial password per week (condition 1) required more login attempts compared to the participants who used one facial password per day (condition 2). Hence the frequency of password usage would significantly affect the ease to login.
- The result indicated that participants accessing four passwords per week (condition 4), were ten times more likely to have an authentication failure compared to participants using a single password per week (condition 1). Thus interference occurring from the use of multiple graphical facial passwords would significantly affect user's memorability.
- The results also demonstrated that the participants who were trained using multiple facial passwords each week during a month (condition 4) were four times more likely to have an authentication failure, than the participants who were trained using one graphical password per week (condition 5). Hence the password training pattern would significantly affect the ease of access. The failure rate in the case of condition 4 was 15.23%.
- In context to long term recall, it was found that the participants using one graphical password throughout a month could remember their password correctly after four months. But, the participants using multiple passwords had problems remembering their passwords due to interference (failure rate 14.29%). Thus, the long term recall is significantly affected as the number of facial passwords increase.

Inferences. The performance of multiple facial passwords is better compared to the results reported in [3] and [8]. However, in [7] participants who were assigned to the condition 4 used each of their four passwords, at least once in a week. This may have helped to retrieve the passwords in subsequent use. The long term recall of the facial passwords also seems promising compared to the other password types. But [] does not report the number of participants in each condition, who took part in the long term recall study. It is also not known whether the participants recorded their passwords, or kept a copy of the same and used them during the long term recall study. This might have helped them to recall the multiple facial passwords after four months. Overall, the study demonstrates that memory interference and frequency of use significantly affected the memorability of multiple facial passwords.

2.4   A Comprehensive Study of the Usability of Multiple Graphical Passwords (INTERACT 2013) – Chowdhury et al. [4]

Chowdhury et al. [4] presented a study with 100 university students, who used multiple image passwords over a period of eight weeks. The study compared the usability of four distinct image types: Mikon, doodle, art and everyday object, when used as graphical passwords.

Study. The study used an independent measure style of experimental design with four conditions (equal number of participants in each condition) namely Mikon, doodle art and everyday objects. Each participant was randomly assigned to only one of the conditions. Each participant in each condition had to choose four passwords from four distinct image collections presented by the system. Each password comprised of four target images, chosen by the participants. Authentication was a four step process. At each step, a challenge set consisting of 15 decoy images and 1 target image was displayed as a 4X4 grid. The participants had to recognize and select the target image at each step. Upon completing the registration, participants had to login with each of their passwords over a period of eight weeks. The frequency of login differed for each week (high frequency-low frequency).

Results

- The findings showed that the memorability of the graphical passwords is significantly affected by the type of images used. In this context, the results revealed that the mean login success percentage over the period of eight weeks is highest for objects (77.31%), closely followed by Mikons (74.17%), then doodles (67.04%) and lowest for the art images (54.90%). The results of the study complement cognitive literature on the picture superiority effect [12], visual search process [16] and nameability of visually complex images [17].
- The results demonstrated that the mean login success percentage for each of the image type drops from week 2 to week 8, as the frequency of usage of the passwords decreases. The mean login success percentage dropped off by 11.44 % in case of Mikon, 12.55 % in case of doodle, 7.74 % in case of art and 14% in case of object, from week 2 to week 8.

Inferences. The performance of the multiple image passwords reported by Chowdhury et al. [4] is better than the results reported by [3] and [8], but inferior compared to [7]. The superior results can be attributed to the fact that all the participants used each of their passwords every week. This may have helped the participants to retain them in the memory through an elaborative encoding. The results reported in the paper clearly demonstrated that multiple image passwords are difficult to remember, even when they are created by the participants and used regularly. The study reported by [4], did not consider the scenario, where multiple image passwords are not used for a considerable period of time. This could have further degraded the performance of the participants, when they are required to remember multiple graphical passwords, without any practice.

3   Discussion

The reviews of the existing studies that have explored the cognitive demands of using multiple graphical passwords clearly demonstrated that users find it difficult to remember the passwords. Hence the memorability problem in case of authentication still exists, and GASs in their current state-of-the-art cannot be considered as a viable alternative to the traditional alphanumeric passwords. There is a need to develop authentication systems that would ease the burden of remembering many passwords. This would help to prevent the use of unsafe coping strategies to store or disclose the passwords, which inherently compromises the security of the system.

In the context of existing interest in image passwords, we propose a hint-based authentication system (PHAS), as a potential solution to address the problem of remembering multiple image passwords. In this system, the users have to choose four images and create hints for each one of them to form a password. During authentication, they have to recognize only the target images, which are displayed with their corresponding hints, among a collection of 15 decoy images, in a four step process. Our system would not rely just on recognition memory, but it would have an additional component, a 'hint', which will act as a cue to recognize the password. The hints can be in any language (we suggest a maximum of 5-6 words), but should be typed in English characters.

In the proposed approach, users give a hint for each target image and can use any strategy to do so. They do not need to create a story or use a mnemonic strategy, nor do they need to remember or reproduce the hints at any stage. This is because all hints are stored in the system and displayed with the challenge set to enhance memorability. We believe that the hints will act as cues while recognizing the images in future, which should enhance memorability [18].

In context to security, i.e. guessability of images using hints, we believe that an image can be guessed easily, if the hint given by a user denotatively describes the elements in it. But if the hint is connotative, where the user relates it to something personal (such as an episode in one's life), a sign or state (how it makes them feel), a context (an idea or event that only has relevance to them), then it might be very difficult for an attacker to guess, without being aware of the relation between the hint and the image [19 and 20]. This also creates a new avenue of research in the field of GASs, i.e. advice that should be given to the users, while they create the hints and select the target images.

We also propose the following features, which could enhance the security of the proposed PHAS:

- PHAS could also offer secure authentication, if an additional lock out policy is implemented not only on a definite number of failed login attempts, but a threshold value of login time. For example, once a user has used the system for certain number of times, then a timer could be set for all the subsequent login sessions. If the user is unable to complete the login session within the set timer, then this will be recorded. After a definite number of failed attempts due to timer expiration, the account could be locked. But, different aspects such as how to customize the timer, the number of attempts before the account is locked have to be considered before this feature could be implemented in practice. The usability of the proposed security component would need to be examined.
- The research on challenge sets in the field of GASs is sparse. Hence we also propose a novel challenge set configuration, which could increase the security of PHAS. Let a user U select four images and give one hint for each one of them in PHAS (x_1- x_4). The system chooses 15 decoy images for each of the target images (x_1- x_4), generating four challenge sets (T_1- T_4). The system would now choose four random images with their corresponding hints (y_1- y_4), which do not belong to user U. Four false challenge sets (F_1- F_4) are generated. The system displays m number of true sets selected from (T_1- T_4) and n number of false sets selected from (F_1- F_4). The value of m and n can either vary for each login attempt or remain constant for all login attempts for the user. Each challenge screen will have 16 images, a hint and a button named "Ignore". This Ignore button could be used by the legitimate user, when a false challenge set is displayed.

If cognitive attacks are carried out to break a PHAS password, we believe that the false challenge sets would make it difficult for an attacker to follow a lead for breaking into the system and the lock out policy based on the login time will put further pressure on making it hard to succeed.

References

1. Adams, A., Sasse, M.A.: Users are not the enemy. Communications of the ACM, 40–46 (CACM December 1999)
2. Florencio, D., Herley, C.: A large-scale study of web password habits. In: Proceedings of International Conference on World Wide Web (WWW 2007), pp. 657–666 (2007)
3. Chiasson, S., Forget, A., Stobert, E., Oorschot, P.C.: Van, and Biddle, R. Multiple Password Interference in Text and Click-Based Graphical Passwords. In: Proc. of CCS, pp. 500–511 (2009)
4. Chowdhury, S., Poet, R., Mackenzie, L.: A comprehensive study of the usability of multiple graphical passwords. In: Kotzé, P., Marsden, G., Lindgaard, G., Wesson, J., Winckler, M. (eds.) INTERACT 2013, Part III. LNCS, vol. 8119, pp. 424–441. Springer, Heidelberg (2013)

5. Davis, D., Monrose, F., Reiter, M.: On user choice in graphical password schemes. In: Proc. of the 13th conference on USENIX Security Symposium, vol. 13, USENIX Association Berkeley, CA (2004)
6. Dhamija, R., Perrig, A.: Deja vu: A user study using images for authentication. In: Proc. USENIX Security Symposium, pp. 45–48 (2000)
7. Everitt, K.M., Bragin, T., Fogarty, J., Kohno, T.: A comprehensive study of frequency, interference, and training of multiple graphical passwords. In: Proc. of CHI, pp. 889–898. ACM, New York (2009)
8. Moncur, W., LePlâtre, G.: Pictures at the ATM - Exploring the usability of multiple graphical passwords. In: Proc. of CHI, pp. 887–894 (2007)
9. Renaud, K.: Web authentication using Mikon images. In: World Congress on Privacy, Security, Trust and the Management of E-Business, pp. 1-10
10. Renaud, K.: On user involvement in production of images used in visual authentication. Journal of Visual Languages and Computing 92, 1–15 (2009)
11. Tao, H.: Pass-Go, a new graphical password scheme. M.S. thesis, School of Information Technology and Engineering, University of Ottawa (2006)
12. Madigan, S.: Picture Memory. In: Yuille, J. (ed.) Imagery, Memory, and Cognition: Essays in Honor of Allan Paivio. Lawrence Erlbaum Associates, Hillsdale (1983)
13. Tulving, E., Pearlstone, Z.: Availaibility Versus Accessibility of Information in Memory for Words. Journal of Verbal Learning and Verbal Behaviour 5, 381–391 (1966)
14. Baddeley, A.: Human Memory:Theory and Practice. Psychology Press, Hove (1997)
15. Jermyn, I., Mayer, A., Monrose, F., Reiter, M., Rubin, A.: The Design and Analysis of Graphical Passwords. In: Proceedings of 8th USENIX Security Symposium (1999)
16. Wolfe, M.: Guided Search 2.0 A Revised Model of Visual Search. Psychonomic Bulletin & Review 1(2), 202–238 (1994)
17. Szekely, A., Bates, E.: Objective Visual Complexity as a Variable in Picture Naming. In: CRL Newsletter Center for Research in Language, University of California, pp. 3–33 (2000)
18. Mantyla, T.: Optimising cue effectiveness. Journal of Experimental Psychology: Learning Memory and Cognition 12, 66–71 (1986)
19. Mathur, P.N.: Barriers to effective visual communication, 3rd edn. Media Asia (1978)
20. Sturken, M., Cartwright, L.: Practices of Looking: An introduction to visual culture. Oxford Press (2012)

E-voting Authentication with QR-codes

Stefanie Falkner[1,2,*], Peter Kieseberg[1], Dimitris E. Simos[1],
Christina Traxler[1,2], and Edgar Weippl[1]

[1] SBA Research, Favoritenstraße 16, 1040 Vienna, Austria
{sfalkner,pkieseberg,dsimos,ctraxler,eweippl}@sba-research.org
[2] University of Applied Sciences Upper Austria, School of Informatics,
Communications and Media, Softwarepark 11, 4232 Hagenberg, Austria
{stefanie.falkner,christina.traxler}@students.fh-hagenberg.at

Abstract. In this paper we propose an e-voting authentication scheme combined with QR-codes and visual cryptography. We focus on the usability, in order to supply voters with less technical experience with a usable scheme. The only requirement is that the user needs to handle a device containing a QR-code reader, most probably a smartphone. This approach is based on visual cryptography as the work horse: The e-voting passwords for authentication are encoded as QR-codes and later encrypted into shadow transparencies. Thus, the transparency by itself conveys no information but when the layers are combined, the secret password is revealed.

Keywords: QR-code, e-voting, usability, visual cryptography, visual secret sharing.

1 Introduction

During the last years a lot of different methods and protocols for e-voting have been proposed, most of them relying on the exchange and/or verification of numbers. Still, for practical use, especially considering older citizens or even people without a good technological background in Information Technology (IT), these schemes are rather impractical.

For example, in a traditional Austrian election the voter has to authenticate himself at the polling place to be allowed to cast a vote. After the polling places have closed, the votes are counted by the poll workers. This process usually takes a considerable amount of time and therefore electronic voting schemes have started to become more and more popular. Especially in online voting systems the authentication is an important factor. In this paper we focus on authentication methods for e-voting which can be combined with QR-codes. To log in at the voting platform, there is no technical background needed, only a QR-code reader i.e. on a smartphone or tablet. We chose QR-codes for encoding the passwords necessary for authentication. The codes are designed for a very

---

* Authors are listed in alphabetical order.

T. Tryfonas and I. Askoxylakis (Eds.): HAS 2014, LNCS 8533, pp. 149–159, 2014.

robust scanning process, incorporating all kinds of methods for detecting and correcting scanning errors, including partially damaged codes, distortions and rotations. The cryptographic primitives used for our scheme come from the field of visual cryptography. The reason for using the latter encryption methods is to gain a high security level while the utilization is still being easily operated. During the encryption process, two shares, which look like random noise and contain no decipherable information, are generated. By overlaying the shares the secret image gets visible to the human eye.

The paper is structured as follows. Section 2 gives a short summary on the background of QR-codes, including the foundation, areas of usage and how they are structured. It also explains visual cryptography as a mechanism for increasing security. The proposed approach for an innovative, robust, secure and above all user-friendly e-voting authentication scheme is explained in detail in Section 3. In Section 4, we evaluate the approach with respect to the usability of our scheme and to the security aspects. Subsequently, in Section 5 we comparing our approach to related works and we conclude the paper in Section 6 by also giving a perspective on further research.

2   Background

2.1   QR-codes

The QR-code is defined as a two-dimensional barcode invented by one of the Japanese Toyota group companies in 1994. The codes have the same function as the traditional barcodes but there is the possibility to store much more data on it. The standard defines 40 versions (sizes) with different capacities. This standard ISO/IEC 18004, an international standard concentrated on QR-codes, has been published in June 2000 [1]. Originally QR-codes were made-up for the application in the production control of automotive parts but since their development they found a wide range of usage in a lot of different areas. In general QR-codes find a popular utilization on advertising, posters and products. In 2010 the International Air Transport Association (IATA) for airports worldwide introduced them for passenger boarding passes. They are also applied in hospitals, i.e. in Hong Kong for patient identification. Some more examples would be QR-codes on bills for e-payment or ticketing systems for trains and airlines. We present below in Figure 1 the structure of a QR-code.

Fig. 1. Structure of version 1 QR-code

A QR-code is divided into modules and each of them is a collection of pixels. For example, version 1 is made of 21x21 modules. In every QR-code there must be three Finder Patterns, which are located in the upper left, upper right and lower left corner. They are used for position detection and identification of possible QR-codes. The Alignment Patterns only occur from version two up to 40, whereby the higher the level is, the more Alignment Patterns exist. For the scanning process a quiet zone, which is defined as a white border, surrounding the QR-code is necessary. This zone is defined in [1] to be at least 4 pixels wide. On a dark background, QR-codes without a quiet zone may be unscannable, because the reader can not distinguish between the dark background and the Finder Patterns. Furthermore, the timing pattern for determining the module coordinates, the Separators for separating the finder patterns from the rest of the code, the data area, the error correction region, and areas which contain the format information as well as the remaining bits are components of a QR-code [1]. The standard defines four different error correction levels (L = 7%, M = 15%, Q = 25%, H = 30%). The error correction is used for recovering the QR-code if parts of the symbol are unreadable or destroyed.

Furthermore, there are also different modes available for encoding the data in QR-codes, depending on which data should be encoded, ranging from plain numbers (numeric mode), simple content like URLs (alphanumeric mode) up to Japanese Kanjis (Kanji mode), amongst others. In particular the 8-bit byte mode, also called binary mode, handles all the character values from $(00)_{HEX}$ to $(FF)_{HEX}$, so far this includes the whole Kana and Latin character set. On the contrary, the alphanumeric mode makes use of a set of 45 characters, containing upper letters, numbers and some predefined special characters.

In order to provide a good contrast for reading a QR-code, it is important that black and white modules are well distributed over the whole symbol. This is done by XORing masks onto the encoded data [1]. Note that, there are eight masks defined in the standard, which are responsible for an optimal distribution of white and black pixels.

2.2   Visual Cryptography

Visual cryptography spawned as a branch of secret sharing cryptography, mainly due to the pioneering idea of Naor and Shamir to split a secret image into n images called shares or transparencies and afterwards if (some) of these shares are stacked using the OR-operation, the original image is revealed [9]. In this paper we use an instantiation of the visual secret sharing (VSS) scheme given in [9], and in particular we use the so-called $(2, 2)$ scheme. The parameters for a (k, n)-threshold scheme [9] are defined as follows.

Let n be the total number of shares and $k \leq n$ the number of shares that need to be stacked in order to reveal the original image. Furthermore, let m be the number of subpixels, v the stacked m-vector, α the relative difference and t be a fixed threshold.

Each share is a collection of subpixels and M are the matrices determining the m subpixels, which are needed for generating the shares. The resulting matrix can be described as a $n \times m$ binary matrix $S = [s_{ij}]$ where $s_{ij} = 1$ if the j-th subpixel in the i-th share is black, and $s_{ij} = 0$ otherwise.

It is important that the stacked shares have a good contrast between the black and the white pixels, because this is needed for a successful scanning process. Therefore the following requirement should be considered; that the parameter m should be as small as possible to gain an optimal resolution. Furthermore, let $w(v)$ be the Hamming weight of a vector v where $v \in \{0, 1\}^s$. The Hamming weight $w(v)$ of the m-vector on which the OR operation is executed, is proportional to the grey level of the stacked shares. While the black pixels remain black in the stacked shares, the white ones are represented with grey color.

For a better visibility the contrast α, which is the relative difference between the minimum and maximum Hamming weight $w(v)$ needs to be as large as possible. The minimum is represented as white (see formula 1) and the maximum as black (see formula 2). For example in the $(2, 2)$ scheme we have used the best contrast α is $\frac{1}{2}$.

$$w(v) \leq t - \alpha \cdot m \tag{1}$$

$$w(v) \geq t \tag{2}$$

The parameter t is the threshold $1 \leq t \leq m$ to construct the shade of grey. The difference between the shades of grey is crucial for the visibility of the stacked shares, to enable the scanning process.

For example in the $(2, 2)$ scheme, two matrices M_0 and M_1 are needed to define the color of the m subpixels in order to generate the two shares S_1 and S_2. We use complimentary matrices to share a black pixel and identical matrices to share a white pixel. Stacking the shares we have all the subpixels associated with the black pixel now black while 50 percent of the subpixels associated with the white pixel remain white. Below we give an example containing two possible matrices for generating the shares.

$$M_0 = \begin{bmatrix} 1 & 0 \\ 1 & 0 \end{bmatrix} \quad M_1 = \begin{bmatrix} 1 & 0 \\ 0 & 1 \end{bmatrix}$$

Following this selection, each pixel of the secret image is selected one by one and the white ones are represented with M_0 and the black ones with M_1 respectively. During this process the columns of the matrices are permuted randomly. From the resulting matrix, each second row is used for creating share number 2 (S_2) and the other rows result in share number 1 (S_1).

For decrypting the secret image in the stacking process, the matrices are stacked using OR-operations, thus revealing the original image.

3   QR-code Based E-voting

The initialization process As can be seen in Figure 2, the first step in our approach is to generate n passwords for the n voters, which are needed for the

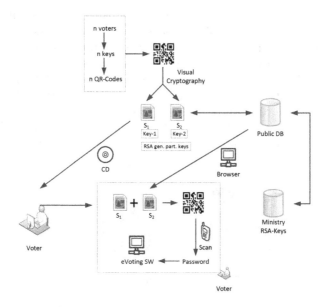

Fig. 2. General structure of the approach

authentication on the voting platform. To create secure passwords we use a pseudorandom number generator (PRNG) [7] with the social security number as unique seed.

Afterwards the n passwords are encoded into n QR-codes. Regarding the QR-code specification, we make use of version 1 and the whole capacity to avoid padding. If there is free space, the QR-code adds fixed binary patterns as padding. Therefore, if voters have the same password length and the same mask, the padding area in the QR-code would appear identical and could therefore be easily spotted, maybe leading to a security breach. For that reason we generate a QR-code without the white border, which is also called the *quiet zone*. Instead of the white border, we use a light uncolored background for the voting platform to further support an unproblematic scanning process.

With regard to the reconstruction of distorted and destructed parts of the code Figure 3 shows the capacity of the binary mode regarding to the ECC (error-correction) levels [1]. For example, the two best combinations for the binary mode would be the ECC Level Q or H and the reasons therefore are explained below.

Version	Modules	ECC Level	Binary
		L	17
1	21 x 21	M	14
		Q	11
		H	7

Fig. 3. Maximum capacity of the QR-code

The main reason for using these combinations is the user friendly password length, while still allowing for a high error correction. There are some advantages especially when using the binary mode. In contrast to the alphanumeric mode, which does not support lower case letters, the required signs for generating a secure password like lower and upper case letters, numbers and special characters are all available in the binary mode. In the next step, with the aid of the $(2, 2)$ VSS scheme, two shares S_1 and S_2 are generated (see Section 2.2), so that either layer by itself conveys no information, but when the layers are combined, the secret image is revealed. An example of the two shares can be seen below in Figure 4.

Fig. 4. Share 1 and share 2

To make the shares assignable there a PKI (public key infrastructure) [7] with a unique RSA key-pair (K_1, K_2) for each voter is needed. A PKI is an infrastructure that allows to verify, which public key belongs to whom. In our approach, K_1 serves as the private key while K_2 is the public key. The public keys have to be certified by a trusted third party. Such an infrastructure for e-government purposes is already provided in some countries, like the Federal Ministry of Labour, Social Affairs and Consumer Protection in Austria.

The Communication and Storing Process. After the setup, the share S_2 and the public key K_2 of each voter are stored in the database, while the share/transparency S_1 and the private key K_1 are stored on a CD and sent separately via post to eligible users to enable them to participate in the election. The letter is sent as an official mail, that means that only the addressed voter is allowed to receive the share S_1 and the key K_1. They are sent separately in order to prevent efficient interception. If the key or the share gets lost while sending them through the post, the voter can report this to the appropriate authorities and get them resent.

Authentication Process. During the election, the voter has to input the username and the private key K_1 from the CD on the voting platform. While the user uploads his share, the system's function is to fetch the correct share S_2 from the database and then stack the shares to reveal the secret QR-code (as this can be seen in Figure 5).

Now the user can scan the QR-code with any QR-code reader to reveal the secret password. Afterwards the user enters the correct password, he is authenticated and finally is allowed to vote.

Fig. 5. Stacked shares

4   Evaluation

In this section we evaluate the usability of our scheme, as well as security related considerations.

4.1   Usability

To achieve as many advantages as possible for voters, our approach emphasizes on the usability. In comparison to scheme [10] which concentrates on stacking the printed shares manually by putting one share on a transparent sheet in front of the screen, our scheme offers an automatic stacking process on the system for revealing the secret image. The procedure of a simultaneously perfect aligning and scanning of the stacked shares is difficult and normally many attempts are necessary. In this point our approach reaches a very good performance in our test case. This test case mainly includes the part of the voter and his interaction with the voting platform, i.e. the duration and effort during the scanning part. Due to the automatic stacking and aligning of the shares by the voting system the voter can save a lot of time, because the stacked image gets recognized in a few seconds by the reader. Moreover, even in the case of distortions or destructed parts, QR-codes can be easily scanned due to the high error correction. Through the use of our scheme people with physical limitations or diseases like tremor also have the possibility to vote without the help of others. Another advantage is that the voter needs no background information about visual cryptography and the structure of QR-codes, thus the proposed scheme is accessible to a broad audience. The only required knowledge the voter needs to have is how to use a QR-code scanner on a smartphone or tablet. Regarding to the QR-code scanning, the voter can decide between all available readers, no specific scanner is needed in this approach.

4.2   Attacker Model

In this section some possible attacks are shown and the impacts on the authentication scheme are explained. This includes a description of all parts and entities that are assumed as trusted parties.

Trusted parties. A party is defined as *trusted* when all included parts and members in this party work trustworthy and without any malicious intents. Figure 6

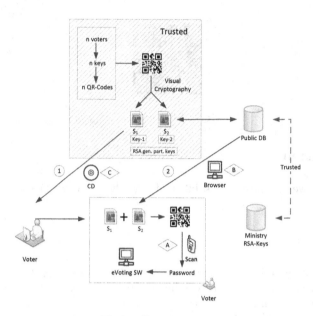

Fig. 6. Attacker model

outlines the two trusted parties: The first one includes the steps during the initialization process in the approach (see Section 3), especially during the initial password generation part, an important assumption is that the passwords and the PRNG-files are not manipulated by the authorities. The same applies for the share and for the RSA-key generation as well as for the trusted third party who certifies them. The second trusted party contains the assignment between the public keys and the shares in the database. The main reason why we assume that this part should be trusted, is to avoid manipulations in the allocation procedure. When this is not the case there is a possibility that the voter receives a wrong share and is not able to reveal the correct password and therefore the authentication process will fail. Furthermore the link between the two trusted parties must also meet the assumptions mentioned above. All this preconditions are perfectly reasonable in an environment where the state is considered trustworthy.

Attack vectors. There exist two major attack vectors against this scheme: (i) Intercepting the shares sent by the post, (ii) Manipulating the shares sent by the browser and (iii) Manipulating the scanning software and sending the password to the attacker. Manipulations and interference on other channels, like e.g. the network layer or a malicious database administrator, are out of the scope of this paper, since these vectors are not specific to our approach and need to be solved by any e-voting solution. Actually, these attack vectors can be translated into two different attacker models: An attacker trying to infiltrate the distribution process of the shares, and an attacker directly targeting the voter.

Resulting Security Requirements. In case of interception (attack vectors (i) and (ii)), our schema is secure in case only one share was derived by the attacker, i.e. only one of the suppliers in the two factor authentication is corrupted. Thus, it is absolutely necessary that the distribution of the two shares is done by completely independent means, as outlined in the approach and that there is no organizational overlap where a single attacker could intercept both shares. Especially the generation process needs to be trusted, as outlined earlier in this Section. As for the attacker that is directly targeting the voter, this could be achieved by either distributing a malicious scanner, or finding security holes in existing, popular scanners and using them through exploits. The intercepted password could then be sent to the attacker. Still, since the hardware the scanner is running on is under the control of the voter, this attack can be avoided: First, our approach does not require the voter to use any kind of special or predefined scanning software, any QR-code scanner can be used, which would require the attacker to either break a large amount of different scanners, or to persuade the voter to use his own. Furthermore, any application wanting to send data needs the respective rights on current smartphone systems. Thus, the users need to be educated by the voting agency, in order not to use any scanning software that requires any network access. Furthermore, this attack vector could be mitigated by supplying a scanner that is under the control of the (trusted) voting agency that does not require any transmission rights. Without network access, the only thing a malicious scanner could do is corrupting the result of the scan. Since our approach supports any scanner and thus does not rely on a specific software, this can be easily mitigated.

Security Limitations. The main security limitation of this approach, aside the need for trusted parties, lies in an attacker who is able to intercept both shares S_1 and S_2. Still, since the underlying VSS is very flexible, the schema could easily be extended to a k-factor authentication scheme, where the only limitation for k lies in the practical usability. Another share could e.g. via MMS from the telecom provider, or several, different, shares could be sent per postal service.

5   Related Work

Authentication, anonymity, confidentiality and non-repudiation are four of the main principles in e-voting schemes. In our scheme we concentrate on authentication because it is an essential part in a voting procedure. We refer to [10], where an authentication scheme for remote voting with visual cryptography is proposed: The voter receives one share from the election office and the second one is shown on the screen. Thus, he has to put the printed transparency in front of the screen image and align it to reveal the secret image. To generate the shares, a unique symmetric key and n random symmetric keys for n voters are needed. With the aid of a RNG (random number generator) the shares are generated. The used seeds are the results of the encryption of n random symmetric keys with the unique key. Our proposed scheme explained in Section 3 differs from the remote voting scheme in some aspects. First of all, we make use of the visual cryptography method given in [9], therefore we do not need predefined keys for generating the shares. In contrast to our scheme, there is no mapping between the voters and the transparencies ([10]). In our scheme, the shares are generated explicitly and one is stored in a database for each voter. With the aid of a PKI we make the shares assignable. If the shares would not be assignable, a man in the middle could fetch the voting packages including the transparencies and vote an arbitrary number of times. In the latter case, the votes are not retractable and hence the voting result can be distorted.

The main purpose of [2] was to introduce an online authentication scheme with visual cryptography in online money transaction systems. In this approach, the users get a special hardware device from their bank with a numbered set of transparencies stored on it. To transact money, the second associated transparency is shown on the screen. By scanning the transparency with the special device the transparencies are stacked and the secret TAN for authentication is revealed. In Germany a similar authentication scheme is already implemented in reality.

Regarding Australia, there also exists a voting scheme using QR-codes [3], which should be ready in November 2014 for the next Victorian State election. During the voting process, the voter has to scan the code to reveal the candidates names.

Finally, in [6] an e-voting scheme combined with secret sharing is proposed. The voting ballot is encrypted and afterwards the private key is divided into n shares. To enable the decryption of the vote, n authorities have to stack their shares to reveal the private key.

6 Conclusions and Future Work

In this paper, we discuss one of the most important security principles in e-voting schemes and therefore we propose a new efficient authentication scheme for e-voting. It is based on QR-codes and visual cryptography schemes. We mainly concentrate on the usability and consider some security aspects. To consider human factors we use QR-codes, which enables a robust scanning process. In combination with visual cryptography and a public key infrastructure we also address some security issues.

The proposed authentication method for an e-voting scheme, raises also some research questions. For example, there are possibilities to extend the authentication scheme to a complete e-voting scheme, including vote casting and tallying [5]. Therefore, other principles such as receipt-freeness, non-repudiation and confidentiality also can be considered. Moreover, watermarking could be introduced to protect shares from cheating attacks [8]. Using digital watermarking provides double security of image shares. Finally, though we have used the $(2, 2)$-threshold scheme there is also the possibility to use more shares or extended schemes [4], [11] in an appropriate use-case scenario.

Acknowledgements. This work has been supported by the Austrian Research Promotion Agency (FFG) under the Austrian COMET Program. In addition, the work of the third author was carried out during the tenure of an ERCIM "Alain Bensoussan" Fellowship Programme. The research leading to these results has received funding from the European Union Seventh Framework Programme (FP7/2007-2013) under grant agreement no. 246016.

References

1. Iso/iec 18004:2000 qr code bar code symbology specification
2. Borchert, B., Reinhardt, K.: Applications of Visual Cryptography. In: Visual Cryptography and secret image sharing, pp. 329–350. CRC Press Taylor & Francis (2012)
3. Burton, C., Culnane, C., Heather, J., Peacock, T., Ryan, P.Y.A., Schneider, S., Srinivasan, S., Teague, V., Wen, R., Xia, Z.: Using pret a voter in victorian state elections. In: Proceedings of the 2012 International Conference on Electronic Voting Technology/Workshop on Trustworthy Elections, EVT/WOTE 2012, p. 1. USENIX Association, Berkeley (2012)
4. Cimato, S., Prsico, R.D., Santis, A.D.: Visual Cryptography for Color Images. In: Visual Cryptography and secret image sharing, pp. 32–56. CRC Press Taylor & Francis (2012)
5. Cramer, R., Franklin, M., Schoenmakers, B., Yung, M.: Multi-authority secret-ballot elections with linear work. In: Maurer, U.M. (ed.) EUROCRYPT 1996. LNCS, vol. 1070, pp. 72–83. Springer, Heidelberg (1996)
6. Cramer, R., Gennaro, R., Schoenmakers, B.: A secure and optimally efficient multi-authority election scheme. In: Fumy, W. (ed.) EUROCRYPT 1997. LNCS, vol. 1233, pp. 103–118. Springer, Heidelberg (1997)
7. Ferguson, N., Schneier, B.: Practical Cryptography. Wiley Publishing, Inc. (2003)
8. Jagdeep Verma, V.K.: A visual cryptographic technique to secure image shares. International Journal of Engineering Research and Applications 2, 1121–1125 (2012)
9. Naor, M., Shamir, A.: Visual Cryptography. In: De Santis, A. (ed.) EUROCRYPT 1994. LNCS, vol. 950, pp. 1–12. Springer, Heidelberg (1995)
10. Paul, N., Evans, D., Rubin, A., Wallach, D.: Authentication for remote voting. In: Workshop on Human-Interaction and Security Systems (2003)
11. Shimizu, T., Isami, M., Terada, K., Ohyama, W., Kimura, F.: Color recognition by extended color space method for 64-color 2-d barcode. In: Proceedings of the IAPR Conference on Machine Vision Applications (IAPR MVA 2011), pp. 259–262 (2011)

I Can't Type That! P@$$w0rd Entry on Mobile Devices[*]

Kristen K. Greene[1], Melissa A. Gallagher[2], Brian C. Stanton[1], and Paul Y. Lee[1]

[1] National Institute of Standards and Technology
100 Bureau Dr, Gaithersburg, MD, USA
{kristen.greene,brian.stanton,paul.lee}@nist.gov
[2] Rice University
6100 Main St, Houston, TX, USA
mg17@rice.edu

Abstract. Given the numerous constraints of onscreen keyboards, such as smaller keys and lack of tactile feedback, remembering and typing long, complex passwords — an already burdensome task on desktop computing systems —becomes nearly unbearable on small mobile touchscreens. Complex passwords require numerous screen depth changes and are problematic both motorically and cognitively. Here we present baseline data on device- and age-dependent differences in human performance with complex passwords, providing a valuable starting dataset to warn that simply porting password requirements from one platform to another (i.e., desktop to mobile) without considering device constraints may be unwise.

Keywords: Passwords, authentication, security, memory, mobile text entry, typing, touchscreens, smartphones, tablets.

1   Introduction

Despite widespread recognition that passwords are a fundamentally broken method of user authentication [1], they will almost certainly remain deeply embedded in today's digital society for quite some time. Unfortunately, the very features of a password that are intended to make it more secure (e.g., increasing length, use of mixed case, numbers, and special characters [2]) generally make it less usable. Remembering and typing long, complex passwords is already a burdensome task on desktop computing systems with full QWERTY keyboards; entering the equivalent text on mobile touchscreen devices will no doubt prove significantly more challenging for users. While this premise seems inarguable—especially given the numerous constraints of onscreen keyboards, such as smaller keys and lack of tactile feedback—it must nonetheless be supported by quantitative human data. Here we present baseline mobile data on device- and age-dependent differences in human performance with complex passwords, complementing the desktop study [3] upon which this work is based.

---

[*] The rights of this work are transferred to the extent transferable according to title 17 U.S.C. 105.

T. Tryfonas and I. Askoxylakis (Eds.): HAS 2014, LNCS 8533, pp. 160–171, 2014.
© Springer International Publishing Switzerland 2014

2   Text Entry

Text entry on mobile devices is a common subroutine in many tasks. Past work has examined the effect of different technologies [4], age [5], motion [6], and a number of different devices [7] [8] when participants are typing words or phrases. While other research (e.g., [9], [10], [11]) has examined non-word strings of random letters, such research did not include the variety of numbers and special characters recommended for passwords, neither for desktop nor for mobile devices. As both the number of accounts users interact with on their mobile devices and the number of passwords required of them increase [12], understanding the input of secure passwords on mobile devices is becoming increasingly important. The predictive algorithms that many users rely on for text entry on mobile touchscreen devices (like autocorrect, autocomplete, and word suggestions), are not useful—indeed, those features are disabled entirely in secure text fields—for password entry. Furthermore, the cost of errors for users differs greatly between text entry for communicative purposes (e.g., composing text messages and emails) versus text entry for authentication to a user account. In other words, the motivation for accuracy, i.e., error-avoidance, is different between tasks: while misspelled words in texts and emails can cause amusement and embarrassment, mistyped passwords can cause a user account to be locked, requiring additional steps, time, and effort to perform an account reset/unlock.

It is likely that users are sensitive to the high cost of error recovery associated specifically with password entry. Those users who are usually fast and inaccurate, relying on predictive text correction algorithms of their smartphones and tablets, may be more likely to intentionally adjust their strategy when entering passwords. In contrast, users who are generally slow and accurate may not need to adjust their speed-accuracy tradeoff function when transitioning between normal text entry and password typing tasks. Regardless, user text entry proficiency should decrease with increasing keyboard screen depth—after all, manufacturers order their screens based on frequency of use. For the more common punctuation symbols, such as a period on iOS[1] devices, it is not even necessary for a user to change screen depth. Double-tapping the space bar will automatically insert a period at the end of a sentence; this is a default keyboard setting on iOS devices, as is automatic capitalization of words following a period. Both of these conveniences are overall quite helpful during normal text entry, but again, cannot be used during password entry.

Visibility of numbers and special characters differs significantly between traditional physical keyboards in the desktop environment and onscreen keyboards on

---

[1] Disclaimer: Any mention of commercial products or reference to commercial organizations is for information only; it does not imply recommendation or endorsement by the National Institute of Standards and Technology nor does it imply that the products mentioned are necessarily the best available for the purpose.

mobile devices. On the former, they are always present and visible, whereas on mobile devices, shifting between multiple screens with different character keyboards is necessary to find these numbers and special characters. While a few of the more common punctuation symbols are on the first screen of the iPad, which are not available from the first screen of the iPhone, all numbers and the majority of special characters are on different screens regardless of device (Figure 1).

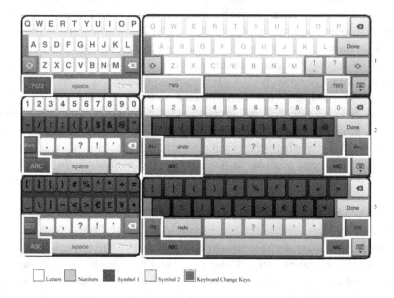

Fig. 1. The three keyboard screen depths (*top to bottom*) for iPhone (*left*) and iPad (*right*). Note that what appears on the Keyboard Change Keys differs by screen depth. Not to scale.

Multiple keyboard screens have significant perceptual-motor and cognitive implications for users. Not only can this double or triple the number of user motor actions (taps) required to input the same symbol with an onscreen keyboard compared to a physical keyboard, but multiple screen depths also carry significant cognitive overhead as well: now users must keep track of a character's position within a password, its spatial location on the visible keyboard, and its relative screen depth location. This becomes even more complicated if the current character is available on multiple screens. To investigate such issues, it is critical to have some record of user shift actions and keyboard changes, as an abundance of extraneous keyboard changes during password entry may indicate that users are indeed unfamiliar with the screen depth of special symbols, and are "losing their place" while visually searching different screens for them.

3   Experiment

3.1   Method

The current work was based heavily on a previously conducted study [11], which examined memorability of ten randomly generated, password-like character strings in the desktop computing environment; unless otherwise noted, current methodology was identical to that of [11]. We replicated this work in two studies with mobile touch screen devices, using a smartphone and tablet, respectively. To facilitate more direct comparisons, mobile device was used as a between-subjects variable in the following consolidated analyses (prerequisite random sampling assumptions were met).

Participants. Participants were recruited from the larger Washington, DC, USA metropolitan area, and were paid $75 for their participation. Participants were fairly diverse in terms of education, ethnicity, and income. A total of 165 people participated. Of these, seven did not make it at least halfway through the study session; their data were not included in any of the following analyses. The remaining 158 participants ranged in age from 19 to 66, with a mean age of 33.2 years ($SD =$ 11). Ninety participants were female, and 68 were male. All were familiar with onscreen keyboards (Table 1), with 75% of participants reporting using the onscreen keyboard multiple times per day.

Table 1. Self-reported onscreen keyboard frequency of use

Frequency of use	N	%
Monthly or less	7	4.4
Weekly	18	11.4
Once a day	14	8.9
Multiple times a day	118	74.7
No report	1	0.6

Design. The experiment was a 10 (strings) x 10 (entry repetitions) x 2 (device) x 2 (age) Mixed Factorial design. All participants typed all 10 strings 10 times each (within-subjects factors of string and entry repetitions, respectively), for a total of 100 string entries per participant. Each participant used either a smartphone (iPhone 4S) or a tablet (iPad 3) to enter the strings; assignment to this between-subjects factor (device) was random. Age was the second between-subjects factor; participants were assigned to the younger or older age group based on whether their age was below or above the median age of 28 years. Eight participants were exactly the median age; they were randomly assigned to the older or younger age category.

Materials. Strings were those used in the desktop study [11], presented in Helvetica font. Participants received the strings in the same randomly determined order shown in Table 2. The data collection application was developed in-house for iOS 6.1.

Table 2. Strings by presentation order and length

Order	String	Length
1	5c2'Qe	6
2	m#o)fp^2aRf207	14
3	m3)61fHw	8
4	d51)u4;X3wrf	12
5	p4d46*3TxY	10
6	q80<U/C2mv	10
7	6n04%Ei'Hm3V	12
8	4i_55fQ$2Mnh30	14
9	3.bH1o	6
10	a7t?C2#	7^2

Procedure. As described in [11], participants saw a series of three screens (Figure 2), corresponding to memorize/practice at will, verify correctly once, enter string 10 times. After completing this sequence for all 10 strings, a surprise recall test followed. Instructions on the surprise recall screen simply asked participants to type as many of the character strings as they could remember (they could be entered in any order). Aside from the instructions, the recall and entry screens were nearly identical, therefore the recall screen is not shown in Figure 2. Typed text was visible during memorize and verify phases, and masked with default iOS bullets during entry and recall phases.

Fig. 2. Screenshots of memorize, verify, and entry screens for iPhone

---

[2] Note that in [11], string 10 was of length 8 rather than 7; it was preceded by the letter "u". Due to a software configuration file change, the leading "u" was omitted in the current study.

3.2   Results

Entry Times. To examine predicted effects of device and age on mean per-string text entry times, a repeated measures ANOVA was run on string by device by age. For each string, the individual 10 entry repetition times were averaged to create mean entry time measures. Observations more than three interquartile ranges (IQRs) below the 25th or above the 75th percentiles of the per-string mean entry time distributions were considered outliers and excluded from the analysis; a total of 19 participants were excluded[3] this way (seven smartphone and 12 tablet) for the following entry times analyses. Despite being unable to include data from these participants, several significant and interesting interactions and main effects were found. While longer strings in general took longer to enter, the pattern of results did not exactly follow those predicted solely by string length, nor by number of keystrokes (Table 3). Compare the two strings of length 14: String 2 requires one fewer keystrokes than String 8, yet its mean entry time is over three seconds slower, perhaps because it requires one extra screen depth change. However, screen depth changes alone do not fully predict times. String 3 requires two fewer screen depth changes than Strings 9 and 1, but is slower than both of them; while number of keystrokes is equivalent, string 3 is longer in length, so it contains more characters for a person to recall. Clearly, a combination of factors account for entry times, with screen depth changes a factor unique to mobile devices..

Not surprisingly, older participants were overall somewhat slower than were younger participants. While these timing differences were negligible and consistent for the easier strings (strings 1, 3, 9, and 10), they were more pronounced for the more difficult strings (2, and 4 through 8). Overall, tablet string entry times were faster than the corresponding smartphone times. Mean entry times between devices did not differ significantly for the hardest string (string 2), suggesting that screen switches may be equally cognitively disruptive regardless of device, and/or that the visual search time for special symbols on the second and third screen depths is problematic regardless of device. Mean entry times were also similar between devices for the easiest strings (strings 1, 3, 9, and 10). The main effect of string on mean entry times (Fig. 3) was significant ($F(5.04, 594.69) = 468.99$, $MSE = 7392.49$, $p < .001$, $\eta_p^2 = .80$, Greenhouse-Geisser adjustment), as was the interaction between string and device (Fig. 4) ($F(5.04, 594.69) = 2.46$, $MSE = 38.77$, $p = .03$, $\eta_p^2 = .02$, Greenhouse-Geisser adjustment). The interaction between string and age was also reliable (Fig. 5) ($F(5.04, 594.69) = 2.23$, $MSE = 35.15$, $p = .05$, $\eta_p^2 = .02$, Greenhouse-Geisser adjustment). The main effect of device was significant ($F(1, 118) = 11.01$, $p = .001$, $\eta_p^2 = .09$), as was the main effect of age ($F(1, 118) = 15.16$, $p < .001$, $\eta_p^2 = .11$).

---

[3] While there were several alternative outlier replacement methods we could have used (e.g., replace the observation with that participant's mean, with that string's entry mean, or with the grand mean), we chose to consistently exclude participants instead, as it was unclear whether any alternative was better justified given the large variability seen in our data.

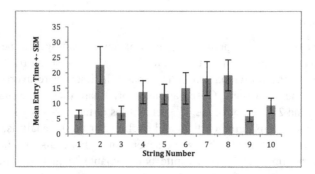

Fig. 3. Significant main effect of string on mean text entry times (seconds)

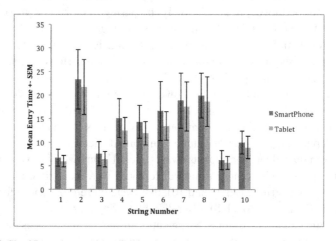

Fig. 4. Significant interaction of string by device on mean text entry times (seconds)

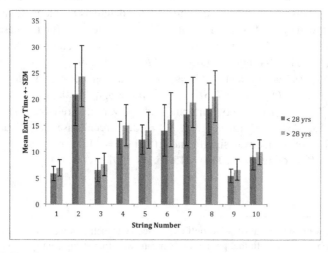

Fig. 5. Significant interaction of string by age on mean text entry times (seconds)

Table 3. Per-string lengths, keystrokes, shifts, and screen depth changes (taps on keyboard change keys), presented from shortest to longest mean entry time (seconds)

Order	String	Mean Entry Time	Length	Key-strokes	Shifts	Screen depth changes
9	3.bH1o	5.97	6	11	1	4
1	5c2'Qe	6.32	6	11	1	4
3	m3)61fHw	6.98	8	11	1	2
10	a7t?C2#	9.45	7	14, 13[*]	1, 2[*]	6, 4[*]
5	p4d46*3TxY	13.13	10	18	2	6
4	d51)u4;X3wrf	13.75	12	19	1	6
6	q80<U/C2mv	15.02	10	19	2	7
7	6n04%Ei'Hm3V	18.20	12	24	3	9
8	4i_55fQ$2Mnh30	19.28	14	25	2	9
2	m#o)fp^2aRf207	22.52	14	24	1	10

[*](iPhone, iPad)

Memorize and Verify Times. Since participants were free to spend as much or as little time on the memorization phase as they pleased, and could revisit the memorize screen at will from the verify screen, the number of visits to both the memorize and verify screens differed widely by participant. Therefore, for these two measures we report total times rather than mean times. Total memorize time and total verify time represent summations of all time (across multiple visits) a participant spent on each screen, respectively. As the patterns of results for total memorize and total verify times were similar to those reported for mean entry times above, we do not present additional figures for significant results in this section. In sharp contrast to the number of extreme entry time observations reported above, only three (two iPhone, one iPad) total memorize time observations were more than three interquartile ranges (IQRs) below the 25th or above the 75th percentile of the memorize total time distribution. These observations were considered outliers and excluded from the following memorize time analyses. The main effect of string on total memorize times was significant, ($F(3.75, 502.07) = 219.05$, $MSE = 1229047.63$, $p < .001$, $\eta_p^2 = .62$, Greenhouse-Geisser adjustment), as was the interaction between string and age, ($F(3.75, 502.07) = 9.30$, $MSE = 52184.44$, $p < .001$, $\eta_p^2 = .07$, Greenhouse-Geisser adjustment). The main effects of device, ($F(1, 134) = 13.48$, $MSE = 282428.253$, $p < .001$, $\eta_p^2 = .09$) and age, ($F(1, 134) = 10.47$, $MSE = 219295.23$, $p = .002$, $\eta_p^2 = .07$) were again significant.

As with entry times, there were numerous extreme observations when examining total verification time. Using the same outlier definition as above, a total of 30 participants (13 smartphone and 17 tablet) were excluded from the following analysis. The average number of failed verify attempts on the iPhone was 7.69 with a standard deviation of 8.65, for the iPad it was 3.65 with a standard deviation of 6.94. The main effect of string on total verify times was significant, ($F(3.33, 356.62) = 63.71$, $MSE = 65166.53$, $p < .001$, $\eta_p^2 = .37$, Greenhouse-Geisser adjustment), as was the interaction between string and device, $(F(3.33, 356.62) = 4.11$, $MSE = 4198.76$, $p = .01$, $\eta_p^2 = .04$, Greenhouse-Geisser adjustment). The main effects of device, $(F(1, 107) = 13.10$, $MSE = 18689.25$, $p < .001$, $\eta_p^2 = .11$) and age $(F(1, 107) = 4.47$, $MSE = 6373.00$, $p = .037$, $\eta_p^2 = .040$) on total verify times were again significant.

Entry Errors. Each string that was typed in the entry phase was analyzed based on the errors it contained at the time of final submission. Based on the common types of errors considered in text entry experiments and the frequency of certain errors types found in this experiment, the following subcategories were created. Extra Character errors occurred when duplicate or additional characters were entered into the field. Missing Character errors occurred when characters were omitted from entry. There were four types of substitution errors: substitution of the correct character with a Wrong Character; with an Incorrectly Shifted character; with an Adjacent Key character (with a character adjacent to it on the keyboard, for example, Q's adjacent keys are A and W); and substituting the number zero for the letter "o" and vice versa (while this could also be considered a Wrong Character error, its high frequency of occurrence warranted giving it a separate category. There were two types of transposition errors: transposition of characters next to one another in the string and characters typed in the wrong place in the string, referred to as Transposition and Misplaced Character, respectively.

Both the frequency and nature of errors varied greatly by device. With the smartphone, there were a total of 2100 errors made, as compared to 1289 errors with the tablet. Most interestingly, the percentage of adjacent key errors was much higher for the smartphone than the tablet (Fig. 6). The onscreen keys are much smaller targets on an iPhone than an iPad overall, and are particularly problematic for the iPhone portrait orientation. Given that participants were forced to use the devices in portrait rather than landscape orientation, the difference in adjacent characters would be expected.

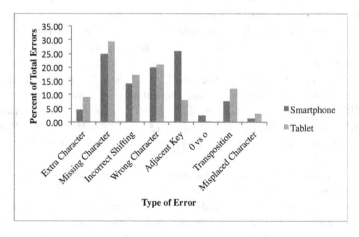

Fig. 6. Percentages of entry errors by error category and device

Surprise Recall. A string was considered correctly (fully) recalled if it exactly matched one of the target strings. Forty-six participants did not recall any of the strings correctly. Most participants were able to recall one or two strings, with one participant able to recall seven strings (Table 4). The most frequently recalled string was the last string memorized, followed by the second-to-last string memorized for each study (Table 5).

Table 4. The frequency of fully-recalled strings

String	Total Times Recalled
a7t?C2#	104
3.bH1o	44
4i_55fQ$2Mnh30	28
q80<U/C2mv	7
6n04%Ei'Hm3V	4
d51)u4;X3wrf	3
p4d46*3TxY	3
m#o)fp^2aRf207	2
5c2'Qe	0
m3)61fHw	0

Table 5. Number of strings fully-recalled by participants during surprise recall task

Number of Strings Recalled	Number of Participants
0	46
1	56
2	37
3	11
4	5
5	2
7	1

Note that in [11], text was visible during the recall phase, whereas in our experiment, text was masked during surprise recall. While this may account for some differences in recall performance between studies, it is more likely that device played a much more significant role.

4   Discussion

In general, main effects are not typically as interesting as interactions, but in this case the underlying explanation behind the main effect of string on both errors and times is at the core of our findings: strings requiring a number of mobile screen depth changes have disproportionately large effects across a variety of dependent measures. They are physically more difficult to type and error-prone, especially for adjacent key characters in the smartphone portrait orientation. Yet mobile devices affect password entry for reasons beyond simply smaller key sizes; these devices can place significantly more demands on working memory for users. Screen depth changes are like mini task interruptions that seem to incur timing costs beyond simply the additional keystrokes (i.e., taps on keyboard change keys) required. People are sensitive to the interruption cost of screen depth changes. As one participant noted, "My brain can't focus on memorizing it. It has to focus on find the right key board. [sic] Now that is a challenge." Clearly, password entry on mobile devices is challenging both cognitively and motorically. We argue that there are platform-dependent cognitive components associated with the interruptive nature of back-and-forth navigation and searching between mobile screen depths. This suggests that simply porting password requirements from one platform to another (i.e., desktop to mobile) without considering device constraints may be unwise.

5   Limitations and Future Work

In the future, we hope to better disentangle typing from memory errors. Our current error analysis has the limitation that it is not utilizing all the data available in the input stream but instead is focused on classified errors that were left unfixed in the text upon submission. A mobile transcription typing experiment that uses password-like text as stimuli, with a full input stream error analysis, would further aid in determining the nature and frequency of typing errors for complex passwords. Ultimately, we need these data to inform and validate predictive, computational cognitive models of password entry on mobile touch screens. Such models can help more objectively evaluate the benefits of additional security requirements against the drawbacks of more onerous passwords for users. To examine the effects of changing password policies over time and across devices, the research community needs fine-grained, baseline human performance data to which we can compare emerging and future technologies and text entry methods.

Working with newer mobile technologies presents interesting challenges that must be addressed in future work. For example, one challenge with using iOS devices is that the only keyboard change event reported by the native iOS keyboard is the show/hide keyboard event; keyboards taps that do not result in changing text are not reported by the OS. This means that taps on the keyboard change keys themselves are not reported, as they do not cause any visible evidence in the text entered. Simply examining interkey intervals in the entered text would not completely address this fundamental piece of password entry that is specific to mobile devices, i.e., that complex passwords force users to deal with numerous screen depth changes. While one can infer that a user had to have tapped on a keyboard change key in order to enter a particular character given the preceding character in the input stream, one would not know how many times the keyboard changed, nor the associated keystroke latencies for each event. This is important future work, as screen depth changes are fundamental differences between password entry with onscreen versus physical keyboards.

Acknowledgements. The authors gratefully acknowledge Clayton Stanley at Rice University. This work was funded by the Comprehensive National Cybersecurity Initiative (CNCI).

References

1. Honan, M.: Kill the password: Why a string of characters can't protect us anymore. Wired (2012)
2. United States Department of Homeland Security: United States Computer Emergency Readiness Team (US-CERT). Security tip (ST04-002): Choosing and protecting passwords (2009), retrieved from website, http://www.us-cert.gov/cas/tips/ST04-002.htm
3. Stanton, B.C., Greene, K.K.: Character strings, memory and passwords: What a recall study can tell us. In: Tryfonas, T., Askoxylakis, I. (eds.) HAS 2014. LNCS, vol. 8533, pp. 195–206. Springer, Heidelberg (2014)
4. Arif, A.S., Lopez, M.H., Stuerzlinger, W.: Two new mobile touchscreen text entry techniques. In: Poster at the 36th Graphics Interface Conference, pp. 22–23 (2010)
5. Nicolau, H., Jorge, J.: Elderly text-entry performance on touchscreens. In: Proceedings of the 14th International ACM SIGACCESS Conference on Computers and Accessibility. ACM, Boulder (2012)
6. Nicolau, H., Jorge, J.: Touch typing using thumbs: understanding the effect of mobility and hand posture. In: Proceedings of the SIGCHI Conference on Human Factors in Computing Systems, pp. 2683–2686 (2012)
7. Castellucci, S.J., MacKenzie, I.S.: Gathering text entry metrics on android devices. In: CHI 2011 Extended Abstracts on Human Factors in Computing Systems, pp. 1507–1512 (2011)
8. Parisod, A., Kehoe, A., Corcoran, F.: Considering appropriate metrics for light text entry. In: Fourth Irish Human Computer Interaction Conference, Dublin City University (2010)
9. Sears, A., Zha, Y.: Data entry for mobile devices using soft keyboards: Understanding the effects of keyboard size and user tasks. International Journal of Human-Computer Interaction 16(2), 163–184 (2003)
10. Allen, J.M., McFarlin, L.A., Green, T.: An in-depth look into the text entry user experience on the iPhone. In: Proceedings of the Human Factors and Ergonomics Society Annual Meeting, vol. 52(5), pp. 508–512 (2008)
11. Salthouse, T.: Effects of age and skill in typing. Journal of Experimental Psychology 113(3), 345–371 (1984)
12. Florencio, D., Herley, C.: A large-scale study of web password habits. In: Proceedings of the 16th international conference on World Wide Web 2007, pp. 657–666 (2007)

Capturing Attention for Warnings about Insecure Password Fields – Systematic Development of a Passive Security Intervention

Nina Kolb, Steffen Bartsch, Melanie Volkamer, and Joachim Vogt

TU Darmstadt, Germany
nina.kolb@stud.tu-darmstadt.de,
{steffen.bartsch,melanie.volkamer}@cased.de,
vogt@psychologie.tu-darmstadt.de

Abstract. Eavesdropping on passwords sent over insecure connections still poses a significant threat to Web users. Current measures to warn about insecure connections in browsers are often overlooked or ignored. In this paper, we systematically design more effective security interventions to indicate insecure connections in combination with password requests. We focus on catching the attention of the user with the proposed security interventions. We comparatively evaluate the three developed interventions using eye-tracking and report how effective these options are in the context of three different website designs. We find that one of the options – red background of the password field – captures significantly more attention than the others, but is less linked to the underlying problem than the yellow warning triangle option. Thus, we recommend a combination of the two options.

Keywords: security warnings, security interventions, morphological approach, attention.

1   Introduction

Business and leisure activities are to a large extent conducted via Internet – including critical tasks, such as online banking. Since most web sites still rely on passwords for authentication, the problem of eavesdropping on passwords over insecure connections, particularly on insecure networks such as airport Wi-Fi, is an imminent threat. Although current browsers offer several possibilities to check whether a connection is secured, many users neglect to do so before logging in with their password [8]. Hence, the user should be further supported in these decisions. So far, several attempts have been made in research to develop browser plug-ins that facilitate secure surfing behavior (e.g., [2, 7]). However, most of these attempts are of a rather exploratory nature and lack a theoretical foundation.

To close this gap, we chose a systematic procedure based on the morphological approach by Zwicky [16] and arrived at three promising security interventions, which follow psychological findings about attention. We comparatively evaluate the interventions using eye-tracking and report how the options play out with respect to

T. Tryfonas and I. Askoxylakis (Eds.): HAS 2014, LNCS 8533, pp. 172–182, 2014.
© Springer International Publishing Switzerland 2014

three different websites as context. We find that one of the options captures significantly more attention than the others, but is linked to the underlying problem to a lesser degree than another, alerting the user in a rather unspecific way. Thus, we recommend a combination of two of the options.

1.1   Security Interventions in the Web Context

Concerning warnings in Web browsers, researchers have particularly focused on the intervention strategies, that is, when and in which form to intervene. For example, Whalen and Inkpen showed how symbols as a passive form of interventions are seen, but not interacted with by the users [12]. Wu et al. argued that the right timing is important for interventions [15]. Similarly, Maurer et al. proposed to display warnings only if the user starts entering sensitive data and right where the data is entered [5].

Generally, active warnings have been shown to be more effective than passive indicators [8]. However, overly frequent active warnings (e.g. from false positives) lead to habituation effects [1]. Thus, there are many situations in which passive indicators seem to be more promising and should therefore be further investigated.

In general, even though new interventions have been proposed and evaluated, their development typically lacked a systematic approach. Therefore, the interventions proposed in this paper are systematically developed and evaluated.

1.2   Psychological Background

We based the development of the security interventions on psychological fundamentals of attention. Wolfe and Horowitz found that certain properties of objects can lead attention already in an early stage of perception [14]. This is particularly the case for color [9, 11, 14]. The color red has been found to have the strongest effect [13]. In addition, so-called "warning colors" – such as the combination of yellow and black – can create a similar level of attention [13]. There is good reason for the use of red and yellow-black for warning and traffic signs.

Biologically, humans perceive red stronger when it occurs in the center of the visual field, while yellow has a stronger effect in the periphery. The reason is the difference in the distribution of receptors for the red and yellow color over the visual field [11]. Moreover, colors also have a meaning: A study on the meaning of colors showed that 100% of the participants associated red with "Stop!" and 90% with "danger", while 81% of participants linked yellow to "Attention!" [11].

Another object property that guides attention is movement [14]. Movement is particularly powerful in the periphery of the visual field since it activates a biological alarm reflex (flank attack). This fundamental reflex makes it difficult for humans to ignore movements in the periphery [10] so that movement should be used sparingly in the Web context. Nielsen showed in an eye-tracking study that people "scan" websites in an "F pattern" – particular attention is thus paid to the upper and left sides of a website [6].

The amount of attention attracted by a stimulus also depends on the environment: The larger the difference among the surrounding distractors, that is, objects close to the stimulus, the smaller is the effect of that stimulus. Conversely, the stimulus is more pronounced in case of a larger difference to the distractors [3]. Accordingly, the goal is to employ a stimulus that is as different to its surrounding as possible. Since the stimulus does not fit with the surrounding, it creates surprise that leads to attention [4].

2   Development of the Security Interventions

Based on the psychological fundamentals laid out in the previous section, we developed security interventions to better protect Web users from eavesdropping on their passwords. The situation is the following: The user visits a web page which contains a password field. There is either no https in place or there is a problem with the https certificate. Since password fields are widespread on websites and often not used to actually login, we decided to develop passive, that is, non-interrupting, interventions. Since our focus at this stage of work lies on the capturing of attention, we developed visual and nonverbal interventions.

We chose a systematic procedure based on the morphological approach by Zwicky [16] – identifying all possible solutions for the different parts of the problem individually and combining them the most promising way – and arrived at the three interventions shown in Figure 1.

In the first intervention, the **password field is highlighted red**. Red creates the most attention as an individual color and is also associated with "Stop!" and "Danger". The intervention is located within the password field, since this should receive attention as part of the login procedure. Moreover, the location creates a semantic connection to the login procedure and, particularly, with entering the password.

The second intervention is a **yellow warning triangle**, containing a black exclamation mark, which should remind of the commonly-used warning sign and should symbolize "Attention!".

The third intervention is a **yellow warning bar**, located below the browser chrome. It shows the above-mentioned warning triangle and the word "Attention!". Text and symbol were added to the bar to provide context and additional information. We deliberately limited the text to a minimum to allow for a comparison between all three interventions. The warning bar is located on the left and upper side of the browsing window, since users look there most while scanning a website, according to Nielsen [6]. To create additional attention, the intervention is only shown 0.5 seconds after the page is displayed and moves into the window from the top left. Since this is a short one-time movement, the movement should not overly distract from the website contents.

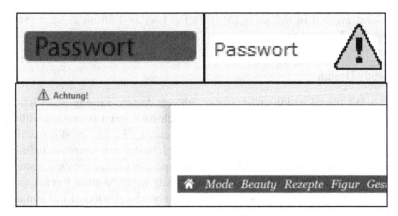

Fig. 1. Passive security interventions tested in our study (red password field, warning triangle, warning bar)

3   Hypotheses

We tested these interventions in a psychological experiment to determine which one attracts the most attention.

Based upon the psychological background given above, we developed the following hypotheses. Color as an object property works best to guide attention [14]. Since the color red has the strongest effect [13], we hypothesize:

H1: Intervention 1 (red password field) generally attracts most attention.

The effect of stimuli furthermore depends on the surrounding of the stimuli [3], so that:

H2: There is an interaction between the attention effect of the individual intervention and the website design. The amount of attention of the interventions thus depends on the website.

Furthermore, we studied for which of the tested interventions potential users understand its meaning best, even without an additional explanatory text.

4   Method

4.1   Participants

In total, 29 people (23 female, 6 male) took part in the study. For technical reasons, the eye-tracking data of only 28 participants could be used in the analysis. All participants are psychology students who took part for course credit. The mean age was 24.21 years (SD=5.76). The participants estimate their experience in using the

Web browser applied in the study (Mozilla Firefox) as 4.86 on average (SD=1.21; scale from 1 to 7, with 1 for very low and 7 for very high experience).

4.2   Study Design

We used a 3x3 mixed within-and-between-subjects design, varying intervention type within and website design between subjects. Each participant interacted with one of three different forum websites designed either in a predominantly red (bfriends.brigitte.de), purist (forum.golem.de) or cluttered way (community.bravo.de). We carefully chose these design criteria for their possible influence on the attentional effect of the interventions. We conducted the study using Mozilla Firefox as this is one of the most common Web browsers. The study was conducted in Germany and therefore in German; the original questions were translated for this publication.

The experiment consisted of two parts. In the first part, participants completed tasks like posting a text or editing their profile (comparable tasks for the different websites), with each task requiring the participants to log in first on the corresponding page with provided credentials. On the login page, the intervention was presented. Each participant saw all three interventions, though in a random order. Due to this within-subjects variation, the consideration of an attentional baseline was not necessary. We used an eye-tracking system (FaceLAB 5.0) to check if the participants had looked at the intervention at all, and – if they had – how long they had focused it.

In the second part of the study, we conducted a semi-structured interview, asking the participants if they had noticed the interventions, how much they had attracted their attention plus several questions about the anticipated meaning of the interventions. To facilitate the interview, we showed the participants screenshots with the different interventions on the websites that they had interacted with in the first part (stimulus recall technique). We carefully referred to the interventions as "modifications" in the attempt to weaken the subjects' tendency to build hypotheses themselves about independent variables. The questions obtaining our dependent variables included:

- "On a scale from 1 to 7, how noticeable did you find this modification [show screenshot], with 1 for very little, 7 for very strong?"
- "What do you think does this modification [show screenshot] mean for you as a user?"
- "If you would be browsing the Web at home and you would notice this modification [show screenshot], would this influence your behavior? If yes, in which way?"
- "The modifications should warn you that the connection is unprotected and thus a third party could eavesdrop e.g. on your password. Would you link this modification [show screenshot] with this situation?"

5   Results

5.1   Eye-Tracking

To determine which intervention attracted the most attention, we measured the total amount of time (in milliseconds) the participants focused on the particular intervention.

In Total. Results show that participants focused longest on the red highlighted password field; followed by the yellow warning triangle and the yellow warning bar (see Table 1). We conducted a repeated measures two-way analysis of variance (ANOVA) with the intervention type as within-subject factor and the website design as between-subjects factor. The analysis showed a significant difference regarding the time that participants focused the interventions, $F(2,50) = 11.41$, $p < .001$, partial $\eta^2=0.31$. In addition, our analysis shows an interaction between the attention effect of the intervention and the website design, $F(4,50) = 4.05$, $p < .05$, partial $\eta^2 = 0.25$.

Table 1. Focus times by intervention

Intervention type	Time (in ms) for focus of intervention	
	M	SD
Intervention 1 (red password field)	2855. 67	2497.76
Intervention 2 (yellow triangle)	1397.07	1013.94
Intervention 3 (yellow warning bar)	894.13	1325.27

Per Website. We also conducted analyses per website design individually. A repeated measures one-way analysis of variance with the intervention type as within-subject factor did not show significant differences for the time of focus for the red design (bfriends). The same analyses for the purist (golem) and the cluttered (bravo) design did show significant and a trend to significant differences, respectively (cf. Table 2). For the latter two designs, participants focused longest on the red password field. Table 3 lists the focus times by website design. Overall, participants spent the most time focusing interventions in the cluttered design.

Table 2. Significance of intervention type as within-subject factor per website design

	df	F	p	partial η^2
Red design (bfriends.brigitte.de)	2, 18	0.30	.785	0.03
Purist design (forum.golem.de)	1.250, 11.247	12.29	.003	0.58
Cluttered design (community.bravo.de)	1.191, 8.339	4.50	.061	0.39

Table 3. Focus times by intervention and website design

	Time (in ms) for focus of intervention	
Intervention type	M	SD
Red design		
Intervention 1 (red password field)	676.80	1236.37
Intervention 2 (yellow triangle)	1033.60	902.08
Intervention 3 (yellow warning bar)	918.40	817.84
Purist design		
Intervention 1 (red password field)	3451.20	2121.85
Intervention 2 (yellow triangle)	1001.60	409.26
Intervention 3 (yellow warning bar)	648.00	996.10
Cluttered design		
Intervention 1 (red password field)	4375.11	2469.06
Intervention 2 (yellow triangle)	2156.00	1282.65
Intervention 3 (yellow warning bar)	992.00	2049.14

5.2   Interviews

Conspicuity. During the interviews, most of the participants rated the red-highlighted password field as the most conspicuous, followed by the yellow warning triangle. The yellow warning bar was rated the least conspicuous. Hence, the results gathered via eye-tracking are in line with the subjective statements. The results from the question are shown in Table 4, also differentiated by website design. The conspicuity of the interventions differs significantly, $F(2, 48) = 43.04$, $p < .001$, partial $\eta^2 = 0.64$. We could not find an interaction between the conspicuity and website design, $F(4, 48) = 2.00$, $p = .110$, partial $\eta^2 = 0.14$.

Meaning. Asked about the anticipated meaning of the interventions, most of the participants (78%) thought the red-highlighted password field indicated an incorrect login, such as a wrong password. For the yellow warning triangle, 56% thought of an incorrect login. 22% of the participants thought they would need to pay more attention to the login and to be more careful with their password. The yellow warning

Table 4. Results from interview question on conspicuity

Intervention type	Conspicuity rating, scale 1 to 7	
	M	SD
Total		
Intervention 1 (red password field)	5.95	1.04
Intervention 2 (yellow triangle)	4.26	1.65
Intervention 3 (yellow warning bar)	2.30	1.92
Red design		
Intervention 1 (red password field)	5.70	1.16
Intervention 2 (yellow triangle)	3.40	1.71
Intervention 3 (yellow warning bar)	1.88	1.73
Purist design		
Intervention 1 (red password field)	6.00	1.05
Intervention 2 (yellow triangle)	4.10	1.45
Intervention 3 (yellow warning bar)	3.10	2.13
Cluttered design		
Intervention 1 (red password field)	6.17	0.94
Intervention 2 (yellow triangle)	5.39	1.22
Intervention 3 (yellow warning bar)	1.78	1.72

bar was most frequently (21%) linked with the detection of malware on the currently visited website, 17% interpreted the symbol as an indication that the website is generally "insecure".

Behavior at Home. In case that the participant would be confronted with the red password field on their own PC at home, 45% would still login and 21% would be irritated and hesitate before entering their password. For the warning triangle, 41% report that they would still login, 21% would look for the reason of the intervention and 14% would be more attentive when entering the password. For the warning bar,

21% would still login, another 21% would close the page and not log in, and 17% would look for the reason of the intervention.

Fit for the Situation. The participants consider the yellow warning triangle as the best fit for the situation of an insecure connection (17% say fitting, 59% not fitting, others are unsure). The warning bar is more often considered fitting than the red password field (14% vs. 7%), but the warning bar is also more often considered not fitting (76% vs. 72%). All participants mentioned that they would like a short explanatory note as an addition for the interventions.

6   Discussion

6.1   Summary of Findings

Overall, the participants spent most eye fixation time on the red password field. We thus can assume that this is the intervention that receives most attention – at least visually.

However, the time participants look at the intervention also depends on the website design. In case of a cluttered design, the interventions are generally looked at longer. Both, for a cluttered and for a purist design, the red password field is the intervention which attracted the longest visual attention. There is no significant difference between the interventions for the red design. The red password field thus appears to be best suited to capture the attention of the user independent of the design: Even for the predominantly red design, it is not significantly shorter looked at than the other interventions, and it is also the most successful attractor of fixation time in the other two designs.

In line with this, we found in the interviews that the red password field is considered the most conspicuous, followed by the yellow triangle. The subjective data thus reflect the eye-tracking data. However, we did not find an interaction with the website design for the subjective rating.

H1 (the red password field generally receives the highest attention) is thus both supported by the eye-tracking and interview data. The assumed interaction between the attention effect of the intervention and the website design (H2) could only be shown for the eye-tracking data, not for the subjective data. One possible explanation could be the fact that the number of participants who interacted with one website is rather small.

None of the interventions appears to be self-explaining. Among the presented solutions all failing to be intuitive, the yellow triangle was considered the best fit to the situation. For this intervention, most participants would try to find the reason for its appearance.

6.2   Implications for the Intervention Design

A possible solution for the final design of the intervention could consist of a combination of the red-highlighted password field to gain attention and the yellow warning triangle for the meaning. Furthermore, we propose to add a short explanatory text, since all participants mentioned that this would be of great use. The question remains, how many words are efficient for this purpose and where to place them.

As follow-up work, we will develop and evaluate the placement of the explanatory texts. Moreover, we will measure whether or not symbol and text actually keep users from logging in over unprotected connections instead of only asking whether or not they would login at home.

6.3   Limitations

An important limitation of this work is that its scope refrains to the effect of the interventions on visual and subjective attention. Since this study is only an intermediate step in the development of the final intervention, we did not investigate whether the interventions actually prevent users from logging in.

Another potential limitation lies in the selection of three intervention types and three website designs. We employed a systematic approach for the design of the interventions and the selection of websites to cover the relevant influence factors. We consider this a good start, however, we cannot exclude that better interventions and other relevant influence factors for the website design exist.

A third limitation is that our study took place in a controlled laboratory environment. Also, the participants used others' login data. Thus, the conclusions which were drawn with respect to everyday handling of one's own login data need further studies. For the time remaining, the password field as elaborated in this study is the best solution.

6.4   Conclusion

This paper contributes to the ongoing effort of developing effective and appropriate interventions for Web browsing. While interventions are typically developed intuitively and then evaluated afterwards in this context, we chose a systematic approach. We developed interventions based on psychological fundamentals regarding human attention, systematically selected the interventions with the morphological approach, and took the final decision based on study results. In this way, we were able to propose a well-founded solution for warning against sending passwords over unprotected connections.

Acknowledgments. The work presented in this paper is supported by funds of the Federal Ministry of Food and Agriculture (BMEL) based on a decision of the Parliament of the Federal Republic of Germany via the Federal Office for Agriculture and Food (BLE) under the innovation support programme.

References

1. Amer, T.S., Maris, J.B.: Signal Words and Signal Icons in Application Control and Information Technology Exception Messages – Hazard Matching and Habituation Effects. Northern Arizona University (2006)

2. Chou, N., et al.: Client-Side Defense Against Web-Based Identity Theft. Presented at the NDSS (2004)
3. Duncan, J., Humphreys, G.W.: Visual search and stimulus similarity. Psychological Review 96(3), 433–458 (1989)
4. Horstmann, G.: Die Unterbrechungsfunktion der Überraschung: ein neues experimentelles Paradigma und eine Überprüfung der Automatizitätshypothese. Uni Bielefeld (2001)
5. Maurer, M.-E., et al.: Using data type based security alert dialogs to raise online security awareness. Presented at the SOUPS 2011, New York, NY, USA (2011)
6. Nielsen, J.: F-Shaped Pattern For Reading Web Content (2006), http://www.nngroup.com/articles/f-shaped-pattern-reading-web-content
7. Ross, B., et al.: Stronger password authentication using browser extensions. Presented at Usenix security 2005, Berkeley, CA, USA (2005)
8. Schechter, S.E., et al.: The Emperor's New Security Indicators. Presented at the IEEE Symposium on Security and Privacy Mai (2007)
9. Treisman, A., Gormican, S.: Feature analysis in early vision: Evidence from search asymmetries. Psychological Review 95(1), 15–48 (1988)
10. Ungerleider, G.L., Mishkin, L.: Two visual cortical systems. MIT Press, Cambridge (1982)
11. Wandmacher, J.: Software-Ergonomie. De Gruyter, Berlin (1993)
12. Whalen, T., Inkpen, K.M.: Gathering evidence: use of visual security cues in web browsers. Presented at the School of Computer Science, University of Waterloo, Waterloo, Ontario, Canada (2005)
13. Wirth, T.: Missing Links. Über gutes Webdesign. Hanser Verlag, München (2002)
14. Wolfe, J.M., Horowitz, T.S.: What attributes guide the deployment of visual attention and how do they do it? Nat. Rev. Neurosci. 5(6), 495–501 (2004)
15. Wu, M., et al.: Do security toolbars actually prevent phishing attacks? Presented at the CHI 2006, New York, NY, USA (2006)
16. Zwicky, F.: Discovery, Invention, Research Through the Morphological Approach. The Macmillian Company, Toronto (1969)

ACCESS: Describing and Contrasting
Authentication Mechanisms

Karen Renaud[1], Melanie Volkamer[2], and Joseph Maguire[1]

[1] University of Glasgow, United Kingdom
[2] T U Darmstadt, Germany
{karen.renaud,joseph.maguire}@glasgow.ac.uk,
melanie.volkamer@cased.de

Abstract. The password the almost universal authentication solution yet is buckling under the strain. It demonstrates insufficiency and weakness due to poor choice, reuse and ease of transfer. Graphical passwords, biometrics, and hardware tokens have been suggested as alternatives. Industry has, unfortunately, not embraced these alternatives. One possible explanation is the complexity of the choice process. To support authentication decision-markers we suggest a framework called ACCESS (Authentication ChoiCE Support System) which captures requirements, consults a knowledge base of existing authentication mechanisms and their properties, and suggests those mechanisms that match the specified requirements.

1   Introduction

The password can provide a high theoretical security, but the security level in practice is compromised by password reuse, use of simple passwords, and recording of passwords [1]. Strict rules for password creation cannot mitigate against human frailty so it seems wise to consider alternatives such as graphical passwords [2–4], biometrics [5–8], hardware tokens [9], two/multi-factor authentication [10], and single sign-on solutions such as OpenID [11].

It is strange that passwords are still so ubiquitous in the light of this range of viable alternatives. It seems to run counter to the natural order of things for an inferior technology to prevail. On the other hand, this level of caution is understandable since authentication is essentially a risk mitigation technique, and organisations have to satisfy their auditors. Passwords are a well-established technique with provable theoretical strength, while alternatives remain an unknown quantity. A few papers have started to emerge [12, 13] which specifically address the strengths of some of these alternatives, but these are unlikely to make an impact on industry in their present format.

As things stand, developers are probably not convinced of the effectiveness of password alternatives as access control mechanisms. The academic literature is probably too obscure and unrealistic to convince them. Successful use of alternatives

T. Tryfonas and I. Askoxylakis (Eds.): HAS 2014, LNCS 8533, pp. 183–194, 2014.
© Springer International Publishing Switzerland 2014

by their contemporaries is likely to carry more weight and might convince them [14, 15], but no one of a high enough profile has, thus far, taken the plunge.

One gets the sense that industry is watching the effects of Apple's recent use of fingerprint biometrics for their iPhone 5S phone very carefully, and this might well be exactly what will make the difference. However, biometrics, while undeniably useful for single owner devices, is not going to be tenable in many a corporate setting.

It might be time for some kind of pro-active intervention, a way to support decision-makers in selecting an appropriate authentication mechanism. The idea would be make it easy for decision makers to access the facts about alternatives, to find answers to their questions and to address their concerns. We propose a framework called ACCESS (Authentication ChoiCE Support System) to capture requirement specifications from decision-makers, consult a knowledge base of existing authentication mechanism properties, and suggest mechanisms that meet the specified requirements.

Our first contribution is the description of this framework. Our second contribution is to identify categories of requirements that will feed into ACCESS based on a literature review in the areas of technology adoption and acceptance, security, usable security, marketing and economics. To confirm these, we conducted a survey with current developers in the field, i.e. target users of ACCESS, to confirm our requirement categories.

As future work, the knowledge base will be created based on existing literature and, where necessary, additional investigations and evaluations of existing proposals carried out to ensure that the knowledge-base supporting ACCESS does indeed deliver value. The remainder of this paper is organised as follows: We first present our proposal for the ACCESS framework to support developers who are interested in considering alternative authentication. The following section presents the results of our literature review: a set of requirements. We then present, in Section 4, the results of an online survey we conducted with developers. We then give an example of how ACCESS might be used before concluding.

2   ACCESS Framework

ACCESS is a decision maker support framework, which encodes and encapsulates a wide range of expert knowledge about authentication mechanisms. Such frameworks have been proposed for use in a wide variety of areas [16–19]. and follow three broad approaches [20]. The first is prior articulation of preferences where the decision maker provides a number of requirements, and the framework then ranks the alternatives from its knowledge base in terms of expected utility. The second is interactive articulation of preferences where the decision maker interacts with the system, and is asked a number of questions in order to guide the user towards one optimal solution. The third approach is the posterior articulation of preferences where the system generates a number of solutions without inputs, and presents these to the decision maker who is then makes a choice.

There is a clear difference between acceptance and adoption. Acceptance is a first step, which includes identifying a technology (here an alternative authentication mechanism) that meets the decision maker's requirements. Then this technology needs to be piloted. If the piloting is a success, the technology is deployed and carefully monitored to ensure that it performs well. If it does, it might, over time, be adopted into full usage by the company. Without the pilot, it is not even accepted, and since acceptance is a necessary pre-requisite to adoption, no long term usage will ensue.

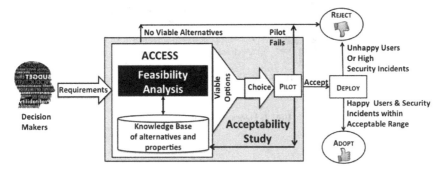

Fig. 1. ACCESS Framework (option 1 according to [20]

An overview of the proposed ACCESS framework is shown in Figure 1. The decision maker provides information about the different requirements either at the beginning or during the Feasibility Assessment. The feasibility assessment tool uses the Knowledge Base, containing descriptive information about a range of authentication mechanisms, to suggest a number of ranked alternatives for consideration. The decision makers would choose one and conduct a pilot study with some real users to determine whether the mechanism meets requirements with the context of use. The pilot's outcome is examined and a decision is made as to whether to deploy the mechanism in the wild or to reject it. The performance of the mechanism will have to be carefully monitored, producing data on the usage experience and security incidents. Should these results show high levels of security incidents or user dissatisfaction, the alternative authentication method is rejected; otherwise, it is very likely to be adopted by the decision makers.

In order to provide an ACCESS tool for decision makers, it is necessary to identify those types of requirements that are relevant in order to select appropriate alternatives for specific situations, services, and users. Once these requirements are identified, the knowledge base can be constructed containing those alternatives proposed in literature together with information about their properties with respect to the identified requirements. It is expected that current evidence available in the literature might well not address all types of requirements. Hence further studies and analyses will be needed to fill the gaps. Furthermore, it will be necessary to dynamically and continuously keep the knowledge base updated as new attacks emerge and new devices become popular. ACCESS can thereby provide support for decision makers in identifying suitable alternative authentication techniques.

3   Requirement Identification

We conducted a research literature review on adoption, acceptance, security, and usable security, as well as business-related publications in order to identify relevant requirements. We identified four categories of requirements (see Figure 2).

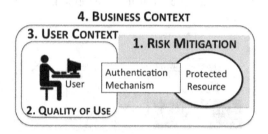

Fig. 2. Users Authenticating

3.1   Risk Mitigation

Authentication is essentially risk mitigation. The value of the protected resource should be matched with the strength of the authentication mechanism being used to protect it. Correspondingly, the framework will need to determine whether the security offered in practise by a particular authentication scheme matches the value of the resource being protected and the assumed attacker capabilities. One possible evaluation scheme has been suggested by De Angeli, Coventry, Johnson and Renaud, who outline the following dimensions to assess the security of authentication mechanisms [21]. They are:

Guessability: How easy it is to guess the secret. No universally accepted security rating method currently exists. One measure that is commonly used as a theoretical strength indicator is theoretical password space, which is a measure of how many possible passwords (whether textual, graphical, or other) exist given certain constraints on the makeup of the password. Since users tend to choose simple passwords that do not take advantage of the entire possible password space, the theoretical password space is a relatively weak measure of offered security. Unfortunately, the results of the user studies cannot be used as a substitute for a universal strength measure either.

Observability: The ease with which entry of the secret can be observed.

Recordability: The ability for an attacker to utilise a user-generated recording, either of or associated with an authentication secret.

These aspects are not used quantitatively, but they do support a comparison between different schemes, so that the best scheme for a particular context, in terms of risk mitigation, can be identified.

3.2   Quality in Use

The traditional technology acceptance (TAM) model suggests that the most influential factors leading to adoption are perceived usefulness and perceived ease- of-use, and these certainly confirm the importance of the usability aspect of this requirement category. This is especially important when users are customers rather than employees [22, 23].

Usability testing is routinely carried out during software development [24]. An equally important aspect of quality in use, which is not encapsulated within traditional usability, is convenience [25]. Users routinely choose based on convenience rather than strength [26, 27].

Moreover, we now arguably inhabit a consumer-era where the real power of the market lies with consumers, not with the service providers. An authentication mechanism designed for the mainstream must match customer expectations and represent a balance between costs and benefits to consumers. A number of aspects are relevant to quality in use:

Memorability: The need to remember them is the password's chief flaw. Humans generate simple secrets to avoid forgetting [28], and this compromises the mechanism's theoretical strength.

Accessibility: Authentication should be accessible to most individuals, even those with disabilities such as dyslexia, colour blindness or mobility issues so as to ensure that the system meets the needs of the end-users [29]. For example, an authentication mechanism reliant on sentences is not suitable if any of the users are likely to be illiterate or to include a significant number of dyslexics. On the other hand, if literacy is a given, and the target audience is elderly, then the deployed authentication mechanism cannot reasonably rely on perfect memory.

Equipment: Some alternative authentication methods require extra hardware, which may reduce the viability of the mechanism. If the target users are employees, this aspect is easily controlled. If they are customers using their own devices, expectations are far more constrained.

Convenience: The effort associated with authentication must be appropriate for the envisioned use. Three aspects [30] are relevant: (1) Enrolment Time: Lengthy enrolment times could deter users but a lengthy enrolment phase may be acceptable if it affords authentication secrets that are used rarely but endure for years. (2) Authentication Time: Time-consuming authentication could deter on-going use of an application or service. However, lengthy authentication may be acceptable in high-risk situations or if it reduces inconvenience in other areas, e.g. password reset. (3) Replacement Time: If employees are locked out of their accounts, their inability to do their jobs costs the organisation money. If customers cannot log into a system, they cannot make a purchase. Thus it is important for replacement to be given due consideration.

It is unlikely that the decision-maker will have a specific mandated time span for these activities. What is reasonable though, is to encode the target user group's tolerance for delays in each of these areas. A simple scheme of Low/Medium/High could suffice.

3.3   Business Context

The reality of the current world economy makes the business environment extremely competitive so businesses want to be sure that any new innovation is going to benefit them ie. not lead to extra expense with no benefit to offset the expense. This can be termed business value. In terms of switching to an alternative the benefit might be reduced calls to the help desk and increased customer satisfaction. The fundamental monetary costs of an authentication approach can be broadly classified into three types [28], as follows:

User cost: If the authentication approach relies on generic hardware and software, e.g. traditional operation system and keyboards, then there are no real costs for the user. However, if the authentication approach is token or biometric-based then the cost of specialised hardware and software for each user would need to be considered.

Infrastructure cost: The cost for the necessary infrastructure to operate the authentication solution. The infrastructure costs for almost any authentication solution are likely to be high. However, the aim is that as more users embrace a system or application, the infrastructure costs are reduced, as an increase in users squeezes value from infrastructure.

Administration cost: The cost associated with the number of professionals required to manage bureaucracy and effectively operate an authentication solution. This is likely to be directly proportional to the number of users.

It will be challenging to estimate some of these costs accurately so perhaps a granular qualitative scheme should be adopted, which supports comparison between different mechanisms but does not attempt to quantify the actual cost.

3.4   User Context

Context includes [30]:

Anticipated Frequency of Use: A mechanism which is used infrequently has greater memorability requirements.

Platform & Place: The envisioned device and/or software of an authentication mechanism and the envisioned environments where an authentication mechanism will be used. The modern mobile computer or smartphone has pushed powerful computation and access to the Internet, onto many more devices. Hence one cannot make any assumptions about platform or place of use.

Purpose: The reason for deploying an authentication mechanism. The mechanism may well serve one purpose in one setting but another, elsewhere. For example, in one setting a person might authenticate to enforce accountability but at other times to authorise purchases.

4   Developer Survey to Confirm Requirements

Having consulted the literature review to identify the requirements relevant to decision making, we noticed that developers are, in general, rarely addressed in the research literature on authentication and technology acceptance and adaption. However, at the end the developers have to agree on new proposed authentication mechanisms as well as being able to implement them and integrate them in existing services and tools. Therefore, we decided to study the different identified requirements further with an online survey with developers. The goal of the survey was, on the one hand, to confirm that the identified requirements were indeed relevant for developers. On the other hand, we wanted to determine whether the list of requirements should be extended in terms of additional aspects. Furthermore, it allowed us to test further types of requirements namely evidence and developer issues which were not mentioned in the authentication literature we reviewed for Section 3 but are often mentioned in literature in related areas.

We posted a link to an online survey on various developer forums. 93 developers responded to our survey, of whom 72% developed systems for the desktop,

2% developed for mobile environments only and the rest developed for both. We asked whether they had had any experience of authentication other than the password. 34% had had some experience of authentication other than the password although 73% were aware that alternatives to passwords existed. 60% said they were aware of situations where the password was not particularly suitable and 96% said they would consider using an alternative mechanism if it were shown to be better for a particular user group.

We asked them what would convince them to switch to an alternative authentication mechanism. We offered them the following possible reasons based on the literature reviewed in Section 3. They could select as many options as they wanted.

1. risk mitigation: strength w.r.t. guessability, observability, recordability;
2. quality in use: easier for users to use and remember;
3. business context: it would reduce costs (either for user, infrastructure or administration);

We did not specifically mention user context because we wanted to see whether the developers mentioned this themselves as aspects of user context are not that obvious and are not mentioned very often in literature. We included 'evidence: other companies have used it successfully' although it has not mentioned in the context of authentication literature we reviewed for Section 3, in order to confirm the importance of stories in convincing organisations to use new technologies [14, 15]. We also included the option 'developer issues: easy to use API'. This type of requirement was added as software engineering researchers in general argue for the benefits of reusable components in software development (see e.g. [31]). We also offered them a text field to add their own reasons or thoughts, in order to get new types or aspects if there are any.

Figure 3 shows the result: User Context did indeed emerge from the developers' comments. In general, all comments could be assigned to at least one of the identified requirements. Sample comments are:

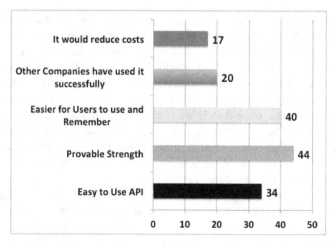

Fig. 3. Confirming Requirements

— Risk Mitigation: "It should resist observation attempts"
— Quality in Use: "Whether it was accessible to blind and deaf users", "Ease of authenticator replacement"
— Business Context: "It must hold value for the company and the end user", "It should not be too costly"
— User Context: "Whether it could be used on multiple platforms"
— Evidence: "Depends on how strong the evidence is", "Ease of implementation"

5   Integration of Requirements into ACCESS

The developer survey led to the decision to include 'evidence' and 'developer issues' in the ACCESS framework although it was not mentioned in the authentication literature. 'Developer issues' is included in business context and evidence is a different kind of element. Evidence encompasses 'risk mitigation', 'quality of use', 'business context', and 'user context' aspects. While decision makers can provide information about requirements in terms of risk, target end-users, business and user context, they might only be willing to trial schemes supported by hard evidence i.e. other organisations have used such a mechanism successfully or the evidence from the academic literature is very convincing.

In Figure 4, the above-mentioned type of requirements are incorporated into the ACCESS framework. While 'risk mitigation', 'quality of use', 'business context', and 'user context' are taken into account for the feasibility analyses and to describe the authentication alternatives in the knowledge base, existence of evidence is a property of schemes included in knowledge base and also added to the output. However, it is not taken into account for the feasibility analysis as only very few of the alternative authentication schemes have been deployed and tested in the wild. If ACCESS is successful this will change in future and then 'evidence' will become part of the feasibility analysis.

In order to support this process and to iteratively extend the framework based on the results for piloting, it is essential for the framework facilitate simple and easy recording of pilot experiences. Such an interface should record the experiences in terms of the core requirements so that it can be matched to scenarios presented by subsequent framework users. If the framework is offered as a web-based decision-support system, this information can immediately be made available to other users. If it is offered as a stand-alone application, it should use a push mechanism to send this knowledge to a central repository for broadcast to other instances of the framework, as recommended by [32]. This will support independent and distributed augmentation of the knowledge repository with authentic and ecologically sound experiences from the field, creating a network of mutually reinforcing systems [33].

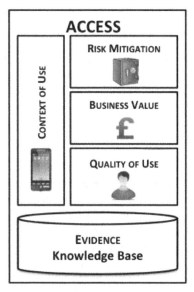

Fig. 4. Feasibility Factors Influencing Acceptance and Adoption of an Alternative Authentication Mechanism

Note, although quality of use is considered in the feasibility analyses, it is necessary to run acceptance studies with the selected alternative afterwards. This is caused by missing evidence from similar settings and the fact that the user studies from literature considering to evaluate quality of use aspects are very limited with respect to having studied a representative group of the population and with respect to long term issues. All this can finally only be assessed in use, in the wild, over time. For example, consider the following requirement specification:

— Risk mitigation: Low risk: essentially a community website.
— Quality of use: Elderly community members, all literate, all with corrected to normal vision, all with reasonable hearing, but with dexterity challenges. Can use basic features on a computer. Convenience is not a concern for these users.
— Business context: Small budget.

— Context of use: They will be using the mechanism from home and library computers, but not from smartphones, or on the move. The purpose of the authentication is to enforce accountability since members can post blog items. There is no current website, and usage is expected to be bi-weekly (fairly infrequent).

If we implement Korhonen et al.'s [20] first approach: eliciting requirements and generating a ranked list of alternatives, the ACCESS framework might feasibly generate the following ranking:

Musical Password [34]. This mechanism has been tested with a wide range of users, and was very favourably received by the elderly participants. It requires users to choose from a number of music clips, all of which feature 1960s music. At authentication users identify "their" clips. In terms of memorability it performed well across all user groups.

Recognition-Based Graphical Authentication [35]. This mechanism was designed specifically for a user group as depicted in the scenario depicted above. Users identify their own PIN, postal code and doodle from subsequent challenge sets composed of image grids. It has proved extremely popular and has been in use for 9 years now.

6   Conclusion

Alternative authentication technologies have not captured the minds and hearts of developers, users, and decision makers. However, the pressures on the (textual) password have increased to such an extent that it is necessary for decision makers to rethink this 'safe' strategy and start thinking of other ways of controlling access to their systems. We cannot realistically expect one alternative to replace the ubiquitous (textual) password, but we propose to use a wider variety of authentication mechanisms. To support decision makers to select appropriate once, trial them, and subsequently to adopt them, we propose the ACCESS framework. Future work will develop the knowledge base and an interface which captures the decision's requirements and matches that to candidate authentication mechanisms to support informed choice.

References

1. Adams, A., Sasse, M.A.: Users are not the enemy. Communications of the ACM 42(12), 40–46 (1999)
2. Chiasson, S., Biddle, R., van Oorschot, P.C.: A Second Look at the Usability of Click-Based Graphical Passwords. In: Proc. 3rd Symposium on Usable Privacy and Security, pp. 1–12 (2007)
3. Moncur, W., Leplatre, G.: Pictures at the ATM: Exploring the Usability of Multiple Graphical Passwords. In: Proc. SIGCHI Conference on Human Factors in Computing Systems (CHI 2007), pp. 887–894 (2007)

4. Stobert, E., Forget, A., Chiasson, S., van Oorschot, P., Biddle, R.: Exploring Usability Effects of Increasing Security in Click-Based Graphical Passwords. In: Proc. 26th Annual Computer Security Applications Conference (ACSAC 2010), pp. 79–88 (2010)
5. Frischholz, R.W., Dieckmann, U.: BioID: A Multimodal Biometric Identification System. IEEE Computer 33(2), 64–68 (2000)
6. Jain, A.K., Ross, A., Prabhakar, S.: An Introduction to Biometric Recognition. IEEE Transactions on Circuits and Systems for Video Technology 14(1), 4–20 (2004)
7. Conti, M., Zachia-Zlatea, I., Crispo, B.: Mind How You Answer Me! Trans parently Authenticating the User of a Smartphone when Answering or Placing a Call. In: Proc. 6th ACM Symposium on Information, Computer, and Communications Security, pp. 249–259 (2011)
8. Frankel, A.D., Maheswaran, M.: Feasibility of a Socially Aware Authentication Scheme. In: Proc. 6th IEEE Consumer Communications and Networking Conference, pp. 1–6 (2009)
9. Corner, M.D., Noble, B.D.: Zero-interaction Authentication. In: Proc. 8th Annual International Conference on Mobile Computing and Networks, pp. 1–11 (2002)
10. Catuogno, L., Galdi, C.: On the security of a two-factor authentication scheme. In: Samarati, P., Tunstall, M., Posegga, J., Markantonakis, K., Sauveron, D. (eds.) WISTP 2010. LNCS, vol. 6033, pp. 245–252. Springer, Heidelberg (2010)
11. Recordon, D., Reed, D.: OpenID 2.0: a platform for user-centric identity management. In: Proceedings of the Second ACM Workshop on Digital Identity Management, pp. 11–16. ACM (2006)
12. Renaud, K., Mayer, P., Volkamer, M., Maguire, J.: Are graphical authentication mechanisms as strong as passwords? In: Frontiers in Network Applications, Network Systems and Web Services (SoFAST-WS 2013), Krakow, Poland, September 8-11 (2013)
13. Schaub, F., Walch, M., Könings, B., Weber, M.: Exploring the design space of graphical passwords on smartphones. In: Symposium on Usable Privacy and Security (SOUPS), Newcastle, UK, July 24-26 (2013)
14. Heath, C., Heath, D.: Made to Stick: Why some ideas take hold and others come unstuck. Arrow Books (2008)
15. Gladwell, M.: The Tipping Point: How Little Things Can Make a Big Difference. Abacus (2001)
16. O'Connor, A.M., Tugwell, P., Wells, G.A., Elmslie, T., Jolly, E., Hollingworth, G., McPherson, R., Bunn, H., Graham, I., Drake, E., et al.: A decision aid for women considering hormone therapy after menopause: Decision support framework and evaluation. Patient Education and Counseling 33(3), 267–280 (1998)
17. Park, J., Simpson, T.W.: Development of a production cost estimation framework to support product family design. International Journal of Production Research 43(4), 731–772 (2005)
18. Dong, J., Du, H.S., Wang, S., Chen, K., Deng, X.: A framework of web-based decision support systems for portfolio selection with OLAP and PVM. Decision Support Systems 37(3), 367–376 (2004)
19. Garg, A.X., Adhikari, N.K., McDonald, H., Rosas-Arellano, M.P., Devereaux, P., Beyene, J., Sam, J., Haynes, R.B.: Effects of computerized clinical decision support systems on practitioner performance and patient outcomes. JAMA: The Journal of the American Medical Association 293(10), 1223–1238 (2005)
20. Korhonen, P., Moskowitz, H., Wallenius, J.: Multiple criteria decision support. A review. European Journal of Operational Research 63(3), 361–375 (1992)

21. De Angeli, A., Coventry, L., Johnson, G., Renaud, K.: Is a picture really worth a thousand words? Exploring the feasibility of graphical authentication systems. International Journal of Human-Computer Studies 63(1), 128–152 (2005)

22. Beal, G.M., Rogers, E.M., Bohlen, J.M.: Validity of the concept of stages in the adoption process. Rural Sociology 22(2), 166–168 (1957)

23. Herley, C., van Oorschot, P.C., Patrick, A.S.: Passwords: If we're so smart, why are we still using them? In: Dingledine, R., Golle, P. (eds.) FC 2009. LNCS, vol. 5628, pp. 230–237. Springer, Heidelberg (2009)

24. Mack, Z., Sharples, S.: The importance of usability in product choice: A mobile phone case study. Ergonomics 52(12), 1514–1528 (2009)

25. Kelley, E.J.: The importance of convenience in consumer purchasing. The Journal of Marketing, 32–38 (1958)

26. Weir, C.S., Douglas, G., Carruthers, M., Jack, M.: User perceptions of security, convenience and usability for ebanking authentication tokens. Computers & Security 28(1-2), 47–62 (2009)

27. Tam, L., Glassman, M., Vanderwauver, M.: The psychology of password management a tradeoff between security and convenience. Behaviour & Information Technology 29(3), 233–244 (2010)

28. O'Gorman, L.: Comparing passwords, tokens, and biometrics for user authentication. Proceedings of the IEEE 91(12), 2021–2040 (2003)

29. Monk, A.: User-centred design. In: Home Informatics and Telematics, pp. 181–190. Springer (2000)

30. Maguire, J.: An ecologically valid evaluation of an observation-resilient graphical authentication mechanism. Ph.D. dissertation, Computing Science (2013)

31. Yang, Y., Bhuta, J., Boehm, B., Port, D.N.: Value-based processes for COTS- based applications. IEEE Software 22(4), 54–62 (2005)

32. Sim, I., Gorman, P., Greenes, R.A., Haynes, R.B., Kaplan, B., Lehmann, H., Tang, P.C.: Clinical decision support systems for the practice of evidence-based medicine. Journal of the American Medical Informatics Association 8(6), 527–534 (2001)

33. Ferguson, J., Bell, M., Chalmers, M.: Mutually reinforcing systems. In: Proceedings of the ACM SIGKDD Workshop on Human Computation. HCOMP 2010, pp. 34–37. ACM, New York (2010)

34. Gibson, M., Renaud, K., Conrad, M., Maple, C.: Musipass: Authenticating me softly with my song. In: Proceedings of the 2009 Workshop on New Security Paradigms Workshop, pp. 85–100. ACM (2009)

35. Renaud, K., Ramsay, J.: Now what was that password again? A more flexible way of identifying and authenticating our seniors. Behaviour & Information Technology 26(4), 309–322 (2007)

Character Strings, Memory and Passwords: What a Recall Study Can Tell Us[*]

Brian C. Stanton and Kristen K. Greene

National Institute of Standards and Technology,
100 Bureau Dr, Gaithersburg, MD, USA
{brian.stanton,kristen.greene}@nist.gov

Abstract. Many users must authenticate to multiple systems and applications, often using different passwords, on a daily basis. At the same time, the recommendations of security experts are driving increases in the required character length and complexity of passwords. The thinking is that longer passwords will result in greater "entropy," or randomness, making them more difficult to guess. The greater complexity requires inclusion of upper- and lower-case letters, numerals, and special characters. How users interact and cope with passwords of different length and complexity is a topic of significant interest to both the computer science and cognitive science research communities.

Using experimental methodology from the behavioral sciences, we set out to answer the following question: how memorable are complex character strings of different lengths that might be used as higher-entropy passwords? In this experiment, participants were asked to memorize a series of ten different character strings and type them repeatedly into a computer program. Character string lengths varied and the random characters were made up of alphanumeric and special characters in order to mimic passwords. Not surprisingly, our findings indicate that the longer a character string is, the longer it takes for a person to recall it, and the more likely they are to make an error when trying to re-type that string. These effects are particularly pronounced for strings of eight to ten characters or longer.

Keywords: passwords, security, character strings, memory, recall.

1 Introduction

As people increasingly interact with multiple computer systems over the course of a day, they are expected to remember an ever-increasing number of passwords [5, 3]. Computer security specialists also want to increase the length of these passwords in order to increase their "entropy," or randomness, making them more difficult to guess. This means users are often forced to remember not only more passwords but longer passwords as well. Increasing password length is not the only method of increasing password entropy; another option is increasing password complexity. The

---

[*] The rights of this work are transferred to the extent transferable according to title 17 U.S.C. 105.

T. Tryfonas and I. Askoxylakis (Eds.): HAS 2014, LNCS 8533, pp. 195–206, 2014.

inclusion of upper- and lower-case letters, numerals, and special characters are often recommended for increasing password security [13]. How users interact and cope with the increasing level of complexity of passwords is an area of interest to the usable security community. This research explored the following question: how memorable are complex character strings of different lengths that might be used as higher-entropy passwords? Password memorability is a multi-faceted concept, affecting the amount of time required to initially commit the password to memory; the time to recall and type the password; and the nature and frequency of errors committed during password entry.

2   Background

In order to provide best practice recommendations for institution-wide password policies, it is critical that the usable security field better understands how various password requirements fundamentally affect human performance. The nature of the interplay between password complexity, errors, timing, and memorability should be more closely examined. It has been long remarked that longer passwords "take longer to enter, have more chance of error when being entered, and are generally more difficult to remember" [12]. It is to be expected that longer passwords should lead to longer entry times and more errors (more characters offer more chances for misremembering) but how many characters are too many? When does the burden of remembering become too much for a user and what types of errors do users make when recalling and typing passwords?

There have been many studies of remembering in general (e.g., [14]) and passwords in particular, addressing such issues as memorability, predictability and attention [6, 7, 15, 16, 17, 18]. In addition, there is a large body of literature examining the factors of skilled typing performance from 1923 [4] through the 1980s [8, 10] including a great deal of literature on the cognitive and perceptual-motor aspects of transcription typing [11]. But, comparatively little research has been done on the fundamentals of password typing. Secure passwords differ greatly from the words used in traditional transcription typing studies; the former are ideally as random as possible, whereas the latter follow orthographic rules and are easily predictable given the surrounding semantic content. Although non-word strings of random letters have been studied in previous transcription typing research (e.g., [10]), such research did not include the variety of numbers and special characters recommended for passwords. The current study is a necessary first step in addressing the fundamentals of passwords.

3   Method

3.1   Participants

Two groups of participants were tested in this study. The first group consisted of 30 participants recruited from the Washington, DC (WDC) metropolitan area in the

United States. Seven WDC participants failed to complete the test in the one-hour time allotted. The second group consisted of 45 participants recruited from the University College London (UCL) in the United Kingdom. All UCL participants completed the test in the time allotted. Ages ranged from 18 to 78 for the two groups with most of the UCL group between the ages of 18 – 27.

3.2   Instructional Materials

The participants were given the following verbal instructions:

You will be working on this computer. You will be presented with 10 character strings with varying lengths, one at a time. Your task is to memorize each string as it's presented to you on the screen. You can take as much time as you need to memorize each string. You may also practice typing the string. After you feel that you have the string memorized, you will be given the chance to verify that you have memorized the string. If you don't pass the verification, you can re-try the verification or go back and memorize the string again. If you do pass the verification, you will be asked to type the character string in ten times. After typing the string in ten times, you will move on to the next character string.

3.3   Materials and Equipment

The strings the participants were asked to memorize consisted of ten strings made up of two strings each of six, eight, ten, twelve, and fourteen character strings. The strings were randomly generated, using a software package1. Each string consisted of upper case, lower case, alphabetic, numeric, and special characters presented in the Consolas font. Strings could not begin with a capital letter, nor could they end with an exclamation mark. The strings are shown in Table 1.

By using randomly generated character strings as stand-ins for user-generated passwords, we hoped to control for effects of different levels of password meaningfulness. Since we only set out to study effects of increasing password length, we wanted to keep other factors, such as meaningfulness, constant across stimuli. Rather than making stimuli equally memorable, we wanted them to be equally unmemorable.

The strings were presented in the above random order for all participants in the WDC group. The last two strings were switched for the UCL group due to a software configuration file change. A custom software program was designed to present the strings, allow the user to enter the strings, and time the user actions.

---

[1] Advanced Password Generator from BinaryMark was used. Disclaimer: Any mention of commercial products is for information only; such identification is not intended to imply recommendation or endorsement by the National Institute of Standards and Technology, nor is it intended to imply that these entities, materials, or equipment are necessarily the best for the purpose.

Table 1. Character string order, string, and length

Order	String	Length
1	5c2'Qe	6
2	m#o)fp^2aRf207	14
3	m3)61fHw	8
4	d51)u4;X3wrf	12
5	p4d46*3TxY	10
6	q80<U/C2mv	10
7	6n04%Ei'Hm3V	12
8	4i_55fQ$2Mnh30	14
9	3.bH1o	6
10	ua7t?C2#	8

Both studies were conducted using a desktop PC with monitor, keyboard and mouse. The WDC study used a standard American QWERTY keyboard, while the UCL study used a standard UK QWERTY keyboard.

3.4   Data Collection Methods

The participant was verbally given the instructions quoted above then was given an informed consent form to sign. The test facilitator started the data collection program and entered the participant number. The participant was given a piece of paper with the first character string. The participant was presented with instructions on the practice screen asking them to memorize the target string (see Fig. 1. Practice Screen). When the participant felt that they had memorized the target string they moved to the next screen (see Fig 2. Verification Screen).

The second screen asked the participant to enter the memorized target string. The string had to be entered correctly in order to move to the third screen where the participant was asked to enter the memorized string ten times (see Fig 3. Entry Screen). If the entered string failed the verification, the user had the opportunity to go back to the practice screen or they could try and enter the string again.

This procedure was repeated for the ten strings. After all ten strings had been tested, the program gave them a surprise recall test to see how many of the ten strings they remembered. During the surprise recall test, if participants asked, they were informed that they didn't have to type the ten strings in the sequence in which they were presented. Typed text was visible during practice and verification (Figs. 1 and 2, respectively), masked with asterisks during entry (Fig. 3), then visible during surprise recall (not shown given its high similarity to the entry screen, Fig. 3).

Fig. 1. Practice Screen

Fig. 2. Verification Screen

Fig. 3. Entry Screen

4   Results

The results were analyzed for the amount and types of errors made during the individual string entry, the amount of time for each individual string entry and the number of strings correctly recalled during the surprise recall task.

4.1   Errors for Entry Tasks

An entered string was in error if it did not exactly match the target string. As long as the entered string contained at least one deviation from the target string, it was deemed to be in error. Fig. 4 and Fig. 5 show the median errors per character string length. The UCL participants made fewer median errors overall than did the WDC group when the character string length reached 10 or greater. Both groups had increases in the variability of error counts as the string length increased.

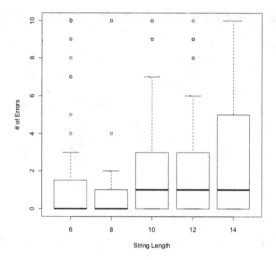

Fig. 4. WDC Errors

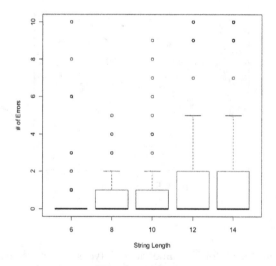

Fig. 5. UCL Errors

4.2   Types of Entry Errors

Each entered string was analyzed as to the type of error or errors it contained. The types of errors made were as follows:

- Extra character
- Missing character
- Incorrect capitalization (shifting)

- Wrong character
- Character typed was adjacent on the keyboard to the target character
- Zero instead of an "O"
- Transposition of characters next to one another in the string
- Character was in the wrong place within the string (misplaced character).

Typing a zero rather than an "O" occurred often enough as to deserve its own category rather than being grouped into the "wrong character" category. The WDC group made 471 errors and the UCL group made 556 for a total of 1,027 errors.

Table 2. Types of entry errors made

Type of error	WDC	UCL	Total
	Percentages	Percentages	Percentages
Extra character	7%	7%	7%
Missing character	25%	10%	17%
Incorrect capitalization	38%	51%	45%
Wrong character	6%	12%	9%
Adjacent key	8%	10%	9%
Zero instead of an "O"	3%	3%	3%
Transposition of characters	10%	6%	8%
Wrong place within the string	3%	1%	2%

4.3   Task Times

The time for a task was calculated from the time the practice screen was first presented until the tenth recalled string was entered on the entry screen. As Fig 6. shows, the average time taken to complete the task increases as the character string

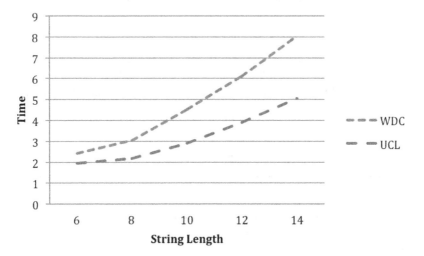

Fig. 6. Average task time (minutes) by character string length

length increases. The figure also shows that the rate of increase increases after the eight character string for both groups, with the WDC group taking somewhat longer overall. Table 3 and Table 4 show the minimum, maximum, mean, and standard deviation (SD) task times for the two groups.

Table 3. WDC task times (minutes) by string length

Length	N	*Min.*	*Max.*	Mean	*SD*
6	24	1.05	4.24	2.4691	0.82538
8	24	1.27	5.17	3.0723	0.99511
10	24	1.65	7.65	4.5305	1.50970
12	24	2.41	9.67	6.1832	1.96270
14	24	3.14	12.83	8.0683	2.55134

Table 4. UCL task times (minutes) by string length

Length	N	Min.	Max.	Mean	SD
6	45	1.43	3.98	2.3410	0.50364
8	45	1.05	2.92	1.7874	0.38765
10	45	1.61	5.79	2.9255	0.86637
12	45	1.98	6.84	3.9296	1.11102
14	45	2.61	10.62	5.0954	1.67292

4.4   Number of Surprise Strings Recalled

Roughly one half of the participants could only remember one string with only one person recalling the maximum number of four strings (see Table 5).

Table 5. Number of surprise strings recalled

Strings Recalled	Number of WDC Participants	Number of UCL Participants
0	5	3
1	12	21
2	5	17
3	2	3
4	0	1

The most recalled string during the surprise recall task was the last string memorized followed by the second to the last memorized string for each group (see Table 6).

Table 6. Surprise strings recalled.

String	Number of times recalled	
	WDC	UCL
ua7t?C2#	17	21
3.bH1o	7	33
q80<U/C2mv	2	2
4i_55fQ$2Mnh30	1	10
6n04%Ei'Hm3V	1	1
m#o)fp^2aRf207	0	1

5   Discussion

In his 1956 paper on human information processing, Miller proposed that human short-term memory could only retain seven plus or minus two items [9]. If we surmise that our participants are working from short-term memory only (or what Baddeley and Hitch called "working memory" [1]), then the results of our study seem to bear out Miller's assertion. This supposition is supported by the final surprise recall results, which show that most participants could only correctly recall the most recent strings they had worked with (see Table 6). We expect that the participants may have been able to recall more strings if the strings had been committed to long-term memory.

As it is likely that the character strings did not go into the participants' long-term memories, we would expect recall success to decrease around the eight- and ten-character string lengths, since that is the point where the number of items to recall would begin exceeding the "seven plus or minus two" range. We found these changes for both timing and errors. Given that, we were not surprised by the finding that the longer the character string was, the more time it took for participants to complete the tasks. What is interesting is that the slope of the timing line increased around the eight-character string length for both the WDC and UCL groups, even though UCL participants were faster overall (see Fig. 6). This would suggest that there is added work involved when the string length exceeds eight characters (as is predicted by [9]). The finding that the UCL participants were faster at completing the tasks may potentially be explained by the fact that they were sampled from a younger participant pool (UCL college students), and may therefore have had better typing skills and/or working memory capacities than the (on average) older WDC participants, who were sampled from the larger Washington DC metropolitan area.

The median number of errors also increased around the eight- to ten-character string lengths. This trend was more visible in the WDC data (see Fig. 4), where the median number of errors increased from zero to one between the eight- and ten-character strings. The variability of the error counts increased at the same point. Even though the median number of errors remained the same for the UCL participants (see Fig. 5), they experienced increased variability of errors around the ten- to twelve-character strings. As with the difference in entry times between the WDC and UCL groups, the difference in the "error variability threshold" may potentially be explained by the younger UCL participants having greater memory capacity and/or better general typing skills. To test these potential explanations, future studies should collect data on whether participants are touch typists and measure their Words Per Minute (WPM) for typing prose passages, in order to account for individual differences in general typing ability. It will also be necessary to capture more granular data on participants' ages; while we know the age ranges from which each group in the current study were recruited, we unfortunately did not have access to ages at the individual participant level. Future studies would also benefit from administering a standardized battery of cognitive ability tests to quantify effects of individual differences in memory capacity.

One of the more interesting findings was the type of errors made. In both participant groups, the largest percentage of errors were capitalization (shifting) errors (see Table 5). Many special characters also require a shift action (e.g., "8" must be shifted to "*"), so these errors are particularly important given the increasing use of special characters in password policies.

6   Conclusions and Future Work

Since capturing real-world password typing data poses significant privacy and security concerns, we instead gathered human performance data in a controlled laboratory experiment using randomly generated, password-like character strings. Admittedly, having randomly generated character strings represent passwords is somewhat artificial, since people often (but not always) create and use passwords that have some meaning for them. Still, we feel that some general recommendations can be derived from our results.

First, the trend towards ever-increasing password lengths is likely to be problematic for users. Our results indicate that the longer a character string is, the longer it takes a person to memorize, recall, and enter it. Longer strings also increase the probability of errors.

Secondly, the trend of requiring special characters and capital letters should be weighed against the increased likelihood of errors, especially for those systems that limit the number of password attempts before lockout. It is possible that longer passwords with more special characters and capital letters may require more attempts to enter them correctly than passwords with fewer (or no) special characters and capital letters. This means that some organizations may need to consider changing the typical "three strikes, you're out" policy for password attempts.

With regards to conducting further research, a natural next step would be to replicate this experiment but have the participants choose their own passwords instead of issuing them random character strings. Participants would likely find chosen (as opposed to assigned) passwords more meaningful and therefore easier to remember. Although challenging from a security and privacy perspective, it would nonetheless be interesting to see whether the "seven plus or minus two" rule would still be in effect in such a case. Another extension of interest would be replicating this experiment on different platforms, such as smartphones. How would working on a different platform affect the input of passwords? Are people using alternative platforms faster or slower when inputting password-like character strings? Do they make more or fewer errors? Are individual differences such as cognitive ability, touch-typing ability, and age more pronounced in the mobile computing environment? These are all questions that bear further investigation.

This study contributes to the usable security community by presenting much-needed human performance data that are difficult to obtain in the real world. This is the first in a series of planned studies exploring effects of password requirements across platforms, starting with the traditional desktop environment and moving on to mobile devices. Only by understanding the fundamental characteristics of password typing may we hope to predict how well users will be able to comply with proposed password policy changes.

Acknowledgments. We would like to thank Dr. Angela Sasse and her colleagues at the University College London for the UCL data collection.

References

1. Baddeley, A.D., Hitch, G.: Working memory. In: Bower, G. (ed.) Recent Advances in Learning and Motivation, vol. 8, pp. 47–90. Academic Press, New York (1974)
2. Chiasson, S., Forget, A., Stobert, E., Van Oorschot, P., Biddle, R.: Multiple password interference in text passwords and click-based graphical passwords. In: Proceedings of the 16th ACM Conference on Computer and Communications Security, pp. 500–511 (2009)
3. Choong, Y., Theofanos, M., Liu, H.: A Large-Scale Survey of Employees' Password Behaviors. Manuscript submitted for publication (manuscript in preparation, 2014)
4. Coover, J.E.: A method of teaching typewriting based upon a psychological analysis of expert typing. National Education Association 61, 561–567 (1923)
5. Florencio, D., Herley, C.: A large-scale study of web password habits. In: WWW 2007, Banff, Canada. ACM Press (2007)
6. Forget, A., Biddle, R.: Memorability of persuasive passwords. In: CHI 2008 Extended Abstracts on Human Factors in Computing Systems, pp. 3759–3764 (2008)
7. Gehringer, E.F.: Choosing passwords: Security and human factors. In: International Symposium on Technology and Society (ISTAS 2002), pp. 369–373 (2002)
8. Gentner, D.: Skilled finger movements in typing. Center for Information Processing, University of California, San Diego. CHIP Report 104 (1981)
9. Miller, G.A.: The magical number seven, plus or minus two: Some limits on our capacity for processing information. Psychological Review 63(2), 81–97 (1956), doi:10.1037/h0043158
10. Salthouse, T.: Effects of age and skill in typing. Journal of Experimental Psychology 113(3), 345–371 (1984)
11. Salthouse, T.: Perceptual, cognitive, and motoric aspects of transcription typing. Psychological Bulletin 99(3), 303–319 (1986)
12. United States Department of Commerce, National Institute of Standards and Technology (NIST), Password usage (FIPS PUB 112) (1985), http://www.itl.nist.gov/fipspubs/fip112.htm (retrieved)

206 B.C. Stanton and K.K. Greene

13. United States Department of Homeland Security, United States Computer Emergency Readiness Team (US-CERT), Security tip (ST04-002): Choosing and protecting passwords (2009), http://www.us-cert.gov/cas/tips/ST04-002.html (retrieved)
14. Unsworth, N., Engle, R.W.: The foundations of remembering: Essays in honor of Henry L. Roedgier III, pp. 241–258. Psychology Press, New York (2007)
15. Vu, K., Bhargav-Spantzel, A., Proctor, R.: Imposing password restrictions for multiple accounts: Impact on generation and recall of passwords. In: HFES 47th Annual Meeting, pp. 1331–1335 (2003)
16. Vu, K., Cook, J., Bhargav-Spantzel, A., Proctor, R.W.: Short- and long-term retention of passwords generated by first-letter and entire-word mnemonic methods. In: Proceedings of the 5th Annual Security Conference, Las Vegas, NV (2006)
17. Vu, K., Proctor, R., Bhargav-Spantzel, A., Tai, B., Cook, J., Schultz, E.: Improving password security and memorability to protect personal and organizational information. International Journal of Human-Computer Studies 65, 744–757 (2006)
18. Yan, J., Blackwell, A., Anderson, R., Grant, A.: Password memorability and security: Empirical results. IEEE Security & Privacy 2(5), 25–31 (2004)

Security Policy and Awareness

From Regulations to Practice: Achieving Information Security Compliance in Healthcare

Subrata Acharya, Brian Coats, Arpit Saluja, and Dale Fuller

Computer and Information Sciences, Towson University, Towson, MD, USA
CIMS, Johns Hopkins Medical Institute, Baltimore, MD, USA
University of Pittsburgh Medical Center Altoona, Altoona, PA, USA
sacharya@towson.edu,
bcoats1@students.towson.edu,
asaluja1@jhmi.edu,
dfuller@altoonaregional.org

Abstract. Access to healthcare is not a new issue, but it has been only in the last few years that it has gained significant traction with the federal government passing a number of laws to greatly enhance the exchange of medical information between all relevant parties: patients, providers, and payers. This research focuses specifically on these issues by examining industry compliance to the Health Insurance Portability and Accountability Act, electronic health record adoption, and the federal Meaningful Use program; all from the healthcare provider's perspective. While many plans have been made, guidelines created, and national strategies forged, there are significant gaps in how actual technology will be applied to achieve these goals. The goal of this research is to bridge the gap from regulation to practice in a number of key technological areas of healthcare information security. Using standardized frameworks, this research proposes how accessibility, efficiency, and integrity in healthcare information security can be improved.

Keywords: Meaningful Use, HIPAA Compliance, Assessment.

1   Introduction

When considering healthcare accessibility, two other issues quickly come to the forefront: efficiency and integrity. Every solution a healthcare provider evaluates related to access, must address these other areas adequately to warrant consideration. The issue of efficiency refers to the organizational impact of delivering and maintaining the chosen solution. Topics such as scalability, support infrastructures, cost, time to market, and functionality all fall under the umbrella of 'efficiency'. Likewise, the area of integrity covers both the privacy and security of the underlying data being accessed.

The Health Insurance Portability and Accountability Act (HIPAA) and the Health Information Technology for Economic and Clinical Health (HITECH) Act are some of the most significant federal actions related to achieving effective electronic

T. Tryfonas and I. Askoxylakis (Eds.): HAS 2014, LNCS 8533, pp. 209–220, 2014.
© Springer International Publishing Switzerland 2014

healthcare access nationally. HIPAA aims to use information technology (IT) to improve health insurance coverage and portability while also lowering costs and improving its quality [1]. Similarly, one of the major aspects of HITECH was designed to provide an incentive program for healthcare providers to implement and utilize electronic health record (EHR) systems to further the original goals of HIPAA [2]. Both of these laws and programs are intended to improve electronic healthcare access but many organizations are struggling to implement them and therefore the industry at large is not fully realizing their theoretical cumulative benefits.

Healthcare providers and payers have been attempting to achieve HIPAA compliance for nearly a decade. The sluggishness of HIPAA compliance is paralleled by the delayed introduction of EHR systems by healthcare organizations. The provisions of the Administrative Simplification, which is part of HIPAA, require the standardization of ePHI transactions to improve efficiency while also safeguarding the privacy and security of their data [3]. In order to achieve this standardization of ePHI and its transactions, many healthcare providers have or are in the process of implementing EHR systems. HIMSS Analytics, the authoritative source on EHR/EMR adoption trends, reports as of Q4 2013 almost 95% of 5,458 providers in the United States were in some stage of an EHR implementation but less than 3% had a complete deployment covering all possible aspects - data capture, storage, access, reporting, and exchange [4]. A high percentage of providers have started the process of adopting an EHR system but very few have actually completed the process.

While the road to HIPAA compliance and EHR adoption is proving elusive and costly, organizations clearly understand the importance and necessity of completing the undertakings. The lack of comprehensive, openly available frameworks for organizations to follow for healthcare information security compliance has become quite obvious. This research aims to fill some the implementation gaps that become readily apparent to all organizations that work towards providing patient access to EHR systems, while working within the HIPAA regulations. To this end, this research provides a comprehensive solution for healthcare providers to assist in the completion of the required attestation for Meaningful Use dictated by the U.S. Department of Health & Human Services (HHS). The product of this research will help organizations successfully review and assess their organization's technology policies and procedures and provide recommendations of how to mitigate potential findings. Specifically, the key contributions of this research to the healthcare information technology industry are:

- The creation of a comprehensive implementation guide for information security policies and procedures at an organizational level,
- A set of assessment tools for healthcare providers to self-evaluate the completeness and effectiveness of their current policies and procedures for attestation and ongoing compliance, and
- Enhanced security and privacy for a national healthcare provider that enabled qualification for Meaningful Use Stage 1.

The remainder of the paper is as follows: Section 2 presents the significance of the research to the healthcare industry and what related work has already been performed; Section 3 describes the framework itself; Section 4 describes how this research is already being applied and benefiting a typical national healthcare organization; finally Section 5 summarizes the goals of this research and its importance to the landscape of information security in healthcare.

2   Background and Related Work

Over the last few years, the healthcare industry has been giving information security special attention with such a focus being put on the implementation of electronic health record (EHR) systems. From the federal government's perspective, EHR systems are the solution to achieving many of the security and privacy measures that HIPAA laid out more than 10 years ago. The federal government has proved its national commitment to universal implementation of EHRs by enticing healthcare providers to start using EHR technology with very lucrative 'carrots' for both hospitals and private practices. In 2009, the federal government passed the HITECH Act which authorizes incentive payments through both Medicaid and Medicare to private practices and hospitals that use certified EHR technology to accomplish specific objectives in care delivery. The incentive program has been labeled 'Meaningful Use' as it rewards providers for demonstrating their meaningful use of EHR systems. In 2011 and 2012, EPs that met the Stage 1 requirements of Meaningful Use could have earned over $100,000 and hospitals over $2 million between Medicaid and Medicare [5]. Stage 1 was just the first of an anticipated 3 stages to ensure full EHR adoption nationally. The requirements for Stage 2 have been released and entities can begin receiving payment for meeting this stage in 2014. Looking ahead, the Stage 3 requirements are already out in a proposed form and it is tentatively scheduled for implementation in 2015. While HHS is offering incentives for early adoption, they are also levying penalties if Stage 1 hasn't been met by 2015.

The financial attraction for healthcare providers to participate in the HHS' Meaningful Use programs is evident, but still many providers have been unable to capitalize on the opportunity. The Centers for Medicare & Medicaid Services (CMS) released reports in June 2012 on the performance of the incentive programs through May 2012 [6]. These reports detailed how nationwide only slightly better than a 35% of all healthcare providers that have registered for the incentive programs are actually receiving the benefits of the Medicare program and barely over 50% are receiving benefits for the Medicaid program. The gap between the number of registered providers and those that are actually getting paid demonstrates that EHR adoption and attestation are considerable challenges.

In an effort to provide organizations a standardized approach for addressing the HIPAA regulations, the National Institute for Standards and Technology (NIST) produced special publication 800-66 that focused on the implementation of the HIPAA Security Rule [7]. This guide gets closer to the concept of mapping regulation to implementation but still does not provide specific actionable recommendations. Unfortunately there are no publically available HIPAA compliance assessment frameworks for organizations to follow. With a lack of clear direction, many entities have difficulty determining the best path for them to follow to satisfy each requirement. Further demonstrating this point is the emergence of numerous consulting firms that offer HIPAA compliance assessment. These companies offer both self and onsite assessment solutions. Kroll and Clearwater are both premier international security firms that offer HIPAA compliance services. Both of these companies state their assessment process includes questionnaires for self-assessment and intensive penetration testing for onsite assessments [8, 9]. These companies further state that their questionnaires and testing is based on the guidelines laid on in the NIST 800-66 publication and the HIPAA regulations themselves. The idea of having actionable plans based off these various publications as well as other industry best practices is not a novel concept in of itself. However, up to this point a solution has not been presented in an open academic format such that organizations can perform both the abstract style assessment from questionnaires and surveys as well as the active penetration testing without assistance. What is also missing from the current commercial offerings is the ability to see specifically the derivation of the all the assessment mechanisms so that they can be updated and adapted if and when regulations are added or changed. This mapping information, tying regulation to practice and assessment, is proprietary to the commercial offerings as it effectively constitutes the entire value of their engagements. Therefore as it stands today, 2 basic options have developed either contract with one of the private security assessment firms that specialize in HIPAA compliance or use the NIST guideline and muddle through alone. With many organizations' budget constraints, unfortunately the latter option tends to become the common option but ultimately without an apparent plan or timeline, it becomes extremely difficult for organizations to generate realistic cost estimates for their compliance efforts and likewise secure the necessary budgetary commitments [10]. This point has been demonstrated consistently since the first HIPAA implementations began. Consequently, national cost estimates of HIPAA efforts have eclipsed a factor of ten higher than what regulators estimated when the law was first enacted.

This research aims to lessen this challenge by providing a comprehensive guide for healthcare providers to follow to implement effective and complete information security policies and procedures. Further, using this research's assessment tools, organizations can evaluate and document the state of their current information security policy and procedure. The operational aspects are given specific attention in the assessment tools to help organizations complete the required Meaningful Use attestation.

3   Methodology

The proposed compliance framework [11] consists of three primary phases that culminate in complete HIPAA compliance for the healthcare provider. A well-documented and repeatable compliance framework will greatly speed up the assessment and testing process, yield more consistent results, present less risk to the normal business operations of the organization, and minimize the resources needed to perform the testing [12]. This research offers a comprehensive solution to organizational assessment and information security testing by providing step-by-step instructions for how to plan and perform information security compliance assessment and testing, how to analyze the results of the tests, and ultimately how to correct and mitigate any findings. The framework is designed to take an organization from the initial recognition of the need for compliance all the way through to implementation of any necessary changes to their environment. Further, the framework provides a post-compliance phase to ensure the healthcare provider maintains their compliance perpetually.

Phase 1 is a high-level assessment involving a thorough review of all policies, procedures, practices, and architectural designs. This first stage uses the Healthcare Information Security Guideline (HISG) produced by this research, to perform an organizational assessment of the healthcare provider. These assessments include a thorough review of the technical architecture, policy, and procedures. The results of these assessments and recommended mitigating actions are combined to produce a Comprehensive Organization Assessment and Roadmap (COAR) report. While the tasks are performed sequentially, there are feedback loops at almost every stage to reflect findings and feedback of successive steps to the preceding steps to ensure the COAR is organizationally relevant. The COAR will eventually serve as a detailed implementation guide for the organization to follow in order to achieve HIPAA compliance. The next phase performs a practical evaluation of the areas covered in the first phase and amends the COAR as necessary.

Phase 2 is a detailed, hands-on technical review and assessment of the IT environment. This phase measures and analyzes the actual performance of the systems and practices both against the theoretical goal of the HISG and the reported state of the organization provided in the assessment stage of Phase 1. The variances found in this effort are reflected in the COAR with appropriate mitigating actions. The technical review includes onsite visits, penetration and vulnerability testing, and a comprehensive review and assessment of all enterprise applications. The onsite visits consist of interviews with the personnel of the organization, both within the IT department and administration. It also involves inspections of various components of the IT environment including physical security controls for the data center and other locations where ePHI data is stored. In addition to the onsite visits, the IT staff is engaged to conduct penetration and vulnerability testing on the network and infrastructure portions of the organization. All associated testing is documented in the Healthcare Information Security Testing Directive (HISTD). The HISTD ensures the testing is standardized and easily repeated not only during the current review period but in future as part of the organization's continued compliance efforts. Additionally, an extensive review, categorization, and analysis of all enterprise applications are conducted in this phase. Each application is examined to determine if it interacts with ePHI and if so, in what way and for what function or purpose. Once each of the technical reviews is complete, the final task of this phase is to update the COAR report with all the findings and corrective actions identified in this phase. At the conclusion of this phase, the organization's entire IT environment has been methodically examined and evaluated.

The final phase involves taking the findings of the first two phases captured in the COAR and performing corrective actions as appropriate. Phase 3 is the implementation stage including changes related to technical configurations, policy, procedures, training, and documentation. At the start of the implementation phase, an implementation plan will be drafted, based off of the final COAR. While the findings and recommendations laid out in the COAR will provide specific tasks to complete, a plan needs to be developed of how to put those changes into operation. Meetings with stakeholders, IT staff, and administrative staff will be necessary to create an effective plan including an appropriate timeline. Once the plan has been developed, the actual implementation can be scheduled and started. In addition to the technical, policy, and procedural changes covered in the COAR implementation plan, this phase will also ensure that necessary documentation is created for both the impending changes and the preexisting environment. Further, this phase will include any necessary training – administrative, technical, or functional – related to the changes implemented, new procedures, and general security awareness training of the organization moving forward.

With the completion of the third phase the organization will have successfully achieved HIPAA compliance. In the efforts to attain compliance, there will also be a number of other tangible accomplishments. This framework presents a standardized Healthcare Information Security Guideline that can be referenced and updated for perpetuity. The HISG will serve as a critical resource for evaluating future enhancements and changes to the environment and ensure compliance is maintained. Additionally, the framework will provides a series of valuable tools for periodic testing of the security configurations. These tools will produce important actionable information as well as save time and effort in regards to the ongoing penetration and vulnerability testing procedures. Lastly, this framework will impart extremely useful training and awareness of security to the organization at all levels. The assessment exercises alone will orient the healthcare practitioners, technical staff and administration alike on the current state of their IT environment. It is often the case in HIPAA compliance efforts, that the simple lack of knowing how to measure compliance can greatly delay the entire effort. This research educates organizations as to what compliance requires, how these requirements translate into their specific environment, and how to satisfy them quickly, efficiently, and at a significantly reduced cost compared to tackling this effort alone.

4   Case Study

In order to validate the effectiveness of this research, it was vital that both the assessment tools and implementation guide be utilized in an actual healthcare provider's environment. In 2011 a partnership was formed with a national HIMSS Stage 6 [13] hospital (Hospital X) for a mutually beneficial relationship. The arrangement allowed this research to be field tested and the hospital would be provided a comprehensive assessment of their entire environment, including specific, actionable tasks to remedy any deficiencies uncovered. The partnership was scoped for a 3 year engagement, with roughly 1 year allocated per phase of a larger information technology assessment framework.

4.1   Organizational Assessment

Starting with Phase 1, a high-level assessment, involving a thorough review of all technology practices and architectural designs, was performed [14]. The information technology staff was interviewed extensively and asked both dichotomous and semantic differential questions. The measurement scale used to quantify the responses is based on the percentage the organization is in compliance with the guidelines laid out in the HIPAA guidelines [15] and NIST's recommendations [16] for HIPAA implementations. The measurement scale used to quantify the responses is based on the percentage the organization is in compliance with the guidelines laid out in the HIPAA guidelines [15] and NIST's recommendations [16] for HIPAA implementations. After all assessments were completed and reviewed, each area was rated based on the organization's degree of compliance. Compliance scores were provided for each section and sub-section to give indications where technical and organizational changes may be necessary. For each assessment, an initial draft, with any potential findings, was presented to the organization for their review and acceptance. The healthcare system either accepted the findings or disputed them and provided supporting documentation that demonstrates the finding was not valid. Following the review and acceptance process, the complete COAR report was produced and submitted to the organization for final review and acceptance.

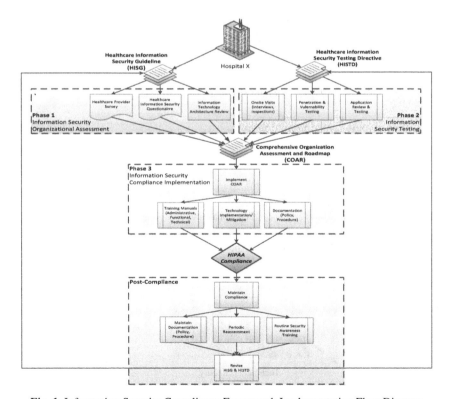

Fig. 1. Information Security Compliance Framework Implementation Flow Diagram

While a significant number of findings were made related to the current policies, practices, and architecture of the organization' IT environment, the partner health system's level of compliance is on par with the industry averages. The industry averages, derived from HIMSS sponsored research [17]; indicate most organizations are closer to full compliance to privacy than security. The partner hospital mirrored this pattern with Privacy Rule compliance at 86% while the Security Rule compliance was approximately 71%. Similar to many healthcare entities, the organization is relatively close to compliance but not at the federally mandated 100% compliance. The functional area that requires the most improvement by the organization is policy and procedures. This deficiency is fairly common throughout all industry with respect to IT and is also one of the hardest areas to correct. Changing policy and procedure requires changes to business practices and it is typically challenging for organizations to secure the leadership commitment and stakeholder buy-in to enact this type of change. Similarly, the organization has the most compliance issues with regard to the human technology interaction element of IT compared to the four solely technical areas.

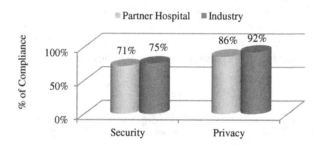

Fig. 2. Overall Compliance Performance

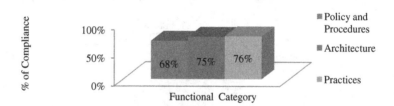

Fig. 3. Compliance per Functional Category

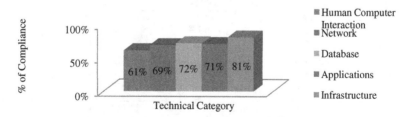

Fig. 4. Compliance per Technical Category

4.2   Security Testing Results

Phase 2 of the framework included a detailed, hands-on technical review and assessment of an organization's IT environment. The technical review included onsite visits, penetration and vulnerability testing, and a comprehensive review and assessment of all enterprise applications. At the conclusion of Phase 2, the organization's entire IT environment had been methodically examined, tested, and documented.

Table 1. Summary of Findings from Security Testing Phase

Subnet	Unique Hosts	Critical	High	Medium	Low	Totals
A	98	66	234	406	93	799
B	171	1583	2155	1611	415	5764
C	11	97	15	95	36	243
D	179	24	43	1025	195	1287
E	192	0	10	1114	187	1311
F	198	15	15	1146	196	1372
G	87	126	291	603	92	1112
H	26	359	436	219	50	1064
I	50	0	54	13	18	85
	1012	2270	3253	6232	1282	13037

Penetration testing and vulnerability scanning by their very nature are an exhaustive, iterative process that many times requires analysis from both operational and security perspectives. One of the most common issues that lead to vulnerabilities or exploitation is merely an ignorance that a particular host is present on the network or a host is running unnecessary or unexpected services [18]. The first step in any penetration test is to create a survey of the hosts that are present on the network and what services that are running. Many of these services are intentional and are functioning as expected. It is those hosts and related services that are unintentional that are of most significance for this initial survey. A number of intensive vulnerability scans were performed of Hospital X's environment. Initially the subnet A was examined exhaustively 98 hosts were discovered with 799 issues ranging from critical to low risk. Following this assessment, the decision was made to expand the network range being tested to include other subnets that held other production and development servers as well as clients and workstations. The expanded subnets included subnets B through I. The summary of the findings from both the initial assessment and the expanded testing can be seen in Table 1.

Through analysis of the security testing results, it was discovered that many of the specific critical and high risk vulnerabilities were found repetitively throughout the environment. Of the 5253 critical and high risk issues found, they are made up only 446 unique vulnerabilities. This finding suggested that enterprise wide patching processes and schedules as well as standardized deployment configurations of servers and workstations could mitigate many of these issues very quickly and reliably. Hospital X's technical staff was able to validate these findings and corresponding mitigation steps to resolve nearly 90% of the findings in a matter of weeks. The final phase of the compliance framework has just begun with the partner hospital. Phase 3 is the implementation stage and includes making changes related to technical configurations, policy, procedures, training, and documentation based on the findings of the earlier phases. Based on the findings that the assessments revealed in the earlier phases, a complete list of recommendations has been prepared and is under review by Hospital X. Once the mitigation recommendations have been analyzed, they will be incorporated into the COAR and become part of the compliance implementation plan. This will enable a final, detailed implementation plan to be prepared. The next step will be to have the healthcare provider review and approve the plan, then ultimately schedule and execute it.

5   Conclusion

The opportunity to apply this research at Hospital X proved to be an excellent exercise. Hospital X was struggling with getting their computing environment to 100% HIPAA compliance. Only just below the national average for compliance for the Security and Privacy rules at 71% and 86% respectively, they were well on their way to full compliance at the beginning of this collaboration. A significant factor that was prohibiting the organization from achieving complete compliance was their lack of a comprehensive procedure to evaluate their environment and reliably identify issues. Their approach to information security was much more reactive than proactive. This stance put their organization at risk legally, financially, and ultimately ethically. Furthermore, not having the ability to periodically assess and test their systems created an unawareness of where to focus their efforts to move forward. Beyond HIPAA, Hospital X was eager to satisfy the Meaningful Use objectives and complete the attestation to qualify for the more than $2 million annual incentive payment. Hospital X had begun an EHR implementation to some extent a number of years prior to the relationship, as they were already a HIMSS Stage 6 hospital, but were unsure of meeting all of the care delivery objectives to in order to complete the MU program.

This research was able to close the gap for Hospital X with regard to both HIPAA and Meaningful Use. Phase 1 of the Healthcare Information Security Compliance Framework provided a quantifiable starting point for the organization. At the completion of this assessment phase, it was clear where the deficiencies were in policy, procedure, and practice. Overall the hospital rated 68% compliant with regard to policy and formal procedures, only slightly better at 75% for architectural design, and approximately 76% for the organization's practices. These results provided a basis upon which to begin Phase 2, the Security Testing stage. The security testing process yielded even more issues with the computing environment by identifying 300 critical and high level findings across 98 production servers. Furthermore, another 5,253 critical and high level issues were found on 914 other systems (workstations and test/development systems) that were on the hospital's production network. Only 16% of the organization's systems did not have at least 1 issue that required attention. This was a concerning discovery as this meant 84% of the hospital's environment was exposed to some degree to unnecessary risk. While finding issues in an environment can oft times not be well received, the Hospital X staff were extremely receptive to working through the analysis of those findings and considering mitigating actions.

Certainly the goal of all organization's information technology staff is to create and maintain flawless, impenetrable systems. Unfortunately the reality is this goal is rarely reached and it is critical to have effective methods to continually evaluate all systems and practices to uncover issues when they are present.

Accessibility is a pillar of healthcare delivery. However, as soon as access is afforded, it is the ethical, legal, and financial responsibility of healthcare providers to ensure the integrity of the care delivery is upheld. HIPAA and EHR systems lay the foundation for satisfying these concerns. Unfortunately, these endeavors have proved challenging to accomplish with the absence of standardized, openly provided, implementation plans. Each HIPAA covered entity has been forced to approach these tasks from their localized, individual perspective and they are spending vast amounts of time, resources, and money trying to determine multiple paths towards the same goals. With a lack of direction, it takes significant effort to determine what needs to be done and how to do it even before organizations can get to the point of actual implementation. As such, most healthcare organizations are expending significant and superfluous effort in the assessment and planning stages. Technology has long thrived on the adoption of standards and this research contends that the issues of accessibility, integrity, and efficiency in healthcare information technology are no exception.

There is overwhelming consensus in the healthcare industry that the spirit of HIPAA is positive and beneficial to both patients and providers. Likewise, the move from paper and film to EHR systems is clearly the natural evolution of health information storage and data exchange. It has not been so much of a struggle for most healthcare providers to find answers to the Why; it has been the How that has kept these issues at the forefront of the healthcare industry for over a decade. The complexity and reach of HIPAA and the Meaningful Use programs across the entire United States has provided a seemingly endless parade of motivations for finding better methods to ensure their implementation. The guides and tools this research has produced will surely assist healthcare providers with the initial implementation of these initiatives as well as better equip organizations to maintain their ongoing compliance.

References

1. United States. Department of Health and Human Services. Office of Civil Rights, HIPAA Administrative Simplification (2006),
   http://www.hhs.gov/ocr/privacy/hipaa/administrative/
   privacyrule/adminsimpregtext.pdf (retrieved November 2011)
2. United States. Department of Health and Human Services. Center for Medicare and Medicaid Services, CMS EHR Meaningful Use Overview (2012), https://www.cms.
   gov/Regulations-and-Guidance/Legislation/EHRIncentive
   Programs/Meaningful_Use.html (last accessed June 2012)
3. United States. Department of Commerce. National Institute of Standards and Technology, An Introductory Resource Guide for Implementing the Health Insurance Portability and Accountability Act (HIPAA) Security Rule (rev 1) (2008),
   http://csrc.nist.gov/publications/nistpubs/800-66-Rev1/
   SP-800-66-Revision1.pdf (retrieved July 2011)

4. HIMSS Analytics, EMR Adoption Trends (2012),
   `http://www.himssanalytics.org/stagesGraph.asp`
   (last accessed October 2012)
5. United States. Department of HHS. The Office of the National Coordinator for Health
   Information Technology, EHR Incentive Programs (2012),
   `http://www.healthit.gov/providers-professionals/`
   `ehr-incentive-programs` (retrieved February 2013)
6. United States. Department of HHS. CMS, Data and Reports (2012),
   `http://www.webcitation.org/6EMwIm36I` (retrieved July 2012)
7. United States. Department of Health and Human Services. Center for Medicare and
   Medicaid Services, HIPAA Security Series – Security Standards: Technical Safeguards
   (2007), `http://www.hhs.gov/ocr/privacy/hipaa/administrative/`
   `securityrule/techsafeguards.pdf` (retrieved September 2011)
8. Kroll, HIPAA Self Risk Assessment (2013),
   `http://www.krollcybersecurity.com/hipaa-risk-assessment/`   (last
   accessed on November 2013)
9. Clearwater Compliance, Achieve HIPAA HITECH Compliance (2013), `https://www.`
   `hipaasecurityassessment.com/` (last accessed on November 2013)
10. Harle, C., Dewar, M.: Factors in Physician Expectations of a Forthcoming Electronic
    Health Record Implementation. In: Proceedings of the 45th Hawaii International
    Conference on System Sciences, pp. 2869–2878 (2012), doi:10.1109/HICSS.2012.277
11. Acharya, A., Coats, B., Saluja, A., Fuller, D.: A Roadmap for Information Security
    Assessment for Meaningful Use. In: Proceedings of the 2013 IEEE/ACM International
    Symposium on Network Analysis and Mining for Health Informatics, Biomedicine and
    Bioinformatics, Shanghai, China (2013)
12. United States. Department of Commerce. NIST, Technical Guide to Information Security
    Testing and Assessment (2008),
    `http://csrc.nist.gov/publications/nistpubs/800-115/`
    `SP800-115.pdf` (retrieved June 2012)
13. HIMSS Analytics, EMR Adoption Model (2011),
    `http://www.webcitation.org/6A1XGCtkJ` (last accessed on November 2011)
14. Coats, B., Acharya, S., Saluja, A., Fuller, D.: HIPAA Compliance: How Do We Get
    There? A Standardized Framework for Enabling Healthcare Information Security &
    Privacy. In: Proceedings of the 16th Colloquium for Information Systems Security
    Education, Orlando, Florida (2012)
15. United States. National Archives and Records Administration, Title 45 – Public Welfare,
    Subtitle A – Department of HHS, Part 164 – Security and Privacy (1996),
    `http://www.access.gpo.gov/nara/cfr/waisidx_07/45cfr164_07.`
    `html` (retrieved April 2012)
16. United States. Department of Commerce. National Institute of Standards and Technology,
    An Introductory Resource Guide for Implementing the Health Insurance Portability and
    Accountability Act (HIPAA) Security Rule, rev 1 (2008),
    `http://csrc.nist.gov/publications/nistpubs/800-66-Rev1/`
    `SP-800-66-Revision1.pdf` (retrieved July 2011)
17. Appari, A., Anthony, D.L., Johnson, M.E.: HIPAA Compliance: An Examination of
    Institutional and Market Forces (2009),
    `http://www.himss.org/foundation/docs/Appari_etal2009_`
    `HIPAAcompliance_20091023.pdf` (last accessed on November 2011)
18. United States. Department of Commerce. NIST, Technical Guide to Information Security
    Testing and Assessment (2008),
    `http://csrc.nist.gov/publications/nistpubs/800-115/SP800-`
    `115.pdf` (retrieved June 2012)

Rethinking the Smart Card Technology

Raja Naeem Akram[1] and Konstantinos Markantonakis[2]

[1] Department of Computer Science, University of Waikato, Hamilton, New Zealand
[2] ISG Smart Card Centre, Royal Holloway, University of London, United Kingdom
rnakram@waikato.ac.nz, k.markantonakis@rhul.ac.uk

Abstract. Creating security architectures and processes that directly interact with consumers, especially in consumer electronics, has to take into account usability, user-experience and skill level. Smart cards provide secure services, even in malicious environments, to end-users with a fairly straightforward limited usage pattern that even an ordinary user can easily deal with. The way the smart card industry achieves this is by limiting users' interactions and privileges on the smart cards they carry around and use to access different services. This centralised control has been the key to providing secure and reliable services through smart cards, while keeping the smart cards fairly useable for end-users. However, as smart cards have permeated into every aspect of modern life, users have ended up carrying multiple cards to perform mundane tasks, making smart card-based services a cumbersome experience. User Centric Smart Cards (UCSC) enable users to have all the services they might be accessing using traditional smart cards on a single device that is under their control. Giving "freedom of choice" to users increases their privileges, but the design requirement is to maintain the same level of security and reliability as traditional architectures while giving better user experience. In this paper, we will discuss the challenges faced by the UCSC proposal in balancing security with usability and "freedom of choice", and how it has resolved them.

1 Introduction

A smart card is a small, resource-restricted and highly security-sensitive device whose fundamental goal is to enable secure services for its users. These devices have been deployed in a large number of heterogeneous industries and used by a huge user base. A smart card has an embedded device which is part of the plastic body of credit cards and SIM cards. The inception of smart cards is rooted in the need to create a highly secure device that is then issued to users, some of whom could be malicious while others may be technologically naive. These represent the two extremes of user competence/knowledge of smart card technology. Since the 1970s, the smart card industry has created successful devices that satisfy the core requirement: a product that is intuitively simple but at the same time has high security assurance[1] - even in the possession of malicious users.

---

[1] Smart cards in certain industries like banking have stringent security requirements, including a detailed third party evaluation based on Common Criteria (CC) [1,2]. In contrast, while smart cards play a crucial role in security for mobile telecom, they do not require CC evaluation [3].

T. Tryfonas and I. Askoxylakis (Eds.): HAS 2014, LNCS 8533, pp. 221–232, 2014.
© Springer International Publishing Switzerland 2014

To balance the security requirements of a particular application and its usability is difficult at best [4]. An application (or device) in the possession of a malicious user makes balance difficult to achieve [5]. The assumption that an increase in usability might negatively affect the overall security of digital systems is not an exaggeration. Along with maintaining security and tamper-resistance while in the possession of a malicious user, a smart card also has to be designed in a manner whereby normal users don't have to perform complicated tasks [6]. An example is the number of steps a user might have to take to access an encrypted/signed email service. Johnny of Whitten and Tygar [7] was troubled by the complicated and technology-intense tasks that he had to perform to achieve the required security goal (i.e. encryption). In smart card deployments, users are not required to perform complicated tasks except for banking [8] or access control [9] applications. In banking and access control applications a user might be required to enter a four (or more) digit Personal Identification Number (PIN). Aside from this input, the user does not have to do anything extra: the smart card then performs the security-related tasks in a seamless manner [10].

To provide a high level of security and require the least user interactions to achieve this, the smart card industry preferred the Issuer Centric Smart Card Ownership Model (ICOM) [11]. The ICOM model enables a centralised authority to manage and issue smart cards to users. Examples of centralised authorities include telecom, banking and transport companies, also referred to as card issuers. Card issuers provide services to their customers via their smart cards; therefore, smart cards act like a secure token that give them access to available services. These card issuers maintain and manage the security features of the smart cards and in most cases do not require the user to perform any technologically challenging tasks (e.g. SIM cards in most of mobile phones) [12].

However, since 2005 technologies like smartphone "Apps" [13] and Near Field Communication (NFC) [14] have changed the smart card technology landscape. Furthermore, Johnny of today requires more features present on a single device. Smart cards can support multiple applications [15] on a single device, but such an initiative did not initially achieve widespread deployment. However, with the advent of NFC and the Apps culture, different organisations have proposed a multiple application smart card initiative termed the Trusted Service Manager (TSM) [16,17]. In addition to the TSM, there are other initiatives including our proposal, the User Centric Smart Card Ownership Model (UCOM) [18]. Furthermore, a model similar to the UCOM has been proposed by GlobalPlatform termed the "Consumer-Centric Model" [19]. In this paper, we discuss the usability and security considerations that we took into account when designing the UCOM.

1.1   Structure of the Paper

In section 2, we discuss the *open card* initiative which was one of the first attempts to offer users "freedom of choice". In subsequent sections, we briefly describe the UCOM and user requirements that became the core of the UCOM design. Section 4 details selected operations of the UCOM to show how the principle of least interaction is used in practice. Finally, in section 5 we conclude the paper.

2 Open Cards

In this section, we briefly discuss the open card initiative and concerns about the usability of this proposal.

2.1 Brief Introduction

It is difficult to give an exact definition of open cards. In general, however, the term "open card" is used to refer to blank smart cards that a user can purchase from a supplier. After purchasing the smart card, the user can perform the role previously performed by the card issuer and either accept or buy applications from different application providers. These applications can be installed onto the user's card and used to access any associated services. The whole card is under the user's control, similar to the card issuer in the ICOM. Therefore, we can say that the open card initiative is an ICOM framework with the user replacing the card issuer.

Traditional smart card frameworks like Java Card, Multos, and GlobalPlatform were considered suitable for such a scenario. Most of these frameworks were built to support the ICOM, and by making the user an issuer, they did not require any substantial changes. However, as implied by Pierre Girard [20], such a mechanism would require an application provider to issue their application to users to install on their smart card. This would require the application provider to trust the user not to reverse engineer or corrupt the application.

Such a scenario does not ensure the security, protection of intellectual property, and reliability of an application, as an application provider does not have any control over the smart card that hosts its application. The main reason for this lack of control on the part of the application provider is the unavailability of any guarantees regarding the security and operational behaviour of smart cards. Similar security issues are raised by Chaumette and Sauveron in [21] and they make the open card initiative in its current form unsuitable for a user-centric framework.

2.2 Issues with Open Card Model

In this section, we will only discuss issues related to the open card model from the usability and least interaction point of view. As discussed in the previous section, the open card model gives a user the ability to download an application to their device of choice (e.g. desktop or laptop). Once the application is downloaded to the user's device, she can then transfer the application to her smart cards. The issue is transferring the application to the smart card: anyone who has worked with installing applications on embedded devices knows that such a task is not trivial. Furthermore, from a security point of view the user has to ensure that during this process no malicious entity can corrupt the application. The user has to perform several tasks and ensure the safe transfer of the application to the smart card, increasing rather than decreasing user interaction. In the UCOM, the least interaction principle requires the user to either not be involved or if required, her involvement to be restricted to the minimum level possible.

3   User Centric Smart Card Model

In this section, we briefly discuss the core design of the UCOM and associated user requirements that became the basis of our subsequent rethinking of smart card technology.

3.1   User: The Core of Design

A user acquires a User Centric Smart Card (UCSC) from a UCSC supplier, and then manages it through software referred to as Card Application Management Software (CAMS): shown in figure 1. The CAMS only provide an interface with the UCSC and there are no security requirements for it (i.e. as part of the design we consider that the CAMS implementation can be modified by a malicious user).

The user can then request a Service Provider (SP): an application provider that utilises the UCSC functionality to provide a secure, reliable and privacy-preserving service. The SP will then request the security and reliability verification and validation of the UCSC [22]. Only after the SP is satisfied with the security and functional-support of the UCSC it will lease its applications. The application lease is governed by a security and functional-support policy of the SP, referred to as an Application Lease Policy (ALP) [11]. The ALP is an SP-specific document and an SP can reject a request for application lease if the requesting UCSC does not support the SP's ALP. Once the application is leased to the UCSC, it can be accessed by the user at any compatible computing platform shown as a Service Access Point (SAP)/Host Platforms in Figure 1.

For the smart card environment, a downloaded application might be a stand-alone application that does not require any accompanying application on the host platform. In the case of a smart card environment, the host platform is the card reader that communicates with the smart card. The reader needs to have an application (of its own) that communicates with the smart card but this requirement is not imposed by the smart card's applications, and is installed separately by the entity that maintains the reader. For example, in the banking and telecom sector the reader only has to conform to a standardised application (e.g. EMV [8]); however, in the transport-service scenario it varies, as different operators install their own readers with customised applications (i.e. TFL [23] and Octopus [24]). However, in case of hand-held and traditional computing devices, applications installed on a UCSC might be part of a larger application that is actually installed on the host platform.

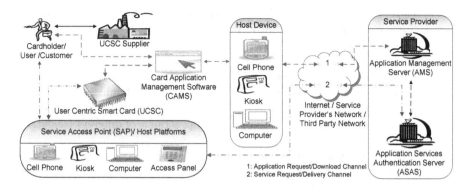

Fig. 1. User Centric Smart Card Framework

3.2   User Requirements

A cardholder is an entity that uses a smart card to access authorised services. In the UCOM, the control of a smart card is with its user. Therefore, cardholders have complete control over the choice of applications on their smart cards. They have the flexibility to change the installed applications on their smart cards. Furthermore, they can install or delete any applications they are entitled to, at their convenience. The framework will provide the mechanism that ensures secure control and ubiquitous management of applications on smart cards. A cardholder's requirements in UCOM are listed below:

1. **Security:** If a smart card is inherently insecure, or if it becomes vulnerable to new threats, it can affect the security of applications installed on the card. We cannot expect that each cardholder is technically capable of ensuring and managing the security of the smart card; therefore, a cardholder would require an assurance that the card platform will be secure and reliable even if it is in the possession of a technologically naive or malicious user.

2. **Privacy:** Applications installed on a smart card represent the identities of the cardholder in different contexts. For example a college card, a health card and a credit card represent a cardholder's identity as a student, a patient, and a consumer respectively. These identities are in the form of applications that have some unique characteristics (e.g. student ID, patient ID, and Primary Account Number: PAN) to identify a particular user. Therefore, applications on a smart card can be treated as the identities of the cardholder. In the ICOM, these identities may not have any connection with each other. However, in the UCOM, any or all of these identities could be on the same card, creating a privacy issue if one application becomes aware of the existence of others on a smart card. Therefore, the identities on a particular card should not have any links between them. For example, a college application should not be able to find out about a medical application(s) installed on the same card.

3. **Least Interaction (Seamless Framework):** Most users do not understand the technology behind a particular product (i.e. mobile phone applications).

Therefore, the framework should not be based on the assumption that an average user can perform technically challenging tasks. The UCOM should be seamless and should perform all necessary tasks by itself, only involving the user when required.

4. **Interoperability:** The smart card user will not want to buy a separate smart card for each application. Smart card suppliers should provide cards that support most of the available functionalities and SPs should offer applications in many formats as possible, to support a range of different execution environments.

5. **Ownership Mechanism:** A mechanism is required that securely authenticates the owner of the smart card and facilitates the exercise of her privileges (i.e. installing and deleting applications).

4   Designing Security for Malicious and Tech-Illiterate Users

In this section, we explore a few of the UCOM operations to show how a secure system can be designed based on minimal user interaction.

4.1   Usability and Security

Selected UCOM operations that had to take into account the security and usability are: User Ownership Acquisition, Application Installation, Application Sharing and Decommissioning Process. Crucially these operations are managed by the card issuer in the ICOM without any user input. However, by giving "freedom of choice" to the user in the UCOM, the outcome of these operations affect the user's device.

4.1.1   User Ownership Acquisition

A UCSC in its pre-issuance state is under the default ownership of the UCSC manufacturer. When a user takes control of the smart card, it will initiate an ownership acquisition process. The process is described below:

1. The user initiates the ownership acquisition process through the Card Application Management Software (CAMS) shown in Figure 1.
2. The UCSC requests the default ownership credentials, which are communicated to the user by the card manufacturer. In response, the user will provide the relevant default credentials.
3. On verification of the credentials, the UCSC checks the mode of platform assurance and validation selected by the user. The supported modes are offline and online attestation [25,26]. Depending upon the user's choice the UCSC proceeds with the security attestation process.
4. Once the assurance validation is communicated to the CAMS, the user can compare the smart card features with those stated by the card manufacturer at the time of purchase. If satisfied, the user will provide her credentials

and they are used to authenticate the user to the UCSC for management operations (e.g. application installation, and deletion). The credentials can be based on a Personal Identification Number (PIN), a password, a passphrase, or biometric data [27] depending upon the card manufacturer, and the user's requirements.

The decommissioning process (section 4.1.4) is used when a user relinquishes control of a UCSC to re-sell or scrap the device. The process is similar to ownership acquisition but this time the user requests ownership delegation that will delete the user's space and any applications she has installed in it.

4.1.2   Application Installation

In this section, the processes that support the secure transmission and installation of an application are discussed. The installation process discussed in this section builds additional checks around the application installation protocols [28,29,30].

The installation request will initiate the process of acquiring an application from an SP's application server (AMS in figure 1) and installing it on a smart card. The entire process can be divided into three sub-processes: 1) Downloading, 2) Localisation, and 3) Application Registration. These sub-processes are explained as below.

1. Downloading: The downloading of an application is initiated by the smart card, through a secure channel protocol [28,29]. At the conclusion of the secure channel protocol, both entities generate a set of keys for application download and domain management. The smart card then generates an SP's domain, provided it has enough space to accommodate it. The SP and smart card will then start the application downloading process. The SP will first generate a signature on the application, then encrypt and MAC it before sending it to the smart card.

   The smart card checks the generated MAC, decrypts the application, and verifies the signature. A decrypted application is not a fully installed application — it is the equivalent of copying an application to a memory location. The next step is to verify whether the application complies with the smart card's operational and security policy. For this purpose an on-card byte code verification is performed [31], which is already mandated by the Java Card 3 [32]; this can be based on well-defined on-card byte code verification proposals [33].

   The UCSC does not mandate the security evaluation of an application. However, certain applications require evaluation due to government or industry regulations (e.g. EMV applications). In these cases, an SP's application(s) provide an evaluation certificate [22]. To verify the certificate the smart card would have to calculate the hash of the downloaded application and compare it with the Application Assurance Certificate (AAC) [22].

2. Localisation: First, the application will be personalised by the SP. Depending upon the relationship between the cardholder and the SP, with the SP's discretion the personalisation can include acquiring user details (in post- and no-registration scenarios), and cryptographic key generation. Furthermore, if the SP is issuing a card-bound lease then it would make sense to generate on-card cryptographic keys. These keys will automatically become device identifiers because each lease of the application will have a specific set of keys. After personalisation, the downloaded application establishes connections with various on-card services (i.e. shareable resources) that are provided by partner applications. To access a partner's application services, the downloaded application will establish an application-sharing relationship that is discussed in detail in [34,35].

3. Application Registration: The final stage of an application installation is application registration by the SP. Registration allows the application to access sanctioned services. Once the SP registers (sanctions) the downloaded application, the smart card will also make it selectable to an off-card entity. By making an application selectable, the smart card allows the application to execute and access on-card services and communicate with off-card entities.

4.1.3   Application Sharing

In this section, we discuss the architecture of the proposed firewall mechanism for UCSCs. The proposed firewall mechanism is based on the Java Card firewall mechanism as illustrated in Figure 2 that is discussed subsequently.

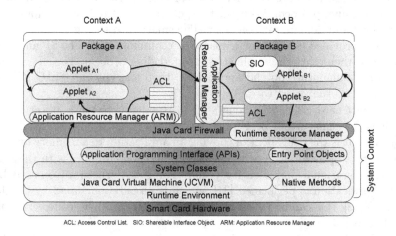

ACL: Access Control List.   SIO: Shareable Interface Object.   ARM: Application Resource Manager

Fig. 2. Architecture of the UCTD firewall mechanism

A request for an application's shareable resource is handled by the application's Application Resource Manager (ARM) and the Runtime Resource Manager (RRM) handles access to the platform's resources (APIs): see figure 2.

The RRM controls access to the entry point objects that are used to access platform services. The resource manager will enforce the security policy for applications as defined by the respective SPs, limiting access to the platform resources as stipulated by the policy.

For each application (package), an Application Resource Manager (ARM) is introduced. This component will act as the authentication and resource allocation point. A client application will request a server application's ARM to enable the sharing of resources. The ARM will decide whether to grant the request based upon the client's credentials (associated privileges). At the time of application installation, the ARM also establishes a shareable interface connection with the platform, enabling the application to access methods that are essential for the application execution. The platform can access any method in the application context only after authorisation from the application's SP. The ARM also receives information regarding the requesting application. If the request is, from the system context, for a method that is not allowed to be accessed by the platform, then the ARM will indicate a security exception.

An Access Control List (ACL) is a private list and it is used to facilitate the implementation of hierarchical access mechanisms and privilege revocations. An ACL can be updated remotely by its corresponding SP (when the application connects with the SP's servers, the SP can update the ACL), changing the behaviour of its application's sharing mechanism. The ACL holds lists of granted permissions, received permissions (permissions to access other application's resources) and a cryptographic certificate revocation list of client applications. The structure of an ACL is under the sole discretion of its SP and it is stored as part of the ARM.

The operations of the firewall can be sub-divided into two distinctive phases. In phase one, a binding is established between the client and the server applications. This process includes authentication of the client's credentials and access privileges by the server's ARM. In the second phase, the client application requests resources in line with the privileges sanctioned by the ARM. In both these phases, the firewall mechanism facilitates individual authorised applications to accomplish the application sharing, while prohibiting unauthorised applications from accessing the resources of an application.

4.1.4   Decommissioning Process

The decommissioning process involves deletion of all applications from a UCSC and removal of any user-specific data stored by the applications and card management system. The decommissioning process is initiated by the user in a manner similar to the ownership acquisition process (section 4.1.1). However, in the decommissioning process the user requests a UCSC to delete all applications in a manner similar to the one discussed in the previous section but this time the UCSC does not check for dependencies. Once all applications are deleted, the card security manager will delete the user-specific cryptographic keys (e.g. user signature key) and associated certificates. It will then request the deletion of ownership credentials that the user has set during the ownership acquisition process. After the decommissioning process is completed, the UCSC reverts to the state it was in when the user acquired it from the card manufacturer (or UCSC suppliers). In other words, it is a blank UCSC.

5   Conclusion

The proposal for the UCOM began with a simple question "can a user have application control on a security-sensitive device like a smart card in a simple but secure manner?". Although work on the UCOM has not yet resolved all the issues and modifications required to move the traditional smart card architecture to the UCOM. However, work to date has a common foundation namely "least interaction". One of the core requirements: "least interaction", requires user's involvement in different UCSC management operations to be kept to a minimum. This enabled us to design a secure, yet user friendly framework to support UCSC.

The work done up till now on the concept of UCOM has shown that a robust and secure system does not have to be difficult for ordinary users to understand/use. We consider that such effects, making the security of a system intuitive, seamless and requiring the minimum of user interaction, might lead the way for better, more reliable and secure systems.

References

1. Dusart, P., Sauveron, D., Tai-Hoon, K.: Some Limits of Common Criteria Certification. International Journal of Security and its Applications 2(4), 11–20 (2008)
2. Sauveron, D., Dusart, P.: Which Trust Can Be Expected of the Common Criteria Certification at End-User Level? Future Generation Communication and Networking 2, 423–428 (2007)
3. Xenakis, C., Merakos, L.: Security in Third Generation Mobile Networks. Computer Communications 27(7), 638–650 (2004)
4. Schultz, E.E.: Research on Usability in Information Security. Computer Fraud & Security 2007(6), 8–10 (2007)
5. Anderson, R., Moore, T.: Information Security Economics – and Beyond. In: Menezes, A. (ed.) CRYPTO 2007. LNCS, vol. 4622, pp. 68–91. Springer, Heidelberg (2007)
6. Askoxylakis, I.G., Pramateftakis, M., Kastanis, D.D., Traganitis, A.P.: Integration of a Secure Mobile Payment System in a GSM/UMTS SIM Smart Card. In: Proceedings of the Fourth IASTED International Conference on Communication, Network and Information Security. CNIS 2007, pp. 40–50. ACTA Press, Anaheim (2007)
7. Whitten, A., Tygar, J.D.: Why Johnny Can'T Encrypt: A Usability Evaluation of PGP 5.0. In: Proceedings of the 8th Conference on USENIX Security Symposium. SSYM 1999, vol. 8, p. 14. USENIX Association, CA (1999)
8. EMV 4.2, Online, EMVCo Specification 4.2 (May 2008),
   http://www.emvco.com/specifications.aspx?id=155
9. Entity Authentication Assurance Framework, ITU-T, Geneva, Switzerland, Recommendation ITU-T X.1254 (September 2012),
   http://www.itu.int/rec/T-REC-X.1254-201209-I

10. Mitrokotsa, A., Sheng, Q.Z., Maamar, Z.: User-driven RFID applications and challenges. Personal and Ubiquitous Computing 16(3), 223–224 (2012)
11. Akram, R.N., Markantonakis, K., Mayes, K.: Application Management Framework in User Centric Smart Card Ownership Model. In: Youm, H.Y., Yung, M. (eds.) WISA 2009. LNCS, vol. 5932, pp. 20–35. Springer, Heidelberg (2009)
12. Petroulakis, N.E., Askoxylakis, I.G., Tryfonas, T.: Life-logging in Smart Environments: Challenges and Security Threats. In: 2012 IEEE International Conference on Communications (ICC), pp. 5680–5684. IEEE (2012)
13. Laugesen, J., Yuan, Y.: What Factors Contributed to the Success of Apple's iPhone? In: Proceedings of the 2010 Ninth International Conference on Mobile Business / 2010 Ninth Global Mobility Roundtable. ICMB-GMR 2010, pp. 91–99. IEEE Computer Society, Washington, DC (2010)
14. Near Field Communications (NFC). Simplifying and Expanding. Contactless Commerce, Connectivity, and Content, ABI Research, Oyster Bay, NY (2006), http://www.abiresearch.com/research/1000885-Near-Field_Communications_(NFC)
15. Sauveron, D.: Multiapplication Smart Card: Towards an Open Smart Card? Inf. Secur. Tech. Rep. 14(2), 70–78 (2009)
16. The GlobalPlatform Proposition for NFC Mobile: Secure Element Management and Messaging, GlobalPlatform, White Paper (April 2009)
17. Mobile NFC Services, GSM Association, White Paper Version 1.0 (2007), http://www.gsmworld.com/documents/nfc_services_0207.pdf
18. Akram, R.N., Markantonakis, K., Mayes, K.: A Paradigm Shift in Smart Card Ownership Model. In: Apduhan, B.O., Gervasi, O., Iglesias, A., Taniar, D., Gavrilova, M. (eds.) Proceedings of the 2010 International Conference on Computational Science and Its Applications (ICCSA 2010), pp. 191–200. IEEE Computer Society, Fukuoka (2010)
19. GlobalPlatform, A.: New Model: The Consumer-Centric Model and How It Applies to the Mobile Ecosystem, GlobalPlatform, Whitepaper (March 2013)
20. Girard, P.: Which Security Policy for Multiplication Smart Cards? In: Proceedings of the USENIX Workshop on Smartcard Technology on USENIX Workshop on Smartcard Technology, p. 3. USENIX Association, Berkeley (1999), http://portal.acm.org/citation.cfm?id=1267115.1267118
21. Chaumette, S., Sauveron, D.: New Security Problems Raised by Open Multiapplication Smart Cards. LaBRI, Université Bordeaux 1, pp. 1332–04 (2004)
22. Akram, R.N., Markantonakis, K., Mayes, K.: A Dynamic and Ubiquitous Smart Card Security Assurance and Validation Mechanism. In: Rannenberg, K., Varadharajan, V., Weber, C. (eds.) SEC 2010. IFIP AICT, vol. 330, pp. 161–172. Springer, Heidelberg (2010)
23. London Underground: Oyster Card. London Underground. United Kingdom, https://oyster.tfl.gov.uk/oyster/entry.do (visited June 2010)
24. EnglishOctopus. Octopus Holdings Ltd. Hong Kong, China, http://www.octopus.com.hk/home/en/index.html (visited December 2010)
25. Akram, R.N., Markantonakis, K., Mayes, K.: Remote Attestation Mechanism based on Physical Unclonable Functions. In: Zhou, C.M.J., Weng, J. (eds.) The 2013 Workshop on RFID and IoT Security (RFIDsec 2013 Asia). IOS Press, Guangzhou (November 2013)
26. Akram, R.N., Markantonakis, K., Mayes, K.: Remote Attestation Mechanism for User Centric Smart Cards Using Pseudorandom Number Generators. In: Qing, S., Zhou, J., Liu, D. (eds.) ICICS 2013. LNCS, vol. 8233, pp. 151–166. Springer, Heidelberg (2013)

27. Bringer, J., Chabanne, H., Kevenaar, T.A.M., Kindarji, B.: Extending Match-On-Card to Local Biometric Identification. In: Fierrez, J., Ortega-Garcia, J., Esposito, A., Drygajlo, A., Faundez-Zanuy, M. (eds.) BioID MultiComm2009. LNCS, vol. 5707, pp. 178–186. Springer, Heidelberg (2009),
    http://www.springerlink.com/content/b16016708315549v/fulltext.pdf
28. Akram, R.N., Markantonakis, K., Mayes, K.: A Privacy Preserving Application Acquisition Protocol. In: Geyong Min, F.G.M. (ed.) 11th IEEE International Conference on Trust, Security and Privacy in Computing and Communications (IEEE TrustCom 2012). IEEE Computer Society, Liverpool (June 2012)
29. Akram, R.N., Markantonakis, K., Mayes, K.: A Secure and Trusted Channel Protocol for the User Centric Smart Card Ownership Model. In: 12th IEEE International Conference on Trust, Security and Privacy in Computing and Communications (IEEE TrustCom 2013). IEEE Computer Society, Melbourne (2013)
30. Akram, R.N., Markantonakis, K., Mayes, K.: Coopetitive Architecture to Support a Dynamic and Scalable NFC Based Mobile Services Architecture. In: Chim, T.W., Yuen, T.H. (eds.) ICICS 2012. LNCS, vol. 7618, pp. 214–227. Springer, Heidelberg (2012)
31. Basin, D., Friedrich, S., Posegga, J., Vogt, H.: Java Bytecode Verification by Model Checking. In: Halbwachs, N., Peled, D.A. (eds.) CAV 1999. LNCS, vol. 1633, pp. 491–494. Springer, Heidelberg (1999)
32. Java Card Platform Specification: Classic Edition; Application Programming Interface, Runtime Environment Specification, Virtual Machine Specification, Connected Edition; Runtime Environment Specification, Java Servlet Specification, Application Programming Interface, Virtual Machine Specification, Sample Structure of Application Modules, Sun Microsystem Inc Std. Version 3.0.1 (May 2009)
33. Basin, D., Friedrich, S., Gawkowski, M.: Verified Bytecode Model Checkers. In: Carreño, V.A., Muñoz, C.A., Tahar, S. (eds.) TPHOLs 2002. LNCS, vol. 2410, pp. 47–66. Springer, Heidelberg (2002)
34. Akram, R.N., Markantonakis, K., Mayes, K.: Firewall Mechanism in a User Centric Smart Card Ownership Model. In: Gollmann, D., Lanet, J.-L., Iguchi-Cartigny, J. (eds.) CARDIS 2010. LNCS, vol. 6035, pp. 118–132. Springer, Heidelberg (2010)
35. Akram, R.N., Markantonakis, K., Mayes, K.: Application-Binding Protocol in the User Centric Smart Card Ownership Model. In: Parampalli, U., Hawkes, P. (eds.) ACISP 2011. LNCS, vol. 6812, pp. 208–225. Springer, Heidelberg (2011)

Compositional Security Modelling
Structure, Economics, and Behaviour

Tristan Caulfield[1], David Pym[1], and Julian Williams[2]

[1] Department of Computer Science,
University College London, UK
{t.caulfield,d.pym}@ucl.ac.uk
[2] Business School,
University of Durham, UK
julian.williams@durham.ac.uk

Abstract. Security managers face the challenge of formulating and implementing policies that deliver their desired system security postures — for example, their preferred balance of confidentiality, integrity, and availability — within budget (monetary and otherwise). In this paper, we describe a security modelling methodology, grounded in rigorous mathematical systems modelling and economics, that captures the managers' policies and the behavioural choices of agents operating within the system. Models are executable, so allowing systematic experimental exploration of the system-policy co-design space, and compositional, so managing the complexity of large-scale systems.

1 Introduction

Security managers in all types of organizations must routinely choose policies and technologies that protect the business-critical infrastructure of their systems. These choices are constrained by both regulatory and economic circumstances and managers necessarily must make trade-offs between security and such operational constraints. When faced with analysing these trade-offs security managers currently have very limited tools to aid them in systematic decision-making. Consequently, managers must rely on their own judgement when selecting their implementation choices. While this approach does not necessarily lead to poor decision-making, it does have some inherent weaknesses. Decisions made in this fashion may or may not be optimal, but typically cannot be shown to be optimal, and their relative effectiveness and value cannot be established, because the manager has no rigorous means of comparison with other approaches. Moreover, any decisions taken by the manager cannot be shared in a meaningful way with other stakeholders, such as operations managers, finance managers, or senior strategists.

Our hypothesis, supported by a body of exploratory (e.g., [1,2]) and theoretical (e.g., [13,14]) work, is that a specific combination of mathematical systems modelling of the structure and dynamics of organizations and their behaviour and economic modelling of their security policy design and decision-making can deliver a framework within which the consequences of security policy and technology co-design decisions can be predicted and explored experimentally. The security systems of interest are often complex

T. Tryfonas and I. Askoxylakis (Eds.): HAS 2014, LNCS 8533, pp. 233–245, 2014.

assemblies of agents, be they software or human, policies, and technology. Handling substantive system complexity is challenging for reasoning tools, as has been observed, for example, in the world of formal methods in software engineering. The lesson that has been learned is that such tools must be compositional.

In Section 2, we summarize the system modelling theory, its implementation in the Julia language, and explain our use of production and utility functions to model policies and decision-making in the context of our experimental methodology. In Section 3, we describe two examples of system security policies and present a range of experimental results. Section 4 explains how our approach allows models to be composed systematically. We summarize our contribution and discuss further work in Section 5.

2   Systems and Security Modelling

2.1   System Modelling

The notion of process has been explored in some detail by the semantics community. Concepts like resource and location have, however, usually been treated as second class ([18] is a partial exception). Whilst there are some good theoretical reasons to do this, in [5] we explore what can be gained by developing an approach in which the structures present in modelling languages are given a rigorous theoretical treatment as first-class citizens. We ensure that each component — location, resource, and process — is handled compositionally. In addition to the structural components of models, we consider also the environment within which a system exists:

Environment: All systems exist within an external environment, which is typically treated as a source of events that are incident upon the system rather than being explicitly stated. Mathematically, environments are represented stochastically, using probability distributions that are sampled in order to provide such events [5].

The key structural components are considered, drawing upon classical distributed systems theory — see, for example, [7] — below.

Location: Places are connected by (directed) links. Locations may be abstracted and refined provided the connectivity of the links and the placement of resources is respected. Mathematically, the axioms for locations [5] are satisfied by various graphical and topological structures, including simple directed graphs and hyper-graphs [5];

Resource: The notion of resource captures the components of the system that are manipulated by its processes (see below). Resources include things like computer memory, system operating staff, or system users, as well as money. Conceptually, the axioms of resources are that they can be combined and compared. We model this notion using *(partial commutative) resource monoids* [19,5]: structures $\mathbf{R} = (\mathbf{R}, \sqsubseteq, \circ, e)$ with carrier set $\mathbf{R}$, preorder $\sqsubseteq$, and partial binary composition $\circ$ with unit e, and which satisfies the *bifunctoriality condition*: $R \sqsubseteq R'$ and $S \sqsubseteq S'$ and $R \circ S$ is defined implies $R' \circ S'$ is defined and $R \circ S \sqsubseteq R' \circ S'$, for all $R, S, R', S' \in \mathbf{R}$.

Process: The notion of process captures the (operational) dynamics of the system. Processes manipulate resources in order to deliver the system's intended services. Mathematically, we use algebraic representation of processes based on the ideas in [17], integrated with the notions of resource and location [5].

Let Act be a commutative monoid of *actions*, with multiplication written as juxtaposition and unit 1. Let $a, b \in$ Act, etc., so that their multiplication is written ab, etc.. The execution of models based on these concepts, as formulated in [5], is described by a transition system with a basic structural operational semantics judgement [17] of the form $L, R, E \xrightarrow{a} L', R', E'$, which is read as 'the occurrence of the action a evolves the process E, relative to resources R at locations L, to become the process E', which then evolves relative to resources R' at locations L''. The meaning of this judgement is given by a structural operational semantics [17]. The basic case, also know as 'action prefix', is the rule

$$\frac{}{L, R, a : E \xrightarrow{a} L', R', E'} \quad \mu(L, R, a) = (L', R').$$

Here μ is a 'modification' function from locations, resources, and actions (assumed to form a monoid) to locations and resources that describes the evolution of the system when an action occurs. Suppressing locations for now, a partial function $\mu : \text{Act} \times \mathbf{R} \to \mathbf{R}$ is a *modification* if it satisfies the following conditions for all a, b, R, S: $\mu(1, R) = R$; if $R \circ S$ and $\mu(a, R) \circ \mu(b, S)$ are defined, then $\mu(ab, R \circ S) = \mu(a, R) \circ \mu(b, S)$.

There are also rules giving the semantics to combinators for concurrent composition, choice, and hiding — similar to restriction in SCCS and other process algebras (e.g., [17]) — as well for recursion. For example, the rule for synchronous concurrent composition of processes is

$$\frac{L, R, E \xrightarrow{a} L', R', E' \qquad M, S, F \xrightarrow{b} M', S', F'}{L \cdot M, R \circ S, E \times F \xrightarrow{ab} L' \cdot M', R' \circ S', E' \times F'},$$

where we presume, in addition to the evident monoidal compositions of actions and resources, a composition on locations (here written as $\cdot$). The rules for the other combinators, with suitable coherence conditions on the modification functions, follow similar patterns [5]. Note that our choice of a synchronous calculus retains the ability to model asynchrony [17,8] (this doesn't work the other way round).

For another example, a key process construct for this paper is non-deterministic choice or sum:

$$\frac{L, R, E_i \xrightarrow{a_i} L', R', E'}{L, R, E_1 + E_2 \xrightarrow{a_i} L', R', E'} \quad i = 1, 2.$$

For example, suppressing location and resource, a process $(a : E) + (b : F) + (c : G)$ will evolve to become E, F, or G depending on the next action being a, b, or c.

Along with the transition system described here comes, in the sense of Hennessy–Milner [11,5], a modal logic [5] with basic judgement $L, R, E \models \phi$, where the proposition ϕ expresses a property of the process E executing with respect to resources R at location L. This logic includes, in addition to the kinds of connectives and modalities usually encounter in process logics, a number of substructural connectives and modalities that are helpful in reasoning compositional about resource-bounded systems. This modal logic can also be extended to the stochastic world. An account of this logic and its extensions is beyond our present scope, but will be of interest in further work.

2.2 Representing the Concepts in Julia

As discussed in Section 2.1, our mathematical modelling framework employs the classical distributed systems concepts of location, resource, process, and environment. In this work, we represent these concepts using the Julia language [15,3]. The language is designed for scientific and numeric computing and also has support for co-routines, making it ideal for process-based simulation. We represent the modelling concepts in Julia as follows:

- Environment is handled by Julia's ability to sample probability distributions;
- Locations are instances of a type with associated links to other locations (and so are graph-like) and associated resources;
- Resources are instances of a type on which algebraic operations (such as those required for a resource monoid) can be defined;
- Processes are represented by co-routines that provide us with the necessary constructs for concurrent execution and choice.

The modelling language Gnosis [6,5] provides, by construction, a reference implementation for the mathematical constructs explained in Section 2.1. However, Julia provides a superior programming environment that is convenient for practical modelling.

Models constructed in Julia are executed in order to explore the consequences of system- and security policy-design decisions, including representations of the behaviour of agents (see subsequent sections). Julia models are designed in layers. At the bottom, they provide functionality for constructing locations, resources, and processes, and executing the latter. On top of this is code for agents and decision-making within the model (again, see subsequent sections). Finally, there is functionality specific to security simulations. This includes a library of standard components, such as implementations of access control mechanisms, that can be configured as required for a particular model.

The full code for the models presented in this paper is available at

`http://www.cs.ucl.ac.uk/staff/D.Pym/FTNCTC-Julia-code.pdf.`

2.3 Productivity and Utility

The processes described above provide a representation for the agents that inhabit and explore a security system.

As they explore the system, agents make decisions about their trajectory through the systems. Decisions are made by agents at specific locations within the system and may depend on the resources that are available at those locations.

Each decision that is made involves a choice between competing alternatives that are available to the agent at its location, given the resources that are available at that location. In economics, this situation can be described using production functions [10]. A leading example is provided by the Cobb-Douglas production function (e.g., [4] for an innovative, and similar, use of production functions in economics). We show how to employ Cobb-Douglas production functions in a way that supports the composition of models (see Section 4).

In its simplest form, the (real-valued) Cobb-Douglas production function, as used in this setting,[1] expresses the value D of a decision in terms of the values, X and Y, of two alternatives whose relative likelihood of occurrence is weighted by parameters α and β such that $\alpha + \beta = 1$; that is, $D = \delta X^{\alpha} Y^{\beta}$, where δ is a scaling factor. Note that the parameter α (and hence β, or vice versa) may be determined stochastically (by sampling a given probability distribution).

In general, a model will include a number of agents, all making a number of decisions during the execution of the model. Thus, associated with an execution of the model is a set D of (values of) decisions, written as follows:

$$D = \{ D_i = \delta_i X_{i_1}^{\lambda_{i_1}} \ldots X_{i_k}^{\lambda_{i_k}} \mid i = 1, \ldots, m \}.$$

The set D describes the space of decisions taken by agents in the model. In each decision D_i, the full space of k choices, $X_{i_1}, \ldots, X_{i_k}$, available is maintained, with their likelihood of being chosen being represent by the λ_i parameters. Associated with the system is another value; that is, the system manager's utility.

The manager determines a security policy that is intended to deliver target values for certain key attributes of the system. For example, the number of security barrier tailgates, the number of database corruptions, or the up-time of a server.

During the operation of the system, the value, V, of an attribute of interest will deviate from its target value, $\bar{V}$, by amounts which depend upon the behaviour of the agents within the system, as represented by the decisions, $D_1, \ldots, D_m$, they make, as described above. The manager assigns value to the deviation from target according to a chosen function f; that is, $f(V - \bar{V})$. The function f is often based on a quadratic or Linex [20] form, and, typically, will incorporate a stochastic component. Overall, the manager will be concerned with a set of such values $\{ V_i \mid i = 1, \ldots n \}$, and the manager will assign a relative importance to each deviation from target by a preference, or weighting, w_i such that $\sum_{i=1}^{n} w_i = 1$.

Thus, the manager's overall expected utility for the system with the given policy — here the policy is represented by the choice of values of interest, their targets, the functional forms valuing deviation from target, and the preference weightings — is given by the following function:

$$\mathbb{E}[U(D_1, \ldots, D_m)] = \mathbb{E}\left[\sum_{r=1}^{n} w_r f_r(V_r(D_1, \ldots, D_m) - \bar{V}_r) \right].$$

Note that here we have expected utility, deriving from the presence of stochastic components in the parameters α and β and the functions f_i.

Note also that in this set-up a separation is maintained between the decisions made by the agents and the manager's overall utility calculation. Moreover, the dependency

---

[1] In a standard economic setting using such a production function, X and Y are inputs (typically capital and labour), δ is the return to scale, and α and β are the elasticities of X and Y. The constraint that $\alpha + \beta = 1$ generally yields tractable solutions. Our use of a production function inspired by Cobb-Douglas to describe security decisions amounts to an hypothesis that security decision-making is log linear (cf. [9], in which exponential decay in losses amounts to this assumption).

of the latter on the former is such that the form of the latter can be used unchanged even if the particular choice of production functions, describing the local value of the agents' decisions, is changed. Similarly, for a fixed model of the agents' decisions, described by given production functions, the manager may vary the functional form of the overall utility in order to reflect changes in policy. As with production functions, this use of utility functions supports the composition of models (see Section 4), allowing managers to consider policies for one part of a system in the context of those for other parts.

This use of multi-attribute utility theory (see [16] for a detailed account) has been employed as a tool for reasoning in a range of security settings; for example, [12,14].

2.4   A Methodology

We have explained how production functions describe the space of decisions that occur in a model and how utility functions describe the system manager's policy and its value.

In an execution of a specific model, a specific agent must make specific choices. In terms of our production functions, this amounts to specific choices of X_is and corresponding λ_is, possibly 0 or 1, with frequency determined by the associated probability distribution. These choices are determined by the agent's maximizing its own subjective utility. This calculation will be determined by the agent's state, including its location and execution trajectory. Here we take a maximization given by

$$choose(D) = \arg\max_{d \in D} \prod_{i=1}^{m} X_{i_d}^{\lambda_i}.$$

In terms of the underlying mathematical system model, this choice determines the action a in an evolution $L, R, E \xrightarrow{a} L', R', E'$, where the agent E evolves at location L relative to available resources R — recalling Section 2.1, think of E as a sum of processes, with each choice guarded by a possible action, determined as above.

We conduct experiments to explore the co-design of systems and security policies. Specifically, we construct models that encompass the following features: the architecture of the system of interest; its security policy, as represented by the system manager's overall utility function; and the behaviour of agents (e.g., people) when they interact with the system in the context of its security policy, as represented by the production functions used to describe agents' decisions.

Based on such a model, we explore the following experimental space: for a range of parameter values that describe the configuration of the system and the preferences of its inhabiting agents, we observe the corresponding range of consequent values for the attributes of interest to the system manager (e.g., breaches of policy and system performance) and so are able, at least in principle, to calculate his utility as a basis for refining system design and policy. In full generality, one would conduct full Monte Carlo simulations of the model for given choices of empirical data.

Our experimental work, reported in the next section, relies on data collected by the 'Productive Security' research project funded by the UK's GCHQ and EPSRC (grant reference EP/K006517/1) that is currently active at UCL. This project has conducted extensive empirical studies within large organizations to elicit the behaviour of staff in a range of security settings.

The data is collated as a collection of rankings, according to the preferences of subjects, of behavioural options in a range of security scenarios used as basis for semi-structured interviews in the organizations.

3   Example Models

We construct models based on two scenarios: one based on tailgating through the access control to a building and one based on access control through screen locking to personal computers within a shared inner office. The former is richer and explored in much more detail than the latter, which is introduced primarily to facilitate our subsequent discussion of composition in Section 4.

This first model looks at tailgating in a business setting. Tailgating is when people without authorization or without the correct credentials follow others through security controls to gain access to a restricted area. In this case, employees arriving at work need an ID badge to gain access to the main office from the foyer. Employees who forget their badges have a choice: to tailgate through security or to gain access through the reception desk. Employees who observe others tailgating also have a choice: to confront the tailgater and send them back to reception, or to ignore them.

Fig. 1. Lobby Tailgating Model   **Fig. 2.** Inner-office Model

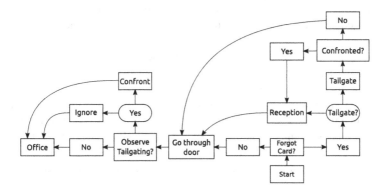

Fig. 3. Agent Processes in the Tailgating Model. Decision Points are Rounded.

Figure 1 shows the locations for the tailgate model, and Figure 3 describes the agents' processes in this model. The two decision points are shown in rounded boxes. Agents start at home and move to the lobby at work, possibly leaving their access cards, a key resource, behind. Agents that have their access cards proceed directly through the security door. Agents that have forgotten their cards have a decision: to tailgate or to go to reception. If the agents choose to go to reception, they queue up until a receptionist is available, and then proceed through the security door. Agents that tailgate wait until the door has opened and follow another agent through. Agents in the 'After Door' location possibly observe other agents tailgating. If they do, they have a decision to confront the tailgating agents, or to ignore them. Agents that are confronted are assumed to return to reception, queue, and then proceed through the security door. Eventually, agents arrive in the office. In this model, nothing happens once the agents are inside the office; they simply wait there until the end of the day and then leave for home.

```
qLen = queue_length(receptionist) + 1          vX_S = max(4 - vX_P, 0.0)
expectedWait = (qLen * mean(dist_receptionist)) / minutes
                                               vX_S *= agent.choice_exponents[SEC]
#get how late we are in minutes                vX_P *= agent.choice_exponents[PROD]
late = get_time_of_day(now(agent.proc)) -      vX_I = agent.choice_exponents[INDIV]
(LEAVE_FOR_WORK_TIME + mean(dist_work_arrival)) vX_M = agent.choice_exponents[MAL]
late /= minutes                                exponents = [lamS, lamP, lamI, lamM]

#get how late we'll arrive in office if we queue #S P I M
reception_arrive = late + expectedWait         d_tailgate = [1.0, 3.0, 1.0, 5.0]
                                               d_reception = [3.0, 1.0, 1.5, 1.0]
vX_P = 0
if reception_arrive > 0                         choose(agent, exponents, [
vX_P += log(reception_arrive ^ 2 + 1)            Choice(d_tailgate, do_tailgate),
end                                              Choice(d_reception, do_reception)])
```

Fig. 4. Julia Code for Tailgating or Reception Decision

Figure 4 shows the Julia code for the choice between tailgating or reception. Here, how much the agent values security or productivity is dependent on whether the agent is early or late to work, and how long the expected wait is for reception.

Agents in this model are considered to be individual subjective utility maximizers for each decision $D = X_S^{\lambda_S} X_P^{\lambda_P} X_I^{\lambda_I} X_M^{\lambda_M}$, where the inputs to this production function are security, productivity, individual cognitive cost, and maliciousness, respectively. Here the return to scale is taken to be 1. In this paper, we do not consider the managers' utility, deferring consideration of policy variation to another occasion.

The tables below show some of the output from the (500) simulation runs. The first four columns are parameters: the average time an agent spends at reception, the number of guards present, and the means of the distributions from which agents' attitudes towards productivity and security are drawn. The remaining columns are outputs, averaged over the simulation runs: the total length of time agents spend waiting for reception, the number of tailgating attempts, success and failures by employees, and the number of malicious tailgating attempts, success, and failures. These attributes reflect aspects of confidentiality, integrity, and availability that are of interest to the managers and other agents.

Tables 1 and 2 show the output from the tailgating model when there is no guard present and with one guard, respectively. In general, high-value attitudes towards security and low-value attitudes towards productivity result in more agents choosing to queue for reception instead of tailgate; in the opposite case, more agents choose to tailgate. When the attitudes are similar, the agents' choices are more evenly split. In the presence of guards (Table 2), the total reception time is higher as more tailgating attempts are caught and the agents are sent back to reception. The number of successful

Table 1. Results from Tailgating Model Simulations, without Guard

rec_mean	num_guards	prod_mean	sec_mean	rec_wait	tail	tail_succ	tail_fail	mal_tail	mal_tail_succ	mal_tail_fail
60	0	0.2	0.2	2538.14	11.0	3.92	7.08	1.46	0.3	1.16
60	0	0.2	0.8	2376.23	7.02	1.38	5.64	1.44	0.02	1.42
60	0	0.8	0.2	1224.59	12.22	8.52	3.7	1.38	0.7	0.68
60	0	0.8	0.8	1396.19	11.12	5.06	6.06	1.46	0.5	0.96
120	0	0.2	0.2	3888.02	12.56	4.0	8.56	1.44	0.42	1.02
120	0	0.2	0.8	4292.42	12.42	2.04	10.38	1.5	0.18	1.32
120	0	0.8	0.2	1450.58	15.34	9.38	5.96	1.44	0.76	0.68
120	0	0.8	0.8	2047.09	13.8	5.5	8.3	1.66	0.52	1.14

Table 2. Results from Tailgating Model Simulations, with Guard

rec_mean	num_guards	prod_mean	sec_mean	rec_wait	tail	tail_succ	tail_fail	mal_tail	mal_tail_succ	mal_tail_fail
60.0	1.0	0.2	0.2	1965.04	9.6	1.3	8.3	1.36	0.18	1.18
60.0	1.0	0.2	0.8	3331.58	8.24	0.42	7.82	1.62	0.06	1.56
60.0	1.0	0.8	0.2	995.04	12.8	4.28	8.52	1.46	0.32	1.14
60.0	1.0	0.8	0.8	1679.81	10.82	1.9	8.92	1.54	0.14	1.4
120.0	1.0	0.2	0.2	4519.47	13.58	1.54	12.04	1.4	0.16	1.24
120.0	1.0	0.2	0.8	5214.63	12.96	0.76	12.2	1.58	0.02	1.56
120.0	1.0	0.8	0.2	1842.76	14.9	3.72	11.18	1.38	0.3	1.08
120.0	1.0	0.8	0.8	2181.14	12.54	1.56	10.98	1.4	0.14	1.26

malicious tailgating attempts is reduced slightly by a higher attitude towards security. The presence of guardsresults in a significant reduction.

Our preliminary results illustrate that small changes in the attitudes of agents can result in substantial changes in behaviour. For example, looking at the case with no guards and the lower reception time, with strong focus on productivity and less on security, the mean number of tailgate attempts is 12.22, with 8.52 success; when the focus is on security over productivity, this drops to 7.02 attempts and just 1.38 successes. But the total time agents spend queueing for reception nearly doubles. The length of time agents have to spend at reception also impacts on the number of tailgating attempts.

Managers employ additional guards in order to further protect confidentiality- and integrity-like attributes. However, the addition of a guard can be seen (Table 2) be have a detrimental effect (see rec_wait) on availability-like attributes (e.g., waiting time).

The second model looks at whether or not employees lock their screens when they leave their computers and how often unlocked computers are accessed. There are only three locations in this model: the start location, the office, and another room. These are shown in Figure 2. The other room represents all other locations agents might be when they are away from their computers, such as meeting rooms, break rooms, and other parts of the building.

While there are fewer locations than in the tailgating model, the agents' processes are more complicated. Upon arriving in the office, agents have a decision to work or to just walk around. Agents that choose to work find a computer — a resource, located in the office, with locked or unlocked state — wait for a while, and eventually leave to go to the other room. When they leave their computer, they have a choice: to lock the computer or to leave it unlocked. As they are walking to the other room they might encounter another computer that has been left unlocked. They then have another choice: ignore the unlocked computer, lock the computer, or access it. The agents then stay in the other room for some time, and then return to their computers, possibly observing another unlocked computer on the way back.

4 Composition

To describe and reason about complex models, it is convenient to describe them in terms of sub-models of which they are composed. That is, it is convenient, under suitable compatibility conditions, to be able to compose two models to form a more complex model. Independent models can also be considered together, with their sets of decisions and utilities simply being the unions and sums, respectively, to give the overall picture. Whilst such simple combinations of production and utility are desirable, it is necessary to understand the circumstances under which models can be combined in useful ways.

This is achieved by describing the interface between two models, so defining what is required for two models to be composable at a specific point. A model can potentially have many interfaces, each with different requirements.

We assume here that for each model we can enumerate the locations and their associated directed links that allow resources to be moved in and out of the model by processes. Figure 5 illustrates two models, each of which has various such locations and links. Among these, location K in Model 1 and location L in Model 2, and their associated links, allow the models to be composed at the point indicated by the interface.

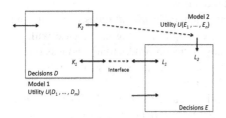
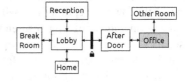

Fig. 5. Composing Models at an Interface   **Fig. 6.** Combined Model

But this description is not yet sufficient to determine a useful composition. For that, we must also require that the agents (processes) that move resources in and out of Model 1 via location K_1 must match with the agents (processes) that move resources in and out of Model 2 via location L_1. That is, any agent that is defined in Model 1 and moves resources across the boundary of Model 1 via location K_1 must also be defined in Model 2 to move the same resources across the boundary of Model 2 via location L_1. Since the links for the illustrated interface are bidirectional, this condition must hold in both directions, but an interface via locations K_2 and L_2 (note that their directions are compatible) would require just the one direction.

Under these constraints, the detailed formulation of which is beyond the scope of this short paper, we have that if $D = \{ D_i = \delta_i X_{i_1}^{\lambda_{i_1}} \ldots X_{i_k}^{\lambda_{i_k}} \mid i = 1, \ldots, m \}$ and $E = \{ E_j = \delta_j Y_{j_1}^{\lambda_{j_1}} \ldots X_{j_k}^{\lambda_{j_k}} \mid j = 1, \ldots, n \}$ then the set of decisions for the composite model is simply $D \cup E$. Similarly, the overall expected utility for the composite model is simply $\mathbb{E}[U(D_1, \ldots, D_m)] + \mathbb{E}[U(E_1, \ldots, E_n)]$.

We can give a simple illustration of of how composition works using the the models described in Section 3. Figure 1 shows the locations and links of the lobby tailgating model. Tailgating is the subject of interest in this model, and what happens once the employees have passed through security into the office is not modelled. Figure 2 shows the locations and links of the office screen-locking model. In this case, the model is designed to study behaviour that occurs within the office.

The office in Figure 1 is a dummy location. Nothing of interest to the model occurs in that location; after getting through security, employees wait there for the end of the work day and then leave. This model can naturally by composed with the office screen-locking model. The dummy office location is removed and replaced with the office location from the second model. Figure 6 shows the resulting locations and links.

Tables 3 and 4 show the output from the composite model without and with a guard. These tables have an additional column: the number of times a computer in the office is accessed by a malicious agent. When agents' attitudes towards security are high and productivity are low, they tend to lock their screens most times when they leave their desks; this results in a low number of malicious accesses. The presence of a guard again reduces the incidences of successful malicious tailgating, and thus also the number of times computers in the office are accessed.

Table 3. Results from Composite Model Simulations, without Guard

rec_mean	num_guards	prod_mean	sec_mean	rec_wait	tail	tail_succ	tail_fail	mal_tail	mal_tail_succ	mal_tail_fail	access
60	0	0.2	0.2	1995.73	9.56	5.42	4.14	1.30	0.52	0.78	8.76
60	0	0.2	0.8	2187.24	8.03	6.93	1.10	1.40	0.65	0.75	0.00
60	0	0.8	0.2	929.68	11.58	5.47	6.12	1.48	0.40	1.08	10.48
60	0	0.8	0.8	1290.88	9.97	7.65	2.32	1.45	0.65	0.80	9.08
120	0	0.2	0.2	3156.48	12.78	5.20	7.58	1.45	0.57	0.88	9.05
120	0	0.2	0.8	3355.64	12.50	7.88	4.62	1.33	0.67	0.67	0.00
120	0	0.8	0.2	1517.90	14.62	6.15	8.47	1.43	0.50	0.93	13.63
120	0	0.8	0.8	1672.00	13.55	8.50	5.05	1.32	0.82	0.50	10.87

Table 4. Results from Composite Model Simulations, with Guard

rec_mean	num_guards	prod_mean	sec_mean	rec_wait	tail	tail_succ	tail_fail	mal_tail	mal_tail_succ	mal_tail_fail	access
60	1	0.2	0.2	1863.38	8.13	1.50	6.63	1.48	0.13	1.35	3.27
60	1	0.2	0.8	2677.96	7.67	2.50	5.17	1.35	0.27	1.08	0.00
60	1	0.8	0.2	1160.51	12.80	2.53	10.27	1.53	0.23	1.30	6.00
60	1	0.8	0.8	1562.94	11.00	3.52	7.48	1.38	0.28	1.10	3.67
120	1	0.2	0.2	4126.91	12.85	2.17	10.68	1.43	0.30	1.13	5.68
120	1	0.2	0.8	4370.40	12.17	3.37	8.80	1.43	0.32	1.12	0.00
120	1	0.8	0.2	1981.08	15.50	2.48	13.02	1.42	0.15	1.27	4.02
120	1	0.8	0.8	2161.73	13.37	3.85	9.52	1.62	0.22	1.40	2.87

In the composite model, when the agents' preferences value security over productivity, there are no times that a computer is accessed by a malicious agent, even if there were successful malicious tailgating attempts. When the preferences are reversed, there are higher numbers of successful malicious tailgating attempts and correspondingly high numbers of computer accesses. The presence of a security guard reduces these greatly: from 0.71 successful malicious attempts and 18.34 accesses, to 0.31 successful tailgating attempts and 8.12 access, in one case. Again, the managers can observe the trade-offs inherent in their policy design choices.

5   Conclusions and Further Work

We suggest that the contribution of this paper is twofold. First, we show how to integrate, compositionally, a mathematically rigorous system modelling technology with a rigorous account of decision-making grounded in utility theory. Second, our experimental results, exploring well-motivated scenarios, provide support for commonly used assumptions in security economics. Specifically, diminishing marginal returns on security investment and trade-offs between confidentiality, integrity, and availability.

We can identify clearly three further lines of work. First, we intend to explore more comprehensively a range of data-rich systems security scenarios investigated in the Productive Security project (EP/K006517/1) at UCL, including managers' utility. Second, we can explore how security and other properties of systems can be expressed logically. As noted in Section 2.1, associated with the process algebraic semantics of our modelling framework is a substructural modal logic that includes connectives and modalities corresponding to system composition and resource-bounded process execution. Third, we can explore the relationship between the preferences and subjective utilities of the agents within models and the preferences and utility of the system manager. This will suggest strategies for promoting the alignment of their incentives, so facilitating security policies that support system productivity while delivering the necessary protection.

References

1. Beautement, A., et al.: Modelling the Human and Technological Costs and Benefits of USB Memory Stick Security. In: Eric Johnson, M. (ed.) Managing Information Risk and the Economics of Security, pp. 141–163. Springer (2008)
2. Beres, Y., Pym, D., Shiu, S.: Decision Support for Systems Security Investment. In: Proc. Business-driven IT Management (BDIM). IEEE Xplore (2010)
3. Bezanson, J., Karpinski, S., Shah, V.B., Edelman, A.: Julia: A fast dynamic language for technical computing (2012), arXiv:1209.5145
4. Bloom, N.: The impact of uncertainty shocks. Econometrica 77(3), 623–685 (2009)
5. Collinson, M., Monahan, B., Pym, D.: A Discipline of Mathematical Systems Modelling. College Publications (2012)
6. Core Gnosis,
   http://www.hpl.hp.com/research/systems_security/gnosis.html
7. Coulouris, G., Dollimore, J., Kindberg, T.: Distributed Systems: Concepts and Design, 3rd edn. Addison Wesley (2000)
8. de Simone, R.: Higher-level synchronising devices in Meije-SCCS. Theoretical Computer Science 37, 245–267 (1985)
9. Gordon, L.A., Loeb, M.P.: The Economics of Information Security Investment. ACM Transactions on Information and Systems Security 5(4), 438–457 (2002)
10. Heathfield, D.F.: Production Functions. Macmillan Press (1971)
11. Hennessy, M., Plotkin, G.: On observing nondeterminism and concurrency. In: de Bakker, J.W., van Leeuwen, J. (eds.) ICALP 1980. LNCS, vol. 85, pp. 299–309. Springer, Heidelberg (1980)

12. Ioannidis, C., Pym, D., Williams, J.: Investments and trade-offs in the economics of information security. In: Dingledine, R., Golle, P. (eds.) FC 2009. LNCS, vol. 5628, pp. 148–166. Springer, Heidelberg (2009)
13. Ioannidis, C., Pym, D., Williams, J.: Information security trade-offs and optimal patching policies. European Journal of Operational Research 216(2), 434–444 (2011)
14. Ioannidis, C., Pym, D., Williams, J.: Fixed costs, investment rigidities, and risk aversion in information security: A utility-theoretic approach. In: Schneier, B. (ed.) Economics of Security and Privacy III, pp. 171–192. Springer (2012)
15. julia, http://julialang.org
16. Keeney, R.L., Raiffa, H.: Decisions with multiple objectives. Wiley (1976)
17. Milner, R.: Calculi for synchrony and asynchrony. Theoret. Comp. Sci. 25(3), 267–310 (1983)
18. Milner, R.: The Space and Motion of Communicating Agents. CUP (2009)
19. O'Hearn, P.W., Pym, D.J.: The logic of bunched implications. Bulletin of Symbolic Logic 5(2), 215–244 (1999)
20. Zellner, A.: Bayesian prediction and estimation using asymmetric loss functions. Journal of the American Statistical Association 81, 446–451 (1986)

End User Development and Information Security Culture

Fredrik Karlsson[1] and Karin Hedström[1,2]

[1] School of Business, Örebro University, Örebro, Sweden
{fredrik.karlsson,karin.hedstrom}@oru.se
[2] Department of Management and Engineering, Linköping University, Linköping, Sweden

Abstract. End user development has grown in strength during the last decades. The advantages and disadvantages of this phenomenon have been debated over the years, but not extensively from an information security culture point of view. We therefore investigate information security design decisions made by an end user during an end user development project. The study is interpretative and the analysis is structured using the concept of inscriptions. Our findings show that end user development results in inscriptions that may induce security risks that organizations are unaware of. We conclude that it is a) important to include end user development as a key issue for information security management, b) to include end user developers as an important group for the development of a security-aware culture, and c) to address information security aspects in end user development policies.

Keywords: Information security, information security culture, information security policy, end user development, inscription.

1   Introduction

End user development grew strong during the 1990s [1, 2]. During this decade end users received powerful desktop tools, such as spreadsheets and easy-to-use databases was used to develop local information systems. This kind of development is highly intertwined with the end users' work. It is, for example, apparent in Brancheau's and Brown's [1] definition of end user development: 'the adoption and use of information technology by personnel outside the information systems department to develop software applications in support of organizational tasks.' Today end user development is a wide spread phenomenon, which exists in almost every organization, although it is not always explicitly recognized, or sanctioned by management or information security specialists. End users are rarely skilled systems developers, and generally lack knowledge about information security practices. End user developed information systems is an important part of many organisations' plethora of information systems, thus making end user development a key issue also when managing information security. In order to develop secure information systems where the organisation's information assets are protected, a security-aware culture, or information security culture, needs to be developed [3]. Information security culture can be viewed as 'the way things are done in the organisations to protect information assets' [4], it is of vital

T. Tryfonas and I. Askoxylakis (Eds.): HAS 2014, LNCS 8533, pp. 246–257, 2014.

importance to include all types of user groups when addressing information security culture. The end user development process and its results are despite this, neither discussed nor addressed as an important issue for an organization's information security culture.

Against this backdrop, the objective of this paper is thus to investigate the role of end user development for an organization's information security culture. We address this objective through the following research questions: (1) does end user(s) make design decisions regarding information security during end user development? and (2) what kind of information security consequences do end users' design decisions result in? Using a case from an international company where an end user developed an information system for price simulation, we illustrate information security consequences that occurred from end user development. This illustration is structured through the use of inscriptions [5] to centre on design decisions (or lack thereof) that have had information security consequences. The conclusions contribute to research on information security culture. Our research acknowledges that end user development has security consequences, illustrating the importance of including end user development as a key issue when working with information security culture. The information security culture becomes an important way of managing information security because end user development is hardly ever controlled as promoted in systems development methods [6]. We also contribute to the end user development field by including information security issues in the on-going debate on pros and cons of end user development.

2   Related Research

2.1   End User Development

The advantages and disadvantages of end user development have been debated. As end users are rarely skilled systems developers they do not have knowledge about 'best practices' in systems development [2] – not on methods, technical solutions or risks. Also, information security risks resulting from end user development are at best discussed briefly in existing research [e.g. 7, 8]. Most of the criticism to date has focused on the quality of the information systems developed [e.g. 9, 10, 11]. Attention has especially been devoted to spreadsheet models and logical errors in these models, since spreadsheets tools are the most commonly used end user development tool [12]. For example, Edberg and Bowman [13] found in a laboratory experiment that end users were outperformed by information systems students on technical quality. Panko and Sprague Jr. [14] confirmed earlier studies on error rates when building spreadsheet models. While concluding that systems developers have much the same error rate as end users, they do however use extensive time for planned test procedures. While these, among others, may be important discoveries, they are limited in terms of understanding end user development from an information security point of view.

2.2   Information Security and Information Security Culture

An important issue for managing information security is the development of an information security culture where employees have the ability to 'integrate acceptable information security practices into their everyday behaviour' [15], i.e., apply a security-aware behaviour to their work [3]. Previous research on information security culture has mainly focused on how to develop or foster 'regular' employees' security-aware behaviour [e.g. 3, 15] or how to improve the systems development processes with regard to information security [e.g. 16, 17, 18]. Information security literature does not explicitly relate to end user development. Instead, this literature either targets end users as consumers of information and information systems or how professional systems developers' work with information security during systems development. In order to make a distinction between use and development we align with Cotterman's and Kumar's [19] definition of development: 'the performance of any or all tasks of the systems development process'. Hence, an end user performing this type of activity differs from end users that consume information and information systems. This means that end user development has to be treated as an activity in its own right. End user developers are thus an important group to address when developing an information security culture, as the end user developed systems could have major information security consequences.

3   Research Design

3.1   Case Description

The empirical base is an end user development project undertaken in an international industrial company. One major challenge for the company was price analysis and simulations. This had become very time consuming since the company was working on many markets. Information had to be retrieved from several enterprise resource planning systems (ERPs) and quite a large amount of manual work had to be done. For example, each time they calculated new sales prices, they had to remove duplicated information since they were using data from several systems. Considering that they have several thousands product items this was a tedious and error-prone task which took a lot of time. The developed information system was supposed to simplify this task, and integrated different information for price analysis and simulation. One example was the possibility to simulate and compare effects from monetary developments in different countries.

The end user initiated this project based on the problems he had experienced. He was working as area sales manager for several markets and had almost 20 years of experience from the companies' products. As an end user he was very experienced in using spreadsheet software, such as Microsoft Excel. Hence, it was a natural choice for him to build a price analysis and simulation system in Excel. The construction of the system followed the common end user development pattern. It means that the end user's current understanding of the problem and the design evolved together with his day-to-day work, and was not structured by any systems development method. The end user made major revisions every other month after using it to analyse current prices. However, since the development work was highly integrated in the end user's daily work it is not possible to tell how many person-hours that were spent on this system. The end user developed information system grew from a simple spreadsheet where calculations could be made using multiple currencies, to a solution that integrated several workbooks using Visual Basic for Application (VBA) scripts. The final version of his system used spreadsheets exported from the ERPs. These files were linked manually to the end user's spreadsheet model where automated scripts, for example, removed duplicates based on product number. The end user developed the information system using his laptop, which was not encrypted. All information that was needed for this application was downloaded from the ERPs to this computer and used locally. Price lists, for the markets within the end user's responsibility, were produced from his system and e-mailed to the sales personal in different countries. Hence, this system contained information about the company's margins with regard to specific markets. Since the development work was done as part of his day-to-day work it meant that it was carried out during extensive traveling.

3.2   Data Collection

Data sources included one logbook, semi-structured interviews, the information system developed by the end user, and the company's information security policy. Triangulation of data sources provided multiple perspectives [20] on the end user development process, and how to interpret the design decisions. The end user was instructed to write a logbook during his development work. The logbook contained what the end user considered as major design decisions, fulfilment of requirements, and arguments for why these requirements were important. The logbook provided us with a time line of these decisions, but also became an effective means for collecting data and cross-checking the informant's interviews. Four semi-structured interviews were carried out with the end user, during various stages of his development work. We used the end user's log book and the functionality of the end user developed information systems as input for the interviews [20]. Questions addressed the design decisions described in the logbook, and the design rationale behind them. This provided the end user perspective on the development processes. We also obtained access to the end user developed information system. It provided an effective means to validate the informant's logbook during data collection. In particular, it allowed us to identify functionality and security mechanisms that had not been mentioned in the logbook or during the interviews. Finally, we had access to the company's information security policy. It provided information on how to interpret the design decisions made during the end user development process in the light of information security. Furthermore, we concluded that the company did not have a policy concerning end user development.

3.3   Data Analysis

The purpose of this paper was to investigate the occurrence of information security consequences resulting from end user development, and to investigate what kind of information security design decisions that an end user make during end user development. It means that we are interested in what types of requirements that are implemented during the development process and why these implementations were made, which makes an interpretative study useful [21, 22]. During the case we unfolded the implementation of requirements through the process of translating [23] design decisions into inscriptions [5, 24]. Inscriptions can be described as a concrete representation of interests and values [25]. The notion of inscription is often used in relation to designers' anticipation of end users' use of a certain technology [24], where the designer delegates patterns of actions, roles, and competencies to future users [26] in for instance an information system. In this study our use of inscription is instead directed towards the end user, and his own vision of future needs and usage. We are interested in a specific type of inscriptions – design decisions concerning information security – taken by the end user. In general terms we define a design decision as an inscription that changes the current version of the end user's information system. As stated above, these decisions are anchored in the end user's interests, what he wanted to achieve through the inscription, which may or may not have been information security related.

The analysis was done in four steps. First we identified design decisions based on the logbook, interviews, and the end user developed information system. For example, the end user added a product name column in the Excel spreadsheet to be able to identify unique products during price analysis and simulations. During the second step we elicited design decisions that had information security consequences. These design decisions could either be implemented as a security mechanism that enhance information security or something that induced security risk/breaches. During this step we used confidentiality, integrity, and availability of information [27], commonly known as the CIA-triad, to classify design decisions as information security related. During the third step we analysed the end user's interest behind each information security-related design decision, i.e. what he intended to achieve from his perspective. Finally, we compared the information security consequence with the company's information security policy in order to analyse if these actions were compliant or non-compliant with the policy. The analysis is presented in Table 1 in Section 4.

4   Inscriptions of Information Security

In this section we take a closer look at the inscriptions made by the end users during his nine months of development work, by analysing the final version of the end user developed information system. In total we identified 253 inscriptions made by the end user. We selected design decisions with information security consequences (see Table 1). The leftmost column in Table 1 contains the number of the design decision, the second column presents the design decision, the third column presents the end users' interest, the fourth column shows the information security consequence, and the rightmost column shows whether or not the design decisions were compliant with the information security policy. When searching for implemented security mechanisms in the end user developed information systems we only identified two. However, we found additional inscriptions that had information security consequences for the organization. These were design decisions that in different ways exposed confidential information for increased risk.

Design decisions 23, 37 and 155 concern downloading information from different ERPs in order to use that information as input in the new system. This information is classified as business critical since it is about current product lines, prices and customers. It was therefore protected in the ERPs using different security mechanisms, such as authorization controls, to keep the information confidential. When accessing these systems from a remote location, i.e. when out traveling, a virtual private network was needed. When the end user downloaded this information as Excel spreadsheet files these security mechanisms became useless. The new information system did not provide any security mechanism to prevent unauthorized access to these files. Moreover, since the laptop was not encrypted these files had no protection at all, beside the login procedure in the Windows operating system.

Table 1 contains six inscriptions (number 28, 65-68 and 74) concerning the margin that the company has on different regions/markets. These design decisions were included in the application to create the simulation functionality and to be able to produce new price lists. Design decisions 189 and 192-193 have a similar purpose in the information system. They were used to create volume discount for different customer segments. Hence, these breakpoints were based on the strategic importance of specific customers. As the developed information systems did not have security mechanisms, and the laptop was unencrypted, it meant that this information was unprotected. The end user used this application in his daily work. The application produced a unique spreadsheet per country (design decision 186). These spreadsheets contained no formulas on how the prices had been calculated; instead they were produced from a second workbook using VBA-scripts. Due to geographic distances the end user e-mailed the relevant price list to the sales personal in each country (design decision 187). Hence, this way of working meant that the end-user implemented a manual security mechanism where a price list for a specific country was treated as confidential information. However, e-mailing the price lists also meant that they were distributed to personnel within the organization that had various, to the end user, unknown security solutions. There is also the risk of entering an incorrect e-mail address, thus disclosing sensitive information to unauthorized people.

Table 1. End user's design decisions

No	Design decision	Interest	Information security consequence	Compliance with information security policy
23	Download product information from ERPs to integrate in the new system.	To have access to up-to-date data for the analysis	This information is protected by the security mechanisms set up by the security adminis-trator. Extracting this information to the unencrypted laptop decreases the protection.	The end user has the authority to use this information, but not on an unencrypted computer.
28	Adding margin for region 1.	Necessary for carrying out simulation	Exposing the company's current margin/markup.	The end user has the authority to use this information.
37	Download product information from ERPs to integrate in the new system.	To have access to up-to-date data for the analysis	This information is pro-tected by the security mechanisms set up by the security administrat-or. Extracting this information to the unencrypted laptop decreases the protection.	The end user has the authority to use this information, but not on an unencrypted computer.
65	Adding margin for region 2.	Necessary for carrying out simulation	Exposing the company's current margin/markup.	The end user has the authority to use this information.
66	Adding margin for region 3.	Necessary for carrying out simulation	Exposing the company's current margin/markup.	The end user has the authority to use this information.
67	Adding margin for region 4.	Necessary for carrying out simulation	Exposing the company's current margin/markup.	The end user has the authority to use this information.
68	Adding margin for region 5.	Necessary for carrying out simulation	Exposing the company's current margin/markup.	The end user has the authority to use this information.
74	Adding margin for region 6.	Necessary for carrying out simulation	Exposing the company's current margin/markup.	The end user has the authority to use this information.
155	Download customer information from ERPs to integrate in the new system.	To have access to up-to-date data for the analysis	This information is protected by the security mechanisms set up by the security admini-strator. Extracting this information to the unencrypted laptop decreases the protection.	The end user has the authority to use this information.

Table 1. (*continued*)

186	Producing one unique price list/country	Keeping confidentiality	Price information is kept confidential for sales people belonging to the specific country	The policy does not state that one country's price information should be kept confidential
187	E-mailing price lists to each country	Keeping confidentiality	Price information is kept confidential for sales people belonging to the specific country	The policy does not state that one country's price information should be kept confidential
190	Adding breakpoint for first volume discount	Incorporating the company's price strategy in the simulation	Exposing the company's discount model and how it is used.	The end user has the authority to use this information.
193	Adding breakpoint for second volume discount	Incorporating the company's price strategy in the simulation	Exposing the company's discount model and how it is used.	The end user has the authority to use this information.
194	Adding breakpoint for third volume discount	Incorporating the company's price strategy in the simulation	Exposing the company's discount model and how it is used.	The end user has the authority to use this information.

5   Discussion

Our analysis shows that the end user made 14 design decisions information security consequences. We only found two design decisions, 186 and 187 in Table 1, that were conscious information security design decisions. The most interesting aspect of design decisions 186 and 187 is that the end user introduced a security mechanism, to keep the price lists separated for each country, which was not necessary according to the information security policy. As we continue examining the design decisions in Table 1 we find inscriptions made into the end user developed information system that decreased information security in existing ERPs. The end user downloaded information about existing products, prices and customers to his laptop, which was stored unencrypted and only protected by a Windows login. Hence, the information was stored in a less secure environment compared to the ERPs. This did not mean that the ERPs as such were compromised. The end user had not disclosed information on how to access them; instead he had moved data outside these systems. From the end user's point of view this was compliant with the information security policy since the Excel exports 'functionality was available in these systems'. According to the information security policy the end user had authorization to use this information, however employees were not allowed to download sensitive information to unencrypted computers. Furthermore, the end user (or any developer) needed clearance from top management in order to combine information from the three ERPs into a new information system. However, this information was only found in the part of the information security policy distributed to systems developers, and hence the end user never made such a request.

From Table 1 we can tell that the end user's design decisions were mainly driven by his needs to solve his current work problems – in this case doing price analysis and simulations when 'creating new or updated price lists'. For example, he added product information from the ERPs to 'have a complete and fresh starting point' in his system. Customer information was downloaded to use the 'different customer categories in the calculations'. The decision to download information as Excel files and linking them manually to his system was preferred 'based on my knowledge of these systems.' However, the end user expressed a concern that this solution was sensitive to 'how these files were created. You end up with nothing but errors if the right data is not found in the right columns'. Hence, this shows that he reflected on the drawbacks of manually extracting data from the ERPs, but not from an information security perspective.

Our findings show that some of the end user's design decisions were non-compliant with the company's information security policy. It means that end user development is not only a quality problem due to end user's limited skills in systems development, which has been the main concern in existing end user development research [e.g. 10, 11, 28, 29], but that end user development also can create information security risks. This illustrates the importance of including end user development as a key issue for a security-aware culture. As we have shown some of the design decisions resulted in increased or new information security risks, exposing information found in the end user developed information system, and information from other, presumed, secure information systems. One problematic aspect of end user development is that it is common in today's organizations, but management rarely controls the development of such applications [6]. Consequently, as end user development results in insecure information systems it means that many organizations, today, have security-compromised systems that they might not even be aware of. When it comes to the information security field it has prioritized end users' use of information and information systems, and how professional systems developers' handle information security during systems development. However, we have identified another area that needs attention: end users' development of information systems. It means that end users are not only consuming information and information systems; they are creating new information and information systems. What complicates matters is that end users have limited knowledge of systems development methods (as in our case), and often do not apply any explicit methods in their endeavors. Consequently, existing contributions in research [e.g. 16, 17, 18, 30] on integrating systems development methods and information security may have limited impact on the situation. It should be acknowledged that an end user (often) develops something only he/she is supposed to use. To some extent this makes the end user's thinking and decisions different from the thinking/decisions made by a professional systems developer. In the former case, when the end user acts as the developer, he/she knows how the 'end user' thinks and reacts to various events since it concerns him/her. This fact may allow the end user to mitigate the need for explicit security measures to some extent, as he/she implicitly rely on the 'end user' to work properly even if no explicit measures are made. On the contrary, professional systems developers lack such luxury and their assumptions on abilities of the 'end user' are naturally limited to some low common denominator, and consequently explicit security measures have to be considered. However, this does not mean that end users, when carrying out end user development, are allowed to violate the information security policy of the organization. Our findings on end user development should have impact on how organizations work with their information security culture, as well as on how they address end user development. Furthermore, our findings should have an impact of the research agenda in both end user development and information security. When it comes to end user development policies existing research [e.g. 31, 32, 33] does not reveal whether or not these policies address information security. Of course, existing research might not have looked into this area, but it should also be acknowledged that end user development policies seem to be rare in practice in the first place. From an information security point of view end user development is not dealt with as a specific area [e.g. 34, 35-37]. Hence, when end users develop information systems they are governed by the general instructions found in the information security policies and the existing information security culture.

6   Conclusion

End user development is a common phenomenon today, where end users develop their own information systems to solve day-to-day problems. Although being extensively researched, the end user development process and its result are neither discussed nor addressed in detail in research on information security culture. In this paper we have therefore investigated the role of end user development for an organisation's information security culture. We address this objective through the following research questions: (1) does end user(s) make design decisions regarding information security during end user development? and (2) what kind of information security consequences do end users' design decisions result in? We traced the inscriptions made by an end user when developing an information system. Only two out of 253 design decisions made by the end user concerned conscious implementation of security mechanisms. However, we did find inscriptions that might cause security breaches. Hence, one could in this case describe them as de-inscriptions from a security point of view. Based on the case findings we propose following tentative propositions:

1. The information security field needs to acknowledge that end users develop information and information systems and explicitly address this as a key issue in information security management, including end user developers as an important group for the development of a security-aware culture.
2. The end user development field needs to acknowledge that end user development has information security as well as information quality consequences, and the former needs to be explicitly addressed in end user development policies.

Every research design has limitations, which should be viewed as opportunities for further research. This study is no exception. Our analysis is based on data from one single case study. Although we triangulated data from one logbook, semi-structured interviews, and code reviews we cannot, and do not claim, that we have identified the complete set of inscriptions of information security requirements. Subsequently, attempts to generalize our results to other end user development projects may not be warranted. However, based on the limited amount of data we have still been able to show lack of conscious information security related design decisions during end user development. We therefore see interesting avenues for future research on the information security consequences of end-user development. We welcome, for instance, future studies mapping the risks of information security breaches in relation to end user development. We have also found that previous research on information security culture commonly view users as a homogenous group, generally as 'employees'. We believe that a lot would be gained if we in future research could differentiate between different user groups and adjust information security measures accordingly.

References

1. Brancheau, J.C., Brown, C.V.: The Management of End-User Computing: Status and Directions. ACM Computing Surveys 25, 437–481 (1993)
2. Taylor, M.J., Moynihan, E.P., Wood-Harper, A.T.: End-user computing and information systems methodologies. Information Systems Journal 8, 85–96 (1998)
3. Da Veiga, A., Eloff, J.H.P.: A framework and assessment instrument for information security culture. Computers & Security 29, 196–207 (2010)
4. Veiga, A.D., Martins, N., Eloff, J.H.P.: Information security culture – validation of an assessment instrument. Southern African Business Review 11, 146–166 (2007)
5. Akrich, M., Latour, B.: A summary of a convenient vocabulary for the semiotics of human and nonhuman assemblies. In: Bijker, W.E., Law, J. (eds.) Shaping Technology/Building Society. Studies in Sociotechnical Change, pp. 259–264. MIT Press, Cambridge (1992)
6. Sutcliffe, A., Mehandjiev, N.: End-User Development. Communication of the ACM 47, 31–32 (2004)
7. McGill, T., Klisc, C.: End-User Perceptions of the Benefits and Risks of End-User Web Development. Journal of Organizational and End User Computing 18, 22–42 (2006)
8. Summer, M., Klepper, R.: Information Systems Strategy and End-User Application Development. ACM SIGMIS Database 18, 19–30 (1987)
9. Ditlea, S.: Spreadsheets can be hazardous to your health. Personal Computing 11, 60–69 (1987)
10. Panko, R.R., Halverson, R.P.: An Experiment In Collaborative Development To Reduce Spreadsheet Errors. Journal of the Association of Information Systems 2, 1–31 (2001)
11. Karlsson, F.: Using Two Heads in Practice. In: Fourth Workshop on End-User Software Engineering (WEUSE IV) ACM Digital Library (2008)
12. Kankuzi, B., Ayalew, Y.: An End-User Oriented Graph-Based Visualization for Spreadsheets. In: Fourth Workshop on End-User Software Engineering (WEUSE IV) ACM Digital Library (2008)
13. Edberg, D.T., Bowman, B.J.: User-developed applications: An empirical study of application quality and developer productivity. Journal of Management Information Systems 13, 167–185 (1996)
14. Panko, R.R., Sprague Jr., R.H.: Hitting the wall: errors in developing and code inspecting a 'simple' spreadsheet model. Decision Support Systems 22, 337–353 (1998)
15. Thomson, K.-L., von Solms, R., Louw, L.: Cultivating an organizational information security culture. Computer Fraud & Security, pp. 7–11 (October 2006)
16. Hitchings, J.: Achieving an Integrated Design: the Way Forward for Information Security. In: The IFIP TC11 11th International Conference on Information Security, pp. 269–283 (1995)

17. James, H.L.: Managing information systems security: a soft approach. In: Proceedings of the 1996 Information Systems Conference of New Zealand (ISCNZ 1996), pp. 10–20. IEEE Society Press (1996)
18. Siponen, M., Baskerville, R.: A new paradigm for adding security into IS development methods. In: Eloff, J., Labuschange, L., Solms, R., Dhillon, G. (eds.) Advances in Information Security Management & Small Systems Security, pp. 99–111. Kluwer Academic Publishers, Boston (2001)
19. Fabian, F., Gürses, S., Heisel, M., Santen, T., Schmidt, H.: A comparison of security requirements engineering methods. Requirements Engineering 15, 7–40 (2010)
20. Patton, M.Q.: Qualitative evaluation and research methods. Sage, Newbury Park (1990)
21. Walsham, G.: Interpretive case studies in IS research: nature and method. European Journal of Information Systems 4, 74–81 (1995)
22. Klein, H.K., Myers, M.D.: A set of principles for conducting and evaluating interpretative field studies in information system. MIS Quarterly 23, 67–94 (1999)
23. Latour, B.: Science in action: how to follow scientists and engineers through society. Harvard University Press, Cambridge (1987)
24. Akrich, M.: The De-Scription of Technical Objects. In: Bijker, W., Law, J. (eds.) Shaping Technology/Building Society. Studies in Sociotechnical Change. The MIT Press, Cambridge (1992)
25. Hanseth, O., Monteiro, E.: Inscribing behaviour in information infrastructure standards. Accounting, Management & Information Technology 7, 183–211 (1997)
26. Latour, B.: Technology is society made durable. In: Law, J. (ed.) A Sociology of Monsters: Essays on Power, Technology and Domination, pp. 103–131. Routledge, London (1991)
27. ISO: ISO/IEC 27001:2005, Information Technology - Security Techniques - Information Security Management Systems - Requirements. International Organization for Standardization (ISO) (2005)
28. Davis, G.B.: The Hidden Costs of End-User Computing. Accounting Horizons 2, 103–106 (1988)
29. Teo, T.S.H., Tan, M.: Spreadsheet development and 'what-if' analysis: quantitative versus qualitative errors. Accounting Management and Information Technologies 9, 141–160 (1999)
30. Sindre, G., Opdahl, A.L.: Eliciting security requirements with misuse cases. Requirements Engineering 10, 34–44 (2005)
31. Galletta, D.F., Hufnagel, E.M.: A model of end-user computing policy – context, process, content and compliance. Information & Management 22, 1–18 (1992)
32. Rittenberg, L.E., Senn, A.: End-user computing. The Intenal Auditor 50, 35–40 (1993)
33. Speier, C., Brown, C.V.: Differences in end-user computing support and control across user departments. Information & Management 32, 85–99 (1997)
34. Howard, P.D.: The Security Policy Life Cycle. In: Tipton, H.F., Krause, M. (eds.) Information Security Management Handbook. CRC Press, Boca Raton (2007)
35. Peltier, T.R.: Information security policies and procedures - a practitioner's reference. Auerbach Publications, Boca Raton (2004)
36. Smith, R.: The Definitive Guide to Writing Effective Information Security Policies and Procedures. Createspace (2010)
37. Wood, C.C.: Information security policies made easy. Information Shield, Huston (2001)

DSAPE – Dynamic Security Awareness Program Evaluation

Charalampos Manifavas[1], Konstantinos Fysarakis[2],
Konstantinos Rantos[3], and George Hatzivasilis[2]

[1] Dept. of Informatics Engineering, Technological Educational Institute of Crete,
Heraklion, Crete, Greece
harryman@ie.teicrete.gr
[2] Dept. of Electronic & Computer Engineering, Technical University of Crete,
Chania, Crete, Greece
{kfysarakis,gchatzivasilis}@isc.tuc.gr
[3] Dept. of Computer & Informatics Engineering, Eastern Macedonia and
Thrace Institute of Technology, Kavala, Greece
krantos@teikav.edu.gr

Abstract. This paper addresses the importance of continuously evaluating an organization's awareness program and provides guidelines that will help organizations assess their efforts, extending the authors' work in [1]. The proposed methodology evaluates an awareness program considering the most common and essential methods used for delivering awareness material. Key awareness-related processes and accompanying quantitative metrics are identified, along with a methodology for dynamically evaluating the metrics and the overall awareness program as a whole. A software tool is developed, to facilitate the deployment and maintenance of the assessment methods and to formalize their aggregation and evaluation. An organization's security awareness posture is modelled as a dynamic system and the awareness level is calculated and monitored through time via Event Calculus. Furthermore, the tool can be deployed in a multi-agent form, to enable its use by organizations operating through remote offices and distributed locations.

Keywords: security awareness, evaluation methodology, security management, event calculus, JESS, JADE, multi-agent.

1   Introduction

In the context of an enterprise environment, security awareness refers to the knowledge and attitude employees possess regarding the protection of the physical and information assets of their organization. Security awareness is a vital element to the orderly and uninterrupted operation of an organization. Even the most efficient security mechanisms have little value in an organization with no security culture, as the human factor often proves to be the weakest link; though, surprisingly, the importance of appropriate awareness and training is often overlooked [2]. Moreover,

T. Tryfonas and I. Askoxylakis (Eds.): HAS 2014, LNCS 8533, pp. 258–269, 2014.
© Springer International Publishing Switzerland 2014

the importance of security awareness is bound to increase with the introduction of smart office environments through the deployment of various embedded computing systems. Employees are already insufficiently educated on the risks introduced by new working behaviors (e.g. working in public spaces and/or involving life-logging applications [3]), as technological advancements have outpaced awareness efforts [4]. This "awareness gap" is bound to be exacerbated as we move towards the Internet of Things (IoT).

At any rate, awareness efforts can be of limited effectiveness unless a needs assessment is conducted prior to deployment, in order to facilitating tailoring the program to the specific organization [5][6]. Moreover, the maturity of the program can play a significant role in its effectiveness; the latter cannot be guaranteed during the first years of deployment. Evaluating the overall information security program of an organization is not enough, as it can only give some indications on the efficacy of its awareness methods; a methodology that focuses specifically on the awareness campaign can provide more detailed and accurate results. Measuring the impact of the awareness campaign is, therefore, vital for ensuring program improvement and continuation through management support, as well as for assessing the awareness team's efforts, providing valuable feedback regarding the effectiveness of the chosen strategy and methods.

There are two factors that have to be considered, in order to assess the effectiveness of a security awareness campaign:

— *Has the information reached the target?* While certain methods provide assurance that the information is bound to reach the target, others rely on the deployment strategy. E.g. asking a person to hand awareness brochures personally to each employee is certainly more effective than leaving them on a desk and asking employees to collect them. On the other hand, awareness material distributed via emails is bound to reach the target.

— *Has the information touched the target?* This is the most important aspect in awareness program evaluation as it assesses how many people actually absorbed the delivered information and, therefore, whether the main aim of the program, which is to create security aware and conscious people, has been achieved.

The above distinction is important and widely cited in related security awareness work, as in [7], where the authors apply a security awareness prototype on an international gold mining company with 25 operations in 11 countries. They use metrics to measure three dimensions of awareness: knowledge (what you know), attitude (what you think) and behavior (what you do). It was identified that the different evaluated factors cannot contribute the same to the final awareness level, thus weights were applied, a technique that is utilized in the work presented here as well.

This paper is structured as follows: Section 2 presents our awareness evaluation framework, along with all the identified metrics, parameters and processes which constitute the "Dynamic Security Awareness Program Evaluation (DSAPE)" methodology, Section 3 describes the accompanying tool, including implementation details and a demonstration of its operation and, finally, the work is concluded in Section 4.

2   The Evaluation Methodology

The evaluation of a program could be based on qualitative or quantitative techniques or a combination of the above.

Qualitative techniques are mainly used to capture employees' sensation regarding awareness and whether they truly exercise security awareness. Although the interpretation of the results obtained by these techniques can sometimes be subjective and might lead to speculations and conjectures, their significance should not be underestimated. Commonly deployed qualitative techniques include users' feedback, independent observations and silent monitoring of employees' reactions (e.g. during an awareness session).

Quantitative techniques attempt to present the evaluation results in a more objective way and provide benchmarks for future evaluations. Methods that can be deployed are metrics, namely key performance indicators (KPI), which can give a clearer view regarding the effectiveness of a program. However, there are neither standardized, universally accepted and validated methods nor exact figures in the industry that can classify a program as successful or not. What is more, defining quantitative metrics appears to be very difficult for most organizations [5]. This is not surprising since these metrics often involve simplifying a complex socio-technical situation down to numbers or partial order [8].

The evaluation methodology presented in this paper will focus on quantitative techniques; quantifiable and repeatable results are an important factor to consider choosing an effective and useful set of metrics for any relevant evaluation, as indicated by all relevant guidelines (e.g. [9]).

2.1   Evaluation Metrics

In the following section, we list some recommended quantitative metrics that will be used in the evaluation methodology, organized in 12 categories. Details on the definition, deployment and marking scheme of the individual metrics can be found in [1].

General metrics
  (a) **Surveys.** Questionnaire-based surveys conducted on technical and security policy issues are one of the most reliable means of measuring a program's effectiveness.
      (i) **M1:** Statistical analysis of monthly surveys on specific organization's divisions
      (ii) **M2:** Statistical analysis of annual surveys
  (b) **Awareness/Security Days:** Security days offer a unique opportunity for the awareness team to directly communicate with employees and get their feedback.
      (i) **M3:** Statistical analysis of security days attendance
  (c) **Independent observations.** Independent observations on the security behaviour of employees are an important indicator of whether the awareness campaign has touched the target audience.

(i) **M4:** Statistical analysis of unsuccessful mock phishing attacks

(ii) **M5:** Statistical analysis of new threat bulletins' readership

(d) **Audit department reports.** Auditing can be used to determine if security awareness related incidents identified by audits are declining. Note that this figure should not include issues that fall within specific roles responsibilities and require training and education, as opposed to awareness [6][10].

(i) **M6:** Number of security issues related to employees security behavior identified by the audit department

(e) **Risk department reports.** Input from the risk department can be used to identify risks related to security awareness. Risks identified during previous risk assessments should be reduced throughout time.

(i) **M7:** Number of security issues related to employees security behaviour identified by the risk department.

(f) **Security incidents.** Security incidents are a valid point of reference regarding awareness program evaluation, and their processing should go beyond a simple check on the volume of incidents.

(i) **M8:** Number of employees who are the source of at least one security incident that stems from non-secure behavior (out of the total number of employees).

(ii) **M9:** Number of employees who are the source of at least one security incident that falls within their responsibilities but were not identified by them (out of the total number of employees).

Individual module metrics

(g) **Awareness sessions (workshops).** This is considered one of the easiest methods to evaluate given the existence of multiple communication paths for getting the required feedback.

(i) **M10:** Statistical analysis of sessions   attendance

(ii) **M11:** Statistical analysis of sessions effectiveness

(h) **Information security website.** The number of employees who visit the website where information security related content is posted demonstrates users' interest in the corresponding topics.

(i) **M12:** Statistical analysis of information security website visits

(i) **e-Learning.** Statistics can provide useful information regarding the number of employees visiting, registering, and completing the e-learning program.

(i)   **M13:** Statistical analysis of e-learning program visits

(ii) **M14:** Statistical analysis of e-learning program registrations

(iii) **M15:** Statistical analysis of completions

(j) **Emails.** Awareness content delivered through emails is bound to reach the target, but the email may be ignored. A simple technique can be used to measure the method's effectiveness: the content can be structured in such a way so that a link is provided as a follow-up for more information regarding the addressed subject and which can be used to measure readers' interest.

(i) **M16:** Statistical analysis of email views

(k) **iNotices.** As with emails where content is delivered electronically, links can be provided in iNotices for follow up information.

   (i) **M17:** Statistical analysis of iNotices readings

(l) **Posters.** Measuring posters contribution to the awareness should involve independent observations, combined with electronic means, e.g. the use of QR codes that provide links to additional resources or the URL where the same poster can be found in electronic form so that employees can download it.

   (i) **M18:** Statistical analysis of poster downloads

2.2   Other Factors

Weighting

Weighting of the metrics and their individual categories is also incorporated in the scheme, so that the system can be tailored to each organization's specific needs and environment. We introduce some sample weight values for demonstrative purposes, but these should be appropriately distributed by higher management in cooperation with the awareness team prior to the initial evaluation. Some guidelines are also included, by giving emphasis on parameters pertaining to assessing the organization's security culture. The latter is the most important aspect in awareness program evaluation as it assesses how many people actually absorbed the delivered information and, therefore, whether the main aim of the program, which is to create security aware and conscious people, has been achieved. Moreover, whatever the exact weights decided upon initial evaluation, further fine tuning is to be expected and, in fact, necessary to optimize the accuracy and efficiency of the evaluation method as the program progresses and new iterations are deployed.

Cost

The proposed framework also considers the cost of implementing and running the various awareness-related mechanisms, to facilitate various types of analyses that will help an organization better evaluate the cost-benefit relationships and other aspects of said mechanisms. This facilitates the comparison of T&A initiatives (e.g. one initiative costing $X and focusing on a subset of awareness mechanisms vs. other initiative costing $Y and focusing on another subset of the mechanisms) and provides valuable information to the decision-making process regarding future directions of the awareness program.

2.3   Evaluation Lifecycle

In order to implement a continuous awareness evaluation program, the processes detailed above need to be executed in a structured and timely manner. This is depicted in the evaluation lifecycle below:

1. Personalize the framework (set weights, identify pertinent metrics etc.)
2. Define the baseline (first run of the evaluation)
3. Set goals and milestones

4. [Optional] Introduce changes and justifications (e.g. new delivery methods/campaigns and pertinent metrics, abandon failed methods)
5. Monitor
6. Re-evaluate (upon milestones) & assess results
7. Repeat from step 3.

3   The Evaluation Tool

A tool is provided for a formally validated aggregation of the individual awareness-related processes' evaluation, through their respective metrics, and their cost, in order to produce an overall score. This is accomplished via a model-based framework for dynamic metrics composition and awareness evaluation. In specific, Event Calculus (EC) [11] is applied for modeling the behavior of a dynamic system and calculating its awareness level through time. The resulting overall score is usable both as a benchmark for future iterations of the evaluation program as well as a figure presentable to higher management. Other features include recommendations based on a metric's record, both in terms of absolute value as well as in terms of the value's change over time. Areas with very poor cost-benefit performance are highlighted, including suggestions about specific changes that could help identify and address the causes behind a mechanism's subpar performance (e.g. "Consider revising T&A session material").

In this section, we describe the implementation details of the DSAPE application, the evaluation process of a security awareness program and the recommendation process. We present how our tool can be utilized by higher management in enterprises and demonstrate a use-case with all the aforementioned metrics.

3.1   Implementation Details

The DSAPE tool implementation is based on Event Calculus (EC) [11]. EC is a logic language for representing and reasoning about actions and their effects. Discrete Event Calculus Knowledge Theory (DECKT) [12] is an implementation of EC with the rule engine Jess [13]. DECKT can perform, among others, automated epistemic, temporal and casual reasoning for dynamic domains. DECKT is extended in [14] with real time events, preferences and priorities. The extended DECKT is transformed to an agent's reasoning behavior with a GUI, which is applied to Java Agent Development framework (JADE) [15]. Different security awareness agents communicate with the standardized Agent Communication Language (ACL) [16].

We model the security awareness program along with its modules and metrics as fluents, and the evaluation of metrics as events of EC and implement them in the extended DECKT. Every program, module and metric contains one method in Java that implements the formulas for evaluating its security awareness level and cost (based on the methodology detailed in Section 2). Moreover, we implement rules in

Jess that trigger the reasoning process of DSAPE for producing recommendations according to the current level of awareness. The security awareness agent maintains this security awareness program and reasoning process for triggering events for the higher management. Moreover, a multi-agent system can be constructed for large enterprises, where each agent monitors the awareness program of a smaller division and communicates with the rest of the agents to produce an aggregated recommendation report. Fig. 1 illustrates the software layers of DSAPE.

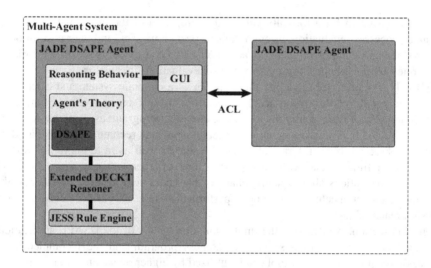

Fig. 1. Software layers of DSAPE

The agent's developer GUI consists of six tabs. The first tab is the agent's *view*. It contains the agent's knowledge base – where the latest changes are indicated with red color; the agent's output – where messages for the reasoning process and communication with other agents are reported; agent's input – where new events can be indicated; and agent's connection – where the agent can connect to other agents and exchange information. The second tab is the agent's *theory*. It consists of rules in Jess, which describe the composition of the security awareness program's modules and metrics, the reasoning process for local recommendations and the communication with other agents. The third tab is the agent's *facts*. They are the basic definitions and facts declarations in Jess that are used in the reasoning process. The fourth tab is the agent's *model*. It traces the latest reasoning process of the extended DECKT. The fifth tab is the agent's *recommendations*. It summarizes the active recommendations of DSAPE along with the remaining budget. The recommendations are grouped in four categories (periodic, temporal, casual and reactive), as described in sub-section 3.3. The last tab is the *DSAPE tab*. It illustrates the local security awareness program as well as its modules and metrics along with their evaluation, their weights (both for individual metrics and their corresponding module weights), as well as their cost values. Low awareness values (less than 30%) are marked with red color, neutral awareness values (30%-70%) are marked with blue color and high awareness values (more than 70%) are marked with green color. The total cost is marked with red color when it reaches a cost threshold, which is specified by the user (as percentage of the organizations budget), to denote the low limited capabilities for performing security awareness activities during the remaining economic period.

DSAPE features a GUI for end-users, implemented in HTML and JavaScript. Users are expected to update the metrics after an awareness event; choosing the metric to be updated and passing the new parameters. Then the agent processes the new event and evaluates the new state of the security awareness program. Users can also view the program's details and receive the latest recommendation report.

3.2   Value Aggregation

A security awareness program is composed of modules and each module is composed of evaluated metrics. When a metric is evaluated there are two functions for calculating its awareness value and cost respectively. The awareness value of a module is the weighted sum of its underlying metrics' value, while its cost is the sum of the costs of these metrics. Respectively, the awareness value of the program is the weighted summation of the program's modules and the total cost is the summation of their costs.

When a metric is evaluated, an event occurs to determine the new program state. The metric's functions for calculating its security awareness level and its cost are executed. The event can change the awareness and cost values of the relevant metric, module and program and can trigger the reasoning process of the awareness agent. Metrics and modules can be deployed or deleted dynamically along with their weights and evaluating functions. The weights can then be re-distributed automatically, or, ideally, via user interaction. The DSAPE application includes 12 modules and 18 metrics, as previously presented, but can be tailored to each organization's needs. For example, an organization can begin with only a small subset of the proposed metrics and modules and add more of them as the security awareness evaluation proceeds. Moreover, it can construct its own metrics and modules according to its business practices and the latest progresses in security awareness.

3.3   Recommendation Reports

The recommendation report procedure is one of the main features of DSAPE. We can model recommendations for periodic, temporal, casual and reactive actions. *Periodic* actions include events that have to be performed in a recurrent manner. Recommendations for periodic actions can include notations for annual and monthly events (e.g. annual surveys and monthly newsletters). A rule is implemented for every periodic action which is triggered after the last update of the relevant metric and determines when the new update has to be performed according to the action's period.

Temporal actions are operations that must be performed at a specific time. For example, the immediate informing of the company's personnel for a serious security incident via an iNotice (and then re-evaluate the security awareness program by performing the relevant metrics). A rule is modeled to erase the notation once the action is performed. *Casual* actions are occasional procedures that are assigned by the management team. An unplanned security audit at a department could be a casual action. A rule is in charge of reporting and erasing the relevant notification. *Reactive* actions are automated activities that are planned by the security management team and determine the organization's reaction based on the current state of the security awareness program. It is a core AI process that performs the organization's strategy for improving the security awareness level. As an example, consider an organization with low security awareness level. First, it should initiate actions to train its employees. Then, it should evaluate the training procedure. If it is acceptable, the organization should proceed to a sampling security audit to its departments. If the audit accents a low enforcement of the security procedures that had been communicated during training, the organization should plan a new training action. Moreover, the reactive plan can take into account an annual budget for security awareness activities. The cost of deploying the periodic actions and the rest actions the have been performed so far is abstracted, and reactive actions are suggested based on the remaining budget.

DSAPE can be used to estimate the effectiveness of an implemented metric through time by tracing its past values. It can also be used to identify the most efficient security awareness operations based on this effectiveness control and a cost-benefit procedure. The framework can, thus, indicate preferable metrics for a specific category and which should be avoided or even eliminated. An analysis of these reports by the management team can lead to a better adjustment of the security awareness program's modules, metrics and their relevant weights for this specific organization.

3.4   Multi-agent DSAPE Application

The single agent DSAPE application can be utilized by small and medium companies for evaluating their security awareness level, as described in the previous sections. However, large enterprises with many divisions and/or offices in various premises or with global reach cannot be effectively evaluated by a single agent.

Thus, a multi-agent DSAPE system is proposed to meet such requirements, where each different division can deploy a DSAPE agent for monitoring and improving its local security awareness level. Other than the recommendations pertinent to this local division, agents can be modeled to communicate high level information to a master agent. The master agent collects all these pieces of knowledge and presents them to the higher levels of management, located in the company headquarters or elsewhere. Thereby, conclusions can be derived about regional security awareness behavior and habits as well as the security awareness status of the organization as a whole. This knowledge can also be combined with other decision making systems (e.g. Management of Information Systems), assessing the upcoming actions in improving the overall security awareness level and the investments in specific countries or geographical regions.

The master DSAPE agent can apply more complex metrics and modules as well as a social reasoning process that runs the DSAPE multi-agent community. The overall security awareness level of a DSAPE multi-agent system is estimated by this master agent and is calculated as the weighted summation of the underlying local security awareness programs and the overall cost as the summation of the costs for evaluating these programs.

3.5   Demonstration

This section presents an application of a single DSAPE agent evaluating the security awareness level of a small organization with 50 employees. For the sake of simplicity, periodic, temporal and casual actions are not included.

Sample weights (as described in subsection 2.2 above) are set and the reactive strategy (described in sub-section 3.3) is modelled. It is assumed that all metrics have been evaluated by the organization at least once. However, the security awareness level is low (28.6%). An e-learning session is performed and its effectiveness is evaluated, updating the e-learning module (metrics M_{13} to M_{15}). For M_{13}, 40 of the 50 employees visit the e-learning web site, increasing the metric's value from 40% to 80%. For M_{14}, 34 of the 40 employees that visit the e-learning site (M_{13}) register to the e-learning program, achieving 85%. For M_{15}, 32 of the 34 registered employees (M_{14}) complete the program successfully, succeeding 95%. Thus, the e-learning module takes the high value 89%. The security awareness level is increased to 33.7% and the program's cost is increased by 60$. DSAPE then indicates an audit action would be beneficial, thus an audit session is performed and the result is evaluated (updating the independent observation module, metrics M_{4-5}, accordingly). A phishing e-mail was sent to each employee (totally 50 e-mails), exhorting the receiver to visit a suspicious web site. For M_4, only 5 employees didn't visit the web site (45 successful phishing attacks), thus the metric achieves a low value of 10%. Moreover, the awareness team sent an e-mail to every employee with a link to a legitimate web site that informs the visitor about new threats and security issues. For M_5, 5 of the total 50 employees eventually visit the web site to get informed about the latest news in security, accomplishing 10%. The pure performance of the personnel reflects to the low value for the independent observation module of only 10%. The security awareness level is decreased to 32.3% and the cost is increased by 30$. DSAPE reveals the low enforcement of the security practices that were learned and suggests planning a new training activity.

Fig. 2 summarizes the security awareness program's state at two of the demonstration phases detailed above. "A" presents the initial state (security awareness level is low and denoted with red color), while "B" is the final state. The corresponding metric and module weighs as well as cost values can also be seen in this figure.

Security Awareness Program
(*Awareness Level:* 28.6, *Cost:* 400.0)
- Surveys (16.0, 60.0) -- 15%
  - o M1 (30.0, 30.0) -- 30%
  - o M2 (10.0, 30.0) -- 70%
- Awareness/security days (30.0, 80.0) -- 5%
  - o M3 (30.0, 80.0) -- 100%
- Independent observations (24.0, 30.0) -- 10%
  - o M4 (20.0, 20.0) -- 60%
  - o M5 (30.0, 10.0) -- 40%
- Audit reports (30.0, 20.0) -- 10%
  - o M6 (30.0, 20.0) -- 100%
- Risk reports (20.0, 20.0) -- 10%
  - o M7 (20.0, 20.0) -- 100%
- Security incidents (20.0, 30.0) -- 10%
  - o M8 (20.0, 20.0) -- 70%
  - o M9 (20.0, 10.0) -- 30%
- Awareness sessions (workshops) (15.0, 30.0) -- 10%
  - o M10 (10.0, 20.0) -- 50%
  - o M11 (20.0, 10.0) -- 50%
- Information security website (30.0, 20.0) -- 5%
  - o M12 (30.0, 20.0) -- 100%
- E-learning (38.0, 60.0) -- 10%
  - o M13 (40.0, 20.0) -- 20%
  - o M14 (50.0, 20.0) -- 30%
  - o M15 (30.0, 20.0) -- 50%
- Emails (40.0, 10.0) -- 5%
  - o M16 (40.0, 10.0) -- 100%
- iNotices (60.0, 20.0) -- 5%
  - o M17 (60.0, 20.0) -- 100%
- Posters (70.0, 20.0) -- 5%
  - o M18 (70.0, 20.0) -- 100%

A.

Security Awareness Program
(*Awareness Level:* 32.3, *Cost:* 490.0)
- Surveys (16.0, 60.0) -- 15%
  - o M1 (30.0, 30.0) -- 30%
  - o M2 (10.0, 30.0) -- 70%
- Awareness/security days (30.0, 80.0) -- 5%
  - o M3 (30.0, 80.0) -- 100%
- Independent observations (10.0, 30.0) -- 10%
  - o M4 (10.0, 20.0) -- 60%
  - o M5 (10.0, 10.0) -- 40%
- Audit reports (30.0, 20.0) -- 10%
  - o M6 (30.0, 20.0) -- 100%
- Risk reports (20.0, 20.0) -- 10%
  - o M7 (20.0, 20.0) -- 100%
- Security incidents (20.0, 30.0) -- 10%
  - o M8 (20.0, 20.0) -- 70%
  - o M9 (20.0, 10.0) -- 30%
- Awareness sessions (workshops) (15.0, 30.0) -- 10%
  - o M10 (10.0, 20.0) -- 50%
  - o M11 (20.0, 10.0) -- 50%
- Information security website (30.0, 20.0) -- 5%
  - o M12 (30.0, 20.0) -- 100%
- E-learning (89.0, 60.0) -- 10%
  - o M13 (80.0, 20.0) -- 20%
  - o M14 (85.0, 20.0) -- 30%
  - o M15 (95.0, 20.0) -- 50%
- Emails (40.0, 10.0) -- 5%
  - o M16 (40.0, 10.0) -- 100%
- iNotices (60.0, 20.0) -- 5%
  - o M17 (60.0, 20.0) -- 100%
- Posters (70.0, 20.0) -- 5%
  - o M18 (70.0, 20.0) -- 100%

B.

Fig. 2. The single DSAPE agent security awareness program

4   Conclusion

The key to a successful awareness program is continuous monitoring and improvement, which can only be proven by applying and following a specific effectiveness measurement approach. Through the use of DSAPE, the evaluation methodology and accompanying model-based tool proposed in this work, the awareness team and higher management will have a dynamic tool providing awareness evaluation and monitoring. DSAPE can, thus, be utilized to provide an assessment and validation of the results of a deployed program, enabling the stakeholders to monitor the level of the program's success with regard to meeting their initial targets and its effect on the organization's actual security awareness culture. The awareness group can then make informed decisions, setting targets for the next awareness program based on the results drawn from the current program's evaluation. Such an ongoing evaluation will provide the means to take corrective actions to ensure the best possible result for their effort and investment.

Acknowledgements. This work was funded by the General Secretarial Research and Technology (G.S.R.T.), Hellas under the Artemis JU research program nSHIELD (new embedded Systems arcHItecturE for multi-Layer Dependable solutions) project. Call: ARTEMIS-2010-1, Grand Agreement No: 269317.

References

1. Rantos, K., Fysarakis, K., Manifavas, C.: How effective is your security awareness program? – An evaluation methodology. Information Security Journal: A Global Perspective 21(6), 328–345 (2012)
2. Tryfonas, T., Kiountouzis, E., Poulymenakou, A.: Embedding security practices in contemporary information systems development approaches. Information Management & Computer Security 9(4), 183–197 (2001)
3. Petroulakis, N.E., Askoxylakis, I.G., Tryfonas, T.: Life-logging in smart environments: Challenges and security threats. In: 2012 IEEE International Conference on Communications (ICC), June 10-15, pp. 5680–5684 (2012)
4. Deloitte, Global Security Survey (2010)
5. European Network and Information Security Agency (ENISA), The new users' guide – How to raise InfoSec Awareness (2010)
6. National Institute of Standards and Technology (NIST), Special Publication 800-50: Building an information technology security awareness and training program (2003)
7. Kruger, H.A., Kearney, W.D.: A prototype for assessing information security awareness. Computers & Security 25, 289–296 (2006)
8. Savola, R.: A Novel Security Metrics Taxonomy for R&D Organizations. In: Proceeding of the ISSA 2008 Innovative Minds Conference, ISSA 2008, Gauteng Region (Johannesburg), South Africa, July 7-9 (2008)
9. National Institute of Standards and Technology (NIST), Special Publication 800-55, Revision 1: Performance Measurement Guide for Information Security (2008)
10. National Institute of Standards and Technology (NIST), Special Publication 800-16: Information technology security training requirements: a role- and performance-based model (1998)
11. Muller, E.T.: Commonsense reasoning. M. Kaufmann (2010)
12. Patkos, T., Plexousakis, D.: DECKT: epistemic reasoning for ambient intelligence. ERCIM News Magazine – Special Theme: Intelligent and Cognitive Systems (84) (January 2011), http://ercim-news.ercim.eu/en84/special/deckt-epistemic-reasoning-for-ambient-intelligence
13. Oracle-Java, JESS: the Rule Engine for the Java Platform, http://herzberg.ca.sandia.gov/
14. Hatzivasilis, G.: Multi-agent distributed epistemic reasoning in ambient intelligence environments. Master Thesis, University of Crete, Computer Science Department, Greece, Crete, Heraklion – Foundation for Research and Technology – Hellas, Institute of Computer Science (FORTH-ICS) (November 2011), http://www.ics.forth.gr/_publications/Hatzivasilis_Master_Thesis.pdf
15. JADE, Java Agent DEvelopnet (JADE) Framework, http://jade.tilab.com/
16. FIPA-ACL, Agent Communication Language (ACL), http://en.wikipedia.org/wiki/Agent_Communication_Language
17. Kruger, H.A., Kearney, W.D.: A prototype for assessing information security awareness. Computers & Security 25, 289–296 (2006)

A Critical Reflection on the Threat from Human Insiders – Its Nature, Industry Perceptions, and Detection Approaches

Jason R.C. Nurse[1], Philip A. Legg[1], Oliver Buckley[1], Ioannis Agrafiotis[1], Gordon Wright[2], Monica Whitty[2], David Upton[3], Michael Goldsmith[1], and Sadie Creese[1]

[1] Cyber Security Centre, Department of Computer Science, University of Oxford, UK
{firstname.lastname}@cs.ox.ac.uk
[2] Department of Media and Communications, University of Leicester, UK
{grw9,mw229}@leicester.ac.uk
[3] Saïd Business School, University of Oxford, UK
david.upton@sbs.ox.ac.uk

Abstract. Organisations today operate in a world fraught with threats, including "script kiddies", hackers, hacktivists and advanced persistent threats. Although these threats can be harmful to an enterprise, a potentially more devastating and anecdotally more likely threat is that of the malicious insider. These trusted individuals have access to valuable company systems and data, and are well placed to undermine security measures and to attack their employers. In this paper, we engage in a critical reflection on the insider threat in order to better understand the nature of attacks, associated human factors, perceptions of threats, and detection approaches. We differentiate our work from other contributions by moving away from a purely academic perspective, and instead focus on distilling industrial reports (i.e., those that capture practitioners' experiences and feedback) and case studies in order to truly appreciate how insider attacks occur in practice and how viable preventative solutions may be developed.

Keywords: insider threats, human factors, technical and psychological indicators, detection approaches, survey reports.

1 Introduction

Corporations today face an increasingly difficult task when it comes to their computer security. On the one hand, there are a plethora of threats (e.g., criminals, hackers, hacktivists) keen to penetrate defences and compromise systems and data. On the other hand, internal (or insider) threats appear to be on the increase and can be particularly debilitating given their privileged access to the enterprise. The insider-threat problem is especially concerning because corporations' defences are arguably still focused on external threats, resulting in inadequate consideration of attacks originating from those with inside knowledge of and access to systems, security processes, and precious company secrets.

T. Tryfonas and I. Askoxylakis (Eds.): HAS 2014, LNCS 8533, pp. 270–281, 2014.

To explore this problem further, and to better understand the various elements involved, this paper engages in a critical reflection upon the threat posed by insiders. We adopt a novel perspective that moves away from a purely theoretical discussion and instead concentrates on distilling the range of industrial reports, which capture broad experiences and feedback from practitioners [1,2,3,4]. We also look at case studies of insider-threat (our own [5] and those from CMU-CERT [6]), in order to further understand how and why insider attacks occur, and how effective detection tools can be developed and deployed.

Our reflection on the insider-threat problem is split into three broad sections. Firstly, we consider the nature of human insider-threats. This includes an investigation into the types of attacks actually being launched against enterprises, an analysis of the motives and psychological aspects surrounding these attacks, and the impact that new technologies may have on the future of insider attacks. We move on to study many of the industry reports that have been published (e.g., [2,7,8]), in order to assess how corporations perceive and are responding to this type of risk. Our findings suggest that there is an underestimation of the risks associated with these threats, particularly evidenced by the minimal investment being made. Finally, we describe techniques that are currently used for detecting insider threats, and explore the state-of-the-art research that is currently being conducted in this area, discussing the effectiveness of techniques and what limitations may exist. To conclude, we discuss own research within the Corporate Insider Threat Detection project (CITD), which aims to address the interdisciplinary nature of insider threat, to provide an enhanced detection tool that addresses both technical and human dimensions of insider threat.

2   The Nature of Insider Threat

In order to understand the nature of the insider-threat problem, there are several fundamental questions of interest. For instance, what exactly is the threat, and what are the most prevalent types? What motivates insiders to attack? Are some insiders more susceptible to becoming a threat? What behaviours may be indicative of an (impending) attack? What is the effect, if any, of new technologies on the problem? These are the questions which we seek to discuss in this section, with a special focus on real-world cases, feedback and reports.

2.1   Types of Insider Threat

There have been many definitions of insider threat throughout the years [9]. Some of these definitions emphasise the active misuse of insider privileges, while others broaden the scope and consider the negative impact of such misuse on the confidentiality, integrity and availability of the organisation's systems and data [6]. The essence of most definitions, however, is that an insider threat is a member of trusted personnel (e.g., employee, contractors, business partners) that used their privileged access for some unauthorised purpose such as revenge or financial gain, and to the detriment of their enterprise. CMU-CERT [6] identifies three types of threat based on observation of typical patterns and on the attacker's purpose and motivation – namely, fraud, theft of Intellectual Property (IP), and sabotage of infrastructure.

Insider fraud is regarded as one the most frequent kinds of attack [2]. Incidents of fraud can range from direct theft of company funds, to complex cases where company services or data is illegitimately traded for personal financial gain. Kroll Advisory's recent fraud report emphasises the strong link between fraud and insiders, in that, of the companies hit by fraud in the last year, more than 67% identified an insider as a leading perpetrator, signalling yet another increase from previous years' studies [10]. While this is concerning, an even more disturbing aspect looking forward is that according to the *Risk of Insider Fraud* report [2], practitioners continue to believe that their enterprises are at a high risk of insider fraud. This is clearly a serious and prevalent problem in companies today and, as hinted above, financial gain is one of the most common motives.

Another threat that causes great concern is IP theft. In this attack, insiders use their access to steal valuable company data, including trade secrets, business information, source code and customer information [11]. There are several key features of this type of attack. First, the target tends to be product information, proprietary software and source code (these are clear targets in CMU-CERT studies [12]). Also, attacks appear more likely to be conducted by technical personnel (e.g., scientists and engineers) [6] and using technical means (54% of insiders used either email, remote access channel or network file transfer [11]) rather than physical theft of prototypes, for example. Finally, a majority of these thefts are committed by employees with legitimate access to the stolen IP; almost 75% stole material they had authorized access to [12]. Although 75% is a strong statistic and it is therefore very tempting to monitor only these individuals for this attack, yet as other articles have highlighted (e.g., the case of the foreign national who stole Ford secrets worth in excess of $50 million [13]), insiders with no legitimate access are also causing a great deal of harm.

Incidents involving IT sabotage, as one might imagine, tend to be more technically sophisticated. These attacks often require privileged access to systems and networks, or particular knowledge of how they are configured. Examples of specific insider attacks range from insertion of malware (most commonly, logic bombs) to tampering and disrupting system hardware components. Moore *et al.* [14] provide one of the more comprehensive points of reference for data on these types of attack. Amongst their findings, some of the most significant include the high proportion of attackers who had system-administrator privileges (90%) and the crucial role of unmet expectations, disgruntlement and stress in the pathways to an attack (for instance, 92% of all the insiders in their sample attacked enterprises following a negative work-related situation or event). In terms of real-world cases, the attempted attack on Fannie Mae [15] is a perfect example of the sabotage threat. Presumably aggrieved after being dismissed, the insider in this case used the last hours of his legitimate access to upload malicious code set to auto-execute 7 days later and designed to erase essential company data on finances, securities and mortgages.

In addition to the focus on malicious insiders (covered above), emphasis on benign or accidental insiders has also grown [16]. These individuals have legitimate access to systems, but through carelessness, neglect or accident introduce a form of insider attack. These accidental attacks have become more important to organisations and researchers because, as studies such as the Credant [17] and Clearswift [18] surveys point out, they occur significantly more often than their malicious counterparts. Unwise email activities and loss of storage devices or laptops are some of the most common sources of these breaches. Further analysis on the different types of benign insiders can be found in several reports, particularly the Symantec's *Data Loss Prevention* white paper [19] where the author distinguishes a number of categories of negligent insiders.

2.2   The Psychology of the Insider

Researchers have argued that insiders have specific psychological traits and characteristics. Turner and Gelles [20], for instance, believe the following types of behavioural indicators need to be considered when examining insider risk: self-centredness, arrogance, risk-taking, manipulativeness, coldness, self-deception and defensiveness. Others have suggested that insider threats score high on the personality traits that make up the 'Dark triad': narcissism, Machiavellianism and psychopathy [11,12,14,20]. The UK's Centre for the Protection of National Infrastructure (CPNI) have identified a number of other personality characteristics they believe are typical of an insider, including: immaturity, low self-esteem, amoral and unethical perspective, superficiality, proneness to fantasy, restlessness and impulsivity, and lack of conscientiousness [21].

If it is indeed the case that insider threats possess specific psychological traits and characteristics, then it might aid detection if employers were able to be privy to their employees' psychological make-ups. However, there is also the possibility that specific personality characteristics are linked to specific attacks rather than all attacks. For example, an insider who scores high on narcissism and Machiavellianism and is a risk taker might be more likely to commit IP theft but less likely to deface Web sites. Moreover, psychological characteristics on their own are clearly not enough to predict that someone is likely to become a malicious insider, and also that there are other personal attributes that should also be considered.

It has been argued that shorter-term psychological or emotional states can also help identify the type of individual who is more likely to attack their organisation. Such psychological states might include stress, depression or anxiety, for instance. It has been theorised, for example, that those under extreme stress are more likely to become threats [11,20]. It might be that the insider instigates the attack to help alleviate the stress that they are encountering. It is argued here, however, that consideration of psychological states in isolation is not sufficient. As is often the case, an external event can trigger a psychological state. Take the case of a person who has experienced financial hardship – such an event may well cause extreme stress; however, in addition, the individual might see an opportunity at work to conduct fraudulent activities which will help them out of their problems. In contrast, someone who is under extreme stress because of marital problems (exhibiting the same behaviours as in the previous case) might be far less likely to conduct fraudulent activities. These examples illustrate the importance of developing a more holistic model on insider-threat psychology.

In addition to external events, psychological disorders have been reported to make some employees more of a risk to an organisation. CPNI have found that those with a gambling or drug addiction are more likely to attack an organisation than those without such addictions [21]. Of course, if an individual is identified as having such a problem, then an organisation might find ways to provide support for that individual, which in turn might reduce the risk they pose.

In considering the psychology of the insider we might want also to consider their attitude towards the workplace. For example, a person who scores high on the dark triad traits and is highly stressed might be less likely to attack an organisation if they have a strong affinity to their workplace. CPNI have found that those who do not follow established procedures, or read or follow announcements and instructions issued by their organisation, are more likely to attack an organisation [21]. Others have identified the 'disgruntled employee' as a real potential risk [22]; that is, someone who believes they have not been fairly treated by their organisation (e.g., missing out on a promotion). Our belief is that those who have a strong identification with their workplace, and then experience an event which leads them to disgruntlement, pose a greater risk. Whilst our preliminary findings have identified important psychological factors in the context of insider-threat, it becomes quite apparent that there is much more work to be done in this space, by considering a more complete view of the attributes that are associated with identifying potential insider-threats.

2.3   The Impact of New Technologies

As new technologies evolve within organisations, so does the potential insider-attack surface [3,18]. Bring Your Own Device (BYOD) is becoming increasingly popular within many organisations, and yet in the survey by Ponemon [2], almost half of the 700 participants state that BYOD has resulted in a significant increase in fraud risk. The same study also reports significant challenges in securing corporate data and networks that are now being accessed through this growing gamut of personal devices. There is a definite trade-off being experienced between the convenience and cost-savings of BYOD, as against the security implications and attack vectors that this also introduces, which organisations will need to consider carefully in the future. Cloud services also introduce difficulties regarding security of information. Credant expands on the risks associated with the cloud, and highlight that although this distributed approach has benefits, it translates into a direct loss of control for the business [17]. This introduces yet another possible attack vector, and could also be exploited as part of an attack by existing employees or by the third parties involved. Again, this raises the trade-off of convenience and cost-savings against maintaining and managing both data and security from within the walls of the organisation.

Social-media use is also generating complex new challenges for enterprises [8,23]. Through sites such as Facebook, Twitter, blogs and forums, sensitive information (e.g., trade secrets, organisation plans and IP) can be leaked much more easily than before and publicised to anyone, anywhere in the world. The literature is full of cases of this happening, and its affect on both private and governmental organisations [24,25]. Malicious or careless insiders are not the only concern either. As a result of the amount of information freely shared on these sites, external entities can now exploit social media to identify, target or recruit prospective insider threats [8]. As social media continue to expand in popularity, organisations appear to underestimate the power and reach that they can have. However, the ethical and legal concerns about monitoring personal communications, and whether this is a breach of privacy, remain to be resolved.

3   Insider Threat from the Organisational Perspective

From the previous section, it is clear that the threat from insiders is real and significant. Despite this fact, however, reports suggest that corporations continue to underestimate the associated risks, as especially evidenced by minimal investment. For example, the findings in the *State of Security* report [7] show that many companies allocate between 11-14% of their annual revenue to their total IT budget, and of this, they spend 10-14% on security-related issues in general. Investment in detecting and preventing insider threats is therefore likely to be much lower. Of course, the appropriate amount to invest must be determined contingently, by individual companies, depending on their circumstances. But there is evidence of general underinvestment in mitigating this risk at the board level. Another article [8] reports that 25% of respondents stated that there was no regular formal review of cybercrime threats by the Chief Executive Officer and the Board. This suggests that security in some corporations still has not reached the level of importance that it warrants, and again, this obviously has knock-on effects for any hope of adequately managing the risk of insider threat.

More specifically, Ponemon's survey concludes that a large number of companies are not attributing the appropriate priority to the risk of insider fraud, while also noting that it is becoming more of a challenge [2]. One of their main observations as it pertains to organisations' views on risk is that, although 61% of respondents rated the threat of insider fraud within their enterprise as very high or high, only 44% believed that their company viewed the prevention of insider threats as a top priority in security. This highlights that even though organisations view themselves as somewhat unprepared, there does not appear to be an overwhelming impetus to address the risks. These findings mirror those in earlier studies such as McAfee's report [7], where 68% of companies recognise insider threat in their security plans but only 48% have actually addressed it.

Another indication that companies may be underestimating insider threat is the lack of awareness demonstrated by employees and the dearth of training programmes offered. In one report [23], it was found that 42% of large companies surveyed do not conduct on-going security awareness training sessions with staff and, worse yet, 10% fail to brief staff on induction. This trend of poor awareness in organisations can also be seen more globally, as highlighted in the *Global*

State of Information Security survey [3]. The issue here is that due to a lack of training, personnel may be unaware of new risks that insider crimes may present to the company or, indeed, may have forgotten about the risks they used to be aware of. Due diligence is also a particularly salient point, as we continue to see evidence (e.g., [1]) of a considerable number of companies not conducting personnel background checks on their employees.

Companies' views on insider risk can also be understood from how they treat them once detected. The first aspect to note is that they are typically under-reported [8,26]. In Kaspersky's article [26], for instance, respondents reported that in 59% of the cases nobody outside the company was notified. PwC's survey [8] supports this point, but also found that for very serious fraud offences, some only issued a warning (18% of respondents) and, in a few incidents, organisations did nothing at all (4% of the cases). While we might assume that failure to report incidents is linked to the fear of negative publicity, it is unclear why, even in the case of serious insider incidents, stricter measures are not undertaken. This might further emphasise an underestimation of the problem within corporate culture, but could equally be due to a dearth of solid evidence.

4   Detecting Insider Threats

As the problem of insider threat continues to escalate, there is a growing focus on how to detect such attacks. Here, we explore the current techniques for detection, and where state-of-the-art research is moving towards in the future.

4.1   Techniques in Use

A variety of approaches have been proposed to mitigate the risk of insider attacks, focusing on prevention, detection and response. Best practices from CMU-CERT include: considering threats from insiders and business partners in enterprise-wide risk assessment; logging, monitoring, and auditing employee's online actions; anticipating and managing negative workplace issues; and developing insider incident-response plans [6]. While a number of these are in common use, the Malicious Insider Threats report notes that many more could be adopted [1]. As discussed in Section 3, what is required is improved education and awareness within enterprise, to encourage active use of such practices.

A key point that arises from published sources (e.g., [12]) is that many attacks are detected by non-technical means (e.g., co-workers noticing suspicious behaviour). Kaspersky's survey article on insiders also identifies reporting by co-workers as the main detection resource as well (indicated in 47% of cases), but also notes the contribution of IT staff in discovering irregularities in system activity logs (41% of cases) [26]. PwC's cybercrime survey identifies three approaches that organisations use to detect threats: corporate controls (e.g., suspicious-transaction monitoring), corporate culture (e.g., whistle-blowing systems), and those beyond the influence of management (e.g., discovering by accident or a third-party) [8]. They found that the effectiveness of corporate-culture methods has declined compared to previous years. From the detection methods reported, the only noteworthy increase in effectiveness compared with previous years was in automated suspicious-transaction monitoring (up from 0% in 2005 to 18% in 2011). It was observed, however, that whistle-blowing and tip-offs are still an important part of detection, contributing to suspicious behaviour being reported rather than overlooked. This does not stop at employees alone, since reports of suspicious behaviour may come from law enforcement, business partners, and even from customers [12,26].

Activity logs are becoming more widely used for detecting suspicious activity conducted on organisations' systems [26]. These can provide detail on a range of activities that employees conduct, from entering buildings and logging-on to systems, through to the e-mail communications that they make and the files that they access on a data server. This mass of data provides a wealth of information on employee usage patterns, including any potentially malicious activity that they may choose to carry out. However, due to the large amount of data that can potentially be logged, actually analysing this can quickly become a laborious and error-prone task. There is growing interest around the notion of automated detection of insider threat, and more recently there have been commercial software tools such as SpectorSoft's Spector360, SureView by Raytheon, and DarkTrace. The *Risk of Insider Fraud* report emphasises this desire for automated tools for detecting and analysing insider risk [2].

Many anomaly-based approaches [27,28] aim to establish what an employee's normal activity may look like, and then analyse how their current behaviour differs from this normal. This opens up a number of challenges, such as how to establish what is actually normal behaviour within an organisation, particularly given that there may already be malicious activity present, and how much of a deviation causes an employee to be classified as a potential insider threat. All organisations will operate differently, as do all humans, and so there will exist many forms of what is deemed to be normal. Likewise, the routine that employees will perform activities on a daily basis will often vary based on their current workload, their personal life, and their mindset, as well as demands made of them by supervisors and co-workers. An employee may well be asked, or need, to perform activities that are outside of their expected normal in order to fulfil their job, and yet this would be flagged as anomalous behaviour. For a system to automatically determine whether an employee is posing a threat or not requires very careful management by the system analyst. An excess of false-positives results in a burden of cases that require investigation, and could result in high resentment by employees. On the other hand, a false-negative would render such a system a failure and could allow the organisation to be severely damaged. It is clear then, that there are many challenges still left to overcome in terms of both detecting, and also analysing, the threat posed by an employee's actions.

4.2   State of the Art in Research

Given the severity of insider threat within many organisations and the strong desire to detect and prevent future attacks, there has naturally been a wealth of research around the problem. Here, we shall examine some of the most notable contributions in the literature and address issues that are currently present.

Brdiczka *et al.* [29] present an approach for proactive detection of insider threats. Their method incorporates structural anomaly-detection, which consists of four stages: graph-structure analysis, graph embedding, dynamic tracking, and anomaly-detection. As they address, this identifies anomalies within the data, not necessarily threats. In order to assess the potential of a threat, they conduct psychological profiling using the Big-5 model, with behavioural, text analysis, and social-networking information as the data used for their profiling. For experimentation, they detect malicious insiders in World of Warcraft data as a proof-of-concept. As acknowledged by the authors, however, in-game malicious behaviour is much more obvious than that of an insider threat in the workplace, who aims to be discrete in their malicious intent. Therefore it would be of great interest to know how the approach copes with more realistic data.

Greitzer *et al.* [30,31] discuss the use of psychological factors for identifying potential insider threats. They propose a Bayesian Network model that consists of a variety of binary observable behaviours (e.g., engagement, accepting criticism, confrontation, performance, stress, absenteeism). Each behaviour has a prior probability that estimates how frequently it occurs, and a weighting term that specifies how significant the behaviour is with regard to monitoring threats. They derive conditional probabilities through a training process, using expert judgement to assess the threat that an employee exhibits based on particular parameters being set to true. Due to the qualitative nature of the behaviours that are modelled, there remains a need for a human observer to assess whether the employee in question is exhibiting such characteristics. The authors note that future work is necessary to develop methods for automatically extracting and inferring psychological factors from employee-data analysis, rather than using subjective behavioural assessment, which is clearly a non-trivial task to achieve.

Kandias *et al.* [32] also present a prediction model that consists of psychological profiling and real-time usage profiling. These two aspects serve as input to a decision manager that determines whether the user is a potential threat, based on scoring their motive, opportunity and capability. Each user is categorized by their system role, their capability, their predisposition and their stress level. The psychological profiling is conducted by questionnaires that cover user sophistication, predisposition and stress level, whilst the usage profiling consists of monitoring system calls, intrusion-detection systems, and honeypots. The authors state that their future work will focus on the implementation of the model, and so there is currently no indication of how well this performs. The use of questionnaires for psychological assessment raises issues such as the accuracy of the answers provided by participants. In addition, a sophisticated insider may well be capable of circumventing traditional monitoring tools as part of their attack.

As we have seen, there are many proposals for managing insider threat. These approaches draw on a wide range of tasks, such as monitoring, detection, prevention, and prediction. Yet still the insider-threat problem persists. One reason for this is the difficulty of implementing such approaches in real-world environments. Proposals that rely on psychological profiling, for instance, may require compliance from the insider at some stage (e.g., accurate completion of questionnaires). Similarly, gathering data on psychological and behavioural factors within a workplace is a challenging task, as it also requires the attention and compliance of other employees (e.g., reporting suspicious behaviour), while also appreciating the related legal and ethical considerations with such monitoring.

Regarding the development of prototype detection systems, the lack of realistic testing data representing the activities monitored still remains a difficult hurdle to overcome. There has been work on the development of synthetic-data generation, such as that by CMU-CERT [33], where malicious-insider threat data is inserted within normal employee-monitoring data. However, they acknowledge that even these datasets lack the noise and variation that would be present in any real-world data. Undoubtedly, however, and as stressed in [1], there is certainly more that could be done by organisations in order to help support and develop the research surrounding insider threats. Previously, we have proposed a conceptual model for insider-threat detection [34]. As part of our on-going research, we have developed an initial system that is capable of reasoning about the threat posed by an individual, based on their observed activities in the technical domain, whilst also incorporating behavioural analysis and psychological assessment. Whilst the system performs well in preliminary experimentation, we are currently at the stage of requiring more complete data, either synthetic or real-world, in order to truly evaluate its effectiveness.

5 Conclusions

Our research in the CITD project recognises the multi-disciplinary nature of insider threat, covering research into the psychological and behavioural aspects that motivate an individual, development of detection systems and analysis tools, and education and awareness-raising within organisations. As a means to detect, prevent, and deter insider threat, the collaboration between these developments is fundamental for addressing the problem effectively. What is clearly apparent, though, is that the insider-threat problem is evident in all types of organisations, can originate in a variety of individuals, ranging from low-level employees through to high-ranking business partners, and can escalate into an attack in many different ways. In this paper, we provide a study on the problem, with the intention of allowing for a better understanding of the nature of insider threats, industry views on the risks faced, and prevention and detection techniques in practice and research. With this critical reflection on current findings and developments, we believe that this serves as an important stage in understanding the ever-persistent and ever-evolving threats that are increasingly occurring within organisations of today.

Acknowledgements. This research was conducted in the context of a collaborative project on Corporate Insider Threat Detection, sponsored by the UK National Cyber Security Programme in conjunction with the Centre for the

Protection of National Infrastructure, whose support is gratefully acknowledged. The project brings together three departments of the University of Oxford, the University of Leicester and Cardiff University.

References

1. Computer Economics: Malicious insider threats (2010),
   http://www.computereconomics.com/page.cfm?name=Insider_Threats
2. Ponemon Institute and Attachmate Corporation: The risk of insider fraud second annual study: Executive summary (2013), http://www.attachmate.com/resources/analyst-papers/bridge-ponemon-insider-fraud-survey.htm
3. PricewaterhouseCoopers: The global state of information security® 2014 (2013), http://www.pwc.com/gx/en/consulting-services/information-security-survey/index.jhtml
4. PricewaterhouseCoopers: US state of cybercrime survey (2013), http://www.pwc.com/us/en/increasing-it-effectiveness/publications/us-state-of-cybercrime.jhtml
5. Whitty, M., Wright, G.: Deliverable 3.1 - Short report of findings from Case Studies (Corporate Insider Threat Detection project), Leicester University Report (2013)
6. Cappelli, D.M., Moore, A.P., Trzeciak, R.F.: The CERT Guide to Insider Threats. Addison-Wesley (2012)
7. McAfee and Evalueserve: State of security (2011), http://www.mcafee.com/us/resources/white-papers/wp-state-of-security.pdf
8. PricewaterhouseCoopers: Cybercrime: Protecting against the growing threat (2012), http://www.pwc.tw/en/publications/events-and-trends/e256.jhtml
9. Hunker, J., Probst, C.W.: Insiders and insider threats – an overview of definitions and mitigation techniques. Journal of Wireless Mobile Networks, Ubiquitous Computing, and Dependable Applications 2(1), 4–27 (2011)
10. Kroll Advisory Solutions and Economist Intelligence Unit: The global fraud report 2012/13 (2012), http://www.kroll.com/library/KRL_FraudReport2012-13.pdf
11. Shaw, E.D., Stock, H.V.: Behavioral risk indicators of malicious insider theft of intellectual property: Misreading the writing on the wall, Symantec Report (2011)
12. Moore, A.P., Cappelli, D.M., Caron, T.C., Shaw, E., Spooner, D., Trzeciak, R.F.: A preliminary model of insider theft of intellectual property. Technical report, CMU-CERT (2011)
13. Kaspersky: Threatpost series: Insider threats (2011),
    http://usa.kaspersky.com/resources/knowledge-center/threatpost
14. Moore, A.P., Cappelli, D.M., Trzeciak, R.F.: The "big picture" of insider IT sabotage across U.S. critical infrastructures. Technical report, CMU-CERT (2008)
15. FBI: Fannie Mae corporate intruder sentenced to over three years in prison for attempting to wipe out fannie mae financial data (2010),
    http://www.fbi.gov/baltimore/press-releases/2010/ba121710.htm
16. Allen, B.: The accidental insider threat: Is your organization ready (expert voices panel) (2012), http://www.boozallen.com/media/file/Accidental-Insider-Threat-Panel-Discussion-Transcript.pdf
17. Credant: Insider threat (2011), http://go.credant.com/campaigns-insider
18. Clearswift: The enemy within: an emerging threat (2013),
    http://www.clearswift.com/blog/2013/05/02/enemy-within-emerging-threat

19. Wall, D.S.: Organizational security and the insider threat: Malicious, negligent and well-meaning insiders. Technical report, Symantec (2011)
20. Turner, J.T., Gelles, M.: Threat assessment: A risk management approach. Routledge (2003)
21. CPNI: CPNI insider data collection study – report of main findings (2013), http://www.cpni.gov.uk/Documents/Publications/2013/2013003-insider_data_collection_study.pdf
22. Holton, C.: Identifying disgruntled employee systems fraud risk through text mining: A simple solution for a multi-billion dollar problem. Decision Support Systems 46(4), 853–864 (2009)
23. The Department for Business, Innovation and Skills (BIS) & PricewaterhouseCoopers: 2013 Information security breaches survey (2013)
24. Sky News: MoD secrets leaked onto the Internet (2010), http://news.sky.com/story/753966/mod-secrets-leaked-onto-the-internet
25. Harrysson, M., Metayer, E., Sarrazin, H.: How not to unwittingly reveal company secrets (Harvard Business Review blog network) (2012), http://blogs.hbr.org/2012/12/how-not-to-unwittingly-reveal/
26. Kaspersky: Threatpost's insider threats survey (2011), http://usa.kaspersky.com/resources/knowledge-center/threatpost
27. Patcha, A., Park, J.M.: An overview of anomaly detection techniques: Existing solutions and latest technological trends. Computer Networks 51(12), 3448–3470 (2007)
28. Salem, M., Hershkop, S., Stolfo, S.: A survey of insider attack detection research. In: Stolfo, S., Bellovin, S., Keromytis, A., Hershkop, S., Smith, S., Sinclair, S. (eds.) Insider Attack and Cyber Security. Advances in Information Security, vol. 39, pp. 69–90. Springer US (2008)
29. Brdiczka, O., Liu, J., Price, B., Shen, J., Patil, A., Chow, R., Bart, E., Ducheneaut, N.: Proactive insider threat detection through graph learning and psychological context. In: IEEE Symposium on Security and Privacy Workshops (2012)
30. Greitzer, F.L., Hohimer, R.E.: Modeling human behavior to anticipate insider attacks. Journal of Strategic Security 4(2), 25–48 (2011)
31. Greitzer, F.L., Kangas, L.J., Noonan, C.F., Dalton, A.C., Hohimer, R.E.: Identifying at-risk employees: Modeling psychosocial precursors of potential insider threats. In: 45th Hawaii International Conference on System Science. IEEE (2012)
32. Kandias, M., Mylonas, A., Virvilis, N., Theoharidou, M., Gritzalis, D.: An insider threat prediction model. In: Katsikas, S., Lopez, J., Soriano, M. (eds.) TrustBus 2010. LNCS, vol. 6264, pp. 26–37. Springer, Heidelberg (2010)
33. Glasser, J., Lindauer, B.: Bridging the gap: A pragmatic approach to generating insider threat data. In: IEEE Symposium on Security and Privacy Workshops (2013)
34. Legg, P.A., Moffat, N., Nurse, J.R.C., Happa, J., Agrafiotis, I., Goldsmith, M., Creese, S.: Towards a conceptual model and reasoning structure for insider threat detection. Journal of Wireless Mobile Networks, Ubiquitous Computing, and Dependable Applications 4(4), 20–37 (2013)

Changing Faces: Identifying Complex Behavioural Profiles

Giles Oatley and Tom Crick

Department of Computing & Information Systems,
Cardiff Metropolitan University,
Cardiff CF5 2YB, UK
{goatley,tcrick}@cardiffmet.ac.uk

Abstract. There has been significant interest in the identification and profiling of insider threats, attracting high-profile policy focus and strategic research funding from governments and funding bodies. Recent examples attracting worldwide attention include the cases of Chelsea Manning, Edward Snowden and the US authorities. The challenges with profiling an individual across a range of activities is that their data footprint will legitimately vary significantly based on time and/or location. The insider threat problem is thus a specific instance of the more general problem of profiling complex behaviours. In this paper, we discuss our preliminary research models relating to profiling complex behaviours and present a set of experiments related to changing roles as viewed through large-scale social network datasets, such as Twitter. We employ psycholinguistic metrics in this work, considering changing roles from the standpoint of a trait-based personality theory. We also present further representations, including an alternative psychological theory (not trait-based), and established techniques for crime modelling, spatio-temporal and graph/network, to investigate within a wider reasoning framework.

1 Introduction

The motivation for this preliminary research is a long-standing interest in determining personality and behaviour from digital data and especially profiling insider threats, a situation where granted access is used illegitimately, often in situations where it is known that actions are scrutinised closely (such as by machine learning algorithms). How best then to develop a profile of an individual (we do not consider group behavior in this paper) so that criminal behavior, which is assumed to be different in some way to normal operating behaviour, can be detected. The data footprint will vary significantly based on either time, location or role, as the individual legitimately passes through their range of activities; for instance, an operator accessing a computer terminal at one location in the morning and another in the afternoon. Likewise, the data footprint will change according to shifting emotional states; for instance, the same operator working at a single terminal differently on different days, one day performing the 'harder' tasks first, and another day, the 'easier' tasks first. Thus, we have the general problem of profiling complex behaviours.

T. Tryfonas and I. Askoxylakis (Eds.): HAS 2014, LNCS 8533, pp. 282–293, 2014.
© Springer International Publishing Switzerland 2014

From collaborations with several UK police forces and crime prevention partnerships, we have seen a wide range of data and problems, with the need to develop models with predictive or classification power, embedded in decision support systems, namely: gun gangs, terrorism networks, retail crime gangs, volume crime, fraud and sex offences. Each problem collected different data, and therefore different techniques were more appropriate to model the criminal behaviour.

Recent research suggests that it may be possible to identify personality traits through textual analysis, that is, analysis of the style and nature of an individuals written expression. A person's identity or personality is reflected in everything they do, including website design [1] and textual communication on the Internet more generally. The growth of social networking websites has put an enormous amount of such written expressions into the public domain for the first time, and investigators have presented frameworks for forensic treatment of this data [2]. Included in our study, we present an unreported set of experiments related to changing roles as viewed through Twitter social media data.

Attempts to characterise personality typologies, include McAdams' intuitively appealing model [3] with the three levels of (i) traits, (ii) mental concerns and strategies (intermediate knowing), and (iii) life story (intimate level). Gosling [4] describes the trait level as painting a portrait in broad brushstrokes but which leaves out much of the finer detail. An example of a trait model is the Big Five or Five Factors (as used in our study), namely: extraversion, emotional stability, agreeableness to other people, conscientiousness and openness to experience [5,6]. There are many ways to be extraverted for instance, and what are these traits able to tell us about a person's values, beliefs, goals and roles; these are the next level of knowing someone. Having worked through the traits and personal concerns of McAdams first two levels, you strike the bedrock of personality – identity. McAdams describes this third level as *"an inner story of the self that integrates the reconstructed past, perceived present, and anticipated future to provide a life with unity, purpose, and meaning."*

For many operational purposes McAdams' lower level of traits can often be sufficient, and certainly, because of its extensive use, it provides a way of comparing research; over the last 50 years the Five Factor model has become a standard in psychology [7], developing a large body of research for comparison.

2   Geospatial, Network and Modus Operandi Data

Working with burglary data from West Midlands Police [8,9,10] in the UK, several new methods were developed, including the composite of geographical range and network connections as shown in Figure 1. Each 'square' is an offender, associated by co-defendant (arrested together) links to other offenders. The map for each offender shows their geographic range of offending. Each offender also had a list of property stolen against each of their crimes, and modus operandi (see Table 1), upon which it was possible to develop predictive models.

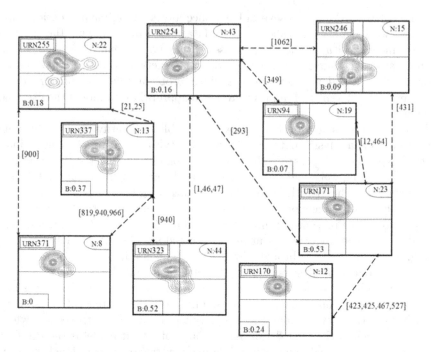

Fig. 1. Geographical networks. Each box is an offender, displaying their codefendent links, and geographical range of offending

The modus operandi data was routinely gathered by scenes of crime officers (SOCOs), and contained a range of 'styles' of burgling, using force or craft and so on [11]. A crucial recommendation to West Midlands Police was that the SOCOs would record richer data that could more adequately distinguish between obviously different crime locations and perpetrators, in order to infer behaviours and traits.

Ewart & Oatley [11] compared models that used just spatio-temporal data (including correlated walk analysis) against modus operandi, and a combination of both. The combined models performed best. Figure 2 shows a geographical plot with triples of [*offender home address, location, victim home address*] for a range of crime types, including woundings, murder, manslaughter, kidnapping and firearms offences. Representing the data in this way, we are able (as in the previous geographical network) to see offending characteristics such as criminal range, and relationships between crime types.

It is clear when looking at crime histories of certain gang members in Greater Manchester, UK, that they committed specific types of crimes, for instance it was unlikely for a career burglar to escalate the severity of their crimes to murder. There were predictors evident of future crimes: the future gun users often including in their histories lack of empathy (evidenced by abduction, rape) and failure to accept responsibility for own actions (aggression against police), and so on. It was clear there were different 'types' of criminal identified within the data.

Table 1. Burglary from dwelling house – modus operandi features

LOCATION OF ENTRY	1. Wall 2. Adjoining Property 3. Below, 4. Front 5. Rear 6. Side7. Roof 8. Window 9. Door 10. Above
ENTRY METHODS AND BEHAVIOUR	1. Smash 2. Cut 3. Cutting equipment 4. Duplicate Key 5. Drill 6.Force 7. Remove Glass 8. Ram 9. Insecure door/window 10. Climbed
TYPE OF DWELLING	1. Old 2. Terrace 3. Maisonette 4. Bungalow 5. Semi-detached 6. Town House 7. Flat
SEARCH BEHAVIOUR	1. Untidy Search 2. Downstairs Only 3. Many Rooms 4. Upstairs Only 5. Tidy Search 6. Search All Rooms
LOCATION OF EXIT	1. Wall 2. Adjoining Property 3. Below 4. Front 5. Rear 6. Side 7. Roof 8. Window 9. Door 10. Exit Same as Entry
ALARM/PHONE	1. Cut Phone 2. Tamper with Alarm 3. Alarm Activated
BOGUS OFFICIAL CRIME	1. Social Services 2. Bogus Official (type unknown) 3. Council 4. DSS 5. Home Help 6. Gardener 7. Other 8. Water

Similar type modus operandi and the geographic and temporal data was available for retail crime gangs in the north-east of England [12]. Retail crime is defined as specifically stealing from retail outlets or shops. We were interested in the most useful way of characterising a network or gang – was it perhaps on the basis of its membership (i.e. its stability, number, type: family or not) or do gangs differ on the basis of their geographical range and modi operandi, for instance falling into groups such a 'local', 'travelling' or not. We explored this by analysing line connectivity and node connectivity over time for particular gangs and the concepts of fragmentation, density, transitivity and core/periphery structures (see Borgatti et al. [13]). Certainly it was intimated from intelligence that within the data there were specialist and highly organised gangs, for instance gangs from eastern Europe specialising in purse theft, or a Malaysian gang targeting cheque fraud, or others favouring mobile phone theft.

3   Personality Theories

3.1   Detection (Covertly) of Personality Type through Game Playing

A set rules of nine rules, representing the nine types of the Enneagram personality typolology [14], was embedded in a game with various 'states' through which a user could navigate [15]; see Figure 3. States in an 'everyday life game' might

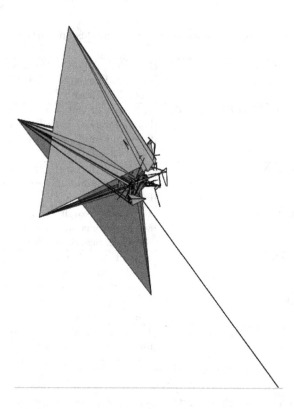

Fig. 2. Offender-Victim-Offence triples. Legend: woundings (light blue), murder (purple), manslaughter (dark blue), kidnapping (green), firearms offences (brown)

include: *'Getting ready for work'*, *'Taking an evening meal'*, *'Walking through a park'* and so on. States are linked according to real life, so you can pass from *'Taking breakfast'* to *'Travelling to work'*, but not from the former to *'Taking an evening meal'*. Questions are asked of the user at each 'state', the answers to which are known to indicate evidence of a certain personality type. For instance, rules for Types 2 and 5 are presented in Listings 1 and 2. Importantly, the player is unaware that the game is slowly determining their personality type (hence the name SNEAK). SNEAK actively searches for the nearest useful 'states' that can quickly lead to a classification, and plots a course towards them. As each state follows coherently from the previous, SNEAK presents the new states to the player, and the player is unaware of the unfolding analysis.

This system was a rapidly developed prototype, to investigate the extent of domain knowledge required to achieve a realistic classification. Commenting on the system, an experienced Enneagram practitioner said of Rule 1 that it was representative of the type but that *"...it could also possibly be a type2Giver. 'sensingPerfection' is too high a concept, probably something that the person is not normally conscious of."*, and of Rule 5, that it was again representative, *"but it is generally an easily recognisable type anyway, at least, by themselves."*

Table 2. Examples of intelligence related to retail crime

Aggression
NPI. Arrested Sunday [DATE] at TK Maxx, Ncle City Centre. Stole clothing valued at £150. Arrested [DATE] at M&S, Newcastle, for £20 theft. DOESN'T LIKE BEING ARRESTED!! MAY RESIST VIOLENTLY.
Modus operandi (what is stolen, from where and how)
Thefts from TKMaxx v £90, Eisenegger, v £64 and Sports Connection v £62, all committed [DATE].
Prolific. 31 Shopthefts recorded since [DATE]. Brief eg's - 240899 Kwik Save,Wallsend, £41 / 130599 Superdrug Ncle, £34 / [CODE] HMV Ncle £49 / [CODE] Disney Store Ncle £15 / [CODE] M&S Ncle £144
Arrested with [PERSON] on [DATE]Theft from HMV,Ncle,val £25, Method – One detags items,passes to other to conceal. Prev Shopthefts '99 - Fenwick [DATE]val £22 & [DATE] val £5, Superdrug [DATE] val £16, Boots v £17 , Bodyshop £5
Sighting by [STAFF], Bhs, Ncle at 1705hrs [DATE]. Suspected attempt Refund Fraud on trousers., val. £25.
At the close of a day's thieving/refunding he collects unused cheques and cash proceeds of fraudulent refunds, having probably allowed deductions for his cohorts' commission. Well organised. Seen in Curry's red Corsa [NUMBERPLATE].
Her last two thefts qualify Tams for a mention in this Target File. On [DATE] She stole clothing from two Newcastle stores - River Island, Eldon Sq (val.stolen £174) and Etams, (val.stolen £230) she has used foil lined bags in the past.
Drug addict, [PERSON] is out daily stealing to feed his habit, and usually steals DURACELL batteries which he can sell on for cash. He has used baskets in Stores/Supermarkets and wanders around with Duracell batteries hidden under a few groceries
Big value clothing theives using big foil lined bags. Make sure you are aware of them because they are very active and very good at their job.
Known associates and gang affiliations
Experienced shopthief and longstanding member of the [GANG], she has recently been arrested together with [PERSON] and [PERSON] (her Partner) on [DATE] for the usual BULK CLOTHING THEFT val.£684, from Littlewoods, Metro Centre.
Thefts from Fenwick and C&A [DATE] with [PERSON], [PERSON], [PERSON], and [PERSON]. VAL £474
Prolific Shopthief in company with partner [PERSON] IDO XXX, in Washington, Metrocentre and other Tyneside areas.

The rules were simple, the states were contrived and of a limited number, in order that every response from every type was able to be coded. This is a long way from automatically diagnosing someone's personality type through user interaction. Indeed, even for a human, administering a personality interview is notoriously difficult; for instance, the standard PCL-R assessment procedure for psychopathy [16] requires a semi-structured interview and a review of available file and collateral information. The purposes of the interview include providing a sample of the individual's interpersonal style, and allowing the user to compare and evaluate the consistency of statements and responses, both within the interview and between the interview and the collateral/file information [16]. Plutchick and Conte [17] confirm this difficulty: *"A simple change in test instructions e.g. 'how do you feel now?' vs. 'how do you usually feel?' generally changes a mood measure into a personality trait measure."*. Without significant structure it is hard to know what is being assessed.

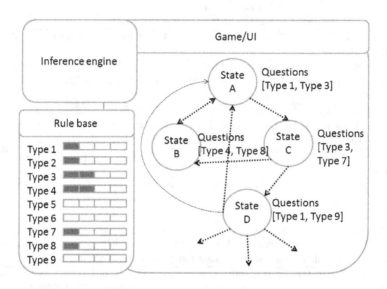

Fig. 3. SNEAK architecture. The rules/classifications are partially instantiated. SNEAK will direct the user to a question that will differentiate between the two most likely current classifications (Type 3 and 4)

Listing 1. Rule for Type 1 Perfectionist

```
Rule1:if
  (Person isa avoidAnger,A) and
  (Person isa postponePleasure,B) and
  (Person isa tryToBeGood,C) and
  (Person isa sensingPerfection,D)
then
  (Person isa type1Perfectionist,E).
```

Listing 2. Rule for Type 5 Observer

```
Rule5:if
  (Person isa needTimeToReflect,A) and
  (Person isa drainedByCommittment,B) and
  (Person isa greedyForKnowledge,C) and
  (Person isa
          detachesAttentionToImpartiallyObserve,D)
  then
  (Person isa type5Observer,E).
```

3.2 Detection of Personality Traits through Textual Analysis of Social Network Data

Advances in psychology research have suggested it may be possible to classify personality through usage of textual analysis of social networking sites rather than the traditional approaches such as interviews or survey self-completion. Studies in the USA have suggested certain key words and phrases can signal underlying tendencies and that this can form the basis of identifying certain aspects of personality [18]. Extrapolating forward suggests that by investigation of an individual's online comments it maybe possible to identify individuals personality traits. Initial evidence in support of this hypothesis was demonstrated in 2012 by a study which analysed Twitter data for signs of psychotic behaviour in respondents [19].

There have been many studies relating to personality and language using the Five Factor model of personality [20,21,22,23]. However, the Five Factor model has known limits [24,25,26]: it has been criticised for its limited scope, methodology and the absence of an underlying theory, and attempts to replicate the Five Factor model in other countries with local dictionaries have succeeded in some countries but not in others [27,28]. Additionally, while Costa and McCrae [5] claim that their Five Factor model "represents basic dimensions of personality", psychologists have identified important trait models, for instance Cattell's 16 Personality Factors [29] and Eysenck's biologically based theory [30]. However, as discussed previously, this model has a significant body of research, which provides useful context for studies.

We have used a top-down dictionary approach [22], as opposed to a bottom-up method, such as collection of words and n-grams. We use two standard psycholinguistic dictionaries: LIWC [1] and MRC [2], and the equations based upon these features, for the Five Factors, based upon the work of Mairesse et al. [7]. MRC category K_F_NSAMP is the Kucera-Francis number of samples (from the Brown Corpus analysis), LIWC categories UNIQUE, ABBREVIATIONS and PRONOUN are the number of unique words, abbreviations and pronouns respectively, and HEARING is a count of words such as 'heard', 'listen', 'sound'. An example equation is presented in Listing 3.

Listing 3. Equation relating to extraversion psychological trait, based on MRC and LIWC psycholinguistic features.

```
Extraversion =
    -0.0379 * MRC.K_F_NSAMP +   -0.0803 * LIWC.UNIQUE +
        -0.6074 * LIWC.ABBREVIATIONS +    0.1445 *
        LIWC.PRONOUN +   -0.3941 * LIWC.HEARING + 17.1407;
```

The data that we have used for this study is from Twitter, and specifically looks at a person's retweet count. This tag is an unofficial way to provide attribution to the original publisher. If a person wishes to share a tweet from someone else (irrespective of whether they agree or disagree with it), it is possible to

---

[1] Linguistic Inquiry and Word Count. Pennebaker and King [20] discuss the individual differences in linguistic styles, and developed the LIWC tool to try and measure these. Their text analysis software calculates the degree to which people use different categories of word, determining the degree any text uses positive or negative emotions, self-references, causal words, and 70 other language dimensions.

[2] The MRC Psycholinguistic Database is a machine-usable dictionary containing 150,837 words with up to 26 linguistic and psycholinguistic attributes for each – psychological measures are recorded for only about 2500 words. This data was empirically derived, which differs from the human judgment of psychological categories that created the LIWC.

re-tweet it and share it on their own Twitter timeline. The retweet count provides the number of times that the tweet has been re-tweeted.

Therefore, a retweet count of zero means the tweet is authored by the user, whereas a value greater than zero means that someone else authored the tweet, although the user has shared the content. A count of zero indicates the user's own words and sentiments, a count greater than zero indicates other's words. Of course we can make further categories, for instance a count of 1 will indicate people being directly followed, and much larger counts will indicate very popular sentiments, and so on. However for this study, we consider only these two categories. In this way, for a single user, we have two different chunks of text, aggregated self-authored tweets and aggregated followed tweets. We perform our Five Factor analysis on these, giving two sets of Five Factor results for each user. In future work we will use multi-dimensional scaling to work out an algorithmic difference between users; however for this study we have selected Chernoff faces [31] for the visual representation. The Five Factors are displayed as five features on a stylised face. Figure 4 shows the Chernoff face representation of the Five Factors (using the R language with the *aplpack* library). A specific facial feature represents each one of the factors. Additionally the height of face (extraversion) has an additional impact also on the colour of the face, the width of eyes influences the eye colour, the width of hair affects the colour of the hair, and the width of nose effects the colour of nose.

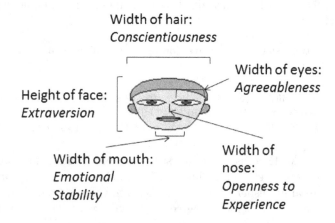

Fig. 4. "Mean" Chernoff face labelled with dimensions

The sample used undergraduate students (n=47) that engaged with a study (to be reported) looking at the correlation between social media profiles (Twitter, Facebook, LinkedIn) and personality typology and affect questionnaires: 44-item Big-Five Inventory, 12-item Dark Triad inventory, 30-item Trait Emotional Intelligence Questionnaire (Short Form), 144-item Riso-Hudson Enneagram Type Indicator Version 2.5 and 48-item Eysenck Personality Questionnaire–revised

(Short Scale). We have only presented eight profiles in Figure 5, deliberately choosing profiles that present significant differences between the self-authored and other-authored faces.

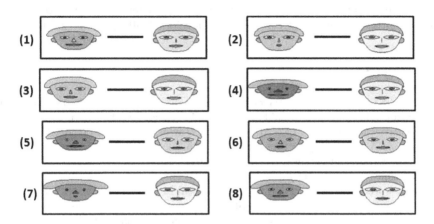

Fig. 5. Pairs of behaviour for a user. Left image of each pair is self-authored, i.e. self-image, and right image is other-authored but liked

4   Conclusions

While we have to be cautious about what we deduce in relation to criminal profiling [32,33], there is no doubt it is possible to determine certain traits of operational value from structured analysis of data from crime investigations. This will be equally true of data aggregated from other sources. Different data lends itself to different forms of analysis. In some circumstances traits and affects can be revealed, in others perhaps even the beliefs, opinions, or notions of identity (McAdams' top and middle levels).

This paper has presented a wide range of operational data and modelling techniques. These have differed with respect to the degree of knowledge inherent in the data itself, the sophistication of the modelling technique and the difficulty of the operational inference. The geospatial and network data (and their standard modelling techniques) are sufficient to characterise certain features of operational usefulness (matching crimes in an area, identifying possible accomplices, determining local versus travelling criminals), but barely reaching McAdams' trait level. Modus operandi data contains greater potential for psychological modelling, for instance whether someone is careful, risk averse, capable of violence, possessing a degree of craft, all indicating traits. The rule-based personality game illustrated the need for a heavily indexed and tightly constrained knowledge to detect personality features best described as McAdams' middle and even highest level. Finally the textual data from Twitter was sufficient to apply psycholinguistic techniques (although we are not able in this paper to consider the limitations of the approach), revealing personality trait knowledge (McAdams' lowest level).

The technique (and future use of multi-dimensional scaling) shows how different high level profiles for an individual can be computed and visualised.

It is hoped that with additional knowledge sources, and solutions from the converging fields of psychology and personality, mindfulness and psychoanalysis, with computer-based models (for instance, using belief-desire-intention (BDI) agents and life-logging) that this field will develop significantly in the future.

References

1. Vazire, S., Gosling, S.D.: e-Perceptions: Personality Impressions Based on Personal Websites. Journal of Personality and Social Psychology 87(1), 123–132 (2004)
2. Haggerty, J., Casson, M.C., Haggerty, S., Taylor, M.J.: A Framework for the Forensic Analysis of User Interaction with Social Media. International Journal of Digital Crime and Forensics 4(4), 15–30 (2012)
3. McAdams, D.P.: Personality, Modernity, and the Storied Self: A Contemporary Framework for Studying Persons. Psychological Inquiry 7(4), 295–321 (1996)
4. Gosling, S.: Snoop: What Your Stuff Says About You. Profile Books (2009)
5. Costa, P.T., McCrae, R.R.: Neo PI-R Professional Manual. Psychological Assessment Resources (1992)
6. Norman, W.T.: Toward an adequate taxonomy of personality attributes: Replicated factor structure in peer nomination personality ratings. Journal of Abnormal and Social Psychology 66(6), 574–583 (1963)
7. Mairesse, F., Walker, M.A., Mehi, M.R., Moore, R.K.: Using Linguistic Cues for the Automatic Recognition of Personality in Conversation and Text. Journal of Artificial Intelligence Research 30, 457–500 (2007)
8. Oatley, G.C., Ewart, B.W.: Crimes Analysis Software: 'Pins in Maps', Clustering and Bayes Net Prediction. Expert Systems with Applications 25(4), 569–588 (2003)
9. Oatley, G.C., McGarry, K., Ewart, B.W.: Offender Network Metrics. WSEAS Transactions on Information Science & Applications 12(3), 2440–2448 (2006)
10. Oatley, G.C., Ewart, B.W., Zeleznikow, J.: Decision support systems for police: Lessons from the application of data mining techniques to "soft" forensic evidence. Artificial Intelligence and Law 14(1-2), 35–100 (2006)
11. Oatley, G.C., Ewart, B.W.: Applying the concept of revictimisation – using burglars' behaviour to predict houses at risk of future victimisations. International Journal of Police Science and Management 5(2), 69–84 (2003)
12. Ewart, B.W., Oatley, G.C.: The criminal patterns of retail offending gangs: Some lessons from the integration of social network and geographical analyses. In: Proceedings of the British Psychological Society's Division of Forensic Psychology Conference (2009)
13. Borgatti, S.P., Mehra, A., Brass, D.J., Labianca, G.: Network Analysis in the Social Sciences. Science 323(5916), 892–895 (2009)
14. Newgent, R.A., Parr, P.E., Newman, I., Higgins, K.K.: The Riso-Hudson Enneagram Type Indicator: Estimates of Reliability and Validity. Measurement and Evaluation in Counseling and Development 36(4), 226–237 (2004)
15. Oatley, G.C.: Computer implementation of indirect questioning techniques for psychological testing. Master's thesis, University of Westminster (1996)
16. Hare, R.D.: Hare Psychopathy Checklist-Revised (PCL-R), 2nd edn. Pearson (2003)

17. Plutchick, R., Conte, H.R.: Measuring emotions and the derivatives of the emotions: Personality traits, ego defenses and coping styles. In: Contemporary Approaches to Psychological Assessment. Brunner Maze, pp. 239–269 (1989)
18. Woodworth, M., Hancock, J., Porter, S., Hare, R., Logan, M., O'Toole, M.E., Smith, S.: The Language of Psychopaths: New Findings and Implications for Law Enforcement. FBI Law Enforcement Bulletin (July 2012)
19. Sumner, C., Byers, A., Boochever, R., Park, G.J.: Predicting Dark Triad Personality Traits from Twitter Usage and a Linguistic Analysis of Tweets. In: Proceedings of the 11th International Conference on Machine Learning and Applications (ICMLA 2012). IEEE Press (2012)
20. Pennebaker, J.W., King, L.A.: Linguistic styles: language use as an individual difference. Journal of Personality and Social Psychology 77, 1296–1312 (1999)
21. Oberlander, J., Gill, A.J.: Individual differences and implicit language: Personality, parts-of-speech and pervasiveness. In: Proceedings of the 26th Annual Conference of the Cognitive Science Society, pp. 1035–1040 (2004)
22. Oberlander, J., Gill, A.J.: Language with character: A stratified corpus comparison of individual differences in e-mail communication. Discourse Processes 42(3), 239–270 (2006)
23. Iacobelli, F., Gill, A.J., Nowson, S., Oberlander, J.: Large Scale Personality Classification of Bloggers. In: D'Mello, S., Graesser, A., Schuller, B., Martin, J.-C. (eds.) ACII 2011, Part II. LNCS, vol. 6975, pp. 568–577. Springer, Heidelberg (2011)
24. Eysenck, H.J.: Four ways five factors are not basic. Personality and Individual Differences 13(6), 667–673 (1992)
25. Paunonen, S.V., Jackson, D.N.: What is beyond the Big Five? Plenty! Journal of Personality 68(5), 821–836 (2000)
26. Block, J.: The Five-Factor Framing of Personality and Beyond: Some Ruminations. Psychological Inquiry 21(1), 2–25 (2010)
27. Szirmák, Z., De Raad, B.: Taxonomy and structure of Hungarian personality traits. European Journal of Personality 8(2), 95–117 (1994)
28. De Fruyt, F., McCrae, R.R., Szirmák, Z., Nagy, J.: The Five-Factor Personality Inventory as a Measure of the Five-Factor Model: Belgian, American, and Hungarian Comparisons with the NEO-PI-R. Assessment 11(3), 207–215 (2004)
29. Cattell, R.B.: The description and measurement of personality. Harcourt, Brace & World (1946)
30. Eysenck, H.J.: Dimensions of Personality. Routledge & Kegan Paul (1947)
31. Chernoff, H.: The Use of Faces to Represent Points in k-Dimensional Space Graphically. Journal of the American Statistical Association 68(342), 361–368 (1973)
32. Alison, L., Bennell, C., Mokros, A., Ormerod, D.: The Personality paradox in offender profiling. A theoretical review of the processes involved in deriving background characterictics from crime scene actions. Psychology, Public Policy, and Law 8(1), 115–135 (2002)
33. Snook, B., Cullen, R.M., Bennell, C., Taylor, P.J., Gendreau, P.: The Criminal Profiling Illusion: What's Behind the Smoke and Mirrors? Criminal Justice and Behavior 35(10), 1257–1276 (2008)

Human Behaviour in Cybersecurity

A Conceptual Framework to Analyze Human Factors of Information Security Management System (ISMS) in Organizations

Reza Alavi[1], Shareeful Islam[1], and Haralambos Mouratidis[2]

[1] The University of East London, United Kingdom
[2] University of Brighton, United Kingdom
{reza,shareeful}@uel.ac.uk,
H.Mouratidis@brighton.ac.uk

Abstract. Safeguarding and securing information assets is critical and challenging for organizations using information system to support their key business processes. *Information Security Management System (ISMS)* defines to setup a solid security framework and regulates systematic way how securely information system can use its resources. However technical advancements of information security do not always guarantee the overall security. All kinds of *human factors* can deeply affect the management of security in an organizational context despite of all security measures. But analyzing, modeling, quantifying and controlling human factors are difficult due to their subjective and context specific nature. This is because individuals tend to have distinct degree of personal and social status. This papers attempts to propose a conceptual framework for analyzing and reasoning three main human factors in an organizational context that supported by goal-modeling language based on concepts of human factors, driving and resisting forces of Force-Field Analysis (FFA) tool, goals, risks, vulnerability, controls, and Threats. This framework is beneficial to better understanding of human factors in the process of ISMS that eventually leads to reasoning a rationale change in organizational context whilst providing reasonable metrics for security. One would be ROI issue that is concern of all organization.

Keywords: Information Security Management System (ISMS), Human Factors, Goal-modeling, Force-Field Analysis (FFA).

1 Introduction

Information Security Management System (ISMS) is necessary prerequisite for business continuity in organizations. To fulfill ISMS goals and objectives, a solid security framework requires ensuring confidentiality, integrity, availability, authenticity and auditability of the critical information assets. Technical mechanism such as authentication mechanism and cryptography, are essential parts of ISMS but people are responsible for design, implementation and operation of these

T. Tryfonas and I. Askoxylakis (Eds.): HAS 2014, LNCS 8533, pp. 297–305, 2014.

technological tools [1]. At the same time information security systems are highly rule-bound, centrally controlled and it is very exclusive. Bringing all other factors together, create an inclusive environment in which they can be more effective.

Therefore, ISMSs should consider non-technical elements, besides technical elements, in order to be inclusive, cooperative, and communicative whilst invite exploration and promote security satisfaction. Consideration of Human factors enables this but human factors at the same time are the most vulnerable part of the system. Human forces, such as irrational behavior and personal gain can adversely affect the function of security systems. For example, as a result of majority of security password policies that require a complex password from employees, people writing their passwords on the sticky note and attach it to their monitors. This keeps the gate open for intruders to organizations' system. It is important that human factors are addressed at the early stage of system design and in line with ISMS requirements. Information security studies generally focus on the effects of information security with less consideration of security threats quantification, human issues, and clear specification of requirements, which could assist senior management to make decisions on resource allocations and deal effectively with security threats [2][7]. Therefore, organizations remain without clear rationale on specifications of how to achieve information security goals and objectives in regards to human factors, which should have been considered from the early stage of design process. In our previous works [2] we defined direct and indirect human factors and initial analysis of three most influential factors. In this paper first we provide an overview analysis of three influential human factors, Communication, Security Awareness, Management Support and their attributes. Then we provide a meta-model to demonstrate the relationship between human factors and their influences on the control measures, which directly address risks and vulnerabilities. In addition, establishment of the relationship between main human factors and control measures enable ISMS for role-based training and awareness program by defining major human factors.

2   Human Factors of ISMS

The human factor domain is a combination of various disciplines including psychology and ergonomics and tends to optimize human performance in organizations [1]. It is a unique scientific discipline in which people's skills, behavior and restraints are applied together to enhance performance and satisfaction as well as overall achievement of organizational objectives. The dependencies between human factors and their attributes and ISMS goal is shown in figure 1. Figure 1 uniquely links the driving and resisting forces with the goal in terms of its satisfaction and obstruction. The satisfaction of factors and attributes provides goal with support and lack of achievement obstruct goal.

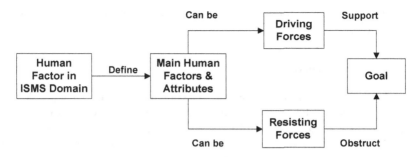

Fig. 1. Dependencies of Human Factor and Goal

There are several researches that highlighted human aspects as main causes of security [2][3][4]. In our previous study, we identified a list of human factors and prioritized three main factors, i.e., security awareness, communication and management support [2]. However the work does not consider the detailed attributes of the identified factors as attributes of human factors. This work provides detailed of these factors, identifying their attributes. Figure 2 provides an overview of three main human factors of ISMS and their attributes. Each single factor also related to other factors as functioning of every factor depends on the effectiveness and integrity of others. We used survey study and Delphi technique for the elicitation and prioritization of the main human factors. Both studies run in two financial organizations.

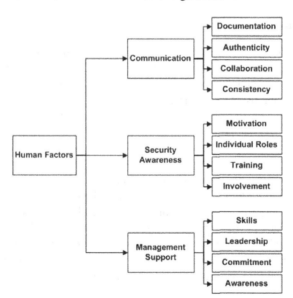

Fig. 2. Human Factors of ISMS

In the proposed conceptual framework we consider a detailed human factors domain analysis and goal-oriented in RE for reasoning the relationship between main human factors and the effectiveness of ISMS. Initially we provide an overview analysis of main human factors and their attributes, and then we present the concepts of the framework.

2.1   Security Awareness

Security Awareness (SA) generally defined as a combination of advising people about information security policies and systems.   Awareness also relates to constantly informed around current threats whilst reinforcing acceptable level of IS practices. Organizations have conventionally focused on technical and procedural security measures when implement their information security solutions and proposals [4]. Managing information security risks is greatly depends on forming an effective and convincing awareness culture. Awareness programs' central point is to generate general observation on IS [5]. However, from the information security perspective, this is inadequate because effective IS requires that users being aware of and use the available security measures as outlined in their respective organizations' ISMS policies and mandates. SA consists of the following attributes: *Motivation:* achieves stakeholders' willingness to participate in any proposed security policy. *Involvement:* ensures all stakeholders are included in the process. *Individual Roles:* provides a clear roles and responsibilities of various stakeholders. And finally *Training:* deliver all necessary and basic skills and knowledge to the stakeholders. For security awareness becomes a driving force, all attributes must be satisfied.

2.2   Communication

Communication (C) in organizational context is the exchange of messages and ideas between people inside and outside of the organization. The development of information and communication technology has played an important role in computer security [6]. Utilizing users in the direction of compliance with security policy, that is part of ISMS tolls and procedures, can be achieved through effective and persuasive communication. The subsequent effective communication involves reaching all employees in an organization at all levels of its hierarchy. Communication factor composed of the following attributes: *Authenticity:* maintains a reliable and necessary communications between stakeholders and ensures all information handled in confidence. *Documentation:* produces an audit trail in the communication process amongst stakeholders for the purpose of continuity and consistency. *Collaboration:* achieves a coherent and trustworthy communication between stakeholders to support mutual understanding. *Consistency:* attains organizations' objectives through stakeholders' steady communication. Achievement of the attributes enables this factor to support goal otherwise the factor would be a resisting factor to obstruct the goal.

2.3   Management Support

Management Support (MS) is essential for effective ISMS [7]. Information security regulations and standards explicitly identified that management should actively support security within the organization through clear direction, demonstrated commitment, explicit assignment and acknowledgement of information security responsibilities. The role of management in ISMS is not only to advocate, but also to deliver a clear message of IS security policy to the rest of the organization. The obvious example of management endorsement of ISMS in organizations is the allocation of an adequate budget, which is entirely under the control of senior management. This factor includes the following attributes: *Awareness:* This is different from SA that directly deals with the individuals SA. Awareness here defines that senior management must understand and be aware of the importance and necessity of ISMS for their respective organizations. Therefore the awareness of management achieves the objectives of all stakeholders. *Commitment:* enables ISMS to be supported by the top organizational hierarchy which important to all stakeholders. *Skills:* Absent of technological skills and knowledge in senior management, deprives ISMS goals from a solid strategic information security planning and understanding. *Leadership:* is one of the important quality factors for senior management to take the responsibility and ownership of strategic information security vision.

3   Proposed Framework

The proposed framework attempts to analyze human factors in ISMS. We followed and adopted two different techniques to identify our concepts and their attributes, the Force Field Analysis (FFA) and Goal-Modeling (GM). Goal-modeling applicability and its relevance to the organizational context have been of interest of software engineering community in recent years [8] [9]. GM is an early of RE for identifying problems and exploring system solutions and alternative. FFA is a decision-making technique to identify driving and resisting forces concepts involved in addressing goals. We used these two concepts from FFA in Human factors domain analysis assist to define the relationships between ISMS goal and human factors in organizational context (environment) on what the system is supposed to do and why. Goal in GM and FFA is an integration point of the concepts of these two techniques. Next section provides a definition of concepts based on this proposed framework.

3.1   Conceptual Model

Conceptual models are formed by concepts for understanding theme they depict [11]. Therefore, the concepts require be defining and presenting by examples. We use different concepts that are relevant for analyzing human factors. We follow force-field analysis and goal-modeling language for this purpose. The following concepts are important for analyzing human factors in ISMS:

- *Human factor*: Human factor is a unique discipline for optimization of human performance in organizations for achievement of organizational objectives. We identified three main human factors in our previous studies, which has four attributes. Each of these factors can be either driving forces or resisting factors.

Awareness, Management Support and Communication are the examples of human factor and each of them are followed by four attributes as mentioned previously. Factors can be driving or resisting forces depending the value of the attributes. If the attributes are adequate or true then the relevant factor is driving forces otherwise they are resisting forces that obstruct goals.

- **Driving forces:** Driving forces are the forces in organizational context that support change in the desired. Each identified human factors can be a driving force if all attributes are true and achieved. For example, if management support achieves all necessary attributes including skills, leadership, commitment and awareness then it becomes a driving force that supports the goal. Lack of management support can affect the allocation of budget that is essential for the continuity of security enforcement.
- **Resisting forces:** They are forces that oppose the positive changes and intending to keep the statue quo or current situation. Human factors become a resisting force if all attributes are false and failed to achieve. For example, E-mail as a communication tool could potentially become a resisting force. Authenticity is one of the attributes of communication and if it is not achieved then obstructs the goal.
- **Goal:** is a high-level objective for achievement that provides a framework for desired system in organizations. In ISMS goal contribute to the achievement of a process to ensure the confidentiality, integrity, availability, authenticity and audibility of the critical information assets in organizational context. For example, to eliminate possible loss and disruption of information due to compromised network for achieving a high level desire of reputational damage.
- **Vulnerability:** is a weakness in system that allows the integrity of system to be violated. For example, SA becomes a resisting force and creates vulnerability if lack of adequate training leads to use of weak password combination by users and pose a potential risk of unauthorized access.
- **Threat:** A Threat is potentially harmful activities that cause destruction, disclosure, modification and/or loss of data [10]. However, specific weakness doesn't create threat but the existing of information systems facilitates threats. Vulnerabilities are contributing to the threats. Threats are pervasive and complex in nature and can be classified as follows: **Internal** and **External** agents. The internal threats cause risks to organizations mainly through employees. Examples are, use of mobile devices or misused of privilege access to system. Examples of external threats can be the theft of employees' mobile devices.
- **Risk:** ISO standard defined risk as a combination of the probability of an event and its consequence [12]. In our meta-model vulnerabilities and threats contribute to risks. Risk is the outcome of the threat multiplies by probability and business impact. An example of risk would be when personal information is passed to unauthorized person.
- **Control:** is defined as any technical and non-technical measure or method that is used for addressing vulnerabilities and influencing human factors in our framework. For example, the support of management is an important factor in the process of ISMS that has been noted in ISO standards but to ensure this is an achievable control the attributes of this control that we listed above should be fulfilled. Control also contribute to the return of investment (ROI) as security expenditure are become an important matter for organizations.

Figure 3 demonstrates the meta-model that combine and model all the defined core concepts in this paper. The objective of this meta-model is to demonstrate and represent: a) main human factors attributes and, b) to demonstrate the relationship between these attributes and control measures in regards to risks and vulnerabilities. The meta-model is used as a technique to structure to analyze human factors in ISMS in a conditioned way so that it can be addressed to meet organizational needs. In this model, human factor is the main concept that consists of three main factors. Each factor has four attributes. If attributes of a factor are fulfilled then the factor becomes a driving force concept that supports goal otherwise it becomes a resisting force, which obstruct the goal concept. For example, the Management Support factor can only be a driving force and support the goal if the management commitment is achieved as well as other attributes. Giving a scenario in which an organization has a solid security policy in place and achieved a security credential, however, senior management is not committed to allocate adequate budget to fulfill the security goals. Lack of budget obstructing goal and creates vulnerability such as, exploiting users weaknesses using social engineering methods. Vulnerability contributes to a potential risk whilst threat causes risk. This risk could be loss of confidential data or reputation damage. In order organizations address vulnerabilities and potential risks, controls are recommended to address the vulnerabilities and risks and meet organizational requirements. This shows the dependency of controls to human factors and therefore controls influence human factors. An example of control would be recognition of adequate training program that conform to each individual organization considering that selection of appropriate and cost effective control itself can be a complex and subjective process. The evidence of the meta-model is the effect of the human factors'

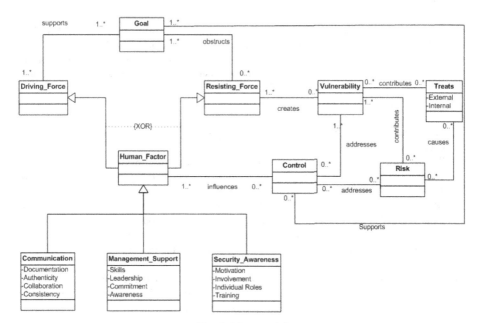

Fig. 3. Meta-model

attributes on individual roles in organizations. Decisions made about controls influence by role-based individuals in various positions, which derived from human factors' attributes. Any control measures assigned to address risks must be affiliated and appropriate to individuals concerning attributes of main factors. The main benefit of this metal model is to analyze and reveals major issues of conflicting desires and expectations in ISMS, which leads to reasoning a rationale change in organizational context. One would be ROI issue that is concern of all organization.

4   Conclusion

Our paper underlines the importance of understanding of main human factors in the effectiveness of ISMS. The proposed conceptual goal-modeling framework attempts to provide ISMS requirements and other related concepts. This framework provides a unique understanding of forces that promotes security posture and satisfaction of ISMS goals in organizational context. Conceptual framework of human domain analysis and GM contribute to the mitigation of risks and the effectiveness of ISMS in organizations. Our future work will be evaluating the proposed framework in two case studies to ensure that the framework can be generalized across the organizational context in real world cases as well as expansion of this work to two major areas of Information Security Assurance (ISA) and Return of Investment (ROI) and their concepts.

References

1. Lacey, D.: Managing the Human Factor in Information Security, How to win over staff and influence business managers. John Wiley & Sons Ltd., Chichester (2009)
2. Alavi, R., Islam, S., Jahankhani, H., Al-Nemrat, A.: Analyzing Human Factors for an Effective Information Security Management System. International Journal Of Secure Software Engineering (IJSSE) 4, 50–75 (2013)
3. Lee, J., Lee, Y.: A holistic model of computer abuse within organizations. Information Management & Computer Security 10(2/3), 57–63 (2002)
4. Puhakainen, P.: Design Theory for Information Security Awareness. University of Oulu, Oulu (2006)
5. Wilson, M., Hash, J.: Building an Information Technology Security Awareness and Training Program. U.S. Department of Commerce, National Institute of Standards and Technology (NIST), Washington (2003)
6. Dhillon, G., Backhouse, J.: Information system security management in the new millennium. Communications of the ACM 43(7), 125–128 (2000)
7. Reddick, C.G.: Management support and information security: an empirical study of Texas state agencies in the USA. Electronic Government, An International Journal 6, 361–377 (2009)
8. Islam, S., Houmb, S.H.: Integrating Risk Management Activities into Requirements Engineering. In: Proceeding of the 4th IEEE International Conference on Research Challenges in Information Science (RCIS 2010), Nice, France (2010)

9. Islam, S., Mouratidis, H., Weippl, E.: An Empirical Study on the Implementation and Evaluation of a Goal-driven Software Development Risk Management Model. Journal of Information and Software Technology 56(2) (February 2014)
10. Mattord, J., Whitman, M.: Management of Information Security, 2nd edn. Thomson Learning Inc., Canada (2008)
11. Mouratidis, H., Giorgini, P.: Integrating Security and Software Engineering: Advances and Future Visions. Idea Group Publication (2007)
12. ISO/IEC: Information technology - Security techniques - Information security management systems - Overview and Vocabulary. ISO/IEC 27000, International Organization for Standardization (ISO) and International Electro technical Commission (IEC) (2009)

Socio-technical Security Analysis
of Wireless Hotspots

Ana Ferreira[1,2], Jean-Louis Huynen[1,2],
Vincent Koenig[1,2], and Gabriele Lenzini[2,*]

[1] Institute of Cognitive Science and Assessment, Univ. of Luxembourg
[2] Interdisciplinary Centre for Security Reliability and Trust, Univ. of Luxembourg

Abstract. We present a socio-technical analysis of security of Hotspot
and Hotspot 2.0. The analysis focuses is user-centric, and aim at understanding which user action can compromise security in presence of a
attacker. We identify research questions about possible factors that may
affect user's security decisions, and propose experiments to answer them.

Keywords: socio-technical security analysis, hotspot ceremonies.

1 Introduction

The increasing demand for WiFi Internet access is pushing several public spaces,
such as hotels and airports, to offer Hotspots. These are open, unencrypted WiFi
networks that may redirect mobile users to web sites where they have to pay a
fee or accept some policy before being allowed to navigate the Internet. Hotspots
are spreading fast for they are believed to be a solution to the overwhelming demand of high-bandwidth services which is presently saturating mobile networks.
Unfortunately, current Hotspots offer little or no security [1][2], therefore Mobile
Network Operators are hailing the newcomer Hotspot 2.0 [3]; this is expected
to rely on a better technology[4], able to overcome present vulnerabilities by
encrypting every interaction and isolating all client's sessions.

Hotspot 2.0 main functionalities are twofold: (1) the seamless roaming enables
Mobile Network Operators to steer some traffic off the 3G and 4G networks to
WiFi networks without user's intervention and (2) access points will be able to
display information about their current load and available services before the
user gains access to the network. The latter being surely useful for venues like
a stadium facing very high demand in bandwidth due to some specific uses, like
instant replays; the network could block unicast streaming traffic on the network
and advertise the use of a multicast streaming service directly from the user's
connection manager [5]. Hotspot 2.0 is thus advertised as a progress, with better
security and better user experience.

However, despite its superior technical security, the *effective security* of this
new technology will depend on how people will make use of it. This aspect is
crucial as it has been proved that security mechanisms are rarely used by users

---

* This research is supported by FNR Luxembourg, project I2R-APS-PFN-11STAS.

T. Tryfonas and I. Askoxylakis (Eds.): HAS 2014, LNCS 8533, pp. 306–317, 2014.

as technically intended [6]. For instance, users may not trust Hotspot 2.0's new technology. Or users can accept it but the new acquired sense of security is no more justified if they switch back to conventional Hotspot, a situation that is possible since the old technology will continue to exist for some time, confusing users on what security risks can be present.

Analysing security issues with people in the loop demands for a *socio-technical* approach. This implies to look at the technical and the human protocols and to consider them together as complex layered ceremonies [7][8][9]. There is no such study for Hotspot and Hotspot 2.0, neither comparatively nor separately.

This paper covers this gap by describing Hotspot and Hotspot 2.0's most salient ceremonies and by studying their security with a user-centric approach. Its main goal is to raise future research questions and priorities about factors and mechanisms (e.g., user awareness, context, perception of security, trust) that may influence a more or less secure user behaviour in Hotspot's WiFi ceremonies. To devise those questions, we worked on four use-cases that cover most of the diversity of those ceremonies. In the next section, we first model the use-cases without any attacker (Section 3) and then perform a security analysis (Section 4). At the end of this paper (Section 5), we outline the setup of experiments allowing to answer the research questions that have emerged throughout this study.

2   Methods

The methods used to analyse socio-technical security of each use-case are: first we model the interaction between the different players of the ceremony with UML sequence diagrams; then we perform a security analysis by systematically devising the possible attacks when these interactions are exposed to threats according to a pre-defined threat model.

2.1   Modeling

We model ceremonies with UML sequence diagrams, a formalism that was successfully applied in socio-technical security analysis of TLS certificates [10]; it visually expresses all the sequential interactions (both Human-Computer and Computer-Computer) run by the players in the ceremony. This modelling is crucial for it defines the sets of interactions that can be analysed individually, in group, or at different levels of inter-dependency.

In order to get an objective analysis of the different use-cases, we divide the Hotspot ceremonies in common phases in which we identify one or more actions. Each action is the result of a decision, taken with or without user's involvement.

Prior is the action that happens before the user enters the ceremony; this is an optional pre-requisite (e.g., getting a SIM card by mail for instance); *Entry* is the entry point of the user, where he performs his initial action (e.g., open a url); *Selection* is the phase where the wireless network to be used is chosen from the list of available networks; *Access* is the action needed to successfully connect to the Hotspot (e.g., pay a fee); *Use* is where the user will actually use the network (e.g., performs again the action he tried in the *Entry* phase).

2.2 Security Analysis

Our analysis takes the user's point of view in the possible presence of an attacker who interferes with the user at *critical decision* points. These *critical decision* points are decision points from which the user can lose data confidentiality and integrity if the attack succeeds. For example, sending sensitive data should only take place when the WiFi is honest or the communication is encrypted. But, at this given *critical decision* point (choosing to send or not sensitive data on a communication channel), the attacker may push the user towards the unsafe behaviour, the *critical action* of sending the data. We first define the feasibility of the attacks through the following *threat model* and *assumptions*; then we identify the ceremonies' *critical actions* by assessing the user's risk in the security-analysis (Section 4).

Threat model: we consider two threats: (1) a Local Attacker (LA) that can read & write in the ether; it means in particular that it can bring up dishonest Access Points and listen to unencrypted messages; (2) a Distant Attacker (DA) that can read & write messages on the Internet; an attacker that provides a phishing link to the user falls in this category. LA and DA can also cooperate.

Assumptions: (1) we assume that all interactions taking place during the *Prior* phase are honest (2) we assume perfect encryption, meaning that the only way to decrypt encrypted information is by knowledge of the key. Under this assumption, HTTPS provides an unbreakable encryption and the honest server exposes a valid, verifiable certificate.

Risk assessment: the risk is described on a four-level scale: *null,* no attack is possible; *low,* the confidentiality or the integrity of user's action is threatened (e.g., when the attacker can listen to user's actions); *medium,* confidentiality of user's data threatened (e.g., when the attacker can listen to user's data); *high,* confidentiality and integrity of user's data threatened (e.g., when the attacker can tamper with the user's data).

Critical actions: are the actions for which the risk is at least medium, and also all other actions that are necessary for them to occur.

Results: we summarize the result of the analysis in tables. For each row – corresponding to a phase of the ceremony– we consider the following information in the columns: (1st) the *information* conveyed to the user, (2nd) the *actions* that the user can perform, (3rd) the *attacks associated* with this action, (4th) the *security property impacted* by these attacks, and (5th) a graphical representation of of the resulting *risk* level. The findings are further discussed in Section 5.

3 Use-Cases

We choose 4 use-cases that we think cover a large variety of situations. We concentrate on main differences like the automation (or lack of) the *selection* and *access* phases, the different types of players (e.g., persons, service providers), the need to pay during the *access* phase, the changes made to the encryption over time, and the information load and quality. We only consider a few types of authentication for the sake of space.

The first two use-cases relate to the Hotspot technology in use (abbreviated as HS1.1 and HS1.2) while the two last ones relate to the Hostpot technology users will encounter in the near future (abbreviated as HS2.1 and HS2.2).

HS1.1: Pay-Per-Use Hotspot. Fig. 1 shows the UML diagram for the pay-per-use ceremony of a typical captive portal Hotspot[1]. The players are a user, a browser, a connection manager, a wireless network provider and a payment platform. The *entry* point is a user who wants to browse the Internet; lacking of Internet connectivity, he proceeds to the *selection* phase where he scans for available networks and connects to the pay-per-use unencrypted wireless network. In the *access* phase, the user is redirected to the payment platform to pay the fee. The browser runs an HTTPS session, which often carries the usual HTTPS browser's cues (🔒), to execute the payment. After this step, the user is then free to *use* the (unencrypted) wireless network to browse the Internet.

HS1.2: Internet Service Provider's Homespot. This use-case is what is commonly called a Homespot. This is a residential router provided by an Internet Service Provider (ISP) that reserves most of its bandwidth for the customer who owns the device, but offers part of its capacity to the passer-by customers. The players are the (passing-by customer) user, his device's connection manager, the wireless network and the ISP. In the *prior* phase, the pre-requisites are that the user receives information (among these, the SSID) and his credentials. Using the same *entry* phase as HS1.1, the user then proceeds to the *selection* phase where he uses his connection manager to list the available Networks, and clicks on the one offered by the ISP. In the *access* phase, the browser is redirected to the ISP's online website, over HTTPS, where the user enters his credentials. As these are valid, the user gets a feedback from the webpage that he is now free to *use* the (unencrypted) wireless network

HS2.1: Mobile Network Operator's Partner Hotspot. Fig. 2 shows the UML diagram for the ceremony of a user connecting to a Hotspot 2.0 through his/her mobile phone. This requires no user interactions except the *entry* phase as the device will follow a pre-defined policy called ANDSF [11] to decide what network to join, and will use its SIM card to authenticate to the Hotspot. The ANDSF policy comprises user's preferences (e.g., always prefer user's home network), the Mobile Network Operator (MNO) preferences (e.g., roaming partners), the application requirements (e.g., steering traffic from VOIP to WiFi) and the Hotspot's conditions (e.g., the device should not switch to an overloaded Access Point). The pre-requisites (*prior* phase) are: the user gets the device pre-configured by his MNO, and sets some ANDSF preferences. The players are the user, the browser, an application, the connection manager, the wireless network and the MNO. In the *entry* phase the user opens a url in the browser which points to the content that requires the use of the application. The connection manager computes the policy bound to this application and concludes that it

---

[1] Captive portal : the user only has access to the Local Area Network until he pays a fee to be freed.

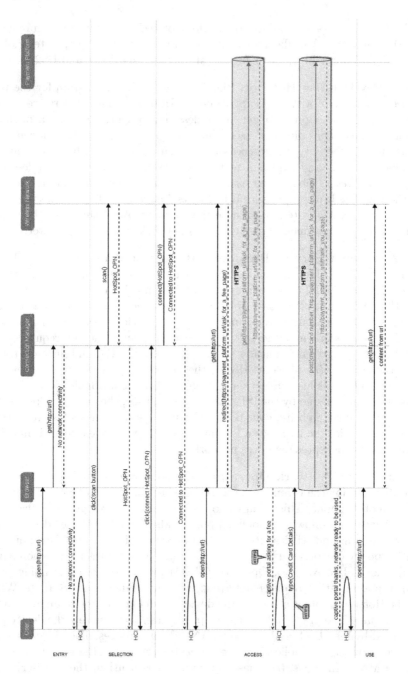

Fig. 1. UML diagram depicting user's interaction when joining a pay-per-use Hotspot. Components are at the top of each line, arrows represent exchanged messages: a plain line is used when a component initiates a message and a dotted line when a component replies to a message. The blue tunnels represent which messages are communicated within an encrypted tunnel with HTTPS.

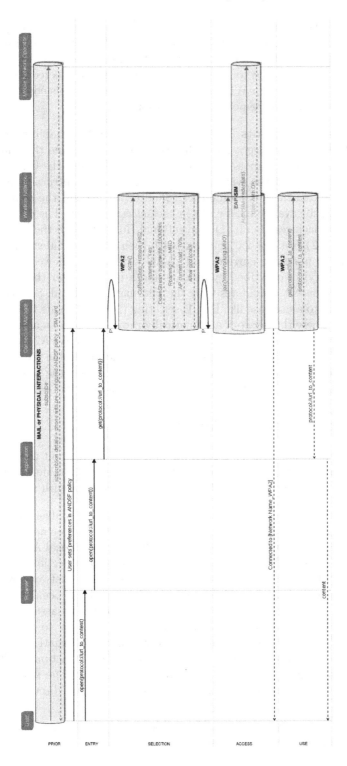

Fig. 2. UML diagram depicting user's interaction when Roaming on a Hotspot 2.0 Hotspot. Components are at the top of each line, arrows represent exchanged messages: a plain line is used when a component initiates a message and a dotted line when a component replies to a message. The blue tunnels represent which messages are encrypted using WPA2 protocol or communicated within an encrypted tunnel with HTTPS.

needs to connect to a WiFi wireless network. As a result, the connection manager automatically proceeds to the *selection* and *access* phases where it authenticates the user to the MNO. Once the connection is ready, the user is notified and, (*use* phase), the traffic corresponding to the content he requested is steered to the wireless network (encrypted with WPA2 Enterprise). Eventually this content is displayed to the user in the corresponding application.

HS2.2: The Future of Hotspots. This use-case focuses on the cohabitation of conventional Hotspots with Hotspot 2.0 with services support[2], when the automatic selection is disabled or impossible. The players are the user, the browser, the connection manager and the wireless network. The user's *entry* action is browsing the Internet; as there is no internet connectivity, he asks the connection manager to scan for available networks in the *selection* phase. The connection manager brings back results of: (1) conventional Hotspots with their SSID and signal strength; (2) Hotspot 2.0 networks with their SSID, signal strength, venue name, roaming partners, current load, WAN bandwidth, allowed ports; and eventually (3) services described by an icon and a url. The user then connects to one of the different candidates from the information at hand. Selecting (1) redirects the user to a use-case like HS1.1; selecting (2) or (3) sends the user to the *access* phase where the network automatically provisions him an account. As a consequence, all following interactions are encrypted with WPA2 Enterprise and the connection manager notifies the user that he joined the network. The *use* phase is different for (2) and (3): in (2) the user browses the Internet, in (3) the user's browser is redirected to the url specified by the service.

4   Socio-Technical Security Analysis

Our security analysis is user-centric, as such, its purpose is to pinpoint the critical actions prone to socio-technical attacks. Ultimately this leads to identifying upcoming research questions and possible laboratory experiments with users.

HS1.1: Pay-per-use Hotspot. Table 1 describes the security analysis of the HS1.1 use-case. In the first phase of interaction the user scans for open networks. As this interaction is not encrypted, it can be eavesdropped by a Local Attacker (LA) so, according to our risk assessment procedure described in Section 2, the risk is set as low. In the *selection* phase, the user picks a dishonest network from the list. By this action, the attacker only knows that his network has been picked; the risk is low. The *access* phase is protected by HTTPS, which by assumption sets the risk to null. In the last phase, *use*, the user decides now to use the network, here the user can give away a lot of possibly valuable information to an eavesdropper and the attacker can even tamper with subsequent actions if the user formerly selected the attacker's network, so the risk is high. The *selection* and *use* phases comprise *critical action* points and will be further discussed in Section 5.

---

[2] We assume the use of the existing CISCO's implementation of Hotspot 2.0 services, called MSAP; see chapter 12 of [12] for additional information.

Table 1. Socio-technical security analysis of the classic pay as you go captive portal

Phase	Information	Actions	Associated Attacks	Security properties impacted	Risk
Entry	No connectivity.	scan()	Eavesdropping scanning action.	Confidentiality.	
Selection	List of available networks.	connect(dishonest)	Eavesdropping picking action.	Authentication of the AP.	
Access	Webpage asking for a fee. HTTPS cues.	enter(credit card details)	-	-	
Use	Network ready.	open(url)	Eavesdropping information. Tampering.	Confidentiality. Integrity.	

HS1.2: Internet Service Provider's Homespot. In the Homespot use-case, the situation is closely related to HS1.1 as the user selects the attacker's network in the *selection* phase (again we set the risk as low). The attacker impersonates the ISP's wireless network but he can not (from assumption) tamper with the *access* phase, as the connection to the ISP relies on the HTTPS protocol (the risk is null). The attacker lets the user authenticate to the ISP, like he would do on a legitimate Homespot. In the *use* phase, the user takes the decision to browse the Internet on this connection, similar to the previous use-case. The risk is high as the user might lose confidentiality and integrity of his data. *Selection* and *use* comprise *critical* actions and will be discussed in Section 5.

HS2.1: Mobile Network Operator's Partner Hotspot. Table 2 describes the security analysis of this use-case. In the *prior* phase, setting a ANDSF policy does not pose any risk. In the *entry* phase, opening a url is considered as low risk because a DA can write a url in the Internet that, when clicked by the user, triggers the network discovery. The *selection* phase's actions are performed by the connection manager following the ANDSF policy (which has been altered by the user). The user can set a preference in the *prior* phase to rate unauthenticated, free Hotspot higher than the authenticated MNO's partners; this can be exploited by a LA which would provide a Hotspot 2.0 with corresponding characteristics. The risk would be high as the LA could eavesdrop and tamper with the user's data. LA and DA can also cooperate: LA can set an appealing hotspot while DA triggers network discovery. Both *critical actions*– setting a loose ANDSF policy and using a dishonest network–will be discussed in Section 5.

HS2.2: The Future of Hotspots. This use-case focuses on the *selection* phase when the automatic selection of an Hotspot is disabled. The user has to deal with different information emanating from different networks. The risk of connecting to a dishonest **network** that exposes appealing properties is high as it would

Table 2. Socio-technical security analysis of an automatic roaming to a Hotspot2.0 through an ANDSF policy

Phase	Information	Actions	Associated Attacks	Security properties impacted	Risk
Prior	SIM card. MNO information.	User sets its ANSDF preferences.	-	-	▯▮▯
Entry	url.	open(dishonnest url)	Trigger Network Discovery.	Authentication of source action.	▯▮
Selection	-	-	Appealing Hotspot2.0.	Authentication of AP.	▯▮
Access	-	-	-	-	▯▯
Use	Network Ready.	open(url)	Eavesdropping. Tampering.	Confidentiality. Data Integrity.	▮

lead the user to compromise his data's confidentiality and integrity in the last phase of the ceremony. The risk of selecting a dishonest **service** is even worse as the user would be automatically redirected to the url set by the LA. The factors that can influence this critical decision will be discussed in Section 5.

5   Discussion

For each *critical action* pointed out in the previous section, we elaborate on the following items: (a) research questions emerging from the *critical actions* about what factors (e.g., user's perception of security and trust, or user's awareness) affect the user's critical decisions; (b) experiments that need to be conducted to answer these questions.

HS1.1: Pay-per-use Hotspot

Selection phase: the user connects to a dishonest Hotspot As the only information conveyed to the user at this point is a list of available WiFi networks, the research question is: (a) what is the influence of the context, the signal strength and the likeliness of the name on the user's preferences? (b) In-vivo experiments based on deception (under strict compliance with ethical requirements like those of American Psychologists' Association - APA) followed by a survey are relevant to assess the importance of these different factors. Surveys and laboratory experiments where participants would have to choose from a network list to fulfil a high-stake task are relevant to refine our findings. Also, contrasting self-reported behaviour (surveys) with observed behaviour (e.g. lab experiments) would be useful to investigate users' awareness.

Use phase: the user uses a dishonest Hotspot As the user just pays a fee through an HTTPS connection before this *critical action*, we focus on the perceived changes of the security properties. (a) Are users aware that security properties change over the course of this ceremony and that after a successful payment, subsequent ceremonies are done in an open/unencrypted connection? If users are aware, what is their degree of awareness and how does that affect their subsequent actions? If users are not aware, do they feel the same sense of security during the whole ceremony or does it change at different stages? Do they perceive the signal and cues that can trigger user awareness for the change? Is there any more adequate contextual information that could improve users' perception of this change? (b) The main challenge here is to investigate how HCI factors impact the awareness and responses to security properties. Laboratory experiments can be set up, e.g., using different security properties as different conditions ideally in a between subjects design. Comparing user behaviour across the conditions would provide strong indicators that could be further understood through interview techniques.

HS1.2: Internet Service Provider's Homespot

Use phase: the user uses a dishonest Homespot We focus here on the impact of an unauthenticated and authenticated interaction with the ISP. (a) Does impersonating an ISP tend to foster a trust relationship with the network? Does interacting with the ISP through a secured-connection foster a trust relationship with the network? Is this true for any player representing authority? (b) Those questions can be investigated with laboratory experiments: users would have to perform critical activities (e.g., e-banking) through different networks–some impersonating ISPs, some authenticated as ISPs. Comparing user behaviour across these different conditions provides indicators that could be further understood through interviewing techniques. One important aspect in these experiments consists in reliably simulating the "risk" without compromising ethical requirements.

HS2.1: Mobile Network Operator's partner Hotspot

Prior phase: the user sets a loose ANDSF policy This decision can be linked to economic considerations, as the MNOs will sign many roaming agreements with different partners, they may keep track of the amount of data consumed by their customers when roaming on WiFi network. If this roaming is not free, users will be tempted to prioritize roaming on free Hotspot whenever they can. (a) How much money are users ready to pay to use the safe roaming partners of their ISP? Are they aware that free Hotspot may be free for dishonest reasons? (b) A laboratory experiment where people would have to do a trade-off between security and money would be relevant to investigate further this question. This could be achieved through a setup where different test conditions require different fees to pay. An alternative approach could consist in having experiment participants match different usage scenarios with different MNO fees and free hotspots. Indeed, various approaches could be set up here or even combined.

Use phase: the user uses a dishonest Hotspot 2.0 The network is chosen automatically by the device (a) Are users aware of which policy rule lead them to use this network? Are users aware of the cost of such a use? Are users aware of the modality of this connection (e.g., 3G/4G/WiFi)? Do users trust a connection after having been notified of its occurrence without having asked for it ? Do users trust their connection on their MNO's network through a third-party as much as a direct connection? What is the effect of the presence of a seam on the user's trust? (b) These usages are new and the technology supporting them is not widely available yet, therefore the experiments can not be easily built on existing "usage" standards. Interviews can be performed either in vivo or in a laboratory setup, with people who just experienced some of these situations, to understand what they are aware of in terms of security.

HS2.2: The future of Hotspots
Selection phase: the user connects to a dishonest Hotspot (a) Does adding more information about the networks help users to select honest WiFi networks? What is the phishing potential of those new information and services? Are users capable of searching for a network to fulfil a task and end up choosing a service instead? (b) Laboratory experiments where participants would have to choose a wireless network to fulfil a high-stake task are relevant to answer these questions. Networks would expose a range of technical qualities; services would be more or less appealing and related to the task.

6   Conclusion

This paper presents a detailed security analysis of hotspots. From this analysis, is possible to identify the various phases of a scenario where the user may affect security. It allows for a better understanding of how each phase may affect the security of subsequent phases or actions.

There is no one-size-fits-all solution. With the implementation of Hotspot2.0, we recommend that it needs to be better tested for socio-technical security. Although technical security has improved in comparison with the previous hotspot version, many issues still need addressing before its full deployment and usage in parallel with that previous version (which will not quickly disappear). We have provided a series of research questions and experiments to face some of the encountered security problems that industry and research will have to deal with.

There are also limitations to our work. The analysis was constrained by the specifications of the documentation that was available at the moment that is was performed. Event though Hotspot2.0 is considered superior with regard to security, our contribution shows such a system can be attacked and further research is needed. This on the other hand is made difficult by the relative lack of documentation on Hotspot2.0 at this stage. Moreover, our proposed research questions do not represent a comprehensive list and are rather a selection of questions we consider important to tackle next. There may be other relevant questions to address once we start answering the proposed ones.

We believe that it is important to analyse security of socio-technical systems, especially of hotspots, in this manner, because many technical attacks can only be fully successful at the user's end. The security analysis presented in this paper can help us focus on understanding what makes a user fall or not for that attack and devise more appropriate defences.

References

1. Chenoweth, T., Minch, R., Tabor, S.: Wireless insecurity: examining user security behavior on public networks. Commun. ACM 53(2), 134–138 (2010)
2. Stakenburg, D., Crampton, J.: Underexposed risks of public wi-fi hotspots (2013), http://ComputerWeekly.Com (accessed April 23, 2014)
3. W.-F. Alliance. Wi-fi certified passpoint: A new program from the wi-fi alliance to enable seamless wi-fi access in hotspots (June 2012), http://www.wi-fi.org (accessed April 23, 2014)
4. 802.11u-2011–Amendment 9: Interworking with External Networks, IEEE Std., http://standards.ieee.org/findstds/standard/802.11u-2011.html (accessed April 23, 2014)
5. Brodkin, J.: Nfl to block mobile streaming video in super bowl stadium (January 2014), http://arstechnica.com/information-technology/2014/01/nfl-to-block-mobile-streaming-video-in-super-bowl-stadium (accessed April 23, 2014)
6. Klasnja, P., Consolvo, S., Jung, J., Greenstein, B.M., LeGrand, L., Powledge, P., Wetherall, D.: "When I am on Wi-Fi, I am Fearless": privacy concerns & practices in everyday wi-fi use. In: Proceedings of the SIGCHI Conference on Human Factors in Computing Systems. CHI 2009, pp. 1993–2002. ACM, New York (2009)
7. Bella, G., Coles-Kemp, L.: Layered Analysis of Security Ceremonies. In: Gritzalis, D., Furnell, S., Theoharidou, M. (eds.) SEC 2012. IFIP AICT, vol. 376, pp. 273–286. Springer, Heidelberg (2012)
8. Ferreira, A., Huynen, J.-L., Koenig, V., Lenzini, G., Rivas, S.: Socio-technical study on the effect of trust and context when choosing wifi names. In: Accorsi, R., Ranise, S. (eds.) STM 2013. LNCS, vol. 8203, pp. 131–143. Springer, Heidelberg (2013)
9. Ferreira, A., Giustolisi, R., Huynen, J., Koenig, V., Lenzini, G.: Studies in Socio-Technical Security Analysis: Authentication of Identities with TLS Certificates. In: Proc. of the 12th IEEE TrustComm 2013, pp. 1553–1558 (2013)
10. Bella, G., Giustolisi, R., Lenzini, G.: Socio-Technical Formal Analysis of TLS Certificate Validation in Modern Browsers. In: Proc. of PST 2013. IFIP, pp. 309–316 (2013)
11. 3GPP Technical Specification 24;312 Access Network Discovery and Selection Function (ANDSF) Management Object (MO), 3GPP Std., Rev. 12.3.0 (December 2013), http://www.3gpp.org/DynaReport/24312.htm (accessed April 23, 2014)
12. Cisco, Cisco context-aware service configuration guide - 7.3, http://www.cisco.com/ (accessed April 23, 2014)

A Conceptual Framework to Study Socio-Technical Security

Ana Ferreira[1,2], Jean-Louis Huynen[1,2]
Vincent Koenig[1,2], and Gabriele Lenzini[2,*]

[1] Institute of Cognitive Science and Assessment, Univ. of Luxembourg
[2] Interdisciplinary Centre for Security Reliability and Trust, Univ. of Luxembourg

Abstract. We propose an operational framework for a social, technical and contextual analysis of security. The framework provides guidelines about how to model a system as a layered set of interacting elements, and proposes two methodologies to analyse technical and social vulnerabilities. We show how to apply the framework in a use case scenario.

Keywords: socio-technical framework, security analysis.

1 Introduction

Systems that are secure even when used by humans –a property that we call *effective security*– are hard to make. A system can embed technical mechanisms that make it technically secure, such as encryption protocols, but those mechanisms can fail if users bypass or misuse them. Such failures are common since humans do not perceive security as a primary goal [1] and do not properly assess risks when using information communication technology [2,3]. There is more: computer system designers, with a few exceptions [4], are not accustomed to count human cognitive and behavioural traits as risk factors in the security requirements. Thus, even systems that have been validated as technically secure, may still be insecure against non-technical attacks (e.g., social engineering) remaining oblivious of socio-technical vulnerabilities.

How can we achieve a better effective security? There is no once-and-for-all solution. Effective security is a complex quality to achieve. It is inherently socio-technical (it depends on how human and technical aspects integrate) and it may be context and culture (incl. education) dependent [5,6]. For example, in hospitals, access control solutions cannot be effective unless designed to fit the nomadic, interrupted, and cooperative nature of the medical work [7]. But, the same access control solutions would be judged differently in a context such as a bank, where employees work mostly alone and where security requirements must consider, for example, threats coming from hackers (e.g., see [8]).

To make a system effectively secure in different scenarios, it likely requires diverse strategies and solutions. However, it is possible to refer to a common framework of analysis. Such a framework should help computer security designers

---

* This research is supported by FNR Luxembourg, project I2R-APS-PFN-11STAS.

T. Tryfonas and I. Askoxylakis (Eds.): HAS 2014, LNCS 8533, pp. 318–329, 2014.

and social scientists to collaborate by providing an operational guideline for an interdisciplinary approach in studying a system's security, as well as tools and methodologies for questioning security at both the technical and the social layers.

Contribution. This paper proposes and describes such framework. STEAL (*Socio-TEchnical Attack AnaLysis*) appears from the need to have a common systematic framework matured from previous experiences the authors had in modelling and analysing socio-technical security [9,10].

2 Related Work

Zhu *et al.* [11] study how an attacker manages to influence the human to take the wrong decision and acquire his private information. They simulate a scenario where an attacker plays successfully the norm of reciprocity (mutual messages exchange with the user) with the victims who are shopping online with mobile devices. However, this study is incipient and does not provide a systematic way to test and mitigate this or other similar norms. STEAL could model the norm of reciprocity scenario with an overview of all the interactions and maybe provide defences that could be applied in different parts of the system, and not only within the human-computer interface dialogue.

Cranor *et al.* [12,13] propose a framework to understand how security failures happen when users misbehave because of flawed human-computer communications. This framework is a sequence of generic steps the designer follows to identify potential failure points for each technical function of the system, where the user participates. The designer needs to mitigate those failures, either by eliminating user's intervention altogether if possible, or improving user's interaction. However, there is no specific model/methodology to reproduce both the sequential or the mitigation process and to enable/operationalize scientific-experimental research. Moreover, Cranor's research assumes to know exactly how a technical function will be used by a human and tries to improve it before its usage. So humans are bound by the technology and how a function can be performed, but this may not always be true. The next two works also assume this. Conti et al. [14] research on visualization systems that typically include the human in the decision-making loop and present a visual taxonomy to identify attacks. Falk et al. [15] examine the prevalence of user-visible security design flaws in high security requirements' financial websites, and present a methodology to testing these issues: selecting the most common five security user-visible flaws of website design and identify them in a set of websites. All the above works study the interactions between the user and the computer interface, mostly clarifying usability questions, and not so much enquire about security in all systems' functions and interactions.

Our framework, instead, provides for the design and analysis of socio-technical attacks to the system's functions, humans, context and all its interactions. An attack may exploit bad communications' design but may also ignore technical functions altogether and focus on the context or the human to perform a successful attack. Moreover, although much research on security usability has been done, these studies are also mostly technology driven.

Other works justify the importance of contextual factors in systems' security in both ATM [16] and hospital authentication solutions [7]. STEAL also integrates context and its interactions in the security analysis.

Regarding social engineering, Janczewski *et al.* [17] review social engineering incidents to give a schematic representation of vulnerabilities usually exploited by social engineers and the attack methodology that better succeeds. Dalpiaz [18] has developed a Socio-Technical Security modelling language which specifies the security and trustworthiness requirements for cross-organizational systems.

Worton *et al.* [19] apply a socio-technical framework to two terrorism scenarios. It groups generic factors like people, goals, technology, culture, buildings, and its characteristics. It is not possible to have a clear overview of how the groups interact and how these interactions could, for instance, generate new threats. Pavkovic and Perkov [20] present SET (for Social Engineering Toolkit), a set of tools to perform advanced attacks against the human element. STEAL could be used to analyse these attacks in more detail.

In summary, we have not found studies that tackle the specific challenge proposed in this paper: to describe a framework providing a common systematic process to analyse the security of socio-technical and contextual factors together with all its interactions. To fulfil this gap, this paper proposes such framework and gives recommendations on how to apply it.

3 A Socio-Technical Security Conceptual Framework

By a socio-technical security conceptual framework, we mean an operational guideline for a systematic approach in modelling and analysing a system's security in its technical and social perspectives. Past research in security validation shows that important elements of such a framework are (I) a *reference model* and (II) a set of procedural *methodologies*. (I) is to describe, at a suitable level of abstraction, the elements of the system that we intend to analyse. (II) is to have tools for a technical and a social experimental analysis of security.

STEAL, our framework, includes them both (see Fig. 1). Its reference model (see Sec. 3.1) suggests a system as composed by interacting elements/actors (human, interfaces, processes, and context). Its set of methodologies (see Sec. 3.2) includes security validation procedures coming from the formal analysis of security protocols and from the applied cognitive sciences and usability research.

3.1 STEAL: Reference Model

It is a variant of the Bella *et al.*'s [21] concertina model (Fig. 1, upper part). A socio-technical system is abstractly seen as layered, each layer made of communicating/interacting elements. There is at least a human persona, say Alice (P_A), and the technology she is using. This is further composed by at least a human interface (UI_A) and some software processes (p_A). Processes can, through a network, communicate with other processes (p_B), behind which may stay one

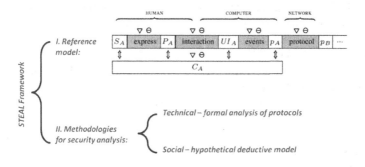

Fig. 1. STEAL Conceptual Framework

or more humans, say Bob (P_B), who are in turn interfaced to human interfaces (UI_B). Layers can be folded, with the effect that not all elements need to be necessarily in place. Representing our system in this way helps the analyst to select the key components for analysis, and to distinguish between the technical, the human components and the context.

STEAL extends this model by adding the context (C_A), and attack and defence models. Context is the physical or social environment where the interactions for '*Alice*' take place. C_A influences how A's *self* $(S_A$, in Fig. 1) expresses into P_A's, the way P_A interacts with the interface, and the software, which can be context-dependent. C_B does the same on B's side, not shown in the figure.

This simple reference model fits many scenarios. For example, in a ATM machine scenario, Alice (P_A) is the client, the user interface (UI_A) is the ATM's set, and p_A is the software executing the client instruction that connects the ATM with the bank (p_B). The context (C_A) is where the ATM is located, a street or the interior of a bank's hall. In a scenario where Alice is accessing a protected web page, the web interface is (UI_A), the browser is the process p_A that runs a protocol with the web server hosting the page, which is process (p_B). The context C_A can be Alice in her office, or in an airport's hall. In a scenario with a few persons collaboratively editing a file in the cloud, the persons are the Alices and Bobs, their screens and keyboards the human-computer interfaces, the software they use to edit and to browse are the processes. The communication happens via the cloud service. The context can be where those persons are, at work, at home, the latter being not only the location but also social environments.

Attack and defence models. STEAL comes also with an attack and with a defence model. They are both relevant for the security analysis, as security is always evaluated with respect to an attacker with specific capabilities (resp., a defender with specific capabilities). The icons ▽ (attacks) and ⊖ (defences) indicate where the model assumes attacks can strike and where defences can act.

Whatever the nature of the channels and the messages they carry, an attacker can intercept, modify and inject messages in any of those channels. These are typical abilities ascribed to a Dolev-Yao intruder [22]. However, differently from the classical Dolev-Yao, in STEAL, the attacker controls not only the network but also the interactions between the application, the user's interfaces, the persona, and the context. Therefore, an attack may be technical and or a social engineering kind of attack.

Defences also act by interfering with the communication channels. This includes the channels with the user. In our framework, users can participate to improve security, a substantial difference between our and other works [13].

Other assumptions. Our reference model assume that the observable behaviour of the system's elements under analysis is (at least at the level of abstraction chosen) known. However, it does not assume, and does not depend on, the reasons, or the logic, behind this behaving be necessarily understood. This assumption endorses a computational approach. A component (whatever it is, human, interface, agent or context) is an entity (an automaton) that behaves according to a certain control logic that determines its input, output and internal *actions* depending on its *state* and on its (previous) inputs.

For example, a user at an ATM machine, behaves according to some beliefs, desires and intentions that he/she has (withdraw money) which, according to his/her state of mind (I have inserted a pin and wait for the money to come out), determine the actions he/she does (taking the money once out). In its turn the ATM machine's logic is its software code, its state is the machine's state (pin inserted, now checking it), and its actions (display selection of banknotes).

In practice, we may not be able to define precisely a component's control logic, or to list the full set of actions it can ever perform, or to know the component's state in time. But, to build a sufficiently consistent picture (i.e., model) of the component's observable behaviour, one can apply indirect methods to inquire properties about an element's state and to test propositions about it, or by observing the actions it does. For example, we can build a model of a browser by looking at its code. In this case we know fully how it works. If the code is proprietary, we may not be able to fully know its logic but we can build a consistent model by walking through its behaviour. Similarly, we can observe a user interacting with our browser, but we may not be able to observe him changing his mental state (e.g., cognitive process), nor knowing why users behave in certain ways. We can only observe and ask him (e.g., questionnaire/interview).

This assumption is also motivated by the tools of analysis we are going to have: tools for a formal analysis such as model checkers, for the technical security, and human computer interactions methodologies, as those used in usability laboratories, for the social security.

3.2   Methodologies for Socio-Technical Security Analysis

STEAL has two methodologies for security analysis. One is apt to understand the security properties without considering a complex model of user's behaviour. The other is apt to question hypotheses on human behaviour and on security properties with the human in the loop.

The two methodologies, together, make the socio-technical analysis possible. The technical analysis helps, against specific threats, discovering if attacks are possible. However, their effectiveness may depend on some user's decisions, exactly as it happens with TLS authentication, where a user may decide to proceed despite a warning flashing that the certificate is invalid. The experimental analysis answers whether those attack would be successful with real users and factual behavioural patterns. The outcomes of the social-oriented analysis also enlighten us on what factors influence critical decisions that may lead to attacks. Such outcomes may therefore suggest defences which, in turn, can be implemented at a technical or a social level or as a combination of them, and understanding their effectiveness triggers another round of analysis. Moreover, it is also possible to perform a security analysis against attacks purely against the human, like social engineering. At the current status of research there is not a stable theory able to model such attacks in a formal model way, thus to study their effect is again done experimentally. This can change in the near future.

To test hypothesis of user's behaviour under socio attacks, we may need to launch such those attacks and harvest the data for analysis. This requires an authorization from an ethical committee and a compliance with a legal framework, assurances that strictly must comply with ethical requirements (APA). In certain situations this may be hard to achieve.

Technical focus - this methodology helps discovering whether an attack is present, within the defined threat model, and mostly with technical interactions and a simple user model. The technical security analysis is applied to elements from UI_A till p_A and possibly p_B till UI_B, including the context(s). P_A is modelled as a non-deterministic process i.e., interacting with process UI_A in every possible way [23,24,9]. The technical analysis, can use formal tools of protocol analysis (e.g., model checking [25]), with the only difference that communications are now multi-layered. In a simple case, the analysis can be pursued informally.

Analysing security in this focus means to verify whether specific security properties remain valid despite an intruder. The technical analysis may reveal vulnerabilities due to a faulty integration between the technical and the human layers, like it happens when a system does not offer users to change a password, when it should (e.g., [21]). The output of the technical analysis gives ground for a successive security analysis with social-focus, as it provides information about what attacks should be considered there.

Social focus - this methodology helps discovering security failures in the human interactions, when a predefined threat model is present, or in presence of specific attacks revealed by the technical analysis. The social analysis focuses on human behaviour and choices, therefore from elements S_A till UI_A and possibly their human-to-human interaction with S_B via UI_B, including the context(s). The social analysis uses the hypothetico-deductive model from empirical social sciences research [26] (Fig. 2).

Briefly, the process starts with the initial definition of *research questions* to be tested. These usually come from previous literature review, insights either

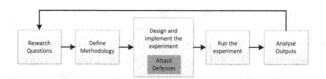

Fig. 2. Social focus: the hypothetico-deductive research model

observed or hinted by human computer interactions. In STEAL they should come from the technical security analysis itself. The process continues with the definition of the most appropriate *research methodology/ies* (i.e., laboratory experiments, interviews, surveys) to answer the research question. Here we also decide on the appropriate threat model and the layers that can be impacted in the reference model. This process is similar if we are testing defences. The next step is to *design and implement the selected methodology(ies)* with the goal of making this process reproducible over a series of experimental tests. After all is set and ready to start, the *experiment is run* and *output data is collected and further analysed*. Usually, data can be analysed using both quantitative (statistical tools can be used to analyse data and test previous defined research questions, and show how significant these are) and qualitative methods (qualitative data gathered from the participants can be correlated with results obtained from statistical analysis and also provide insight or explanation on user's behaviour).

4   Running Example: Applying STEAL

We describe how STEAL works with a scenario of a visitor at the Univ. of Luxembourg trying to get WiFi Internet access by choosing an *open* SSID name from the list he is presented by his device's network manager.

4.1   Reference Model

STEAL reference model highlights the elements of the scenario (Fig. 3), comprising the network manager and all the network communication protocols (p_A), the interface on the user's mobile device (UI_A) and the user trying to select a wireless network name to connect to the Internet (P_A). The premises of the University of Luxembourg, the place where all is happening, is the context C_A.

About the interactions, *express* would be the expression of all the human traits of a persona into how P_A takes security decisions when interacting with a human-computer interface in that particular scenario. (We are not able to model those expressions, but we may want to consider them in the analysis). Then, *interaction* are the actions performed by the user, to access the wireless network manager's list and select an SSID name to connect; *events* are the communications exchanged between the user's interface on the mobile device and the wireless network manager application and the wireless access point, which manages calls to its network; *protocol* are the network protocols and messages

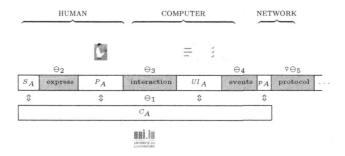

Fig. 3. Reference model for WiFi connection to the Internet

exchanged between the wireless network manager application and wireless access point, which manages all accesses to the services that its network provides.

4.2 Socio-Technical Security Analysis

Technical Analysis - We model the technical layers in a UML diagram. It illustrates the sequence of actions between those elements during an attack in this scenario (Fig. 4). In theory is possible to run a formal analysis against a Dolev-Yao attacker. Here, it is immediately evident that an intruder can open a rogue wireless access point because the SSID is not authenticated.

The success of the attack relies only on the user's choice, precisely on whether a user will actually choose the rogue access point or not. This cannot be understood with this technical analysis only. However, we elaborate more on the attack before passing to the social analysis. We hypothesise that the context plays a very important role in this scenario as the attacker can use the University's visual identity –and all that is connected with it such as knowledge, reputation, etc– to lure a victim to choose a rogue but meaningful name, such as "uni.lu", over the University's official SSID names (actually "uni-visitor" and "eduroam"). The attacker can also set up a second SSID, "secure_AP", a name recalling "security" and test which name has more appeal for the user. Fig. 4 shows the attack.

Social Analysis - to apply the hypothetico-deductive model for this analysis we devised the following stages (more detail in [10]): (1) *Research question*: do context and trust influence users' choice of a wireless network name? Alias do names reminding security influence that choice? (2) *Methodology*: on-line survey with two different groups of questions (one relating to context and the other to trust) each together with open questions to provide further explanation of the participant's selection. The groups of questions must be answered by two different groups of participants (in a between subjects design) regarding wireless network names preferences and graded using a Likert scale (1 - less trusted/less preferred to 5 - highly trusted/preferred); (3) *Design and implement the experiment*: the survey included a list of 12 wireless network names is compiled based on: they exist in the region where the study was conducted, non-existing, evocative of security or freeness and location/context-specific. The participants should be randomly associated with either the first or the second group of questions (between subjects design); (4) *Run the experiment*: send an email to the staff of the University of Luxembourg; (5) *Analysis*: Data was collected, then analysed using R statistical tool. Basic descriptive statistics were applied followed by t-test and wilcoxon rank test. We actually run such an experiment in [10]).

Main results: The social analysis confirms the hypothesis that SSID names reminding the context influence choices, but when users are unaware, or have not been instructed to use the official SSIDs. However, the study refutes the hypothesis that users trust names recalling "security".

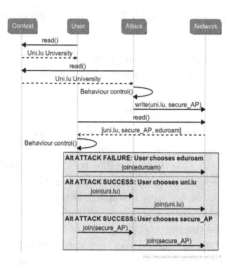

Fig. 4. Technical Focus: the UML sequence diagram for the WiFi connection to the Internet with an intruder attacking the network

4.3 Adding Defences

After having identified possible attacks, we may devise possible defences. We sketch some of them in the reminder of this paragraph. Defences can act at the technical layers or at the social layers. For example, if all wireless access points were strongly authenticated by the user's device, then the identified attack would not occur. This is likely the case with the new Hotspot 2.0, where the device's SIM card embeds the certificate of proprietary access points. The network manager, p_A, can be programmed to disable the 'join()' action on all networks that have not been vouched by the university's system administrator ($\ominus_4$, Fig. 3). Another technical defence can be implemented at the Network layer by monitoring the live SSIDs, and spot whether some new SSID is trying to use the name of the context (e.g., the "uni.lu" SSID). Technically it is possible to disrupt the joining process to newcomer SSID by sending spoofed deauth packets. This action has the effect of disabling the 'join()' function ($\ominus_5$).

If no technical solution is feasible, defences can be applied at the social layers or to the context. For example, stickers can be left all over the University campus, advertising the legitimate access point of the University ($\ominus_1$). This may likely increase user's awareness. The University can give training to its employees to help them recognize rogue SSIDs ($\ominus_2$). The network manager and the user interface can have a trust indicator displayed aside each SSID ($\ominus_3$).

Whether these defences are effective in successfully decreasing the number of people that fall victim of the attack herein described, is a research question that should be tested by new runs of our framework.

5 Discussion

Conflicts between security and usability are a well known problem. What this paper intends to highlight is that effective security should be the result of a multidisciplinary research. Computer scientists and social scientists must collaborate on similar ground and terminology to study a system's security in an integrated fashion. Security analysis must comprise technical, social and contextual elements. Although the literature has plenty of interesting studies on usability and security, we miss a common operational framework to systematically perform an analysis of security tackling both technical and social aspects.

STEAL comprises a model of a socio-technical scenario and suggests methodologies to analyse and test the same scenario for its security. It helps modelling socio-technical attack scenarios too. At the moment, the methodologies for both technical and social security analysis are working in a pipeline, and allows more runs of analysis. The technical analysis justifies the presence of technical attacks, and the social analysis give ground to evaluate the effectiveness when user's decisions are in place with those attacks. The technical analysis cannot, at the moment, help with attacks of purely social nature, because there is no model able to express and simulate them. The same relates to mature human behaviour: there are no stable human behavioural models that can be used within an automatic security validation tool. Defining such a model must, however, be supported by experimental research.

It is not a primary goal of STEAL to build a model for understanding why users behave the way they do. However, it is possible to use STEAL to design and perform experiments that focus on understanding why some users fall victims of a specific socio-technical attack, by following some behavioural patterns. Such findings may inspire defences, whose effectiveness can be tested in STEAL.

We showed here how to apply our framework in a specific socio-technical scenario. However, we need more examples to be more confident about the flexibility of the approach. Regarding our reference model, this has been shown as we applied it to model socio-technical scenario about users accessing the Internet [9,10], but more scenarios are needed to validate the actual flexibility. About the technical security analysis, it can be applied generically once all components of a socio-technical system, together with its interactions, are modelled as suggested. The main issue to consider is the human behavioural analysis, and if

STEAL can help to generalize this analysis for a large set of scenarios. We believe that the methodology used for the social analysis (hypothetico-deductive experimental model) is generic enough to be applied in the design and implementation of user related experiments for socio-technical systems. In order to perform the security analysis, all the steps of that process need to be clearly and objectively defined. It may be the case that we can only test one interaction, and therefore, one hypothesis at a time. Still, its analysis uses methods that either confirm or dismiss that hypothesis. Once we know this answer we can step to the next question or generate some conclusion. This is still generic and prone to be adapted to different socio-technical scenarios. As discussed in the methodology, some experiment may need authorization from an ethical committee, compliance with a legal framework, and with ethical requirements (APA), before being set.

6   Conclusion

We believe that STEAL is a good first step in the integration of socio-technical security analysis by a multidisciplinary team. Nevertheless, there is the need to apply STEAL to model and analyse more socio-technical scenarios. Only this way will it be possible to improve STEAL and enrich its flexibility and generalization. As future work we plan to use STEAL to design and test the devised socio-technical defences for each scenario and verify whether they work or need further revision.

References

1. West, R.: The Psychology of Security. Communication of the ACM 51(4), 34–38 (2008)
2. Tversky, A., Kahneman, D.: Judgment under uncertainty: Heuristics and biases. Science 185, 1124–1131 (1974)
3. Kumaraguru, P., Sheng, S., Acquisti, A., Cranor, L.F., Hong, J.: Teaching johnny not to fall for phish. ACM Trans. Internet Technol. 10(2), 7:1–7:31 (2010)
4. Parkin, S., van Moorsel, A., Inglesant, P.G., Sasse, M.A.: A Stealth Approach to Usable Security: Helping IT Security Managers to Identify Workable Security Solutions. In: Proc. of NSPW 2010, Sept. 21-23, pp. 33–50. ACM (2010)
5. Tembe, R., Hong, K.W., Murphy-Hill, E., Mayhorn, C., Kelley, C.: American and indian conceptualizations of phishing. In: Proc. of STAST 2013, pp. 37–45. IEEE (2013)
6. Volkamer, M., Stockhardt, S., Bartsch, S., Kauer, M.: Adopting the cmu/apwg anti-phishing landing page idea for germany. In: Proc. of STAST 2013, pp. 46–52. IEEE (2013)
7. Bardram, J.E.: The trouble with login: on usability and computer security in ubiquitous computing. Personal and Ubiquit. Comput. 9(6), 357–367 (2005)
8. Weerasinghe, D., Rakocevic, V., Rajarajan, M.: Security framework for mobile banking. In: Trustworthy Ubiquitous Computing, Atlantis Ambient and Pervasive Intelligence, vol. 6, pp. 207–225 (2012)

9. Ferreira, A., Giustolisi, R., Huynen, J., Koenig, V., Lenzini, G.: Studies in socio-technical security analysis: Authentication of identities with tls certificates. In: Proc. of the 12th IEEE TrustComm 2013, pp. 1553–1558 (2013)
10. Ferreira, A., Huynen, J.-L., Koenig, V., Lenzini, G., Rivas, S.: Socio-technical study on the effect of trust and context when choosing wifi names. In: Accorsi, R., Ranise, S. (eds.) STM 2013. LNCS, vol. 8203, pp. 131–143. Springer, Heidelberg (2013)
11. Zhu, F., Carpenter, S., Kulkarni, A., Kolimi, S.: Reciprocity attacks. In: Proc. of the SOUPS 2011, pp. 9:1–9:14. ACM, New York (2011)
12. Arce, I.: The weakest link revisited. IEEE Security Privacy 1(2), 72–76 (2003)
13. Cranor, L.F.: A Framework for Reasoning About the Human in the Loop. In: Proc. of the 1st Conf. on Usability, Psychology, and Security, pp. 1–15. USENIX Association (2008)
14. Conti, G., Ahamad, M., Stasko, J.: Attacking information visualization system usability overloading and deceiving the human. In: Proc. of the SOUPS 2005, pp. 89–100. ACM (2005)
15. Falk, L., Prakash, A., Borders, K.: Analyzing websites for user-visible security design flaws. In: Proceedings of SOUPS 2008, pp. 117–126. ACM, New York (2008)
16. De Luca, A., Langheinrich, M., Hussmann, H.: Towards understanding atm security: a field study of real world atm use. In: Proc. of SOUPS 2010, pp. 16:1–16:10. ACM, New York (2010)
17. Janczewski, L., Lingyan, F.: Social engineering-based attacks: Model and new zealand perspective. In: Proc. of IMCSIT 2010, pp. 847–853 (2010)
18. Dalpiaz, F., Giorgini, P., Mylopoulos, J.: Adaptive Socio-Technical Systems: a Requirements-Based Approach. Requirements Engineering 18, 1–24 (2013)
19. Worton, K.: Using socio-technical and resilience frameworks to anticipate threat. In: Proc. of STAST 2012, pp. 19–26 (2012)
20. Pavkovic, N., Perkov, L.: Social engineering toolkit x2014; a systematic approach to social engineering. In: Proc. of MIPRO 2011, pp. 1485–1489 (2011)
21. Bella, G., Coles-Kemp, L.: Layered Analysis of Security Ceremonies. In: Gritzalis, D., Furnell, S., Theoharidou, M. (eds.) SEC 2012. IFIP AICT, vol. 376, pp. 273–286. Springer, Heidelberg (2012)
22. Dolev, D., Yao, A.: On the security of public-key protocols. IEEE Transaction on Information Theory 29(2), 198–208 (1983)
23. Bella, G., Giustolisi, R., Lenzini, G.: Socio-Technical Formal Analysis of TLS Certificate Validation in Modern Browsers. In: Proc. of PST 2013. IFIP, pp. 309–316 (2013)
24. Bella, G., Giustolisi, R., Lenzini, G.: A Socio-Technical Understanding of TLS Certificate Validation. In: Fernández-Gago, C., Martinelli, F., Pearson, S., Agudo, I. (eds.) Trust Management VII. IFIP AICT, vol. 401, pp. 281–288. Springer, Heidelberg (2013)
25. Clarke, E.M., Grumberg, O., Peled, D.: Model Checking. MIT Press (1999)
26. Godfrey-Smith, P.: Theory and Reality: An Introduction to the Philosophy of Science. Science and Its Conceptual Foundations. Univ. of Chicago Press (2003)

An Evaluation of Behavioural Profiling
on Mobile Devices

Fudong Li[1], Ross Wheeler[1], and Nathan Clarke[1,2]

[1] Centre for Security, Communications and Network Research (CSCAN), Plymouth University,
Portland Square, Plymouth, PL4 8AA, United Kingdom
[2] Security Research Institute, Edith Cowan University, Perth, Western Australia, Australia
{fudong.li,N.Clarke}@plymouth.ac.uk,
ross.wheeler2@students.plymouth.ac.uk

Abstract. With more than 6.3 billion subscribers around the world, mobile devices play a significant role in people's daily life. People rely upon them to carry out a wide variety of tasks, such as accessing emails, shopping online, micro-payments and e-banking. It is therefore essential to protect the sensitive information that is stored on the device against misuse. The majority of these mobile devices are still dependent upon passwords and Personal Identification Numbers (PIN) as a form of user authentication. However, the weakness of these point-of-entry techniques is well documented. Furthermore, current point-of-entry authentication will only serve to provide a one-off authentication decision with the time between an authentication and access control decision effectively becoming independent. Through transparent authentication, identity verification can be performed continuously; thereby more closely associating the authentication and access control decisions. The challenge is in providing an effective solution to the trade-off between effective security and usability.

With the purpose of providing enhanced security, this paper describes a behavioural profiling framework, which utilizes application or service usage to verify individuals in a continuous manner. In order to examine the effectiveness a series of simulations were conducted by utilising real users' mobile applications usage. The dataset contains 76 users' application activities over a four-week period, including 30,428 log entries for 103 unique applications (e.g. telephone, text message and web surfing). The simulations results show that the framework achieved a False Rejection Rate (FRR) of 12.91% and a False Acceptant Rate (FAR) of 4.17%. In contrast with point of entry approaches, the behavioural profiling technique provides a significant improvement in both device security and user convenience. An end-user trial was undertaken to assist in investigating the perceptions surrounding the concept of behavioural profiling technique – an approach that is conceptually associated with privacy concerns. The survey revealed that participants were strongly in favour (71%) of using the behavioural approach as a supplement of the point-of-entry technique to protect their devices. The results also provided an interesting insight into the perceived privacy issues with the approach, with 38% of the participants stating they do not care about their personal information being recorded.

Keywords: behavioural profiling, authentication, non-intrusive, transparent.

T. Tryfonas and I. Askoxylakis (Eds.): HAS 2014, LNCS 8533, pp. 330–339, 2014.
© Springer International Publishing Switzerland 2014

1   Introduction

With more than 6.8 billion subscribers around the world, mobile devices certainly play a significant role in people's daily life (ITU, 2014). Indeed, people rely upon them to carry out a wide variety of tasks, such as accessing emails, shopping online, micro-payments and transferring money via e-banking. These activities are inevitably associated with a certain level of personal and/or business information, such as corporate email, customer data, bank account numbers and personal contact details (Lazou and Weir, 2011; Checkpoint, 2013). Therefore, it is essential to protect the sensitive information that is stored on the device against threats such as when it is lost or stolen, infected by a virus or attacked using social engineering.

With the aim of protecting these mobile devices from user misuse, two forms of authentication techniques (i.e. Personal Identification Number (PIN) and biometrics) can be utilised. Currently, the majority of mobile devices are dependent upon the PIN as the first line of defence against unauthorised usage. However, the weakness of the PIN is well documented in the literature (Clarke and Furnell, 2005; Kurkovsky and Syta, 2010; Huth et al, 2012). For example, PINs can be poorly chosen, written down on a paper, shared with others or never changed. Biometric authentication is an automatic process to uniquely identify individuals based upon their physical (e.g. face) or behavioural (e.g. keystroke) characteristics and traits (Prabhakar et al, 2003). Recently, biometrics have begun to gain attention in the area of mobile authentication due to its ease of use. Indeed, a number of physiological biometric techniques have already been commercially implemented on mobile devices as an alternative security control, such as the Touch ID on the iPhone 5S and FaceLock on Google Android (Apple Inc., 2014; FaceLock, 2014).

As the existing PIN and biometrics techniques are implemented as a point-of-entry approach on mobile devices, they will only serve to provide a one-off authentication decision where the time between an authentication and a subsequent access control decision effectively becoming independent. Through transparent authentication, identity verification can be performed continuously; thereby more closely associating the authentication and access control decisions. The challenge in providing an effective solution is determining an optimal level between effective security and usability. To this end, this paper presents a novel behavioural profiling framework that provides continuous and transparent authentication for mobile devices, an experiment to underpin its capabilities and an evaluation of the technique based upon end users.

The remainder of the paper is structured in the following manner: Section 2 provides an insight into the current state of the art; Section 3 and 4 present the behavioural profiling framework and a preliminary evaluation of the framework through real user's application activities respectively. Based upon the promising simulation result, Section 5 presents the development of a prototype (called Sentinel). An end-user evaluation of the behavioural profiling approach is discussed in section 6. The paper concludes by highlighting future research directions.

2   Transparent Authentication on Mobile Devices

The concept of transparent authentication has become an area of active research since the turn of the millennium; however, with the significant enhancement of mobile device functionality, it has grown significantly in recent years (Clarke and Furnell, 2006; Clarke and Mekala, 2007; DARPA, 2011). It is also commonly referred to as continuous or active authentication. There are a number of authentication approaches that lend themselves to transparent authentication, such as behavioural profiling, keystroke analysis, facial recognition, speaker verification, gait and handwriting (Li et al, 2013; Clarke and Furnell, 2006; Weinstein et al 2002; Woo et al, 2006; Derawi et al, 2010; Clarke and Mekala, 2007).

Whilst much research has been undertaken in some biometric approaches, the transparent nature of the authentication approach requires further research – achieving point-of-entry authentication represents a significantly different problem to performing it transparently. Typically, variables that tend to be fixed in a point-of-entry scenario are not in a transparent mode of operation. For example, facial recognition would typically operate within an environment with fixed illumination with a facial image that is a fixed distance from the camera, with a fixed orientation. Within a transparent environment none of these aspects can be fixed – requiring a more flexible yet still secure approach.

As shown in Table 1, research is being undertaken to develop transparent biometric approaches and their performance is within the expectations of traditional behavioural-based biometrics in terms of Equal Error Rate (EER).

Table 1. The performance comparison of behavioural techniques on mobile devices

Behavioural Techniques	EER (%)
Behaviour profiling (Li et al, 2013)	10
Gait recognition (Derawi et al, 2010)	20.1
Keystroke analysis (Clarke and Furnell, 2006)	13
Handwriting recognition (Clarke and Mekala, 2007)	1
Speaker verification (Woo et al, 2006)	7.8

It is the purpose of this paper to focus upon and extend the current state of the art within one such area, behavioural profiling.

3   A Behavioural Profiling Framework

Based upon the foundation laid by the Transparent Authentication System (TAS) that utilises a mixture of biometric techniques to verify a mobile user's identity in a continuous and transparent manner (Clarke, 2011), the behavioural profiling framework was initially proposed by Li et al (2013). By employing the behavioural profiling technique as the authentication method, the framework is designed to work in the following style: verifies the user via their app usage in a continuous manner and ensures the verification process is carried out in a user-friendly way (i.e. the user is mainly verified transparently). The framework can operate in one of the following modes: as a standalone security control, within an Intrusion Detection System (IDS) or within a TAS. A number of components have been devised to fulfil the purpose of the behavioural profiling framework (as illustrated in Figure 1). Details of them are described in the following sections.

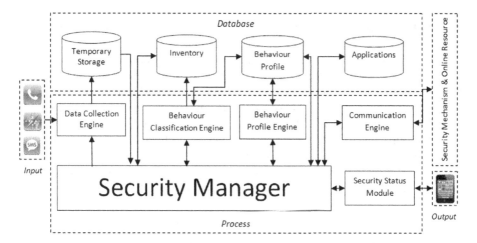

Fig. 1. A behavioural profiling framework (Li et al, 2013)

The Data Collection Engine is designed for capturing user's apps activities. It automatically collects various app features when an app is utilised. The Behaviour Profile Engine is used for the generation of various templates via the combination of user's historical data, a dynamic profiling technique and a smoothing function. With the aim of maintaining the accuracy of the templates, the dynamic profiling technique updates user's profile on a daily basis. The Behaviour Classification Engine performs the verification process whenever is required.

The Security Status Module is utilised to indicate how secure the system is. The framework can provide or deny access to the user when the system is at high or low security respectively. The security level of the system is calculated based upon the verification result and the quality of the sample being used. The quality factor is dynamically allocated to each app based upon their uniqueness (i.e. a higher factor is given to the app which is more unique/discriminative to the user). After the activity of an app is verified, the security level is increased (verified successfully) or decreased (verified unsuccessfully) by the performance factor of the app.

The Security Manager is central node of the framework as it co-operates with other components to complete various tasks, such as continuous verification and automatic profile updates. Among these tasks, the key responsibility of the Security Manager is to maintain the security level and make subsequent decisions when the user requests access to an app; this can be achieved by employing the System Security Status Monitor And Response (SMAR) algorithm that is designed to provide a high level of user convenience and improved security (Li et al, 2013). The algorithm employs both transparent and intrusive methods to verify a user, with three main checking stages before the user is locked out by the device. Hence, it is envisaged that legitimate users will mainly experience transparent phases and intrusive challenges will only be utilised to ensure a user's legitimacy when access to the device is requested but the security level is below the requirement.

4   Empirical Simulation

With the aim of evaluating the performance of the framework, a simulation process was conducted. The simulation utilised a subset of the Massachusetts Institute of Technology Reality Mining dataset as its simulating data (Eagle et al, 2009). The subset contains 76 users' 103-app activities during the period of 24/10/2004-20/11/2004 as illustrated in Table 2. Each user's data was divided into two halves, containing first and second two-week activities respectively. A user's profile was initially obtained by using their first two-week activities; the profile was then dynamically updated on a daily basis. The rest of users' activities were employed to evaluate the performance of the behaviour profiling framework.

Table 2. The simulation dataset

	Normal Apps	Telephony	SMS
Users	76	71	22
Unique apps / telephone numbers	101	2,317	258
Logs	30,428	13,599	1,381

In order to evaluate the effectiveness of the Behaviour Profiling framework, the PIN based technique was chosen as a baseline method. Therefore, the framework was configured to verify a user's identity as soon as an app is utilised, similarly to the way how the PIN functions. Based upon this configuration, all users' activities were put through the framework.

With the aim of maximising the security, it is assumed that a PIN is required after the device has been idle for more than one minute. By utilising this setting, users are required to enter a PIN for every single app usage (i.e. no transparent authentication at all) if the PIN based technique was applied to the same simulation data. In comparison, the simulation result shows that the Behaviour Profiling framework achieved an overall FRR of 12.91%, indicating 87.09% of the time legitimate user will be transparently verified and automatically obtain access to the device. With the same configuration, the imposter has only a 4.17% opportunity to abuse an app and conversely 95.83% of the time they will be denied access. Based upon the above discussion, it demonstrates that the Behaviour Profiling framework is capable of offering continuous and transparent security for majority of the time and is able to do so in a more secure and user convenient fashion. Nonetheless, the Behaviour Profiling framework should have a small footprint upon the device, permitting it to be possibly adopted by users. With this aim, a prototype of the framework is described in the following section.

5   Sentinel – A Prototype of the Behaviour Profiling Framework

Based upon the encouraging simulation results, a working prototype of the Behaviour Profiling framework, Sentinel, was developed to demonstrate the concept of the behavioural profiling technique on a real mobile device. Sentinel, designed specially to have a small memory footprint, is capable of monitoring user's app activities and then identifying the legitimacy of the actions accordingly.

A Google Nexus smartphone with Android 4.0 was chosen as the development platform because the open source nature of the operating system provides a flexible environment and also the large amount of market share of the Android presents huge number of potential users for the prototype (IDC, 2013). As the Behaviour Profiling framework utilises user's app activities to identify individuals, the initial barrier of implementing the Sentinel was whether the prototype can collect features of each apps. This was achieved by the support of several Android API classes as demonstrated in Table 3. As a result, Sentinel is able to collect various features of the app, such as time of usage, name of the app, the location of usage. Sentinel utilises the SQLite as its database to store user's app activities. All users' app activities are stored in the SQLite database initially until enough data is collected for building the user's behavioural profile. By utilising the user's profile and a dynamic rule-based classifier (Li et al, 2013), Sentinel can determine the legitimacy of each user's app activity and deal the classification result accordingly.

Table 3. Android API class for data collection process of the Sentinel

Android API class	Description
Activity Manager	Interacts with overall activities running on a device
Telephony Manager	Accesses telephony data relating to cellular location
Location Manager	Accesses location data relating to geo-location
Broadcast Receiver	Listens for outgoing call state changes
Phone State Listener	Monitors for incoming call state changes

Once the development of the Sentinel backbone was completed, a graphical user interface was also designed and developed, permitting user to perform various tasks. As illustrated by Figure 2, user can start the Sentinel by clicking on the "Start Service" button, browse various log files (e.g. an overview of user's app activities is presented by the Application Logs function) and review the classification results (i.e. 0 and 1 indicate unsuccessful and successful verifications respectively).

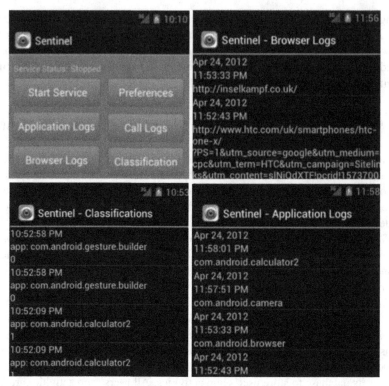

Fig. 2. A selection of screenshots of Sentinel

As demonstrated above, the prototype of the Behaviour Profiling framework, can identify user's identity based upon their apps usage. In addition, the user will not notice its existence because it not only mainly runs as a background service but also has a tiny footprint (i.e. 6KB) on the device's overall memory as illustrated in Table 4.

Table 4. An overview of Sentinel's memory

Services	Memory
Logging Service	4.9KB
Sentinel Activity	896B
State Listener	80B
Outcall Receiver	64B
Reminder	96B
Total	**6KB**

6   Evaluation of Behavioural Profiling on Mobile Devices

As user acceptance is crucial to the adoption of new technologies and processes, a survey was designed to obtain end-user perceptions on the behavioural profiling technology. The survey contains 9 questions, covering participants' background of Information Technology (IT), how they utilise and secure their devices, and their opinion upon the behavioural profiling technique. As the behavioural profiling is a novel authentication technique, a brief description of its working principle was also provided to assist participants to understand how the technique provides transparent and continuous protection for mobile devices. The survey was conducted over the Internet and advertised through the use of social networking and word of mouth.

In total 55 participants completed the survey. The results shows that the participants have a wide range of technical experience with 9.1% classifying themselves with the beginner knowledge of IT category, 56.4% with intermediate knowledge and 32.7% with advanced or greater knowledge of IT systems. As illustrated in Figure 3, participants utilise several operating systems on their mobile phones: Android, iOS, Symbian, BlackBerry and Windows with 44%, 23%, 5%, 4% and 4% of users respectively. Despite 80% of the participants utilised smartphones, the SMS and telephony functions still remain as the most frequent used apps with 45% and 24% of the users accordingly, followed by email and internet browsing with 16% and 9% of the participants respectively.

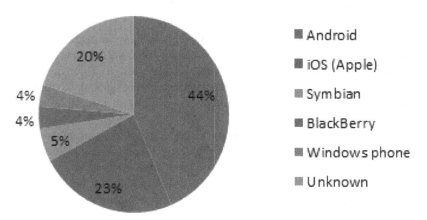

Fig. 3. Comparison of participants' mobile device operating systems

The survey also revealed that only 56.4% of the participants utilised the point-of-entry technique (e.g. PIN) and 54.5% of the participants believe they store important information (e.g. email messages and personal contacts) on their mobile devices. It all likelihood a far larger proportion of users have sensitive data but merely do not recognise it. Interestingly, 62% of the participants stated they do care about their personal information being recorded, revealing that privacy concerns may not be as great as literature suggests. The majority of participants were strongly in favour (71%) of using the behavioural approach as a supplement of the point-of-entry technique to protect their devices. For those who were reluctant in adopting the behavioural profiling technique, privacy was their primary concern (as illustrated in Figure 4).

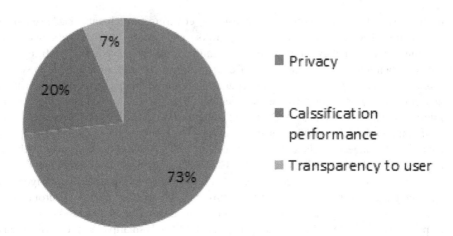

Fig. 4. Reasons for not adopting the behavioural profiling technique

7   Conclusion

The first part of the paper identified that authentication is an essential service that underpins the security of systems; however, current solutions fail to take appropriate consideration of the human-factors of good security design. Through behavioural profiling, transparent and continuous authentication provides the opportunity to overcome the systematic usability issues that exist offering an acceptable, more robust and more secure approach.

Based upon the promising simulation result, a proof of concept and end-user evaluation, the approach has demonstrated significant merit. However, care, particularly on issues of privacy need to be taken in consideration. In the future, a most robust and comprehensive version of the Sentinel should be developed with built-in privacy protection. This will also allow for a complete and longitudinal end user trial to be conducted.

References

1. Apple Inc., iPhone 5s: Using the touch ID kb/HT5883 (2014),
   http://support.apple.com/ (accessed: January 09, 2014)
2. Checkpoint, The impact of mobile devices on information security (2013),
   http://www.checkpoint.com/downloads/products/check-point-mobile-security-survey-report2013.pdf (accessed: January 05, 2014)
3. Clarke, N.: Transparent User Authentication. Springer, Berlin (2011)
4. Clarke, N.L., Furnell, S.M.: Authentication of users on mobile telephones—a survey of attitudes and practices. Computer Security 24(7), 519–527 (2005)
5. Clarke, N.L., Mekala, A.R.: The application of signature recognition to trans-parent handwriting verification for mobile devices. Information Management & Computer Security 15(3), 214–225 (2007)

6. Clarke, N.L., Furnell, S.M.: Authenticating Mobile Phone Users Using Keystroke Analysis. International Journal of Information Security, 1–14 (2006) ISSN:1615-5262
7. DARPA, Active Authentication, DARPA (2011),
   `http://www.darpa.mil/OurWork/I2O/Programs/Active Authentication.aspx` (accessed: January 17, 2014)
8. Derawi, M.O., Nickel, C., Bours, P., Busch, C.: Unobtrusive User-Authentication on Mobile Phones Using Biometric Gait Recognition. In: Sixth International Conference on Intelligent Information Hiding and Multimedia Signal Processing (2010)
9. Eagle, N., Pentland, A., Lazer, D.: Inferring social network structure using mobile phone data. Proceedings of the National Academy of Sciences (PNAS) 106, 15274–15278 (2009)
10. FaceLock (2014), `http://www.facelock.mobi/` (date accessed: January 08, 2014)
11. Gartner, Gartner Says Mobile App Stores Will See Annual Downloads Reach 102 Billion in 2013 (2013), `http://www.gartner.com/newsroom/id/2592315` (accessed: October 10, 2014)
12. Huth, A., Orlando, M., Pesante, L.: Password Security, Protection, and Management (2012), `https://www.uscert.gov/sites/default/files/ publications/PasswordMgmt2012.pdf` (accessed: January 09, 2014)
13. IDC, Android Pushes Past 80% Market Share While Windows Phone Shipments Leap 156.0% Year over Year in the Third Quarter (2013),
    `http://www.idc.com/getdoc.jsp?con-tainerId=prUS24442013` (accessed: January 23, 2014)
14. ITU, Global ICT developments (2014),
    `http://www.itu.int/en/ITUD/Statistics/Pages/stat/default. aspx` (accessed: January 06, 2014)
15. Kurkovsky, S., Syta, E.: Digital natives and mobile phones: A survey of practices and attitudes about privacy and security. In: Proceedings of the IEEE International Symposium on Technology and Society (ISTAS), pp. 441–449 (2010)
16. Lazou, A., Weir, G.: Perceived risk and sensitive data on mobile devices. Cyberforensics. University of Strathclyde, Glasgow, pp. 183–196 (2011) ISBN 9780947649784
17. Li, F., Clarke, N.L., Papadaki, M., Dowland, P.S.: Active authentication for mobile devices utilising behaviour profiling. International Journal of Information Security (2013), doi:10.1007/s10207-013-0209-6
18. Portioresearch, Fast growth of apps user base in booming Asia Pacific market (2013), `http://www.portioresearch.com/en/blog/2013/fast-growth-of- apps-user-base-in-booming-asia-pacific-market.aspx` (accessed January 10, 2014)
19. Prabhakar, S., Pankanti, S., Jain, A.K.: Biometric recognition: security and privacy concerns. IEEE Security & Privacy 1(2), 33–42 (2003)
20. Weinstein, E., Ho, P., Heisele, B., Poggio, T., Steele, K., Agarwal, A.: Handheld face identification technology in a pervasive computing environment. In: Pervasive 2002, Zurich, Switzerland, pp. 48–54 (2002)
21. Woo, R., Park, A., Hazen, T.: The MIT Mobile Device Speaker Verification Corpus: Data collection and preliminary experiments. In: Proceeding of Odyssey, The Speaker & Language Recognition Workshop, San Juan, Puerto Rico (June 2006)

Nudging for Quantitative Access Control Systems

Charles Morisset, Thomas Groß, Aad van Moorsel, and Iryna Yevseyeva

Centre for Cybercrime and Computer Security,
Newcastle University, NE1 7RU, U.K.
firstname.lastname@newcastle.ac.uk

Abstract. On the one hand, an access control mechanism must make a conclusive decision for a given access request. On the other hand, such a mechanism usually relies on one or several decision making processes, which can return partial decisions, inconclusive ones, or conflicting ones. In some cases, this information might not be sufficient to automatically make a conclusive decision, and the access control mechanism might have to involve a human expert to make the final decision. In this paper, we formalise these decision making processes as *quantitative access control systems*, which associate each decision with a measure, indicating for instance the level of confidence of the system in the decision. We then propose to explore how nudging, i.e., how modifying the context of the decision making process for that human expert, can be used in this context. We thus formalise when such a delegation is required, when nudging is applicable, and illustrate some examples from the MINDSPACE framework in the context of access control.

1 Introduction

An *access control mechanism* (ACM) takes as input an access request, and returns a decision describing whether this request should be performed or not. We consider here an access request to contain all information that can be required to make the decision, following the attributed-based access control approach [22,23,7]. For instance, an RBAC request [9] would contain the user, the object, but also the roles of the user, the potential role hierarchy, the permission associated with the object, etc. In general, the final decision needs to be *conclusive*, i.e., either **accept** or **deny**, since the request either goes through or not.

In general, an ACM relies on one or several decision making processes, which indicate what decision should be made. Typically, an *access control policy* is a structured document associating each request with a decision, ranging from an access matrix [14] to sets of XACML policies [18]. Other decision processes can also be used, such as Machine Learning approaches [21,17] or Markov Decision Processes [15]. However, these decision processes do not always return a conclusive decision to the ACM, for instance: a policy might not be applicable to the

T. Tryfonas and I. Askoxylakis (Eds.): HAS 2014, LNCS 8533, pp. 340–351, 2014.

request, thus yielding the decision **na** [18]; missing attributes can create *inde-terminacy*, and return a set of all possible decisions instead of a single one [7]; different decision processes can return conflicting decisions [2].

In such situations, the access control mechanism might be able to still make a conclusive decision, for instance by using resolving algorithms (such as the XACML permit-unless-deny and deny-unless-permit algorithms, which, by defi-nition, can only return a conclusive decision), otherwise it might be required to involve a human expert, who will make the final decision.

In this paper, we introduce the notion of *quantitative access control system* (QACS), which represents a decision process, such that each decision is associ-ated with some quantity, for instance indicating the weight of one decision over another. We then postulate that when no conclusive decision can be made au-tonomously, it might be possible to use the quantitative information to know in which direction the human expert should be *nudged*, following the observation that the way the information is presented to a decision maker has an influence on the final decision made [25]. Intuitively, if the access control mechanism be-lieves that a request should be accepted more than it should be denied, but is not confident enough to make an autonomous decision, then the human expert can be nudged into accepting the request. This approach relies on the assump-tion that the human expert is more apt to resolve the uncertainty, and thus can ignore any nudge if needed, but could benefit from being provided with a *choice architecture* [24], i.e., a structured context in which the choice is made.

The main contribution of this paper are the following ones: we propose a gen-eral notion of access control mechanism, instantiated with several examples from the literature (Section 2); we describe the nudging approach in the context of access control (Section 3); and we propose an evaluation strategy for nudging, identifying the possible choices and their consequences, and we illustrate our approach with an example inspired from conference reviewing (Section 4). This paper is exploratory in nature, and focuses on presenting the different concepts within a common architecture, hopefully accessible to computer scientists, se-curity experts and psychologists, with the intent to open the discussion on this research problem, rather than to bring a concrete solution for a specific problem.

2   Quantitative Access Control Mechanisms

We consider here the set of decisions $\mathcal{D} = \{\textbf{accept}, \textbf{deny}, \textbf{na}\}$, and given a set of requests $\mathcal{R}$, a quantitative access control system (QACS) is a function $\kappa : \mathcal{R} \rightarrow (\mathcal{D} \rightarrow [0,1])$, i.e., given a request, returns a function $\delta : \mathcal{D} \rightarrow [0,1]$. In other words, a QACS associates each possible decision with a *quantity*, such that $\delta(\textbf{accept}) + \delta(\textbf{deny}) + \delta(\textbf{na}) \leq 1$.

Our notion of QACS is inspired to some extent by subjective logic [13], which has been used, among others, in trust networks [12]. Indeed, in subjective logic, a truth value is given by a triple (b, d, u), where b represents the level of belief, d the level of disbelief and u the level of uncertainty, such that $b + d + u = 1$. However, our approach differs in that we do not impose the sum of all quanti-ties to equal 1, and we consider the difference between this sum and 1 as the measure of uncertainty. In other words, we could represent the function δ as a tuple (a, d, na, u), representing the quantities for **accept**, **deny**, **na** and for the uncertainty, respectively, such that $a + d + na + u = 1$. We do not consider here the composition of quantitative access decisions, and we leave for future work a further exploration of subjective logic, and other fuzzy logic in general, in the context of QACS.

We now present some concrete examples of QACS, based on majority-voting [20], Markov Decision Process [15] and machine learning [17]. These examples do not aim at representing an exhaustive list of such systems, but rather to illustrate their diversity.

2.1 Majority Voting Policy

Ni et al. propose in [20] the D-Algebra to encode the semantics of an access control model, where the underlying logics is not necessarily limited to the classical one, and can for instance be the Łukasiewicz one, which comes with a rational number interpretation. Hence, given a policy consisting of several sub-rules, the evaluation of this policy can be defined as true (or permit) if there are more rules evaluating to true than rules evaluating to false.

In particular, they propose an encoding of XACML [18], where each rule can evaluate to one of the following: P, D, NA, P-NA, D-NA, where P stands for Permit, D for Deny and NA for Not-Applicable[1], and given a policy consisting of several, respectively associate the values v_0, v_1, v_2, v_3 and v_4 for the number of rules evaluating for each decision. A policy evaluates to:

- P if $v_0 > v_1 + v_4$, i.e., when the number of permit is higher than the sum of deny and possible deny,
- D if $v_1 > v_0 + v_3$,
- P-NA if $v_0 \leq v_1 + v_4$ and $v_0 + v_3 > v_1 + v_4$,
- D-NA if $v_1 \leq v_0 + v_3$ and $v_1 + v_4 > v_0 + v_3$,
- NA otherwise.

We can define a quantitative access control system as the function

$$\delta(d) = \begin{cases} v_0 + v_3/2 & \text{if } d = \textbf{accept}, \\ v_1 + v_4/2 & \text{if } d = \textbf{deny}, \\ v_2 + v_3/2 + v_4/2 & \text{if } d = \textbf{na}, \end{cases}$$

More recently, Huth et al. introduced the Peal language [6,11], in which access control decisions are made based on numerical evidence, such as trust. In other words, each basic target identifying a condition of interest is associated with a quantity, which can be easily aggregated and selected through numerical operators. Although Peal somehow abstracts the different quantities in the final decision by using some thresholds, we could easily use them to define a QACS.

---

[1] This interpretation of the XACML decision set is somehow slightly between the standard set of XACML 2 and the extended set of XACML 3, but this discussion is outside of the scope of this paper and not particularly relevant for the notion of majority voting.

2.2   Markov Decision Process

A Markov Decision Process (MDP) [1] is a state machine, transitioning from one state to another through actions, such that transitions are probabilistic (i.e., given one state and one action, we know the probability of reaching each other state) and are associated with rewards. In this context, a *policy* is a function deciding which action to take in each state, and the *optimal policy* is that maximising the expected reward.

Martinelli and Morisset extended this notion in [15] with that of Access Control Markov Decision Process (AC-MDP), which, roughly speaking, is an MDP where each state contains both all relevant security information (levels of security, access matrix, roles, etc) and each action corresponds to a decision. For the sake of conciseness, we do not recall here the formal definition of an AC-MDP, but it is worth pointing out that Bellman's equations [1] allow us to return the expected reward of each decision in each state.

In general, the values of decisions as calculated by an AC-MDP need to be normalised in order to define a QACS, since they do not necessarily belong to [0, 1]. An interesting question is whether the normalisation should be done for each state or for the entire model. In the former case, we ensure that the sum of the values of all decisions equal 1, while in the latter case, the highest and lowest possible values in the entire model are likely not to be reachable in all states, meaning that the sum of the values of all decisions might not equal 1, which could account for uncertainty and/or non-applicability.

2.3   Classifier Based

Roughly speaking, a classifier can be seen has an hyper-plane, separating a set of data points into two distinct classes. Once this classifier is built, any new point is mechanically on one side or the other of the plane, and thus classified, assuming of course that the way the new point should be classified is somehow similar to the way the previous points have been classified.

Such an approach has been used in the context of access control policies [21], where a Role-Based Access Control policy is learned using different techniques. This approach is later refined in [17], showing that the distance to the hyper-plane can be used as a measure of uncertainty, the closer to the plane the higher the uncertainty. Following this idea, we could define a QACS which would return, for each decision, its normalised distance to the hyper-plane. Note that this approach is mostly tailored for only two decisions, **accept** and **deny**.

An important common aspect of the three examples described above is that they do not directly integrate an explicit notion of uncertainty, i.e., the sum of all decisions should normally equal 1. However, some of these examples could be extended to include such a notion, for instance, a majority-voting based QACS could consider any policy that could not be retrieved or evaluated at all as uncertain, or an MDP based QACS could compute the variance of the values of each decision in order to represent some notion of uncertainty, with the intuition that the higher the variance, the higher the uncertainty.

3   Nudging

Thaler and Sunstein define in [24] the notion of *choice architect*, who, in a system where its users have the choice between several options, has the responsibility for organizing the context in which these users make decisions. They give the example of a doctor, who must describe the alternative treatments available to a patient. In this case, the doctor does not make the decision for the patient, but presents the characteristics of each possible treatment, often by including some probabilities of success or failure. However, the way the probabilities are *framed*, i.e., emphasising the positive or negative side, can have an impact on the final decision made by the user [25]. For instance, presenting the survival rate of surgery rather than the mortality rate (one being simply the opposite of the other) often leads patients to prefer surgery to other treatments [19].

In the context of access control systems, the choice architect is the entity responsible to present the different possibilities when a decision has to be delegated. This entity is likely to be a human being with a good knowledge of the system, apt to understand the consequences of allowing or denying a given request. As described above, this *decision maker* is prone to bias, and might be influenced by the way the delegation is presented.

In this context, a nudge is "any aspect of the choice architecture that alters peoples behavior in a predictable way without forbidding any options or significantly changing their economic incentives" [24]. Some examples of nudges provided in this book include: *Give More Tomorrow*, where people tend to agree to increase donations in the future; *Filters for air conditioners; the helpful red light*, which proposes to have a red light notifying when the filter of an air conditioner should be changed; or *The Civility Check*, which would prompt the user with a warning when an email appears to be rude or inappropriate, in order to save the user from regretting to have sent it after a few hours or days.

A particularly important point of a nudge is the behavorial effect it uses in order to effectively influence people, and Dolan et al. define in [8] the MINDSPACE framework, recalled in Table 1, which presents nine classes of behavorial effects, based on the reason why each effect works.

Selecting a nudge requires a precise methodology [5], and we do not main here at defining which nudges or behavorial effects are the most relevant. However, intuitively speaking, some effects could be particularly worth exploring. For instance, consider the case where the decision is made by composing several sub-policies and by using a majority voting strategy (see Section 2.1), but a conclusive decision cannot be made autonomously because some sub-policies fail to evaluate. In order to influence the decision maker towards a decision, we could, according to the *Messenger* effect, indicate *who* issued the sub-policies returning that decision, assuming these entities are somehow trusted by the decision-maker.

Similarly, uncertainty in XACML can be due to missing attributes in the request, and XACML comes with an optional mechanism to identify which are those attributes. Returning these attributes to the decision maker, emphasizing

Table 1. The MINDSPACE framework for behavior change [8]

MINDSPACE cue	Behaviour
Messenger	We are heavily influenced by who communicates information to us
Incentives	Our responses to incentives are shaped by predictable mental shortcuts such as strongly avoiding losses
Norms	We are strongly influenced by what others do
Defaults	We go with the flow of pre-set options
Salience	Our attention is drawn to what is novel and seems relevant to us
Priming	Our acts are often influenced by sub-conscious cues
Affect	Our emotional associations can powerfully shape our actions
Commitments	We seek consistency with our public promises, and reciprocate acts
Ego	We act in ways that make us feel better about ourselves

their *salience*, could help justify why there is uncertainty about the request, and whether a conservative approach might be needed.

On a different aspect, Molloy et al. suggest in [16] to use market mechanisms in access control policies, showing that the *Incentive* effect can be used to enhance the decisions made by employees. This effect can be used at two different levels: the decision maker can receive some incentive to make the best decisions, possibly by adapting the incentive to the impact of the request, and the decision maker can take into account the incentive of the user for making the original request.

Another way of influencing the decision maker could be through the *Norm* effect, i.e., to compare how other decision makers would behave in the same situation. Such an approach has been proposed for instance in theorem-proving [3,10], by offering a user stuck with a proof the possibility of seeing different strategies followed by experts. In a similar fashion, a decision maker could be informed that in similar situations, known experts would accept or deny the request.

An important point to consider is that quite often, the choice architecture is not neutral to start with. For instance, the *Defaults* effect indicates that when facing different options, the one offered by default is more likely to be selected. Hence, proposing the decision maker with a pre-selected decision is not neutral. In addition, the *Salience* of the information plays an important role. It could for instance be the case that, when presenting an attribute request, the attributes presented first have an impact on the decision, e.g., presenting the attribute Secret first might lead the decision maker to be more conservative, while presenting the attribute Urgent first might lead the decision maker to be more flexible.

Clearly, the examples above are only intuitions of which nudges and effects could be useful, based on the idea that the decision maker is, in the end, a human being who needs to make a decision, and could be therefore influenced. It is also worth mentioning that nudges are often studied over an entire population rather than for a single individual, and little guarantee can be provided that a particular nudge will work for a given individual. Nevertheless, we believe that involving human decision makers in security mechanisms is required by the complexity of existing systems, especially when dealing with uncertainty, and that any approach aiming at helping or influencing such a decision maker is worth exploring.

There is however a very important ethical aspect to consider. Indeed, it could be argued that if we merely provide the decision maker with more information, then we simply help making a rational decision; on the other hand, we can also influence the decision making process by adding, removing or changing some information. For instance, informing a decision maker that 90% of known experts would accept a particular request is very likely to have an impact, whether it is true or not. Highlighting or hiding some particular pieces of information might not be considered as lying, but can nevertheless highly influence the decision maker.

4   Nudging for Quantitative Decisions

Let δ be a function returned by a QACS for a given request. There are up to two choices to be made: first, whether the final decision can be made autonomously or should be delegated to the decision maker, and in the latter case, whether the decision maker should be influenced in some way.

4.1   When to Delegate

Perhaps the simplest case is when $\delta(\textbf{accept}) = 1$ or $\delta(\textbf{deny}) = 1$, i.e., when the QACS is effectively behaving as a regular ACM, and provides a conclusive decision, with no uncertainty. In this case, the QACS can make the decision autonomously, and there is no particular need for nudging.

Otherwise, the QACS could not reach a conclusive decision with certainty, in which case, it is hard to generalise whether the decision should be delegated to a human expert or not. For instance, consider the case $\delta(\textbf{accept}) = 0.99$, $\delta(\textbf{deny}) = 0$ and $\delta(\textbf{na}) = 0.01$: one could argue that the decision **accept** can be taken autonomously. For instance, thresholds can be used to decide when the measure of a decision is good enough, in a similar way than when dealing with risk-based access control [4]. However, we could equally argue that in case of doubt, the decision should be delegated, especially if the impact of making the wrong decision is important.

4.2   Nudge Selection

Once we have decided that the decision should be delegated, the next question is to know whether the choice architecture of the decision maker should be organised in order to influence the outcome. For instance, if $\delta(\textbf{accept}) + \delta(\textbf{na}) + \delta(\textbf{deny}) = 1$, then there is no uncertainty (i.e., there is no missing information) and if $\delta(\textbf{accept}) = \delta(\textbf{deny})$, then the QACS does not favour any particular conclusive decision. In this case, no particular nudge needs to be enforced, but it might be however worth notifying the decision maker that there is no uncertainty, meaning that there is just no helpful rule encoded in the QACS, or that there are equal chances of both decisions to be correct.

Table 2. Influenced Decision Maker (IDM) Versus Neutral Decision Maker (NDM)

	NDM correct	NDM incorrect
IDM = NDM	Non-blocking	Ineffective
IDM ≠ NDM	Counterproductive	Effective

On the other hand, if $\delta(\textbf{accept}) + \delta(\textbf{na}) + \delta(\textbf{deny}) = 1$ and either $\delta(\textbf{accept})$ or $\delta(\textbf{deny})$ is strictly maximal, i.e., the value for a conclusive decision is strictly higher than the others, then it might be worth nudging the decision maker towards that decision. In particular, the value of each decision can be used to select a nudge with an appropriate "strength", i.e., with an appropriate chance of effectively influencing the decision maker.

For instance, in the case described above, $\delta(\textbf{accept}) = 0.99$, $\delta(\textbf{deny}) = 0$ and $\delta(\textbf{na}) = 0.01$, the confidence that the request should be accepted is quite high, and for instance, a strong financial incentive could be offered as a nudge to the decision maker. On the other hand, in a case where $\delta(\textbf{accept}) = 0.51$, $\delta(\textbf{deny}) = 0.49$ and $\delta(\textbf{na}) = 0$, we could simply make sure that **accept** is the first decision proposed to the decision maker. Clearly, such a flexibility in the nudge selection requires a detailed study of the effect of a catalogue of nudge proposed for a particular decision maker.

Finally, if $\delta(\textbf{accept}) + \delta(\textbf{na}) + \delta(\textbf{deny}) < 1$, then there is some uncertainty in the QACS. In this case, in addition to nudging to the maximal conclusive decision, if any, it could also be worth highlighting this uncertainty, which could denote some problems in the system, such as an ongoing attack.

4.3   Evaluation of Nudging

Applying nudging in the context of access control naturally leads to the question of the evaluation of the approach, and whether we improve the situation or not. In order to define an evaluation model, let us assume an oracle, able to decide (possibly afterwards) if the final decision was correct or not[2].

In addition, we need to consider two different decision makers: the Neutral Decision Maker (NDM), who represents how the decision maker would have behaved without explicit nudging (we abuse the term neutral here, since, as we said above, defining a bias-free environment is not an easy task), and the Influenced Decision Maker (IDM), who represents how the decision maker behaves after being influenced by one or several nudges. In the following, we say that an IDM or an NDM are *correct* whenever they behave as the oracle. For the sake of simplicity, we also assume that the oracle returns a single decision, meaning that when two decision makers behave differently, at most one of them is correct.

Table 2 summarises the different possibilities when nudging. Note that this table does not directly depend on the actual decision taken by a decision maker,

---

[2] Clearly, such an oracle would not be available at run-time, otherwise it would be used in lieu of the ACM.

but rather on wether the IDM behaves similarly to the NDM, and whether the NDM was correct in the first place.

Roughly speaking, when the IDM behaves similarly to the NDM (first row), the nudge had no direct effect on the decision maker. Hence, two cases are possible: either the NDM was right in the first place, in which case the nudge is *non-blocking*, or the nudge is *ineffective*, as it failed to prevent the NDM from making the wrong decision. Two reasons can lead to the latter case: either a nudge leading to the correct decision was used but ignored by the decision maker, indicating that the nudge was not powerful enough, or the nudge was coinciding with the decision of the NDM, meaning that the QACS did not return a quantitative decision allowing to predict the correct decision. In either case, nudging is not worse than the neutral approach.

The main impact of nudging comes when the IDM behaves differently than the NDM (second row). Here again, two cases are possible: if the NDM was correct in the first place, then by assumption, the IDM is not correct, meaning that the nudge was *counterproductive*, or the NDM was incorrect, and therefore the IDM is correct, making the nudge *effective*. The second case is clearly the reason why we want to nudge in the first place, to help the decision maker to make the best decision. However, the first case is not to be ignored, and as with inefficient nudges, two reasons can lead to counterproductive nudges. First, the nudge could have been in the right direction, but confusing to the decision maker, who thus went against his own intuition and chose the incorrect decision (for instance by displaying an unexpected message box). Second, the QACS could have been wrong in predicting the decision, leading to intentionally nudging the decision maker away from his original decision, even though it was correct.

4.4   Example

As an example of our approach, let us consider a special case of access control policy with the reviewing mechanism of a conference: a paper submitted to a conference is eventually either accepted or denied, usually by considering quantitative decisions made by several reviewers, which fits with the idea of QACS.

For the sake of simplification, let us consider that each paper is reviewed by four different reviewers, each of them having up to 0.25 points to give for the paper, in a form of a triple (a, d, na), where a represents the number of points given to accept the paper, d the number of points given to reject the paper and na the number of points given to indicate that the reviewer is not apt to review the paper. A sum $a + d + na$ below 0.25 indicates some uncertainty from the reviewer. For instance, a review $(0.1, 0.1, 0.05)$ might indicate that the paper has both good and bad points, but that the reviewer is not a top expert in the field but has a good confidence; a review $(0.1, 0, 0.1)$ might indicate that the reviewer is not particularly confident, but found some good points; a review $(0, 0, 0)$ might indicate that the paper was not understood at all by the reviewer, etc.

In order to make a final decision, the triples returned by all the reviewers for each paper are added in a point-wise way, which creates a triple (a, d, na) corresponding to the final score of the paper. By construction, we have $a + d +$

$na \leq 1$, and therefore we can consider this score as returned by a QACS (note that a missing review would be automatically considered as a triple $(0, 0, 0)$, thus denoting full uncertainty). The Programme Committee Chair (PCC) of the conference sets up the rule that any paper with a score such that $a \geq 0.8$ is automatically accepted while any paper with a score such that $d \geq 0.8$ is automatically rejected; any other paper has to be processed by the PCC.

Neutral decision. If $a = d$, meaning that the paper has received an equal number of points for accepting and denying it, then no particular nudge is applied to influence one or the other decision, and the paper is presented in a neutral format (e.g., black text over white background). In addition, the names of the reviewers can be omitted, in order to remove Messenger influencer. If $a + d + na < 0.5$, then there is a lot of uncertainty about the paper, perhaps indicating that it is not well written, and an automatic spelling check could be performed, thus providing a quantitative indicator of the poor quality of the writing, if there are indeed many errors. If $na > 0.5$, it could be the case that the paper is off-topic for the conference, and the keywords of the paper could be highlighted, together with a comparison of the key-phrases of the paper (as Easychair [26] offers) with the call for papers of the conferences.

Nudging towards acceptance/rejection. If $a > d$ (and conversely when $a < d$), then the paper is presented in a positive format, for instance with a green background, and the names of the reviewers who accepted the paper are highlighted to the PCC. To some extent, Easychair is already using different colours to represent different potential decisions during the programme committee phase. Papers are also put in a by-default category, such that if no action is taken, the paper is accepted automatically. Finally, if the number of accepted papers is at this point lower than that of the previous edition of the conference, then the PCC can be reminded that the conference normally accepts more papers.

Altogether, one could argue that we are simply presenting the PCC with the most relevant information to make a final decision, without forcing her hand to accept or reject a paper, which is the general approach of nudging: organising the context in which the choice is made while leaving freedom of choice. It could be equally argued that, in practice, the PCC is influenced by multiple biases, some intentional (e.g., the colours of the options), some perhaps less (the order in which papers are presented can have an impact), and our approach could also provide a frame aiming at removing such unintentional biases. Finally, other aspects could be integrated in the nudging process, such as favouring more submissions coming from some countries, to encourage diversity, or even to favour less submissions coming from members of the programme committee.

5   Discussion

We have presented an abstract approach for nudging in the context of quantitative access control systems (QACS). This approach is based on two observations: human beings might be involved in the security decision making process, and human beings can be influenced. The notion of QACS introduced in Section 2 is general enough to cover several kind of systems, and illustrates why a conclusive decision might not always be made autonomously, thus requiring the intervention of a human expert. We have seen in Section 3 that it could be possible to nudge the behaviour of this expert, using different techniques, for instance following the MINDSPACE framework, and we have discussed in Section 4 when nudging should be used and how to evaluate a nudging approach.

An initial observation can be taken from this discussion: a nudge can be inefficient or counterproductive both when the QACS is not accurate enough (and thus predicts the wrong decision) and when the nudge is not followed by the decision maker. Hence, nudging is not necessarily the best approach, and needs to be properly evaluated before being deployed. The example of the conference reviewing system could serve as an interesting basis for a study, especially since it is data that is often accessible to academics. However, this is not strictly speaking a security policy, and the effect of nudges in one context might not be applicable to others.

In addition to conducting several rigorous studies to evaluate nudging approaches in specific context, several leads are interesting to explore further. If the effects of a nudge can be quantified, then we can design an MDP to calculate the optimal decision at each step. However, the repeated usage of nudges leads to the *habituation* of this nudge for a user, and it might be worth considering using a nudge only when it is worth it, which could be done by integrating a notion of value in the above MDP. Finally, it could be worth studying how larger sets of decisions (e.g., including obligations) can impact the nudging approach, since the decision maker has more than two options to choose from.

Acknowledgements. This research is supported by EPSRC Grant EP/K006568 Choice Architecture for Information Security, part of the GCHQ/EPSRC Research Institute in Science of Cyber Security, and the authors warmly thank Pam Briggs, Lynne Coventry, Debora Jeske, Christopher Laing and James Turland for the fruitful discussions on nudging in the security context.

References

1. Bellman, R.: A markovian decision process. In. Univ. Math. J. 6, 679–684 (1957)
2. Bruns, G., Huth, M.: Access-control policies via belnap logic: Effective and efficient composition and analysis. In: Proc. of CSF 2008, pp. 163–176 (2008)
3. Bundy, A., Grov, G., Jones, C.: Learning from experts to aid the automation of proof search. In: AVoCS 2009, vol. CSR-2-2009, pp. 229–232 (September 2009)
4. Cheng, P.-C., Rohatgi, P., Keser, C., Karger, P.A., Wagner, G.M., Reninger, A.S.: Fuzzy multi-level security: An experiment on quantified risk-adaptive access control. In: Proceedings of S&P 2007, pp. 222–230. IEEE (2007)
5. Coventry, L., Briggs, P., Jeske, D., van Moorsel, A.: SCENE: A structured means for creating and evaluating behavioral nudges in a cyber security environment. In: Marcus, A. (ed.) DUXU 2014, Part I. LNCS, vol. 8517, pp. 229–239. Springer, Heidelberg (2014)

6. Crampton, J., Huth, M., Kuo, J., Morisset, C.: Policy-based access control from numerical evidence. Technical Report 2013/6, Imperial College London, Department of Computing (October 2013)
7. Crampton, J., Morisset, C.: PTaCL: A language for attribute-based access control in open systems. In: Degano, P., Guttman, J.D. (eds.) Principles of Security and Trust. LNCS, vol. 7215, pp. 390–409. Springer, Heidelberg (2012)
8. Dolan, P., Hallsworth, M., Halpern, D., King, D., Metcalfe, R., Vlaev, I.: Influencing behaviour: The mindspace way. Journal of Economic Psychology 33(1), 264–277 (2012)
9. Ferraiolo, D.F., Kuhn, D.R.: Role-based access control. In: Proceedings of the 15th National Computer Security Conference, pp. 554–563 (1992)
10. Freitas, L., Whiteside, I.: Proof Patterns for Formal Methods. In: Jones, C., Pihlajasaari, P., Sun, J. (eds.) FM 2014. LNCS, vol. 8442, pp. 279–295. Springer, Heidelberg (2014)
11. Huth, M., Kuo, J.: PEALT: A reasoning tool for numerical aggregation of trust evidence. Technical Report 2013/7, Imperial College London, Department of Computing (October 2013) ISSN 1469-4166 (Print), ISSN 1469-4174 (Online)
12. Jøsang, A., Hayward, R., Pope, S.: Trust network analysis with subjective logic. In: Proceedings of ACSC 2006, Darlinghurst, Australia, pp. 85–94 (2006)
13. Jøsang, A., Bondi, V.: Legal reasoning with subjective logic. Artificial Intelligence and Law 8(4), 289–315 (2000)
14. Lampson, B.: Protection. In: Proceedings of the 5th Annual Princeton Conference on Information Sciences and Systems, pp. 437–443. Princeton University (1971)
15. Martinelli, F., Morisset, C.: Quantitative access control with partially-observable markov decision processes. In: CODASPY 2012, pp. 169–180. ACM (2012)
16. Molloy, I., Cheng, P.-C., Rohatgi, P.: Trading in risk: Using markets to improve access control. In: NSPW (2008)
17. Molloy, I., Dickens, L., Morisset, C., Cheng, P.-C., Lobo, J., Russo, A.: Risk-based security decisions under uncertainty. In: Proceedings of CODASPY 2012, pp. 157–168. ACM, New York (2012)
18. Moses, T.: eXtensible Access Control Markup Language TC v2.0, XACML (2005)
19. Moxey, A., O'Connell, D., McGettigan, P., Henry, D.: Describing treatment effects to patients. Journal of General Internal Medicine 18(11), 948–959 (2003)
20. Ni, Q., Bertino, E., Lobo, J.: D-algebra for composing access control policy decisions. In: Li, W., Susilo, W., Tupakula, U.K., Safavi-Naini, R., Varadharajan, V. (eds.) ASIACCS, pp. 298–309. ACM (2009)
21. Ni, Q., Lobo, J., Calo, S., Rohatgi, P., Bertino, E.: Automating role-based provisioning by learning from examples. In: Proceedings of SACMAT 2009, pp. 75–84. ACM, New York (2009)
22. OASIS. eXtensible Access Control Markup Language (XACML) Version 3.0, Committee Specification 01 (2010)
23. Rao, P., Lin, D., Bertino, E., Li, N., Lobo, J.: An algebra for fine-grained integration of xacml policies. In: Proceedings of SACMAT 2009, pp. 63–72 (2009)
24. Thaler, R., Sunstein, C.: Nudge: Improving Decisions about Health, Wealth, and Happiness. Yale University Press (2008)
25. Tversky, A., Kahneman, D.: The framing of decisions and the psychology of choice. Science 211(4481), 453–458 (1981)
26. Voronkov, A.: Easychair. In: Kovacs, L., Kutsia, T. (eds.) WWV 2010. EPiC Series, vol. 18, p. 2. EasyChair (2013)

Social Information Leakage: Effects of Awareness and Peer Pressure on User Behavior

Mariam Nouh[1], Abdullah Almaatouq[1], Ahmad Alabdulkareem[1],
Vivek K. Singh[2], Erez Shmueli[2], Mansour Alsaleh[1], Abdulrahman Alarifi[1],
Anas Alfaris[1,2], and Alex 'Sandy' Pentland[2]

[1] Center for Complex Engineering Systems (CCES),
King Abdulaziz City for Science and Technology (KACST),
Riyadh, Saudi Arabia
{mnouh,aalmaatouq,aabdulkareem,maalsaleh,aarifi}@kacst.edu.sa
[2] Massachusetts Institute of Technology (MIT),
Cambridge, MA, USA
{singhv,shmueli,anas,pentland}@mit.edu

Abstract. Today, users share large amounts of information about themselves on their online social networks. Besides the intended information, this sharing process often also "leaks" sensitive information about the users - and by proxy - about their peers. This study investigates the effect of awareness about such leakage of information on user behavior. In particular, taking inspiration from "second-hand smoke" campaigns, this study creates "social awareness" campaign where users are reminded of the information they are leaking about themselves and their friends. The results indicate that the number of users disallowing the access permissions doubles with the social awareness campaign as compared to a baseline method. The findings are useful for system designers considering privacy as a holistic social challenge rather than a purely technical issue.

Keywords: Social information leakage, Online social networks, Privacy, Peer pressure.

1 Introduction

The growing popularity of Online Social Networks (OSNs), such as Facebook, Twitter and LinkedIn, has made them integral parts of contemporary online activities. Although OSNs are widely used and represent a rich source of information, much of their data is also sensitive and personal (e.g., demographic, interests, etc.) [1]. OSN users usually disclose such personal information in order to participate in social communities or in return of services [2,3]. However, disclosing personal information in this case can be a double-edged sword. For example, such exposure might make the user vulnerable to personalized attacks such as stalking, identity theft, reputation slander, personalized spamming and phishing. While most of the OSN services offer various levels of privacy protection (e.g., allowing only authorized list of other OSN users, applications and

T. Tryfonas and I. Askoxylakis (Eds.): HAS 2014, LNCS 8533, pp. 352–360, 2014.

third parties, etc.), users' information may extend beyond the defined bounds, which in a privacy context is referred to as information leakage [4].

Information leakage is the phenomena where explicit information provided to a third party can be used to derive implicit and previously hidden information about an entity. Many of the literature suggest some reactive measures to be taken to minimize the effects of information leakage. Such measures include suggesting some friends to un-friend in order to minimize the amount of leakage [5]. In this study, we would like to address this issue in a preemptive way rather than in a reactive way. Since the user is the entity in charge of such decision, we would like to test whether informing the user before sharing personal information can minimize this effect preemptively. Additionally, we examine the extent to which peer pressure influences user's behavior. We present the design of our experiment as well as the results and drawn conclusions. The experiment goal is to investigate how different users behave when they know that they are leaking sensitive information about themselves or their peers and how this affects their decisions. Our study was conducted on an online social network platform with around 200 participants. The results show that users were more responsive to the peer pressure variable, and thus, gives an indication that if users consider their peers when making their online privacy decisions they will most probably leak less information and increase their privacy level.

2   Related Work

Social information leakage (SIL) in OSN has different types and forms. Information leakage may occur from a user's network (friends) to the user, from a user to himself, or from a user to his network. The first has been heavily studied in the literature [6,7]; mainly it occurs by correlating and aggregating information from a user's network to reveal sensitive information about the user. The second is when a user shares different pieces of information (attributes) in one or more OSNs. By correlating these pieces of information one can construct a user's social print, which may pose several threats to the user's privacy and aids in launching several targeted attacks (e.g., social engineering, password recovery) [8]. The last type, as yet understudied scenario, is when a user leaks information about his network (friends) by explicitly sharing his own information.

As individual decisions are known to be sub-optimal in social settings [9], we need to provide incentivization as seen in [10] or peer-pressure mechanisms as seen in [11,12] in order to nudge users towards better social outcomes.

Moreover, previous research showed that relying on traditional ways for managing privacy, such as textual privacy management settings, proven to be inconvenient. Either due to the user's inexperience in dealing with these settings, or due to the high complexity of the privacy settings. Lipford et al. [13] performed an experiment to study this issue. They designed a privacy management interface focused on showing audience point of view. Their results showed that providing visual feedback of the outcome of privacy settings can improve users' understanding of their privacy and help them make more accurate decisions.

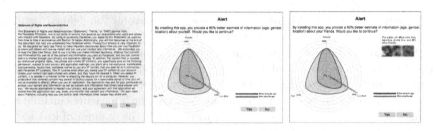

Fig. 1. Types of SIL Messages

In designing our experiment, we incorporate visual elements as well as peer-pressure mechanisms in order to study their effects on users' privacy decisions.

3   SIL Experiment Design

The main question that this study aims to answer is whether users knowing the implication of sharing pieces of information may make them change their behavior. We design our experiment by defining the hypothesis that we want to test, how participants are allocated to different groups, who are our targeted population, and what are the evaluation metrics that we want to measure. Specifically, in this study we try to answer the following questions:

1. If the user is presented with a numerical quantification of the amount of information leaked, does this affect his/her behavior?
2. What are the differences in user behavior when informed about leaking information about themselves, as opposed to leaking information about their peers.

This is especially interesting because: a) it grants the user a sense of 'agency' and b) it brings out the effect of direct and indirect peer pressure on user behavior. Previous results in smoking campaigns (e.g. second hand smoke affects your dear ones) as well as healthy behavior adoption [14] have suggested an impact of social peer pressure on user behavior. This affect is as yet not studied or quantified from a behavioral privacy aspect.

3.1   User Groups

In order to test our hypothesis we design the experiment such that users are randomly assigned to one of three groups. The social information leakage message consists of three main components: text message, visual message, and social message. Each group is presented with a different combination of these components (see Figure 1).

Control Group: This group is presented with only a text-based message shown as a typical terms and conditions page. This group acts as our control group (baseline). Users have two options either to accept and proceed to the app page, or decline and exit the app.

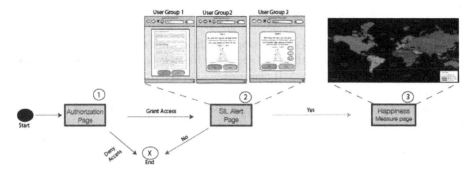

Fig. 2. The Sequence of Steps

User to User Group: This group is presented with both a text and a visual message. The text message states that using the app will result in leakage of some of the user's sensitive information. A spider graph is shown to visually emphasize the before/after effect on leaking the user's information. Users have two options either to accept and proceed to the app page, or decline and exit the app.

User to Network Group: This group is presented with all three components of the SIL alert message (i.e., text, visual, and social messages). The text message states that using the app will result in leakage of sensitive information about the user's friends. Similar to the previous group a spider graph is shown to visualize the amount of leakage. Additionally, profile pictures of user's friends are pulled and displayed as part of the social message to add the social pressure and test the peer effect on user's behavior. Users have two options either to accept and proceed to the app page, or decline and exit the app.

3.2 Population and Metrics

Our goal is to have population representation from different age groups, gender, and ethnic backgrounds. For each participants, we measure two variables: (1) user's action when presented with the information leakage alert message. (2) How much time it takes the user to respond to the message.

4 Experiment Setup

Due to it's popularity, we chose Facebook as a platform to conduct our experiment. We built a Facebook app and assigned each user who participated in the experiment to one of the three user groups presented earlier. The Facebook app is called Happiness Measure, which shows how happy the user is according to his/her current location. The app presents the users with a heat map of the world's happiest countries according to the 2013 World Happiness Report [15].

The actual functionality of the app was selected for simplicity and mainly to attract users to participate.

When the user first connects to the app, he/she is presented with an authorization request to allow the application access to his/her basic profile information (e.g., name, age, location, etc.). If the user grants the application access to her information, she is counted as part of our experiment and proceeds to the SIL alert page, otherwise their information is discarded. At this stage we measure the time it takes the user to respond to the SIL message (i.e., decision time), as well as record his response to the message (i.e., decision). Figure 2 shows the sequence of steps the users follow in the experiment.

For the sake of data collection, we utilized the Facebook advertisement services to promote the app and encourage people to participate in the study. The data collection started from November 23rd to December 5th, 2013. The advertisement campaign targeted 30 countries from different continents to allow for a diverse set of participants. A list of the targeted countries is shown in Table 1.

5   Experiment Results

We divided our analysis to two main parts. First is the decision analysis, where we look at the different decisions users made in each group. Second, we study the time factor to know how much time elapsed before users reached their decisions. The application received around 300 users' clicks, of those around 200 users completed the experiment while the rest decided to close the application before answering the SIL message. In this section, we analyze and discuss the results of those users, and we aim to answer the two questions stated previously in Section 3.

5.1   Decision Analysis

Table 2 summarizes the number of users per group together with their decisions. Decision analysis focuses on studying the differences between each group in terms of user's response to the SIL message. In Group 1, 91% of the users agreed to the terms and conditions page and thus responded with Yes to grant the app access, while 9% responded with No. Similarly, in Group 2 90% of the users responded with Yes knowing that the app will leak some of their personal information and only 10% responded with No. However, in Group 3 when presented with their friends' pictures 20% of the users decided to deny the application access and

Table 1. List of Targeted Countries

Tunisia	Algeria	Brazil	Canada	Chile	China	Egypt
India	Iraq	Mexico	Morocco	Pakistan	Qatar	Switzerland
Turkey	Colombia	UK	Jordan	Russia	Italy	France
UAE	USA	Saudi Arabia	Greece	Germany	Ghana	Slovakia

Table 2. Data Description

Groups	Num. of Users	Yes	No
Group1: Control Group	82	91%	9%
Group2: User to User Group	63	90%	10%
Group3: User to Network Group	54	80%	20%

Table 3. Median Time in Seconds

Groups	Median Yes	Median No	Median Total
Group1: Control Group	6s	8s	6s
Group2: User to User Group	9s	6s	8s
Group3: User to Network Group	9s	13s	10.5s

responded with No. The results show that the third group behaves differently than the other two groups. Thus, this indicate that peer pressure have an effect on user's decisions. Figure 3 shows the percentages of each decision per user group.

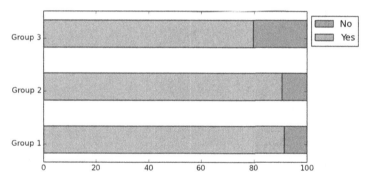

Fig. 3. Decisions per User Group

5.2 Decision Time Analysis

Decision time analysis focuses on studying the differences between user groups in terms of the time spent to make a decision on the SIL message. Again the results show that users in Group 3 behaved differently than users in the other two groups. The median total time elapsed to make a decision for users in Group 3 was 10.5 seconds (either yes or no), 8 seconds for users in Group 2, and 6 seconds for users in Group 1 (See Table 3). Moreover, we studied the behavior of each group based on the type of decision they took (i.e., Yes or No decision). Again, the analysis showed that Group 3 spent more time to make a decision than the other two groups. In the case of No decision, the median time of users in Group 2 was significantly less than the other two groups. Figures 4 and 5 represent a

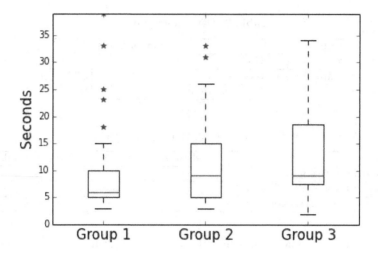

Fig. 4. Time to Take the "Yes" Decision

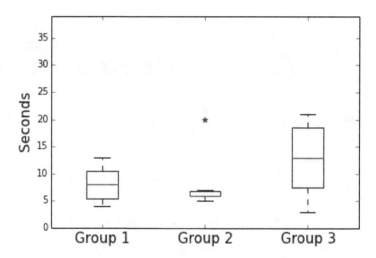

Fig. 5. Time to Take the "No" Decision

box plot of the time spent by each group to make a Yes and No decisions. The box plot representation gives a good overview of the distribution of the data, the median, minimum, maximum, and outliers. The box contains 50% of the data points, with the red line inside the box represent the median time for each experiment group.

6   Discussion

We can see that in both kinds of analysis Group 3 behaved differently than the other two groups. Additionally, unlike our initial expectation Group 1 and Group 2 were fairly similar in making their decisions. Thus, the quantification of information leaked seems not to have the major effect on user's decisions and behavior which answers the first question in our hypothesis. Moreover, when users are informed that they are leaking sensitive information about themselves they were more willing to proceed with the app as opposed to when their friends or peers were affected. This behavior was consistent in both the decisions they took and in spending more time to think when they were aware that their decision will affect their friends. This observation was also consistent among subpopulations. We looked at two demographic features, age and gender. We analyzed how each subpopulation responded to the experiment and the results were fairly consistent. Thus, this suggests that users intend to leak less information when they consider the effects on their peers.

7   Conclusion

In this paper we presented a user study on how knowing that you are compromising your friends' privacy may affect your decision-making. We discussed the experiment design, procedure, and results. Our analysis showed that peer pressure has influence on users' behavior. As a future work, we intend to study further what made Group 3 behave differently by conducting a second experiment with variations of Group 3 SIL message components. To the best of our knowledge, this is the first attempt to study peer pressure and its effects on users' behavior with regard to privacy. We hope the presented results will bring useful insights for policy and application design of future social applications with respect to privacy.

Acknowledgments. The authors would like to thank King Abdulaziz City for Science and Technology (KACST) for funding this work. In addition, the authors thank the Center for Complex Engineering Systems (CCES) at KACST and MIT for their support.

References

1. Chaabane, A., Kaafar, M.A., Boreli, R.: Big friend is watching you: Analyzing online social networks tracking capabilities. In: Proceedings of the 2012 ACM Workshop on Workshop on Online Social Networks, WOSN 2012, pp. 7–12. ACM, New York (2012)
2. Lampe, C.A., Ellison, N., Steinfield, C.: A familiar face(book): Profile elements as signals in an online social network. In: Proceedings of the SIGCHI Conference on Human Factors in Computing Systems, CHI 2007, pp. 435–444. ACM, New York (2007)

3. Strater, K., Lipford, H.R.: Strategies and struggles with privacy in an online social networking community. In: Proceedings of the 22nd British HCI Group Annual Conference on People and Computers: Culture, Creativity, Interaction, BCS-HCI 2008, vol. 1, pp. 111–119. British Computer Society, Swinton (2008)
4. Becker, J., Chen, H.: Measuring Privacy Risk in Online Social Networks. In: Proceedings of W2SP 2009: Web 2.0 Security and Privacy (May 2009)
5. Heatherly, R., Kantarcioglu, M., Thuraisingham, B.: Preventing Private Information Inference Attacks on Social Networks. IEEE Transactions on Knowledge and Data Engineering 25(8), 1849–1862 (2013), doi:10.1109/TKDE.2012.120
6. Blenn, N., Doerr, C., Shadravan, N., Van Mieghem, P.: How much do your friends know about you?: reconstructing private information from the friendship graph. In: Proceedings of the Fifth Workshop on Social Network Systems (SNS 2012), Article 2, 6 p. ACM, New York (2012), http://doi.acm.org/10.1145/2181176.2181178, doi:10.1145/2181176.2181178
7. Singla, P., Richardson, M.: Yes, there is a correlation: - from social networks to personal behavior on the web. In: WWW 2008: Proceeding of the 17th International Conference on World Wide Web, pp. 655–664. ACM, New York (2008)
8. Irani, D., Webb, S., Pu, C., Li, K.: Modeling unintended personal-information leakage from multiple online social networks. IEEE Internet Computing 15(3), 13–19 (2011)
9. Hardin, G.: The Tragedy of the Commons. Science 162(3859), 1243–1248 (1968)
10. Singh, V.K., Jain, R., Kankanhalli, M.S.: Motivating contributors in social media networks. In: Proceedings of the First SIGMM Workshop on Social Media, WSM 2009, pp. 11–18. ACM, New York (2009)
11. Mani, A., Rahwan, I., Pentland, A.: Inducing Peer Pressure to Promote Cooperation. Sci. Rep. 3, 1735 (2013)
12. Bond, R.M., Fariss, C.J., Jones, J.J., Kramer, A.D., Marlow, C., Settle, J.E., Fowler, J.H.: A 61-million-person experiment in social influence and political mobilization. Nature 489(7415) (September 2012)
13. Lipford, H.R., Besmer, A., Watson, J.: Understanding privacy settings in facebook with an audience view. In: UPSEC. USENIX Association (2008)
14. Aharony, N., Pan, W., Ip, C., Khayal, I., Pentland, A.: Social fmri: Investigating and shaping social mechanisms in the real world. Pervasive Mob. Comput. 7(6), 643–659 (2011)
15. John Helliwell, R.L., Sachs, J.: World Happiness Report (2013), http://unsdsn.org/files/2013/09/WorldHappinessReport2013_online.pdf

The Curious Incidence of Security Breaches by Knowledgeable Employees and the Pivotal Role of Security Culture

Karen Renaud and Wendy Goucher

School of Computing Science, University of Glasgow,
Glasgow, United Kingdom
karen.renaud@glasgow.ac.uk, wendy@goucher.co.uk

Abstract. Computer users are often referred to, rather disparagingly as "the weakest link" in information security. This resonates with the frustration experienced by organisations who are doing their best to secure their systems, only to have an employee compromise everything with an insecure act. Organisations put a great deal of effort into education and training but it has become clear that this, on its own, is not sufficient. A wide range of relevant literature has been consulted in order to produce a model that reflects the process from ignorance to actual behaviour, and to highlight the factors that play a role in this pathway. This is the primary contribution of this paper. The model introduces the notion of two gulfs. The gulf of evaluation has the undecided user at one side, at the other a user with an intention to behave securely. A set of factors that help to bridge the gulf have been identified from the research literature. The second gulf is called the gulf of execution, which has to be bridged, assisted or deterred by a number of factors, so that users will convert intentions to actual behaviours. Interestingly, one of the factors that play a role in bridging both gulfs is security culture. Particular attention is paid to this factor and its role in encouraging secure behaviour.

1 Introduction

In days gone by "computer" security was something someone else took care of and the term mostly referred to physical access control. This was a viable approach when security entailed controlling access to the huge mainframes that did most of the computing work for the organisation. Everything changed with the advent of the Internet, connecting everyone to a vast invisible network stretching across the globe. A Google Ngrams search shows that the term "information security" first appeared in the literature in 1975, with an exponential leap manifesting from 1997 to the present time. The Internet ushered in a new era of global collaboration and easy communication but it also opened up the way for hackers to target many more machines, and to exploit the naïvety of their users and owners. This gave a hacker located in, for example, Suriname the ability to hack a Romanian computer user, without the need for physical proximity. This advance

T. Tryfonas and I. Askoxylakis (Eds.): HAS 2014, LNCS 8533, pp. 361–372, 2014.

escalated the range and number of threats as well as the difficulties of securing systems and information and made "security" far more challenging.

It soon became clear that responsibility for security was now shared by every employee in an organisation. So, instead of security being the responsibility of a select few highly trained individuals, it has now moved away from the hub and outwards to every leaf and branch of the organisation. In fact this was a positive move, because as Chia et al. [1] point out, involvement of employees in a process can, in fact, actually reduce the overall cost of security.

Organisations have responded to this reality with a two-pronged strategy. The first prong is to write and disseminate a variety of acceptable use policies which attempt to encapsulate a list of behaviours that the employees should, or should not, engage in. The second prong is the education of their employees so that they are aware of the contents of the policies, and understand how they should act to secure the information they have access to. This is reflective of the prevalent view in business: that operational training is a straightforward process of putting information in and getting the required behaviour out. In theory this sounds reasonable. In practice it hasn't worked as well as expected [2].

The new, shared, responsibility for security has not always been embraced with undiluted enthusiasm [3, 4]. Many employees see security as a hurdle [5]; something that gets in the way of their being able to satisfy their goals quickly and efficiently. It has become clear that employees, even those who have the required knowledge, sometimes still compromise the security of an organisation's systems and information by behaving insecurely. This apparent anomaly demands closer inspection.

2   Employees and Security

It is essential to understand exactly how employees are expected to assist in keeping the organisation's information secure.

If one examines acceptable use policies it becomes evident that the instructions all relate to usage. There is generally no mention of technical measures. This is an acknowledgement that many security-related activities can only be carried out by well-qualified individuals. So, for example, the IT department will install virus protection on all machines but the security policy will instruct users not to disable it. Hence it is secure usage of IT resources that is in the hands of non-IT employees. They are able to subvert security, and thereby, often unwittingly, compromise the system.

The key word in the previous sentence is unwittingly. In the first place it suggests that the employees are well intentioned and not doing this deliberately. In the second place it suggests that they simply don't know how to behave securely. Organisations thus routinely educate, run awareness campaigns, write and disseminate policies [6]. Based on the two assumptions organisations expect that employees will subsequently practice secure usage.

2.1   Security Breaches

Unfortunately, moderate to severe infractions of basic information security still happen. The Privacy Rights Clearinghouse Website[1] maintains a list of data breaches in the USA. It supports searching in order to examine breach antecedents. A search was carried out to extract only non-deliberate breaches that occurred in 2013. 281 (53%) breaches were returned by the search engine out of a total of 533 during 2013, the rest are attributed either to external hackers or to compromises caused by malicious insiders.

Some of the breaches were caused by errors of omission (laptops not encrypted: 36%), some are due to errors of commission (sending personal data to the wrong people: 20%) and some are due to insufficient care being taken (improper disposal of personal records 9%). Some are simply due to human fallibility: eg. loss of thumb drives (11%) and information accidentally posted on the web server (11%) and thus unwittingly made available online. Some of these seem to be a consequence of human fallibility (misdirected data) that cannot be addressed by any interventions. Others, though, could reasonably have been prevented, such as the use of unencrypted laptops outside the organisation, and improper disposal of records. It is probable that at least some of the affected organisations had policy edicts covering these aspects, that employees did not comply with.

2.2   Summary

This brief review suggests that a myopic focus on training efforts is probably not sufficient in and of itself. Organisations are keen to understand how to make their approaches more effective since breaches are damaging to their reputation and often expensive to recover from. If evidence of a better way can be provided, it is likely that they will embrace it, since they are as perplexed as researchers are by the failure of their best efforts to encourage secure usage by their employees.

It is time for us to reconsider the de facto education-based approach and formulate a new strategy. The obvious first step is to understand the employee actions, and the reasons behind them. The question that has to be answered is: "Why do employees behave insecurely despite the fact that they seem to know better?". The literature on human motivation provides insights to answer this question.

The rest of this paper is structured as follows. Human motivation is discussed in Section 3 taking a closer look at human factors that underlie behaviour. Section 4 then considers security behaviour in particular. The discussion reveals a clear distinction between behavioural intention and actual behaviour, arguing that the former doesn't necessarily lead to the latter. Sections 4.1 and 4.2 discuss these aspects in greater detail. Section 4.3 then explores the mitigating role of security culture. Section 5 concludes.

---

[1] http://www.privacyrights.org/data-breach/new

3   Human Motivation

There is a need to understand human motivation before it can be influenced. Many believe that human behaviour is easy to influence: simply incentivise the behaviour you want and punish the behaviour you don't want [8]. John Locke wrote [9]:

> "Good and evil, reward and punishment, are the only motives to a rational creature: these are the spur and reins whereby all mankind are set on work, and guided."

Although Locke was writing about children, this is the view ascribed to by organisations who believe that employees can be incentivised by money on the one hand, and by punishment on the other. This is a widely held belief, even in 2013, as evidenced by the many organisations who incentivise their employees by offering bonuses [10, 11]. This idea may have originated from Taylor [12] who in the early 1900s, advocated motivating workers by using external rewards. Some years later, further research revealed that when staff were paid enough to fulfill their basic financial needs [13], other aspects of the work environment also became important, such as working conditions, career prospects and flexible working hours. It turned out that Taylor was working in a time of deep depression with workers who were exerting themselves physically. His findings do not necessarily apply to knowledge-based workers in a different era.

Humans are far more complicated than is suggested by a model where extrinsic rewards motivate effort, and the greater the reward, the greater the effort. The importance of intrinsic needs must be acknowledged. Various authors have reported on a wide variety of intrinsic needs, as opposed to the extrinsic needs fulfilled by monetary rewards, which are fulfilled by employment, such as relatedness [14, 15] , moral good [16], autonomy [14, 17, 18, 15], mastery & purpose [18], personal growth & self-acceptance [19], emotional needs such as status and certainty [15] and fairness [15, 20].

There is a wealth of literature that can be consulted about what people derive from working, but since this is not the focus of this paper we will merely conclude by highlighting the oft-overlooked role of intrinsic needs, and the need to acknowledge their impact on human behaviour.

Section 2 points out that organisations' current efforts to avoid security incidents are built on two assumptions, that employees (1) are well intentioned, and (2) that insecure behaviour is due to a lack of knowledge. The rest of this paper will consider the first assumption to be true. It can be argued that fraudulent insiders have already made their minds up not to behave securely, and addressing the problems posed by these employees is outwith the focus of this paper. The second assumption has been challenged above. The rest of the paper will discuss the factors that will play a role in motivating employees to behave more securely.

4   Progressing to Secure Behaviour

Human behaviour is goal-seeking and actions are directly controlled by intentions [21]. Ajzen says "... not all intentions are carried out; some are abandoned altogether while others are revised to fit changing circumstances" (p. 2). Research suggests that, although people may formulate an intention to adhere to a behaviour in practice, they will not always do so [2]. There is thus a difference between behavioural intention and actual behaviour. An intention to behave securely is obviously a necessary prerequisite of secure behaviour, but, as becomes evident in reality, this intention sometimes does not convert to actual behaviour. Hence these two aspects should be explored separately.

In terms of information security, evidence suggests that despite the best efforts of organisations, and probably of employees themselves, these intentions do not convert to secure behaviour. If this situation is going to be ameliorated, all the antecedents, both of behavioural intention and of actual behaviour, must be understood.

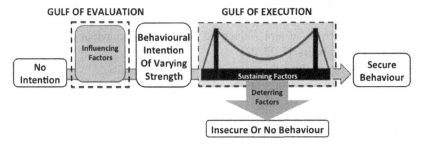

Fig. 1. Antecedents of Secure Behaviour

Figure 1 depicts the progression towards secure behaviour, with a number of factors mediating the process. The gulf nomenclature is borrowed from Norman [22] because it seems to describe the concepts expressed here so well. These two gulfs need to be traversed successfully if secure behaviour is to be realised:

- The Gulf of Evaluation: a number of factors will determine whether the person formulates the intention to behave securely or not. Section 4.1 will explore this gulf in more detail.
- The Gulf of Execution: here, too, a number of factors will determine whether the person converts the intention to actual secure behaviour. Section 4.2 will advance a number of factors that play a role here.

The factors that play a role in bridging these gulfs will probably interact with each other either to sustain or deter progress. There is no suggestion that all factors have to be active in order for the gulfs to be bridged: some may be more powerful than others, and others may only play a role in conjunction with others. Moreover, it is important to note that the behavioural intention that appears centrally is not a binary intention: it has varying strength, and this strength (valence), too, will influence whether or not the intention converts to behaviour [23]. The other aspect of intention that plays a role in how powerful it will be is its stability — how well it endures. Cooke and Sheeran [24] argue that stability might be more powerful than valence in predicting actual behaviour. As a final proviso it must be acknowledged that, in dealing with predicting human behaviour, one can never predict anything with certainty. Humans retain their uniqueness and unpredictability, which is what distinguishes them from machines.

4.1   Gulf of Evaluation

The research literature was consulted to identify the factors that could mediate in terms of encouraging formulation of the desirable behavioural intention of sufficient strength (Figure 2). To identify these factors we searched for publications that reported on the fostering of behavioural intentions in a security-related, risk-related or precautionary context. The following factors were identified:

- Knowledge [7] and Awareness [25].
- Security Culture/Norms [7, 3]
- Attitude [7] which is, in turn, influenced by previous behaviour [26].
- Perceived Vulnerability [7, 27, 28]
- Perceived Severity [7, 29, 30]
- Response Efficacy (trusting in the effectiveness of the required behaviour to make a difference) [7, 31, 32]
- Response Cost [7, 33]
- Self-Efficacy (trusting in your own abilities) [7, 27]

4.2   Gulf of Execution

We carried out a search of the literature to identify the factors that would mediate in this gulf (Figure 3). We did not restrict our search to security-related publications since non-conversion of good intentions seemed to be a more wide-spread problem, and we felt that we could learn from the literature in other areas as well as the security area (diet, finance, conservation, etc.). It became clear, as we worked our way through the literature, that two kinds of factors were emerging, the first serving to increase resistance, the second acting to sustain the intention to behave securely. We therefore report these two separately.

- Deterring Factors
  - Response Cost [28]
  - Lack of Expertise (knowing what needs to be done, but not how to do it) [34]
  - Conflict between demands of job and security requirements [2]

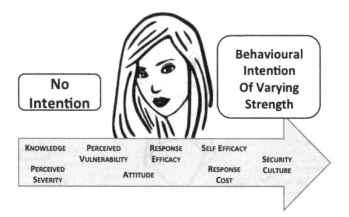

Fig. 2. Gulf of Evaluation Factors

— Scarcity of Resources supporting secure behaviour [35].
— Time lapsed since behavioural intention was formed [36, 37]
— Work Pressure [38, 34, 39, 40].
— Lack of Leadership in Organisation [41–43].
— Lack of trust in Expertise of Person advocating particular secure behaviour [44].
— Inappropriate Training eg. issuing policies without formal training [45].

- Sustaining Factors
  — Commitment to security values [38, 45].
  — Verbal Feedback on Security Performance [46]
  — Social Norms [27] and Behavioural expectations [47].
  — Employee Participation & Involvement in formulating security processes and policies [48, 1] and existence of a Feedback channel [49].
  — Visibility of Monitoring Activities [50].
  — Autonomy (having control over own actions) [47].
  — Habit (previous habitual secure behaviours make future behaviours more likely) [51].
  — Implementation intention (a plan for how the intention will be implemented) [52]

4.3   The Role of Security Culture

There is one factor that plays a role in helping the user to bridge both gulfs: security culture. It is worth taking a closer look at this particular factor since it seems to have significant potential in playing a strong role in propelling employees all the way across both gulfs to secure behaviour.

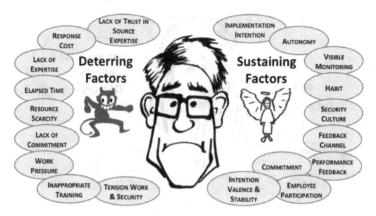

Fig. 3. Gulf of Execution Factors

A strong security culture suggests that people behave securely as a matter of course, without consciously thinking about each decision [53]. This implies that a descriptive norm exists of behaving securely, and that employees, both new and old, will be able to see evidence of this, and be influenced by it [43]. This alludes to the powerful impact of the social environment [40] and the need for active promotion of secure behavioural norms.

Van Niekerk and Von Solms [42] identify escalating levels of security culture. Knowledge constitutes the first level and this is what it makes it essential. Yet knowledge, by itself, does not constitute culture, and this is perhaps why the knowledge and training efforts of organisations have failed. Ensuring that people have the knowledge, according to the model of human motivation depicted in Figure 1 does not guarantee that a secure intention will result.

The next level, according to [42], is "shared tacit assumptions". They explain that these are shared beliefs that are taken for granted, and not necessarily verbalised. The third level is "espoused values" which are strategies, goals and philosophies which are necessarily recorded in policies that address the organisation's security needs. The final level is that of artefacts. This is in the nature of a descriptive norm [54]. Policies encode injunctive norms but these have far less impact than descriptive norms on employee behaviour.

New employees are likely to observe artefacts (cultural indicators) as soon as they start working in an organisation. These, then, constitute behavioural expectations that are very powerful in terms of guiding actual behaviour. Sheppard [55] argues that expectations might well be more influential than intentions in predicting actual behaviour.

So, how do organisations foster such norms? Feldman [56] explains that norms are constructed "through explicit statements by supervisors or co-workers, critical events in the group's history, primacy, or carry-over behaviors from past situations". Thus, verbalised behaviours coming from supervisors [43] and co-workers are important, and this is confirmed by Knapp et al. [57]. One cannot discount the impact of observed behaviour. It seems that, in addition to education and training efforts, organisations should also put some effort into discovering the descriptive norms in their organisations, especially those that have been habituated. If these are insecure, then this is an area for focused attention, in order to break the cycle before it leads to a negative security event. This can only be done effectively by observing real behaviour [57] and so short-cut approaches like employee questionnaires are unlikely to succeed.

On the other hand, the benefits of really understanding your organisation's security culture is the first step in improving it and fostering the culture you want to have. Chia et al. [1] studied security culture in organisations and make the important point that organisations should act by "emphasising that improving security is an incremental process. Instead of trying to set a short-time goal based on the level of security that you would like to achieve, set a long-term goal based on the direction that the organisation would like to follow".

The current approach of educating first and often will not, given the influencing factors uncovered in our review, change habitual behaviours that are actually descriptive norms (artifacts), which is why they propagate. It will re-quire targeted education efforts to change such behaviours. Deliberately seeking out undesirable descriptive norms will be a valuable way of identifying areas for attention. This, then, can be followed up by deliberate interventions to bring behaviours into line with secure usage, i.e. acting deliberately to establish a security culture.

5   Conclusion

This paper has examined human motivation in general, and security behaviour in particular. Two gulfs have been identified and described: that of evaluation (formulating behavioural intent) and execution (converting intent to actual behaviour). Security culture seemed particularly efficacious since it played a role in both gulfs, so it was examined in more detail. Empirical research in this area is challenging to carry out because the stakes are so high and organisations are afraid of the consequences should an experimental new approach be harmful to security in the organisation. However, carrying out a longitudinal study of the impact of fostering clear security cultures is the obvious next step in this research now that the concept of the gulfs has been formulated and the mitigating factors identified and enumerated.

References

1. Chia, P., Maynard, S., Ruighaver, A.: Understanding organizational security culture. In: Proceedings of PACIS 2002, Japan (2002)
2. Albrechtsen, E.: A qualitative study of users' view on information security. Computers & Security 26(4), 276–289 (2007)
3. Pahnila, S., Siponen, M., Mahmood, A.: Employees' behavior towards is security policy compliance. In: 40th Annual Hawaii International Conference on System Sciences, HICSS 2007, p. 156b. IEEE (2007)

4. Siponen, M., Pahnila, S., Mahmood, A.: Employees adherence to information security policies: an empirical study. In: Venter, H., Eloff, M., Labuschagne, L., Eloff, J., von Solms, R. (eds.) New Approaches for Security, Privacy and Trust in Complex Environments. IFIP, vol. 232, pp. 133–144. Springer, Boston (2007)

5. Ross, B., Jackson, C., Miyake, N., Boneh, D., Mitchell, J.C.: Stronger password authentication using browser extensions. In: Proceedings of the 14th Usenix Security Symposium, vol. 1998 (2005)

6. Gaunt, N.: Practical approaches to creating a security culture. International Journal of Medical Informatics 60(2), 151–157 (2000)

7. Gundu, T., Flowerday, S.V.: The enemy within: A behavioural intention model and an information security awareness process. In: Information Security for South Africa (ISSA), pp. 1–8. IEEE (2012)

8. Skinner, B.F.: Beyond freedom and dignity. Bantam Vintage (1972)

9. Locke, J.: Some thoughts concerning education. In: Eliot, C.W. (ed.) The Harvard Classics, ch. XXXVII. P.F. Collier & Son, New York (1909-1914)

10. Gloucestershire Citizen, Poundland staff in Gloucester given 10p discount for Christmas bonus (December 22, 2013),
http://www.gloucestercitizen.co.uk/Poundland-staff-Gloucester-given-10p-discount/story-20353454-detail/story.html

11. Hawkes, S.: IKEA rewards thousands of staff with pension bonus. The Telegraph (December 19, 2013)

12. Taylor, F.W.: The principles of scientific management, New York, vol. 202 (1911)

13. Maslow, A.H.: A theory of human motivation. Psychological Review 50(4), 370 (1943)

14. Roe, A.: Section of psychology: Personality and vocation. Transactions of the New York Academy of Sciences 9(7 Series II), 257–267 (1947)

15. Rock, D.: SCARF: a brain-based model for collaborating with and influencing others. NeuroLeadership Journal 1(1), 44–52 (2008)

16. Lopes, H.: Why do people work? Individual wants versus common goods. Journal of Economic Issues 45(1), 57–74 (2011)

17. Deci, E.L.: Intrinsic motivation, extrinsic reinforcement, and inequity. Journal of Personality and Social Psychology 22(1), 113 (1972)

18. Pink, D.H.: The surprising truth about what motivates us. Soundview Executive Book Summaries (2010)

19. Ryff, C.D., Keyes, C.L.M.: The structure of psychological well-being revisited. Journal of Personality and Social Psychology 69(4), 719 (1995)

20. Adams, J.S.: Inequity in social exchange. Advances in Experimental Social Psychology 2, 267–299 (1965)

21. Ajzen, I.: From intentions to actions: A theory of planned behavior. Springer (1985)

22. Norman, D.A.: Cognitive engineering. In: User Centered System Design, pp. 31–61 (1986)

23. Webb, T.L., Sheeran, P.: Integrating concepts from goal theories to understand the achievement of personal goals. European Journal of Social Psychology 35(1), 69–96 (2005)

24. Cooke, R., Sheeran, P.: Moderation of cognition-intention and cognition-behaviour relations: A meta-analysis of properties of variables from the theory of planned behaviour. British Journal of Social Psychology 43(2), 159–186 (2004)

25. Dinev, T., Hu, Q.: The centrality of awareness in the formation of user behavioral intention toward preventive technologies in the context of voluntary use. In: The Fourth Annual Workshop on HCI Research in MIS, International Conference of Information Systems, ICIS (2005)
26. Bentler, P.M., Speckart, G.: Models of attitude–behavior relations. Psychological Review 86(5), 452 (1979)
27. Herath, T., Rao, H.R.: Protection motivation and deterrence: a framework for security policy compliance in organisations. European Journal of Information Systems 18(2), 106–125 (2009)
28. Hedstrom, K., Karlsson, F., Kolkowska, E.: Social action theory for understanding information security non-compliance in hospitals: The importance of user rationale. Information Management & Computer Security 21(4), 266–287 (2013)
29. Maddux, J.E., Rogers, R.W.: Protection motivation and self-efficacy: A revised theory of fear appeals and attitude change. Journal of Experimental Social Psychology 19(5), 469–479 (1983)
30. Vroom, V.H., Yetton, P.W.: Leadership and decision-making. University of Pittsburgh Press (1973)
31. Liu, C., Marchewka, J.T., Lu, J., Yu, C.-S.: Beyond concern: a privacy–trust–behavioral intention model of electronic commerce. Information & Management 42(1), 127–142 (2004)
32. Damond, M.E., Breuer, N.L., Pharr, A.E.: The evaluation of setting and a culturally specific HIV/AIDS curriculum: HIV/AIDS knowledge and behavioral intent of african american adolescents. Journal of Black Psychology 19(2), 169–189 (1993)
33. Goo, J., Yim, M.-S., Kim, D.J.: A path way to successful management of individual intention to security compliance: A role of organizational security climate. In: 2013 46th Hawaii International Conference on System Sciences (HICSS), pp. 2959–2968. IEEE (2013)
34. Renaud, K., Goucher, W.: Health service employees and information security policies: an uneasy partnership? Information Management & Computer Security 20(4), 296–311 (2012)
35. Shelton, D.: Commitment and compliance: The role of non-binding norms in the international legal system. Oxford University Press (2003)
36. Steel, R.P., Ovalle, N.K.: A review and meta-analysis of research on the relationship between behavioral intentions and employee turnover. Journal of Applied Psychology 69(4), 673 (1984)
37. Christophel, D.M.: The relationships among teacher immediacy behaviors, student motivation, and learning. Communication Education 39(4), 323–340 (1990)
38. Whitby, M., McLaws, M.-L., Ross, M.W.: Why healthcare workers don't wash their hands: a behavioral explanation. Infection Control and Hospital Epidemiology 27(5), 484–492 (2006)
39. Bakker, A.B., Demerouti, E., Verbeke, W.: Using the job demands-resources model to predict burnout and performance. Human Resource Management 43(1), 83–104 (2004)
40. Furnell, S., Rajendran, A.: Understanding the influences on information security behaviour. Computer Fraud & Security 2012(3), 12–15 (2012)
41. Ashenden, D., Sasse, A.: CISOs and organisational culture: Their own worst enemy? Computers & Security 39, 396–405 (2013)
42. Van Niekerk, J., Von Solms, R.: Information security culture: A management perspective. Computers & Security 29(4), 476–486 (2010)

43. Leach, J.: Improving user security behaviour. Computers & Security 22(8), 685–692 (2003)
44. Pornpitakpan, C.: The persuasiveness of source credibility: A critical review of five decades' evidence. Journal of Applied Social Psychology 34(2), 243–281 (2004)
45. Furnell, S., Thomson, K.-L.: From culture to disobedience: Recognising the varying user acceptance of it security. Computer Fraud & Security 2009(2), 5–10 (2009)
46. Schelly, C., Cross, J.E., Franzen, W.S., Hall, P., Reeve, S.: Reducing energy consumption and creating a conservation culture in organizations: A case study of one public school district. Environment and Behavior 43(3), 316–343 (2011)
47. Webb, T.L., Sheeran, P.: Does changing behavioral intentions engender behavior change? a meta-analysis of the experimental evidence. Psychological Bulletin 132(2), 249 (2006)
48. Walton, R.E.: From control to commitment in the workplace. In: The Sociology of Organizations: Classic, Contemporary, and Critical Readings, pp. 114–122. Sage Publications, California (2003)
49. Singh, A.N., Picot, A., Kranz, J., Gupta, M., Ojha, A.: Information security management (ism) practices: Lessons from select cases from India and Germany. Global Journal of Flexible Systems Management 14(4), 225–239 (2013)
50. Foubert, J.D.: The longitudinal effects of a rape-prevention program on fraternity mens attitudes, behavioral intent, and behavior. Journal of American College Health 48, 158–163 (2000)
51. Ouellette, J.A., Wood, W.: Habit and intention in everyday life: the multiple processes by which past behavior predicts future behavior. Psychological Bulletin 124(1), 54 (1998)
52. Gollwitzer, P.M., Bayer, U.C., McCulloch, K.C.: The control of the unwanted. In: The New Unconscious, pp. 485–515 (2005)
53. Thomson, K.-L., von Solms, R., Louw, L.: Cultivating an organizational information security culture. Computer Fraud & Security 2006(10), 7–11 (2006)
54. Rivis, A., Sheeran, P.: Descriptive norms as an additional predictor in the theory of planned behaviour: A meta-analysis. Current Psychology 22(3), 218–233 (2003)
55. Sheppard, B.H., Hartwick, J., Warshaw, P.R.: The theory of reasoned action: A meta-analysis of past research with recommendations for modifications and future research. Journal of Consumer Research, 325–343 (1988)
56. Feldman, D.C.: The development and enforcement of group norms. Academy of Management Review 9(1), 47–53 (1984)
57. Knapp, K.J., Marshall, T.E., Rainer, R.K., Ford, F.N.: Information security: management's effect on culture and policy. Information Management & Computer Security 14(1), 24–36 (2006)

Privacy Issues

User Acceptance of Privacy-ABCs:
An Exploratory Study

Zinaida Benenson[1], Anna Girard[1], Ioannis Krontiris[2], Vassia Liagkou[3],
Kai Rannenberg[2], and Yannis Stamatiou[2]

[1] Friedrich-Alexander-University Erlangen-Nuremberg, Germany
[2] Goethe University Frankfurt, Germany
[3] Computer Technology Institute Patras, Greece

Abstract. In this work, we present the first statistical results on users'
understanding, usage and acceptance of a privacy-enhancing technology
(PET) that is called "attribute-based credentials", or Privacy-ABCs. We
identify some shortcomings of the previous technology acceptance models
when they are applied to PETs. Especially the fact that privacy-enhancing
technologies usually assist both, the primary and the secondary goals of
the users, was not addressed before. We present some interesting relationships between the acceptance factors. For example, understanding of
the Privacy-ABC technology is correlated to the perceived usefulness of
Privacy-ABCs. Moreover, perceived ease of use is correlated to the intention to use the technology. This confirms the conventional wisdom that
understanding and usability of technology play important roles in the user
adoption of PETs.

Keywords: privacy enhancing technologies, user acceptance model.

1 Introduction

Using the Internet in a great multitude of settings, people leave various digital
tracks that are being used for profiling and identification [13]. Although privacy-
enhancing technologies (PETs) can help online users to protect their privacy, not
many PETs found their way into the everyday life [18]. Most frequently stated
reasons for the poor adoption are the difficulties for non-specialists to grasp the
purpose of the technologies and the necessity of privacy protection, and also
poor usability of the tools.

Privacy Attribute-Based Credentials (Privacy-ABCs) is a specific PET that
allows users to minimally disclose certified information when authenticating with
online service providers [5, 2–4]. In general, Privacy-ABCs are issued just like ordinary cryptographic credentials (e.g., X.509 credentials) using a digital (secret)
signature key. However, Privacy-ABCs allow their holder to transform them into
a new token, called *presentation token*, in such a way that the privacy of the user
is protected. Still, these transformed tokens can be verified similarly to ordinary
cryptographic credentials (using the public verification key of the issuer) and
offer the same strong security.

T. Tryfonas and I. Askoxylakis (Eds.): HAS 2014, LNCS 8533, pp. 375–386, 2014.
© Springer International Publishing Switzerland 2014

Two prominent examples of Privacy-ABC systems available today are IBM's Idemix [10] and Microsoft's U-Prove [15]. The EU-funded project ABC4Trust [1] has built a unified architecture for Privacy-ABCs that abstracts away the differences between the specific implementations and ensures their interoperability. Most importantly, the project is the first to deploy Privacy-ABCs in real-life environments through pilot scenarios. This motivated us to study the problem of adoption of Privacy-ABCs by users.

Contribution. In this work, we are the first to investigate the user acceptance of Privacy-ABCs. We use the pilot deployment of Privacy-ABCs at the University of Patras, Greece to explore the experiences of users with the technology and to build a first, tentative model of user acceptance. We identify some shortcomings of the previous technology acceptance models when they are applied to PETs and present some interesting relationships between the considered user acceptance factors. For example, understanding of the Privacy-ABC technology is correlated to the perceived usefulness of Privacy-ABCs. Moreover, perceived ease of use is correlated to the intention to use the technology. This confirms the conventional wisdom that understanding and usability of technology play important roles in the user adoption of PETs.

Roadmap. This paper is organized as follows. We first discuss related work in Section 2 and then explain the concept of Privacy-ABCs and the course evaluation system in Section 3. We present our research methodology in Section 4. Descriptive statistics on the usage and acceptance of the Privacy-ABCs are discussed in Section 5. We present the resulting user acceptance model in Section 6, discuss limitations of this work in Section 7 and conclude in Section 8.

2   Related Work

User acceptance studies for security- or privacy-enhancing technologies are rare. We are only aware of two explorations that are similar to our topic, although they focus on different technologies. Spiekermann [17] investigates the consumer acceptance of PETs for RFIDs in the hypothetical scenario of RFID-based retail. Sun et al. [19] conducted a laboratory experiment and a qualitative study about user acceptance of single sign-on for websites.

Our study focuses on the adoption of Privacy-ABCs in a real scenario of course evaluation in contrast to Spiekermann's hypothetical scenario of PET usage for RFID. Thus, our users actually have experience with a Privacy-ABC prototype, which places them in a more realistic position to assess the technology. We note, however, that the demographic distribution of the participants in our study is very restricted in comparison to Spiekermann's representative sample of German population, as all our users are computer science students that participated in the ABC4Trust pilot.

Sun et al. investigate single sign-on, an existing mature security technology that is already being used for some time on the web sites, such that users have some experience with it. In comparison, Privacy-ABCs are a pilot development that is not ready for the market yet. The qualitative study by Sun et al. resulted in a tentative user acceptance model for single sign-on. We considered this model when developing our explorative quantitative study.

User acceptance of technology has been a very active research topic in information science. Starting in late 80-ties, the Technology Acceptance Model (TAM) [7, 8] has been developed and refined for different technology types [16, 11]. We used the TAM in our study as a starting point of investigations.

Graf et al. investigate in the scope of the EU project PrimeLife [9] challenges in designing HCI for PETs. Understanding PET-related terms and the complex background mechanisms are identified as factors influencing the interaction of the users with the technology. Wästlund et al. [21, 20] study the users' mental models of the data minimization property of Privacy-ABCs. However, the adoption of Privacy-ABCs by users has not been studied so far.

3   Privacy-ABCs for the Course Evaluation

User trial performed by ABC4Trust took place at University of Patras in Greece. Privacy-ABCs were used by the university students in order to anonymously access an electronic course evaluation system at the end of the semester. The first round of the pilot was conducted during the winter term 2012, and this work is based on the data collected during that round.

3.1   Course Evaluation with Privacy-ABCs

Course evaluations have become standard practice in most universities around the world. They are usually conducted anonymously in order to ensure credible results. Privacy-ABC technology is employed in the pilot to guarantee that no identifying information about the students that submit the evaluations is sent to the system. At the same time, the Privacy-ABC system guarantees that only eligible students can have access to the evaluation of a course. That is, the system verifies that a student (1) is enrolled in the university, (2) has registered to the course and (3) has attended most of the lectures of that course.

Although the above conditions can be partly satisfied by paper-based and by other electronic course evaluation systems, it is difficult (and sometimes impossible) to ensure all of them. For example, in the paper-based evaluation, students can be de-anonymized by their handwriting. When the evaluations are conducted through computers, the students often need to put a lot of trust into the systems and into the technical staff. In both cases, ensuring that only the students that attended most of the lectures can evaluate the course requires quite a lot of effort.

To satisfy the above requirements, each student in the ABC4Trust pilot obtains a smart card that is used to receive credentials issued by the university, as shown in Fig. 1. These credentials will be used by students at the end of the semester to prove the desirable properties, i.e., to verify their enrollment in the university and their registration for the course without revealing their identity. The students utilize the same smart card to anonymously collect evidence for

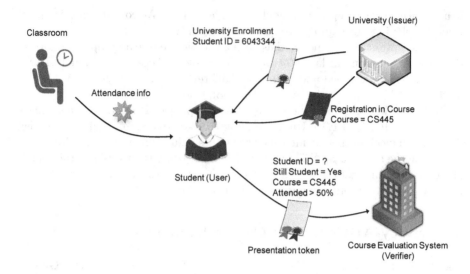

Fig. 1. The participating entities and the information flow in the Patras pilot

their class attendance throughout the semester by waving the card in front of a NFC (near field communication) device installed in the lecture room.

At the end of the semester, they *anonymously* authenticate from their PCs to the online evaluation website of the corresponding course by combining the credentials they have collected. That is, the students authenticate by proving that they are registered to the course and they have attended more than 50% of the lectures for the specific course. The technology behind the scene does not allow the card owners to exchange their obtained credentials or submit more than one evaluation for the same course. The students can make periodic backups of their smartcards such that in case of loss they can restore their credentials content to a new smartcard.

3.2   Properties of Privacy-ABCs

The ABC4Trust course evaluation system has the following properties:

- *Pseudonymity:* A student can authenticate to the system under a pseudonym. No one else (including a malicious issuer) can present a matching pseudonym to hijack the user's identity.
- *Selective Disclosure:* The students are able to prove the desirable properties, e.g. to verify their enrollment to the course, without disclosing more information.
- *Untraceability:* The evaluation system cannot connect the evaluation of two different courses back to the same student.
- *Unlinkability:* The system cannot connect a presentation token with the issuance of any of the underlying credentials.

– *Consumption Control:* The students cannot submit more than one evaluation for the same course.

4   Research Methodology

4.1   Research Questions

Our main research objective is to investigate the factors that drive user acceptance of Privacy-ABCs. Taking into account the extensions made by Pavlou [16] to the original technology acceptance model [7, 8], and also considering extensions proposed by Sun et al. [19], we identified the following factors and their relationships with each other, see also Fig. 2.

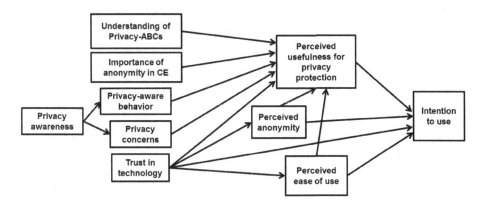

Fig. 2. Hypothetical Technology Acceptance Model for Privacy-ABCs

Perceived usefulness and perceived ease of use are the most important influencing factors on the intention to use the technology according to the original TAM. As the goal of Privacy-ABCs is to protect privacy of the users, we consider the perceived usefulness of Privacy-ABCs for privacy protection in our TAM. Pavlou [16] integrated trust into the online vendor and perceived risk of transactions into the TAM in order to investigate user acceptance of e-commerce. We also think that trust into the Privacy-ABC technology is going to positively influence perceived usefulness for privacy protection and perceived ease of use. The latter influence is justified by Pavlou with the argument that the users feel that they do not need to monitor their transactions with the system closely if they trust the system, and thus their mental effort in using the system decreases.

Instead of perceived risk that negatively influences intention to use the system, we consider perceived anonymity as a reverse construct in the context of Privacy-ABCs. The reason behind this is that the users are exposed to the risk of de-anonymization during and after the course evaluation. Thus, we assume that perceived anonymity will positively influence intention to use. Just as perceived risk is negatively influenced by trust in Pavlou's model, we assume that perceived anonymity will be positively influenced by trust in our TAM.

Moreover, we think that understanding the privacy-protecting properties of Privacy-ABCs will positively influence perceived usefulness of Privacy-ABCs. This agrees with the observation by Sun et al. [19] that the misunderstanding of the singel sign-on technology negatively impacts adoption intentions. We also assume that the perceived usefulness for privacy protection will be positively influenced by the subjective importance of anonymity protection for course evaluations.

We also hypothesize that privacy awareness and privacy concerns will play an important role in perceived usefulness of Privacy-ABCs. We decided also to measure privacy-aware behavior (i.e., user's behavior that protects user's privacy), as we assume that privacy awareness manifests itself through privacy concerns and privacy-aware behavior.

The above influencing factors were measured either using adapted measurement scales from the literature or single questions, see section 4.3 below.

4.2   Sample and Data Collection

80 computer science students that enrolled in the course "Distributed Systems I" were given an introductory lecture on Privacy-ABCs and 48 of them decided to take part in the trial. They were given smartcards and corresponding readers, as well as supporting material (manual and videos). The printouts of the questionnaire were distributed to the pilot participants at the end of the semester. We received 41 filled out questionnaires. Thus, all further descriptions relate to the sample size of 41 subjects (28 male, 12 female, 1 not specified, 23 years old on average).

4.3   Measurement Scales

In the first data analysis step, we run an exploratory factor analysis with a Varimax rotation to ensure the one-dimensionality and hence the validity of the measured reflective constructs. Secondly, we conducted several reliability tests to assure the reliability of each measurement scale. Due to space limit we cannot present our scales here, but they are available on request from the authors.

The *perceived ease-of-use* as well as the *perceived usefulness for privacy protection* of the Privacy-ABC technology were measured with items adapted from Davis [7] on a 5-point Likert scale ranging from "strongly disagree" to "strongly agree". Whereas the adapted items of the perceived ease of use scale used almost the exact wording of the original items (for example, "I would find the Privacy-ABC system easy to use"), the perceived usefulness scale had to be adapted much more heavily, as the original scale concentrates very much on productivity, such as quickness, effectiveness and efficiency of task execution. As we measure the usefulness not for task execution but for privacy protection, we had to remove four items and to add four new ones that were adapted from Spiekermann [17]. However, during the analysis we had to drop two reverse coded items in order to ensure validity and reliability. Both constructs are one-dimensional (KMO > 0.679, total variance explained > 51.59%) and reliable (Cronbach α > 0.676).

The *behavioral intention to use* was assessed with the single question about the intention to use the Privacy-ABC system in future course evaluations. *Importance of anonymity in course evaluation* and *perceived anonymity* were also assessed with single questions.

To measure the *privacy concerns* of the participants we used the Westin Index [12] to classify them into privacy fundamentalist, pragmatic or unconcerned. Measured on a 5-point Likert scale the construct shows one-dimensionality (KMO = 0.539, total variance explained = 50.68%). Unfortunately, the reliability is low (Cronbach α = 0.449).

Understanding of the concepts underlying the Privacy-ABCs was measured with six knowledge statements that refer to different aspects of the concept, such as pseudonymity, minimal disclosure or untraceability as discussed in section 3.2. For example, the statement "When I authenticate to the system, the smartcard transmits its unique serial number" was designed to test the understanding that interactions with the system are pseudonymous, that is, the system cannot identify the users (and their cards), and thus no serial number can be transmitted. The statements could be marked with "true", "false" and "don't know".

Similarly, *privacy awareness* was also measured with knowledge questions about privacy issues, for example about the usage of cookies, or about connections between IP address and user's location and personal data. To measure *privacy-aware behavior*, we asked the participants about their usage of different privacy protection mechanisms, such as cleaning cookies or browsing in private mode.

To measure *trust*, we constructed an new formative scale that asked about the trust into the different stakeholders: the developers of the system, the ABC4Trust project, the environment (University of Patras) and the underlying cryptographic algorithms.

5   Descriptive Results

Understanding of Privacy-ABCs. According to the results (see Fig. 3), most participants had difficulties with understanding of the underlying concepts, as more than 50% of them answered 4 out of 6 questions incorrectly or indicated that they do not know the right answer. The majority of the students believed that the smartcard transmits more information than it actually does, including the information that can eventually identify them, e.g. the smartcard serial number or the number of class attendances.

Perceived Ease of Use. Most participants found the system easy to use (m=3.658, σ=0.656 on a 5-points Likert scale). One aspect of the usability of the technology is the involvement of a smartcard that the users had to carry with them and where class attendance information is stored. Therefore, it is important that the

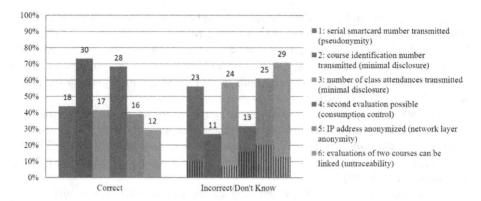

Fig. 3. Understanding of Privacy-ABCs. The left side of the graph shows the percentage of the students that answered the knowledge questions correctly. The right side shows both those who answered incorrectly or chose 'don't know'. The latter is shown by the bars filled with vertical lines.

user does not lose the smartcard. We asked the users whether they were worried that they might lose the smartcard during the semester. Most of them (68%) replied that they were not or little worried about it, while 29% appeared to be more worried. However, only 14% of the users stated that they used the backup tool for the smartcard information during the semester.

Perceived Usefulness. Most participants found the system useful for protecting their online privacy (m=3.689, σ=0.627 on a 5-point Likert scale). In addition, we explored how useful students found Privacy-ABCs in the specific scenario of course evaluation. Whereas 58.5% of the users had experience with paper-based course evaluation, only 7.3% had used an electronic course evaluation system before the trial. All students strongly agreed that protecting their anonymity in a course evaluation is important to them (mean 4.39 on a 5-point Likert scale). Comparing the paper-based evaluation with the evaluation using Privacy-ABCs, students found that using Privacy-ABCs is both more convenient and guarantees their anonymity better. Overall, 87.8% of the students declared that they would prefer a course evaluation system based on Privacy-ABCs, as opposed to 12.2% of the students that would prefer a paper-based system.

Privacy Concerns, Privacy Awareness, Privacy-aware behavior. Participants expressed a relatively high level of privacy concerns, as 34.1% were classified as privacy fundamentalist and the rest as pragmatic according to Westin Index. Privacy awareness was generally high: on average, 84.55% of the questions were answered correctly. The results of privacy-aware behavior varied a lot between different privacy protection actions. For example, while 88% of the students responded that they sometimes clean the cookies and history from their browser, only 29% of them have ever encrypted an email. 49% sometimes use the private mode in their browser, while 66% stated that they sometimes refrained from creating a web account or making an online purchase because of privacy concerns.

Trust into the Privacy-ABC technology. The participants also had a high level of trust into the system (m=3.378, σ=0.761 on a 5-points Likert scale) that varied very marginally between the different stakeholders.

6   Tentative User Acceptance Model for Privacy-ABCs

We looked into correlations between the variables in order to build a first, tentative acceptance model for Privacy-ABCs. The resulting user acceptance model is depicted in Fig. 4 and only partly confirms the hypothetical TAM from the Fig. 2. The perceived ease of use is the most important factor in user acceptance, whereas the perceived usefulness does not directly influence the intention to use the system. Although the users have high level of trust into the system, it is not correlated to any other variables. Understanding of the technology is connected to the perceived usefulness, as expected.

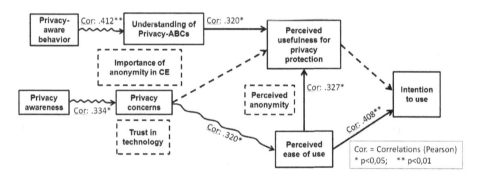

Fig. 4. Technology Acceptance Model for Privacy-ABCs resulting from the data analysis. Constructs that are not correlated to the core concepts of TAM (perceived usefulness, perceived ease of use and intention to use) are depicted in dashed rectangles. Some of the hypothetical, but not confirmed correlations are depicted with dashed lines, and some of such correlations are omitted for clarity of presentation. New (not anticipated) correlations are depicted with curly lines.

Quite surprisingly, trust is not connected to perceived usefulness and perceived ease of use. Probably another kind of trust should be measured here. We measured trust into stakeholders, but there is also a notion of trust into the specific technology as developed by McKnight et al. [14] that is probably more appropriate in our context.

Most interesting is the absence of the correlation between perceived usefulness for privacy protection and intention to use. However, security- and privacy-enhancing technologies have a property that is not characteristic for all other technology types: it usually serves not only the primary goals of the users, but also their secondary goals [6]. Primary goal of the users in the Patras pilot is the course evaluation. However, we only measure perceived usefulness of Privacy-ABCs for the secondary goal which is the privacy protection. Considering perceived usefulness for both primary and secondary goals may favorably change the relationships between the variables in our TAM.

The correlation between privacy-aware behavior and the understanding of Privacy-ABCs is also quite interesting. It seems that people that use PETs in their everday life also better understand the ideas underlying privacy-protecting technologies.

7   Limitations

This work has several limitations that make it difficult to generalize the results. For example, all participants are computer science students, meaning that they are technically savvy and interested in technology. With other user groups, especially the results on ease of use might be quite different. Moreover, the pilot system was not actually designed with usability in mind. Better usability might have improved the understanding of system properties, as showed by Wästlund et al. [20].

8   Conclusion and Future Work

In this work, we present the first statistical results on users' understanding, usage and acceptance of attribute-based credentials, also called Privacy-ABCs. When trying to build and verify a technology acceptance model for Privacy-ABCs, we met with several difficulties that were not present in the previous TAM-related works. Especially the fact that security- and privacy-enhancing technologies usually assist both, the primary and the secondary goal of the users, was not addressed in the previous and in the presented models. On the other hand, we found some interesting relationships between the considered constructs. Thus, understanding of the Privacy-ABC technology is correlated to the perceived usefulness of Privacy-ABCs. Moreover, perceived ease of use is correlated to the intention to use the technology. We hypothesize that the strong influence of usability will even increase for users with the lower levels of privacy concerns and with less technological experience. Based on the findings from this work, we developed an improved version of the TAM for Privacy-ABCs that is going to be tested in the second run of the University of Partras pilot deployment in winter term 2014.

Acknowledgments. The research leading to these results has received funding from the European Community's Seventh Framework Programme (FP7/2007-2013) under Grant Agreement no. 257782 for the project Attribute-based Credentials for Trust (ABC4Trust) and was also supported by the Bavarian State Ministry of Education, Science and the Arts within the scope of research association ForSEC (www.bayforsec.de).

References

1. ABC4Trust: Attribute-based Credentials for Trust. EU-funded research and development project (accessed on April 26, 2013)
2. Brands, S.A.: Rethinking public key infrastructures and digital certificates: building in privacy. The MIT Press (2000)
3. Camenisch, J.L., Lysyanskaya, A.: An efficient system for non-transferable anonymous credentials with optional anonymity revocation. In: Pfitzmann, B. (ed.) EUROCRYPT 2001. LNCS, vol. 2045, pp. 93–118. Springer, Heidelberg (2001)
4. Camenisch, J., Lysyanskaya, A.: Signature schemes and anonymous credentials from bilinear maps. In: Franklin, M. (ed.) CRYPTO 2004. LNCS, vol. 3152, pp. 56–72. Springer, Heidelberg (2004)
5. Chaum, D.: Security without identification: transaction systems to make big brother obsolete. Commun. ACM 28(10) (October 1985)
6. Cranor, L.F., Garfinkel, S.: Security and Usability: Designing Secure Systems that People Can Use. O'Reilly (2008)
7. Davis, F.D.: Perceived usefulness, perceived ease of use, and user acceptance of information technology. MIS Quarterly, 319–340 (1989)
8. Davis, F.D.: User acceptance of information technology: system characteristics, user perceptions and behavioral impacts. International Journal of Man-Machine Studies 38(3), 475–487 (1993)
9. Graf, C., Wolkerstorfer, P., Hochleitner, C., Wästlund, E., Tscheligi, M.: HCI for PrimeLife Prototypes. In: Camenisch, J., Fischer-Hübner, S., Rannenberg, K. (eds.) Privacy and Identity Management for Life, ch. 11, pp. 221–232. Springer (2011)
10. IBM Research Zurich. Idemix, http://www.zurich.ibm.com/security/idemix
11. King, W.R., He, J.: A meta-analysis of the technology acceptance model. Information & Management 43(6), 740–755 (2006)
12. Kumaraguru, P., Cranor, L.F.: Privacy indexes: A survey of Westin's studies. Institute for Software Research. Paper 856 (2005)
13. Mayer, J., Mitchell, J.: Third-party web tracking: Policy and technology. In: 2012 IEEE Symposium on Security and Privacy, SP (2012)
14. Mcknight, D.H., Carter, M., Thatcher, J.B., Clay, P.F.: Trust in a specific technology: An investigation of its components and measures. ACM Transactions on Management Information Systems (TMIS) 2(2), 12 (2011)
15. Microsoft Research. U-Prove,
    http://research.microsoft.com/en-us/projects/u-prove
16. Pavlou, P.A.: Consumer acceptance of electronic commerce: integrating trust and risk with the technology acceptance model. International Journal of Electronic Commerce 7(3), 101–134 (2003)
17. Spiekermann, S.: Privacy enhancing technologies for RFID in retail- an empirical investigation. In: Krumm, J., Abowd, G.D., Seneviratne, A., Strang, T. (eds.) UbiComp 2007. LNCS, vol. 4717, pp. 56–72. Springer, Heidelberg (2007)
18. Spiekermann, S., Cranor, L.: Engineering privacy. IEEE Transactions on Software Engineering 35(1) (2009)
19. Sun, S.-T., Pospisil, E., Muslukhov, I., Dindar, N., Hawkey, K., Beznosov, K.: What makes users refuse web single sign-on?: an empirical investigation of OpenID. In: Proceedings of the Seventh Symposium on Usable Privacy and Security, p. 4. ACM (2011)

20. Wästlund, E., Angulo, J., Fischer-Hübner, S.: Evoking comprehensive mental models of anonymous credentials. In: Camenisch, J., Kesdogan, D. (eds.) iNetSec 2011. LNCS, vol. 7039, pp. 1–14. Springer, Heidelberg (2012)
21. Wästlund, E., Fischer-Hübner, S.: The users' mental models' effect on their comprehension of anonymous credentials. In: Camenisch, J., Fischer-Hübner, S., Rannenberg, K. (eds.) Privacy and Identity Management for Life, ch. 12, pp. 233–244. Springer (2011)

"My Life Doesn't Have to Be an Open Book": A Model to Help Designers to Enhance Privacy Controls on Social Network Sites

Francine B. Bergmann and Milene S. Silveira

Faculdade de Informática – Pontifícia Universidade Católica do Rio Grande do Sul
Avenida Ipiranga 6681, Prédio 32, 90619-900 – Porto Alegre/RS, Brazil
francine.bergmann@acad.pucrs.br, milene.silveira@pucrs.br

Abstract. Social network sites (SNS) are powerful technologies to bring people together and share information, changing the way society interacts in contemporary days. SNS such as Facebook have grown in popularity in recent years, reaching 1,3 billion monthly active users. However, as this network helps to make the world more open and connected, participants inevitably end up losing control over the extent that their personal information may reach among people that belong to their social circle or not. In this context we present +PrivacyCTRL, a model to enhance privacy controls on SNS, which supports the design of privacy settings in order to give users more autonomy over what they publish in these networks. +PrivacyCTRL was applied – via paper prototype technique – to three well-known SNS and showed promise in clarifying the privacy settings and improving the user's choice about what to reveal and to whom.

Keywords: +PrivacyCTRL, privacy model, social network sites, Facebook.

1 Introduction

Social Network Sites (SNS) are powerful technologies that enable their users to share information and stay connected with friends and the world. They have gained popularity in recent years and are now considered to be one of the fast-growing internet sites in the world [17]. To build this network, SNS allow the creation of online profiles in which users can exchange messages, tag photos/videos, "Like" and "Comment" on friends posts and share publications. Among all, Facebook is considered to be the largest and most famous site with more than 1,3 billion users and approximately 125 billion connections between friends and 300 million photos posted per day [7]. This explains Facebook's mission to make the world more open and connected [7].

Since SNS are virtual spaces that allow several possibilities for self-expression and social interaction, their use ends up creating significant challenges regarding the management of the users' privacy. There are many cases in which it is possible to find personal information of individuals in SNS and use it for malicious and/or illegal

T. Tryfonas and I. Askoxylakis (Eds.): HAS 2014, LNCS 8533, pp. 387–399, 2014.

purposes [1]. For example, photo albums may contain personal data in subtitles, places people visit, geolocation or information about friends. Nevertheless, because of the inherent desire to share their moments, people often prefer to be relied to the existing settings on SNS than not publishing content [3,8]. As a consequence, users can be not only putting their privacy at risk, but also their friends' privacy.

Following this subject and assuming that current SNS have insufficient manners to rule the privacy of their users, the objective of this work is to propose a model[1] called +PrivacyCTRL, in order to help the designer to build and develop SNS enhancing the privacy controls, and also to allow the users to understand and configure their social network account in an intuitive way that they can choose the amount of information they want to reveal and the people who can have access to it.

Next chapter of this paper addresses related researches, followed by the presentation of the model. The work ends with conclusions and future work.

2   Literature Review

Johnson [10] discussed privacy even before the diffusion of SNS, demonstrating there are several ways in which information can be created, collected, moved and used by computational technologies, all this motivated by public and private companies who want (and use for profitable purposes) information about individuals.

A group of researchers [1,8,14] discovered that SNS users frequently publish personal information such as address, phone number and photos. Most of them are aware of the privacy settings available, but some just relied and remained with the default settings or had not even read them. The small group that made changes complained about the lack of control over the material others post about them. Also, there is a serious discrepancy between the users' intentions and reality when speaking about privacy definitions of SNS [12, 14].

One study [20] investigated users' strategies to avoid unauthorized access to their profile contents, like sharing private messages rather than public comments and even falsify data to restrict the possibility of strangers to gather sensitive information. In other research [13], approximately 90% of users accepted the invitation of fake profiles, demonstrating the lack of concern by adding a stranger as friend in SNS.

The study by Pimenta and Freitas [16] discusses the privacy issue from the point of view of SNS developers, focusing in problems such as time pressure and cost. Thus, the authors explore several SNS and list the main privacy issues found in order to create a "manual" of standard procedures and solutions that would help professionals to build a secure platform prioritizing the privacy rights of the end users.

The work of Dhia [5] affirms that it is necessary to increase the users control over the distribution of their personal data, since they generally do not want to share life details with everyone. Thus, the author proposes a model of access control for social networks based on the characteristics of connections between users. The model

---

[1] The term model [19] was chosen because represents processes, variables and relationships without providing specific guidelines for implementation, which are at the discretion of the developer.

provides conditional access to shared resources based on limitations of scope between the owner and the requestor of a piece of information, showing the results through social graphs. All studies presented in this chapter show that we cannot ignore the vulnerability inherent to the growth and popularization that these sites are having today.

3 The Proposed Model

This chapter describes three sections of investigative procedures. Only the most relevant results to create +PrivacyCTRL will be presented.

3.1 Investigating Privacy-Related Issues

First, we spread an online survey [2] which had the collaboration of 255 volunteers from all ages, 30 questions and was available for 10 days, useful for understanding what information users protect more, what kind of privacy issues they have, their interests in changing existing settings and their concern about having their privacy violated when using SNS. Based on the results, people seem to be aware of the existence of privacy settings, however, their responses suggest they do not use the help systems or maybe the SNS is failing to provide easy and safer solutions. For example, users were asked if they had any information completely public in their profiles, and 28% (72) of the participants said "No". The first 15 of these 72 people had their Facebook profiles analyzed, and surprisingly, they all had at least one public information such as birth date, relationship status, workplace, photos or wall posts. Through other similar questions, it was observed that there were controversial points between what people perceive as private and what the SNS really provide [2].

After the survey, we applied the Semiotic Inspection Method (SIM) and the Communicability Evaluation Method (CEM) over the interface of Facebook (chosen because it is one of today's most popular SNS), in order to identify the settings offered by the SNS, what they allow to protect and how they are distributed in the interface. These methods were selected because assess in greater depth the communication quality, since it is through the interface that the designer tries to transmit to the users what they can do and how to perform their actions [18]. For its application, 9 people [18] were selected and 7 were aged between 19 to 29 years old. Also, 2 participants aged between 40 to 50 years old were invited to the tests to verify if their behavior would be distinct from the younger ones. The application of both methods was performed with the creation of five scenarios inspired by the most important features of Facebook's privacy settings (according to the online survey):

1. Local Settings: who can see users' posts in the Timeline and News feed area;
2. General Settings: who can see posts from users and their friends in the Timeline;
3. Photo Tagging Settings: who can see tags, automatic tagging and tagging removal;
4. Possibility to hide activities on News feed and Timeline;
5. Preservation of personal identity in Facebook's search system.

Through the application of these methods, we identified several communication breaks in the interface, such as: decisive icons for privacy control with low visibility; inconsistency between options along the interface (often 3 or 4 ways to do the same thing); lack of metalinguistic signs to alert the user during interaction (and existing ones are sometimes confusing to interpret), among others. Also, we found problems related to the control over the information published, such as: privacy settings scattered throughout the interface; content published in News feed to strangers without users' knowledge; initial Facebook settings defined as public by default; tutorials that appear only once in the system, without the possibility of new access; unclear explanations about external search systems (which expose users' data on the Web); inability to disable functions such as "Like" and "Share" (which are mainly responsible to spread the information on SNS) and automatic features like geolocation (list of places that users visited) and tags; settings that cover many items that should be individual. Finally, it is understood that the user needs to be experienced and enjoy exploring the interface to find (and understand) all existing settings and possibilities.

With all these items explored, the next stage of this work addresses how the information obtained was arranged to create +PrivacyCTRL.

3.2   Building the Model

Gundecha et. al. [9] affirm that an individual is vulnerable if any of his social network friends has insufficient privacy settings, impacting in the protection of the entire network. For all exposed until now, it is noted that current SNS are not fully adequate to manage the privacy settings of its users. Simple cases such as initial settings on Facebook being public are enough to cause serious damage to the integrity of users who do not usually explore the environment they interact. In this ambit we present +PrivacyCTRL, which attempts to minimize users' exposure and increase control over their content on SNS, supporting the design and improvement of privacy settings.

Through the results of the survey and the application of SIM and CEM over Facebook, added to the literature review and the practical exploration of common social networks like Twitter, YouTube, LinkedIn, Orkut and Google+, it was possible to make several assertions with regard to the composition of social networks, which are the main ways to interact in them, what types of content are published therein, how their privacy settings are and what they should (or may) protect.

To support creation and diagramming of +PrivacyCTRL, some terms related to the main features that compose SNS are presented, helping to organize all the information collected until now. They were created based on practical and theoretical research and also incorporated from other existing works. The terms are as follows:

- Resources: characterized by all sorts of content that the user can publish on the network, such as photos, videos, messages, map locations, lists of friends etc.;
- Activities: refer to what the user can do with the resources, as, for example, share, favorite, like, post, comment, tag, follow etc.;
- Individual Attributes: actions that the user makes on his profile and in the general interaction areas of the SNS [9];

- Community Attributes: actions that other people do on user's profile or in the general interaction areas of the SNS that involves the user somehow [9];
- Local Settings: made directly in publications, usually when the user performs some Activity over a Resource;
- General Settings: made once and valid for all profile items and publications;
- Help: detailed and complete explanation about Resources, Activities and Settings.

Then these described, the elements were grouped in a diagram (Fig. 1) according to their relationships, and to what is essential to have in a social network that allows the users to control their privacy and autonomy on SNS.

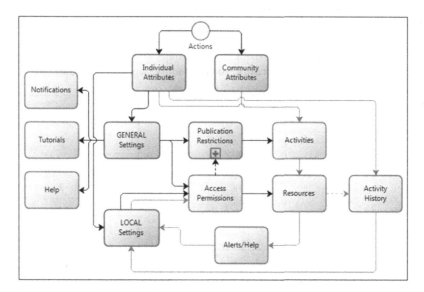

Fig. 1. +PrivacyCTRL, a model to enhance privacy controls on social network sites

This diagram represents the proposed model, which helps the designer to enhance privacy controls on SNS. The green circle refers to the beginning of an action by the user, and the blue squares are steps taken until reaching a final phase, this last one represented by orange squares. The arrows, which flow according to their type and color, represent the relationship between each square. Dotted arrows represents only system actions, not user's, unlike the others. The gray square is an optional function.

To better understand the flow among the elements and how to use +PrivacyCTRL, the model will be described in parts in the following sections. Some design recommendations proposed by other authors are cited to complement the model.

Settings. In Fig. 2-A, which is a cut of Fig. 1, we observe the flow of the General and Local Settings. It is important to keep these two areas separated, since there are many configurable items on SNS and exposing them all together to the user may be confusing. During the application of CEM it was seen that the first place user seeks for privacy solution is in a local area (easiest and fastest way possible). If he fails, he looks for a more complete area which will ensure his privacy more broadly, encompassing all publications.

The action in Fig. 2-A starts with the Individual Attributes, i.e., with the possibility of the user makes actions over his own profile. In this case, the path he has to follow would be the General or Local Settings. Following the flow of both, the user would be taken to the most basic configurations: the Access Permissions over the Resources, better seen in Fig. 2-B. The Access Permissions are composed by [11]:

- Private: the resources are private to the user;
- Friends: the resources will be visible to all friends of the user;
- Friends of Friends: the resources will be displayed for user's friends of friends;
- Public: the feature will be visible to anyone on the social network;
- Custom: the action may be viewed by specific friends the user defines;
- Groups: the resources will be visible to the groups that the user creates or that are recommended by the social network, such as family, work, college etc.

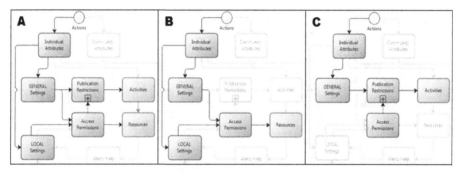

Fig. 2. A – Flow of General and Local Settings. **B** – Access Permissions. **C** – Publication Restrictions (this image's purpose is to focus the colored areas from Fig.1 to be discussed).

The orange item Resources (Fig. 2-B) represents the completion of the action. Then, this part of the model allows the user to access the Local Settings of a Resource on SNS. For example, the user can set that only his "Family" (Access Permission) could view a photo (Resource), and then go back surfing on the site. He could do a similar action through General Settings, selecting that only his "Friends" can view his publications. Due to problems stemming from privacy settings defined as Public by default on SNS, it is recommended Access Permissions be set for "Friends" by default. This would prevent the spread of information, bringing the user some kind of trouble. Later, if the user wants, he can any time make all its resources Public through settings.

Looking at Fig. 2-C, we see the items related to General Settings, which are the Publication Restrictions, to be applied exclusively over the Activities. The Publication Restrictions determines who can perform any Activity over the user's Resources, and shall comprise three main items:

- Disable: indicates the user could disable completely the possibility of any person to accomplish any Activity over his Resources;

- Enable: indicates the user could allow anyone who is viewing his Resources to perform Activities over them;
- Enable with Permissions: indicates the user could allow the execution of Activities over his Resources by certain people, and this can be set through the item Access Permissions, which is "embedded" in Publication Restrictions and can be seen through the "[+]" in Fig. 2-C, also indicated with a dotted arrow.

This feature allows the user to control unauthorized actions over his publications. For example, the user can set friends to comment his photo albums or that only one group can favorite his posts. One of the users interviewed during the application of CEM had his whole photo album shared at once by a friend, and to manage the situation, he changed the visibility of the album to "Private" on Facebook's general settings. Through +PrivacyCTRL, the user would have control to restrict the group of people that can share his resources, and would not have to hide them permanently.

The item Enable with Permissions could also include broader solutions for specific activities, such as Tagging. Added to the fact that shall be an option on SNS that allow users to "disable" this functionality, another research [15] proposes a "hiding" feature, which allows the tag visualization only by the photo's owner and the user tagged, not needing to be deleted. Thus, the user does not lose the interaction with the photo and can have more control over the publication, allowing or not the tag to be visible to others. If the tag is hidden, he turns it difficult for others to trace his profile data, avoiding the visitors to obtain information about him without authorization.

Another solution found in literature [4,15] suggest that when a user upload photos of people to the SNS, the system keeps all the faces blurred and the only person that can undo this action is the face's owner (not the photo's owner), after he is tagged. Then, the face will be allowed or not to be displayed to other people by its real owner.

Notifications, Tutorials and Help. An important point of any interactive system refers to help, which must assist the user when he interacts to the interface, when he needs to change settings to ensure his privacy and mainly to alert about the consequences (and range) of the configurations he has made.

+PrivacyCTRL provides three help approaches through General Settings: Notifications, Tutorials and Help (Fig. 3-A).

Notifications are areas of the interface designed to inform the user about updates on the SNS when he is involved somehow, for example when he is mentioned (or tagged) in groups, events, publications, applications, communities etc. The user shall be able to set *what, how, when* and *if* he wants to receive warnings about his profile, and they may be displayed by the interface of the social network, by email or even by phone. Another feature of the notifications area is to alert users of any kind of changes relating to privacy issues in the interface (e.g., to notify when there is a change on the user settings page in a transition of interfaces, or inform future updates on site policies).

The Tutorials cover quick access to areas of little help, by which users quickly learn about the features of the network, how to use them properly and how the items related to privacy work, always having easy access to them when visiting the General

Settings. Moreover, the tutorials may also pop up during the user interaction, in order to help when he is using the SNS for the first time, for example. We observed during the application of CEM that users do not lose more than 30 seconds on the same screen looking for help, so the more focused, clear and direct the tutorial steps are the better and more interesting they will be for the users.

Recently Facebook has implemented tutorial boxes to teach their users quickly how to use the system. This shows that these changes come to reinforce what is suggested in this work through +PrivacyCTRL. The only problem that has been noticed is that, once the access to these tutorials are lost, or if the user chose to stop reading it (button "Close") after the first time it is displayed, he can no longer go back and view it again.

Help areas of the SNS must always be of easy access to the users, allowing them to find the solution of their problems through topics, FAQs (Frequently Asked Questions) or search mechanisms, for example. This is the way the designer will pass to the user his main message about the interface, therefore, it must be clear and cover (if possible) all areas of interaction of the social network.

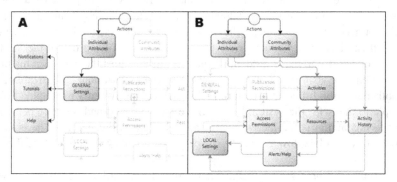

Fig. 3. A - Notifications, Tutorials and Help. **B** - Activity History and Alerts (this image's purpose is to focus the colored areas from Fig.1 to be discussed).

Activity History and Alerts. It is necessary to specify the actions related to the Activities and Settings area on SNS. In Fig. 3-B we note two possibilities of interaction: one through the Individual Attributes and the other through Community Attributes.

We found during the application of SIM that it is important to keep a record of all the activities made by the user on the SNS: people he adds, posts he comments, groups he joins, publications he makes etc. Thus, starting the flow with the Individual Attributes, we see that this record would occur every time the user performs an Activity over a Resource, and it would automatically be part of an Activity History, shown in Fig. 3-B with a dotted arrow (see better details in Fig. 1). This history (every move the user makes on the SNS) would be displayed in the user's profile to be set locally, choosing what to display to whom. Or else, the Activity History could be in a separate area of the interface, keeping user's personal profile only for displaying the main activities related to himself (for example, a comment he leaves on a friend's post would appear only in the Activity History, not in his profile). The most important is the Activity History function shall be present in some area of the interface, so the user can easily control which of his activities should be visible to others.

Alerts/Help (gray square in Fig. 3-B) are optional under certain conditions, and should appear when the user perform an Activity over a Resource. The purpose of this function is to alert the user about the risk of privacy violation when doing any activity on SNS. If the user posts a photo and his settings were previously set as "Public", it is important that the interface alerts the publication will be visible to anyone, and immediately offers a path to Local Configurations for the user to change its Access Permissions settings, giving him the choice to control the exhibition of his information.

Further, we need to address the Community Attributes, i.e., what other people make in the user profile and elsewhere in the SNS involving the user. Since the main items of +PrivacyCTRL have been described in the previous section, watching the flow of steps in Fig. 3-B we can exemplify an action: if a user's friend makes a comment (Activity) in a photo (Resource), he (the visitor) can also set the privacy level of this activity. However, it will always be subjected to the original settings established by the owner of the content, i.e.: if the user sets the Access Permissions of his photos to Friends, the person who wants to leave a comment cannot turn publication "Public" somehow, but can further restrict his comment viewing for "Only me and the owner".

Through +PrivacyCTRL, we expect that developers can better build and develop an interface, since the model covers the essential parts of SNS and how they can be protected. Thus, with a well designed and comprehendible interface that offers more ways to control personal data, users could easily understand the system, configure their settings and thus have an intentional choice about disclosing their information.

3.3   Analysis with Users

The analysis of the model was made through the redesign (via paper prototype technique) of the interfaces of three well-known social networks in Brazil (Facebook, Orkut and Twitter). The users who participated were the same of the CEM (9 people).

The tests were made individually, and to each user was explained the actions allowed by the model, its utility for developers and how an interface could have its settings improved through its use, becoming a suitable environment to protect users' information. The interfaces were presented in its original form and after the application of +PrivacyCTRL, having some privacy issues fixed.

The following sections describe some interfaces presented to the participants and their most significant responses to the survey.

Redesigned Interfaces. Eight examples of redesigned interfaces were presented to the users, and the personal profile area of Orkut was one of them. Currently, the privacy setting applies to the overall contents in the users profile and cannot be restricted individually according to the users preference. Then, if the user wants only his coworkers to see his e-mail, for example, he can do nothing about that. As stated by the model (Fig. 1), a user must have the possibility to set, through the Local

Settings, the Access Permissions of an Activity over a Resource. Thus, the proposed solution in this example occurs through the introduction of small icons (padlocks) along the interface, allowing the user to configure the Access Permissions for each of the personal data in the page, such as address, birthday, relationships status etc.

In Fig. 2-C, we have the explanation of the item "Enable with Permissions" that belongs to the square Publication Restrictions, which brings suggestions for better controlling tags, like the face obfuscation feature (Fig. 4).

Fig. 4. A photo on Facebook with blurred faces. The photo's owner (who published it) lies in the center of the image (Source: adapted from Google Images).

In the example of Fig. 4, when a user uploads a photo with several people in it, the faces in it are blurred until the owner of each face is tagged by the user. This manner, each one can authorize (and control) his face to be displayed or not. Other tagging features suggested by +PrivacyCTRL, like "disable" and "hide" (explained in Fig. 2-C) were flagged during the tests via quick access to Facebook and Twitter settings (this last one has the tagging feature similar to Facebook), showing that this type of configuration could be applied along the interface with other tagging options.

The next section presents the survey applied to users after the presentation of the redesigned interfaces.

Post-test Survey. The survey was divided into two main parts: the first one consists of general questions about privacy and the second part were questions about +PrivacyCTRL. Only the main questions and results are commented.

One of the questions was if users would publish more content if they could better manage their privacy in social networks, and 6 out of 9 participants (67%) said "Yes". Next, 8 people (89%) think it is important to receive notifications about all activities involving their profiles on SNS, and 7 people (78%) say they have already deleted posts or didn't publish content for not knowing how to protect them. All 9 participants said they would not want complete strangers seeing what they publish.

The following questions comprehends specifically the functions proposed in the model. In the case of tagging, 8 out of 9 users (89%) said they would like to use the mechanism to "blur faces" in photos they were tagged, or totally disable photo tagging. All 9 participants would use the "hiding tags" feature suggested in the model, which makes the tag visible only to the owner of the photo and the person tagged.

When asked whether with +PrivacyCTRL users would have the opportunity to better control their privacy and the content that their friends post about them on SNS, all participants said "Yes". A problem cited by one volunteer was he couldn't hide his Likes and Comments updates from Facebook's Timeline. Using the model to redesign the interface, he'd have more autonomy to control his actions, activities and those who can see what he shares. Other user commented: "*Some strangers were commenting my photos and I think it's quite unpleasant. If the network was properly suited to the model, I could control this kind of activity*". About the redesigned interfaces, one user said that "*these few examples we saw were enough to better control the privacy of our publications and see that the model appears to be very promising*".

As the results shown here, we observe that users are concerned about who has access to their information and they want to have more control over their exposure on SNS. The redesigned interfaces through the application of +PrivacyCTRL demonstrated to be very useful for users, who saw in practice how a secure interface would looks like. Simple problems like photo tagging had easy and quick solutions for users who do not like to be labeled. The study indicates that the model shows promise in improving the interfaces and helping to correct some existing privacy problems.

4   Conclusions and Future Works

Social networks sites became part of human culture and totally changed the way society interacts today. However, the consequence of their popularization gives rise to frequent privacy problems, highlighting the need for actions and solutions that will help the user to better control their exposure online.

Thus, this work presented a series of procedures, researches and tests performed to understand how people have faced the privacy-related issues in SNS, what are the main existing problems and why they occur. With these results in hand, we proposed +PrivacyCTRL, model to enhance privacy controls on SNS which helps the designer to better build and develop the interface, allowing the user to understand and configure the system according to his needs and preferences. At the same time, the tests with users indicated that the model shows promise to help fixing several existing privacy problems and could be used to help building safer SNS in the future.

With all these exposed, we see that it is still a challenge for social networks being suited to the privacy demands of its users, and alternatives such +PrivacyCTRL proposes are crucial to help in the evolution of privacy treatment of SNS. Also, the model cannot yet be the solution for all privacy problems, but it certainly helps the designer to focus on the points that should gain more attention to build a safer system.

It is also known that the activities and resources present are constantly evolving, since the demand for content is always increasing. It is crucial that these networks should enhance their system to serve people better and ensure that new features are equipped with good privacy settings like the ones suggested through +PrivacyCTRL.

In 2013, reinforcing the results of this work, Facebook casually updated its privacy settings. The main changes were the addition of local help and tour areas along the interface, explaining more about features and privacy, and the centralization of the privacy settings, that were previously scattered in different areas of the interface.

There is still the human factor in the history: social networks are composed of content that others choose to share and distribute, and, at these times, wondering if this type of information will harm someone or not remains a question. As said by Eric Schmidt, CEO of Google [6]: *"If you have something you do not want anyone to know, maybe you should not do this in the first place"*. This could prevent a lot of problems, and educating users to use their common sense in SNS is a difficult and challenging task, but basic to success.

As future work, +PrivacyCTRL could be applied more deeply in the studied SNS, trying to cover a wider range of issues and thus see how it could be refined and complemented. It would be important that the model was applied by other specialists than the authors, to verify if the instructions are comprehensible for the designers who may want to follow it, for example.

At the same time, the implementation and reformulation of the model presented here to build safer mobile interfaces would be an interesting alternative, since the use of social networks on smartphones and tablets is increasing nowadays.

References

1. Ai, H., Maiga, A., Aimeur, E.: Privacy protection issues in social networking sites. In: IEEE/ACS International Conference on Computer Systems and Applications (AICCSA 2009), pp. 271–278 (2009)
2. Bergmann, F.B., Silveira, M.S.: Eu vi o que você fez.. e eu sei quem você é!": uma análise sobre privacidade no facebook do ponto de vista dos usuários. In: 11th Brazilian Symposium on Human Factors in Computing Systems (IHC 2012), pp. 109–118. Brazilian Computer Society, Porto Alegre (2012)
3. Besmer, A., Lipford, H.R.: Moving beyond untagging: photo privacy in a tagged world. In: 28th International Conference on Human Factors in Computing Systems (CHI 2010), pp. 1563–1572. ACM, New York (2010)
4. Cutillo, L.A., Molva, R., Önen, M.: Privacy preserving picture sharing: enforcing usage control in distributed on-line social networks. In: 15th Workshop on Social Network Systems (SNS 2012), p. 6. ACM, New York (2012)
5. Dhia, I.B.: Access control in social networks: a reachability-based approach. In: 15th Joint EDBT/ICDT Workshops (EDBT-ICDT 2012), pp. 227–232. ACM, New York (2012)
6. Dwyer, C.: Privacy in the Age of Google and Facebook. IEEE Technology and Society Magazine 30(3), 58–63 (2011)
7. Facebook Newsroom, http://newsroom.fb.com
8. Faliagka, E., Tsakalidis, A., Vaikousi, D.: Teenagers' Use of Social Network Websites and Privacy Concerns: A Survey. In: 15th Panhellenic Conference on Informatics (PCI 2011), pp. 207–211 (2011)
9. Gundecha, P., Barbier, G., Liu, H.: Exploiting vulnerability to secure user privacy on a social networking site. In: 17th ACM SIGKDD International Conference on Knowledge Discovery and Data Mining (KDD 2011), pp. 511–519. ACM, New York (2011)

10. Johnson, D.G.: Computer Ethics. Prentice Hall, Englewood Cliffs (1999)
11. Liu, Y., Gummadi, K.P., Krishnamurthy, B., Mislove, A.: Analyzing facebook privacy settings: user expectations vs. reality. In: 11th ACM SIGCOMM Conference on Internet Measurement (IMC 2011), pp. 61–70. ACM, New York (2011)
12. Madejski, M., Johnson, M., Bellovin, S.M.: A study of privacy settings errors in an online social network. In: 10th IEEE International Conference on Pervasive Computing and Communications Workshops (PerCom 2012), pp. 340–345 (2012)
13. Michalopoulos, D., Mavridis, I.: Surveying Privacy Leaks Through Online Social Network. In: 14th Panhellenic Conference on Informatics (PCI 2010), pp. 184–187. IEEE Computer Society, Washington (2010)
14. Osman, F.Y., Ab Rahim, N.Z.: Self-disclosure and Social network sites users' awareness. In: 2nd International Conference on Research and Innovation in Information Systems (ICRIIS 2011), pp. 1–6 (2011)
15. Pesce, J.P., Casas, D.L., Rauber, G., Almeida, V.: Privacy attacks in social media using photo tagging networks: a case study with Facebook. In: 1st Workshop on Privacy and Security in Online Social Media (PSOSM 2012), p. 8. ACM, New York (2012)
16. Pimenta, P.C., de Freitas, C.M.: Security and privacy analysis in social network services. In: 5th Iberian Conference on Information Systems and Technologies (CISTI 2010), pp. 1–6 (2010)
17. Rauber, G., Almeida, V.A.F., Kumaraguru, P.: Privacy Albeit Late. In: 7th Brazilian Symposium on Multimedia and the Web (WebMedia 2011), p. 8. ACM, New York (2011)
18. de Souza, C.S., Leitão, C.F.: Semiotic Engineering Methods for Scientific Research in HCI. Morgan and Claypool Publishers, San Francisco (2009)
19. Tomhave, B.: Alphabet Soup: Making Sense of Models, Frameworks, and Methodologies. George Washington University (2005)
20. Young, A.L., Quan-Haase, A.: Information revelation and internet privacy concerns on social network sites: a case study of facebook. In: 4th International Conference on Communities and Technologies (C&T 2009), pp. 265–274. ACM, New York (2009)

Paper Audit Trails and Voters' Privacy Concerns

Jurlind Budurushi, Simon Stockhardt, Marcel Woide, and Melanie Volkamer

TU Darmstadt / CASED, Darmstadt, Germany
name.surname@cased.de

Abstract. Advances in information technology have simplified many processes in our lives. However, in many cases trust issues arise when new technology is introduced, and voting is one prominent example. To increase voters' trust, current e-voting systems provide paper audit trails (PATs) which enable automatic tally and/or manual audit of the election result. PATs may contain only the encrypted vote or the plaintext vote in human-readable and/or machine-readable format. Previous studies report voter privacy concerns with PATs containing additional information (e.g. QR-Codes) other than the human-readable plaintext vote. However, omitting such PATs negatively influences security and/or efficiency. Hence, to address these concerns we applied the coping and threat appraisal principles of the protection motivation theory in the communication process. We evaluated them in separate surveys focused on the EasyVote system [15]. Results show that the coping appraisal is more promising than the threat appraisal approach. While our findings provide novel directions on addressing privacy concerns in the e-voting context, corresponding limitations need to be considered for future user studies.

Keywords: electronic voting, paper audit trails, privacy, user study.

1 Introduction

The introduction and the continuous advances in information technology have simplified many processes in our lives, for example traveling has become much easier because of navigation systems. Recently, voting has also joined the family of the processes improved by information technology, as a large number of electronic voting systems have been proposed and are already in use for legally binding polling station elections, for instance in the US. However, in many cases (including voting) trust issues arise when new technology is introduced. In order to increase voters' trust and detect malicious voting systems, many of these proposals provide voters with paper audit trails (PATs) of their cast votes. PATs are used for tallying and/or auditing the election result and remain in a ballot box in the polling station.[1] PATs differ from system to system and they may contain: only the encrypted vote [5], the encrypted permutation of candidates

---

[1] For example, in [5] and [6] voters can take copies of their PATs and audit the election result independent form time and place.

T. Tryfonas and I. Askoxylakis (Eds.): HAS 2014, LNCS 8533, pp. 400–409, 2014.

together with the position of the selected candidate [6], the plaintext vote in a human-readable format [17], or the plaintext vote in a human-readable and a machine-readable (e.g. QR-Code [14] and [15], or RFID chip [16]) format.

Beside enabling the detection of malicious voting systems, PATs also enable an automatic tallying of cast votes. Thus, less time and human resources are required. However, previous studies [3] and [10] report that voters have concerns regarding vote secrecy, when PATs with additional information (e.g. encryption of the vote or a QR-Code that encodes the plaintext vote) other than the plaintext vote are used. Voters are concerned that this information might reveal their selections, i.e. voters believe that the encryption helps others to guess their selections, or that the QR-Code contains a time stamp of their cast vote. Hence, enabling voters to verify (i.e. detect a malicious voting system), decreases their trust regarding vote secrecy.

Refraining from PATs with additional information is not in the interest of security and/or efficiency, therefore our goal is to identify an adequate approach to address these concerns. In order to achieve our goal, we use the protection motivation theory [12] as the underlying theoretical foundation. Thereby, we focus on its two key principles, namely the coping and the threat appraisal. Respectively, we developed two approaches: The first approach, which is based on the coping appraisal, provides a technical solution. While based on the threat appraisal, the second approach describes the necessary effort an attacker needs in order to violate vote secrecy. We evaluated both approaches in a user study with two online surveys, and focused on the EasyVote system proposed by Volkamer et al. [15]. We report the findings from our user study and analyzed the impact of both approaches regarding voters' privacy concerns. The coping appraisal approach is more promising than the threat appraisal approach. However, the two approaches provide new and important insights into addressing voters' privacy concerns and how these concerns can be positively influenced (decreased) to increase voters' trust regarding new voting technology.

This work is structured as follows: In section 2 we briefly introduce the EasyVote system. Section 3 provides an overview of voters' privacy concerns reported in previous studies. Section 4 presents the methodology and describes the design of the user study. In section 5 we present the results. Section 6 summarizes our findings and provides directions for future research.

2   The EasyVote Voting System

The EasyVote system proposed by Volkamer et al. [15] focuses on voting challenges introduced by complex ballots and voting rules, e.g., some local elections in Germany or parliamentary elections in Belgium. Many other electronic voting systems, for example [2], [4], [14] and [16], are based on the same general concepts. We only describe here the voting phase, and omit the description of the tallying phase which is beyond the scope of this paper.

Voting phase. The voter first identifies herself to the poll workers, similar to traditional paper-based system. Afterwards, the voter enters the voting booth and uses the electronic voting device to prepare her ballot. When the voter confirms her selections, the electronic voting device starts the printing process and all electronic data are deleted, i.e. all voter's selections.[2] The printout (PAT), which contains voter's selections, consists of two parts: a human-readable and a machine-readable (a QR-Code) part, see Figure 1.[3] The voter verifies that the human-readable part contains the made on the electronic voting device. Finally, the voter leaves the voting booth and deposits the folded printout into the ballot box.

Fig. 1. The EasyVote paper ballot (printout/PAT)

3   Privacy Concerns in Previous Studies

The studies conducted by Budurushi et al. [3] and Llewellyn et al. [10] showed that voters have concerns regarding privacy of their votes, when PATs containing information other than the plaintext vote are used [3] and [10]. Llewellyn et al. [10] conducted a user study at the University of Surrey, UK in June/July 2011. The user study was repeated five times. In each repetition, which consisted of six sequentially rounds, took part 12 different participants. The electronic voting system used in the user study implemented the system proposed by Ryan et al. [11]. The goal of this user study was to evaluate voters' understanding regarding privacy of the vote and the subsequent impact on verifiable voting technologies. In the user study participants cast a vote in a fictitious election, and were additionally required to select on the ballot (receipt) whether they wish to "post" their receipt (anonymously) on the bulletin board. Afterwards, participants (including themselves) attempted to guess the selection of every

---

[2] Note that here voter's selections are deleted from the vote casting software, i.e. on the software level.

[3] The machine-readable part (the QR-Code) contains the exact information as the human-readable part and enables an automatic tallying of the printouts. Further, if two voters select the same candidates the QR-Codes are identical.

participant, independent whether or not that participant published her receipt. Participants who chose to post their receipts received a reward of £1. Further, for each correct guess the participant received a reward of £.50 and lost an amount of £.50 for every participant who correctly guessed her selection. The economic incentives revealed participants' understanding of the security mechanisms, i.e. privacy of the vote. Thus, in case a participant was confident that the receipt does not reveal any information on her selection, she would always post her ballot in each and every round. Otherwise, she would not publish her receipt. In the study 23 out of 60 participants did not post their receipts in at least one round, i.e. were concerned regarding privacy of the vote.

Budurushi et al. [3] report about the results of a test election, which was combined with an exit survey and took place alongside the university elections at Technische Universität Darmstadt in June 2013. The electronic voting system used in the user study implemented the EasyVote system proposed by Volkamer et al. [15]. The general goals of this study were: 1) To evaluate the system from a technical and practical perspective; 2) To find out participants' (voters) perception regarding privacy of the vote. In order to measure participants' perception with respect to privacy, of the vote, the exit survey contained two specific items: First, the statement, "I think that vote secrecy might be violated by the use of the QR-Code.". Thereby, participants indicated their agreement with this statement on a five-point Likert scale anchored in "strongly disagree" and "strongly agree". Second, a text box where participants could justify their selections. In the study 79 out of 198 participants were concerned regarding privacy of the vote due to the use of QR-Codes. Further, the most comprehensive justification whose parts include most of all other justifications, was the following: "In the election poll workers recorded names on the electoral register, sequentially. In addition to my selections, the time and the sequential order of vote casting can be stored on the QR-Code.".

4   User Study

In this section we describe the different approaches (two online surveys) which were used in order to increase voters' trust and decrease voters' privacy concerns with respect to PATs that contain additional information (e.g. encryption of the vote or a QR-Code that encodes the plaintext vote) other than the human-readable plaintext vote. We also report about recruiting and sampling of participants.

4.1   Online Surveys

Both surveys shared the same general structure and differed only in the part that addressed voters' privacy concerns. Thus, the general structure of the surveys was the following: First participants were asked if they would cast their vote electronically in the upcoming federal election in September 2013. Second, participants were asked if they know what is a QR-Code. In the third question, participants were asked if they have a QR-Code reader application on their smartphone. Then, participants were provided with the survey's specific approach. In addition the surveys collected some demographic data (gender, age and education degree).

4.2 Recruiting and Sampling

The participants were recruited via E-Mail and social networks, for example Facebook. In the first survey participated 99 subjects (38 female, 61 male). 38 participants were between 18 and 25 years old, 41 participants were between 26 and 35 years old, 8 participants were between 36 and 45 years old, 10 participants were between 46 and 60 years old, and 2 participants were older than 60 years. The education level was as follows: 1 participant had a secondary school certificate, 13 had an advanced technical certificate, 34 had a general qualification for university entrance, 14 had a bachelor degree, 29 had a master degree or equivalent like diploma, 3 had a Ph.D. and 5 had an alternative educational degree.

In the second survey participated 94 subjects. There were 61 male and 33 female participants. 44 participants were between 18 and 25 years old, 26 participants were between 26 and 35 years old, 8 participants were between 36 and 45 years old, 14 participants were between 46 and 60 years old, and 2 participants were older than 60 years. The participants' education levels were the followings: 8 participant had a secondary school certificate, 11 had an advanced technical certificate, 38 had a general qualification for university entrance, 18 had a bachelor degree, 12 had a master degree or equivalent like diploma, 4 had a Ph.D. and 3 had an alternative educational degree. Note that difference of the education level between both groups was not significant.

4.3 Approaches to Address Participants' Privacy Concerns

In order to address participants' privacy concerns we used the protection motivation theory [12]. This theory, which predicts participants behavior when confronted with a threat and has been applied to other security contexts e.g. [8] and [9], but not electronic voting, provides the foundation for our approaches. For further information regarding the protection motivation theory, refer to [1] and [7].

First Approach: Coping Appraisal After the initial questions participants were first confronted with a summary of the concerns that was deduced from the results of the study conducted by Budurushi et al. [3]. The concern statement in the survey was the following: "In the election poll workers recorded names on the electoral register, sequentially. In addition to my selections, the time and the sequential order of vote casting can be stored on the QR-Code.": Then, participants were confronted with a technical approach: First, the approach requires that in the pre-voting phase one ore more trustworthy authorities generate sample PATs, i.e. all possible QR-Codes that can be generated in an election.[4] These

---

[4] Note that this approach is only feasible for "simple" elections.

sample QR-Codes encode only the corresponding selected candidate(s) and no other information like a time stamp or the sequential order of cast votes. Second, to ensure privacy of the vote, i.e. to detect a malicious voting system that has included additional information in the QR-Codes rather than only voter selections, all QR-Codes generated in the voting phase have to be compared with the sample QR-Codes.

Participants were asked to rank different comparison procedures according to their preference. This ranking included also the option, which enabled participants to indicate that this approach does not ensure privacy of the vote. The ranking contained the following items:

A: Voters have a specific application on their smartphone that compares the generated QR-Codes with the sample QR-Codes.
B: A trustworthy, external institution, for example the German Federal Office for Information Security or OSCE/ODHIR, compare all generated QR-Codes with the sample QR-Codes.
C: A combination of both procedures, namely A and B, is provided.
D: The approach does not ensure vote privacy. QR-Codes have to be removed.

In the next step participants were asked if they would use the electronic voting system in the upcoming federal election. To answer this question, participants could chose all or none of the items from the ranking. Finally, participants had to justify the comparison procedure they had ranked in the first position.

Second Approach: Threat Appraisal In this approach participants were confronted with the description of a possible attack to violate vote privacy. After the initial questions the survey described the voting process step by step for both the electronic voting system and the paper-based system.[5] Then, participants were confronted with a specific attack with respect to each systems. From an abstract perspective both attacks described adversaries' capabilities, i.e. the necessary effort an adversary needs for violating privacy of the vote. These are the sequential steps of the attacks presented to the participants:

Attack steps in the electronic voting system.

1. The attacker needs to get access and manipulate the electronic voting system (the voting device or the printer) such that timestamps are encoded on the QR-Codes.
2. The attacker must be physically present in the polling station to record the name and time of voters casting their vote.
3. The attacker needs to have access to the QR-Codes (PATs) in order to violate vote privacy. This can only be done after the public tallying phase:

---

[5] In this survey we did not include the privacy concerns regarding the electronic voting system that were identified in [3], because they are covered in the corresponding attack.

either during transport or by accessing the storage room in the corresponding municipality.[6]

Attack steps in the paper-based system.

1. The attacker needs to attach a unique identifier to each paper ballot. This identifier should not be visible to the human eye.
2. Then, the attacker must be physically present in the polling station to keep track which voter gets which paper ballot.
3. Similar to the electronic voting system.

Afterwards, participants were asked to indicate which of the systems is more vulnerable with respect to the corresponding attack, and justify their selection. Then, participants had to indicate their understanding of the described attacks and their agreement that these attacks are possible in practice, on a five-point Likert scale anchored in "strongly disagree" and "strongly disagree". Further, participants had to answer six questions which evaluated their perception of vulnerability and risk with respect to the electronic voting and the paper-based system. The last question in the second survey required participants to indicate if they would cast their vote with the electronic voting system.

Note that we intentionally repeated this question in order to evaluate the impact of the approach regarding participants' security behavior and compare both surveys. In the first survey this question was implicitly asked, while participants chose their preferred option to cast a vote with the electronic voting system.

5   Results

In this section we report the results of our user study. The results of each survey are presented separately. We first present the results of the first survey (technical approach), and then the results of the second survey (attack to violate privacy of the vote).

In the first survey 51 out of 99 participants would cast their vote electronically in the upcoming federal election in September 2013. 81 out of 99 participants knew what a QR-Code is, and 44 of all participants had a QR-Code reader application on their smartphone. Table 1 presents the ranking of the different comparison procedures according to the participants' preference.

The option that was ranked on the first place by most of the participants, namely 51 out of 99, is D. However after the survey, 90 participants would cast a vote with the electronic voting system in the upcoming elections if at least one of the options (A, B, C and D) is provided. Thereby, 26 out of 90 participants would cast a vote only if the QR-Code is removed This means that about 64 out of 90 participants would cast a vote with the electronic voting system if option A, B or C is provided. Furthermore, from the 26 participants, seven stated in

---

[6] In this work we address the parliamentary elections in Germany. Thereby, the tallying process is public, and votes are physically stored at most six month before the upcoming election. Thus, this needs to be considered when designing user studies.

Table 1. Ranking of the comparison procedures by number of participants

Ranking	A: Smartphone application	B: Trustworthy, external institution	C: A and B	D: No QR-Code
1	9	18	21	51
2	21	27	42	9
3	29	41	21	8
4	40	13	15	31

the beginning of the survey that they would cast a vote with the electronic voting system, and 19 would not. Finally, only nine out of 99 participants would not cast a vote with the electronic voting system. Thereof, five had stated at the beginning of the survey that they would not cast a vote with the electronic voting system, and four that they would.

In the second survey 59 out of 94 participants would cast their vote electronically in the upcoming federal election in September 2013. 72 out of 94 participants knew what a QR-Code is, and 45 of all participants had a QR-Code reader application on their smartphone. At the end of the survey 60 participants would cast their vote electronically. Thereof, stated six in the beginning of the survey that they would not do so. Further, 34 would not cast their vote electronically, while five of them stated the contrary in the beginning. 82 out of the 94 participants understood the attack description regarding the electronic voting system, while 84 out of all participants understood the attack regarding the paper-based system. Further, 30 out of 94 participants agreed that the electronic voting system is vulnerable with respect to the described attack. Thereof, 10 had stated in the beginning of the survey that they would cast their vote electronically, while at the end of the survey only seven of them would still accept the "risk". In contrast, 38 out of 94 participants agreed, or strongly agreed that the electronic voting system is not vulnerable with respect to the corresponding attack. In comparison only 12 out of 94 participants agreed that the paper-based voting system is vulnerable to the described attack, while 58 did not agree. From the 12 participants that agreed, nine of them would like to cast a vote with the electronic voting system.

6   Discussion and Future Work

The results show that in the first approach a considerable number of participants still have privacy concerns, because some of them would only cast a vote if the QR-Code is removed, and others chose to not do so only after the survey. The percentage of participants that have privacy concerns is smaller compared to the study conducted by Budurushi et al. [3], 21% v.s. 39.9% respectively, however not sufficient in the context of electronic voting. Furthermore, half of the participants that were "against" electronic voting in the beginning of the survey, are willing to cast a vote electronically if they have an application on their smartphone that verifies the content of the QR-Code, or a trustworthy, external institution verifies the content of QR-Codes, or both procedures are provided. This shows that the first approach is a promising method towards increasing voters' trust and decreasing voters' privacy concerns with respect to PATs with additional information or more generally regarding new voting technologies. In contrast, the second approach has a lower impact on participants' security behavior, as no significant changes were identified before and after the survey. Hence, this indicates that the coping appraisal has a higher impact on security behavior than the threat appraisal. However, the results of the second approach reflect the current participants' perception regarding new voting technologies in general, i.e. their insecurity towards understanding and perception of the corresponding risks.

Our findings provide novel directions on addressing privacy concerns in the context of electronic voting. However, both approaches to address voters' privacy concerns are tailored to the EasyVote system [15]. Furthermore, we are aware that the sample does not represent the entire population. These limitations need to be considered for the design of future user studies. Nevertheless, the results of this work lead future work in many different directions. In particular, more research is needed to better understand voters' mental models regarding trust and privacy concerns with respect to new voting technologies. The coping appraisal seems a promising method, however more research is needed in order to improve this method in the context of electronic voting.

Acknowledgements. This paper has been developed within the project 'VerkonWa' - Verfassungskonforme Umsetzung von elektronischen Wahlen - which is funded by the Deutsche Forschungsgemeinschaft (DFG, German Science Foundation). We would like to thank everyone who supported us by participating in the user study.

References

1. Anderson, C., Agarwal, R.: Practicing safe computing: a multimedia empirical examination of home computer user security behavioral intentions. MIS Q. 34, 613–643 (2010)
2. Ben-Nun, J., Fahri, N., Llewellyn, M., Riva, B., Rosen, A., Ta-Shma, A., Wikström, D.: A New Implementation of a Dual (Paper and Cryptographic) Voting System. In: Kripp, M., Volkamer, M., Rüddiger, G. (eds.) EVOTE 2012. LNI, vol. 205, pp. 315–329. GI (2012)
3. Budurushi, J., Volkamer, M.: Implementing and evaluating a software-independent voting system for polling station elections. Journal of Information Security and Applications (2014), http://dx.doi.org/10.1016/j.jisa.2014.03.001
4. Board of Elections City of New York: Ballot Marking Device, http://www.votethenewwayny.com/en/using-the-new-voting-system
5. Chaum, D.: Secret-Ballot Receipts: True Voter-Verifiable Elections. In: Schneider, F. (ed.) IEEE S&P 2004, vol. 2, pp. 38–47. IEEE (2004)

6. Chaum, D., Ryan, P.Y.A., Schneider, S.: A Practical Voter-Verifiable Election Scheme. In: De Capitani di Vimercati, S., Syverson, P.F., Gollmann, D. (eds.) ESORICS 2005. LNCS, vol. 3679, pp. 118–139. Springer, Heidelberg (2005)

7. Floyd, D., Prentice-Dunn, S., Rogers, D.: A Meta-Analysis of Research on Protection Motivation Theory. JASP 30, 407–429 (2000)

8. Johnston, A.C., Warkentin, M.: Fear Appeals and Information Security Behaviors: An Empirical Study. MIS Q. 34, 548–566 (2010)

9. Lee, Y., Larsen, K.R.: Threat or Coping Appraisal: Determinants of SMB Executives' Decision to Adopt Anti-Malware Software. EJIS 18, 177–187 (2009)

10. Llewellyn, M., Schneider, S., Xia, Z., Culnane, C., Heather, J., Ryan, P.Y., Srinivasan, S.: Testing Voters' Understanding of a Security Mechanism Used in Verifiable Voting. JETS 1, 53–61 (2013)

11. Ryan, P.Y., Bismark, D., Heather, J., Schneider, S., Xia, Z.: Prêt à Voter: a Voter-Verifiable Voting System. IEEE Transactions on Information Forensics and Security (Special Issue on Electronic Voting) 4(4), 662–673 (2009)

12. Rogers, R.: A Protection Motivation Theory of Fear Appeals and Attitude Change. Journal of Psychology: Interdisciplinary and Applied 9, 93–114 (1975)

13. Rivest, R., Wack, J.: On the notion of "software independence" in voting systems. Technical report, Information Techonolgy Laboratroy, National Institute of Standards and Technology (2006)

14. Vegas, C.: The New Belgian Evoting System. In: Kripp, M., Volkamer, M., Rüddiger, G. (eds.) EVOTE 2012. LNI, vol. 205, pp. 199–211. GI (2012)

15. Volkamer, M., Budurushi, J., Demirel, D.: Vote Casting Device with VV-SV-PAT for Elections with Complicated Ballot Papers. In: Grimm, R., Schneider, S., Volkamer, M., Weldemariam, K. (eds.) REVOTE 2011, pp. 1–8. IEEE (2011)

16. Vot.ar, http://www.vot-ar.com.ar/en/system-votation/

17. VOTE-TRAKKER, http://www.avantetech.com/products/elections/dre/

Mental Models for Usable Privacy: A Position Paper

Kovila P.L. Coopamootoo and Thomas Groß

School of Computing Science, Newcastle University, United Kingdom
{kovila.coopamootoo,thomas.gross}@newcastle.ac.uk

Abstract. In this position paper, we propose a new approach to privacy decision-making that relies on conceptual representations of mental models. We suggest that helping users to construct mental models of privacy will facilitate privacy decisions and hence contribute towards usable privacy. We advance that usable privacy research will benefit from qualitative and quantitative user studies that first elicit users' mental models of privacy and second aim to build a composite model of the concept maps of users' mental models. The links between the concept maps and deductive and inductive reasoning, and System 1 and 2 of the dual-process theory, are thought to potentially provide valuable insights for future usable privacy research. We also propose that the composite model might provide routes to privacy decisions and enable us to develop strategies akin to nudges aimed towards facilitating privacy behaviour.

Keywords: Usable privacy, mental models, dual-process, System 1, System 2, deductive, inductive, privacy decision-making.

1 Introduction

A privacy dichotomy is often observed online that is although users have privacy concerns, observed online behaviour often does not match their claimed concerns [1,2]. An explanation for the dichotomy could be that the increasing use of the Internet and accompanying technologies in society is blurring the distinction between the public and private online leading to fuzziness when evaluating privacy. This in turn contributes to the difficulty in making privacy decisions, an issue that is not corroborated with the offline world.

Online privacy designs vary with contexts and include two main approaches. First the privacy-by-policy approach that provides notice and choice, such as via the privacy policy in E-Commerce and second, the privacy-by-architecture approach that targets privacy protection at the design phase through minimisation of data collection, anonymity and unlinkability of individuals [3]. This approach is also referred to as privacy-by-design [4,5]. The privacy-by-policy approach is often found to be too legalistic, confusing, un-usable and, at best, a substitute for more meaningful privacy protection [6]. It relies on the self-regulation approach [7] that views privacy as a commodity that can be traded in the market place. The self-regulation approach assumes rational behaviour from users who are expected to conduct a risk assessment.

T. Tryfonas and I. Askoxylakis (Eds.): HAS 2014, LNCS 8533, pp. 410–421, 2014.

The evaluation of one's privacy and associated risks and benefits requires high cognitive effort and rational decisions that conflict with research on psychological biases and attributions that underpin the behaviour of individuals [8]. The privacy-by-design approach aims to enable users to protect their privacy by providing appropriate tools including access control, encryption and anonymous credentials mechanisms. While these abstract the technical complexity such as through eIDs, users still need to have transparent choices and be able to engage in an intuitive way.

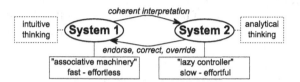

Fig. 1. The Dual-Process Model

Therefore, whilst privacy evaluation is embedded within social behavior offline [9] and can be thought to be part of effortless interactions, in the online environment users are expected to make complex decisions. These decisions may be governed by different cognitive processes, for which we introduce the dual-process model as abstraction, that distinguishes between effortless intuitive and effortful analytical cognition. Hence, investigation into the type of thinking users engage in can provide valuable insights for usable privacy research. Moreover the human-computer interaction (HCI) community believes that users build and use mental models to guide the way they learn and interact with computers [10]. Research has previously tapped into conceptual representations of mental models to help users better understand and predict system behaviour [10,11,12].

In the following sections we first provide an exposé that highlights the differences in modes of offline versus online privacy with the help of the dual-process model. This is followed with a review of mental models literature, of the use of mental models in HCI and existing privacy and security research's links with mental models. We then establish our research questions and elaborate on approaches to elicit, analyse and represent mental models of privacy while proposing links with deductive-inductive studies and findings. We suggest investigations of the effects of privacy mental models on users' dual-process thinking methods. We discuss how our approach aligns with established mental models research together with the usefulness of mental models for usable privacy research before concluding the paper.

2   Background

In this section we first discuss the links between online and offline privacy with dual-processing modes of thinking and decision-making. Second we review mental models literature, and in particular its use within HCI. This section ends with a brief of previous mental models research related to privacy and security.

The Dual-Process Model. In our approach to systematically analyse privacy decisions we use the so called *dual-process model* as a basis (see Figure 1), which is used within cognitive psychology literature to explain that people have the ability to employ dual-process thinking and reasoning [13,14,15,16]. The model states that there exist two systems in human cognition, called System 1 and System 2. System 1 is effortless and includes intuitive operations; System 2 is effortful and includes analytical operations. System 1 facilitates many automated processes of cognition including processing of visual input and cues and aims to create a coherent representation and interpretation of the world. System 2 is often described as 'lazy' as it only intervenes at times, by endorsing, correcting or rejecting decisions.

Privacy in Relation to the Dual-Process Model. Privacy is a concept with behavioural dimension in that individuals dynamically manage their privacy according to different situations in social life. Whilst users are able to manage their privacy effortlessly offline, in the online environment they are expected to make complex decisions [7]. Privacy enables a dialectical state [9] that allows individuals to be both connected and autonomous. The interplay of needing both privacy and openness influences the decisions individuals make about the way they manage their information. As a consequence, they do not usually require complete privacy. Rather, they are happy to share information with others as long as certain social norms are met, that is contextual integrity of the shared information is maintained [17]. Therefore individuals' privacy requirements vary according to contexts and over time and are very much linked to how people present their identity. Privacy elaboration offline is implicit within behaviour [18,9] and by conjecture happens intuitively and effortlessly, linking offline privacy decision-making to System 1 method of thinking which is quick and automatic [13,14,15,16]. System 1 uses associative memory to help construct a coherent interpretation when making sense of the world in an instantaneous and effortless fashion. During associative activation, evoked ideas trigger other ideas in a spreading cascade of mental activity that is bounded together by coherence. Each element of the association connects, supports and strengthens each other and can in turn quickly generate emotions and expressions or behaviour [16].

However in the online environment the focus of interactions is often explicitly on the primary task making privacy the secondary goal. To make a correct privacy evaluation online that adheres to offline privacy decision-making, users need to fully assimilate what personal information is shared to whom in which manner, who will own the information, what does disclosing personal information in a particular context means that is how it affects their self-presentation [19], how it relates to or modifies their identity [20], whether there is a risk of conflict between roles played by identities and how to resolve these conflicts. Current designs expect users to understand what privacy mechanisms are available at their disposal and how to use these to their benefit. Therefore online privacy designs also expect users to elaborate about their privacy by allocating attention to the effortful mental activities that demand to consciously reason and construct thoughts in an orderly series of steps that is via System 2. System 2 helps to follow rules, compare objects on several attributes and to make deliberate and systematic choices [16].

Individuals make countless decisions involving various thought processes every day. These decisions can range from ones that are barely noticed and soon forgotten to others that are highly consequential. The classical view of decision-making in literature refers to 'rational theory of choice' that postulates that individuals have orderly preferences that obey certain rules [21]. Therefore when faced with making a choice, decision makers are assumed to gauge subjective utility and to choose the alternative with the highest utility. In the event of uncertainty about the outcomes, decision makers are believed to calculate an option's expected utility. However this standard view is an inadequate model of how decisions are actually made. Models that account for a variety of human resource constraints such as bounded attention and memory capacity and limited time have instead been proposed including prospect theory [22] and status quo or regret theory [23]. Moreover, individuals' preferences are heavily shaped by particular perceptions of risk and value, by influences on attribute weights, by the tendency to avoid conflicts, by salient factors and emotions leading to the literature on judgment and decision-making and heuristics and biases [16]. As shown in Figure 1, System 1 quickly proposes intuitive judgments to problems as they arise and System 2 monitors the quality of these proposals that it may endorse, correct or override [24]. Since the capacity for mental effort is limited [25], effortful processes tend to disrupt each other whilst effortless processes neither cause nor suffer much interference and the effect of concurrent cognitive tasks can provide a useful indication of whether a mental process belongs to System 1 or 2.

Mental Models. Mental models are 'small-scale models' of reality constructed by the mind to help anticipate events, to reason and underlie explanations [26]. They are therefore internalised, mental representations of a device or idea that facilitates reasoning [27]. Johnson-Laird developed the mental models theory that explains deductive and inductive reasoning [27,28]. Although the theory has suffered criticisms [29], it is still considered an important part of mental models research and has been linked to dual-process approaches through conditional reasoning [30]. This sub-section reviews these aspects of mental models and introduces means that help users form mental models, and methods of eliciting, analysing and representing mental models that are further explored in later sections.

The mental model theory makes several assumptions aimed at relieving the load models place on working memory [31]. During reasoning, individuals can understand the meaning of assertions, envisage corresponding situations and ascertain whether a conclusion holds in them. Mental models theory however postulates that reasoning is not based on syntactic derivations of logical forms but rather on manipulations of mental representations of situations [32,33] that yield both deductive and inductive inferences [34].

Deductive reasoning involves making inferences on the basis of some given premises: a conclusion must be true given that the premises are true. Mental model theory postulates that deduction is a semantic process akin to the search for counterexamples that does not increase semantic information. Deductive mental models include logical and causal mental models [35]. Causal models differ from logical ones by drawing on information in long-term memory structures as opposed to logical models that are created on the spot and only involve information active in working memory [35].

Compared to deduction, induction is a process that increases semantic information. Given a set of premises, inductive conclusions might go beyond what is given in the premises to eliminate possibilities. Johnson-Laird postulates that since induction depends on knowledge, it is constrained by availability and representativeness heuristic [36]. Moreover, some inductions are implicit in that they are rapid, involuntary and unconscious whereas others are explicit having slow, voluntary and conscious properties. Mental models theory has suffered criticisms such as for example Evans et al. [29] argue that the mental models theory for conditional reasoning [37] is flawed for not accounting for suppositional theory. Gauffroy and Barouillet [30] propose to resolve the theoretical conflict by differentiating between two kinds of reasoning and links to a dual-process theory that integrates heuristic-analytical modes within conditional mental model theory [38].

A variety of methods exist for forming, eliciting, analysing and displaying users' mental models as reviewed by Sasse [39]. Analogies that are types of similarities in which analogous situations share common patterns of relationships [40] and metaphors that use the same principle but involve semantically distant domains [10] can be used to help users form mental models. Although users' mental models can be elicited via interviews or think aloud methods, the concepts and relations between the concepts present within users' mental models need to be identified and extracted to depict users' mental models. Concept mapping is one such approach that can show concepts as vertices and relationships as edges within a graph that can be directed, weighted or labelled or a combination of these [41]. Exploration of the concept map could give an indication of the thought processes or reasoning approaches users are engaged in. A more detailed discussion of these methods is provided in the following sections.

Mental Models in HCI. In HCI, models are used for various purposes and Norman [10] offers some distinctions between the different models of a system including the target system, the conceptual model of the target system, the system image, users' mental models and scientists' or researchers' conceptualisation of a mental model. The system image can be thought to have the most direct and immediate influence on the user since it is through the systems' image, its appearance and behaviour that the user interacts with the system.

It is thought that users build and use models to guide the way they learn and interact with computers. Mental models enable them to predict and explain the operation of a target system through internal representations of themselves and the objects they interact with [10]. Evidence suggests that giving users a conceptual model of a system before using a system or rather than procedural instruction enhances user learning with the model suggested to serve as a knowledge organiser that prevents confusion and promotes understanding of the system [11,12]. Users given models also perform better in complex tasks compared to those not provided with a model [11] and are expected to be more apt at troubleshooting and problem solving [42].

Mental Models in Privacy and Security. Analogies and metaphors function as tools of thought that help structure unfamiliar domains [40] and are useful when forming mental models. Metaphors have been proposed in privacy research, for instance Lederer et al. [43] proposed a 'situational faces' metaphor that aims to provide guidance for supporting notice and consent. Richter-Lipford et al. [44] proposed the 'audience-view' metaphor to help users form a model of the recipients of their information disclosure in Facebook. The Primelife project explored approaches to help users form mental models of the data minimisation property of the concept of anonymous credentials [45]. Although the research found that an adapted card-based approach metaphor evoked better mental models of anonymous credentials there was also a suggestion for the need for a better design paradigm to improve user understanding [46].

Moreover, metaphors are often used within information security to communicate risk to users. Camp [47] reviews metaphors currently in use within security including the physical security model through control of perimeters, the medical model that refers to worms and viruses, the criminal model with reference to malicious codes and breach, the warfare model with the idea of firewalls and DMZs and vulnerabilities leading to downtimes and failures such as through denial of service akin to a market model. They also recommend the need for further mental models research in the area of privacy and security.

3   Research Questions

In light of the previous sections we propose research in the area of mental models for online privacy. We believe such approach will contribute to the research space covering effectiveness and usability of online privacy.

Since mental models are small-scale representations of reality consisting of relations and semantic information about objects, we believe it will help to address the gap in usable privacy research by assisting to channel user perceptions, to form judgment and to guide decision-making. The conceptual representations of mental models will help users better understand how the system works and enhance their ability to predict system behaviour and in doing so help them towards making intuitive judgments. We first assume that System 1 and System 2 of Figure 1 can be active concurrently during privacy decision-making. The contribution of the two systems in determining judgments can depend on task features (such as the type of privacy design including the system image characteristics), characteristics of tasks privacy evaluation is secondary to (such as online shopping, social networking or micro-blogging) and individual characteristics such as time available for deliberation, mood, cognitive impulsiveness, intelligence. As System 2 monitors the proposals made by System 1, it can endorse it or expend mental effort to evaluate the context such as by comparing models, analysing and discarding unmatched models, and restructuring and ameliorating existing models. Moreover as evidenced with chess masters who perform more intuitively with experience [48], by conjecture we propose that users will be able to more intuitively identify privacy design models with experience. Thus our main research question is: 'how do mental models of privacy affect privacy decision-making?' The question includes mental models derived via inductive or deductive reasoning and judgments involving System 1 or 2. Our research problem therefore involves the need to: establish the contents of mental models, the concepts comprised in users' models and their relationship for different privacy design approaches and contexts; analyse the models with respect to strength and weights of connections, the type of reasoning involved, effort required, and compare with expert models; develop a composite conceptual representation of mental models that can potentially show different links to decisions; make use of the composite model to infuse designs with triggers and interventions aimed at enhancing usable privacy; and investigate the effect of particular interventions on performance (such as the number of errors in understanding privacy operations, users' feeling of certainty, type of privacy related behaviour), user effort required and reasoning approach used.

4   Mental Models of Privacy

In this section we first look at methods for eliciting mental models of privacy followed with analysis methods and approaches to represent conceptualisations of users' mental models. We also propose study designs aimed at assessing the impact of the conceptual representation of privacy mental models or of links within the conceptual representation that can act as triggers.

User Mental Models of Online Privacy. As privacy designs are often claimed to be un-usable, determining the contents and structure of users' mental models of different privacy designs could lead to in-depth understanding of privacy HCI. This could hint to ways of tuning the system image to users' expectations and potentially enhance their predictive power. Users' mental models have been gathered before via a variety of methods including interviews [41], problem-solving tasks, teach back procedure [49] or having users draw their mental models [50]. The quality in terms of complexity and structure of the model elicited can be thought to be primed by data collection design including the type of questions set to study participants (such as open versus closed-ended questions), the content of the questions (such as whether privacy is explicitly mentioned), the task associated with the information gathering process and potentially other heuristics. Therefore data collection methods for privacy mental models might benefit from a mix of approaches that generate rich indicative data that informs research on better suited approaches to design specific user studies. For instance interviews might be linked with structural knowledge elicitation [51] or network task analysis [52], procedural knowledge analysis and think aloud protocol analysis for problem solving for troubleshooting and teach back data [49].

However, we posit to start with open questionnaires or think aloud data that can be analysed via grounded theory coding techniques including open and axial coding [53]. This approach has been used before to first identify concepts, define relationships between concepts, display the resultant coded mental representation graphically within mental models research [41]. The depiction of relations between concepts and their semantic relationship can adhere to a concept mapping approach [41]. Concept mapping is common to investigation of students' mental models [54,55,56]. As a portrayal of the users' mental model, the concept map can contain propositional and visual type information such as strings and symbols corresponding to natural language, analogies of the world and images that are perceptual correlates from a particular point of view. The concept map can be measured quantitatively based on a scoring protocol [57] with edges weighted or analysed qualitatively. For instance labelled edges and vertices can potentially lead to understanding of the strength of concepts in influencing others and also in the type of reasoning involved. Performance and effort data can also be collected to later relate the model generated with dual-process theory.

Composite Conceptual Model. A compilation and analysis of the concept maps obtained above can lead to a composite model. This composite conceptual model might in turn provide indications on the strength of particular concepts, their occurrence in different context, their relationship to other concepts and the paths to specific privacy decisions. The composite model can be compared to experts' model of privacy design and further lead to proposal for privacy designs that better match users' mental models. The composite model might also lead us to a series of inferences that suggest triggers or interventions that make use of System 1's intuitive and effortless approach.

User Studies. The impact of these particular interventions can then be investigated with user experiments. The experimental observations might not only provide data on improving usability of privacy designs but also on fine-tuning the composite model.

This part of our research will aim to identify the influence of specific interventions from the composite model on users' dual-process model mode of thinking as depicted in Figure 1 such as whether privacy within an E-Commerce context as opposed to a social network environment engenders effortless and intuitive methods of thinking of privacy or lead to effortful and analytical interactions. System 2 thinking competes for mental effort that users have of limited capacity. Therefore in conducting an experiment we would for instance design a condition that cognitively depletes users (such as via attempts to hold a long number in memory, ADD-3 to a 4 digit number or via participation in Wason's selection task [58]) and observe the effort required (or ease) to correctly conduct a privacy related task (in terms of time, number of errors made, certainty in actions, pupil dilation, correctness of think aloud account). If the privacy task also requires high effort, users might be prone to errors or not able to correctly assess their privacy. The impact of our interventions could then also be compared with existing methods of notifying or warning users.

5   Discussion

We pursue the discussion of our research approach for mental models for usable privacy in three strands. We first discuss the state of mental model research and methods as a basis for this research. Second, we review the paper's approach and, third, the possible outcomes for usable privacy.

We perceive that there is no unified theory of mental models and associated methodologies in sight. There are multiple approaches to elicit, analyse and represent mental models with the goal of establishing a conceptual model. Specific methodologies for user studies can give rise to dedicated analysis methods and representations of the conceptual model. For instance, on one hand think-aloud or verbal methods to elicit user input are particularly suited for concept maps, which can in turn be represented as undirected weighted graph with vertices modelling concepts and edges the relationships between them. On the other hand, inductive and deductive models can be elicited with premise-consequence completion tasks and likely modelled in a logic representation. Observing this panoply of approaches, we also need to account for their strengths as well as the criticisms they received for their shortcomings.

At this point, it is uncertain which particular methodology will benefit usable privacy decision-making the most. As established in Section 4, we perceive that the user's concept map, insights into deductive and inductive reasoning and the involvement of the dual-process systems may all be meaningful for privacy decision-making. The concept map seems promising as the associations encoded therein can give rise to priming and triggers activating adjacent concepts. The dual-process model and deductive-inductive reasoning link has been made in the critique of mental models by Evans et al. [29] and propositions by Gauffroy and Barouillet [30]. Given that recent research in the privacy space has linked bounded rationality concepts with privacy decision-making, such as the research pursued by Acquisti and Grossklags [2], it is a natural step to investigate the involvement of System 1 and System 2 in privacy decision-making. Hence, we are considering multiple methodologies to establish a conceptual model for privacy decision-making, each coming with its own user study, analysis and representation methods. The final conceptual model is likely to be a composite of the outcomes of each approach. We find it conceivable that an abstracted representation may encode all outcomes in one model, for instance, in a directed, weighted, labelled graph, in which edges do not only encode associations, but also deduction and induction between concept vertices.

Finally, we need to consider how this research would support usable privacy. We observe that privacy design has mainly been influenced by expert models and we see a necessity to complement those with insights in user mental models. We follow the rationale that interventions such as stimuli, triggers or nudges should speak the user's language and we consequently attempt to gain insights in that with a multi-pronged approach of concept maps, deductive and inductive strategies and dual-process activation. We aim to make the resulting conceptual model a tool to plan interventions. Consider the hypothetical example that the concept 'best friends' and the concept 'consideration in disclosure' (or 'don't talk behind my back') are closely linked in the concept map. Then, priming with the 'best friends' concept can nudge towards privacy-friendly disclosure decisions. Therefore, the conceptual model can act as guidance to choose interventions from a larger portfolio, such as the nudge inventory of MINDSPACE [59]. Similarly, typical deductions observed in the user study can make the premise a suitable trigger. If we see evidence that privacy decision-making is largely governed by the automated and effortless System 1, as suggested in the theory on the formation of mental models as proposed by Gauffroy and Barouillet [30], then an artificial invocation of System 2 is likely to change users' approach.

6   Conclusion

In this position paper, we make a case that research into user mental models is beneficial for usable privacy. Observing that mental model research has seen a diverse set of approaches and various criticisms, we focus on three areas that we deem most promising for the privacy domain: concept maps, deductive and inductive reasoning, and the activation of System 1 and System 2 according to the dual-process model. There exists a body of literature in mental model methodology as well as related areas such as behavioural economics that give us foundations in theory and modelling user studies. The research aims to establish a composite conceptual model, which will in turn inform design for usable privacy. In particular, the conceptual model will allow educated choices on the placement of interventions to support the privacy decision-making of the user.

Acknowledgement. This research on usable privacy is currently supported by the EU FP7 FutureID project http://futureid.eu) under GA n° 318424.

References

1. Spiekermann, S., Grossklags, J., Berendt, B.: E-privacy in 2nd Generation E-Commerce: Privacy preferences vs. actual behavior. In: Proc. ACM Conf. E-Commerce, pp. 38–47 (2001)
2. Acquisti, A., Grossklags, J.: Privacy and rationality in individual decision making. IEEE S & P 3(1), 26–33 (2005)
3. Spiekermann, S., Cranor, L.: Engineering privacy. IEEE Trans. on S/W Eng. 38(1), 67–82 (2009)
4. Langheinrich, M.: Privacy by Design - Principles of Privacy-Aware Ubiquitous Systems. In: Abowd, G.D., Brumitt, B., Shafer, S. (eds.) UbiComp 2001. LNCS, vol. 2201, pp. 273–291. Springer, Heidelberg (2001)
5. Cavoukian, A.: Privacy by Design... Take the Challenge. Information (2009)
6. Milne, G.R., Culnan, M.J.: Strategies for reducing privacy risks: why consumers read (or don't read) online privacy notices? Journ. of Interactive Marketing 18(3), 15–29 (2004); and Privacy Commissioner of Ontario, Canada (2009)
7. Zwick, D., Dholakia, N.: Models of privacy in the digital age: implications for marketing and e-commerce. Research Inst. for Telecom. and Information Marketing (1999)
8. Tversky, A., Kahneman, D.: Judgement under uncertainty: heuristics and biases. Science 185(4157), 1124–1131 (1974)
9. Palen, L., Dourish, P.: 'Unpacking' privacy for a networked world. In: Proceedings of the CHI Conference on Human Factors in Computing Systems, pp. 126–136. ACM, NY (2003)
10. Norman, D.A.: Some observations on mental models. In: Human-computer Interaction, pp. 241–244. Morgan Kaufmann Publishers Inc., CA (1983, 1987)

11. Borgman, C.L.: The user's mental model of an information retrieval system: effects on performance. Dissertation abstract internations, 45, 4a (1984)
12. Halasz, F.G.: Mental models and problem solving in using a calculator. Doctoral dissertation, Standord University, CA, USA (1984)
13. Stanovich, K.E.: Who is Rational? Studies of Individual Differences in Reasoning, Elrbaum (1999)
14. Stanovich, K.E., West, R.F.: Individual differences in reasoning: Implications for the rationality debate. Behav. Brain Sci. 23, 645–726 (2000)
15. Evans, J.B.T.: Dual-processing accounts of reasoning, judgment and social cognition. Annual Review of Psychology 59, 255–278 (2008)
16. Kahneman, D.: Thinking fast and slow. Farrar, Strauss (2011)
17. Nissenbaum, H.F.: Privacy as contextual integrity. Washington Law Review 79(1), 119–158 (2004)
18. Altman, I.: The Environment and Social Behaviour: Privacy, Personal Space, Territory and Crowding. Brooks/Cole Publishing, Monterey (1975)
19. Coles-Kemp, L., Kani-Zabihi, E.: On-line privacy and consent: a dialogue, not a monologue. In: NSPW 2010 (2010)
20. Bennett, L.: Reflections on privacy, identity and consent in on-line services. Information Security Technical Report 14, 119–123 (2009)
21. LeBoeuf, R.A., Shafir, E.: Decision Making. In: Holyoak, K.J., Morrisson, R.G. (eds.) The Cambridge Handbook of Thinking and Reasoning (2005)
22. Kahneman, D., Tversky, A.: Prospect theory: an analysis of decision under risk. Econometrica 47(2), 262–292 (1979)
23. Kahneman, D., Jack, L.K., Thaler, R.: Anomalies: The endowment effect, loss aversion and the status quo bias. Journal of Economic Perspectives 5(1), 193–206 (1991)
24. Kahneman, D., Frederick, S.: A model of Heuristic Judgment. In: Holyoak, K.J., Morrisson, R.G. (eds.) The Cambridge Handbook of Thinking and Reasoning (2005)
25. Baumeister, R.F., Vohs, K.D., Tice, D.M.: The strength model of self-control. Current Directions in Psychological Science (2007)
26. Craik, K.: The nature of explanation. Cambridge University Press, Cambridge (1943)
27. Johnson-Laird, P.N.: Mental Models: Towards a Cognitive Science of Language, Inference, and Consciousness. Cambridge University Press, Cambridge (1983)
28. Johnson-Laird, P.N.: How we reason. Oxford University Press (2006)
29. Evans, J.B.T., Over, D.E., Handley, S.J.: Suppositions, extensionality, and conditionals: a critique of the mental model theory of Johnson-Laird and Byrne. Psychological Review 112(4), 1040–1052 (2002)
30. Gauffroy, C., Barouillet, P.: Heuristic and analytic processes in mental models for conditionals: an integrative development theory. Develop. Review 29(4), 249–282 (2009)
31. Johnson-Laird, P.N.: Mental models and human reasoning. Proceedings of the National Academy of Sciences of the USA, 107(43) (2007)
32. Johnson-Laird, P.N., Byrne, R.M.J.: Deduction. Erlbaum, Hillsdale (1991)
33. Polk, T.A., Newell, A.: Deduction as verbal reasoning. Psychol. Rev. 102, 533–566 (1995)
34. Rogers, Y., Rutherford, A., Bibby, P.A.: Models in the Mind: Theory, Perspective and Application, London (1992)
35. Markman, A.B., Gentner, D.: Thinking. Annual Review of Psychology 52, 223–247 (2001)
36. Johnson-Laird, P.N.: Mental models and thought. In: Holyoak, K.J., Morrisson, R.G. (eds.) The Cambridge Handbook of Thinking and Reasoning (2005)
37. Johnson-Laird, P.N., Byrne, R.M.J.: Conditionals: A theory of meaning, pragmatics, and inference. Psychological Review 109, 646–678 (2002)
38. Barrouillet, P., Gauffroy, C., Lecas, J.F.: Mental models and the suppositional account of conditionals. Psychological Review 115(3), 760–771 (2008)

39. Sasse, M.A.: Eliciting and Describing Users' Models of Computer Systems. Ph.D. Thesis, Computer Science, University of Birmingham (1997)
40. Gentner, D., Gentner, D.R.: Flowing waters or teemings crowds: mental models of electricity. In: Gentner, D., Stevens, A.L. (eds.) Mental Models, pp. 99–130. Lawrence Erlbaum Associate, Hilsdale (1983)
41. Carley, K., Palmquist, M.: Extracting, representing, and analyzing mental models. Social Forces 70(3), 601–636 (1992)
42. DeKleer, J., Brown, J.S.: Assumptions and ambiguities in mechanistics mental models. In: Gentner, D., Stevens, A.L. (eds.) Mental Models, pp. 155–190. Lawrence Erlbaum Associate, Hilsdale (1983)
43. Lederer, S., Mankoff, J., Dey, A.K.: Who Wants to Know What When? Privacy Preference Determinants in Ubiquitous Computing. In: CHI 2003. ACM, New York (2003)
44. Richter-Lipford, H., Besmer, A., Watson, J.: Understanding privacy settings in Facebook with an audience view. In: Proc. 1st Conf. on Usability Psych., & Sec., pp. 1–8. USENIX Association (2008)
45. PRIME WP06.1, HCI Guidelines, D06.1.f (2008), https://www.primeproject.eu/prime_products/reports/arch/pub_del_D06.1.f_ec_wp06.1_v1_final.pdf
46. Wästlund, E., Angulo, J., Fischer-Hübner, S.: Evoking comprehensive mental models of anonymous credentials. In: Camenisch, J., Kesdogan, D. (eds.) iNetSec 2011. LNCS, vol. 7039, pp. 1–14. Springer, Heidelberg (2012)
47. Camp, L.J.: Mental models of privacy and security. IEEE Technology and Society Magazine 28(3) (2009)
48. Simon, H.A., Chase, W.G.: Skill in chess. American Scientist 61, 394–403 (1973)
49. van der Veer, G.C.: Individual differences and the user interface. Ergonomics 32, 1431–1449 (1989)
50. Otter, M., Johnson, H.: Lost in hyperspace: metrics and mental models. Interacting with Computers 13, 1–40 (2000)
51. Kraiger, K., Salas, E.: Measuring mental models to assess learning during training. Paper presented at the Annual Meeting of the Society for Industrial/Organizational Psychology, San Francisco, CA (1993)
52. Diesner, J., Kumaraguru, P., Carley, K.M.: Mental models of privacy and security from interviews with Indians. In: 55th Annual Conference of the International Communication Association, New York, NY (2005)
53. Adams, A., Lunt, P., Cairns, P.: A qualitative approach to HCI research. In: Cairns, P., Cox, A.L. (eds.) Research Methods for Human-Computer Interaction, 1st edn., pp. 138–157. Cambridge University Press, Cambridge (2008)
54. Kinchin, I.M., Hay, D.B.: How a qualitative approach to concept map analysis can be used to aid learning by illustrating patterns of conceptual development. Educational Research 42(1) (2000)
55. Halford, G.S.: Children's Understanding: The Development of Mental Models. Lawrence Erlbaum, Hillsdale (1993)
56. Novak, J.D.: Learning, Creating and Using Knowledge: Concept Maps as Facilitative Tools in Schools and Corporations. Lawrence Erlbaum, Hillsdale (1998)
57. Novak, J.D., Gowin, D.B.: Learning How to Learn. Cambridge University Press, Cambridge (1984)
58. Wason, P.C.: Reasoning. In: Foss, B.M. (ed.) New Horizons in Psychology, Penguin, Harmondworth (1966)
59. Dolan, P., Hallsworth, M., Halpern, D., King, D., Metcalfe, R., Vlaev, I.: Influencing behaviour: The mindspace way. Journal of Economic Psychology 33(1), 264–277 (2012)

Web Privacy Policies in Higher Education:
How Are Content and Design Used to Provide Notice
(Or a Lack Thereof) to Users?

Anna L. Langhorne

University of Dayton, Department of Communication,
300 College Park, Dayton, Ohio 45469-1410
Alanghorne1@udayton.edu

Abstract. This paper explores the content themes and provision structures of
the website privacy policies of a nonrandom sample of comparable universities
across the United States. Because these organizations collect, analyze, and
manage personal information via digital media, it is important to evaluate the
legal content and usability of their privacy policies. The issue is complex,
because technology continues to advance, privacy policy standards continue to
evolve, and the law is unclear on many aspects of privacy. Furthermore, the
education sector lags industry in its implementation of privacy and security
programs. A content analysis was conducted to identify patterns in legal
provisions, general usability, and communication of sixteen university web
privacy policies. This approach revealed what universities disclose about their
information practices and user rights. The results reveal the commonalities of
how web privacy policies are structured, what concepts are presented, and what
information is absent. Additionally, recommendations are shared regarding how
to develop comprehensive online privacy policies appropriate for higher
education.

Keywords: Privacy, privacy policy, privacy law, information practices,
security, usability, higher education, information sharing, communication,
cyber security.

1   Introduction

Higher education websites serve as global communication vehicles, connecting
content and materials with domestic and international audiences (e.g., prospective
students/parents, enrolled students and their parents, employees, alumni, and
community members). Interactions between users and university websites create
many opportunities for data generation and collection. For example, many websites
passively collect data about users, such as page visits and referring websites. These
data may be anonymous or identified. In addition, data may be actively collected. An
example is when a user voluntarily shares data through site registration to complete an
information request. The nature of these data may be nonspecific but may involve
personal information (PI). PII data is involved when a user shares personally

T. Tryfonas and I. Askoxylakis (Eds.): HAS 2014, LNCS 8533, pp. 422–432, 2014.
© Springer International Publishing Switzerland 2014

identifiable information (e.g., prospective student discloses her Social Security Number in an online application), something that occurs when a tax return is submitted for financial aid consideration, or perhaps health the submission of immunization records

These examples represent a limited sample of the many ways in which university websites touch user data. The situation becomes more complex when one considers how and with whom information is shared. Higher education institutions share information with third parties with increasing frequency. These associations include, but are not limited to, parties such as advertising providers, vendor partnerships, or law enforcement. For example, the University of Iowa had a data sharing relationship with the local sheriff's office. After the sheriff notified the university that a student applied for a gun permit, the university allowed the sharing of information related to academic performance and emotional state [1]. Through these kinds of arrangements and data generating activities, universities have become custodians of massive amounts of PI and non-PI. As stewards, they assume a duty to protect that information.

Privacy policies (PPs) are official communications through which organizations disclose their information practices and approaches to privacy and data protection. Given current societal concerns, higher education websites should provide and be governed by online PPs. These policies can be designed to meet university legal compliance needs as well as provide meaningful notice to users. When they are effective and successful, they also have the potential to build user trust. In essence, PPs are communication opportunities to inform, assure, and empower users. Therefore, PPs may aid relationship development between institutions and users. Trust and relationship building are important as higher education continues to learn lessons about the impact of inadequate (or nonexistent) privacy and security programs. The 2006 hack of Ohio University's databases and theft of 173,000 Social Security numbers illustrate how brand erosion, relationship damage, and diminished profitability may result. Ohio University sustained a class action lawsuit and an 8% decline in donations compared to the previous year [2]. More recently on February 19, 2014, the University of Maryland announced it was hacked [3]. The records of 309,079 student, faculty, and staff were compromised, many of whom were affiliated as long ago as 1998. Their names, Social Security Numbers, birthdates, and university IDs were divulged.

These concerns about privacy and security and the impact on university brand and user trust are now part of the higher education privacy landscape, in which several factors are relevant. First, there is a trend to move information and documents to an electronic format, and as the University of Maryland example illustrates, these records are attractive to potential criminals and wrongdoers. As a result, there are risks and vulnerabilities associated with collecting, using, managing, and storing records in digital environments, regardless of whether the records comprise PI or non-PI. Privacy and security concerns are well founded due to an increase in breaches across sectors; however, higher education contributed "nearly 160 breaches and more than 2.3 million records breached since 2008" [4].

Unfortunately, the current legal structure is unprepared to cope with privacy and security needs. Currently, forty-six states, the District of Columbia, Guam, Puerto Rico and the Virgin Islands have enacted data breach notification legislation [5]. Many laws stipulate aspects of breach disclosures such as procedures and timing, although they vary in terms of specificity. In 2011, FERPA allowed authorized representatives to share student personal information without consent, making it easier to share information with nongovernmental actors [6]. However, regulatory changes are moving toward expanded requirements for the private and public sectors (e.g., HIPAA requires institutions to have a privacy officer). California recently passed a privacy law which prohibits public and private postsecondary educational institutions from requiring or requesting student disclosure of social media information including: 1) username or password, 2) access in the presence of the institution's member, or 3) personal social media information [7]. Changes are inevitable as the FTC clarifies standards for industry.

Third, there is an expanding focus on big data and analytics and new technologies that challenge traditional notions of privacy. Social media, for example, blur the lines of organizational boundaries and create complexities in information management and protocol. Not only are there diverse types of data and invasive technologies, but higher education, and universities in particular, have complex interactions with data. Given the numerous potential university units that touch website data (e.g., marketing, admissions, financial aid, student affairs, human resources, institutional research, information security, campus police, and library services), privacy issues are both highly sensitive and extremely important.

The purpose of this descriptive study is to determine the nature and extent of information practice disclosure via university website privacy policies. A content analysis was conducted of sixteen university PPs. The objectives are: 1) Describe commonalities in web privacy policy content and design, 2) Identify differences in approaches to privacy, 3) Contrast the policies with FTC recommendations for fair information practices, and 4) Provide recommendations for improving higher education online privacy.

2   Literature Review

2.1   Usable Online Privacy Policies and Their Value

Usability refers to the ease of use, learnability, efficiency, memorability and satisfaction of a system. It is the measure of quality of a user's experience. In the context of online privacy policies, usability means a policy should be easy to locate, easy to read, and quickly digestible. It should provide useful information that is needed by users. Finally, it should empower users to make informed decisions about their online behavior.

Unfortunately, most PPs are overwhelmingly unsatisfactory. Many policies are dense and written in legalese, exceeding the reading level of users [8]. The resulting incomprehensibility of PPs prevents the organization from successfully giving notice to the user. The challenges associated with online privacy policy design include the understandability of jargon and privacy preference complexity [9], user fatigue issues due to reading difficulty and time consumption [10], improving organization trustworthiness [11], policy effectiveness related to brevity, clarity, and breadth [12], and format effect on comprehension [13].

PP effectiveness is based on several factors. The Article 29 Data Protection Working Party recommends a multilayered format in which an initial webpage provides summary notice with primary information, where detailed information is provided via subsequent webpages [14]. Alternatively, Kelley et al. (2009) suggest modeling privacy policies after nutrition labels to improve the accuracy and efficiency of locating relevant information [15]. Angulo et al (2012) articulated an approach for designing user-friendly privacy policy interfaces which incorporated a nutrition label format with the added features of privacy alerts (e.g., notification of identified third-party data sharing and usage) and parallel privacy management (i.e., users could adjust privacy settings "on the fly") [16]. They found users valued the ability to manage their privacy during web interactions. However, results also revealed the difficulty in balancing design, content, and attention demands. Similarly, a study of online behavioral advertising notices (OBAs) found notices go unnoticed by users, ineffectively communicate user choices, and fail to inform users about the choice mechanisms OBAs provide [17].

When effectively designed, PPs provide organizational value. In addition to satisfying legal compliance, it may influence user attitudes about the organization and choices about disclosure. In an examination of privacy, Xu et al (2011) determined organizational factors, such as privacy policies, and user attitudes and perceptions are related to privacy concerns [18]. In a related study of consumer trust, Flavian & Guinaliu (2006) found "trust in the Internet is particularly influenced by the security perceived by consumers regarding the handling of their private data by the website (p. 612) [19]. Privacy policies may function to alleviate user privacy concerns.

3   Methodology

3.1   Sample

A nonrandom sample of twenty-eight higher education institutions was selected (See Table 1). All university websites' homepages were reviewed for a link to a privacy policy. If no link was provided, the website was searched internally to identify whether a privacy policy existed. Fordham University, Loyola University Chicago, and Saint Louis University were excluded after a search of their websites yielded no results. Although the remaining twenty-five websites provided privacy policies, many addressed areas unrelated to the focus of this research paper (e.g., alumni relations, library services, health center, registrar, and online programs). Only sixteen university websites provided a web or combination privacy policy (i.e., a privacy policy that addressed numerous areas, including the website) (See Table 3).

Table 1. Sample of university websites

University	URL	Privacy Policy Type
American University	www.american.edu	Combination
Baylor University	www.baylor.edu	Combination
Bradley University	www.bradley.edu	Other
Creighton University	www.creighton.edu	Other
Depaul University	www.depaul.edu	Other
Drexel University	www.drexel.edu	Web
Duquesne University	www.duq.edu	Web
Fordham University	www.fordham.edu	N/A
Hofstra University	www.hofstra.edu	Other
Lehigh University	www4.lehigh.edu	Web
Loyola Marymount University	www.lmu.edu	Web
Loyola University Chicago	www.luc.edu	N/A
Marquette University	www.marquette.edu	Web
Miami University	miamioh.edu	Combination
Ohio University	www.ohio.edu	Other
St. John's University	www.stjohns.edu	Other
St. Joseph University	www.sju.edu	Other
Saint Louis University	www.slu.edu	N/A
Santa Clara University	www.scu.edu	Web
Seton Hall University	www.shu.edu	Web
The Catholic University of America	www.cua.edu	Other
The Ohio State University	www.osu.edu	Web
University of Cincinnati	www.uc.edu	Other
University of Dayton	www.udayton.edu	Web
University of Denver	www.du.edu	Combination
University of San Diego	www.sandiego.edu	Web
Villanova University	www.villanova.edu	Web
Xavier University	www.xavier.edu	Web

3.2   Data

Two types of data were gathered from the selected university website privacy policy pages. First, the policies received a usability score based on whether a policy feature or design characteristic was present according to a 16-point checklist (See Table 2). Second, the text of the privacy policy text was captured and the content was analyzed. The data collection was performed from November 2013 to February 2014.

3.3   Content Analysis

Content analysis was used to examine the website and combination PPs of sixteen universities. The content was analyzed using a coding scheme that incorporated measures of usability, communication, fair information practice compliance, and legal concepts. The unit of analysis was the concept or feature. If a concept (e.g., a legal provision) or feature (e.g., a homepage link to PP) was present, it was coded as a one. Absent concepts/features were coded as zeros.

Table 2. Privacy Policy Coding Scheme – Abridged Version

SAMPLE MEASURES	
General categories	**Examples of concepts/features**
Usability	Homepage link, privacy policy label, layered format, contrast, font size, heading/sub-headings, bullets, clear policy purpose, critical information above fold, icons
Communication	Policy steward, contact information, links – related policies, links – related resources, definitions, notifications, plain language
Fair Information Practices	Notice/awareness, choice/consent, access/participation, integrity/security, enforcement/redress
Legal	Provision types, obligations, user rights, consent mechanisms, procedures, policy violation, regulations/frameworks, standards

The coding scheme addressed PP usability, communication openness, fair information practices, and legal orientation. The usability measures ranged from navigation (e.g., whether there was a direct path to the PP) to page and content design (e.g., PP layout, scannability, and chunking). Communication focused on openness (e.g., identifying a named privacy officer), clarity of concepts (e.g., definition usage), and facilitation of interactions (e.g., contact phone number or email address). The fair information practices category comprised concepts related to data collection, usage, storage, protection, sharing, and management (e.g., user access to stored data). The legal category facilitated classification of PP provision types, whether procedures were stated, and what regulatory frameworks were identified.

3.4   Coding Process and Data Analysis

Policies were coded for the presence or absence of features, concepts, themes, and provisions. A present entity was coded as 1. Absent entities received a 0. Policies occasionally referenced third-party privacy policies. In those examples, it was noted there was third-party policy content, but it was not coded as part of the university policy. Similarly, online PPs solely focused on specific departments (e.g., spirit, library use, alumni networks, health center, or student records) were excluded from coding, although it was noted the policy existed for the department/function. The focus of this analysis was web PPs and comprehensive PPs.

After coding the PPs, a percentage was calculated of PP entities present within each of the categories. The total number of possible features/concepts follows: Usability (16), communication (30), fair information practices (164), and legal (49).

The percentage represents the PP emphasis of certain concepts, features, and focuses. For example, a usability score of 100% indicates the PP addressed or met 16 of the 16 possible measures. Although a high percentage is expected to correlate with satisfactory usability, it does not represent a passing or failing score.

4   Results and Discussion

Overall, the results illustrate too many universities have no website/combination PP (43% of the universities sampled for this study), which prevent universities from reassuring their customers and building their brands and images [20]. Equally troubling is the serious need for improvement across all focus areas: Usability, communication, fair information practices, and legal content. No PP excelled in every area. In fact, usability is the only category where some PPs showed strength. All PPs were weak in the areas of communication, fair information practices, and legal concepts.

Table 3. Privacy Policy Content Analysis Results

University	Usability (16 items)	Communication (30 items)	Fair Information Practices (164 items)	Legal (49 items)
American University	50%	3%	13%	4%
Baylor University	50%	7%	18%	6%
Drexel University	69%	3%	10%	4%
Duquesne University	38%	7%	12%	4%
Lehigh University	31%	7%	15%	4%
Loyola Marymount University	69%	0%	15%	2%
Marquette University	56%	3%	15%	4%
Miami University	63%	7%	18%	6%
Santa Clara University	0%	7%	12%	0%
Seton Hall University	0%	3%	8%	0%
The Ohio State University	31%	0%	4%	0%
University of Dayton	44%	7%	14%	8%
University of Denver	38%	10%	12%	2%
University of San Diego	63%	10%	12%	4%
Villanova University	56%	0%	13%	2%
Xavier University	6%	7%	17%	10%
Mean percentage across PPs for each category:	**43%**	**5%**	**13%**	**4%**

Regarding usability, the mean score was 43% with a range from 0% to 69% (See Table 3). Most PPs used high text/background contrast and headings (87.5% and 69%, respectively), and adopted plain language (81%). However, a minority of policies provided a clear path to contact information (37.5%), used a layered format (0%), used subheadings (6%) and icons (0%), placed critical content above the fold (12.5%), or provided concise provisions (25%). Thirty-eight percent of universities had no homepage link to the PP, forcing users to search for, and perhaps not find, the PP. The good news is the aforementioned inadequacies have simple solutions: Add a homepage link, place a summary of important information above the fold, reduce the amount of text in provisions, and use bullet points to make information digestible.

Communication focused on whether a PP provided openness, concept clarity, and means for interaction. All PPs lacked a communication focus, shown by the overall mean score of 5% and a high score of 10%. Few PPs provided links to related policies (31%) and resources (0%). None of the policies identified a privacy officer or privacy office. Perhaps this indicates an absence of a dedicated, formalized approach to privacy. Although 62.5% provided contact information, it was usually a generic email (e.g., webmaster@university.edu) or a mailing address. Only 12.5% of the PPs provided definitions of key terms like personal information, education record, and third-party. Finally, every PP failed to address communication related to breaches, violations, and corrective action. In general, universities failed to use the PP as a communication opportunity. To improve, PPs should identify the privacy officer and provide multiple methods for communication. They should define jargon and share information about university communication and notifications.

The fair information practices category showed university PPs do not adequately reflect the FTC concepts of notice, choice, access, integrity, and enforcement. The university PPs, with a mean score of 13%, neglected to address many important topics. Although 87.5% of PPs mentioned data collection such as general cookies (62.5%), log files (37.5%), and web servers (25%), no policies differentiated among cookie types, explained the collection process, or provided detailed information about the collection process. Similarly, PPs frequently referred to PI (75%), web page visitation (62.5%), and IP address (81%), but few if any PPs were specific about the PI or provided information on other data types such as health, education, and social media. PPs also failed to provide notice about data usage (e.g., marketing - 19%, behavioral advertising – 0%, and association with other data – 19%) or data storage. PPs generally omitted information about what information is stored, how long data are retained, and archival/destruction methods. In terms of data protection, PPs mentioned general safeguarding (44%) and encryption (50%), but neglected the concepts of compliance reviews (0%), audits (6%), physical security (6%), privacy programs (0%), verifications (0%), vulnerability testing (0%), and anonymizing data (0%). The policies also sparsely referenced or discussed data management. No PP discussed general opting out. Few data management options were presented and were limited to opting out of third-party sharing (6%) and communication (25%). Data sharing was another troubling area. Only 56% of PPs stated there was no selling of data and no policies were clear about how data was shared across the university. All PPs failed to discuss how a user could access his data or recourse methods. University

PPs could better reflect fair information principles by providing more transparency and detail about data collection, management, sharing, and storage practices.

The legal category allowed classification of PP provision types, procedures, PP history, and regulatory frameworks. University PPs, with a mean score of 4%, did not address legal concepts as defined here. Although 81% addressed miscellaneous provisions, the focus was on disclaiming responsibility for the university website (62.5%) or external websites (62.5%). No PPs stated procedures for general inquiries, reporting incidents, filing complaints, or requesting status updates. No policies addressed prohibited activities such as identity theft, and policy violation remedies were absent (termination, expulsion, training, ID theft prevention protection). Regarding PP history, only 31% shared an effective date and a revision date. Finally, PPs infrequently referred to regulatory frameworks, with mentions solely of HIPAA (12.5%), general state law (12.5%), or the Ohio Public Records Act (6%).

5   Future Research and Limitations

This research establishes a comprehensive framework for evaluating PPs in terms of usability, communication, fair information practices, and legal perspectives. Although the content analysis provided a broader and deeper investigation of PP content than other content analyses [2, 21, 22, 23], the coding scheme can benefit from additional refinement. In future research, the coding scheme will be revised to provide an assessment of how well the PP addressed concepts. In addition, experimental research should be conducted to determine PP effectiveness.

In terms of limitations, capturing PPs presents challenges. As this study showed, many organizations fail to include a direct link to the PP from the homepage. This forced the use of internal and external search engines to locate PPs. It is possible that an organization may have a PP even though it was not located. Of course, this raises an important issue: Users need to be able to locate PPs in order to have notice of the information practices. Another limitation relates to the disorganization of PP content. Because there are limited PP best practices and no standards, content is highly variable and policies differ in provisions placement and sequence. In fact, many policies use vague, informal language and have no defined provisions. This presents an issue content coding. In the present study, if a concept was present, it received credit.   This issue can be addressed by including subjective measures in future coding frameworks.

6   Conclusion and Recommendations

University website/combination PPs provide inadequate notice to users. They fail to address the complex issues and situations that originate from universities assuming the role of information steward. The duties that accompany the steward role are not reflected in the language or structure of privacy policies. This was demonstrated by the tendency of university PP content to ignore communication standards, fair information practices, and important legal information.

Good privacy policy design is an expectation and a requirement, especially given the level of sensitivity of some information activities in higher education. Institutions should develop PPs that address the needs of their constituents. They need to be written in plain language, organized, comprehensive, and informative. A few areas to improve: 1.) Provide transparency about the collection, usage, sharing, and storage of information, 2.) Provide access to the information and articulate the mechanism for addressing privacy issues (e.g., correcting data, reporting violations), and 3.) Give users choice regarding the disposition of their data. Higher education institutions also should provide information on privacy topics of specific concern to education (e.g., affiliation of education record data with browsing behavior).

Usable PPs are feasible for all education institutions as they can be economically developed and produced [24]. It is a low investment that may alleviate user privacy concerns and improve user perceptions of risk and control. This preventive measure is an investment in reputation management and proactive alleviation of harm/damage. There are several easy, low-cost ways to create or improve policies.

A concise, comprehensive privacy policy that meaningfully addresses user needs is an opportunity for an institution to demonstrate its commitment to user privacy, an understanding of its data governance, accountability, and an interest in trust building. Given the relatively low cost of developing and communicating such a policy, universities would be well advised to invest a small amount of resources in exchange for a significant return in the future.

References

1. DeSantis, N.: U. of Iowa Shares Data With Local Sheriff on Students Seeking Gun Permits. The Chronicle of Higher Education (December 17, 2013)
2. Culnan, M., Carlin, T.: Online Privacy Practices in Higher Education: Making the Grade? Communications of the ACM 52(2), 126–130 (2009)
3. Loh, W.: UMD Data Breach (2014), http://uhr.umd.edu/2014/02/umd-data-breach
4. Cox, J.: Are Colleges and Universities at Greater Risk of Data Breaches? Network World (2010), http://www.networkworld.com/news/2010/091510-higher-ed-data-breaches.html
5. National Conference of State Legislatures, http://www.ncsl.org/research/telecommunications-and-information-technology/security-breach-notification-laws.aspx (retrieved February 2, 2014)
6. FERPA, 34 C.F.R. section 99.3 (2011)
7. California Social Media Privacy Law S.B. 1394 (2012)
8. Jensen, C., Potts, C.: Privacy Policies as Decision-making Tools: An Evaluation of Online Privacy Notices. Paper presented at the CHI 2004, Vienna, Austria (2004)
9. Cranor, L., Guduru, P., Arjula, M.: User Interfaces for Privacy Agents. ACM Transactions on Computer-Human Interaction 13(2), 135–178 (2006)
10. McDonald, A.M., Reeder, R.W., Kelley, P.G., Cranor, L.F.: A Comparative Study of Online Privacy Policies and Formats. In: Goldberg, I., Atallah, M.J. (eds.) PETS 2009. LNCS, vol. 5672, pp. 37–55. Springer, Heidelberg (2009)

11. Au, N., Law, R.: Presentation Formats of Policy Statements On Hotel Websites and Privacy Concerns: A Multimedia Learning Theory Perspective. Journal of Hospitality & Tourism Research (2012)
12. Goel, S., Chengalur-Smith, I.N.: Metrics for Characterizing the Form of Security Policies. The Journal of Strategic Information Systems 19(4), 281–295 (2010)
13. Vail, M.W., Earp, J.B., Antón, A.I.: An Empirical Study of Consumer Perceptions and Comprehension of Web Site Privacy Policies. IEEE Transactions on Engineering Management 55(3), 442–454 (2008)
14. Article 29 Data protection Working Party, Opinion on More Harmonised Information Provisions 1198704/EN WP 100, European Commission (2004)
15. Kelley, P., Cesca, L., Bresee, J., Cranor, L.: Standardizing Privacy Notices: An Online Study of the Nutrition Label Approach. In: Proceedings of the 28th International Conference on Human Factors in Computing Systems, p. 1573. ACM, New York (2010)
16. Angulo, J., Fishcer-Hübner, S., Wästlund, E., Pulls, T.: Toward Usable Privacy Policy Display and Management. Information Management & Computer Security 20(1), 4–17 (2012)
17. Leon, P., Cranshaw, J., Cranor, L., Graves, J., Hastak, M., Ur, B., Guzi, X.: What Do Online Behavioral Advertising Disclosures Communicat to Users? Carnegie Mellon University CyLab (2012)
18. Heng, X., Dinev, T., Smith, J., Hart, P.: Information privacy Concerns: Linking Indivdiual Perceptions with Institutional Privacy Assurances. Journal of the Association for Information Systems 12(12), 798–824 (2011)
19. Flavián, C., Guinalíu, M.: Consumer Trust, Perceived Security and Privacy Policy: Three Basic Elements of Loyalty to a Web Site. Industrial Management & Data Systems 106(5), 601–620 (2006)
20. McRobb, S., Rogerson, S.: Are They Really Listening? An Investigation Into Published Online Privacy Policies at The Beginning of The Third Millennium. Information Technology & People 17(4), 442–461 (2004)
21. Reay, I., Beatty, P., Dick, S., Miller, J.: Privacy Policies and National Culture on the Internet. Inf. Syst. Front. 15, 279–292 (2013)
22. Jensen, C., Potts, C.: Private Policies Examined: Fair Warning or Fair Game? (2003)
23. Earp, J.B., Antón, A.I., Aiman-Smith, L., Stufflebeam, W.H.: Examining Internet Privacy Policies within the Context of User Privacy Values. IEEE Transactions on Engineering Management 52(2), 227–237 (2005)
24. Meinert, D., Peterson, D., Criswell, J., Crossland, M.: Privacy Policy Statements and Consumer Willingness to Provide Persona Information. Journal of Electronic Commerce in Organizations 4, 1–17 (2006)

Privacy Protection Based Privacy Conflict Detection and Solution in Online Social Networks

Arunee Ratikan[1] and Mikifumi Shikida[2]

[1] School of Information Science
[2] Research Center for Advanced Computing Infrastructure,
Japan Advanced Institute of Science and Technology, Ishikawa, Japan 923-1211
{a.ratikan,shikida}@jaist.ac.jp

Abstract. Online Social Networks (OSNs) such as Facebook, Twitter, and so on recently are major impact in communication and social interaction. Users can share any information with others. However, they have concerns about losing privacy due to lack of an adequate privacy protection provided by the OSNs. The information posted by the user (owner) might leak to unwanted target users. Especially, when collaborative information (e.g. text, photo, video, link), which has associated with the owner and multiple users (co-owners) in the real world, is posted into the OSNs, the co-owners do not have permission to control and might not be aware their information that is being managed by others. To overcome, collective privacy protection (CPP) is proposed to balance between the collaborative information sharing and the privacy protection for the owner and co-owners by majority vote. It enables the owner to create the privacy policy and the co-owners to make a decision in the privacy policy by vote. It additionally identifies and solves the privacy conflicts because at least one co-owner intends to keep private.

Keywords: Online Social Networks, Information sharing, Privacy protection.

1 Introduction

OSNs such as Facebook, Google+, Twitter refer to "online communities whose main goal is to make available an information space, where each social network participant can publish and share information" defined by [1]. This leads to communication and social interaction each other. For example, when the user can share personal stories, interests, activities, services and so on, other users can comment or press like button on this information.

The user in the OSNs can be both reader and creator according to the information consuming and the information sharing. The creator can additionally refer to an owner and a co-owner. The owner creates and posts the collaborative information to the OSNs. The co-owner has participated in creating the collaborative information or can referred by the owner such as tagging or mention. Nonetheless, the co-owner does not post it to the OSNs.

T. Tryfonas and I. Askoxylakis (Eds.): HAS 2014, LNCS 8533, pp. 433–445, 2014.

In case of the collaborative information, the owner can tag and mention the co-owners on the information. Moreover, the OSNs allow the user, who is not the owner of the information to share the information. If the collaborative information leaks to unwanted target users (referring to whom the owner and the co-owner are not willing to share with), it is hard to solve. This is because the owner and co-owners cannot command those users to stop spread the information via mobile phone, word of mouth and so on. Therefore, this causes the owner and co-owners, who have associated with the collaborative information, lose privacy thanks to lack of an adequate privacy protection.

Our goal is to balance between the collaborative information sharing and the privacy protection for the owner and co-owners. Therefore, this research proposes the CPP by applying majority vote concept. The proposed CPP allows the owner to create the privacy policy and the co-owners to make a decision in the privacy policy by vote whether or not the collaborative information should be posted. This is because the owner or co-owners have difficulty with setting the privacy policy [2]. This makes the proposed CPP differ from other research works [3] [4]. The proposed CPP additionally identifies and solves the privacy conflicts because at least one co-owner intends to keep private. The privacy conflict comes from different privacy concerns over the collaborative information by the owner and the co-owners. Furthermore, when the co-owners want to share the information, they also can perform themselves as the owner. This is because the owner and co-owners have right in the collaborative information and each owner might have different privacy preference.

2   Background and Related Works

2.1   Cause of Losing Privacy

The losing privacy in the OSNs can generally cause from four possible ways as follows:

1. The information is shared by the user or other users with poor privacy setting or no privacy setting. Several research works indicated that the users have difficulty with the privacy setting or do not use it [5] [6].
2. The information is tagged or mentioned by other users. These actions are meaningless in privacy protection because the tagged or mentioned users do not have permission the control the information before the information was spread in the OSNs.
3. When the user posted the information via own space provided by the OSNs, it might be shared or re-shared by other users without permission such as retweet in Twitter or share in Facebook.
4. Privacy setting provided by the OSN is not adequate for privacy protection because it allows only the user, who posts the information, to privilege in control the information. This means the other users, who have associated with this information, cannot do anything for their information.

Posting the collaborative information might lead to a crime problem because the OSNs allow the creator to use "Check-in" feature. This feature can reveal actual location where the activities are being performed or were done by many users, therefore a criminal can take advantage from this information within little time to find victim's location available on the SNP.

2.2   Access Control Models and Other Solutions for Privacy Protection

In order to protect the user's privacy, most of research works have been proposed the access control model. Gollu et al. [7] presented a social-networking-based access control mechanism for the information sharing. Identities between the users were viewed as key pair and social relationship. They provided access control list to determine who can access the information. Carminati et al. [8] proposed a rule-based access control mechanism for the OSNs. Type, depth and trust level of existing relationship between the users were used for expressing the complex privacy policy. Hart et al. [9] used the relationship information, which had exist in the OSNs, in a content-based access control model. This model could authenticate the user for accessing the information. Hu et al. [3] proposed a mechanism that detected and resolved the privacy conflict among the users, who had shared ownership of the collaborative information. Their research works enabled these users to provide the policy then calculated the privacy risk and sharing loss. Hu et al. [4] presented collaborative privacy management for shared data in Google+. This research introduced the concept of circle and trust to their model. Squicciarini et al [10] considered that the information might not belong to only one user in some cases, therefore they made a mechanism that supported the information sharing in the OSNs based on the notion of content ownership.

Besides the access control models, there are other solutions for privacy protection. Dinh et al. [11] attempted to construct a circle of trust by proposing the hybrid algorithm from investigating the maximum circle of trust problem. Thus, the user can safely share the information with others or the information will not be leaked to unwanted target users. Li et al. [2] used machine learning techniques and structured semantic knowledge in the ONS to learn the users' privacy setting pattern in the past and users' profiles. Then, this research made recommendation for the privacy setting to the user. Adu-Oppong et al. [12] applied automatically extracted network communities to make privacy policies easier by grouping friends into lists.

Although many access control models and other solutions have been proposed for privacy protection, they allow only the owner to control the privacy setting. Only few research works realized losing privacy of the co-owners, who has associated with the collaborative information. In some research works [3] [4], the owner and co-owners can create the privacy policy; but it cannot satisfy everyone. Possibility of violating privacy remains if at least one co-owner intends to keep private.

3   Research Methodology

Figure 1 depicts the proposed CPP for the privacy protection of owner and co-owners. It composes of five main components: social graph, privacy policy, co-owner invitation, majority vote, and conflict identification and provided solution. The work-flow of the proposed CPP begins at the owner creates the privacy policy. Then, the co-owners are detected in order to send the invitation that they are owned a part of the information and this information is being posted to the owner in the OSNs. The co-owners can vote on the privacy policy whether or not this collaborative information should be posted on the OSNs. The co-owner can be one of three statuses: acceptance, rejection and no response. No response status presents that the co-owner does not accept or reject in time. Nevertheless, when the time is over, the co-owner with no response will be moved to rejection status because the privacy is considered as a high priority. Next, the proposed CPP finds the privacy conflict among the owner and the co-owners, and provides the solution for each conflict. A list of the target users, who can see this information, is suggested to the owner to re-check before uploading it to the OSNs.

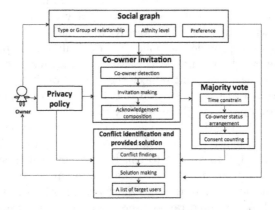

Fig. 1. The proposed collective privacy protection for the owner and co-owners in the information sharing

4   Proposed Collective Privacy Protection

The proposed CPP composes of five main components, which are social graph, privacy policy, co-owner invitation, majority vote, and conflict identification and provided solution. More details are explained as follows.

1. **Social graph**

   It is to create a graph that represents the social relationship among the users in the OSNs as demonstrated in Fig. 2. A node refers to a user in the OSNs. An edge presents relationship between two nodes. Label between nodes indicates type or group of relationship and affinity level. In this research, preference of user is added in the social graph. This graph supports the notion about importance of relationship quality [6] because relationship between users influences making privacy decision.

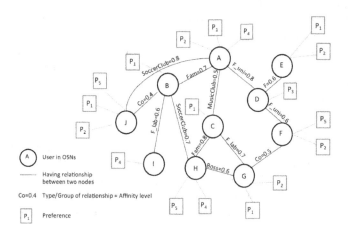

Fig. 2. The simple social graph in the OSNs

2. Privacy policy

The privacy policy is designed for limit the number of the users, who can see the collaborative information. Idea of this policy is that the owner tries to match this information to the target users, who might be interested in it. Nonetheless, when the co-owner wants to share the collaborative information, they can change the position to the owner position then create the privacy policy. The privacy policy helps alleviate the information overload by reducing amount of information and the owner can control the distance of the information, which is spread in the OSNs. The owner constructs the privacy policy by using four useful factors obtained from the social graph: type or group of relationship, affinity level, preference and distance for information distribution.

– **Type or group of relationship** (T/G_Rela)
   In the OSNs, the users have ability to create a group for different purposes. It is fact that members in a contact list cannot have the same role in both the OSNs world and the real-world. Therefore, the T/G_Rela is subjected to each user such as friend, family, boss, co-worker and so on.
– **Affinity level** (AL)
   This factor refers to how familiar two users are. Generally, the user is not able to give everyone in the contact list with same closeness level. The AL can range from 0.1 to 1.0 (denoting 0.1 is very unfriendly, 1.0 is very familiar)

- **Preference** (Pref)
  The user's preference presents the interests of the user such as music, movie, sport and so on. Using the user's preference is a good way because the information will not leak to other users, who are not interested in that information and does not cause the users annoyance.
- **Distance for information distribution** (Dist)
  It indicates how far the information can be spread to the other users. Controlling the distance can limit the number of the users, who can see the information. Nevertheless, it relies on the purpose of the owner. If the owner intends to spread the information as much as possible without privacy setting, it is possible that the information will be consumed by large number of users.

3. **Co-owner invitation**
   This component is proposed to inform the co-owners that they are a part of the collaborative information. It differs from previous works [8] [11] because this component makes the co-owners know that their information is being managed by others. In many cases, the co-owners lose the privacy that causes from the owner share the collaborative information without permission. This component additionally is important since it helps the co-owners realize whether or not posting this collaborative information might cause them trouble in the future. Then, the co-owner can make a decision by vote on the privacy policy created by the owner. After that the vote result will be collected and transferred to the majority vote component. The vote result of each co-owner is considered as the co-owner's status. The co-owner can be one of three statuses: acceptance, rejection and no response. Acceptance status means the co-owner agrees with the privacy policy. Rejection status indicates the co-owner denies the privacy policy or he/she needs to keep this information private. No response status presents the co-owner does not accept or reject in time.

4. **Majority vote**
   It has a duty to seek the consent of all co-owners as much as possible because allowing all of owner and co-owners to create the privacy policy is difficult to meet all of desires in one times. This component starts with gathering all of co-owners' status from the co-owner invitation component. Nonetheless, it takes time for collecting the vote results; so it needs to specific time. When the time is over, the co-owner with no response status will be moved to rejection status to protect the privacy. After status arrangement, the vote results will be counted if the number of acceptances is more than half of the vote results, this means that the collaborative information can be posted to the OSNs. The advantage of the majority vote is that if there is one co-owner rejects this privacy policy, he/she is still provided the privacy protection.

5. **Conflict identification and provided solution**
   It is designed for finding the cause of conflicts among the co-owners, who accept and reject the privacy policy, and making solution for those conflicts. Then, a list of target users is recommended to the owner. The owner can verify it before uploading the information. The conflicts are also identified

when sharing and re-share are occurred. In order to find the conflicts, the social graph is required because it can indicate how each user connects or has associated with. Moreover, it can represent the mutual friends as depicted in Fig. 2. User C is a mutual friend of user A and user B, while user H is a mutual friend of user B and user C. The mutual friend is necessary for detecting the conflict between the co-owners, who accept and reject the privacy policy. The proposed CPP shows the co-owners the list of users, who can see the collaborative information. These users have direct relationship with the owner and pass a condition of the privacy policy.

5   Experiment and Results

The experiment aims to analyze the factor and combination of factors, which help the information not leak to unwanted target users and to investigate the opinion of co-ownership by using the proposed architecture as shown in Fig. 1 and a questionnaire. The analysis results in this experiment will be used in the privacy policy, which is a part of the proposed CPP.

5.1   Experimental Setup

In order to study the factor and the combination of factors, which have influential on sharing sensitive information, a virtual social graph was built that helped the respondents imagined the flow of the information when it was shared in the OSNs. In this experiment, it was not created by the real data due to permission requirement. The virtual social graph consisted of 88 nodes, 201 edges as shown in Fig. 4. Each node referred to a user in the OSNs and one user had few preferences e.g. sport, music, game, food, travel. The edge presented a relationship and 10 affinity levels (ranging from 0.1 (very unfriendly) to 1.0 (very familiar)) between two nodes. In this experiment, the collaborative information additionally was assumed that it has associated with one owners and five co-owners. Three co-owners accepted the privacy policy created by the owner so that the vote results had a majority. There are 15 types for investigation, which compose of four groups according to the number of factors as follows in Table 1.

Each respondent were shown many scenarios as denoted in Fig. 3 according to types of information e.g. text, photo, video and link. The respondents then imagined that they were the owner and created the privacy policy that composed of the one factor and combination of factors. Also, they observed the flow of information with consideration of co-owners, who rejected the privacy policy. At the same privacy policy, the respondent swapped a position to co-owners and observed the flow of information again. Moreover, the co-owner could change a position from the co-owner to the owner in order to post this collaborative information.

Figure 4 indicates that the owner 0 created the privacy policy by using the combination of T/G_Rela and Dist (setting as 1 hop) factors. The co-owner 1 and 4 rejected this privacy policy. Therefore, the users, who have relationship with the owner 0 and co-owner 1, and the owner 0 and the co-owner 4, could not see this information due to conflicts (user 20 and 13). Figure 5 shows the position change from the co-owner 2 in Fig. 4 to the owner 2. The owner 2 also created the privacy policy policy by using the same combination of factors. Nonetheless, the co-owner 4 and 6 rejected this policy. By consideration of results, it can be divided into two main groups. Firstly, users could not see the information because of rejection of the owner 4 (user 3) and not consistency with this policy (user 8 and 43), Secondly, the user can see the information due to acceptance of the co-owner 1 (user 20 and 42) and consistency with this policy (user 9, 10, 11, 22, 23, 24, 39, 45, 47).

Fig. 3. An example of scenarios

After the experiment, the respondents did the questionnaire to evaluate the performance of each factor and combination of factors. The questions in the questionnaire were answered by 24 respondents: 14 male and 10 female. All respondents were asked about general questions, privacy in the OSNs, opinion of co-ownership as described in next Sect. 5.2

5.2 Results

Each question about the privacy in the OSNs and the opinion of co-ownership in the questionnaire was answered by Yes/No, explanation and a 5-point Likert scale. The performance of each factor and combination of factors was investigated by Mean and Standard deviation.

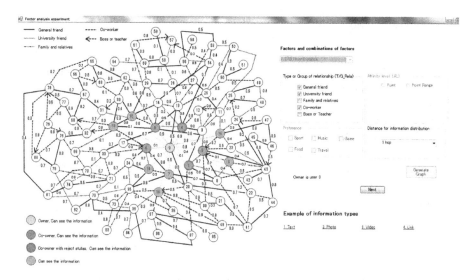

Fig. 4. An example of changing the position from the co-owner to the owner and results (before)

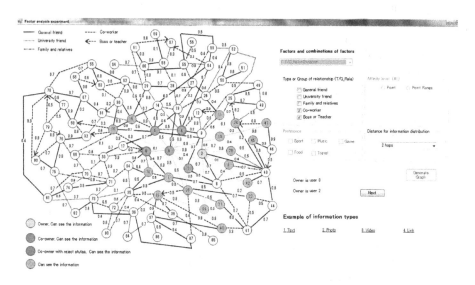

Fig. 5. An example of changing the position from the co-owner to the owner and results (after)

1. General questions

Most of the respondents age range from 21 to 40 years old and have good experience in using the OSNs. They normally have more than one account. 62.5% of them spend time on using the OSNs about 1-4 hours a day. Purposes of using the OSNs generally are entertainment, information sharing, consuming and relationship maintenance.

2. **Privacy in the OSNs**

The results show that most of the respondents concerned the privacy with 3.91 ± 0.99. 62.5% of them made an effort to avoid the sensitive information leak by using a custom setting. The remaining respondents use a default setting provided by the OSNs. However, they still complained that the privacy setting was difficult to understand [2] [13]. Moreover, it had many steps to complete setting. Some of them state that they would not post much information via the OSNs, which little provided the privacy setting such as Line (Timeline) or Instagram.

Photo and text were considered that they easily leak to unwanted target users. This is because they were easy to recognize by others and using tagging and mention on the information can be done without permission.

Family and Boss are the group of people, who the respondents did not want the sensitive information leak to. Although the respondents care feeling of them, the respondents still need private. Some opinion was expressed that if some sensitive information leaks to their family, it could lead to misunderstanding, worry, or disputation. Boss influenced career because several decisions relied on the boss. Posing the information sometimes could refer to an image of organization.

Further interesting analysis, the respondents would not be worried much if the sensitive information leaked to people, who the respondents did not have relationship with [14].

From Table 1, the number of factors influenced the privacy protection that if the number of factors increased, it helped the sensitive information not leak to unwanted target users. A combination of T/G_Rela, AL, Pref and Dist is considered as the most important for the privacy protection because it could filter unwanted target users. Although the performance of Pref factor or combinations containing this factor dropped, minority of the respondents believed that combinations with the Pref factor would scope the number of users, who had similar point of view.

From the respondents' opinions, the T/G_Rela and the AL factors were a basis that the privacy setting should have. This was relevant to the results in Table 1. If the combination of factors contains the T/G_Rela and the AL factors, the performance increased.

3. **Opinion of co-ownership**

Almost all respondents have experience in losing privacy because the owner posted the collaborative information without their permission. Around 64% of these respondents faced trouble after the collaborative information, which was sensitive, was posted to the OSNs. They were worried about information leak with 3.86 ± 0.77.

There are two different opinions when the respondents were asked about asking the co-owner's permission before posting the collaborative information. The respondents imagined that they were the co-owner. 83.33% of them think that asking the permission was necessary with four reasons.

– The respondents did not want the information leak to others, whom the respondent do not want to share with.

Table 1. Influence of factors on privacy protection

Factor	Personal information	Confidential business information	Freedom of expression	Improper morality	Behavior embarrassing
1. T/G_Rela	3.54±1.47	3.29±1.60	3.25±1.50	3.75±1.92	3.46±2.00
2. AL	3.42±1.50	2.92±1.53	3.29±1.30	3.46±1.50	3.33±1.34
3. Pref	2.63±1.73	2.67±1.61	3.63±1.38	2.75±1.39	2.54±1.25
4. Dist	3.63±1.12	2.88±1.56	2.92±1.05	3.08±1.21	3.04±1.23
5. T/G_Rela+AL	4.04±1.30	3.58±1.47	3.75±0.98	4.13±1.03	3.71±1.12
6. T/G_Rela+Pref	3.46±1.47	3.33±1.43	3.88+1.08	3.50±1.06	3.17±0.96
7. T/G_Rela+Dist	3.88±1.15	3.38±1.50	3.45±1.30	3.42±1.28	3.29±1.33
8. AL+Pref	3.30±1.31	2.98±1.43	3.83±1.12	3.29±1.23	3.13±1.26
9. AL+Dist	3.46±1.22	3.08±1.50	3.29±1.27	3.38±1.20	3.33±1.17
10. Pref+Dist	3.25±1.22	2.92±1.50	3.25±1.29	2.83±1.17	2.79±1.10
11. T/G_Rela+AL+Pref	3.92±1.32	3.63±1.44	4.08±0.97	4.17±1.00	3.96±1.00
12. T/G_Rela+AL+Dist	4.25±0.85	3.71±1.30	3.79±1.14	4.04±0.95	3.95±1.04
13. T/G_Rela+Pref+Dist	3.83+1.12	3.46±1.38	3.92±1.18	3.92±0.88	3.79±0.78
14. AL+Pref+Dist	3.67±0.96	3.50±1.35	3.96±1.20	3.77±0.95	3.58±1.06
15. T/G_Rela+AL+Pref+Dist	**4.50±0.93**	**3.79±1.44**	**4.21±1.22**	**4.38±0.71**	**4.21±0.72**

- They should have right to decide whether or not this information could be posted because the could not know which the information would cause them trouble in the future.
- Sensitivity level of privacy toward each information relied on person. In other words, each person has different privacy concern when seeing the same information.
- They should know their information is being managed by whom because they were worried who would see the information.

Nonetheless, the remaining respondents state that no need to ask their permission when they were the co-owner. Three reasons are explained below.

- They could not expect the owner to use the privacy setting, thus the co-owner should have to be careful the collaborative information by themselves.
- Giving the permission every times was boring task.
- They did not care much the privacy.

6   Discussion

Analysis results can imply that the respondents are worried when the collaborative information, which is sensitive, leak to the users, who the respondents have relationship with especially family and boss. They generally have many roles depending on society. They thus perform different behaviors when are in different societies. Although they want to post the collaborative information to the OSNs, they need private by not revealing some information to others because of negative feedback. As a result, most of the respondents believe that the combination of T/G_Rela, AL, Pref and Dist factors helps protect the privacy for leaking the information. On the other hand, they do not care much if the collaborative information will leak to other users, who the respondents have no relationship with or not familiar with because they might not meet in the real world. Asking the co-owner's permission is expressed that the owner takes responsibility to the co-owners' privacy and it is suitable way although sometimes waiting for the permission might make the information not fresh or up to date.

7   Conclusion and Future Works

The CPP is proposed to balance between the collaborative information sharing and the privacy protection for the owner and co-owners by majority vote. It enables the owner to create the privacy policy and the co-owners to make a decision in the privacy policy by vote. It additionally identifies and solves the privacy conflicts because at least one co-owner intends to keep private. We have analyzed the factors, which help protect the privacy, the privacy in the OSNs, and opinion of co-ownership via the survey. Asking permission from the co-owners is necessary because it helps the collaborative information not leak to unwanted target users. For the future work, we plan to classify the sensitive information in order to help remind the owner before posting.

References

[1] Dhia, I.B.: Access control in social networks: A reachability-based approach. In: Proceedings of the 2012 Joint EDBT/ICDT Workshops, EDBT-ICDT 2012, pp. 227–232. ACM, New York (2012)

[2] Li, Q., Li, J., Wang, H., Ginjala, A.: Semantics-enhanced privacy recommendation for social networking sites. In: 2011 IEEE 10th International Conference on Trust, Security and Privacy in Computing and Communications (TrustCom), pp. 226–233 (2011)

[3] Hu, H., Ahn, G.J., Jorgensen, J.: Detecting and resolving privacy conflicts for collaborative data sharing in online social networks. In: Proceedings of the 27th Annual Computer Security Applications Conference, ACSAC 2011, pp. 103–112. ACM, New York (2011)

[4] Hu, H., Ahn, G.J., Jorgensen, J.: Enabling collaborative data sharing in google+. In: 2012 IEEE Global Communications Conference (GLOBECOM), pp. 720–725 (2012)

[5] Acquisti, A., Grossklags, J.: Privacy and rationality in individual decision making. IEEE Security Privacy 3(1), 26–33 (2005)

[6] Banks, L., Wu, S.: All friends are not created equal: An interaction intensity based approach to privacy in online social networks. In: International Conference on Computational Science and Engineering, CSE 2009, vol. 4, pp. 970–974 (2009)

[7] Gollu, K., Saroiu, S., Wolman, A.: A social networking-based access control scheme for personal content. In: Proceeding of the 21st ACM Symposium on Operating Systems Principles, SOSP 2007 (2007) (Work-in-Progress Session)

[8] Carminati, B., Ferrari, E., Perego, A.: Rule-based access control for social networks. In: Meersman, R., Tari, Z., Herrero, P. (eds.) OTM 2006 Workshops. LNCS, vol. 4278, pp. 1734–1744. Springer, Heidelberg (2006)

[9] Hart, M., Johnson, R., Stent, A.: More content- less control: Access control in the web 2.0. In: IEEE Web 2.0 Privacy and Security Workshop (2007)

[10] Squicciarini, A.C., Shehab, M., Wede, J.: Privacy policies for shared content in social network sites. The VLDB Journal 19(6), 777–796 (2010)

[11] Dinh, T.N., Shen, Y., Thai, M.T.: The walls have ears: optimize sharing for visibility and privacy in online social networks. In: CIKM, pp. 1452–1461 (2012)

[12] Adu-Oppong, F., Gardiner, C., Kapadia, A., Tsang, P.: Social circles: Tackling privacy in social networks. In: Symposium on Usable Privacy and Security, SOSP (2008)

[13] Church, L., Anderson, J., Bonneau, J., Stajano, F.: Privacy stories: Confidence in privacy behaviors through end user programming. In: Proceedings of the 5th Symposium on Usable Privacy and Security, SOUPS 2009. ACM, New York (2009)

[14] Wellman, B., Salaff, J., Dimitrova, D., Garton, L., Gulia, M., Haythornthwaite, C.: Computer networks as social networks: Collaborative work, telework, and virtual community. Annual Review of Sociology 22(1), 213–238 (1996)

Author Index